African Americans

A CONCISE

VOLUME

SECOND EDITION

DARLENE CLARK HINE
Northwestern University

WILLIAM C. HINE
South Carolina State University

STANLEY HARROLD
South Carolina State University

PEARSON
Prentice
Hall

Upper Saddle River, New Jersey 07458

Library of Congress Cataloging-in-Publication Data

Hine, Darlene Clark.
  African Americans : a concise history / Darlene Clark Hine, William C. Hine, Stanley Harrold.—2nd ed.
    p. cm.
  "Combined volume."
  Includes bibliographical references and index.
  ISBN 0-13-192583-0 (combined volume)
  1. African Americans—History.   I. Hine, William C.   II. Harrold, Stanley.   III. Title.
  E185.H534 2006
  973'.0496073—dc22

                                                                                        2005049286

Vice President/Editorial Director: Charlyce Jones Owen
Associate Editor: Emsal Hasan
Editorial Assistant: Maureen Diana
Director of Production and Manufacturing: Barbara Kittle
Senior Managing Editor: Joanne Riker
Production Liaison: Louise Rothman
Prepress and Manufacturing Manager: Nick Sklitsis
Prepress and Manufacturing Buyer: Benjamin Smith
Director of Marketing: Heather Shelstad
Electronic Artist: Mirella Signoretto
Composition and Full-Service Project Management: GGS Book Services, Atlantic Highlands
Cover Design: Bruce Kenselaar
Printer/Binder: Courier Companies, Inc.
Cover Printer: Phoenix Color Corporation

Credits and acknowledgments borrowed from other sources and reproduced, with permission, in this textbook appear on appropriate page within text.

Pearson Education LTD.
Pearson Education Australia PTY, Limited
Pearson Education Singapore, Pte. Ltd
Pearson Education North Asia Ltd

Pearson Education, Canada, Ltd
Pearson Educación de Mexico, S.A. de C.V.
Pearson Education–Japan
Pearson Education Malaysia, Pte. Ltd

10 9 8 7 6 5 4 3 2 1
ISBN 0-13-192582-2

To

CARTER G. WOODSON & BENJAMIN QUARLES

Contents

CHAPTER 3 • **Black People in Colonial North America, *1526–1763***

38

CHAPTER 6 • **Life in the Cotton Kingdom**   **104**

CHAPTER 7 • **Free Black People in Antebellum America**   **123**

CHAPTER 8 • **Opposition to Slavery, *1800–1833***   **145**

CHAPTER 9 • **Let Your Motto Be Resistance,** *1833–1850*   **161**

CHAPTER 10 • **And Black People Were at the Heart of It:** *The United States Disunites over Slavery*   **179**

CHAPTER 11 • **Liberation:** *African Americans and the Civil War*   **201**

CHAPTER 13 • **The Meaning of Freedom:** *The Failure of Reconstruction*   **251**

CHAPTER 14 • **White Supremacy Triumphant:** *African Americans in the South in the Late Nineteenth Century*   **273**

CHAPTER 15 • **Black Southerners Challenge
White Supremacy**   **296**

CHAPTER 17 • **African Americans and the 1920s**   **361**

CHAPTER 18 • **Black Protest, the Great
Depression, and the New Deal**   **384**

CHAPTER 19 • **Meanings of Freedom:** *Culture and Society in the 1930s and 1940s*   **408**

CHAPTER 20 • **The World War II Era and the Seeds of a Revolution**   **432**

CHAPTER 21 • **The Freedom Movement,** *1954–1965*   **454**

CHAPTER 22 • **The Struggle Continues,** *1965–1980*   **483**

CHAPTER 23 • **Black Politics, White Backlash,
*1980 to the Present***

514

Ronald Reagan and the Conservative Reaction   514
Dismantling the Great Society   514

CHAPTER 24 • **African Americans at the Dawn of a New Millennium**   **537**

Preface

"One ever feels his two-ness,—an American, a Negro; two souls, two thoughts, two un-reconciled strivings; two warring ideals in one dark body." So wrote W. E. B. Du Bois in 1897. African-American history, Du Bois maintained, was the history of this double-consciousness. Black people have always been part of the American nation that they helped to build. But they have also been a nation unto themselves, with their own ex-periences, culture, and aspirations. African-American history cannot be understood except in the broader context of American history. American history cannot be un-derstood without African-American history.

Since Du Bois's time our understanding of both African-American and American history has been complicated and enriched by a growing appreciation of the role of class and gender in shaping human societies. We are also increasingly aware of the complexity of racial experiences in American history. Even in times of great racial po-larity some white people have empathized with black people and some black people have identified with white interests.

It is in light of these insights that we tell the story of African Americans. That story begins in Africa, where the people who were to become African Americans began their long, turbulent, and difficult journey, a journey marked by sustained suffering as well as perseverance, bravery, and achievement. It includes the rich culture—at once splendidly distinctive and tightly intertwined with a broader American culture—that African Americans have nurtured throughout their history. And it includes the many-faceted quest for freedom in which African Americans have sought to counter white oppression and racism with the egalitarian spirit of the Declaration of Independence that American society professes to embody.

Nurtured by black historian Carter G. Woodson during the early decades of the twentieth century, African-American history has blossomed as a field of study since the 1950s. Books and articles have appeared on almost every facet of black life. Yet this survey is the first comprehensive college textbook of the African-American experi-ence. It draws on recent research to present black history in a clear and direct manner, within a broad social, cultural, and political framework. It also provides thorough cov-erage of African-American women as active builders of black culture.

African Americans: A Concise History balances accounts of the actions of African-American leaders with investigations of the lives of the ordinary men and women in black communities. This community focus helps make this a history of a people rather than an account of a few extraordinary individuals. Yet the book does not neglect im-portant political and religious leaders, entrepreneurs, and entertainers. And it gives extensive coverage to African-American art, literature, and music.

African-American history started in Africa, and this narrative begins with an ac-count of life on that continent to the sixteenth century and the beginning of the forced migration of millions of Africans to the Americas. Succeeding chapters present the struggle of black people to maintain their humanity during the slave trade and as slaves in North America during the long colonial period.

The coming of the American Revolution during the 1770s initiated a pattern of black struggle for racial justice in which periods of optimism alternated with times of repression. Several chapters analyze the building of black community institutions, the antislavery movement, the efforts of black people to make the Civil War a war for emancipation, their struggle for equal rights as citizens during Reconstruction, and the strong opposition these efforts faced. There is also substantial coverage of African-American military service, from the War for Independence through American wars of the nineteenth and twentieth centuries.

During the late nineteenth century and much of the twentieth century, racial segregation and racially motivated violence that relegated African Americans to second-class citizenship provoked despair, but also inspired resistance and commitment to change. Chapters on the late nineteenth and early twentieth centuries cover the great migration from the cotton fields of the South to the North and West, black nationalism, and the Harlem Renaissance. Chapters on the 1930s and 1940s—the beginning of a period of revolutionary change for African Americans—tell of the economic devastation and political turmoil caused by the Great Depression, the growing influence of black culture in America, the racial tensions caused by black participation in World War II, and the dawning of the civil rights movement.

The final chapters tell the story of African Americans during the second half of the twentieth century and beginning of the twenty-first century. They portray the successes of the civil rights movement at its peak during the 1950s and 1960s and the efforts of African Americans to build on those successes during the more conservative 1970s, 1980s, and 1990s. Finally, there are discussions of black life at the turn of the twenty-first century and of the continuing impact of African Americans on life in the United States.

In all, *African Americans: A Concise History* tells a compelling story of survival, struggle, and triumph over adversity. It will leave students with an appreciation of the central place of black people and black culture in this country and a better understanding of both African-American and American history.

NEW TO THE SECOND EDITION

For the second edition, we have broadened the text's international perspective, expanded coverage of interaction among African Americans and other ethnic groups, and added new material on African Americans in the western portion of the United States. We have also added a new chapter on the evolution of black politics since the 1980s.

In early chapters there is additional material concerning the growth of the Atlantic slave trade and on black life in New Spain's northern borderlands. There is also an extended comparison of slavery in the American South with slavery in Latin America. African-American interaction with American Indians in the colonial era receives increased attention. We also have more information on African Americans on the western frontier during and after Reconstruction including their often uneasy, if not hostile, relationships with Native Americans. The discussion of black towns in the west has been enhanced. We have added material on black Roman Catholics by including a discussion of the nineteenth-century Healy family.

In chapters dealing with the twentieth century there is a new international account of black migration from the Caribbean. There are also international approaches to the African-American reaction to the Italian invasion of Ethiopia in 1935, to black entertainer and political activist Paul Robeson, and to the HIV/AIDS crisis in Africa and the United States. Our discussion of the Supreme Court's decision in *Brown v. Topeka Board of Education* has been revised and consolidated. The new chapter on late-twentieth twentieth century politics portrays African Americans developing from a special interest group into the core of the Democratic Party. Our final chapter includes broadened coverage of contemporary culture, immigration and ethnic tension, black feminism, black mega-churches, and hip hop.

SPECIAL FEATURES

The special features and pedagogical tools integrated within *African Americans: A Concise History* are designed to make the text accessible to students. They include a variety of tools to reinforce the narrative and help students grasp key issues.

- **Brief chronologies** provide students with a snapshot of the temporal relationship among significant events.
- **End-of-chapter timelines** establish a chronological context for events in African-American history by relating them to events in American history and in the rest of the world.
- **Review questions** encourage students to analyze the material they have read and to explore alternative perspectives on that material.
- **Recommended Reading** and **Additional Bibliography** lists direct students to more information about the subject of each chapter.

SUPPLEMENTARY INSTRUCTIONAL MATERIALS

The supplements that accompany *African Americans: A Concise History* provides instructors and students with resources that combine sound scholarship, engaging content, and a variety of pedagogical tools to enrich the classroom experience and students' understanding of African-American history.

Instructor's Manual with Tests

The Instructor's Manual with Tests provides summaries, outlines, learning objectives, lecture and discussion topics, and audio/visual resources for each chapter. Test materials include multiple choice, essay, identification and short-answer, chronology, and map questions. To help with the assignment of supplementary material offered with the text, the Test Item File includes test questions in multiple choice, true/false and essay format for this material.

History Notes (Volumes I and II)

This student study aid includes a summary for each chapter, reviews key points and concepts, and provides multiple choice, essay, chronology, and map questions.

Documents Set (Volumes I and II)

The *Documents Set* supplements the text with additional primary and secondary source material covering the social, cultural, and political aspects of African-American history. Each reading includes a short historical summary and several review questions. The documents are included on the student CDROM and many are referenced throughout the text with special call outs to call attention to related textual material.

African American Stories

This collection of brief biographical sketches of the many African-American figures represented in the text serves as an indispensable companion to *African Americans*. Students can use this as a reference to learn more about the people who have helped to shape both American and African American history.

Prentice Hall and Penguin Bundle Program

Prentice Hall and Penguin are pleased to provide adopters of *African Americans: A Concise History* with an opportunity to receive significant discounts when orders for *African Americans: A Concise History* are bundled together with Penguin titles in American history. Contact your local Prentice Hall representative for details.

Research Navigator™

This unique resource helps your students make the most of their research time. From finding the right articles and journals, to citing sources, drafting and writing effective papers, and completing research assignments, **Research Navigator**™ simplifies and streamlines the entire process. Access to **Research Navigator**™ is available with every copy of the *OneSearch guide*. For more information, contact your local Prentice Hall representative.

Acknowledgments

Each of us enjoyed the support of family members, particularly Barbara A. Clark, Robbie D. Clark, Emily Harrold, Judy Harrold, Carol A. Hine, Peter J. Hine, Thomas D. Hine, and Alma J. McIntosh.

We gratefully acknowledge the essential help of the superb editorial and production team at Prentice Hall: Charlyce Jones Owen, Vice President and Editorial Director for the Humanities, whose vision got this project started and whose unwavering support saw it through to completion; Editorial Assistant, Maureen Diana; Louise Rothman, Production Editor, who saw it efficiently through production; Stephen Forsling, Photo Researcher; Heather Shelstad, Director of Marketing; Emsal Hasan, Associate Editor, who pulled together the book's supplementary material; and Nick Sklitsis, Manufacturing Manager, Benjamin Smith, Manufacturing Buyer, and Joanne Riker, Managing Editor, who kept the whole team on schedule.

About the Authors

DARLENE CLARK HINE

Darlene Clark Hine is Board of Trustees Professor of African American Studies and Professor of History at Northwestern University. She is past-president of the Organization of American Historians (2001–2002) and of the Southern Historical Association (2002–2003). Hine received her BA at Roosevelt University in Chicago, and her MA and Ph.D. from Kent State University, Kent, Ohio. Hine has taught at South Carolina State University, Purdue University, and at Michigan State University. In 2000–2001 she was a fellow at the Center for Advanced Study in the Behavioral Sciences at Stanford University, and in 2002–2003 she was a fellow at Radcliffe Institute for Advanced Studies. She is the author and/or editor of fifteen books, most recently, with David Barry Gaspar, *Beyond Bondage: Free Women of Color in the Americas* (Urbana: University of Illinois Press, 2004), and *The Harvard Guide to African American History* (Cambridge: Harvard University Press, 2000) coedited with Evelyn Brooks Higginbotham and Leon Litwack. She coedited a two-volume set with Earnestine Jenkins, A *Question of Manhood: A Reader in Black Men's History and Masculinity* (Bloomington: Indiana University Press, 1999, 2001); and with Jacqueline McLeod, *Crossing Boundaries: Comparative History of Black People in Diaspora* (Bloomington: Indiana University Press, 2000pk). With Kathleen Thompson she wrote *A Shining Thread of Hope: The History of Black Women in America* (New York: Broadway Books, 1998), and edited with Barry Gaspar, *More Than Chattel: Black Women and Slavery in the Americas* (Bloomington: Indiana University Press, 1996). She won the Dartmouth Medal of the American Library Association for the reference volumes coedited with Elsa Barkley Brown and Rosalyn Terborg-Penn, *Black Women in America: An Historical Encyclopedia* (New York: Carlson Publishing, 1993). She is the author of *Black Women in White: Racial Conflict and Cooperation in the Nursing Profession, 1890–1950* (Bloomington: Indiana University Press, 1989). Her forthcoming book is entitled *Black Professional Class and Race Consciousness: Physicians, Nurses, Lawyers, and the Origins of the Civil Rights Movement, 1890–1955.*

WILLIAM C. HINE

William C. Hine received his undergraduate education at Bowling Green State University, his master's degree at the University of Wyoming, and his Ph.D. at Kent State University. He is a professor of history at South Carolina State University. He has had articles published in several journals, including *Agricultural History, Labor History,* and the *Journal of Southern History.* He is currently writing a history of South Carolina State University.

STANLEY HARROLD

Stanley Harrold, Professor of History at South Carolina State University, received his bachelor's degree from Allegheny College and his master's and Ph.D. degrees from Kent State University. He is coeditor with Randall M. Miller of *Southern Dissent*, a book series published by the University Press of Florida. He received during the 1990s two National Endowment for the Humanities Fellowships to pursue research dealing with the antislavery movement. His books include: *Gamaliel Bailey and Antislavery Union* (Kent, Ohio: Kent State University Press, 1986), *The Abolitionists and the South* (Lexington: University Press of Kentucky, 1995), *Antislavery Violence: Sectional, Racial, and Cultural Conflict in Antebellum America* (co-edited with John R. McKivigan, Knoxville: University of Tennessee Press, 1999), *American Abolitionists* (Harlow, U.K.: Longman, 2001); *Subversives: Antislavery Community in Washington, D.C., 1828–1865* (Baton Rouge: Louisiana State University Press, 2003), and *The Rise of Aggressive Abolitionism: Addresses to the Slaves* (Lexington: University Press of Kentucky, 2004). He has published articles in *Civil War History, Journal of Southern History, Radical History Review,* and *Journal of the Early Republic.*

CHAPTER TWELVE

THE MEANING OF FREEDOM

THE PROMISE OF RECONSTRUCTION, 1865–1868

THE END OF SLAVERY

With the collapse of slavery, many black people were quick to inform white people that whatever loyalty, devotion, and cooperation they might have shown as slaves had never been a reflection of their inner feelings and attitudes. Near Opelousas, Louisiana, a Union officer asked a young black man why he did not love his master, and the youth responded sharply, "When my master begins to lub me, den it'll be time enough for me to lub him. What I wants is to get away. I want to take me off from dis plantation, where I can be free."

In North Carolina, planter Robert P. Howell was deeply disappointed that a loyal slave named Lovet fled at the first opportunity. "He was about my age and I had always treated him more as a companion than a slave. When I left I put everything in his charge, told him that he was free, but to remain on the place and take care of things. He promised me faithfully that he would, but he was the first one to leave . . . and I did not see him for several years."

Emancipation was a traumatic experience for many former masters. A Virginia freedman remembered that "Miss Polly died right after the surrender, she was so hurt that all the negroes was going to be free." Another former slave, Robert Falls, recalled that his master assembled the slaves to inform them they were free. "I hates to do it, but I must. You all ain't my niggers no more. You is free. Just as free as I am. Here I have raised you all to work for me, and now you are going to leave me. I am an old man, and I can't get along without you. I don't know what I am going to do." In less than a year, he was dead. Falls attributed his master's death to the end of slavery. "It killed him."

Differing Reactions of Former Slaves

Other slaves bluntly displayed their reaction to years of bondage. Aunt Delia, a cook with a North Carolina family, revealed that for a long time she had secretly gained retribution for the indignity of servitude. "How many times I spit in the biscuits and peed in the coffee just to get back at them mean white folks." In Goodman, Mississippi, a slave named Caddy learned she was free and rushed from the field to find her owner. "Caddy threw down that hoe, she marched herself up to the big house, then, she looked around and found the mistress. She went over to the mistress, she flipped up

225

her dress and told the white woman to do something. She said it mean and ugly. This is what she said: 'Kiss my ass!'"

In contrast, some slaves, especially elderly ones, were fearful and apprehensive about freedom. On a South Carolina plantation, an older black woman refused to accept emancipation. "I ain' no free nigger! I is got a marster and mistiss! Dee right dar in de great house. Ef you don' b'lieve me, you go dar an' see."

Reuniting Black Families

As slavery ended, the most urgent need for many freed people was finding family members who had been sold away from them. Slavery had not destroyed the black family. Husbands, wives, and children went to great lengths to reassemble their families after the Civil War. For years and even decades after the end of slavery, advertisements appeared in black newspapers appealing for information about missing kinfolk. The following notice was published in the *Colored Tennessean* on August 5, 1865:

> Saml. Dove wishes to know of the whereabouts of his mother, Areno, his sisters Maria, Neziah and Peggy, and his brother Edmond, who were owned by Geo. Dove of Rockingham County, Shenandoah Valley, Va. Sold in Richmond, after which Saml. and Edmond were taken to Nashville, Tenn., by Joe Mick; Areno was left at the Eagle Tavern, Richmond. Respectfully yours, Saml. Dove, Utica, New York.

In North Carolina a northern journalist met a middle-age black man "plodding along, staff in hand, and apparently very footsore and tired." The nearly exhausted freedman explained that he had walked almost six hundred miles looking for his wife and children who had been sold four years earlier.

There were emotional reunions as family members found each other after years of separation. Ben and Betty Dodson had been apart for twenty years when Ben found her in a refugee camp after the war. "Glory! glory! hallelujah," he shouted as he hugged his wife. "Dis is my Betty, shuah. I foun' you at las'. I's hunted and hunted till I track you up here. I's boun' to hunt till I fin' you if you's alive."

Other searches had more heart-wrenching results. Husbands and wives sometimes learned that their spouses had remarried during the separation. Believing his wife had died, the husband of Laura Spicer remarried—only to learn after the war that Laura was still alive. Sadly, he wrote to her but refused to meet with her. "I would come and see you but I know I could not bear it. I want to see you and I don't want to see you. I love you just as well as I did the last day I saw you, and it will not do for you and I to meet."

Tormented, he wrote again pledging his love. "Laura I do not think that I have change any at all since I saw you last—I thinks of you and my children every day of my life. Laura I do love you the same. My love to you never have failed. Laura, truly, I have got another wife, and I am very sorry that I am. You feels and seems to me as much like my dear loving wife, as you ever did Laura."

One freedman testified to the close ties that bound many slave families when he replied bitterly to the claim that he had had a kind master who had fed him and never used the whip. "Kind! yes, he gib men corn enough, and he gib me pork enough, and he neber gib me one lick wid de whip, but whar's my wife?—whar's my chill'en? Take away de pork, I say; take away de corn, I can work and raise dese for myself, but gib me back de wife of my bosom, and gib me back my poor chill'en as was sold away."

LAND

As freed people embraced freedom and left their masters, they wanted land. Nineteenth-century Americans of virtually every background associated economic security with owning land. Families wanted to work land and prosper as self-sufficient yeomen. Former slaves believed their future as a free people was tied to the possession of land. But just as it had been impossible to abolish slavery without the intervention of the U.S. government, it would not be possible to procure land without federal assistance. At first, federal authorities seemed determined to make land available to freedmen.

Special Field Order #15

Shortly after his army arrived in Savannah—after having devastated Georgia—Union general William T. Sherman announced that freedmen would receive land. On January 16, 1865, he issued Special Field Order #15. This military directive set aside a 30-mile-wide tract of land along the Atlantic coast from Charleston, South Carolina, 245 miles south to Jacksonville, Florida. White owners had abandoned the land, and Sherman reserved it for black families. The head of each family would receive "possessory title" to forty acres of land. Sherman also gave the freedmen the use of army mules, thus giving rise to the slogan, "Forty acres and a mule."

Former slaves assembled in a village near Washington, D.C. Black people welcomed emancipation, but without land, education, or employment, they faced an uncertain future.
Courtesy of the Library of Congress

Within six months, forty thousand freed people were working 400,000 acres in the South Carolina and Georgia low country and on the Sea Islands. Former slaves generally avoided the slave crops of cotton and rice and instead planted sweet potatoes and corn. They also worked together as families and kinfolk. They avoided the gang labor associated with slavery. Most husbands and fathers preferred that their wives and daughters not work in the fields as slave women had had to do.

The Port Royal Experiment

Meanwhile, hundreds of former slaves had been cultivating land for three years. In late 1861 Union military forces carved out an enclave around Beaufort and Port Royal, South Carolina, that remained under federal authority for the rest of the war. White planters fled to the interior, leaving their slaves behind. Under the supervision of U.S. Treasury officials and northern reformers and missionaries who hurried south in 1862, ex-slaves began to work the land in what came to be known as the "Port Royal Experiment." When Treasury agents auctioned off portions of the land for nonpayment of taxes, freedmen purchased some of it. But northern businessmen bought most of the real estate and then hired black people to raise cotton.

White owners sometimes returned to their former lands only to find that black families had taken charge. A group of black farmers told one former owner, "We own this land now, put it out of your head that it will ever be yours again." And on one South Carolina Sea Island, white men were turned back by armed black men.

THE FREEDMEN'S BUREAU

As the war ended in early 1865, Congress created the Bureau of Refugees, Freedmen, and Abandoned Lands—commonly called the Freedmen's Bureau. Created as a temporary agency to assist freedmen to make the transition to freedom, the bureau was placed under the control of the U.S. Army and General Oliver O. Howard was put in command. Howard, a devout Christian who had lost an arm in the war, was eager to aid the freedmen.

The bureau was given enormous responsibilities. It was to help freedmen obtain land, gain an education, negotiate labor contracts with white planters, settle legal and criminal disputes involving black and white people, and provide food, medical care, and transportation for black and white people left destitute by the war. However, Congress never provided sufficient funds or personnel to carry out these tasks.

The Freedmen's Bureau never had more than nine hundred agents spread across the South from Virginia to Texas. Mississippi, for example, had twelve agents in 1866. One agent often served a county with a population of ten thousand to twenty thousand freedmen. Few of the agents were black because few military officers were black. John Mercer Langston of Virginia was an inspector of schools assigned to the bureau's main office in Washington, D.C.; Major Martin R. Delany worked with freedmen on the South Carolina Sea Islands.

The need for assistance was desperate as thousands of black and white Southerners endured extreme privation in the months after the war ended. The bureau established camps for the homeless, fed the hungry, and cared for orphans and the sick as best it could. It distributed more than thirteen million rations—consisting of flour, corn meal, and sugar—by 1866. The bureau provided medical care to a half million freedmen and thousands of white people who were suffering from smallpox, yellow fever, cholera, and pneumonia. Many more remained untreated.

In July 1865 the bureau took a first step toward distributing land when General Howard issued Circular 13 ordering agents to "set aside" forty-acre plots for freedmen. But the allocation had hardly begun when the order was revoked, and it was announced that land already distributed under General Sherman's Special Field Order #15 was to be returned to its previous white owners.

The reason for this reversal in policy was that President Andrew Johnson, who had become president after Lincoln's assassination in April 1865, began to pardon hundreds and then thousands of former Confederates and restore their lands to them. General Howard was forced to tell black people that they had to relinquish the land they thought they had acquired. In a speech before some two thousand freedmen on South Carolina's Edisto Island in October 1865, Howard pleaded with his audience to "lay aside their bitter feelings, and to become reconciled to their old masters." A black

OFFICE OF THE FREEDMEN'S BUREAU, MEMPHIS, TENNESSEE.
[See Page 346.]

Freedmen's Bureau agents often found themselves in the middle of angry disputes over land and labor that erupted between black and white Southerners. Too often the Bureau officers sided with the white landowners in these disagreements with former slaves.
Harper's Weekly, June 2, 1866.

man shouted a response, "Why, General Howard, why do you take away our lands? You take them from us who are true, always true to the Government! You give them to our all-time enemies. This is not right!"

A committee rejected Howard's appeal for reconciliation and forgiveness and they insisted the government provide land:

> You ask us to forgive the landowners of our island. You only lost your right arm in war and might forgive them. The man who tied me to a tree and gave me 39 lashes and who stripped and flogged my mother and my sister and who will not let me stay in his empty hut except I will do his planting and be satisfied with his price and who combines with others to keep away land from me well knowing I would not have anything to do with him if I had land of my own—that man I cannot well forgive.

Howard was moved by these appeals. He returned to Washington and attempted to persuade Congress to make land available. Congress refused, and President Johnson was determined that white people would get their lands back. It seemed so sensible to most white people. Property that had belonged to white families for generations simply could not be given to freedmen. Freedmen saw matters differently. They deserved land that they and their families had worked without compensation for generations. Freedmen believed it was the only way to make freedom meaningful and to gain independence from white people. As it turned out, most freedmen were forced off land they thought should belong to them.

Southern Homestead Act

In early 1866 Congress attempted to provide land for freedmen with the passage of the Southern Homestead Act. More than three million acres of public land were set aside for black people and southern white people who had remained loyal to the Union. Much of this land, however, was unsuitable for farming and consisted of swampy wetlands or unfertile pinewoods. More than four thousand black families—three-quarters of them in Florida—did claim some of this land, but many of them lacked the financial resources to cultivate it. Eventually southern timber companies acquired much of it, and the Southern Homestead Act largely failed.

Sharecropping

To make matters worse, by 1866 bureau officials tried to force freedmen to sign labor contracts with white landowners—putting black people once again under white authority. Black men who refused to sign contracts could be arrested. Theoretically, these contracts were legal agreements between two equals: landowner and laborer. But they were seldom freely concluded. Bureau agents usually sided with the landowner and pressured freedmen to accept unequal terms.

Occasionally, the landowner would pay wages to the laborer. But because most landowners lacked cash to pay wages, they agreed to provide the laborer with part of the crop. The laborer, often grudgingly, agreed to work under the supervision of the landowner. The contracts required labor for a full year; the laborer could neither quit nor strike. Landowners demanded that the laborers work the fields in gangs. Freedmen resisted this system. They sometimes insisted on making decisions involving planting, fertilizing, and harvesting as they sought to exercise independence.

Thus it took time for a new form of agricultural labor to develop. But by the 1870s, the system of sharecropping had emerged and dominated most of the South. There were no wages. Freedmen worked land as families—not in gangs—and not under direct white supervision. When the landowner provided seed, tools, fertilizer, and work animals (mules, horses, oxen), the black family received one-third of the crop. There were many variations on these arrangements, and frequently black families were cheated out of their fair share of the crop.

THE BLACK CHURCH

In the years after slavery, the church became the most important institution among African Americans other than the family. Not only did it fill deep spiritual and inspirational needs, it offered enriching music, provided charity and compassion to those in need, developed community and political leaders, and was free of white supervision. Before slavery's demise, free black people and slaves often attended white churches where they were encouraged to participate in religious services conducted by white clergymen and where they were treated as second-class Christians.

Once liberated, black men and women organized their own churches with their own ministers. Most black people considered white ministers incapable of delivering a meaningful message. Nancy Williams recalled, "Ole white preachers used to talk wid dey tongues widdout sayin' nothin', but Jesus told us slaves to talk wid our hearts."

Northern white missionaries were sometimes appalled by the unlettered and ungrammatical black preachers who nevertheless communicated effectively and emotionally with their parishioners. A visiting white clergyman was genuinely impressed and humbled on hearing a black preacher who lacked education, but more than made up for it with devout faith. "He talked about Christ and his salvation as one who understood what he said. . . . Here was an unlearned man, one who could not read, telling of the love of Christ, of Christian faith and duty in a way which I have not learned."

Other black and white religious leaders anguished over what they considered moral laxity and displaced values among the freed people. They preached about honesty, thrift, temperance, and elimination of sexual promiscuity. They demanded an end to "rum-suckers, bar-room loafers, whiskey dealers and card players among the men, and to those women who dressed finely on ill gotten gain."

Church members struggled, scrimped, and saved to buy land and to build churches. Most former slaves founded Baptist and Methodist churches. These denominations tended to be more autonomous and less subject to outside control. Their doctrine was usually simple and direct without complex theology. Of the Methodist churches, the African Methodist Episcopal (AME) church made giant strides in the South after the Civil War.

In Charleston, South Carolina, the AME church was resurrected after an absence of more than forty years. In 1822, during the turmoil over the Denmark Vesey plot, the AME church was forced to disband and its leader had to flee (see Chapter 8). But by the 1870s, three AME congregations were thriving in Charleston. In Wilmington,

North Carolina, the sixteen hundred members of the Front Street Methodist Church decided to join the AME church soon after the Civil War ended. They replaced the longtime white minister, the Reverend L. S. Burkhead, with a black man.

White Methodists initially encouraged cooperation with black Methodists and helped establish the Colored (now Christian) Methodist Episcopal church (CME). But the white Methodists lost some of their fervor after they tried but failed to persuade the black Methodists to keep political issues out of the CME church and to dwell solely on spiritual concerns.

The Presbyterian, Congregational, and Episcopal churches appealed to the more prosperous members of the black community. Their services tended to be more formal and solemn. Black people who had been free before the Civil War were usually affiliated with these congregations and remained so after the conflict. Well-to-do free black people in Charleston organized St. Mark's Protestant Episcopal Church when they separated from the white Episcopal church. But they retained their white minister Joseph Seabrook as rector. Poorer black people of darker complexion found churches like St. Mark's decidedly unappealing. Ed Barber visited, but only one time.

> When I was trampin' 'round Charleston, dere was a church dere called St. Mark, dat all de society folks of my color went to. No black nigger welcome dere, they told me. Thinkin' as how I was bright 'nough to git in, I up and goes dere one Sunday, Ah, how they did carry on, bow and scrape and ape de white folks. . . . I was uncomfortable all de time though, 'cause they were too "hifalootin" in de ways, in de singin', and all sorts of carryin' ons.

The Roman Catholic Church made modest in-roads among black Southerners. There were all-black parishes in St. Augustine, Savannah, Charleston, and Louisville after the Civil War. For generations prior to the conflict, large numbers of well-to-do free people of color in New Orleans had been practicing Catholics, and their descendants remained faithful to the church. On Georgia's Skidaway Island, Benedictine monks established a school for black youngsters in 1878 that survived for nearly a decade.

This unidentified photograph depicts the quality of housing that most former slaves inhabited in the decades after the Civil War. The black family shown here is attired in their best clothes as they pose for the photograph.
Courtesy of the Library of Congress

Religious differences among black people not-withstanding, the black churches, their parishioners, and clergymen would play a vital role in Reconstruction politics. More than one hundred black ministers were elected to political office after the Civil War.

EDUCATION

Freedom and education were inseparable. To remain illiterate after emancipation was to remain enslaved. One ex-slave master bluntly told his former slave, Charles Whiteside, "Charles, you is a free man they say, but Ah tells you now, you is still a slave and if you lives to be a hundred, you'll STILL be a slave, cause you got no education, and education is what makes a man free!"

Almost every freed black person—young or old—desperately wanted to learn. Elderly people were especially eager to read the Bible. Even before slavery ended, black people began to establish schools. In 1861 Mary Peake, a free black woman, opened a school in Hampton, Virginia. On South Carolina's Sea Islands, a black cabinetmaker began teaching openly after having covertly operated a school for years. In 1862 northern missionaries arrived on the Sea Islands to begin teaching. Laura Towne, a white woman, and Charlotte Forten, a black woman, opened a school on St. Helena's Island as part of the Port Royal Experiment. They enrolled 138 children and 58 adults. By 1863 there were 1,700 students and 45 teachers at 30 schools in the South Carolina low country.

With the end of the Civil War, northern religious organizations in cooperation with the Freedmen's Bureau organized hundreds of day and night schools. Classes were held in stables, homes, former slave cabins, taverns, churches, and even—in Savannah and New Orleans—in the old slave markets. Former slaves spent hours in the fields and then trudged to a makeshift school to learn the alphabet and arithmetic. In 1865 black ministers created the Savannah Educational Association, raised $1,000, employed fifteen black teachers, and enrolled six hundred students.

In 1866 the Freedmen's Bureau set aside $500,000 for education. The bureau furnished the buildings while former slaves hired, housed, and fed the teachers. By 1869 the Freedmen's Bureau was involved with 3,000 schools and 150,000 students. Even more impressive, by 1870 black people had contributed $1 million to educate their people.

Black Teachers

Although freedmen appreciated the dedication and devotion of the white teachers affiliated with the missionary societies, they usually preferred black teachers. The Reverend Richard H. Cain, an AME minister who came south from Brooklyn, New York, said that black people needed to learn to control their own futures. "We must take into our own hands the education of our race. . . . Honest, dignified whites may teach ever so well, but it has not the effect to exalt the black man's opinion of his own race, because they have always been in the habit of seeing white men in honored positions, and respected."

Black men and women responded to the call to teach. Virginia C. Green, a northern black woman, felt compelled to go to Mississippi. "Though I have never known servitude they are . . . my people. Born as far north as the lakes I have felt no freer because so many were less fortunate. . . . I look forward with impatience to the time when my people shall be strong, blest with education, purified and made prosperous by virtue and industry." Hezekiah Hunter, a black teacher from Brooklyn, New York, commented in 1865 on the need for black teachers. "I believe we best can instruct our own people, knowing our own peculiarities—needs—necessities. Further—I believe we that are competent owe it to our people to teach them our speciality." And in Malden, West Virginia, when black residents found that a recently arrived eighteen-year-old black man could read and write, they promptly hired him to teach.

In some areas of the South, the sole person available to teach was a poorly educated former slave equipped primarily with a willingness to teach his or her fellow freedmen. One such teacher explained, "I never had the chance of goen to school for I was a slave until freedom. . . . I am the only teacher because we can not doe better now." Many northern teachers, black and white, provided more than the basics of elementary education. Black life and history were occasionally read about and discussed. Abolitionist Lydia Maria Child wrote *The Freedmen's Book*, which offered short biographies of Benjamin Banneker, Frederick Douglass, and Toussaint Louverture. More often northern teachers, dismayed at the backwardness of the freedmen, struggled to modify behavior and to impart cultural values by teaching piety, thrift, cleanliness, temperance, and timeliness.

Many former slaves came to resent some of these teachers as condescending, selfrighteous, and paternalistic. Sometimes the teachers, especially those who were white, became frustrated with recalcitrant students who did not readily absorb middle-class values. Others, however, derived enormous satisfaction from teaching freedmen. A Virginia teacher commented, "I think I shall stay here as long as I live and teach this people. I have no love or taste for any other work, and I am happy only here with them."

Black Colleges

Northern churches and religious societies established dozens of colleges, universities, academies, and institutes across the South in the late 1860s and the 1870s (see Map 12–1). Most of these institutions provided elementary and secondary education. Few black students were prepared for actual college or university work. The American Missionary Association—an abolitionist and Congregationalist organization—worked with the Freedmen's Bureau to establish Berea in Kentucky, Fisk in Tennessee, Hampton in Virginia, Tougaloo in Alabama, and Avery in South Carolina. The primary purpose of these schools was to educate black students to become teachers.

In Missouri, the black enlisted men and the white officers of the 62nd and 65th Colored Volunteers raised $6,000 to establish Lincoln Institute in 1866, which would become Lincoln University. The American Baptist Home Mission Society founded Virginia Union, Shaw in North Carolina, Benedict in South Carolina, and Morehouse in Georgia. Northern Methodists helped establish Claflin in South Carolina, Rust in Mississippi, and Bennett in North Carolina. The Episcopalians were responsible for St. Augustine's in North Carolina and St. Paul's in Virginia. These and many other similar institutions formed the foundation for the historically black colleges and universities.

MAP 12–1   The Location of Black Colleges Founded before and during Reconstruction.
Three black colleges were founded before the Civil War. In Pennsylvania, Cheyney University opened in 1837, and it was followed by the establishment of Lincoln University in 1854. In 1856, Wilberforce University was founded in Ohio. After the Civil War, northern black and white missionary groups fanned out across the South and—frequently with the assistance of Freedmen's Bureau officials—founded colleges, institutes, and normal schools in the former slave states.

Response of White Southerners

White Southerners considered efforts by black people to learn absurd. For generations, white Americans had looked on people of African descent as abjectly inferior. When significant efforts were made to educate former slaves, white Southerners reacted with suspicion, contempt, and hostility. One white woman told a teacher, "I do assure you, you might as well try to teach your horse or mule to read, as to teach these niggers. They can't learn."

Most white people were well aware that black people could learn. Otherwise, the slave codes that prohibited educating slaves would have been unnecessary. After slavery's end, some white people went out of their way to prevent black people from learning. Countless schools were burned, mostly in rural areas. In Canton, Mississippi, black people collected money to open a school—only to have white residents inform them that the school would be burned and the prospective teacher lynched if it opened. The female teacher at a freedmen's school in Donaldsonville, Louisiana, was shot and killed.

Other white Southerners grudgingly tolerated the desire of black people to acquire an education. One planter bitterly conceded in 1870, "Every little negro in the county is now going to school and the public pays for it. This is one hell of [a] fix but we can't help it, and the best policy is to conform as far as possible to circumstances."

Most white people adamantly refused to attend school with black people. No integrated schools were established in the immediate aftermath of emancipation. Most black people were more interested in gaining an education than in caring whether white students attended school with them. When black youngsters tried to attend a white school in Raleigh, North Carolina, the white students stopped going to it. For a brief time in Charleston, South Carolina, black and white children attended the same school, but they were taught in separate classrooms.

VIOLENCE

In the days, weeks, and months after the end of the Civil War, an orgy of brutality and violence swept across the South. White Southerners—embittered by their crushing defeat and unable to adjust to the end of slave labor and the loss of millions of dollars worth of slave property—lashed out at black people. There were beatings, murders, rapes, and riots, often with little or no provocation.

Black people who demanded respect, wore better clothing, refused to step aside for white people, or asked to be addressed as "mister" or "missus" were attacked. In South Carolina, a white clergyman shot and killed a black man who protested when another black man was removed from a church service. In Texas, one black man was killed because he failed to remove his hat in the presence of a white man and another for refusing to relinquish a bottle of whiskey. A black woman was beaten for "using insolent language," and a black worker in Alabama was killed for speaking sharply to a white overseer. In Virginia, a black veteran was beaten after announcing he had been proud to serve in the Union Army.

In South Carolina, a white man asked a passing black man whom he belonged to. The black man replied that he no longer belonged to anybody. "I am free now." With that, the white man roared, "Sas me? You black devil!" He then slashed the freedman with a knife, seriously injuring him. The sheriff of DeWitt County, Texas, shot a black man who was whistling "Yankee Doodle." A Freedmen's Bureau agent in North Carolina explained the intense white hostility. "The fact is, it's the first notion with a great many of these people, if a Negro says anything or does anything that they don't like, to take a gun and put a bullet into him, or a charge of shot." In Texas another Freedmen's Bureau officer claimed that white people simply killed black people "for the love of killing."

There was also large-scale violence. In 1865 University of North Carolina students twice attacked peaceful meetings of black people. Near Pine Bluff, Arkansas, in 1866, a white mob burned a black settlement and lynched twenty-four men, women, and children. An estimated two thousand black people were murdered around Shreveport, Louisiana. In Texas, white people killed one thousand black people between 1865 and 1868.

In May 1866 in Memphis, white residents went on a brutal rampage after black veterans forced local police to release a black prisoner. The city was already beset with economic difficulties and racial tensions caused in part by an influx of rural refugees. White people, led by Irish policemen, invaded the black section of Memphis and destroyed hundreds of homes, cabins, and shacks as well as churches and schools. Forty-six black people and two white men died.

On July 30, 1866, in New Orleans, white people—angered that black men were demanding political rights—assaulted black people on the street and in a convention hall. City policemen, who were mostly Confederate veterans, shot down the black delegates as they fled in panic waving white flags in a futile attempt to surrender. Thirty-four black people and three of their white allies died. Federal troops eventually arrived and stopped the bloodshed. General Philip H. Sheridan characterized the riot as "an absolute massacre."

Little was done to stem the violence. Most Union troops had been withdrawn from the South and demobilized after the war. The Freedmen's Bureau was usually unwilling and unable to protect the black population. Black people left to defend themselves were usually in no position to retaliate. Instead, they sometimes attempted to bring the perpetrators to justice. In Orangeburg, South Carolina, armed black men brought three white men to the local jail who had been wreaking violence in the community. In Holly Springs, Mississippi, a posse of armed black men apprehended a white man who had murdered a freedwoman.

For black people, the system of justice was thoroughly unjust. Although black people could now testify against white people in a court of law, southern juries remained

Black and white land-grant colleges stressed training in agriculture and industry. In this late-nineteenth-century photograph, Hampton Institute students learn milk production. The men are in military uniforms, which was typical for males at these colleges. Military training was a required part of the curriculum.
Courtesy of Hampton University Archives

all white and refused to convict white people charged with harming black people. In Texas in 1865 and 1866, five hundred white men were indicted for murdering black people. Not one was convicted.

THE CRUSADE FOR POLITICAL AND CIVIL RIGHTS

In October 1864 in Syracuse, New York, 145 black leaders gathered in a national convention. Some of the century's most prominent black men and women attended, including Henry Highland Garnet, Frances E. W. Harper, William Wells Brown, Francis L. Cardozo, Richard H. Cain, Jonathan J. Wright, and Jonathan C. Gibbs. They embraced the basic tenets of the American political tradition and proclaimed that they expected to participate fully in it.

Anticipating a future free of slavery, Frederick Douglass optimistically declared "that we hereby assert our full confidence in the fundamental principles of this government . . . the great heart of this nation will ultimately concede us our just claims, accord us our rights, and grant us our full measure of citizenship under the broad shield of the Constitution."

Even before the Syracuse gathering, northern Republicans met in Union-controlled territory around Beaufort, South Carolina, and nominated the state's delegates to the 1864 Republican national convention. Among those selected were Robert Smalls and Prince Rivers, former slaves who had exemplary records with the Union Army. The probability of black participation in postwar politics seemed promising indeed.

But northern and southern white leaders who already held power would largely determine whether black Americans would gain any political power or acquire the same rights as white people. As the Civil War ended, President Lincoln was more concerned with restoring the seceded states to the Union than in opening political doors for black people. Yet Lincoln suggested that at least some black men deserved the right to vote. On April 11, 1865, he wrote, "I would myself prefer that [the vote] were now conferred on the very intelligent, and on those who serve our cause as soldiers." Three days later Lincoln was assassinated.

PRESIDENTIAL RECONSTRUCTION
UNDER ANDREW JOHNSON

Vice President Andrew Johnson then became president and initially seemed inclined to impose stern policies on the white South while befriending the freedmen. He announced that "treason must be made odious, and traitors must be punished and impoverished." In 1864 he had told black people, "I will be your Moses, and lead you through the Red Sea of War and Bondage to a fairer future of Liberty and Peace." Nothing proved to be further from the truth. Andrew Johnson was no friend of black Americans.

Born poor in eastern Tennessee and never part of the southern aristocracy, Johnson strongly opposed secession and was the only senator from the seceded states to remain loyal to the Union. He had nonetheless acquired five slaves and the conviction that black people were so thoroughly inferior that white men must forever govern them. In 1867 Johnson argued that black people could not exercise political power and they had "less capacity for government than any other race of people. No independent government of any form has ever been successful in their hands. On the contrary, wherever they have been left to their own devices they have shown a constant tendency to relapse into barbarism."

Johnson quickly lost his enthusiasm for punishing traitors. Indeed, he began to placate white Southerners. In May 1865 Johnson granted blanket amnesty and pardons to former Confederates willing to swear allegiance to the United States. The main exceptions were high former Confederate officials and those who owned property in excess of $20,000, a large sum at the time. Yet even these leaders could appeal for individual pardons. And appeal they did. By 1866 Johnson had pardoned more than seven thousand high-ranking former Confederates and wealthier Southerners. Moreover, he had restored land to those white people who had lost it to freedmen.

Johnson's actions blatantly encouraged those who had supported secession, owned slaves, and opposed the Union. He permitted longtime southern leaders to regain political influence and authority only months after the end of America's bloodiest conflict. As black people and radical Republicans watched in disbelief, Johnson appointed provisional governors in the former Confederate states. Leaders in those states then called constitutional conventions, held elections, and prepared to regain their place in the Union. Johnson merely insisted that each Confederate state formally accept the Thirteenth Amendment (ratified in December 1865, it outlawed slavery) and repudiate Confederate war debts.

The southern constitutional conventions gave no consideration to the inclusion of black people in the political system or to guaranteeing them equal rights. As one Mississippi delegate explained, "'Tis nature's law that the superior race must rule and rule they will."

BLACK CODES

After the election of state and local officials, white legislators gathered in state capitals across the South to determine the status and future of the freedmen. With little debate, the legislatures drafted the so-called black codes. Southern politicians gave no thought to providing black people with the political and legal rights associated with citizenship.

The black codes sought to ensure the availability of a subservient agricultural labor supply controlled by white people. They imposed severe restrictions on freedmen. Freedmen had to sign annual labor contracts with white landowners. South Carolina required black people who wanted to establish a business to purchase licenses costing from $10 to $100. The codes permitted black children ages two to twenty-one to be apprenticed to white people and spelled out their duties and obligations in detail. Corporal punishment was legal. Employers were designated "masters" and employees "servants." The black codes also restricted black people from loitering or vagrancy, using alcohol or firearms, hunting, fishing, and grazing livestock. The codes did guarantee rights that slaves had not possessed. Freedmen could marry legally, engage in contracts, purchase property, sue or be sued, and testify in court. But black people could not vote or serve on juries. The black codes conceded—just barely—freedom to black people.

BLACK CONVENTIONS

Alarmed by these threats to their freedom, black people met in conventions across the South in 1865 and 1866 to protest, appeal for justice, and chart their future. Men who had been free before the war dominated the conventions. Many were ministers, teachers, and artisans. Few had been slaves. Women and children also attended—as spectators, not delegates—but women often offered comments, suggestions, and criticism. These meetings were hardly militant or radical affairs. Delegates respectfully insisted that white people live up to the principles and rights embodied in the Declaration of Independence and the Constitution.

At the AME church in Raleigh, North Carolina, delegates asked for equal rights and the right to vote. At Georgia's convention they protested against white violence and appealed for leaders who would enforce the law without regard to color. "We ask not for a Black Man's Governor, nor a White Man's Governor, but for a People's Governor, who shall impartially protect the rights of all, and faithfully sustain the Union."

Delegates at the Norfolk meeting reminded white Virginians that black people were patriotic. "We are Americans. We know no other country. We love the land of our birth." But they protested that Virginia's black code caused "invidious political or legal distinctions, on account of color merely." They requested the right to vote and added that they might boycott the businesses of "those who deny to us our equal rights."

Two conventions were held in Charleston, South Carolina—one before and one after the black code was enacted. At the first, delegates stressed the "respect and affection" they felt toward white Charlestonians. They even proposed that only literate men be granted the right to vote if it were genuinely applied to both races. The second convention denounced the black code and insisted on its repeal. Delegates again asked for the right to vote and the right to testify in court. "These two things we deem necessary to our welfare and elevation." They also appealed for public schools and for "homesteads for ourselves and our children." White authorities ignored these and other black conventions and their petitions. Instead they were confident they had effectively relegated the freedmen to a subordinate role in society.

By late 1865 President Johnson's reconstruction policies had aroused black people. One black Union veteran summed up the situation. "If you call this Freedom, what do you call Slavery?" Republicans in Congress also opposed Johnson's policies toward the freedmen and the former Confederate states.

THE RADICAL REPUBLICANS

Radical Republicans, as more militant Republicans were called, were especially disturbed that Johnson seemed to have abandoned the ex-slaves to their former masters. They considered white Southerners disloyal and unrepentant, despite their military defeat.

Moreover, radical Republicans—unlike moderate Republicans and Democrats—were determined to transform the racial fabric of American society by including black people in the political and economic system.

Among the most influential radical Republicans were Charles Sumner, Benjamin Wade, and Henry Wilson in the Senate and Thaddeus Stevens, George W. Julian, and James M. Ashley in the House. Few white Americans have been as dedicated to the rights of black people as these men. They had fought for the abolition of slavery. They were reluctant to compromise. They were honest, tough, and articulate but also abrasive, difficult, self-righteous, and vain. Black people appreciated them; many white people excoriated them. One black veteran wrote Charles Sumner in 1869, "Your name shall live in our hearts forever." A white Philadelphia businessman commented on Thaddeus Stevens, "He seems to oppose any measure that will not benefit the nigger."

Bearing a remarkable resemblance to a slave auction, this scene in Monticello, Florida, shows a black man auctioned off to the highest bidder shortly after the Civil War. Under the terms of most southern black codes, black people arrested and fined for vagrancy or loitering could be "sold" if they could not pay the fine. Such spectacles infuriated many Northerners and led to demands for more rigid Reconstruction policies.
The Granger Collection, New York

Radical Proposals

Stevens, determined to provide freedmen with land, introduced a bill in Congress in late 1865 to confiscate 400 million acres from the wealthiest 10 percent of Southerners and distribute it free to freedmen. The remaining land would be auctioned off in plots no larger than 500 acres. Few legislators supported the proposal. Even those who wanted fundamental change considered confiscation a gross violation of property rights.

Instead, radical Republicans supported voting rights for black men. They were convinced that black men—to protect themselves and to secure the South for the Republican Party—had to have the right to vote.

Moderate Republicans, however, found the prospect of black voting almost as objectionable as the confiscation of land. They preferred to build the Republican Party in the South by cooperating with President Johnson and attracting loyal white Southerners.

The thought of black suffrage appalled northern and southern Democrats. Most white Northerners—Republicans and Democrats—favored denying black men the right to vote in their states. After the war, proposals to guarantee the right to vote to black men were defeated in New York, Ohio, Kansas, and the Nebraska Territory. In the District of Columbia, a vote to permit black suffrage lost 6,951 to 35. However, five New England states as well as Iowa, Minnesota, and Wisconsin did allow black men to vote.

As much as they objected to black suffrage, most white Northerners objected even more strongly to defiant white Southerners. Journalist Charles A. Dana described the attitude of many Northerners. "As for negro suffrage, the mass of Union men in the Northwest do not care a great deal. What scares them is the idea that the rebels are all to be let back . . . and made a power in government again, just as though there had been no rebellion."

In December 1865 Congress created the Joint Committee on Reconstruction to determine whether the southern states should be readmitted to the Union. The committee investigated southern affairs and confirmed reports of widespread mistreatment of black people and white arrogance.

The Freedmen's Bureau Bill and The Civil Rights Bill

In early 1866 Senator Lyman Trumball, a moderate Republican from Illinois, introduced two major bills. The first was to provide more financial support for the Freedmen's Bureau and extend its authority to defend the rights of black people.

The second proposal was the first civil rights bill in American history. It made any person born in the United States a citizen (except Indians) and entitled them to rights protected by the U.S. government. Black people would possess the same legal rights as white people. The bill was clearly intended to invalidate the black codes.

Johnson's Vetoes

Both measures passed in Congress with nearly unanimous Republican support. President Johnson vetoed them. He claimed that the bill to continue the Freedmen's Bureau would greatly expand the federal bureaucracy and permit too "vast a number

FEDERAL RECONSTRUCTION LEGISLATION, 1865–1867	
1865	Freedmen's Bureau established
1865	Thirteenth Amendment passed and ratified
1866	Freedmen's Bureau Bill and the Civil Rights Act of 1866 passed over Johnson's veto
1866	Fourteenth Amendment passed (ratified 1868)
1867	Reconstruction Acts passed over Johnson's veto

of agents" to exercise arbitrary power over the white population. He insisted that the civil rights bill benefited black people at the expense of white people. "In fact, the distinction of race and color is by the bill made to operate in favor of the colored and against the white race."

The Johnson vetoes stunned Republicans. Although he had not meant to, Johnson drove moderate Republicans into the radical camp and strengthened the Republican Party. The president did not believe Republicans would oppose him to support the freedmen. He was wrong. Congress overrode both vetoes. The Republicans broke with Johnson in 1866, defied him in 1867, and impeached him in 1868 (failing to remove him from office by only one vote in the Senate).

THE FOURTEENTH AMENDMENT

To secure the legal rights of freedmen, Republicans passed the Fourteenth Amendment. This amendment fundamentally changed the Constitution by compelling states to accept their residents as citizens and to guarantee that their rights as citizens would be safeguarded.

Its first section guaranteed citizenship to every person born in the United States. This included virtually every black person. It made each person a citizen of the state in which he or she resided. It defined the specific rights of citizens and then protected those rights against the power of state governments. Citizens had the right to due process (usually a trial) before they could lose their life, liberty, or property.

All persons born or naturalized in the United States, and subject to the jurisdiction thereof, are citizens of the United States and of the State wherein they reside. No State shall make or enforce any law which shall abridge the privileges or immunities of citizens of the United States; nor shall any State deprive any person of life, liberty, or property, without due process of law; nor deny to any person within its jurisdiction the equal protection of the laws.

Eleven years after Chief Justice Roger Taney declared in the Dred Scott decision that black people were "a subordinate and inferior class of beings" who had "no rights that white people were bound to respect," the Fourteenth Amendment vested them with the same rights of citizenship other Americans possessed.

The amendment also threatened to deprive states of representation in Congress if they denied black men the vote. The end of slavery had also made obsolete the three-fifths clause in the Constitution, which had counted slaves as only three-fifths (or 60 percent) of a white person in calculating a state's population and determining the number of representatives each state was entitled to in the House of Representatives. Republicans feared that southern states would count black people in their populations without permitting them to vote, thereby gaining more representatives than those states had had before the Civil War. The amendment mandated that the number of representatives each state would be entitled to in Congress (including northern states) would be reduced if that state did not allow adult males to vote.

Democrats almost unanimously opposed the Fourteenth Amendment. Andrew Johnson denounced it, although he had no power to prevent its adoption. Southern states refused to ratify it except for Tennessee. Women's suffragists felt badly betrayed because the amendment limited suffrage to males. Despite this opposition, the amendment was ratified in 1868.

RADICAL RECONSTRUCTION

By 1867 radical Republicans in Congress had wrested control over Reconstruction from Johnson, and they then imposed policies that brought black men into the political system as voters and officeholders. It was a dramatic development, second in importance only to emancipation and the end of slavery.

Republicans swept the 1866 congressional elections despite the belligerent opposition of Johnson and the Democrats. With two-thirds majorities in the House and Senate, Republicans easily overrode presidential vetoes. Two years after the Civil War ended, Republicans dismantled the state governments established in the South under President Johnson's authority. They instituted a new Reconstruction policy.

Republicans passed the First Reconstruction Act over Johnson's veto in March 1867. It divided the South into five military districts, each under the command of a general (see Map 12–2). Military personnel would protect lives and property while new civilian governments were formed. Elected delegates in each state would draft a new constitution and submit it to the voters.

Universal Manhood Suffrage

The Reconstruction Act stipulated that all adult males in the states of the former Confederacy were eligible to vote, except for those who had actively supported the Confederacy or were convicted felons. Once each state had formed a new government and approved the Fourteenth Amendment, it would be readmitted to the Union with representation in Congress.

The advent of radical Reconstruction was the culmination of black people's struggle to gain legal and political rights. Since the 1864 black national convention in Syracuse and the meetings and conventions in the South in 1865 and 1866, black leaders had argued that one of the consequences of the Civil War should be the inclusion of black men in the body politic. The achievement of that goal was due to their

MAP 12–2 Congressional Reconstruction. Under the terms of the First Reconstruction Act of 1867, the former Confederate states (except Tennessee) were divided into five military districts and placed under the authority of military officers. Commanders in each of the five districts were responsible for supervising the reestablishment of civilian governments in each state.

persistent and persuasive efforts, the determination of radical Republicans, and, ironically, the obstructionism of Andrew Johnson who had played into their hands.

Black Politics

Full of energy and enthusiasm, black men and women rushed into the political arena in the spring and summer of 1867. Although women could not vote, they joined men at the meetings, rallies, parades, and picnics that accompanied political organizing in the South. For many former slaves, politics became as important as the church and religious activities. Black people flocked to the Republican Party and the new Union Leagues.

The Union Leagues had been established in the North during the Civil War, but they expanded across the South as quasi-political organizations in the late 1860s. The Leagues were social, fraternal, and patriotic groups in which black people often, but not always, outnumbered white people. League meetings featured ceremonies, rituals, initiation rites, and oaths. They gave people an opportunity to sharpen leadership skills and gain an informal political education by discussing issues from taxes to schools.

Sit-Ins and Strikes

Political progress did not induce apathy and a sense of satisfaction and contentment among black people. Gaining citizenship, legal rights, and the vote generated more expectations and demands for advancement. For example, black people insisted on equal access to public transportation. After a Republican rally in Charleston, South Carolina, in April 1867, several black men staged a "sit-in" on a nearby horse-drawn streetcar before they were arrested. In Charleston, black people were permitted to ride only on the outside running boards of the cars. They wanted to sit on the seats inside. Within a month, due to the intervention of military authorities, the streetcar company gave in. Similar protests occurred in Richmond and New Orleans.

Black workers also struck across the South in 1867. Black longshoremen in New Orleans, Mobile, Savannah, Charleston, and Richmond walked off the job. Black laborers were usually paid less than white men for the same work, and this led to labor unrest during the 1860s and 1870s. Sometimes the strikers won, sometimes they lost. In 1869 a black Baltimore longshoreman, Isaac Myers, organized the National Colored Labor Union.

THE REACTION OF WHITE SOUTHERNERS

White Southerners grimly opposed radical Reconstruction. They were outraged that black people could claim the same legal and political rights they possessed. Such a possibility seemed preposterous to people who had an abiding belief in the absolute inferiority of black people. A statement by Benjamin F. Perry, whom Johnson had appointed provisional governor of South Carolina in 1865, captures the depth of this

With the adoption of radical Republican policies, most black men eagerly took part in political activities. Political meetings, conventions, speeches, barbecues, and other gatherings also attracted women and children.
Courtesy of the Library of Congress

racist conviction. "The African," Perry declared, "has been in all ages, a savage or a slave. God created him inferior to the white man in form, color and intellect, and no legislation or culture can make him his equal. . . . His hair, his form and features will not compete with the caucasian race, and it is in vain to think of elevating him to the dignity of the white man. God created differences between the two races, and nothing can make him equal."

Some white people, taking solace in their belief in the innate inferiority of black people, concluded they could turn black suffrage to their advantage. White people, they assumed, should easily be able to control and manipulate black voters just as they had controlled black people during slavery. White Southerners who believed this, however, were destined to be disappointed, and their disappointment would turn to fury.

TIMELINE

AFRICAN-AMERICAN EVENTS	NATIONAL EVENTS
1862	
March 1862 The beginning of the Port Royal Experiment in South Carolina	**February 1862** Julia Ward Howe publishes the first version of "Battle Hymm of the Republic" in the "Atlantic Monthly"
	July 1862 Morrell Land-Grant College Act signed into law by Abraham Lincoln
1864	
October 1864 Black national convention in Syracuse, New York	**November 1864** Abraham Lincoln reelected
1865	
January 1865 General Sherman's Special Field Order #15	**April 1865** Abraham Lincoln is assassinated; Andrew Johnson succeeds to presidency
March 1865 Freedmen's Bureau established	**May 1865** Andrew Johnson begins presidential Reconstruction
Sept.–Nov. 1865 Black codes enacted	**June–August 1865** Southern state governments are reorganized
	December 1865 Thirteenth Amendment to the Constitution is ratified

continued

AFRICAN-AMERICAN EVENTS	NATIONAL EVENTS
1866	
February 1866 Southern Homestead Act **March 1866** President Johnson's vetoes of bill to extend the Freedman's Bureau and the Civil Rights bill **April 1866** Override of Johnson's veto of the Civil Rights bill by Congress **May 1866** Memphis riot **July 1866** New Freedmen's Bureau bill enacted by Congress over Johnson's veto; New Orleans Riot	**November 1866** Republican election victories produce greater than two-thirds majorities in House and Senate
1867	
Spring–Summer 1867 Union Leagues and the Republican Party organized in southern states	**March 1867** The first Reconstruction Act passes over President Johnson's veto The United States agrees to buy Alaska from Russia
1868	
	February 1868 House impeaches President Johnson **May 1868** Senate acquits Johnson by one vote **July 1868** Fourteenth Amendment to the Constitution is ratified **November 1868** Ulysses S. Grant elected president
1869	
1869 The National Colored Labor Union established under the leadership of Isaac Myers	**May 1869** Transcontinental railroad completed

CONCLUSION

Why were black Southerners able to gain citizenship and access to the political system by 1868? Most white Americans did not suddenly abandon 250 years of deeply ingrained beliefs that people of African descent were their inferiors. The advances that African Americans achieved fit into a series of complex political developments after the Civil

War. Black people themselves had fought and died to preserve the Union, and they had earned the grudging respect of many white people and the open admiration of others. Black leaders in meetings and petitions insisted that their rights be recognized.

White Northerners—led by the radical Republicans—were convinced that President Andrew Johnson had made a serious error in supporting policies that permitted white Southerners to retain pre–Civil War leaders while the black codes virtually made freedmen slaves again. Republicans were determined that white Southerners realize their defeat had doomed the prewar status quo. Republicans established a Reconstruction program to disfranchise key southern leaders while providing legal rights to freedmen. The right to vote, they reasoned, would give black people the means to deal more effectively with white Southerners while simultaneously strengthening the Republican Party in the South.

The result was to make the mid to late 1860s one of the few high points in African-American history. During this period, not only was slavery abolished, but black Southerners were able to organize schools and churches, and black people throughout the South acquired legal and political rights that would have been incomprehensible before the war. Yet black people did not stand on the brink of utopia. Most freedmen still lacked land and had no realistic hope of obtaining much if any of it. White violence and cruelty continued almost unabated across much of the South. Still, for millions of African Americans, the future looked more promising than it had ever before in American history.

REVIEW QUESTIONS

1. How did freedmen define their freedom? What did freedom mean to ex-slaves? How did their priorities differ from those of African Americans who had been free before the Civil War?

2. What did the former slaves and the former slaveholders want after emancipation? Were these desires realistic? How did former slaves and former slaveholders disagree after the end of slavery?

3. Why did African Americans form separate churches, schools, and social organizations after the Civil War? What role did the black church play in the black community?

4. How effective was the Freedmen's Bureau? How successful was it in assisting ex-slaves to live in freedom?

5. Why did southern states enact black codes?

6. Why did radical Republicans object to President Andrew Johnson's Reconstruction policies? Why did Congress impose its own Reconstruction policies?

7. Why were laws passed to enable black men to vote?

8. Why did black men gain the right to vote but not possession of land?

9. Did congressional Reconstruction secure full equality for African Americans as American citizens?

RECOMMENDED READING

Ira Berlin and Leslie Rowland, eds. *Families and Freedom: A Documentary History of African-American Kinship in the Civil War Era.* New York: Cambridge University Press, 1997. A collection of documents that conveys the aspirations and frustrations of freedmen.

W. E. B. Du Bois. *Black Reconstruction in America: An Essay toward a History of the Part Which Black Folk Played in the Attempt to Reconstruct Democracy in America, 1860–1880.* New York: Russell & Russell, 1935. A classic account of Reconstruction challenging the traditional interpretation that it was a tragic era marked by corrupt and inept black rule of the South.

Eric Foner. *Reconstruction: America's Unfinished Revolution, 1863–1877.* New York: Harper & Row, 1988. The best and most comprehensive account of Reconstruction.

Herbert G. Gutman. *The Black Family in Slavery and Freedom, 1750–1925.* New York: Oxford University Press, 1976. An illustration of how African-American family values and kinship ties forged in slavery endured after emancipation.

Steven Hahn. *A Nation under Our Feet: Black Political Struggles in the Rural South from Slavery to the Great Migration.* Cambridge, MA: Harvard University Press, 2003. In a sophisticated analysis, Hahn explores the ways in which African Americans conceived of themselves as political people and organized from slavery through Reconstruction and disfranchisement to the growth of Marcus Garvey's Universal Negro Improvement Association in the 1920s.

Tera W. Hunter. *To 'Joy My Freedom: Southern Black Women's Lives and Labors after the Civil War.* Cambridge, MA: Harvard University Press, 1997. An examination of the interior lives of black women, their work, social welfare, and leisure.

Gerald D. Jaynes. *Branches without Roots: Genesis of the Black Working Class in the American South, 1862–1882.* New York: Pantheon, 1986. The changes in work and labor in the aftermath of slavery.

Leon F. Litwack. *Been in the Storm Too Long: The Aftermath of Slavery.* New York: Alfred A. Knopf, 1979. A rich and detailed account of the transition to freedom largely based on recollections of former slaves.

CHAPTER THIRTEEN

THE MEANING OF FREEDOM

THE FAILURE OF RECONSTRUCTION

CONSTITUTIONAL CONVENTIONS

Black men as a group first entered politics as delegates to constitutional conventions in the southern states in 1867 and 1868. Each of the former Confederate states, except Tennessee, which had already been restored to the Union, elected delegates to these conventions. Most southern white men were Democrats. They boycotted these elections to protest both Congress's assumption of authority over Reconstruction and the extension of voting privileges to black men. Thus the delegates to the conventions that met to frame new state constitutions to replace those drawn up in 1865 under President Johnson's authority were mostly Republicans joined by a few conservative southern Democrats. The Republicans represented three constituencies. One consisted of white northern migrants who moved to the South in the wake of the war. They were disparagingly called carpetbaggers, because they were said to have arrived in the South with all their possessions in a single carpetbag. A second group consisted of native white Southerners, mostly small farmers in devastated upland regions of the South who hoped for economic relief from Republican governments. This group was known derogatorily as scalawags, or scoundrels, by other southern white people. African Americans made up the third and largest Republican constituency.

Of the 1,000 men elected as delegates to the ten state conventions, 265 were black. Black delegates were a majority only in the South Carolina and Louisiana conventions. In most states, including Alabama, Georgia, Mississippi, Virginia, North Carolina, Arkansas, and Texas, black men made up 10 percent to 20 percent of the delegates. At least 107 of the 265 had been born slaves; about 40 had served in the Union Army. Several were well-educated teachers and ministers; others were tailors, blacksmiths, barbers, and farmers. Most went on to hold other political offices in the years that followed.

These delegates produced impressive constitutions. Unlike previous state constitutions in the South, the new constitutions ensured that all adult males could vote, and except in Mississippi and Virginia, they did not disfranchise large numbers of former Confederates. They conferred broad guarantees of civil rights. In several states they provided the first statewide systems of public education. These constitutions were progressive, not radical. Black and white Republicans hoped to attract support from white Southerners for the new state governments these documents created by encouraging state support for private businesses, especially railroad construction.

Southern black men cast ballots for the first time in 1867 in the election of delegates to state constitutional conventions. The ballots were provided by the candidates or political parties, not by state or municipal officials. Most nineteenth-century elections were not by secret ballot.
The Granger Collection, New York

Elections

Elections were held in 1868 to ratify the new constitutions and elect officials. The white Democratic response varied. In some states, Democrats boycotted the elections. In others, they participated, but voted against ratification, and in still other states they supported ratification and attempted to elect as many Democrats as possible to office. Congress required only a majority of those voting—not a majority of all registered voters—to ratify the constitutions. In each state a majority of those voting eventually did vote to ratify, and in each state, black men were elected to political offices.

BLACK POLITICAL LEADERS

Over the next decade, 1,465 black men held political office in the South. Although black leaders individually and collectively enjoyed significant political leverage, white Republicans dominated politics during Reconstruction. In general the number of

Table 13–1
African-American Population and Officeholding during Reconstruction in the States Subject to Congressional Reconstruction

	African-American Population in 1870	African Americans as Percentage of Total Population	Number of African-American Officeholders during Reconstruction
South Carolina	415,814	58.9	314
Mississippi	444,201	53.6	226
Louisiana	364,210	50.1	210
North Carolina	391,650	36.5	180
Alabama	475,510	47.6	167
Georgia	545,142	46.0	108
Virginia	512,841	41.8	85
Florida	91,689	48.7	58
Arkansas	122,169	25.2	46
Texas	253,475	30.9	46
Tennessee	322,331	25.6	20

Source: Eric Foner, *Freedom's Lawmakers: A Directory of Black Officeholders during Reconstruction* (1993), xiv; The Statistics of the Population of the United States, Ninth Census (1873), xvii.

black officials in a state reflected the size of that state's African-American population. Black people were a substantial majority of the population in just Mississippi and South Carolina, and most of the black officeholders came from those two states and Louisiana, where black people were a bare majority. In most states, such as Arkansas, North Carolina, Tennessee, and Texas where black people made up between 25 percent and 40 percent of the population, far fewer black men were elected to office (see Table 13–1).

Initially, black men chose not to run for the most important political offices because they feared their election would further alienate already angry white Southerners. But as white Republicans swept into office in 1868, black leaders reversed their strategy, and by 1870 black men had been elected to many key political positions. No black man was elected governor, but Lieutenant Governor P. B. S. Pinchback served one month (from December 1872 to January 1873) as governor in Louisiana after the white governor was removed from office. Blanche K. Bruce and Hiram Revels represented Mississippi in the U.S. Senate. Beginning with Joseph Rainey in 1870 in South Carolina, fourteen black men served in the U.S. House of Representatives during Reconstruction. Six men served as lieutenant governors. In Mississippi and South Carolina, a majority of the representatives in state houses were black men, and each of these states had two black speakers of the house in the 1870s. Jonathan J. Wright served seven years as a state supreme court justice in South Carolina. Four black men served as state superintendents of education, and Francis L. Cardozo served as South Carolina's secretary of state and then treasurer. During Reconstruction,

112 black state senators and 683 black representatives were elected. There were also 41 black sheriffs, 5 black mayors, and 31 black coroners. Tallahassee, Florida, and Little Rock, Arkansas, had black police chiefs.

Many of these men—by background, experience, and education—were well qualified. Others were not. Of the 1,465 black officeholders, at least 378 had been free before the Civil War, 933 were literate, and 195 were illiterate (we lack information about the remaining 337). Sixty-four had attended college or professional school. In fact, 14 of the leaders had been students at Oberlin College in Ohio, which began admitting both black and female students before the Civil War.

Black farmers and artisans—tailors, carpenters, and barbers—were well represented among those who held political office. There were also 237 ministers and 172 teachers. At least 129 had served in the Union Army, and 46 had worked for the Freedmen's Bureau.

Several black politicians were wealthy, and a few were former slave owners. Antoine Dubuclet, who became Louisiana's treasurer, had owned more than one hundred slaves and land valued at more than $100,000 before the Civil War. Former slave Ferdinand Havis became a member of the Arkansas House of Representatives. He owned a saloon, a whiskey business, and two thousand acres near Pine Bluff, where he became known as "the Colored Millionaire."

Although black men did not dominate any state politically, a few did dominate districts with sizable black populations. Before he was elected to the U.S. Senate, Blanche K. Bruce all but controlled Bolivar County, Mississippi, where he served as sheriff, tax collector, and superintendent of education. Former slave and Civil War hero Robert Smalls was the political "kingpin" in Beaufort, South Carolina. He served successively in the South Carolina house and senate, and in the U.S. House of Representatives. He was also a member of the South Carolina constitutional conventions in 1868 and 1895. He was a major figure in the Republican Party and served as customs collector in Beaufort from 1889 to 1913.

THE ISSUES

Many, but not all, black and white Republican leaders favored increasing the authority of state governments to promote the welfare of all the state's citizens. Before the Civil War, most southern states did not provide schools, medical care, assistance for the mentally impaired, or prisons. Such concerns—if attended to at all—were left to local communities or families.

Education and Social Welfare

Black leaders were eager to increase literacy and promote education among black people. Republican politicians created statewide systems of public education throughout the South. It was a difficult and expensive task, and the results were only a limited success. Schools had to be built, teachers employed, and textbooks provided. To pay for it, taxes were increased in states still reeling from the war.

In some communities and in many rural areas, schools were not built. In other places, teachers were not paid. Some people—black and white—opposed compulsory education laws, preferring to let parents determine whether their children should attend school or work to help the family. Some black leaders favored a poll tax on voting if the funds it brought in were spent on the schools. Thus, although Reconstruction leaders established a strong commitment to public education, the results they achieved were uneven.

Furthermore, white parents refused to send their children to integrated schools. Although no laws required segregation, public schools during and after Reconstruction were invariably segregated. Black parents were usually more concerned that their children should have schools to attend than whether the schools were integrated. New Orleans, however, was an exception; it provided integrated schools.

Reconstruction leaders also supported higher education. In 1872 Mississippi legislators took advantage of the 1862 federal Morrill Land-Grant Act, which provided states with funds for agricultural and mechanical colleges, to found the first historically black state university: Alcorn A&M College. Although the university was named after a white Republican governor, James L. Alcorn, former U.S. senator Hiram Revels was its first president. The South Carolina legislature created a similar college and attached it to the Methodist-sponsored Claflin University.

Black leaders in the state legislature compelled the University of South Carolina, which had been all white, to admit black students and hire black faculty. Many, but not all, of the white students and faculty left. Several black politicians enrolled in the law and medical programs at the university. Richard Greener, a black Harvard graduate, served on the university's faculty and was its librarian.

Despite the costs, Reconstruction leaders also created the first state-supported institutions for the insane, the blind, and the deaf in the South. Some southern states during Reconstruction began to offer medical care and public health programs. Orphanages were established. State prisons were built. Black leaders also supported revising state criminal codes, eliminating corporal punishment for many crimes, and reducing the number of capital crimes.

Civil Rights

Black politicians were often the victims of racial discrimination when they tried to use public transportation and accommodations such as hotels and restaurants. Rather than provide separate arrangements for black customers, white-owned businesses simply excluded black patrons. This was true in the North as well as the South. Robert Smalls, for example, the Civil War hero who had commandeered a Confederate supply ship to escape from Charleston in 1862 (see Chapter 11), was unceremoniously ejected from a Philadelphia streetcar in 1864. After protests, the company agreed to accept black riders. In Arkansas, Mifflin Gibbs and W. Hines Furbish successfully sued a local saloon after they had been denied service. In South Carolina, Jonathan J. Wright won $1,200 in a lawsuit against a railroad after he had purchased a first-class ticket but had been forced to ride in the second-class coach.

Black leaders were determined to open public facilities to all people, in the process revealing deep divisions between themselves and white Republicans. In several southern states they introduced bills to prevent proprietors from excluding black people from restaurants, barrooms, hotels, concert halls, and auditoriums, as well as railroad coaches, streetcars, and steamboats. Many white Republicans and virtually every Democrat attacked such proposals as efforts to promote social equality and gain access for black people to places where they were not welcome. The white politicians blocked these laws in most states. Only South Carolina—with a black majority in the house and many black members in the senate—enacted such a law, but it was not effectively enforced. In Mississippi, the Republican governor James L. Alcorn vetoed a bill to outlaw racial discrimination by railroads. In Alabama and North Carolina, civil rights bills were defeated, and Georgia and Arkansas enacted measures that encouraged segregation.

ECONOMIC ISSUES

Black politicians sought to promote economic development in general and for black people in particular. For example, white landowners sometimes arbitrarily fired black agricultural laborers near the end of the growing season and then did not pay them. Some of these landowners were dishonest, but others were in debt and could not pay their workers. To prevent such situations, black politicians secured laws that required laborers to be paid before the crop was sold or at the time when it was sold. Some black leaders who had been slaves also wanted to regulate the wages of laborers, but these proposals invariably failed because most Republicans did not believe states had the right to regulate wages and prices.

Legislators also enacted measures that protected the land and property of small farmers against seizure for nonpayment of debts. Black and white farmers who lost land, tools, animals, and other property because they could not pay their debts were unlikely ever to recover financially. "Stay laws" prohibited, or "stayed," authorities from taking property. Besides affording financial protection to hard-pressed poor farmers, Republicans hoped these laws would attract political support from white yeomen and draw them away from their attachment to the Democratic Party.

Land

Black leaders were unable to initiate programs that would provide land to landless black and white farmers. Many black and white political leaders believed the state had no right to distribute land. Again, South Carolina was the exception. Its legislature created a state land commission in 1869.

The commission could purchase and distribute land to freedmen. It also gave the freedmen loans on generous terms to pay for the land. Unfortunately, the commission was corrupt, inefficiently managed, and it had little fertile land to distribute. However, despite its many difficulties, the commission enabled more than fourteen thousand black families and a few white families to acquire land in South Carolina. Their descendants still possess some of this land today.

Although some black leaders were reluctant to use the states' power to distribute land, others had no qualms about raising property taxes so high that large landowners would be forced to sell some of their property to pay their taxes. Abraham Galloway of North Carolina explained, "I want to see the man who owns one or two thousand acres of land, taxed a dollar on the acre, and if they can't pay the taxes, sell their property to the highest bidder . . . and then we negroes shall become the land holders."

Business and Industry

Black and white leaders had an easier time enacting legislation to support business and industry. Like most Americans after the Civil War, Republicans believed that expanding the railroad network would stimulate employment, improve transportation, and generate prosperity. State governments approved the sale of bonds supported by the authority of the state to finance railroad construction. In Georgia, Alabama, Texas, and Arkansas, the railroad network did expand. But the bonded debt of these states soared and taxes increased to pay for it. Moreover, railroad financing was often corrupt. Most of the illegal money wound up in the pockets of white businessmen and politicians. Black politicians rarely had access to truly large financial transactions.

So attractive were business profits that some black political leaders formed corporations. They invested modest sums and believed—like so many capitalists—that the rewards outweighed the risks. In Charleston, twenty-eight black leaders (and two white politicians) formed a horse-drawn streetcar line they called the Enterprise Railroad to carry freight between the city wharves and the railroad terminal. Black leaders in South Carolina also created a company to extract the phosphate used for fertilizer from riverbeds and riverbanks in the low country. Neither business lasted long. Black men found it far more difficult than white entrepreneurs to finance their corporations.

BLACK POLITICIANS: AN EVALUATION

Southern black political leaders on the state level did create the foundation for public education, for providing state assistance for the blind, deaf, and insane, and for reforming the criminal justice system. They tried, but mostly failed, to outlaw racial discrimination in public facilities. They encouraged state support for economic revival and expansion.

But black leaders could not create programs that significantly improved the lives of their constituents. Because white Republicans almost always outnumbered them, they could not enact an agenda of their own. Moreover, black leaders often disagreed among themselves about specific issues and programs. Class and prewar status frequently divided them. Those leaders who had not been slaves and had not been raised in rural isolation were less likely to be concerned with land and agricultural labor. More prosperous black leaders showed more interest in civil rights and encouraging business. Even when they agreed about the need for public education, black leaders often disagreed about how to finance it and whether or not it should be compulsory.

REPUBLICAN FACTIONALISM

Disagreements among black leaders paled in comparison to the internal conflicts that divided the Republican Party during Reconstruction. Black and white Republicans often disagreed on political issues and strategy, but the lack of party cohesion and discipline was even more harmful. The Republican Party in the South constantly split into factions as groups fought with each other. Most disagreements were over who should run for and hold political office.

During Reconstruction, hundreds of would-be Republican leaders—black and white—sought public offices. If they lost the Republican nomination in county or state conventions, they often bolted and formed a competing slate of candidates. Then Republicans ran against each other and against the Democrats in the general election. It was not a recipe for political success.

These bitter and angry contests were based less on race and issues than on the desperate desire to gain an office that would pay even a modest salary. Most black and white Republicans were not well off; public office assured them a modicum of economic security.

Ironically, these factional disputes led to a high turnover in political leadership and the loss of that very economic security. It was difficult for black leaders (and white leaders too) to be renominated and reelected to more than one or two terms. Few officeholders served three or four consecutive terms in the same office during Reconstruction. This made for inexperienced leadership and added to Republican woes.

OPPOSITION

Even if black and Republican leaders had been less prone to internecine conflict and more effective in adopting a political platform, they might still have failed to sustain themselves for long. Most white Southerners led by conservative Democrats remained absolutely opposed to letting black men vote or hold office. As a white Floridian put it, "The damned Republican Party has put niggers to rule us and we will not suffer it." Of course, because black people voted did not mean they ruled during Reconstruction, but many white people failed to grasp that. Instead, for most white Southerners, the only acceptable political system was one that excluded black men and the Republican Party.

As far as most white people were concerned, the end of slavery and the enfranchisement of black men did not make black people their equals. They did not accept the Fourteenth Amendment. They attacked Republican governments and their leaders unrelentingly. White Southerners blamed the Republicans for an epidemic of waste and corruption in state government. But most of all, they considered it preposterous and outrageous that former slaves could vote and hold political office.

James S. Pike spoke for many white people when he ridiculed black leaders in the South Carolina House of Representatives in 1873:

> The body is almost literally a Black Parliament. . . . The Speaker is black, the Clerk is black, the door-keepers are black, the little pages are black, the chairman of the Ways and Means is black, and the chaplain is coal-black. At some of the desks sit colored men whose types it would be hard to find outside of Congo; whose costume, visages, attitudes, and expression only befit the forecastle of a buccaneer. It must be remembered, also, that these men, with not more than a half a dozen exceptions, have been themselves slaves, and that their ancestors were slaves for generations.

Pike's observations circulated widely in both North and South.

White Southerners were determined to rid themselves of Republicans and the disgrace of having to live with black men who possessed political rights. White Southerners would "redeem" their states by restoring white Democrats to power. This did not simply mean defeating black and white Republicans in elections; it meant removing them from any role in politics. White Southerners believed any means—fair or foul—were justified in exorcising this evil.

THE KU KLUX KLAN

If black men in politics was illegitimate—in the eyes of white Southerners—then it was acceptable to use violence to remove them. This thinking gave rise to militant terrorist organizations, such as the Ku Klux Klan, the Knights of the White Camellia, the White Brotherhood, and the Whitecaps. Threats, intimidation, beatings, rapes, and murder

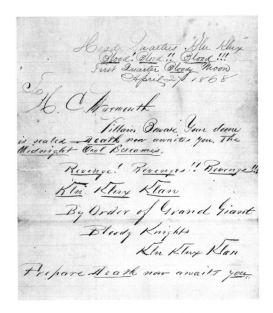

The flowing white robes and cone-shaped headdresses associated with the Ku Klux Klan today are mostly a twentieth-century phenomenon. The Klansmen of the Reconstruction era, like these two men in Alabama in 1868, were well armed, disguised, and prepared to intimidate black and white Republicans. The note is a Klan death threat directed at Louisiana's first Republican governor, Henry C. Warmoth.

Rutherford B. Hayes Presidential Center (left); from the Henry Clay Warmoth Papers #752, Southern Historical Collection, Wilson Library, University of North Carolina at Chapel Hill (right)

would restore conservative white Democratic rule and force black people back into subordination.

The Ku Klux Klan was founded in Pulaski, Tennessee, in 1866. It was originally a social club for Confederate veterans who adopted secret oaths and rituals—similar to the Union Leagues, but with far more deadly results. One of the key figures in the Klan's rapid growth was former Confederate general Nathan Bedford Forrest, who became its grand wizard. The Klan drew its members from all classes of white society, not merely from among the poor. Businessmen, lawyers, physicians, and politicians were active in the Klan as well as farmers and planters.

The Klan and other terrorist organizations functioned mainly where black people were a large minority and where their votes could affect the outcome of elections. Klansmen virtually took over areas of western Alabama, northern Georgia, and Florida's panhandle. The Klan controlled the up country of South Carolina and the area around Mecklenburg County, North Carolina. However, in the Carolina and Georgia low country where there were huge black majorities, the Klan never appeared.

Although the Klan and similar societies were neither well organized nor unified, they did reduce support for the Republican Party and helped eliminate its leaders. Often wearing hoods and masks to hide their faces, white terrorists embarked on a campaign of violence rarely matched and never exceeded in American history.

Mobs of marauding terrorists beat and killed hundreds of black people—and many white people. Black churches and schools were burned. Republican leaders were routinely threatened and often killed. The black chairman of the Republican Party in South Carolina, Benjamin F. Randolph, was murdered as he stepped off a train in 1868. Black legislator Lee Nance and white legislator Solomon G. W. Dill were murdered in 1868 in South Carolina. In 1870 black lawmaker Richard Burke was killed in Sumter County, Alabama, because he was considered too influential among "people of his color."

As his wife looked on, Jack Dupree—a local Republican leader—had his throat cut and was eviscerated in Monroe County, Mississippi. In 1870 North Carolina senator John W. Stephens, a white Republican, was murdered. After Alabama freedman George Moore voted for the Republicans in 1869, Klansmen beat him, raped a girl who was visiting his wife, and attacked a neighbor. An Irish-American teacher and four black men were lynched in Cross Plains, Alabama, in 1870. Notorious Texas outlaw John Wesley Hardin openly acknowledged he had killed several black Texas state policemen.

White men attacked a Republican campaign rally in Eutaw, Alabama, in 1870 and killed four black men and wounded fifty-four other people. After three black leaders were arrested in 1871 in Meridian, Mississippi, for delivering what many white people considered inflammatory speeches, shooting broke out in the courtroom. The Republican judge and two of the defendants were killed, and in a wave of violence, thirty black people were murdered, including every black leader in the small community. In the same year, a mob of five hundred men broke into the jail in Union County, South Carolina, and lynched eight black prisoners who had been accused of killing a Confederate veteran.

Nowhere was the Klan more active and violent than in York County, South Carolina. Almost the entire adult white male population joined in threatening, attacking, and murdering the black population. Hundreds were beaten and at least eleven killed. Terrified families fled from their homes into the woods. Appeals for help were sent to Governor Robert K. Scott.

But Scott did not send aid. He had already sent the South Carolina militia into areas of Klan activity, and even more violence had resulted. The militia was made up mostly of black men, and white terrorists retaliated by killing militia officers. Scott could not send white men to York County because most of them sympathized with the Klan. Thus Republican governors like Scott responded ineffectually. Republican-controlled legislatures passed anti-Klan measures that made it illegal to appear in public in disguises and masks, and they strengthened laws against assault, murder, and conspiracy. But enforcement was weak.

A few Republican leaders did deal harshly and effectively with terrorism. Governors in Tennessee, Texas, and Arkansas declared martial law and sent in hundreds of well-armed white and black men to quell the violence. Hundreds of Klansmen were arrested, many fled, and three were executed in Arkansas. But when Governor William W. Holden of North Carolina sent the state militia after the Klan, he succeeded only in provoking an angry reaction. Subsequent Klan violence in ten counties helped Democrats carry the 1870 legislative elections, and the North Carolina legislature then removed Holden from office.

Outnumbered and outgunned, black people in most areas did not retaliate against the Klan, and the Klan was rarely active where black people were in a majority and prepared to defend themselves. In the cause of white supremacy, the Klan usually attacked those who could not defend themselves.

THE WEST

During the 1830s the U.S. government forced five tribes—the Cherokee, Chickasaw, Choctaw, Creek, and Seminole—from their southern homelands to Indian territory in what is now Oklahoma. By 1860 Native Americans held 7,367 African Americans in slavery. Many of the Indians fought for the Confederacy during the Civil War. Following the war, the former slaves encountered nearly as much violence and hostility from Native Americans as they did from southern white people. Indians were reluctant to share their land with freedmen, and they vigorously opposed policies that favored black voting rights.

Gradually and despite considerable Indian prejudice, some African Americans managed to acquire tribal land. Also, the Creeks and the Seminoles permitted former

FEDERAL RECONSTRUCTION LEGISLATION: 1868–1875
1869   Fifteenth Amendment passed (ratified 1870)
1870   Enforcement Act passed
1871   Ku Klux Klan Act passed
1875   Civil Rights Act of 1875 passed

slaves to take part in tribal government. Black men served in both houses of the Creek legislature—the House of Warriors and the House of Kings. An African American, Jesse Franklin, served as a justice on the Creek tribal court in 1876. In contrast, the Chickasaw and Choctaw were absolutely opposed to making concessions to freed people, and thus the U.S. government ordered federal troops onto Chickasaw and Choctaw lands to protect the former slaves.

Elsewhere on the western frontier, black people struggled for legal and political rights and periodically participated in territorial governments. In 1867 two hundred black men voted—although white men protested—in the Montana territorial election. In the Colorado territory, William Jefferson Hardin, a barber, campaigned with other black men for the right to vote, and they persuaded 137 African Americans (91 percent of Colorado's black population) to sign a petition in 1865 to the territorial governor appealing for an end to a white-only voting provision. In 1867 black men in Colorado finally did gain the right to vote. Hardin later moved to Cheyenne and was elected in 1879 to the Wyoming territorial legislature.

THE FIFTEENTH AMENDMENT

The federal government under Republican domination tried to protect black voting rights and defend Republican state governments in the South. In 1869 Congress passed the Fifteenth Amendment, which was ratified in 1870. It stipulated that a person could not be deprived of the right to vote because of race: "The right of citizens of the United States to vote shall not be denied or abridged by the United States or by any State on account of race, color, or previous condition of servitude." Black people, abolitionists, and reformers hailed the amendment as the culmination of the crusade to end slavery and give black people the same rights as white people.

Northern black men were the amendment's immediate beneficiaries because before its adoption, black men could vote in only eight northern states. Yet to the disappointment of many, the amendment said nothing about women voting and did not outlaw poll taxes, literacy tests, and property qualifications that could disfranchise citizens.

THE ENFORCEMENT ACTS

In direct response to the terrorism in the South, Congress passed the Enforcement Acts in 1870 and 1871, and the federal government expanded its authority over the states. The 1870 act outlawed disguises and masks and protected the civil rights of citizens. The 1871 act—known as the Ku Klux Klan Act—made it a federal offense to interfere with an individual's right to vote, hold office, serve on a jury, or enjoy equal protection of the law. Those accused of violating the act would be tried in federal court. For extreme violence, the act authorized the president to send in federal troops and suspend the writ of habeas corpus. (Habeas corpus is the right to be brought before a judge and not be arrested and jailed without cause.)

Black congressmen, who had long advocated federal action against the Klan, endorsed the Enforcement Acts. Representative Joseph Rainey of South Carolina wanted to suspend the Constitution to protect citizens. "I desire that so broad and liberal a construction be placed on its provisions, as will insure protection to the humblest citizen. Tell me nothing of a constitution which fails to shelter beneath its rightful power the people of a country."

Armed with this new legislation, the Justice Department and Attorney General Amos T. Ackerman moved vigorously against the Klan. Hundreds of Klansmen were arrested—seven hundred in Mississippi alone. Faced with a full-scale rebellion in late 1871 in South Carolina's up country, President Ulysses S. Grant declared martial law in nine counties, suspended the writ of habeas corpus, and sent in the U.S. Army. Mass arrests and trials followed, but federal authorities permitted many Klansmen to confess and thereby escape prosecution. The government lacked the human and financial resources to bring hundreds of men to court for lengthy trials. Some white men were tried, mostly before black juries, and were imprisoned or fined. Comparatively few Klansmen, however, were punished severely, especially considering the enormity of their crimes.

THE NORTH LOSES INTEREST

Although the federal government did reduce Klan violence for a time, white Southerners remained convinced that white supremacy must be restored and Republican governments overturned. Klan violence did not overthrow any state governments, but it gravely undermined freedmen's confidence in the ability of these governments to protect them. Meanwhile, radical Republicans in Congress grew frustrated that the South and especially black people continued to demand so much of their time and attention year after year. There was less and less sentiment in the North to continue support for the freedmen and involvement in southern affairs.

Many Republicans in the North lost interest in issues and principles and became more concerned with elections and economic issues. By the mid-1870s there was more discussion in Congress of patronage, veterans' pensions, railroads, taxes, tariffs, the economy, and monetary policy than civil rights or the future of the South.

The American political system was awash in corruption by the 1870s, which detracted from concerns over the South. Although President Ulysses S. Grant was a man of integrity and honesty, many men in his administration were not. They were implicated in an assortment of scandals involving the construction of the transcontinental railroad, federal taxes on whiskey, and fraud within the Bureau of Indian Affairs. Nor was the dishonesty limited to Republicans. William Marcy "Boss" Tweed and the Democratic political machine that dominated New York City were riddled with corruption as well.

Many Republicans began to question the necessity for more moral, military, and political support for African Americans. Others, swayed by white Southerners' views of black people, began to doubt the wisdom of universal manhood suffrage. Many white people who had nominally supported black suffrage began to believe the exaggerated complaints about corruption among black leaders and the unrelenting claims that freedmen were incapable of self-government. Some white Northerners began to conclude that Reconstruction had been a mistake.

Economic conditions contributed to changing attitudes. A financial crisis—the Panic of 1873—sent the economy into a slump for several years. Businesses and financial institutions failed, unemployment soared, and prices fell sharply. In 1874 the Democrats recaptured a majority in the House of Representatives for the first time since 1860 and also took political control of several northern states.

THE FREEDMEN'S BANK

One of the casualties of the financial crisis was the Freedmen's Savings Bank, which failed in 1874. Founded in 1865 when hope flourished, the Freedmen's Savings and Trust Company had been chartered by Congress but was not connected to the Freedmen's Bureau. However, the bank's advertising featured pictures of Abraham Lincoln, and many black people assumed it was a federal agency. Freedmen, black veterans, black churches, fraternal organizations, and benevolent societies opened thousands of accounts in the bank. Most of the deposits totaled under $50, and some amounted to only a few cents.

Although the bank had many black employees, its board of directors consisted of white men. They unwisely invested the bank's funds in risky ventures, including Washington, D.C. real estate. With the Panic of 1873, the bank lost large sums in unsecured railroad loans. To restore confidence, its directors asked Frederick Douglass to serve as president and persuaded him to invest $10,000 of his own money to help shore up the bank. Douglass lost his money, and African Americans from across the South lost more than $1 million when the bank closed in June 1874. Eventually about half the depositors received three-fifths of the value of their accounts, but many African Americans believed the U.S. government owed them a debt. Well into the twentieth century, they wrote to Congress and the president to retrieve their hard-earned money.

THE CIVIL RIGHTS ACT OF 1875

Before Reconstruction finally expired, Congress made one final—some said futile—gesture to protect black people from racial discrimination when it passed the Civil Rights Act of 1875. Strongly championed by Senator Charles Sumner of Massachusetts, it was originally intended to open public accommodations including schools, churches, cemeteries, hotels, and transportation to all people regardless of race. It passed in the Republican-controlled Senate in 1874 shortly before Sumner died. But House Democrats held up passage until 1875 and deleted bans on discrimination in churches, cemeteries, and schools.

The act stipulated "That all persons . . . shall be entitled to the full and equal enjoyment of the accommodations, advantages, facilities, and privileges of inns, public conveyances on land or water, theaters, and other places of public amusement." After its passage, no attempt was made to enforce these provisions, and in 1883 the U.S. Supreme Court declared it unconstitutional. Justice Joseph Bradley wrote that the Fourteenth Amendment protected black people from discrimination by states but not by private businesses. Black newspapers likened the decision to the Dred Scott case a quarter century earlier.

As Reconstruction drew to an end in 1876, black men from across the country assembled in Nashville, Tennessee, for the Colored National Convention. They spent three days in April discussing their prospects for a future that did not look promising. Black and white Republican leaders had lost political control in each of the southern states except Florida, Louisiana, and South Carolina.
Corbis–NY

THE END OF RECONSTRUCTION

Reconstruction ended as it began—in violence and controversy. Democrats demanded "Redemption"—a word with biblical and spiritual overtones. They wanted southern states restored to conservative, white political control. By 1875 those Democrats had regained authority in all the former Confederate states except Mississippi, Florida, Louisiana, and South Carolina (see Map 13–1). Democrats had redeemed Tennessee in 1870 and Georgia in 1871. Democrats had learned two valuable lessons. First, few black men could be persuaded to vote for the Democratic Party—no matter how much white leaders wanted to believe former slaves were easy to manipulate. Second, intimidation and violence would win elections in areas where the number of black and white voters was nearly equal. The federal government had stymied Klan violence in 1871, but by the mid-1870s, the government had become reluctant to send troops to the South to protect black citizens.

Violent Redemption

In Alabama in 1874, black and white Republican leaders were murdered, and white mobs destroyed crops and homes. On Election Day in Eufaula, white men killed seven and injured nearly seventy unarmed black voters. Black voters were also driven from the polls in Mobile. Democrats won the election and redeemed Alabama.

MAP 13–1   Dates of Readmission of Southern States to the Union and Reestablishment of Democratic Party Control. Once conservative white Democrats regained political control of a state government from black and white Republicans, they considered that state "redeemed." The first states the Democrats "redeemed" were Georgia, Virginia, and North Carolina. Louisiana, Florida, and South Carolina were the last. (Tennessee was not included in the Reconstruction process under the terms of the 1867 Reconstruction Act.)

White violence accompanied every election in Louisiana from 1868 to 1876. After Republicans and Democrats each claimed victory in the 1872 elections, black people seized the small town of Colfax along the Red River to protect themselves against a Democratic takeover. They held out for three weeks, and then on Easter Sunday in 1873, a well-armed white mob attacked the black defenders, killing 105 in the worst single day of bloodshed during Reconstruction. In 1874 the White League almost redeemed Louisiana in an astonishing wave of violence. Black people were murdered, courts were attacked, and white people refused to pay taxes to the Republican state government. Six white and two black Republicans were murdered at Coushatta. In September, President Grant finally sent federal troops to New Orleans after 3,500 White Leaguers attacked and nearly wiped out the black militia and the Metropolitan Police. But the stage had been set for the 1876 campaign.

The Shotgun Policy

In 1875 white Mississippians, no longer fearful the national government would intervene in force, declared open warfare on the black majority. The masks and hoods of the Klan were discarded. One newspaper publicly proclaimed that Democrats would carry the election, "peaceably if we can, forcibly if we must." Another paper carried a bold banner: "Mississippi is a white man's country, and by the eternal God we'll rule it."

White Mississippi unleashed a campaign of violence known as the "Shotgun Policy" that was extreme even for Reconstruction. Many Republicans fled and others were murdered. In late 1874 an estimated three hundred black people were hunted down outside Vicksburg after black men armed with inferior weapons had lost a "battle" with white men. In 1875 thirty teachers, church leaders, and Republican

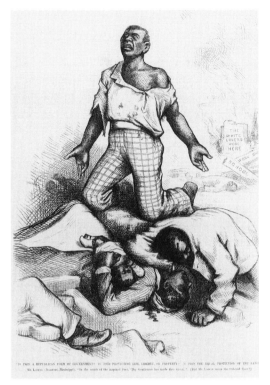

Editorial cartoonist Thomas Nast chronicled the travails of freedmen during the twelve years of Reconstruction in the pages of *Harper's Weekly*. Here Nast deplores the violence and intimidation that accompanied the 1876 election campaign and questions the willingness of white Americans to respect the rights of black Americans.
Courtesy of the Library of Congress

officials were killed in Clinton. The white sheriff of Yazoo County, who had married a black woman and supported the education of black children, had to flee the state.

Mississippi governor Adelbert Ames appealed for federal help, but President Grant refused: "The whole public are tired out with these annual autumnal outbreaks in the South . . . [and] are ready now to condemn any interference on the part of the Government." No federal help arrived. The terrorism intensified, and many black voters went into hiding on Election Day, afraid for their lives and the lives of their families. Democrats redeemed Mississippi and prided themselves that they—a superior race representing the most civilized of all people—were back in control.

In Florida in 1876, white Republicans noted that support for black people in the South was fading. They nominated an all-white Republican slate and even refused to renominate black congressman Josiah Walls.

The Hamburg Massacre

South Carolina Democrats were divided between moderate and extreme factions, but they united to nominate former Confederate general Wade Hampton for governor after the Hamburg Massacre. The prelude to this event occurred on July 4, 1876—the nation's centennial—when two white men in a buggy confronted the black militia that was drilling on a town street in Hamburg, a small, mostly black town. Hot words were exchanged, and days later, Democrats demanded the militia be disarmed. White rifle club members from around the state arrived in Hamburg and attacked the armory, where forty black members of the militia defended themselves. The rifle companies brought up a cannon and reinforcements from nearby Georgia. After the militia ran low on ammunition, white men captured the armory. One white man was killed, twenty-nine black men were taken prisoner, and the other eleven fled. Five of the black men identified as leaders were shot down in cold blood. The rifle companies invaded and wrecked Hamburg. Seven white men were indicted for murder. All were acquitted.

The Hamburg Massacre incited South Carolina Democrats to imitate Mississippi's "Shotgun Policy." It also forced a reluctant President Grant to send federal troops to South Carolina. In the 1876 election campaign, hundreds of white men in red flannel shirts turned out on mules and horses to support Wade Hampton in his contest against incumbent Republican governor Daniel Chamberlain and his black and white allies. When Chamberlain and fellow Republicans tried to speak in Edgefield, they were ridiculed, threatened, and shouted down by six hundred Red Shirts, many of them armed.

Democrats attacked, beat, and killed black people to prevent them from voting. Democratic leaders instructed their followers to treat black voters with contempt. "In speeches to negroes you must remember that argument has no effect on them. They can only be influenced by their fears, superstition, and cupidity. . . . Treat them so as to show them you are a superior race and that their natural position is that of subordination to the white man."

As the election approached, black people in the up country of South Carolina knew it would be exceedingly dangerous if they tried to vote. But in the low country, black people went on the offensive and attacked Democrats. In Charleston, a white man was killed in a racial melee. At a campaign rally at Cainhoy, a few miles outside Charleston, armed black men killed five white men.

A few black men supported Wade Hampton and the Red Shirts. Hampton had a paternalistic view of black people and, although he considered them inferior to white people, promised to respect their rights. Martin Delany believed Hampton and the Democrats were more trustworthy than unreliable Republicans; Delany campaigned for Hampton and was later rewarded with a minor political post. A few genuinely conservative black men during Reconstruction also supported the Democrats and curried their favor and patronage. Most black people despised them. When one black man threw his support to the Democrats, his wife threw him and his clothes out, declaring she would prefer to "beg her bread" than live with a "Democratic nigger."

The "Compromise" of 1877

Threats, violence, and bloodshed accompanied the elections of 1876, but the results were confusing and contradictory. Samuel Tilden, the Democratic candidate, won the popular vote by more than 250,000, and he had a large lead over Republican Rutherford B. Hayes in the electoral vote. Hayes had won 167, but Tilden had 185, and the 20 remaining electoral college votes were in dispute. Both Democrats and Republicans claimed to have won in Florida, Louisiana, and South Carolina, the last three southern states that had not been redeemed. (There was also one contested vote from Oregon.) Whoever took the twenty electoral votes of the three contested states (and Oregon) would be the next president (see Map 13–2).

There was a prolonged controversy, and the constitutional crisis over the outcome of the 1876 election was not resolved until shortly before Inauguration Day in March 1877. Although not a formal compromise, an informal understanding ended the dispute. Democrats accepted a Hayes victory, but Hayes let southern Democrats know he would not support Republican governments in Florida, Louisiana, and South Carolina.

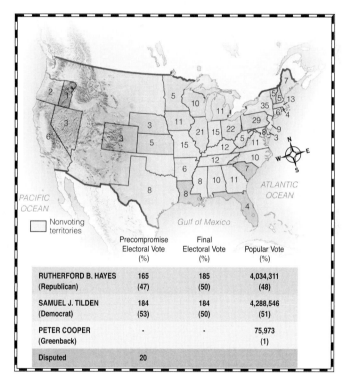

	Precompromise Electoral Vote (%)	Final Electoral Vote (%)	Popular Vote (%)
RUTHERFORD B. HAYES (Republican)	165 (47)	185 (50)	4,034,311 (48)
SAMUEL J. TILDEN (Democrat)	184 (53)	184 (50)	4,288,546 (51)
PETER COOPER (Greenback)	-	-	75,973 (1)
Disputed	20		

MAP 13–2   The Election of 1876. Although Democrat Samuel Tilden appeared to have won the election of 1876, Rutherford B. Hayes and the Republicans were able to claim victory after a prolonged political and constitutional controversy involving the disputed electoral college votes from Louisiana, Florida, and South Carolina (and one from Oregon). In an informal settlement in 1877, Democrats agreed to accept electoral votes for Hayes from those states, and Republicans agreed to permit those states to be "redeemed" by the Democrats. The result was to leave the entire South under the political control of conservative white Democrats. For the first time since 1867, black and white Republicans no longer effectively controlled any former Confederate state.

Hayes withdrew the last federal troops from the South, and the Republican administration in those states collapsed. Democrats immediately took control.

Redemption was now complete. Each of the former Confederate states was under the authority of white Democrats. Henry Adams, a black leader from Louisiana, explained what had happened. "The whole South—every state in the South had got into the hands of the very men that held us as slaves."

T I M E L I N E

AFRICAN-AMERICAN EVENTS	NATIONAL EVENTS
1865	
1865 The Freedmen's Savings Bank and Trust Company is established	**1865** Freedmen's Bureau established **1866** President Johnson vetoes Freedmen's Bureau Bill and civil rights bill. Congress overrides both vetoes Ku Klux Klan is founded in Pulaski, Tennessee
1867	
1867–1868 Ten southern states hold constitutional conventions **1867** Howard University established in Washington, DC **1868** Black political leaders elected to state and local offices across the South	**1867** Congress takes over Reconstruction and provides for universal manhood suffrage **1868** Fourteenth Amendment to the Constitution is ratified Ulysses S. Grant elected president
1869	
1870 Hiram R. Revels is elected to the U.S. Senate and Joseph H. Rainey is elected to the U.S. House of Representatives Congress passes the Enforcement Act	**1869** Knights of Labor founded in Philadelphia **1870** Fifteenth Amendment to the Constitution is ratified John D. Rockefeller incorporates Standard Oil Co. in Cleveland
1871	
1871 Congress passes the Ku Klux Klan Act	**1871** William Marcy "Boss" Tweed indicted for fraud in New York City Much of Chicago burns in a fire **1872** Ulysses S. Grant reelected Yellowstone National Park established

continued

AFRICAN-AMERICAN EVENTS	NATIONAL EVENTS
1873	
1873	**1873**
The Colfax Massacre occurs in Louisiana	Financial panic and economic depression begin
1875	
1875	**1875**
Blanche K. Bruce is elected to the U.S. Senate Congress passes the Civil Rights Act of 1875 Democrats regain Mississippi with the "Shotgun Policy"	Whiskey Ring exposes corruption in federal liquor tax collections
	1876
1876	Presidential election between Samuel J. Tilden and Rutherford B. Hayes is disputed
Hamburg Massacre occurs in South Carolina	Gen. George A. Custer and U.S. troops defeated by Sioux and Cheyenne in Battle of Little Big Horn
1877	
1877	**1877**
Last federal troops withdrawn from South	The "Compromise of 1877" ends Reconstruction

CONCLUSION

The glorious hopes that emancipation and the Union victory in the Civil War had aroused among African Americans in 1865 appeared forlorn by 1877. To be sure, black people were no longer slave laborers or property. They lived in tightly knit families that white people no longer controlled. They had established hundreds of schools, churches, and benevolent societies. The Constitution now endowed them with freedom, citizenship, and the right to vote. Some black people had even acquired land.

But no one can characterize Reconstruction as a success. The epidemic of terror and violence made it one of the bloodiest eras in American history. Thousands of black people had been beaten, raped, and murdered since 1865, simply because they had acted as free people. Too many white people were determined that black people could not and would not have the same rights that white people enjoyed. White Southerners would not tolerate either the presence of black men in politics or white Republicans who accepted black political involvement. Gradually most white Northerners and even radical Republicans grew weary of intervening in southern affairs and became convinced again that black men and women were their inferiors and were not prepared to participate in government. Reconstruction, they concluded, had been a mistake.

Furthermore, black and white Republicans hurt themselves by indulging in fraud and corruption and by engaging in angry and divisive factionalism. But even if Republicans had been honest and united, white southern Democrats would never have accepted black people as worthy to participate in the political system.

Southern Democrats would accept black people in politics only if Democrats could control black voters. But black voters understood this, rejected control by former slave owners, and were loyal to the Republican Party—as flawed as it was.

But as grim a turn as life may have taken for black people by 1877, it would get even worse in the decades that followed.

REVIEW QUESTIONS

1. What issues most concerned black political leaders during Reconstruction?

2. What did black political leaders accomplish and fail to accomplish during Reconstruction? What contributed to their successes and failures?

3. Were black political leaders unqualified to hold office so soon after the end of slavery?

4. To what extent did African Americans dominate southern politics during Reconstruction? Should we refer to this era as "Black Reconstruction"?

5. Why was it so difficult for the Republican Party to maintain control of southern state governments during Reconstruction?

6. What was "redemption"? What happened when redemption occurred? What factors contributed to redemption?

7. How did Reconstruction end?

8. How effective was Reconstruction in assisting black people to make the transition from slavery to freedom? How effective was it in restoring the southern states to the Union?

RECOMMENDED READING

Eric Foner. *Freedom's Lawmakers: A Directory of Black Officeholders during Reconstruction.* New York: Oxford University Press, 1993. Biographical sketches of every known southern black leader during the era.

John Hope Franklin. *Reconstruction after the Civil War.* Chicago: University of Chicago Press, 1961. An excellent summary and interpretation of the postwar years.

William Gillette. *Retreat from Reconstruction, 1869–1879.* Baton Rouge: Louisiana State University Press, 1979. An analysis of how and why the North lost interest in the South.

Thomas Holt. *Black over White: Negro Political Leadership in South Carolina.* Urbana: University of Illinois Press, 1979. A masterful and sophisticated study of black leaders in the state with the most black politicians.

Michael L. Perman. *Emancipation and Reconstruction, 1862–1879.* Arlington Heights, IL: Harlan Davidson, 1987. Another excellent survey of the period.

Howard N. Rabinowitz, ed. *Southern Black Leaders of the Reconstruction Era.* Urbana: University of Illinois Press, 1982. A series of biographical essays on black politicians.

Frank A. Rollin. *Life and Public Services of Martin R. Delany.* Boston: Lee and Shepard, 1883. This is the first biography of a black leader by an African American. The author was Frances A. Rollin, but she used a male pseudonym.

WHITE SUPREMACY TRIUMPHANT

AFRICAN AMERICANS IN THE SOUTH IN THE LATE NINETEENTH CENTURY

POLITICS

In the late nineteenth century, black people remained important in southern politics. Black men served in Congress, state legislatures, and local governments. They received federal patronage appointments to post offices and custom houses. But as southern Democrats steadily disfranchised black voters in the 1880s and 1890s, the number of black politicians declined until the political system was virtually all white by 1900.

When Reconstruction ended in 1877 and the last Republican state governments collapsed, black men who held major state offices were forced out. In South Carolina, Lieutenant Governor Richard H. Gleaves resigned in 1877, but not without a protest. "I desire to place on record, in the most public and unqualified manner, my sense of the great wrong which thus forces me practically to abandon rights conferred on me, as I fully believe by a majority of my fellow citizens of this State."

For a time, some conservative white Democrats accepted limited black participation in politics as long as no black leader had power over white people and black participation did not challenge white domination. South Carolina's governor Wade Hampton even assured black people that he respected their rights and would appoint qualified black men to minor political offices.

Paternalistic Democrats like Hampton did appoint black men to lower-level positions. Hampton, for example, appointed Richard Gleaves and Martin Delany trial justices. In turn, some black men supported the Democrats. A few black Democrats were elected to state legislatures in the 1880s. Some had been Democrats throughout Reconstruction; others had abandoned the Republican Party.

Most black voters, however, remained loyal Republicans even though the party had become a hollow shell of what it had been during Reconstruction. Its few white supporters usually shunned black Republicans. The party rarely fielded candidates for statewide elections, limiting itself to local races in regions where Republicans remained strong.

Black Congressmen

Democrats skillfully created oddly shaped congressional districts to confine much of the black population of a state to one district, such as Mississippi's third district, South Carolina's seventh, Virginia's fourth, and North Carolina's second. A black Republican usually represented these districts while the rest of the state elected white Democrats to Congress. This diluted black voting strength, and it reduced the number of white people represented by a black congressman. Thus Henry Cheatham of North Carolina, John Mercer Langston of Virginia, Thomas E. Miller of South Carolina, and George H. White of North Carolina were elected to the House of Representatives long after Reconstruction had ended (see Table 14–1).

Table 14–1
Black Members of the U.S. Congress, 1870–1901

Dates	Name	State	Occupation	Prewar Status
1. 1870–1879	Joseph H. Rainey	South Carolina	Barber	Slave, then free
2. 1870–1873	Jefferson Long	Georgia	Tailor, storekeeper	Slave
3. 1870–1873	Hiram Revels*	Mississippi	Barber, minister, teacher, college president	Free
4. 1871–1877	Josiah T. Walls	Florida	Editor, planter, teacher, lawyer	Slave
5. 1871–1873	Benjamin Turner	Alabama	Businessman, farmer, merchant	Slave
6. 1871–1873	Robert C. DeLarge	South Carolina	Tailor	Free
7. 1871–1875	Robert B. Elliott	South Carolina	Lawyer	Free
8. 1873–1879	Richard H. Cain	South Carolina	AME minister	Free
9. 1873–1875	Alonzo J. Ransier	South Carolina	Shipping clerk, editor	Free
10. 1873–1875	James T. Rapier	Alabama	Planter, editor, lawyer, teacher	Free
11. 1873–1877, 1882–1883	John R. Lynch	Mississippi	Planter, lawyer, photographer	Slave
12. 1875–1881	Blanche K. Bruce*	Mississippi	Planter, teacher, editor	Slave
13. 1875–1877	Jeremiah Haralson	Alabama	Minister	Slave
14. 1875–1877	John A. Hyman	North Carolina	Storekeeper, farmer	Slave
15. 1875–1877	Charles E. Nash	Louisiana	Mason, cigar maker	Free
16. 1875–1887	Robert Smalls	South Carolina	Ship pilot, editor	Slave
17. 1883–1887	James E. O'Hara	North Carolina	Lawyer	Free
18. 1889–1893	Henry P. Cheatham	North Carolina	Lawyer, teacher	Slave
19. 1889–1891	Thomas E. Miller	South Carolina	Lawyer, college president	Free
20. 1889–1891	John M. Langston	Virginia	Lawyer	Free
21. 1893–1897	George W. Murray	South Carolina	Teacher	Slave
22. 1897–1901	George H. White	North Carolina	Lawyer	Slave

*Revels and Bruce served in the Senate, and the twenty remaining black legislators served in the House of Representatives.

But like their predecessors during Reconstruction, these black men wielded only limited power in Washington. They could not persuade their white colleagues to enact significant legislation to benefit their black constituents. They did, however, get Republican presidents to appoint black men and women to federal positions in their districts—including post offices and custom houses—and they spoke out about the plight of African Americans.

Democrats and Farmer Discontent

Black involvement in politics survived Reconstruction, but it did not survive the nineteenth century. Divisions within the Democratic Party and the rise of a new political party—the Populists—accompanied successful efforts to remove black people entirely from southern politics.

Militant Democrats stridently opposed the more moderate and paternalistic conservatives who took charge after Reconstruction. In the eyes of the militants, these redeemers seemed too willing to tolerate even limited black participation in politics while showing little interest in the needs of white yeoman farmers. Dissatisfied independents, "readjusters," and other disaffected white people resented the domination of the Democratic Party by former planters, wealthy businessmen, and lawyers who often favored limited government and reduced state support for schools, asylums, orphanages, and prisons while encouraging industry and railroads. Nor did the redeemer and paternalistic Democrats always agree among themselves. Some did favor agricultural education, the establishment of boards of health, and even separate colleges for black students. This lack of redeemer unity permitted insurgent Democrats and even Republicans sometimes to exploit economic and racial issues to undermine Democratic solidarity.

Many farmers felt betrayed as the industrial revolution transformed American society. They fed and clothed America, but large corporations, banks, and railroads increasingly dominated economic life. Wealth was concentrated in the hands of big industrialists and financiers. Farmers were no longer self-sufficient, admired for their hard work and self-reliance. They now depended on banks for loans, were exploited when they bought and sold goods, and found themselves at the mercy of railroads when they shipped their agricultural commodities. As businessmen got richer, farmers got poorer.

Small independent (yeoman) farmers in the South suffered from a sharp decline in the price of cotton between 1865 and 1890. Overwhelmed by debt, many lost their land and were forced into tenant farming and sharecropping. In response to their economic woes and political weakness, farmers organized. In the 1870s they formed the Patrons of Husbandry, or Grange. Initially a social and fraternal organization, the Grange promoted the formation of cooperatives and involvement in politics. Grangers especially favored government regulation of the rates railroads charged to transport crops. By the early 1880s, many hard-pressed small farmers turned to farmers' alliances. These organizations further encouraged farmers to buy and sell products cooperatively and to unite politically. They favored railroad regulation, currency inflation (to increase crop prices and ease debt burdens), and support for agricultural education. By 1888 many of them joined in the National Farmers' Alliance.

The Colored Farmers' Alliance

Although the alliances were radical on economic issues, they were conservative on racial issues. The Southern Alliance did not include black farmers, who instead formed their own Colored Farmers' Alliance. Even if it did not have that many supporters, the Colored Farmers' Alliance was one of the largest black organizations in American history. When the white alliances met in St. Louis in 1889, so did the black alliance—in a separate convention. The alliances maintained strict racial distinctions but promised to cooperate to resolve their economic woes. However, black and white alliance members did not always see their economic difficulties from the same perspective. Some of the white farmers owned the land that the black farmers lived on and worked. Black men saw their alliance as a way of getting a political education.

But white people were less certain that they wanted black men to vote at all—intelligently or otherwise. Many white alliance members harbored serious doubts about the right of black men to vote, and they opposed electing black men to office. Paradoxically, they also encouraged black men to vote as long as the black voters supported candidates the alliances backed. By the late 1880s, alliance-backed candidates in the South were elected to state legislatures, to Congress, and to four governorships.

The Populist Party

By 1892 many alliance farmers threw their political support to a new political party—the People's Party, generally known as the Populist Party—that mounted a serious challenge to the Democrats and Republicans. The Populists hoped to wrestle political control of the nation's economy from bankers and industrialists and their allies in the Republican and Democratic parties and to let the "people" shape the country's economic destiny. The Populists favored no less than the federal government takeover of railroads, telegraph, and telephone companies. The new party wanted the government to operate a loan and marketing program known as a Subtreasury system to benefit farmers. The Populists ran candidates for local and state offices and for Congress. In 1892 they nominated James B. Weaver of Iowa for president. The Populists urged southern white men to abandon the Democratic Party and southern black men to reject the Republican Party and to unite politically to support the Populists.

The foremost proponent of black and white political unity was Thomas Watson of Georgia. He and other Populist leaders believed economic and political cooperation could transcend racial differences. During the 1892 campaign, Watson explained that black and white farmers faced the same economic exploitation, but that they failed to cooperate with each other because of race. "The white tenant," he said,

> lives adjoining the colored tenant. Their homes are almost equally destitute of comforts. Their living is confined to bare necessities. They are equally burdened with heavy taxes. They pay the same high rent for gullied and impoverished land. . . .
>
> Now the Peoples' Party says to these two men. You are kept apart that you may be separately fleeced of your earnings. You are made to hate each other because upon that hatred is rested the keystone of the arch of financial despotism which enslaves you both. You are deceived and blinded that you may not see how this race antagonism perpetuates a monetary system which beggars both.

Despite such remarks, Watson was not calling for improved race relations. He opposed economic exploitation that was disguised by race, but when Democrats accused him of promoting racial reconciliation, he denied it.

Years after the failure of the Populists, Watson became a racial demagogue who warmly and thoroughly supported white supremacy. But in 1892 Watson and the Populists desperately wanted black and white voters to support Populist candidates. Southern Democrats, furious and outraged at the Populist appeal for black votes, resorted again to fraud, violence, and terror to prevail. When a biracial coalition of black and white Populists succeeded in taking political control of Grimes County in east Texas, Democrats massacred first the black and then the white leaders in 1900.

The Populist challenge heightened the fears of southern Democrats that black voters could tip the balance of elections if the white vote split. But many black people were suspicious of the Populist appeals and remained loyal to the Republican Party. The Republican Party in the South, however, was a much weaker organization than it had been during Reconstruction because many of its supporters could no longer vote. Years before the alliances and the Populists emerged, southern Democrats had begun to eliminate the black vote.

DISFRANCHISEMENT

As early as the late 1870s, southern Democrats had found ways to undermine black political power. Violence and intimidation, so effective during Reconstruction, continued in the 1880s and 1890s. Frightened, discouraged, or apathetic, many black men stopped voting. Black sharecroppers and renters could sometimes be intimidated or bribed by their white landlords not to vote, or to vote for candidates the landlord favored.

More militant and determined Democrats in the South were not content to rely on an assortment of unreliable methods to curtail the black vote. Some "legal" means had to be found to prevent black men from voting. However, the Fifteenth Amendment to the Constitution was a serious obstacle to this goal. It explicitly stated that the right to vote could not be denied on "account of race, color, or previous condition of servitude."

White leaders worried that if they imposed what were then legally acceptable barriers to voting—literacy tests, poll taxes, and property qualifications—they would disfranchise many white as well as black voters. But resourceful Democrats committed to white supremacy found ways around this problem. In 1882, for example, South Carolina passed the Eight Box Law, a primitive literacy test that required voters to deposit separate ballots for separate election races in the proper ballot box. Illiterate voters could not identify the boxes unless white election officials assisted them.

Mississippi

Mississippi made the most concerted and successful effort to eliminate black voters without openly violating the Fifteenth Amendment. Black men had continued to vote in Mississippi despite hostility and intimidation. In 1889 black leaders from forty Mississippi counties protested the "violent and criminal suppression of the black vote." In response white men called a constitutional convention to do away with the black vote.

With a single black delegate and 134 white delegates, the convention adopted complex voting requirements that—without mentioning race—disfranchised black voters. Voting required proof of residency and payment of all taxes, including a two-dollar poll tax. A person who had been convicted of arson, bigamy, or petty theft—crimes the delegates associated with black people—could not vote. People convicted of so-called white crimes—murder, rape, and grand larceny—could vote.

Above all, the new Mississippi constitution required voters to be literate, but with a notable exception. Illiterate men could still qualify to vote by demonstrating that they understood the constitution if the document was read to them. It was taken for granted that white voting registrars would accept almost all white applicants and fail most black applicants seeking to register under this provision.

South Carolina

Black voting had been declining in South Carolina since the end of Reconstruction. In the 1876 election, 91,870 black men voted; in the 1888 election, only 13,740 did. Unhappy that even so few voters might decide an election, U.S. senator Benjamin R. Tillman won approval for a constitutional convention in 1895. The convention followed Mississippi's lead and created an "understanding clause," but not without a vigorous protest from black leaders.

Six black men and 154 white men were elected to the South Carolina convention. Two of the black men—Robert Smalls and William Whipper (see Chapter 13)—had been delegates to the 1868 constitutional convention. The six black men protested black disfranchisement. Thomas E. Miller explained it was not just a matter of black power, but that the basic rights of citizens were at stake.

It was all for naught. Black voters were disfranchised in South Carolina. White delegates did not even pretend that elections should be fair. William Henderson of Berkeley County admitted

> We don't propose to have fair elections. We will get left at that every time. . . . I tell you, gentlemen, if we have fair elections in Berkeley we can't carry it. There's no use to talk about it. The black man is learning to read faster than the white man. And if he comes up and can read you have got to let him vote. Now are you going to throw it out. . . . We are perfectly disgusted with hearing so much about fair elections. Talk all around, but make it fair and you'll see what'll happen.

The Grandfather Clause

In 1898 Louisiana added a new twist to disfranchisement. Its grandfather clause stipulated that only men who had been eligible to vote before 1867—or whose father or grandfather had been eligible before that year—would be qualified to vote. Because virtually no black men had been eligible to vote before 1867—most had just emerged from slavery—the law immediately disfranchised almost all black voters.

Except for Kentucky and West Virginia, each southern state had enacted elaborate restrictions on voting by the 1890s. The federal government demonstrated a fleeting willingness to protect black voting rights. Republican senator Henry Cabot Lodge of

THE SPREAD OF DISFRANCHISEMENT

	State	Strategies
1889	Florida	Poll tax
	Tennessee	Poll tax
1890	Mississippi	Poll tax, literacy test, understanding clause
1891	Arkansas	Poll tax
1893, 1901	Alabama	Poll tax, literacy test, grandfather clause
1894, 1895	South Carolina	Poll tax, literacy test, understanding clause
1894, 1902	Virginia	Poll tax, literacy test, understanding clause
1897, 1898	Louisiana	Poll tax, literacy test, grandfather clause
1899, 1900	North Carolina	Poll tax, literacy test, grandfather clause
1902	Texas	Poll tax
1908	Georgia	Poll tax, literacy test, understanding clause, grandfather clause

Source: Goldfield et al., *The American Journey* (Upper Saddle River, NJ: Prentice Hall, 2004), p. 550.

Massachusetts introduced a bill in 1890 to send federal supervisors to states and congressional districts where election fraud was alleged. But southern Democrats blocked it.

SEGREGATION

When black attorney T. McCants Stewart visited Columbia, South Carolina, in 1885, he told readers of the New York Age that he had been pleasantly received and had encountered little discrimination. "I can ride in first class cars on the railroads and in the streets. I can go into saloons and get refreshments even as in New York. I can stop in and drink a glass of soda and be more politely waited upon than in some parts of New England." Stewart's visit occurred before most segregation laws requiring separation of the races in public places had been enacted. In fact, the word *segregation* was almost never used before the twentieth century.

Jim Crow

The term *Jim Crow* originated with a minstrel show routine called "Jump Jim Crow" that a white performer, Thomas "Daddy" Rice, created in the 1830s and 1840s. Rice blackened his face with charcoal and ridiculed black people. How Rice's character came to be synonymous with segregation and discrimination is not clear. What is clear is that by the end of the nineteenth century, Jim Crow and segregation were rapidly expanding in the South, greatly restricting the lives of African Americans.

In the decades following slavery's demise, segregation evolved gradually as an arrangement to enforce white control and domination. Many white Southerners resented the presence of black people in public facilities, places of entertainment, and business establishments. If black people were—as white Southerners believed—a subordinate race, then their proximity in shops, parks, and on passenger trains suggested an unacceptable equality in public life.

Moreover, many black people acquiesced in some facets of racial separation. During Reconstruction, people of color formed their own churches and social organizations. Black people were invariably more comfortable around people of their own race than they were among white people. Furthermore, black Southerners often accepted separate seating in theaters, concert halls, and other facilities that previously had been closed to them. Segregation represented an improvement over exclusion.

Segregation on the Railroads

Many white people particularly objected to the presence of black people in the first-class coaches of trains. Before segregation laws, white passengers and railroad conductors sometimes forced black people who had purchased first-class tickets into second-class coaches.

The first segregation laws involved passenger trains. Despite the spirited opposition of black politicians, the Tennessee legislature mandated segregation on railroad coaches in 1881. Florida passed a similar law in 1887. The railroads opposed these laws, but not because they wanted to protect the civil rights of black people. Rather, they were concerned about the expense of maintaining separate cars or sections within cars for black and white people. Whether they could pay for a first-class ticket or not, most black passengers found themselves confined to grimy second-class cars crowded with smoking and tobacco-chewing black and white men. Hitched at the head of the train just behind the smoke-belching locomotive, these cars were filthy with soot and cinders.

Plessy v. Ferguson

In 1891 the Louisiana legislature required segregated trains within the state, despite opposition from a black organization, the American Citizens' Equal Rights Association of Louisiana, the state's eighteen black legislators, and the railroads.

In a test case, black people challenged the Louisiana law and hoped to demonstrate its absurdity by enlisting the support of a black man who was almost indistinguishable from a white person. In 1892 Homer A. Plessy bought a first-class ticket and attempted to ride on the coach designated for white people. Plessy, who was only one-eighth black, was arrested for violating the new segregation law.

The case—*Plessy v. Ferguson*—wound its way through the judicial system. Plessy's lawyers argued that segregation deprived their client of equal protection of the law guaranteed by the Fourteenth Amendment. But in 1896 the U.S. Supreme Court in an 8 to 1 decision upheld Louisiana's segregation statute. Speaking for the majority, Justice Henry Brown ruled that the law, merely because it required separation of the races, did not deny Plessy his rights, nor did it imply he was inferior. The lone dissenter from this "separate but equal" doctrine, Justice John Marshall Harlan, whose father had owned slaves, likened the majority opinion to the *Dred Scott* decision thirty-nine years earlier. Thus with the complicity of the Supreme Court, the Fourteenth

Amendment no longer afforded black Americans equal treatment under the law. After the *Plessy* decision, southern states and cities passed hundreds of laws that created an elaborate system of racial separation.

Streetcar Segregation

In the late nineteenth century, before the automobile, the electric streetcar was the primary form of public transportation in American cities and towns. Beginning with Georgia in 1891, states and cities across the South segregated these vehicles. In some communities, the streetcar companies had to operate separate cars for black and white passengers; in other towns they designated separate sections within individual cars. The companies often resisted segregation, citing the expense of duplicating equipment and hiring more employees.

But black people were even more bitterly opposed to Jim Crow streetcars. During Reconstruction, they had fended off streetcar discrimination with boycotts and sit-ins. Thirty years later, they tried the same techniques. There were streetcar boycotts in at least twenty-five southern cities between 1891 and 1910. Black people refused to ride segregated cars in Atlanta, Augusta, Jacksonville, Montgomery, Mobile, Little Rock, and Columbia. They walked or took horse-drawn hacks. Initially, the boycotts succeeded in Atlanta and Augusta, where segregation was briefly abandoned. The boycotts seriously hurt the streetcar companies.

Segregation Proliferates

Jim Crow proceeded inexorably. "White" and "colored" signs appeared in railroad stations, theaters, auditoriums, and rest rooms and over drinking fountains. Southern white people were willing to go to any length to keep black and white people apart. Courtrooms maintained separate Bibles for black and white witnesses "to swear to tell the truth." By 1915 Oklahoma mandated white and colored public telephone booths. New Orleans attempted to segregate customers of black and white prostitutes, but only achieved mixed results.

Although *Plessy v. Ferguson* required "separate but equal" facilities for black and white people, when facilities were made available to black people, they were inferior to those afforded white people. Often, no facilities at all were provided for people of color. They were simply excluded. Few hotels, restaurants, libraries, bowling alleys, public parks, amusement parks, swimming pools, golf courses, or tennis courts would admit black people. The only exceptions would be black people who accompanied or assisted white people. For example, a black woman caring for a white child could visit a "white-only" public park with the child, but she dare not visit it with her own child.

RACIAL ETIQUETTE

Since slavery, white people had insisted that black people act in an obedient and subservient manner. Such behavior made white dominance clear. After emancipation, white Southerners sought to maintain that dominance through a complex pattern of racial etiquette that determined how black and white people dealt with each other in their day-to-day affairs.

Black and white people did not shake hands. Black people did not look directly into the eyes of white people. They were supposed to stare at the ground when addressing white men and women. Black men removed their hats in the presence of white people. White men did not remove their hats in a black home or in the presence of a black woman. Black people went to the back door, not the front door, of a white house. A black man or boy was never to look at a white woman. A black man in Mississippi observed, "You couldn't smile at a white woman. If you did you'd be hung from a limb." It was a serious offense if a black male touched a white woman, even inadvertently.

White customers were always served first in a store, even if a black customer had been the first to arrive. Black women could not try on clothing in white businesses. White people did not use titles of respect—mister, missus, miss—when addressing black adults. They used first names, or "boy" or "girl," or sometimes even "nigger." Older black people were sometimes called "auntie" or "uncle." But black people were expected to use mister, missus, and miss when addressing white people, including adolescents. "Boss" or "cap'n" might do for a white man.

VIOLENCE

In the late nineteenth century, the South was a violent place. Political and mob violence, so prevalent during Reconstruction, continued unabated into the 1880s and 1890s as Democrats often used armed force to drive the dwindling number of black and white Republicans out of politics.

Washington County, Texas

In 1886 in Washington County in eastern Texas, Democrats were determined to keep the political control that they had only won in 1884 through fraud. Masked Democrats tried to seize ballot boxes in a Republican precinct. But armed black men resisted and, with a shotgun blast, killed one of the white men. Eight black men were arrested. A mob of white men in disguise broke into the jail, kidnapped three of the black men, and lynched them. Three white Republicans fled for their lives, but convinced federal authorities to investigate. The U.S. Attorney twice tried to secure convictions for election fraud. The first trial ended in a hung jury, the second in acquittal. The white Democratic sheriff did not investigate the lynching. But the black man charged with firing the shotgun was sentenced to twenty-five years in prison.

The Phoenix riot

In the tiny South Carolina community of Phoenix in 1898, a white Republican candidate for Congress urged black men to fill out an affidavit if they were not permitted to vote. This produced a confrontation with Democrats. Words were exchanged, shots were fired, and the Republican candidate was wounded. White men then went on a rampage through rural Greenwood County. Black men were killed—how many is unknown. Others had to humiliate themselves by bowing down and saluting white men.

The Wilmington Riot

While white men roamed Greenwood County in search of black victims, an even bloodier riot erupted in Wilmington, North Carolina. Black and white men shared power as Republicans and Populists in Wilmington's city government, and white Democrats bitterly resented it. The Democrats were determined to drive the legitimately elected political leaders from power and would not hesitate to use violence to do so.

In the midst of this tense situation, the young editor of a local black newspaper, Alex Manly, published an editorial condemning white men for the sexual exploitation of black women. Manly also suggested that black men had sexual liaisons with rural white women, which infuriated the white community. "Poor white men are careless in the matter of protecting their women, especially on the farms. . . . Tell your men that it is no worse for a black man to be intimate with a white woman than for a white man to be intimate with a colored woman. . . . Don't think ever that your women will remain pure while you are debauching ours."

A white mob that included some of Wilmington's business and professional leaders destroyed the newspaper office. Black and white officials resigned in a vain attempt to prevent further violence. But at least a dozen black men—and perhaps many more—were murdered. Some 1,500 black residents of Wilmington fled. White people then bought up black homes and property at bargain rates. Black congressman George H. White, who represented Wilmington and North Carolina's second district, served the remainder of his term and then moved north. He ruefully remarked, "I can no longer live in North Carolina and be a man." White was the last black man to serve in Congress from the South until the election of Andrew Young in Atlanta in 1972.

The New Orleans Riot

Robert Charles was a 34-year-old literate laborer who had migrated to New Orleans from rural Mississippi. Infuriated by lynching, he was tantalized by the prospect of emigration to Liberia promoted by AME Bishop Henry M. Turner. On July 23, 1900, Charles and a friend were harassed by white New Orleans police officers. One of the officers attempted to beat Charles with a nightstick. Failing to subdue the large black man, the officer then drew a gun. Charles pulled out his own gun, and each man wounded the other. Charles fled and for a time evaded authorities. He was tracked down to a rooming house where he had secluded himself with a Winchester rifle with which he proceeded to shoot his tormentors. Eventually, a white mob that numbered as many as twenty thousand gathered. In the meantime, Charles—an expert marksmen—methodically shot twenty-seven white people, killing seven, including four policemen. Finally, burned out of the dwelling, Charles was shot and his corpse stomped beyond recognition by enraged white people. Four days of rioting ensued in which at least a dozen black people were killed and many more injured.

Lynching

Lynching had become common in the South by the 1890s. Between 1889 and 1932, 3,745 people were lynched in the United States. An average of two to three people were lynched every week for thirty years. Most lynchings happened in the South, and

Lynchings were common and public events in the South at the turn of the century. Often hundreds of people took part in and witnessed these gruesome spectacles.
Courtesy of the Library of Congress

black men were usually the victims. Sometimes white people were lynched. In 1891 in New Orleans eleven Italians were lynched for alleged involvement with the Mafia and for the murder of the city's police chief. For black Southerners, violence was an ever-present possibility.

The people who carried out the lynchings were never apprehended, tried, or convicted. Prominent community members frequently encouraged and even participated in lynch mobs. White political leaders, journalists, and clergymen rarely denounced lynching in public. The Atlanta *Constitution* dismissed lynching as relatively inconsequential. "There are places and occasions when the natural fury of men cannot be restrained by all the laws in Christendom."

There was no such thing as a civilized lynching. Lynchings were barbaric, savage, and hideous. Such mob brutality was another manifestation of white supremacy. Black people were murdered, beaten, burned, and mutilated for trivial reasons—or for no reason. Most white Southerners justified lynching as a response to the raping of white women by black men. But many lynchings involved no alleged rape, and even when they did, the victims often had no connection to the alleged offense.

Mobs often attacked black people who had achieved economic success. In Memphis, Thomas Moss with two friends opened the People's Grocery Company in a black neighborhood. The store flourished, but it competed with a white-owned grocery. "[T]hey were succeeding too well," one of Moss's friends observed. After the white grocer had had the three black men indicted for conspiracy, black people organized a protest and violence followed. The three black men were jailed. A white mob attacked the jail, lynched them, and then looted their store. Ida B. Wells, a newspaper editor and a friend of Moss, was heartbroken. "A finer, cleaner man than he never walked the streets of Memphis." She considered his lynching an "excuse to get rid of Negroes who were acquiring wealth and property and thus keep the race terrorized and keep the nigger down." Responding to the incident in her paper, Wells began a lifelong crusade against lynching.

Although less often than men, black women were also lynched. In 1914 in Wagoner County, Oklahoma, seventeen-year-old Marie Scott was lynched because her brother had killed a white man who had raped her. In Valdosta, Georgia, in 1918 after Mary Turner's husband was lynched, she publicly vowed to bring those responsible to justice. Although she was eight months pregnant, a mob considered her determination a threat. They seized her, tied her ankles together, and hanged her upside down from a tree. A member of the mob slit her abdomen, and her nearly full-term child fell to the ground. The mob stomped the infant to death. They then set her clothes on fire and shot her.

Rape

Although white people often justified lynching as a response to the presumed threat black men posed to the virtue of white women, white men routinely harassed and abused black women. There are no statistics on such abuse, but it surely was more common than lynching. Like lynching, rape inflicted pain and suffering, and it demonstrated the power of white men over black men and women. Black men tried to keep their wives and daughters away from white men. They refused to permit black women to work as maids and domestics in homes where white men were present. A black man could not easily protect a black woman. He might be killed trying to do it.

Many white people believed black women "invited" white males to take advantage of them. Black women were considered inferior, immoral, and lascivious. White people reasoned it was impossible to defend the virtue of black women because they had none. Governor Coleman Blease of South Carolina pardoned black and white men found guilty of raping black women. "I am of the opinion," he said in 1913, "as I have always been, and have very serious doubts as to whether the crime of rape can be committed upon a negro."

MIGRATION

In 1900 AME minister Henry M. Turner despaired for black people in America. "Every man that has the sense of an animal must see that there is no future in this country for the Negro. [W]e are taken out and burned, shot, hanged, unjointed and murdered in every way. Our civil rights are taken from us by force, our political rights are a farce."

It is, therefore, not surprising that thousands of African Americans fled poverty, powerlessness, and brutality in the South. What is perhaps surprising is that more did not leave. In the 1910s, 90 percent of black Americans still lived in the southern states.

And of those who left the South, most did not head north along the old Underground Railroad. The Great Migration to the northern industrial states did not begin until about 1915. Emigrants of the 1870s, 1880s, and 1890s were more likely to strike out for Africa or move west to Kansas, Oklahoma, and Arkansas, or move from farms to southern towns or cities.

The Liberian Exodus

When white Democrats redeemed Mississippi in 1875 with the "Shotgun Policy," a group of black people from Winona, Mississippi, wrote to Governor Adelbert Ames "to inquire about the possibility of moving to Africa. [W]e the colored people of Montgomery County are in a bad fix for we have no rights in the county and we want to know of you if there is any way for us to get out of the county and go to some place where we can get homes . . . so will you please let us know if we can go to Africa?"

They did not go to Africa, but some black Georgians and South Carolinians did. In 1877 black leaders in South Carolina, including AME minister and congressman Richard H. Cain, probate judge Harrison N. Bouey, and Martin Delany urged black people to migrate to Liberia. Many black communities and churches caught "Liberia Fever" while black people in upper South Carolina still felt the trauma of the political terror that had ended Reconstruction.

Several black men organized the Liberian Exodus Joint Stock Steamship Company. They raised $6,000 and hired a ship, the *Azor*, for the trip to Africa. The ship left Charleston in April 1878 with 206 migrants aboard and 175 left behind because there was not enough room for them. With inadequate food and fresh water and no competent medical care, twenty-three migrants died at sea. The ship arrived in Liberia on June 3.

Once settled in Liberia, several of the migrants prospered. Sam Hill established a seven hundred-acre coffee plantation, and C. L. Parsons became the chief justice of the Liberian Supreme Court. But others did less well, and some returned to the United States. The Liberian Exodus Company experienced financial difficulties and could not pay for further voyages.

The Exodusters

In May 1879 black delegates from fourteen states met in a convention in Nashville presided over by Congressman John R. Lynch of Mississippi. The convention resolved to support migration. The delegates declared that "the colored people should emigrate to those States and Territories where they can enjoy all the rights which are guaranteed by the laws and Constitution of the United States." They also asked Congress—in vain—to appropriate $500,000 for this venture.

Nevertheless, black people headed west. Between 1865 and 1880, 40,000 black people known as "Exodusters" moved to Kansas. Several hundred were persuaded to migrate by Benjamin "Pap" Singleton, a charismatic ex-slave and cabinetmaker from Tennessee. Six black men were instrumental in founding the Kansas town of Nicodemus in 1877. Named after an African prince who bought his freedom, Nicodemus thrived for a few years in the 1880s with a hotel, two newspapers, a general store, a drugstore, a school, and three churches. Several of the businesses were white owned. By 1890, however, Nicodemus went into a decline from which it never recovered. Three separate railroads were built across Kansas, but each avoided Nicodemus, spelling economic ruin for the community. In 1889 Congress had enacted legislation eliminating Indian Territory in Oklahoma, dispossessing the Five Civilized tribes of their land and dismantling tribal government. More than two dozen black towns including Boley and Liberty were founded in Oklahoma. There were nearly fifty black towns in the west by the early twentieth century including Allensworth, California; Blackdom, New Mexico; and Dearfield, Colorado. Other black migrants settled in rural and isolated portions of Nebraska, the Dakotas, Colorado as well as elsewhere on the Great Plains and in the Rocky Mountains.

Many black and white people who moved west after the Civil War took advantage of the 1862 Homestead Act that provided 160 acres of federal land free to those who would settle on it and farm it for at least five years. (Alternatively, a settler could buy the land for $1.25 per acre and possess it after six months' residency.) Life on the frontier was often a bleak, dreary, and lonely existence where trees were few and rain infrequent. People lived in sod houses and relied on cow (or buffalo) chips for heat and cooking fuel as they struggled to endure.

Railroads encouraged migration by offering reduced fares. Some western farmers and agents were eager to sell land, but some of it was of little value. Some of the white residents of Mississippi and South Carolina, which had large black majorities in their population, were glad to see the black people go. Others were alarmed at the loss of cheap black labor.

Some black leaders opposed migration and urged black people to stay put. In 1879 Frederick Douglass insisted that more opportunities existed for black people in the South than elsewhere. Robert Smalls urged black people to come to his home county of Beaufort, South Carolina, "where I hardly think it probable that any prisoner will ever be taken from jail by a mob and lynched."

Migration Within the South

Many black people left the poverty and isolation of farms and moved to nearby villages and towns in the South. Others went to larger southern cities including Atlanta, Richmond, and Nashville, where they settled in growing black neighborhoods. Urban areas offered more economic opportunities than rural areas. Although black people were usually confined to menial labor—from painting and shining shoes to domestic service—city work paid cash on a fairly regular basis, whereas rural residents received no money until their crops were sold. Towns and cities also afforded more entertainment and religious and educational activities. Black youngsters in towns spent more time in school than rural children, who had to help work the farms.

Black women had a better chance than black men of finding regular work in a town, although it was usually as a domestic or cleaning woman. This economic situation adversely affected the black family. Before the increase in migration, husband and wife headed 90 percent of black families. But with migration, many black men remained in rural areas where they could get farm work while women went to urban communities. Often these women became single heads of households.

BLACK FARM FAMILIES

Most black people did not leave the South or move to towns. They remained poverty-stricken sharecroppers and renters on impoverished land white people owned. They were poorly educated. They lacked political power. They were always in debt. Many rural black families remained precariously close to involuntary servitude in the decades after Reconstruction.

Sharecroppers

Most black farm families (and many white families as well) were sharecroppers. Sharecropping had emerged during Reconstruction as landowners allowed the use of their land for a share of the crop. The landlord also usually provided housing, horses or mules, tools, seed, and fertilizer as well as food and clothing. Depending on the agreement or contract, the landowner received from one-half to three-quarters of the crop.

Sharecropping lent itself to cheating and exploitation. By law, verbal agreements were considered contracts. In any case, many sharecroppers were illiterate and could not have read written contracts. The landowner informed the sharecropper of the

For more than a century—from the early 1800s until the 1920s—cotton was *the* crop across much of the deep South. First as slaves, then as sharecroppers, renters, and landowners, generations of black people toiled in the cotton fields.
Corbis/Bettmann

value of the product raised—typically cotton—as well as the value of the goods provided to the sharecropping family. Black farmers who disputed white landowners put themselves in peril. Although many sharecroppers were aware the proprietor's calculations were wrong, they could do nothing about it. Also, cotton brokers and gin owners routinely paid black farmers less than white farmers per pound for cotton. Black men were forced to accept the white man's word.

Renters

When they could, black farmers preferred renting to sharecropping. As tenants, they paid a flat charge to rent a given number of acres. Payment would be made in either cash—perhaps $5 per acre—or, more typically, in a specified amount of the crop—two bales of cotton per twenty acres. Tenants usually owned their own animals and tools. As Bessie Jones explained, "You see, a sharecropper don't ever have nothing. Before you know it, the man done took it all. But the renter always have something, and then he go to work when he want to go to work. He ain't got to go to work on the man's time. If he didn't make it, he didn't get it."

Crop Liens

In addition to the landowner, many sharecroppers and renters were also indebted to a local merchant for food, clothing, tools, and farm supplies. The merchant advanced the merchandise but took out a lien on the crop. If the sharecropper or renter failed to repay the merchant, the merchant was legally entitled to all or part of the crop once the landowner had received his payment. Merchants tended to charge high prices and high interest rates. They usually insisted that farmers plant cotton before they would agree to a lien. Cotton could be sold quickly for cash.

Peonage

Many farmers fell deeply into debt to landowners and merchants. They were cheated. Bad weather destroyed crops. Crop prices declined. Farmers who were in debt could not leave the land until the debt was paid. If they tried to depart, the sheriff pursued them. This was called peonage, and it amounted to enslavement, holding thousands of black people across the South in a state of perpetual bondage. Peonage violated federal law, but the law was rarely enforced. When landowners and merchants were prosecuted for keeping black people in peonage, white juries acquitted them.

Black Landowners

Considering the incredible obstacles against them, black farm families acquired land at an astonishing rate after the Civil War. Many white people refused to sell land to black buyers, preferring to keep them dependent. Black people also found it difficult to save enough money to purchase land even when they could find a willing seller. Still, they steadily managed to accumulate land.

Some black families had kept land that had been distributed in the Carolina and Georgia low country under the Port Royal Experiment and Sherman's Special Field Order #15 (see Chapter 11). In 1880 black people on South Carolina's Sea Islands held ten thousand acres of land worth $300,000.

By 1900 more than 100,000 black families owned their own land in the eight states of the deep South. Black land ownership increased more than 500 percent between 1870 and 1900. Most black people possessed small farms of about twenty acres. In many cases these small plots of land were subsequently subdivided among sons and grandsons, making it more difficult for their families to prosper. But some black farmers owned impressive estates. Prince Johnson had 360 acres of excellent Mississippi Delta land. Freedman Leon Winter was the richest black man in Tennessee, with real estate worth $70,000 in 1889. Florida farmer J. D. McDuffy had an 800-acre farm near Ocala and raised cantaloupes, watermelons, cabbages, and tomatoes. Texas freedman Daniel Webster Wallace had a 10,000-acre cattle ranch. Few black people inherited large estates. Most of these landowners had been born into slavery. In the decades after emancipation, they managed to accumulate land—usually just a few acres at a time.

White Resentment of Black Success

Many white Southerners found it difficult to tolerate black economic success. They resented black progress and lashed out at those who had achieved it. When one rural black man built an attractive new house, local white people told him not to paint it— lest it look better than theirs. He accepted the advice and left the dwelling bare.

When automobiles arrived in the early twentieth century, Henry Watson, a well-to-do black farmer in Georgia, drove a new car to town. Enraged white people surrounded the car, forced Watson and his daughter out at gunpoint, and burned the vehicle. Watson was told, "From now on, you niggers walk into town, or use that ole mule if you want to stay in this city."

AFRICAN AMERICANS AND SOUTHERN COURTS

The southern criminal justice systems yielded nothing but injustice to black people who ran afoul of it. Southern lawmakers worried incessantly about what they considered the growing black crime problem, and they worked diligently to control the black population. They enacted laws and ordinances to regulate the behavior of black people. Vagrancy laws made it easy to arrest any idle black man or one who was passing through a community. Contract evasion laws ensnared black people who attempted to escape peonage and perpetual servitude.

Segregated Justice

The legal system also became increasingly white after Reconstruction. Black police officers were gradually eliminated, and white policemen acquired a deserved reputation for brutality. Fewer and fewer black men served on juries, which were all white by 1900. (No women served on southern juries.) When black men were accidentally called for jury duty, they were rejected. In Alabama, a black man called for a local grand jury insisted on serving until he was beaten and forced to step down. Judges were white men. Most attorneys were white. The few black lawyers faced daunting hurdles. Some black defendants believed—correctly—that they would be found guilty and sentenced to a longer term if they retained a black attorney rather than a white one. Court personnel treated black plaintiffs, defendants, and witnesses with contempt.

A black defendant could not get justice. Black men and women were more often charged with crimes than white people. They were almost always convicted, regardless of the strength of the evidence or the credibility of witnesses. In one of the few instances when a black man was found not guilty of killing a white man, the defendant's attorney advised him to leave town because local white people were unlikely to accept the verdict. He fled, but returned twenty years later and was castrated by two white men.

Race was always the priority with jurors. Even when black people were the victims of crime, they were punished. In 1897 in Hinds County, Mississippi, a white man beat a black woman with an axe handle. She took him to court only to have the justice of the peace rule that he knew of "no law to punish a white man for beating a negro woman."

Juries rarely found white people guilty of crimes against black people. In a Georgia case in 1911, the evidence against several white people for holding black families in peonage was so overwhelming that the judge virtually ordered the jury to return a guilty verdict. Nonetheless, after five minutes of deliberation, the jury found the defendants not guilty. Many black and white people were astonished in 1898 in Shreveport, Louisiana, when a jury actually found a white man guilty of murdering a black man. He was sentenced to five years in prison.

Black people could receive leniency from the judicial system, but it was not justice. They were much less likely to be charged with a crime against another black person, like raping a black woman, than against a white person. Black people often were not charged with crimes such as adultery and bigamy because white people considered such offenses typical of black behavior.

Black defendants who had some personal or economic connection to a prominent white person were less likely to be treated or punished the same way as black people who had no such relationship. In Vicksburg, Mississippi, a black woman watched as the black man who had murdered her husband was acquitted because a white man intervened. Those black people known as "a white man's nigger" had a decided advantage in court.

Black people received longer sentences and larger fines than white people. In Georgia, black convicts served much longer sentences than white convicts for the same offense—five times as long for larceny, for example. An eighty-year-old black preacher went to prison "for what a white man was fined five dollars." In New Orleans, a black man was sentenced to ninety days in jail for petty theft. According to a local black newspaper, it was "three days for stealing and eighty-seven days for being colored."

The Convict Lease System

Conditions in southern prisons were indescribably wretched. Black prisoners—many incarcerated for vagrancy, theft, disorderly conduct, and other misdemeanors—spent months and years in oppressive conditions and were subjected to the unrelenting abuse of white authorities. But conditions could and did get worse.

Southern politicians devised the convict lease system in the late nineteenth century. Businesses and planters leased convicts from the state to build railroads, clear swamps, cut timber, tend cotton, and work mines. The company or planter had to feed, clothe, and house the prisoners. Of course, the convicts were not paid. The state and local community was not only freed of the burden of maintaining prisons and jails but also received revenue. For example, South Carolina was paid three dollars per month per prisoner. Some states and counties found this so remunerative that law enforcement officials were encouraged to charge even more black men with assorted crimes so they could contribute to this lucrative enterprise.

Leased convicts endured appalling treatment and conditions. They were shackled and beaten. They were overworked and underfed; they slept on vermin-infested straw mattresses and received little or no medical care. They sustained terrible injuries on the job and at the hands of guards; diseases proliferated in the camps. Hundreds died, meaning they had, in effect, been sentenced to death for their petty crimes.

Businessmen and planters found such cheap labor almost irresistible, and black prisoners found it "nine kinds of hell." It was worse than slavery because these black lives had no value to either the government or the businesses involved in this sordid system. As one employer explained in 1883, "But these convicts; we don't own em. One dies, get another." The inhumanity of convict leasing became such a scandal that states outlawed it by the early twentieth century. Convicts were returned to state-operated penitentiaries.

T I M E L I N E

AFRICAN-AMERICAN EVENTS	NATIONAL EVENTS
1875	
	1877
	Reconstruction ends
1880	
1880	**1880**
Cadet Johnson C. Whittaker is assaulted at West Point	James Garfield elected President
	1880s
1881	Southern Farmers' Alliance forms, beginning
Tennessee enacts the first law segregating passenger trains	Farmers' Alliance movement
	1881
Tuskegee Institute founded	President James Garfield assassinated
	Clara Barton establishes the Red Cross
1885	
1886	**1886**
Riot occurs in Washington County, Texas	Haymarket affair in Chicago kills seven police and four strikers

continued

AFRICAN-AMERICAN EVENTS	NATIONAL EVENTS
1887 National Colored Farmers' Alliance is formed **1889–1908** Southern states disfranchise black voters Florida segregates passenger trains	**1887** Congress creates the Interstate Commerce Commission Dawes Act permits individual Indian families to own reservation land **1889** *Wall Street Journal* established
1890	
1891 Georgia segregates streetcars **1892** 235 people are lynched in the United States, 155 of them African American, the most in American history	**1890** 11 Italians lynched in New Orleans James A. Naismith invents basketball in Springfield, Massachusetts **1892** The Populist Party challenges the Democrats and Republicans in national elections Homestead strike at the Carnegie steel plant near Pittsburgh Grover Cleveland elected to a second term as president **1893** Panic of 1893 begins a serious economic depression
1895	
1896 In *Plessy v. Ferguson*, the U.S. Supreme Court upholds legal segregation **1898** The Phoenix riot occurs in South Carolina The Wilmington riot occurs in North Carolina **1899–1901** Term of George H. White of North Carolina ends—the South's last black congressman until 1972	**1896** Republican William McKinley is elected president; Populist Party holds last national campaign **1898** Eugene V. Debs helps found what will become the Socialist Party U.S. annexes Hawaii **1899** William McKinley reelected president
1900	
1900 New Orleans riot	

CONCLUSION

With the end of the Civil War and slavery in 1865, more than four million Americans of African descent had looked with hope and anticipation to the future. Four decades later, there were more than nine million African Americans, and more than eight million of them lived in the South. The crushing burden of white supremacy increasingly limited their hopes and aspirations. The U.S. government abandoned black people to white Southerners and their state and local governments. The federal government that had assured their rights as citizens during Reconstruction ignored the legal, political, and economic situation that entrapped most black Southerners.

Although the Thirteenth Amendment abolished slavery, thousands of black people were hopelessly trapped in peonage; thousands of others labored as sharecroppers and renters, indebted to white landowners and merchants. Yet more than 100,000 black families managed to acquire farms of their own by 1900. Many black farmers had also organized and participated in the Colored Farmers' Alliance and the Populist Party, although it brought few tangible benefits.

The Fourteenth Amendment had guaranteed the rights of citizenship that included due process of law. No state could deprive a person of life, liberty, or property without a court proceeding. The amendment also ensured each citizen equal protection of the law. But the Supreme Court had ruled that racial segregation in public places did not infringe on the right to equal protection of the law. And as for the right to life, hundreds of black people had lost their lives at the hands of lynch mobs by the early 1900s.

The Fifteenth Amendment stipulated that race could not be used to deprive a man of the right to vote. Nevertheless, southern states circumvented the amendment with poll taxes, literacy tests, and the grandfather clause. Thus, by 1900, after black men had held political offices across the South for the previous thirty years, no black person served in any elected political position in any southern state.

White people clearly regarded black Americans as an inferior race not entitled to those rights that the Constitution so emphatically set forth. What could black people do about the intolerance, discrimination, violence, and powerlessness they had to endure? What strategies, ideas, and leadership could they use to overcome the burdens they were forced to bear? What realistic chances did they have of overcoming white supremacy? How could black people organize to gain fundamental rights that were guaranteed to them?

REVIEW QUESTIONS

1. How were black people prevented from voting despite the provisions of the Fifteenth Amendment?

2. What legal and ethical arguments did white Americans use to justify segregation?

3. Why did the South experience an epidemic of violence and lynching in the late nineteenth century?

4. Why didn't more black people migrate from the South in this period?

RECOMMENDED READING

Edward L. Ayers. *The Promise of the New South: Life after Reconstruction.* New York: Oxford University Press, 1992. An excellent overview of how people lived in the late-nineteenth-century South.

Leon Litwack. *Trouble in Mind: Black Southerners in the Age of Jim Crow.* New York: Alfred A. Knopf, 1998. In moving words and testimony, black people describe what life was like in a white supremacist society.

Rayford Logan. *The Negro in American Life and Thought: The Nadir, 1877–1901.* New York: Dial Press, 1954. Explorations of the contours and oppressiveness of racism.

Benjamin E. Mays. *Born to Rebel: An Autobiography.* New York: Charles Scribner, 1971. Eloquent and graphic recollection of what it was like to grow up black in the rural South at the turn of the century.

C. Vann Woodward. *The Strange Career of Jim Crow.* New York: Oxford University Press, 1955. The evolution of legal segregation in the South.

BLACK SOUTHERNERS CHALLENGE WHITE SUPREMACY

SOCIAL DARWINISM

Pseudoscientific evidence and academic scholarship bolstered the conviction of many Americans that white people, especially those of English and Germanic descent—Anglo-Saxons—were culturally and racially superior to nonwhites and even other Europeans. Sociologists Herbert Spencer and William Graham Sumner drew on Charles Darwin's theory of evolution and concluded that life in modern industrial societies mirrored life in the animal kingdom. This theory, called social Darwinism, held that through a process of natural selection, the strong would thrive, prosper, and reproduce while the weak would falter, fail, and die. Life was a struggle; only the fittest survived.

Social Darwinism applied to both individuals and "races." It conveniently justified great disparities in wealth, suggesting that such men as John D. Rockefeller and Andrew Carnegie were rich because they were "fit," whereas many European immigrants and most African Americans were poor and unlikely to succeed because they were "unfit." The same logic explained the strength and prosperity of the United States, Great Britain, and Germany compared to countries such as Spain and Italy and conveniently explained why African, Asian, and Latin American societies seemed so backward and primitive. In absorbing this ideology of class and race, many Americans and Europeans came to believe they had a responsibility—a duty—to introduce the political, economic, and religious benefits and values of Western cultures to the "less advanced" and usually darker peoples of the globe. This presumed responsibility was summed up in the words of the English poet Rudyard Kipling as "the white man's burden."

Social Darwinism increasingly influenced the way most Protestant white Americans perceived their society, leading them to believe people could be ranked from superior to inferior based on their race, nationality, and ethnicity. Black people were invariably ranked at the bottom of this hierarchy, and the eastern and southern European immigrants who were flooding the country only slightly above them. Black people were capable, so the reasoning went, of no more than a subordinate role in a complex and advanced society as it rushed into the twentieth century. And if their position was biologically ordained, why should society devote substantial resources to their education?

EDUCATION AND SCHOOLS

A black youngster who wanted an education in the late nineteenth century faced formidable obstacles. Most black people were poor farmers who had few opportunities for an education and even fewer prospects for a career in business or one of the professions. It is remarkable—and a testimony to black perseverance—that so many black people did manage to acquire some education and to free themselves from illiteracy.

Gaining even a rudimentary education was not easy. Rural schools for black children rarely operated for more than thirty weeks a year. Because of the demands of fieldwork, most black youngsters could not attend school on a regular basis. Brothers and sisters sometimes alternated work and school with each other on a daily basis.

Schools were often dilapidated shacks. They lacked plumbing, electricity, books, and teaching materials. Some schools were in churches and homes. Teachers were poorly paid and often poorly prepared. Septima Clark remembered her first teaching experience on Johns Island on the South Carolina coast in the early twentieth century:

> Here I was, a high-school graduate, eighteen years old, principal in a two-teacher school with 132 pupils ranging from beginners to eighth graders, with no teaching experience, a schoolhouse constructed of boards running up and down, with no slats on the cracks, and a fireplace at one end of the room that cooked the pupils immediately in front of it but allowed those in the rear to shiver and freeze on their uncomfortable, hard, back-breaking benches.

Segregated Schools

Although southern states could not afford to support even one first-rate public school system, each of them operated separate schools for black and white children (see Table 15–1). The South had almost no public black high schools. In 1915 in 23 southern cities with populations of more than 20,000, including Tampa, New Orleans, Charleston, and Charlotte, there was not one black public high school. But these 23 cities had 36 high schools for white youngsters. In 1897 over the vehement protests of the black community, white school officials in Augusta, Georgia, closed Ware High School, the black secondary school, and transformed it into a black primary school. The U.S. Supreme Court in 1899 in *Cumming v. Richmond County [Georgia] Board of Education* unanimously refused to accept the contention of black parents that the elimination of the black high school violated the "separate but equal" doctrine announced in the *Plessy v. Ferguson* case three years earlier. Augusta was left with two white high schools—one for males and one for females, and none for black people.

Young black people who sought more than a primary education often had to travel to a black college or university that offered a high school program. For example, in 1911, at the age of sixteen, Benjamin Mays boarded a train and traveled one hundred miles to South Carolina State College and enrolled in the seventh grade. He graduated from high school there in 1916 at the age of twenty-two and then graduated from Maine's Bates College four years later.

In many communities, black people, with the assistance of churches and northern philanthropists, operated private academies and high schools, such as Fort Valley High and Industrial School in Georgia and Mather Academy in Camden, South Carolina, to fill the void created by the lack of public schools. Typically students were charged a modest tuition, and those who attended came from the more prosperous families of the black community. In 1890 the number of black youngsters between the

Table 15–1
South Carolina's Black and White Public Schools, 1908–1909

Black Schools		White Schools
2,354	Public Schools	2,712
894	Men Teachers	933
1,802	Women Teachers	3,247
181,095	Total Pupils	153,807
123,481	Average Attendance	107,368
77	Pupils per School	55
63	Pupils per Teacher	35
14.7	Average Number of Weeks of School	25.2
$118.17	*Average Yearly Salary for Men Teachers*	$479.79
$91.45	*Average Yearly Salary for Women Teachers*	$249.13
$308,153.16	*Total Expenditures*	$1,590,732.51

School for most southern black students and teachers was a part-time activity. Because of the demands of agriculture, few rural students, black or white, attended school more than six months a year. Very few teachers were graduates of four-year college programs. The situation was better in urban communities and upper South schools, where the school year lasted longer and education was better financed. But all public schools were segregated in the South.

Source: Department of Education Annual Report, South Carolina, 1908–09, pp. 935, 961.

ages of fifteen and nineteen attending black public or private high schools in the South was 3,106. By 1910 that number had risen to 26,553.

The Hampton Model

Some black people and many white people regarded education for black youngsters a pointless exercise. Benjamin Mays's father put little value in education: "My greatest opposition to going away to school was my father. When I knew that I had learned everything that I could in the one-room Brickhouse School and realized how little that was, my father felt that this was sufficient—that it was all I needed. . . . He was convinced that education went to one's head and made him a fool and dishonest." In 1911 South Carolina's governor Coleman Blease was even more blunt: "Instead of making an educated negro, you are ruining a good plow hand and making a half-trained fool."

Many of those who did value schooling were convinced the most appropriate education for a black child was industrial or domestic training. Black youngsters, these people maintained, should learn skills they could teach others and use to make themselves productive members of the community.

Hampton Normal and Agricultural Institute was founded in 1868 in Virginia and was dominated for decades by Samuel Chapman Armstrong, a white missionary with strong paternalistic inclinations. Hampton trained legions of African Americans and

Native Americans to teach skills and to embrace the importance of hard work, diligence, and Christian morality. Armstrong stressed learning trades, such as shoemaking, carpentry, tailoring, and sewing. Hampton placed little emphasis on critical or independent thinking. Students were taught to conform to middle-class values. Armstrong cautioned against black involvement in politics, and he acquiesced in Jim Crow racial practices.

Washington and the Tuskegee Model

Armstrong's prize student and Hampton's foremost graduate was Booker T. Washington, who became the nation's leading apostle of industrial training and one of the preeminent leaders and most remarkable men—black or white—in American history. Washington was born a slave in western Virginia in 1856. His father was a white man whose identity is unknown. He was raised by his mother, Jane, in an unimpressive, but tidy, cabin of split logs on a small farm. As a child, he was employed at a salt works and in coal mines. He was also a houseboy for a prominent white family. He attended a local school where he learned to read and write.

Intensely ambitious, Washington set off for Hampton Institute in 1872. While there, he was much affected by Armstrong and his curriculum and method of instruction. He worked his way through school and taught for two years at Hampton after

Booker T. Washington, looking regal in this portrait, was the most influential black leader in America by 1900. White business and political leaders were reassured by his message that black people themselves were responsible for their economic progress and that people of color should avoid a direct challenge to white supremacy.
The Granger Collection, New York

graduating. In 1881 he accepted an invitation to found a black college in Alabama—Tuskegee Institute. The result was an institution, which he forged almost single-handedly, that reflected his experience at Hampton and the influence of Armstrong.

From the day he arrived at Tuskegee until his death in 1915, Washington worked tirelessly to persuade black and white people that the surest way for black people to advance was by learning skills and demonstrating a willingness to do manual labor. Washington believed that if black people acquired skills and became prosperous small farmers, artisans, and shopkeepers, they would in time earn the respect and acceptance of white Americans and eventually eradicate the race problem—all without unseemly protest and agitation.

Washington's message earned accolades from white political leaders and philanthropists, who were more inclined to support the promotion of trades and skills among black people than an academic and liberal education. Disciples of Washington and graduates of Tuskegee fanned out across the South as industrial and agricultural educational training for black youngsters proliferated.

The Morrill Act, which Congress passed in 1862, entitled each state to the proceeds from the sale of federal land (most of it in the West) for establishing land-grant colleges to provide agricultural and mechanical training. However, southern states did not admit black students to their A&M (Agricultural and Mechanical) schools. A second Morrill Act, however, passed in 1890 that permitted states to establish and fund separate black land-grant colleges. By 1915 there were sixteen black land-grant colleges.

Most of the institutions were not actually colleges. Few of their students graduated with bachelor's degrees, and many of them were enrolled in primary and secondary programs. Virtually all the students at the black land-grant schools had to take courses in trades, agriculture, and domestic sciences. Most of the schools required students to do manual labor for which they were paid small sums. Students built and maintained the campuses, and they raised the food served in the school cafeteria. Some of the students were in the "normal" curriculum, which prepared them to teach at a time when most states did not require a college degree for a teaching certificate.

Critics of the Tuskegee Model

Not everyone shared Washington's stress on industrial and agricultural training for young black men and women to the near exclusion of the liberal arts, including literature, history, philosophy, and languages. Washington's program, some critics charged, seemed to be designed to train black people for a subordinate role in American society. Black people, they worried, would continue to labor much as they had in slavery.

W. E. B. Du Bois, a Fisk- and Harvard-trained scholar, and AME Bishop Henry M. Turner believed education went beyond mere training and the acquisition of skills. It involved intellectual growth and development. It would confront racial problems. It would create wise men. According to Du Bois, "The function of the Negro college, then, is clear, it must maintain standards of popular education, it must seek the social regeneration of the Negro, and it must help in the solution of problems of race contact and cooperation. And finally, beyond all this, it must develop men."

Many of the private black colleges resisted the emphasis on agricultural and mechanical training, promoted the liberal arts, and taught Latin, Greek, mathematics, and natural sciences. Henry L. Morehouse of the American Baptist Home Missionary Society explained the purpose of education was to develop strong minds. He believed gifted intellectuals—a "talented tenth" as he characterized them in 1896—could lead people forward. Du Bois likewise stressed the need for the best educated 10 percent of the black population to promote progress and to advance the race.

In fairness to Washington, he did not deny the importance of a liberal arts education, but he also believed industry was the foundation to progress:

> On such a foundation as this will grow habits of thrift, a love of work, economy, ownership of property, bank accounts. Out of it in the future will grow practical education, professional education, and positions of public responsibility. Out of it will grow moral and religious strength. Out of it will grow wealth from which alone can come leisure and the opportunity for the enjoyment of literature and the fine arts.

Ultimately, however, Washington was wrong to believe education for black people that focused on economic progress would earn the respect of most white Americans. As Du Bois explained, most white people preferred ignorant and unsuccessful black people to educated and prosperous ones:

> If my own city of Atlanta had offered it to-day the choice between 500 Negro college graduates—forceful, busy, ambitious men of property and self-respect—and 500 black cringing vagrants and criminals, the popular vote in favor of the criminals would be simply overwhelming. Why? Because they want Negro crime? No, not that they fear Negro crime less, but that they fear Negro ambition and success more. They can deal with crime by chain gang and lynch law, or at least they think they can, but the South can conceive neither machinery nor place for the educated, self-reliant, self-assertive black man.

As Chapter 16 discusses, the conflict among black leaders over the most suitable form of education would expand by the early twentieth century into a larger controversy. What began as a disagreement over the value of practical education would become a passionate debate among Washington, Du Bois, and others over the most effective strategy—accommodation or confrontation—for overcoming Jim Crow and white supremacy.

CHURCH AND RELIGION

In a world in which white people otherwise so thoroughly dominated the lives and limited the possibilities of black people, the church had long been the most important institution—after the family—that African Americans controlled for themselves. After the Civil War, black people organized their own churches and religious denominations, which grew and thrived as sources of spiritual comfort and centers of social activity. Black clergymen were often the most influential members of the black community.

In 1890 the South had more black Baptists than all other denominations combined. Baptist congregations were more independent and under less supervision by

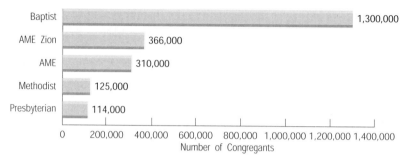

Figure 15–1   **Church Affiliation among Southern Black People: 1890**
The vast majority of black Southerners belonged to Baptist, Methodist, and
Presbyterian congregations in the late nineteenth century, although there were
about 15,000 black Episcopalians and perhaps 200,000 Roman Catholics.
Source: Edward L. Ayers, *The Promise of the New South*, pp. 160–61.

church hierarchy than other denominations. Bishops, for example, in the African
Methodist Episcopal Zion church and the African Methodist Episcopal (AME) church
exercised considerable authority over congregations, as did Methodist and Presbyterian
leaders. Many black people (and many southern white people as well) preferred the
autonomy of the Baptist churches (Figure 15–1).

But whatever the denomination, the church was integral to the lives of most black
people. It fulfilled spiritual needs through sermons and music. It gave black people
the opportunity, free from white interference, to plan, organize, and lead. It was especially a sanctuary for black women, who immersed themselves in church activities.
Although church members usually had little money to spare, they helped the sick, the
bereaved, and people displaced by fires and natural disasters. Black congregations also
helped thousands of youngsters attend school and college.

The church service itself was the most important aspect of religious life for most
black congregations. Parishioners were expected to participate in the service and not
merely listen quietly to the minister's sermon. Black people had long considered white
church services too sedate. One black school principal believed black people gave
added meaning to Christianity: Whereas "the white man gives it system, logic and ab-
straction, the Negro is necessary to impart feeling, sanctioned emotions, heart throes
and ecstasy." In most black churches, members punctuated the minister's call with
many an "Amen." They testified, shouted, laughed and cried, and sometimes fainted.
Choirs provided joyful music and solemn songs.

Most congregations did not want scholarly sermons or theologically sound addresses. When Frederick Jones, a well-dressed new black minister in North Carolina,
offered a deliberate message brimming with rationality, he was met with silence and re-
buked by a senior member of the congregation. "Dese fellers comes out heah wid dere
starched shirts, and dey' beaver hats, and dere kid gloves, but dey don't know nuffin
b[o]ut 'ligion." The next time Jones preached, he had changed his clothes and delivered a passionate sermon.

Many black ministers had little or no education. Benjamin E. Mays's father told him the clergy did not need an education. "God called men to preach; and when He called them, He would tell them what to say!" Poorly prepared and unqualified clergymen who relied on ungrammatical and rhetorical appeals disturbed some black leaders. In 1890 Booker T. Washington claimed that "three-fourths of the Baptist ministers and two-thirds of the Methodists are unfit, either mentally or morally, or both, to preach the Gospel to any one or to attempt to lead any one." W. E. B. Du Bois wanted black churches free of "the noisy and unclean leaders of the thoughtless mob" and the clergy replaced by thoughtful "apostles of service and sacrifice." But a black Alabama farmer observed that solemn and erudite preachers would not survive: "You let a man preach de true Gospel and he won't git many nickels in his pocket; but if he hollers and jumps he gits all the nickels he can hold and chickens besides."

Although infrequently, black women sometimes led congregations. Nannie Helen Burroughs established Women's Day in Baptist churches. Women delivered sermons and guided the parishioners. But Burroughs complained that Women's Day quickly became more an occasion to raise money than to raise women.

The Church as Solace and Escape

For many black people, the emotional involvement and enthusiastic participation in church services was an escape from their dreary and oppressive daily lives. Growing up in rural Greenwood County, South Carolina, Benjamin E. Mays admitted that his Baptist preacher, James F. Marshall, who barely had a fifth-grade education, "emphasized the joys of heaven and the damnation of hell" and that the "trials and tribulations of the world would all be over when one got to heaven." But Mays understood the need for such messages to assuage the impact of white supremacy. "Beaten down at every turn by the white man, as they were, Negroes could perhaps not have survived without this kind of religion."

Black clergymen like Marshall refused to challenge white supremacy. Even veiled comments might invite retaliation or even lynching. When a visiting minister began to criticize white people to Marshall's congregation, Marshall immediately stopped him. Despite the reluctance of many black clergymen to advocate improvement in race relations, many white people still viewed black religious gatherings as a threat. Black churches were burned and black ministers assaulted and killed with tragic regularity in the late-nineteenth-century South.

Black clergymen, like their white counterparts, often stressed middle-class values to their congregations while suggesting that many black people found themselves in shameful situations because of their sinful ways. They urged them to improve their behavior. Black people who had acquired sinful reputations sometimes received funeral sermons that consigned them to eternal damnation in a fiery hell.

There were black religious leaders who publicly and vigorously opposed white supremacy and insisted that black people stand up for their rights. AME Bishop Henry M. Turner persistently spoke out on racial matters. In 1883 after the U.S. Supreme Court declared the 1875 Civil Rights Act unconstitutional, Turner called the Constitution "a dirty rag, a cheat, a libel and ought to be spit upon by every Negro in the land."

The Holiness Movement and the Pentecostal Church

Not all black people belonged to mainline denominations. The Holiness movement and the emergence of Pentecostal churches affected Methodist and Baptist congregations. Partly in reaction to the elite domination and stiff authority of white Methodism, the Holiness movement gained a foothold among white people and then spilled over among black Southerners. Holiness churches ordained women such as Neely Terry to lead them. Holiness clergy preached that sanctification allowed a Christian to receive a "second blessing" and to feel the "perfect love of Christ." Believers thus achieved an emotional reaffirmation and a new state of grace.

The Church of God in Christ (COGIC) became the leading black Holiness church. After a series of successful revivals in Mississippi and Memphis, two black former Baptists—Charles Harrison Mason and C. P. Jones—founded COGIC in 1907. However, Mason was expelled after reporting that "a flame touched [his] tongue," and his "language changed." He had spoken in tongues. Mason then organized the Pentecostal General Assembly of the Church of God in Christ, and he assigned several black men to serve as bishops in Mississippi, Arkansas, Texas, Missouri, and California. In 1911 Mason appointed Lizzee Woods Roberson to lead the Woman's Department, a post she held until 1945. She transformed that department into a financial powerhouse for COGIC.

In the meantime, Charles Fox Parham, a dynamic white minister, had founded the Pentecostal church in the early twentieth century in the Houston-Galveston area of Texas. William J. Seymour, who was born a slave in Louisiana, played a key role in the development of the church. After hearing black people speak in tongues in Houston, he went to Los Angeles where he and others also began to speak in tongues. There he founded the highly evangelistic church that became the Pentecostal church. It attracted enormous interest and grew rapidly.

Charles Harrison Mason joined the Pentecostal movement, and under his leadership the Reorganized Church of God in Christ became the leading Pentecostal denomination. It soon spread across the South among black and white people. Although there were tensions between black and white believers, the Pentecostal church was the only movement of any significance that crossed the racial divide in early twentieth-century America.

Roman Catholics and Episcopalians

Most African Americans belonged to one of the Baptist or Methodist churches. Booker T. Washington reportedly observed that "If a black man is anything but a Baptist or Methodist, someone has been tampering with his religion." Nevertheless, black people also belonged to other churches and denominations—or occasionally belonged to no organized religious group.

As many as 200,000 African Americans were Roman Catholic in 1890. They were rarely fully accepted by the church or white Catholics. They were segregated in separate churches with separate parish schools in the South.

The most prominent black Catholics in nineteenth-century America came from the Healy family. Eliza Clark was a slave who had nine children by Michael Healy, an

Irish-Catholic plantation owner in Georgia. Unlike many white men, Healy genuinely cared for Eliza and their children, although by law he could not marry a black woman. The children were educated in northern schools. James A. Healy graduated from the Jesuit-run Holy Cross College in Massachusetts and was ordained a priest at Notre Dame Cathedral in Paris in 1854. He later became a bishop in Portland, Maine.

Patrick Healy also attended Holy Cross and became the first black Jesuit priest in the United States. He served eight years as president of Georgetown University in Washington. Eliza Healy took vows as a nun and was the headmistress of a Catholic school in Vermont. Most white people were unaware of the racial ancestry of the Healys, and members of the family did not openly acknowledge being African American even when other black Catholics asked for their support. Bishop James Healy, for example, refused on three occasions to speak to the Congress of Colored Catholics, an association of black Catholics that met at least four times in northern cities between 1889 and 1893. Its members were mainly concerned with the discrimination they faced in the Roman Catholic Church and with the educational opportunities that were available—or more often that were not available—to black Catholic children in church schools.

Augustus Tolton was another African-American priest, and there was no question about his color. Because no American seminary would accept him, he was educated and ordained in 1886 in Rome. For a time, he presided over a parish in Quincy, Illinois, made up mainly of Irish and German Catholics. Unlike Bishop Healy, Tolten did speak to the Congress of Colored Catholics in Philadelphia in 1892.

Mother Mathilda Beasley came from a prominent free black family in Savannah. Her efforts to establish a community of Franciscan sisters in rural Georgia ultimately failed. In New Orleans, where there were sizable numbers of black Catholics of French and Spanish descent, the Sisters of Blessed Sacrament established a black high school in 1915 that became Xavier University in 1925.

Fairly or unfairly, most African Americans identified black Episcopalians with wealth and privilege. Many of those Episcopalians traced their heritage to free black families before the Civil War. By 1903 approximately 15,000 members of black Episcopal parishes worshipped in Richmond, Raleigh, Charleston, and other urban communities in the North and South.

RED VERSUS BLACK: THE BUFFALO SOLDIERS

After the Civil War, the U.S. Army was reduced to fewer than 30,000 troops. Congressional Democrats tried to eliminate black soldiers and their regiments from this small force, but radical Republicans, led by Massachusetts senator Henry Wilson, prevailed to keep the military open to black men. The Army Reorganization Act of 1869 maintained four all-black regiments: the 9th and 10th Cavalry Regiments and the 24th and 25th Infantry Regiments. These four regiments spent most of the next three decades on the western frontier. Nearly 12,500 black men served during the late nineteenth century in these segregated units commanded—as black troops had been during the Civil War—by white officers. Unlike in the Civil War, however, many of these white officers were Southerners, and all too frequently, they held black men in low regard.

Military service in the West was wretched for white troops and invariably worse for black soldiers. Too often officers considered black troops lazy, undisciplined, and cowardly. Black regiments were assigned mainly to the New Mexico and Arizona territories and to west Texas because the army thought black people tolerated heat better than white people did.

Discrimination in the Army

Black troops faced more than adverse weather. The army routinely provided them inferior food and inadequate housing. Whereas white soldiers received dried apples and peaches, canned tomatoes, onions, and potatoes, black troops were given foul beef, bad bread, and canned peas unfit for human consumption. In 1867 white troops at Fort Leavenworth in Kansas lived in barracks while black troops were forced to sleep in tents on wet ground. Black regiments were allotted used weapons and equipment. The army sent its worst horses—often old and lame—to the black cavalry.

Long stretches of boredom, tedious duty, and loneliness marked army life for black and white men in the West. Weeks and months might pass without combat. Commanders constantly had to deal with desertion and alcoholism. Black soldiers were much less likely to desert or turn to drink than were white troops. For example, in 1877 eighteen men deserted from the all-black 10th Regiment, and 184 white soldiers deserted from the all-white 4th Regiment. Black troops realized that although army life could be harsh and dangerous, it compared favorably to the civilian world, which held few genuine opportunities for them. Army food was poor, but the private's pay of $13 per month was regular. Moreover, black troops developed immense pride in themselves as professional soldiers.

The Plains Indians who fiercely resisted U.S. forces were so impressed with the performance of their black adversaries that they called them "buffalo soldiers." Indians associated the hair of black men with the shaggy coat of the buffalo, a sacred animal. Black troops considered it a term of respect and began to use it themselves. The 10th Cavalry displayed a buffalo in their unit emblem.

The Buffalo Soldiers in Combat

It was ironic that white military authorities would employ black men to subdue red people. Most black soldiers, however, had no qualms about fighting Indians, protecting white settlers and railroad construction gangs, or apprehending bandits and cattle rustlers. From the late 1860s to the early 1890s, the four black regiments repeatedly engaged hostile Indians. In September 1867, seven hundred Cheyenne attacked fifty U.S. Army scouts along a dry riverbed in eastern Colorado. The scouts held out for over a week until the 10th Cavalry rescued them. For more than twelve months in 1879 and 1880, the 9th and 10th Cavalry fought the Apaches under Chief Victorio in New Mexico and Texas in a campaign of raid and counterraid. The Apaches slipped across the Mexican border and then returned to southwest Texas. In clashes at Rattlesnake Springs and near Fresno Spring, the 10th killed more than thirty Apaches before Victorio fled again to Mexico where he was killed by the Mexican Army. But the 9th and 10th Cavalry deserve most of the credit for Victorio's defeat with their dogged pursuit of the Apaches for months over hundreds of miles of rugged terrain.

In 1879, however, 10th Cavalry troops protected Kiowa women and children from Texas Rangers. In other instances black troops protected Chickasaw and Cherokee farmers from an attack by Kiowa and Comanche bands.

In late 1890 military units including the 9th Cavalry were sent to the Pine Ridge Reservation in South Dakota where Sioux Indians were holding an intense religious ceremony known as the Ghost Dance. Confined to reservations, some Indians—out of desperation and yearning for the past—believed their fervent participation in the Ghost Dance would bring both their ancestors and the almost extinct buffalo back to the Great Plains. Then white people would vanish, and Indian life would be restored to what it had been decades earlier. But white authorities considered the Ghost Dance a dangerous act of defiance.

On December 29, the 7th Cavalry attempted to disarm a band of Sioux at Wounded Knee on the Pine Ridge Reservation. Shooting erupted, and 146 Indian men, women, and children, and 26 soldiers were killed. The 9th Cavalry, 108 miles away in the Badlands, rode the next day through a blizzard and arrived tired and freezing to come to the aid of elements of the 7th Cavalry. The 9th spent the remainder of the bitter winter guarding the surviving Sioux. A black private, W. H. Prather, observed, "The Ninth, the Ninth were the first to come, will be the last to leave, we poor devils, and the Sioux are left to freeze."

Civilian Hostility to Black Soldiers

Despite the gallant performance of the buffalo soldiers, civilians frequently treated them with hostility. In southern Texas in 1875, Mexicans ambushed five black soldiers, killed two of them, and mutilated their bodies. The next day the infuriated white commander of the 9th Cavalry, Colonel Edward Hatch, rode out with sixty soldiers and apprehended the Mexicans. A local grand jury indicted nine of them for murder, but the only one tried was acquitted, and the other eight were released without a trial. Hatch, another white officer, and three buffalo soldiers were then indicted for breaking into and burglarizing the shack where the Mexicans had sought refuge. The charges were eventually dropped, but the five men had to hire their own lawyers.

In 1877 fifty-four black troops from the 9th Cavalry intervened successfully in a tense political and ethnic dispute between white and Mexican residents of El Paso, Texas. The 9th also found itself dispatched to police the so-called Johnson County War in Wyoming between big and small ranchers in 1890. The black troops deployment was arranged by one of the state's U.S. senators, who favored the big ranchers, and the presence of black soldiers angered small ranchers, as it was intended to do. Racial violence and bloodshed soon erupted between residents of the town of Suggs, who had run two black soldiers out of town, and several of the soldiers who had disobeyed orders. The troops were withdrawn after the town was shot up and one soldier killed.

A west Texas newspaper, the *Bellville Countryman*, summarized the attitudes of many white westerners when it complained that "the idea of a gallant and high-minded people being ordered and pushed around by an inferior, ignorant race is shocking to the senses."

Brownsville

One of the worst examples of hostility to black troops, the so-called Brownsville affair, also occurred in Texas. In 1906 the 1st Battalion of the 25th Infantry was transferred from Fort Niobrara, Nebraska, to Fort Brown in Brownsville, Texas, along the Rio Grande. The black soldiers immediately encountered discrimination from both white people and Mexicans in this border community. More than four out of five of Brownsville's residents were Hispanic. Black people were not permitted in public parks, and white businesses refused to serve them. Several times civilians provoked and attacked individual black soldiers.

Shortly after midnight on August 14, shooting erupted in Brownsville. About 150 shots were fired. One man died, and an Hispanic policeman and the editor of a Spanish-language newspaper were injured. Black troops were blamed for the violence when clips and cartridges from the army's Springfield rifles were found in the street. Two military investigations concluded that black soldiers did the shooting. The army could not identify the specific soldiers responsible because no one would confess or name the alleged perpetrators.

With no hearing or trial, President Theodore Roosevelt dismissed three companies of black men—167 soldiers—from the army. They were barred from rejoining the military and from government employment and were denied veterans' pensions or benefits. The black community, which had supported Roosevelt, reacted angrily. Booker T. Washington, a Roosevelt supporter, privately wrote, "There is no law, human or divine, which justifies the punishment of an innocent man." Washington added, "I have the strongest faith in the President's honesty of intention, high mindedness of purpose, sincere unselfishness and courage, but I regret for all these reasons all the more that this thing has occurred."

Republican senator James B. Foraker of Ohio later led a Senate investigation that upheld Roosevelt's dismissals. But Foraker, a strong opponent of Roosevelt, questioned the guilt of the black men. The clips and cartridges that served as evidence were apparently planted. After Roosevelt left office in 1909, the War Department reinstated fourteen of the soldiers. In 1972 the Justice Department determined that an injustice had occurred. The black soldiers were posthumously awarded honorable discharges. The only survivor of the Brownsville affair—Dorsie Willis—received $25,000 from Congress and the right to treatment at veterans' facilities.

AFRICAN AMERICANS IN THE NAVY

Naval service was even more unappealing than life in the army. In the late nineteenth century, as the navy made the transition from timber and sail to steam and steel, approximately one sailor in ten was a black man. Although the navy's ships were technically integrated, in that black and white sailors served on them together, white sailors were hostile to black sailors. They would not eat or bunk with them or take orders from them. Increasingly, and to enforce a de facto shipboard segregation, black sailors were restricted to stoking boilers in the bowels of naval vessels and to cooking and serving food to white sailors.

Although several black men enrolled as midshipmen at the Naval Academy in the 1870s, they faced social ostracism and none of them graduated. Not until 1949 did a black man graduate from the academy.

THE BLACK COWBOYS

Black men before, during, and after the Civil War were familiar with horses and mules. As slaves, they tended and cared for animals. Some black men served with the 9th and 10th U.S. Cavalry Regiments and gained experience with horses. By the 1870s and 1880s, black men joined several hundred Mexicans, Native Americans, and white men on the long cattle drives from Texas to Kansas, Nebraska, and Missouri. There were probably no more than a few hundred black cowboys in the late nineteenth and early twentieth centuries.

Managing cattle was monotonous, difficult, and dirty work. Yet it required considerable skill as a rider to manage hundreds of head of ornery and stinking animals. Cowboys had to tolerate weather that ranged from incredibly hot to bitter cold. They had to be willing to consume unappetizing food for weeks at a time. There was no bed to sleep in each night, and their closest companion most days and nights was the horse they rode.

Black cowhands sometimes endured discrimination and abuse. They had to tame the toughest horses, work the longest hours, and face hostility in saloons, hotels, brothels, and shops in towns like Dodge City, Abilene, or Cheyenne. Still, many black cowboys earned the respect of white ranchers and cattle barons.

THE SPANISH-AMERICAN WAR

With the western frontier subdued by 1890, many Americans concluded that the United States should expand overseas. European nations had already carved out extensive colonies in Africa and Asia. Many, but by no means all, Americans favored the extension of U.S. political, economic, and military authority to Latin America and the Pacific. In 1893 the U.S. Navy and American businessmen toppled the monarchy in Hawaii, and the United States annexed that chain of islands in 1898.

The same year, the United States went to war to liberate Cuba from Spanish control. As in the Civil War, black men enlisted, fought, and died. Twenty-two black sailors were among the 266 men who died when the battleship USS *Maine* blew up in Havana harbor, the event that helped trigger the war. Many black Americans were convinced, as they had been in previous wars, that the willingness of black people to support the war against Spain would impress white Americans sufficiently to reduce or even eliminate white hostility. E. E. Cooper, editor of the Washington *Colored American*, declared that the war would bring black people and white people together in "an era of good feeling the country over and cement the races into a more compact brotherhood through perfect unity of purpose and patriotic affinity." The war, he asserted, would help white Americans "unloose themselves from the bondage of race prejudice."

Many black and white Americans, however, questioned the American cause. Some black people saw the war as an effort to extend American influence and racial practices, including Jim Crow, beyond U.S. borders. The Reverend George W. Prioleau, chaplain of the Ninth Cavalry, wondered why black Americans supported what he considered a hypocritical war:

> Talk about fighting and freeing poor Cuba and of Spain's brutality. . . . Is America any better than Spain? Has she not subjects in her very midst who are murdered daily without a trial of judge or jury? Has she not subjects in her own borders whose children are half-fed and half-clothed, because their father's skin is black. . . . Yet the Negro is loyal to his country's flag.

Whether or not they harbored doubts, black men by the thousands served in the Spanish-American War and in the Philippine Insurrection that followed it. Shortly before war was declared, the army ordered its four black regiments of regular troops transferred from their western posts to Florida to prepare for combat in Cuba. President William McKinley also appealed for volunteers. The War Department designated four of the black volunteer units "immune regiments" because it believed black men would tolerate the heat and humidity of Cuba better than white troops and black people were immune or at least less susceptible to yellow fever, which was endemic to Cuba. (Yellow fever was carried by mosquitoes, but this was unknown in 1898. Most people believed the disease was caused by the tropical Caribbean climate.)

State militia (national guard) units were also called into federal service, and several states, including Alabama, Ohio, Massachusetts, Illinois, Kansas, Virginia, Indiana, and North Carolina, sent all-black militias, as well as white units. But Georgia's governor refused to permit that state's black militia to serve, and New York would not permit black men to enlist in its militia. The states typically followed the federal example and kept black men confined to all-black units commanded by white officers, but there were exceptions.

Black Officers

The buffalo soldiers of the 9th and 10th Cavalry and the 24th and 25th Infantry remained under the leadership of white officers. But the men of several volunteer units insisted they be led by black officers: "No officers, no fight." So for the first time in American military history, black men commanded all-black units: the 8th Illinois, the 23rd Kansas, and the 3rd North Carolina. Mindful that many people doubted the ability of black men to lead, the colonel of the 8th Illinois cautioned his men, "If we fail, the whole race will have to shoulder the burden." The War Department also permitted black men to serve as lieutenants with other black volunteer units, but all higher ranking officers were white men. Charles Young, a black graduate of West Point who was serving as a military science instructor at Wilberforce University in Ohio, was given command of Ohio's 9th Battalion, and he served with distinction and was promoted from captain to colonel.

As black and white troops assembled in Georgia and Florida before departing for Cuba, black men soon realized a U.S. uniform did not lessen white racial prejudice. White civilians in Georgia killed four black men of the 3rd North Carolina. All-white juries acquitted those who were charged with the murders. After the white proprietor of a drug store in Lakeland, Florida, refused to serve a black soldier at the soda fountain, a mob of black troops gathered. The proprietor was pistol whipped, and another white man was killed by a stray bullet before the troops were disarmed. In Tampa, where the troops were embarking for Cuba, a bloody all-night riot broke out after drunken white soldiers from Ohio decided to shoot at a black child for target practice. Twenty-seven black soldiers and three white soldiers were seriously injured. It is not surprising that when the men of the all-black 3rd Alabama adopted an injured crow as the unit mascot, they named it Jim.

Most of the black units never saw combat. White military authorities considered black men unreliable and inadequately trained for combat. Black volunteer units stayed behind in Florida when white units embarked for Cuba. However, the four regiments of regular black troops, the buffalo soldiers, did go to Cuba, where they performed well despite the doubts and persistent criticism of some white men. The Spanish troops were impressed enough to give the black men the nickname "smoked yankees."

A Splendid Little War

In the summer of 1898, U.S. troops arrived in Cuba. Black men of the 10th Cavalry fought alongside Cuban rebels, many of whom were themselves black. Four black American privates earned the Congressional Medal of Honor for their part in an engagement in southwestern Cuba. Black and white troops were best remembered for their role in the assault on San Juan and Kettle Hills overlooking the key Cuban port of Santiago in eastern Cuba. Santiago was the main Spanish naval base in Cuba and its capture would break Spain's hold over the island.

In this assault, black soldiers from the 24th Infantry and the 9th and the 10th Cavalry Regiments fought alongside white troops including Theodore Roosevelt's volunteer unit, the Rough Riders. In the fiercest fighting of the war and amid considerable confusion, black and white men were thrown together as they encountered withering Spanish fire. Although for a time the outcome was in doubt, they took the high ground overlooking Santiago harbor. White soldiers praised the performance of the black troops. One commented, "I am not a negro lover. My father fought with Mosby's Rangers [in the Confederate Army] and I was born in the South, but the negroes saved that fight." In his campaign for vice president in 1900, Theodore Roosevelt stated that black men saved his life during the battle. Later, however, Roosevelt reversed himself and accused several black men of cowardice.

As hostilities concluded, men of the 24th Infantry agreed to work in yellow fever hospitals after white regiments refused the duty. About half the black soldiers—some 471 men—contracted yellow fever. Other black troops arrived in Cuba after the war to serve garrison duty. The 8th Illinois and the 23rd Kansas built roads, bridges, schools, and hospitals. The black men were especially pleased at the lack of discrimination and absence of Jim Crow in Cuba. Some black soldiers discussed the possibility of organizing emigration to Cuba, but nothing came of it. Still other black troops from the 6th Massachusetts joined in the invasion of Puerto Rico as the United States took that island from Spain.

The Philippine Insurrection

With the resounding victory in the Spanish-American War, many Americans decided their nation had an obligation to uplift those less fortunate peoples who had been part of the Spanish Empire. Thus, President William McKinley and American diplomats insisted the United States acquire Guam, Puerto Rico, and the Philippines from Spain in the Treaty of Paris that ended the war in December 1898. The Filipinos, like the Cubans, had long opposed Spanish rule and fully expected the American government to support their independence. Instead, they were infuriated to learn that the United States intended to annex the Philippines. The Filipinos, under Emilio Aguinaldo, switched from fighting the Spanish to fighting the occupying U.S. forces.

Many black and white Americans denounced the U.S. effort to take the Philippines. They were unconvinced the Filipinos would benefit from American benevolence. AME Bishop Henry Turner termed it an "unholy war of conquest," and Booker T. Washington believed the Filipinos "should be given an opportunity to govern themselves."

Opposition to U.S. involvement in the Philippines notwithstanding, black men in the military served throughout the campaign in the Pacific islands. The black troops included the regular 25th Infantry and 24th Infantry, the 9th Cavalry, and the 48th and 49th Volunteer Regiments. Through propaganda, the Filipino rebels attempted to convince black troops to abandon the cause. Posters reminded "The Colored American Soldier" of injustice and lynching in the United States. White troops did not help by calling Filipinos "niggers." Although many black soldiers had reservations about the fighting, they remained loyal. By the time the conflict ended with an American victory in 1902, only five black men had deserted. David Fagen of the 24th Infantry joined Filipino forces and became an officer, fighting American troops for two years before he was killed. Two black men from the 9th Cavalry were executed for desertion; fifteen white soldiers who deserted had their death sentences commuted.

Although black men had served with distinction as professional soldiers for forty years after the Civil War—on the frontier, in Cuba, and in the Philippines—the army little valued their achievements and sacrifice, as the Brownsville affair showed. White military and political leaders persistently relied on passions and prejudices over evidence of achievement. Time and again, these circumstances dashed the hopes of those black civilians and soldiers who believed the performance of black troops would challenge white supremacy and demonstrate that black citizens had earned the same rights and opportunities as other Americans.

Black Businesspeople and Entrepreneurs

Well-educated black men and women stood no chance of gaining employment with any major business or industrial corporation at the turn of the century. White males not only monopolized management and supervisory positions, but also occupied nearly every job that did not involve manual labor. In 1899 black novelist Sutton E. Griggs described the frustrations that an educated black man encountered:

> He possessed a first class college education, but that was all. He knew no trade nor was he equipped to enter any of the professions. . . . He would have made an excellent drummer,

salesman, clerk, cashier, government official (county, city, state, or national), telegraph operator, conductor, or anything of such a nature. But the color of his skin shut the doors so tight that he could not even peep in. . . . It is true that such positions as street laborer, hod carrier, cart driver, factory hand, railroad hand were open to him; but such menial tasks were uncongenial to a man of his education and polish.

Although white supremacy and the proliferation of Jim Crow severely restricted opportunities for educated black people, those same limitations enabled enterprising black men and women to open and operate businesses that served black clientele. By the early twentieth century, black Americans not only had their own churches and schools, but they had also established banks, newspapers, insurance companies, retail businesses, barbershops, beauty salons, and funeral parlors. Virtually every black community had its own small businesses, markets, street vendors, and other entrepreneurs.

Some black men and women established thriving and substantial businesses. In Atlanta, Union Army veteran Alexander Hamilton was a successful building contractor. He supervised construction of the Good Samaritan Building, oversaw the erection of buildings on the Morris Brown College campus, and built many of the impressive houses on Peachtree Street. Hamilton employed both black and white workmen on his projects.

Alonzo Herndon was a former slave who also achieved financial success in Atlanta. He operated a fashionable barbershop on Peachtree Street that served well-to-do white men. The shop had crystal chandeliers and polished brass spittoons. Herndon expanded and opened two other shops, eventually employing seventy-five men. He also founded the Atlanta Life Insurance Company, the largest black stock company in the world.

In Montgomery, Alabama, H. A. Loveless, a former slave, became a butcher and then diversified his business operations by opening an undertaking establishment and operating a hack and dray company. By 1900 Loveless also ran a coal and wood yard and sold real estate.

In Richmond, Virginia, Maggie Lena Walker—the secretary–treasurer of the Independent Order of St. Luke, a mutual benefit society, and a founder of the St. Luke's Penny Savings Bank—became the wealthiest black woman in America. Also in Richmond, former slave John Dabney owned an exclusive catering business that served wealthy white Virginians. He catered two state dinners for President Grover Cleveland. He used his earnings to purchase several houses and to invest in real estate.

Madam C. J. Walker may have been the most successful black entrepreneur of them all. Born Sarah Breedlove in 1867 on a Louisiana cotton plantation, she married at age fourteen and was a widowed single parent by age twenty. She spent the next two decades struggling to make ends meet. In 1905 with $1.50, she developed a formula to nourish and enrich the hair of black women. She insisted it was not a process to straighten hair.

She sold the product door to door in Denver but could not keep up with the demand. The business rapidly expanded and became a thriving enterprise that employed hundreds of black women. She established the company's headquarters in Indianapolis. In the meantime, she married Charles Joseph Walker and took his name and the title Madam. As she accumulated wealth, she shared it generously with Bethune Cookman College, Tuskegee Institute, and the NAACP. She was a major contributor to the NAACP's antilynching campaign. When she died of a stroke at age fifty-one in 1919, she was reportedly a millionaire.

Despite such successes, most black people who went into business had difficulty surviving, and many failed. Too often they depended on black customers who were themselves poor. White-owned banks were unlikely to provide credit to aspiring black businesspeople. And even the wealthiest black entrepreneurs did not come close to possessing the wealth the richest white Americans accumulated.

AFRICAN AMERICANS AND LABOR

Thousands of black Southerners worked in factories, mills, and mines. Although most textile mills refused to hire black people except for janitorial duties, many black laborers toiled in tobacco and cigarmaking facilities, flour mills, coal mines, sawmills, turpentine camps, and on railroads. Black women worked for white families as cooks, maids, and laundresses. Black workers usually were paid less than white men employed in the same capacity. Conversely, white working people frequently complained they were not hired because employers retained black workers who worked for less pay. In 1904 in Georgia white railroad firemen went on strike in an unsuccessful attempt to compel railroad operators to dismiss black firemen. Invariably, there was persistent antagonism between black and white laborers.

Unions

When white workers formed labor unions in the late nineteenth century, they usually excluded black workers. The Knights of Labor, however, founded in 1869, was open to all workers (except whiskey salesmen, lawyers, and bankers), and by the mid-1880s counted 50,000 women and 70,000 black workers among its nearly 750,000 members. But by the 1890s, after unsuccessful strikes and a deadly riot in Chicago, the Knights had lost influence to a new organization, the American Federation of Labor (AFL). Founded in 1886, the AFL was ostensibly open to all skilled workers, but most of its local craft unions barred women and black tradesmen. In contrast, the United Mine Workers (UMW), formed in 1890, encouraged black coal miners to join the union rather than serve as strikebreakers. By 1900 approximately 20,000 of the 91,000 members of the UMW were black men. The Industrial Workers of the World (IWW), a revolutionary labor organization founded in 1905, brought black and white laborers together in, among other places, the Brotherhood of Timber Workers in the Piney Woods of east Texas.

In 1869 a Baltimore ship caulker, Isaac Myers, organized the National Colored Labor Union, which lasted for seven years. It discouraged strikes and encouraged its members to work hard and be thrifty. It lost whatever effectiveness it had when it was largely taken over by Republican leaders during Reconstruction.

Strikes

During the late nineteenth and early twentieth centuries, although some strikes by unions won concessions from business owners, most failed because owners could rely on strikebreakers and the police or national guard to intervene and bring the strikes

Although most southern black people worked long hours in cotton fields, thousands toiled in factories, mills, and mines. Here black women stem tobacco in a Virginia factory under the supervision of a white man.
Valentine Richmond History Center

to an often violent end. For a time, black shipyard workers in southern ports did achieve some success. Black stevedores who loaded and unloaded ships endured oppressive conditions and long hours for low pay. They periodically went on strike in Charleston, Savannah, and New Orleans. The Longshoremen's Protective Union in Charleston won several strikes in the 1870s. In Nashville in 1871 black dockyard workers went on strike, demanding twenty cents an hour. Steamboat owners broke the strike by hiring state convicts for fifteen cents an hour.

Black and white laborers who toiled in the Louisiana sugarcane fields earned an average of $13 a week in the 1880s. They were paid in scrip—not cash—that was redeemable only in stores the planters owned where prices were exorbitant. Workers lived in 12' × 15' cabins that they rented from the planters. In some ways, it was worse than slave labor.

Although the state militia had broken previous strikes, 9,000 black and 1,000 white workers responded to a call for a new strike in 1887 by organizers from the Knights of Labor. They quit the sugar fields in four parishes (as Louisiana counties are called) to demand more pay. The strike was peaceful, but planters convinced the governor to send in the militia. The troops fired into a crowd at Pattersonville and killed four people. The next day local officials killed several strikers who had been taken prisoner. In the town of Thibodaux, "prominent citizens" organized and armed themselves and had martial law declared. More than thirty-five unarmed black people, including women and children, were killed in their homes and churches. Two black strike leaders were lynched. The strike was broken.

Black washerwomen went on strike in Atlanta in 1881. The women, who did laundry for white families, refused to do any more until they were guaranteed $1 per twelve pounds of laundry. The strike was well organized through black churches, and it spread to cooks and domestics. A strike committee used persuasion and intimidation to ensure support. Some three thousand black people joined the strike. White families went two weeks without clean clothes. However, Atlanta's white community broke the strike. Police arrested strike leaders for disorderly conduct. Several black women were fined from $5 to $20. The city council threatened to require each member of the Washer Women's Association of Atlanta to purchase a city business license for $25. Although the strike gradually ended without having achieved its goal, it did demonstrate that poor black women could organize effectively.

BLACK PROFESSIONALS

Like business and labor, the medical and legal professions were strictly segregated. Most black physicians, nurses, and lawyers attended all-black professional schools in the late nineteenth century. Black people in need of medical care were either excluded from white hospitals or confined to all-black wards. Black physicians were denied staff privileges at white hospitals. Thus black people in many communities formed their own hospitals. Most were small facilities with fifty or fewer beds.

Medicine

In 1891 Dr. Daniel Hale Williams established Provident Hospital and Training Institute in Chicago, the first black hospital operated solely by African Americans. In 1894 the Freedmen's Hospital was organized in Washington, D.C., and it later affiliated with Howard University. Frederick Douglass Memorial Hospital and Training School was founded in Philadelphia in 1895. Dr. Alonzo McClennan in cooperation with several other black physicians established the Hospital and Training School for Nurses in Charleston, South Carolina, in 1897.

In 1900 Williams, explaining why black medical institutions were necessary, wrote,

> In view of this cruel ostracism, affecting so vitally the race, our duty seems plain. Institute Hospitals and Training Schools. Let us no longer sit idly and inanely deploring existing conditions. Let us not waste time trying to effect changes or modifications in the institutions unfriendly to us, but rather let us seek to promote the doctrine of helping and stimulating our race.

By 1890 there were 909 black (most of whom were male) physicians practicing in the United States. They served a black population of 7.5 million people. Barred from membership in the American Medical Association, black doctors organized the National Medical Association in Atlanta in 1895.

In 1910, in a report issued by the Carnegie Foundation for the Advancement of Teaching, Abraham Flexner recommended improving medical education in the United States by eliminating weaker medical schools. He suggested raising admission standards and expanding laboratory and clinical training in the stronger schools. As a result of the implementation of these recommendations, 60 of 155 white medical schools closed, and among black medical schools, only Howard and Meharry survived. By 1920 there were 3,885 black physicians. Many had completed medical school before the Flexner report was compiled.

The number of black women physicians was actually declining. In 1890 there were ninety black women practicing medicine, and by 1920 there were sixty-five. The number of medical schools had decreased, and most black and white men considered medicine an inappropriate profession for women. But black women also had to contend with the opposition of white women. Isabella Vandervall was a 1915 graduate of New York Medical College and Hospital who was accepted for an internship at the Hospital for Women and Children in Syracuse. When she appeared in person, however, the hospital's female administrator rejected Vandervall, ". . . we can't have you here! You are colored!"

Nursing was another matter. By 1920 there were 36 black nurse training schools and 2,150 white nursing schools. White nurses resented the competition from black nurses for positions as private duty nurses. And the black physicians who ran nurse training schools exploited their students by hiring them out, as part of their training, for private duty work but requiring them to relinquish their pay to the schools. Moreover, many people—black and white—regarded black nurses more as domestics than as trained professionals. Unlike white nurses, for example, black nurses were usually addressed by their first names. To confront such obstacles, fifty-two black nurses met in New York City in 1908 and formed the National Association of Colored Graduate Nurses (NACGN). By 1920 the NACGN had five hundred members.

Black physicians and nurses struggled to provide medical care to people who were often desperately ill and sought treatment only as a last resort. Disease and sickness flourished among people who were ill nourished, poorly clad, and inadequately housed. Tuberculosis, pneumonia, pellagra, hookworm, and syphilis afflicted many poor black people—as they also did poor white people. Bessie Hawes, a 1918 graduate of Tuskegee Institute's Nurse Training program, described the kind of situation she faced in rural Alabama:

> A colored family of ten were in bed and dying for the want of attention. No one would come near. I was glad of the opportunity. As I entered the little country cabin, I found the mother in bed. Three children were buried the week before. The father and the remainder of the family were running a temperature of 102–104. Some had influenza, others had pneumonia. No relatives or friends would come near. I saw at a glance I had work to do. I rolled up my sleeves and killed chickens and began to cook. . . . I milked the cow, gave medicine, and did everything I could to help conditions. I worked day and night trying to save them for seven days. I had no place to sleep. In the meantime the oldest daughter had a miscarriage and I delivered her without the aid of any physicians. . . . I only wished that I could have reached them earlier and been able to have done something for the poor mother.

The Law

Unlike black physicians and nurses, who were excluded from white hospitals, black lawyers were permitted to practice in what was essentially a white male court system. But white judges and attorneys did not welcome them. Rather than create additional problems for themselves, black defendants and plaintiffs often retained

Howard University in Washington, D.C. provided education for African Americans in many professions, including dentistry. Howard first opened its doors in 1867 as a public university.
Courtesy of the Library of Congress

white lawyers in the hope that white legal counsel might improve their chances of receiving justice. As a result, many black attorneys had a hard time making a living from the practice of law.

The American Bar Association (ABA) would not admit black attorneys to membership. Attorney William H. Lewis, a graduate of Amherst College and the Harvard Law School who was appointed an assistant U.S. attorney general by President William Howard Taft in 1911, was expelled by the ABA in 1912 when its leaders discovered he was black. The leaders defended his expulsion by claiming the association was mainly a social organization. In 1925 black lawyers—led by Howard Law School graduate George H. Woodson—organized the National Bar Association. In 1910 the United States had about eight hundred black lawyers.

Very few black women were lawyers. Charlotte Ray was the first. In 1900 there were ten black women practicing law. There were over 700 black men and 112,000 white men engaged in the legal profession. Lutie A. Lytle, who graduated from Central Tennessee Law School in 1879, later returned to that black institution and became the first black woman to be a law professor in the United States.

MUSIC

In the half century after the Civil War, music created and performed by black people evolved into the uniquely American art forms of ragtime, jazz, and blues. The roots of these extraordinary musical innovations are obscure and uncertain. Some late-nineteenth-century music can be traced to African musical forms and rhythms. One source is slave work songs; another is the spirituals of the slavery era.

Traveling groups of black men, some of them ex-slaves, put on minstrel shows that featured "coon songs" after the Civil War. Many black Americans resented these popular shows as caricatures and exaggerations of black behavior. At least six hundred "coon songs" that attracted a predominantly white audience were published by 1900 including "All Coons Look Alike to Me," "Mammy's Little Pickaninny," and "My Coal Black Lady."

Most black people did not perform in or enjoy the demeaning minstrel shows. They had other forms of musical entertainment. "The Civil Rights Juba," published in 1874, was a precursor to ragtime. In 1871 the Fisk University Jubilee Singers began the first of many fund-raising concert tours that entertained black and white audiences in the United States and Europe for years thereafter with slave songs and spirituals. Other black colleges and universities also sent choirs and singers on similar trips.

Ragtime

Ragtime, which emerged in the 1890s, was composed music, written down for performance on the piano. Ragtime pieces were not accompanied by lyrics and not meant to be sung. The creative genius of the form, Scott Joplin, was born in Texarkana, Texas, in 1868. He learned to play on a piano his mother bought from her earnings as a maid, and he may have had some training in classical music. Joplin subsequently learned to transfer complex banjo syncopations to the piano as he fused European harmonies and African rhythms. He traveled to Chicago in 1893 and played at the Columbian Exposition. He soon began to write ragtime sheet music that sold well. In 1899 he composed his best-known tune, the "Maple Leaf Rag," named after a social club (brothel) in Sedalia, Missouri. It sold an astonishing one million copies.

Jazz

Jazz gradually replaced ragtime in popularity in the early twentieth century. Unlike ragtime, jazz was mostly improvised, not composed, and it was not confined to the piano. Jazz incorporated African and European musical elements drawn from such diverse sources as plantation bands, minstrel shows, riverboat ensembles, and Irish and Scottish folk tunes. The first jazz bands emerged in and around New Orleans where they played at parades, funerals, clubs, and outdoor concerts. Instead of the banjos, pipes, fifes, and violins of earlier black musical groups, these bands relied more on brass, reeds, and drums.

Ferdinand J. La Menthe, regarded as the first prominent jazz musician, was born in 1890 and grew up in a French-speaking family in New Orleans. Young La Menthe played several musical instruments before settling on the piano. He was also a superb composer and arranger. Later he changed his name to Morton and came to be known as Jelly Roll Morton. He played in the "red light" district of New Orleans known as Storeyville where he was also a pool shark and gambler. He moved to Los Angeles in

1917 and to Chicago in 1922 where he subsequently led and recorded with "Morton's Red Hot Peppers." He died in 1941.

The Blues

In rural, isolated areas of the South, poor black people composed and sang songs about their lives and experiences. W. C. Handy, the father of the blues, later recalled, "Southern Negroes sang about everything. Trains, steamboats, steam whistles, sledge hammers, fast women, mean bosses, stubborn mules." They accompanied themselves on anything from a guitar, to a harmonica, to a washboard. They played in juke joints (rural nightclubs), at picnics, lumber camps, and urban nightclubs.

Handy, who was born in Florence, Alabama, in 1873, took up music despite the opposition of his devoutly Christian parents. He learned to play the guitar, although his mother and father regarded it as the "devil's plaything." He later led his own nine-man band. In the Mississippi Delta in 1903, Handy encountered "primitive," or "boo-gie," music unlike anything he had heard before. Handy was not initially impressed by the mostly unskilled and itinerant musicians whose lives swirled around cheap whiskey, gambling, prostitution, and violence. "Then I saw the beauty of primitive music. They had the stuff people wanted. It touched the spot. Their music wanted polishing, but it contained the essence. People would pay money for it." Handy went on to compose many tunes including "Memphis Blues" and "St. Louis Blues."

Handy was not the only musician to "discover" the blues. Gertrude Pridget sang in southern minstrel shows. In 1902 she heard a young black woman in a small Missouri town sing forlornly about a lover who had left her. Pridget took the song and included it in her shows. In 1904 she married William "Pa" Rainey and became "Ma" Rainey. Rainey proceeded to create other "blues" songs based on ballads, hymns, and the experiences of black people. As "Mother of the Blues," she recorded extensively and continuously in the 1920s and 1930s.

By 1920 two forms of American music were well along in their evolution—jazz and the blues. Both drew on African and American musical elements as well as on European styles. But most of all, jazz and the blues represented the experiences of African Americans and the creativity of the exceptional musicians who developed and performed the music.

SPORTS

While talented black men and women were making dramatic musical innovations, black athletes found that white athletes and sports entrepreneurs were increasingly opposed to the presence of black men in the boxing ring and on the playing field. In boxing, black men regularly fought white men through the end of the nineteenth century. But many white people, especially Southerners, were offended by the practice. In 1892 George Dixon, a black boxer, won the world featherweight title, and some white men cheered his victory, distressing a Chicago journalist. "It was not pleasant," he complained, "to see white men applaud a negro for knocking another white man out. It was not pleasant to see them crowding around 'Mr.' Dixon to congratulate him on his victory, to seek an introduction with 'the distinguished colored gentleman' while he puffed his cigar and lay back like a prince receiving his subjects." Despite such opinions, there was never any official prohibition of interracial bouts.

Jack Johnson

The success of another black boxer, heavyweight Jack Johnson, angered many white Americans. Johnson was born in Galveston, Texas, in 1878 and became a professional boxer in 1897. Between 1902 and 1907 he won fifty-seven bouts against black and white fighters. In 1908 he badly beat the white heavyweight champion, Tommy Burns, in Australia. Many white boxing fans were unwilling to accept Johnson as the champion and looked desperately for "a great white hope" who could defeat him. Jim Jeffries, a former champion, came out of retirement to take on Johnson. In a brutal fight under a scorching sun in Reno, Nevada, in 1910, Johnson knocked Jeffries out in the fifteenth round.

Johnson's personal life, as well as his prowess in the ring, provoked white animosity. Having divorced his black wife, he married a white woman in 1911. Several months later, overwhelmed by social ostracism, she committed suicide. After Johnson married a second white woman, he was convicted of violating the Mann Act, which made it illegal to transport a woman across state lines for immoral purposes. In Johnson's case the "immorality" was his marriage to white women. Sentenced to a year in prison and fined $1,000, Johnson fled to Canada and then to France to avoid punishment. He lost his title to Jesse Willard in 1915 in Havana in the twenty-sixth round in a fight many people believe that Johnson threw. He returned to the United States in 1920 and served ten months in Leavenworth Prison.

Baseball, Basketball, and Other Sports

Baseball was a relatively new sport that became popular after the Civil War. As professional baseball developed in the 1870s and 1880s, both black and white men competed to earn money playing the game. It was not easy. They were the nation's first professional athletes, but professional baseball was unstable. Teams were formed and dissolved with depressing regularity. Players moved from team to team. Some thirty black men played professional baseball in the quarter century after the Civil War.

White players led by Adrian Constantine "Cap" Anson of the Chicago White Stockings tried to get baseball club owners to stop signing black men to contracts. Anson, who was from Iowa, bitterly resented having to play against black men. In 1887 International League officials rescinded a rule that had permitted them to sign black baseball players. One black player, Weldy Wilberforce Walker, protested the exclusion in a letter to *Sporting Life*. He insisted black men be judged by their skills, not by their color. "There should be some broader cause—such as lack of ability, behavior, and intelligence—for barring a player, rather than his color. It is for these reasons and because I think ability and intelligence should be recognized first and last—at all times and by everyone—I ask the question again, 'Why was the law permitting colored men to sign repealed, etc.?'" There was no intelligent answer to Walker's question. But Jim Crow was now on the baseball diamond. Moses Fleetwood Walker—Weldy's brother— was the last black man to play major league baseball in the nineteenth century as a catcher with Toledo of the American Association. No black men would be allowed to play with white men in major league baseball until Jackie Robinson joined the Brooklyn Dodgers in 1947.

In reaction to their exclusion, black men formed their own teams. By 1900 there were five black professional teams including the Norfolk Red Stockings, the Chicago Unions, and the Cuban X Giants of New York. The Negro Leagues would be an integral (but not integrated) part of sports for the next half century.

James Naismith invented basketball in 1891 in Springfield, Massachusetts. Black youngsters were playing organized basketball by 1906 in YMCAs and later YWCAs in New York City, Philadelphia, and Washington, D.C. By 1910–1911 Howard University and Hampton Institute had basketball teams. In horse racing, black jockeys regularly won major races. Willie Simms won the Kentucky Derby in 1894, 1895, 1896, and 1898. Bicycling and bicycle racing were enormously popular by the 1890s, and in 1900 a black rider, Marshall W. "Major" Taylor, won the U.S. sprint championship.

College Athletics

Generally, white colleges and universities in the North that admitted black students would not let them participate in intercollegiate sports. (Southern colleges and universities did not admit black students.) There were, however, exceptions. In 1889 W. T. S. Jackson and William Henry Lewis played football for Amherst College. Lewis was the captain of the team in 1890. As a law school student, Lewis played for Harvard and was named to the Walter Camp All-American team in 1892. (Lewis became a distinguished attorney who was forced out of the American Bar Association because of his color. See the section "The Law" in this chapter.) White institutions with black players often encountered the racism so rampant during the era. In 1907 the University of Alabama baseball team canceled a game with the University of Vermont after learning the Vermont squad had two black infielders. Moreover, black players were frequently subjected to abuse from opposing teams and their fans.

Intercollegiate athletics emerged at black colleges and universities in the late nineteenth century. White schools occasionally played black institutions. The Yale Law School baseball team, for example, played Howard in 1898. But black college teams were far more likely to play each other. The first football game between two black colleges took place on December 27, 1892, when Biddle University (today Johnson C. Smith University) defeated Livingston College in Salisbury, North Carolina.

Eventually black athletic conferences were formed. The Central Intercollegiate Athletic Association (CIAA) was organized in 1912 with Hampton, Howard, Virginia Union, and Shaw College in Raleigh, North Carolina, among its early members. The Southeastern Conference was established in 1913 and consisted of Morehouse, Fisk, Florida A&M, and Tuskegee among others. In Texas, in 1920, five black colleges founded the Southwestern Athletic Conference: Prairie View A&M, Bishop College, Paul Quinn College, Wiley College, and Sam Houston College.

TIMELINE

AFRICAN-AMERICAN EVENTS	NATIONAL EVENTS
1860	
	1862 Morrill Land-Grant Act is passed to support agricultural and mechanical education
1865	
1867 Independent Order of St. Luke is founded in Baltimore	**1867** U.S. purchases Alaska from Russia
1868 Hampton Institute is founded	**1869** Cincinnati "Red Stockings" is organized as the first professional baseball team
1869–1898 Four regiments of black soldiers serve on the western frontier	Rutgers and Princeton play the first college football game
1870	
1870 Howard University Law School is established	**1873** Panic of 1873 is followed by major depression
1875	
1880	
1881 Tuskegee Institute is founded	**1881** Clara Barton establishes the Red Cross
1885	
1887 Black players are barred from major league baseball	
1890	
1891 Dr. Daniel Hale Williams founds Provident Hospital in Chicago	**1890** Second Morrill Act is passed
1892 First black college football game: Biddle vs. Livingstone	**1891** John D. Rockefeller funds the establishment of the University of Chicago
	1892 Grover Cleveland elected to a second term as president

continued

AFRICAN-AMERICAN EVENTS	NATIONAL EVENTS
1895	
1895 Booker T. Washington addresses the Cotton States Exposition in Atlanta	**1895** Sears Roebuck and Company form a retail mail order business
1899 Scott Joplin composes the "Maple Leaf Rag"	**1899** *Cumming v. Richmond County [Georgia] Board of Education* eliminates Augusta's black high school
1900	
1903 St. Luke Penny Savings Bank is established in Richmond with Maggie Lena Walker as president	**1901** President William McKinley assassinated. Vice President Theodore Roosevelt becomes president
	1903 Henry Ford organizes the Ford Motor Co. Wilbur and Orville Wright launch the first powered aircraft at Kitty Hawk, N.C.
1905	
1908 National Association of Colored Graduate Nurses is founded in New York City. Jack Johnson wins the heavyweight championship in boxing	**1908** William Howard Taft elected president
1910	
1915	

CONCLUSION

White supremacy was debilitating, discouraging, and dangerous, but black Americans were sometimes able to turn Jim Crow to their advantage. To lessen the effects of white racism and to improve the economic status of black people, educators like Samuel Chapman Armstrong and Booker T. Washington recommended agricultural and mechanical training for most black Americans. But critics such as W. E. B. Du Bois stressed the need to cultivate the minds as well as the hands of black people to develop leaders.

Black men served with distinction in all-black military units in the Indian wars, the Spanish-American War, and the Philippine Insurrection. But no matter how loyal or how committed black men in uniform were, the white majority never fully trusted nor displayed confidence in them. African Americans could only react with dismay and outrage when President Theodore Roosevelt dismissed 167 black soldiers in 1906 in the Brownsville affair.

As they tried to shape their own destinies in the late nineteenth century, black Americans organized a variety of institutions. Mostly barred from white schools, churches, hospitals, labor unions, and places of entertainment, they developed businesses and facilities to serve their communities. Black businesses, organizations, and institutions functioned in an environment mostly free from white control and interference. Black people relied on their own experiences and imaginations to create new forms of music. They participated in sports with white athletes but more often played separately from them as segregation and white hostility spread.

Although black people recognized their churches, hospitals, schools, and businesses were often inadequately financed and usually less imposing than those of white people, they also knew that at a black school or church, in a black store, or in the care of a black physician or nurse, they would not be abused, mistreated, or ridiculed because of their color.

REVIEW QUESTIONS

1. How and why did the agricultural and mechanical training offered by Hampton Institute and Tuskegee Institute gain so much support among both black and white people? Why did black colleges and universities emphasize learning trades and acquiring skills?

2. How compatible was the educational philosophy of the late nineteenth century with the racial ideology of that era?

3. Of what value was an education for a black person in the 1890s or early 1900s? To what use could a black person put an education? What exactly was the benefit of an education?

4. What purpose did the black church serve? What were the strengths and weaknesses of the black church? What roles did black clergymen play in late-nineteenth-century America?

5. How could a black man in the U.S. Army justify participating in wars against Native Americans, the Spanish, and the Filipinos? What motivated black soldiers to serve? How well did they serve?

6. Did black people derive any benefits from the growth and expansion of segregation and Jim Crow?

7. Why did ragtime, jazz, and the blues emerge and become popular?

8. How did segregation affect the development of amateur and professional athletics in the United States?

RECOMMENDED READING

James D. Anderson. *The Education of Blacks in the South, 1860–1931.* Chapel Hill: University of North Carolina Press, 1988. Anderson is highly critical of the education and philosophy promoted and provided by Hampton Institute and Tuskegee Institute.

Edward L. Ayers. *The Promise of the New South: Life after Reconstruction.* New York: Oxford University Press, 1992. This wide-ranging study encompasses almost every aspect of life in the late-nineteenth-century South, including religion, education, sports, and music.

Sutton E. Griggs. *Imperium in Imperio.* New York: Arno Press reprint, 1899. This novel describes the formation of a separate black nation in Texas at the end of the nineteenth century.

Leon Litwack. *Trouble in Mind: Black Southerners in the Age of Jim Crow.* New York: Alfred A. Knopf, 1998. The author lets the words of black people of the time, including lawyers, physicians, and musicians, explain what life was like in an age of intense white supremacy.

Leon Litwack and August Meier, eds. *Black Leaders in the Nineteenth Century.* Urbana: University of Illinois Press, 1988. This volume contains eighteen brief but valuable biographical essays.

Benjamin E. Mays. *Born to Rebel.* New York: Scribner, 1971. Mays's autobiography includes penetrating insights into religion and education among rural black Southerners.

Howard N. Rabinowitz. *Race Relations in the Urban South, 1865–1890.* New York: Oxford University Press, 1978. The author examines black life in Atlanta, Montgomery, Nashville, Raleigh, and Richmond.

Quintard Taylor. *In Search of the Racial Frontier.* New York: W. W. Norton, 1998. This is a fine survey and analysis of the role of African Americans in the West from the 16th century to 1990.

CHAPTER SIXTEEN

CONCILIATION, AGITATION, AND MIGRATION

AFRICAN AMERICANS IN THE EARLY TWENTIETH CENTURY

RACE AND THE PROGRESSIVE MOVEMENT

By the first decade of the twentieth century, many Americans were concerned and even alarmed about the rapid economic and social changes that confronted the United States, including industrialization, the rise of powerful corporations, the explosive growth of cities, and the influx of millions of immigrants. Their apprehensions spawned a disparate collection of efforts at reform known as the progressive movement. In general, progressives believed America needed a new social awareness to deal with the new social and economic problems. But most of the middle- and upper-class white people who formed the core of the movement showed little interest in white racism and its impact. Indeed, many were racists themselves. They were primarily concerned with the concentration of wealth in monopolies such as Standard Oil, with pervasive political corruption in state and local governments, and with the plight of working-class immigrants in American cities. They cared deeply about the debilitating effects of alcohol, tainted food, and prostitution, but little about the grim impact of white supremacy. When Upton Sinclair wrote his muckraking novel *The Jungle* to expose the exploitation of European immigrants in Chicago meatpacking houses, he depicted black people as brute laborers and strikebreakers.

The reforms of the progressive movement nonetheless offered at least a glimmer of hope that racial advancement was possible. If efforts were made to improve America, was it not possible that there be some advances achieved in policies and conditions affecting black Americans? But how much militancy or forbearance was necessary to achieve significant racial progress? Did it even make sense for black people to demand a meaningful role in a nation that despised them? Perhaps it was wiser to turn inward and rely on each other rather than plead for white recognition and respect.

BOOKER T. WASHINGTON'S APPROACH

Booker T. Washington's commitment to agricultural and industrial education served as the basis for his approach to "the problem of the color line." By the beginning of the twentieth century, Washington was convinced that black men and women who had mastered

327

skills acquired at institutions like Tuskegee and Hampton would be recognized, if not welcomed, as productive contributors to the southern economy. Washington believed economic acceptance would lead in due course to political and social acceptance.

The Tuskegee leader eloquently outlined his philosophy in a speech he delivered at the opening ceremonies of the Cotton States Exposition in Atlanta in 1895. Black people, he told his segregated audience, would find genuine opportunities in the South. "[W]hen it comes to business, pure and simple, it is in the South that the Negro is given a man's chance in the commercial world." Washington added that black people should not expect too much but should welcome menial labor as a first step in the struggle for progress. Ever optimistic, he looked for opportunities while deprecating those who complained. "Nor should we permit our grievances to overshadow our opportunities." He told white listeners that the lives of black and white Southerners were historically linked and black people were far more loyal and steadfast than newly arrived immigrants. "[I]n our humble way, we shall stand by you with a devotion that no foreigner can approach, ready to lay down our lives, if need be, in defence of yours, interlacing our industrial, commercial, civil, and religious life with yours in a way that shall make the interests of both races one."

Then, in a striking metaphor, Washington reassured white people that cooperation between the races in the interest of prosperity did not endanger segregation. "In all things that are purely social we can be as separate as the fingers, yet one as the hand in all things essential to mutual progress." Finally, Washington implied that black people need not protest because they were denied rights white men possessed. Instead, he urged his black listeners to struggle steadily rather than make defiant demands. "The wisest among my race understand that the agitation of questions of social equality is the extremest folly, and that progress in the enjoyment of all the privileges that will come to us must be the result of severe and constant struggle rather than of artificial forcing." Washington was convinced that as African Americans became productive and made economic progress, white people would concede them their rights.

The speech was warmly received by both white and black listeners and by those who read it when it was widely reprinted. T. Thomas Fortune, the black editor of the New York *Age*, told Washington he had replaced Frederick Douglass (who died in 1895) as a leader. "It looks as if you are our Douglass, the best equipped of the lot of us to be the single figure ahead of the procession."

But not everyone was complimentary. The black editor of the Washington *Bee*, W. Calvin Chase, complained, "He said something that was death to the Afro-American and elevating to white people." Bishop Henry M. Turner of the AME church added that Washington "will have to live a long time to undo the harm he has done our race."

White people regarded Washington's speech as moderate, sensible, and altogether praiseworthy. Almost overnight he was designated the spokesman for African Americans. Washington accepted the recognition and took full advantage of it.

Washington's Influence

Booker T. Washington was a complex man. Many people found him unassertive, dignified, and patient. Yet he was ambitious, aggressive, and opportunistic as well as shrewd, calculating, and devious. He had an uncanny ability to determine what he might say to other people that would elicit a positive response from them. He became extraordinarily powerful. In the words of his assistant, Emmett J. Scott, Washington was "the Wizard of Tuskegee."

After the Atlanta speech, Washington's influence soared. He received extensive and mostly positive coverage in black newspapers. Some of that popularity stemmed from admiration for his leadership and agreement with his ideas. But Washington also cultivated and flattered editors, paid for advertisements for Tuskegee, and subsidized struggling journalists.

He was especially effective in dealing with prominent white businessmen and philanthropists. William H. Baldwin, vice president of the Southern Railroad, was so impressed with Washington's management of Tuskegee that Baldwin agreed to serve as the chairman of Tuskegee's board. Washington developed support among the nation's industrial elite including steel magnate Andrew Carnegie and Julius Rosenwald, the head of Sears, Roebuck, and Company. They trusted Washington's judgment and invariably consulted him before contributing to black colleges and universities. Washington assured them of the wisdom of investing in the training of black men and women in agricultural and mechanical skills. These students, he repeatedly reminded donors, would be self-sufficient and productive members of southern society.

The Tuskegee Machine

Washington advised black people to avoid politics, but he ignored his own advice. Although he never ran for office or was appointed to a political position, Washington was a political figure to be reckoned with. His connections to white businesspeople and politicians gave him enormous influence. Critics and admirers alike referred to him as "the Wizard of Tuskegee." With his influence, his connections, and his organizational skills, Washington operated what came to be known as "The Tuskegee Machine." In 1896 he supported winning Republican presidential candidate William McKinley over the Democratic and Populist William Jennings Bryan. Washington got along superbly with McKinley's successor, Theodore Roosevelt. Although Roosevelt subscribed to social Darwinism (see Chapter 15) and regarded black Americans as inferiors, he liked and respected Washington.

In 1901 Roosevelt invited Washington to dinner at the White House, where Roosevelt's wife, daughter, three sons, and a Colorado businessman joined them. Black people applauded, but the white South, alarmed by such a flagrant breach of racial etiquette (black people did not dine with white people), recoiled in disgust. Mississippi senator James K. Vardaman was so angry that he claimed the White House was "so saturated with the odor of the nigger than the rats have taken refuge in the stable." Roosevelt was unmoved, and a few days later the two men dined again together at Yale University. Still, Roosevelt never invited Washington for another meal at the Executive Mansion.

Washington and Roosevelt regularly consulted each other on political appointments. In the most notable case, Washington urged Roosevelt to appoint William D. Crum, a black medical doctor, as the collector of customs for the port of Charleston, South Carolina. White Southerners, led by Senator Benjamin R. Tillman, a South Carolina Democrat, opposed Crum's appointment and delayed final confirmation by the Senate for nearly three years. With Washington's assent, Roosevelt appointed black attorney and former all-American football player William Lewis to be U.S. district attorney in Boston. Several years later, President William Howard Taft appointed Lewis assistant attorney general of the United States. (For more details on Lewis, see Chapter 15.)

Most of Washington's political activities were not public. He secretly helped finance an unsuccessful court case against the Louisiana grandfather clause. (The statute disfranchised those voters—black men—whose grandfathers had not possessed the right to vote; see Chapter 14.) Washington provided funds to carry two cases challenging Alabama's grandfather clause to the U.S. Supreme Court, which ultimately rejected both on a technicality. He tried to persuade railroad executives to improve the conditions on segregated coaches and in station waiting rooms. He worked covertly with white attorneys to free a black farm laborer imprisoned under Alabama's peonage law. In many of these secret activities, Washington used code names in correspondence to hide his involvement. In the Louisiana case he was identified only as X.Y.Z.

Washington was a conservative leader who did not directly or publicly challenge white supremacy. He was willing to accept literacy and property qualifications for voting if they were equitably enforced regardless of race. He also opposed women's suffrage. He attacked lynching only occasionally. But he did write an annual letter to white newspapers filled with data on lynchings that had been compiled at Tuskegee. Washington let the grim statistics speak for themselves rather than denounce the injustice himself.

Washington founded the National Negro Business League in 1900 and served as its president until he died in 1915. The league brought together merchants, retailers, bankers, funeral directors, and other owners and operators of small enterprises. It helped promote black businesses in the black community and brought businessmen together to exchange information. Moreover, the league's annual meetings allowed Washington to develop support for the Tuskegee Machine from black businessmen who were community leaders from across the nation. Similarly, he worked closely with leaders in black fraternal orders such as the Odd Fellows and Pythians.

Opposition to Washington

Years before Washington rose to prominence, there were black leaders who favored a direct challenge to racial oppression. In 1889 delegates representing twenty-three states met to form the Afro-American League in Chicago. The league's main purpose was to press for civil and political rights guaranteed by the U.S. Constitution. "The objects of the League are to encourage State and local leagues in their efforts to break down color bars, and in obtaining for the Afro-American an equal chance with others in the avocations of life . . . in securing the full privileges of citizenship." But the league did not flourish, and it was eventually displaced by the Niagara Movement.

Opposition to Washington's conciliatory stance on racial matters steadily intensified. William Monroe Trotter became the most vociferous critic of Booker T. Washington and the Tuskegee Machine. Trotter was the Harvard-educated editor of the Boston *Guardian,* and he savagely attacked Washington as "the Great Traitor," "the Benedict Arnold of the Negro Race," and "Pope Washington." At a 1903 meeting of the National Negro Business League in Boston, Trotter stood on a chair and interrupted a speech by Washington, defiantly asking, "Are the rope and the torch all the race is to get under your leadership?" Washington ignored him, and the police arrested the editor for disorderly conduct. He spent thirty days in jail for what newspapers labeled "the Boston Riot."

W. E. B. DU BOIS

William Edward Burghardt Du Bois, who was twelve years younger than Booker T. Washington, would eventually eclipse the influence and authority of the Wizard of Tuskegee. Du Bois emerged as the most significant black leader in America during the first half of the twentieth century. Whereas Washington's life had been shaped by slavery, poverty, and the industrial work ethic fostered at Hampton Institute, Du Bois was born and raised in the largely white New England town of Great Barrington, Massachusetts. It was a small community where he encountered little overt racism and developed a passion for knowledge.

Du Bois possessed, as he put it, "a flood of Negro blood, a strain of French, a bit of Dutch, but, thank God! no Anglo-Saxon." He graduated from Great Barrington High School at a time when few white and still fewer black youngsters attended more than primary school. He went south to Fisk University in Nashville and graduated at age twenty. He was the first black man to earn a Ph.D. (in history) at Harvard in 1895, and he pursued additional graduate study in Germany.

Du Bois was perhaps the greatest scholar-activist in American history. He was an intellectual, at ease with words and ideas. He wrote sixteen nonfiction books, five novels, and two autobiographies. He was a fearless activist determined to confront disfranchisement, Jim Crow, and lynching. Whereas Washington solicited the goodwill of powerful white leaders and was comfortable with a gradual approach to the eradication of white supremacy, Du Bois was impatient with white people who accepted or ignored white domination. Moreover, he had little tolerance for black people who were unwilling to demand their civil and political rights.

Du Bois was well aware that he and Washington came from dissimilar backgrounds:

> I was born free. Washington was born a slave. He felt the lash of an overseer across his back. I was born in Massachusetts, he on a slave plantation in the South. My great-grandfather fought with the Colonial Army in New England in the American Revolution. I had a happy childhood and acceptance in the community. Washington's childhood was hard. I had many more advantages: Fisk University, Harvard, graduate years in Europe. Washington had little formal schooling.

The Souls of Black Folk

Du Bois was not always critical of Washington. Following Washington's speech at the Cotton States Exposition in 1895, Du Bois, then a young Harvard Ph.D. teaching at Ohio's Wilberforce University, wrote to praise him. "Let me heartily congratulate you upon your phenomenal success at Atlanta—it was a word fitly spoken." But in 1903, the same year as Trotter's arrest in the "Boston Riot," Du Bois, by then an Atlanta University professor, published *The Souls of Black Folk.* One of the major literary works of the twentieth century, it contained the first formal attack on Washington and his leadership.

In a provocative essay, "Of Booker T. Washington and Others," Du Bois conceded it was painful to challenge Washington, a man so highly praised and admired. "One hesitates, therefore, to criticise a life which, beginning with so little, has done so much. And yet the time is come when one may speak in all sincerity and utter courtesy of the mistakes and shortcomings of Mr. Washington's career, as well as the triumphs." Du Bois attacked Washington for failing to stand up for political and civil rights and higher education for black Americans. Du Bois found even more infuriating Washington's willingness to compromise with the white South and Washington's apparent agreement with white Southerners that black people were not their equals. "Mr. Washington represents in Negro thought the old attitude of adjustment and submission . . . and Mr. Washington's programme practically accepts the alleged inferiority of the Negro races."

Washington worried the opposition of Trotter, Du Bois, and others would jeopardize the flow of funds from white philanthropists to black colleges and universities. In an effort to reconcile with his opponents, he organized a meeting with them, funded by white philanthropists, at Carnegie Hall in New York City in 1904. But Du Bois and other opponents of Washington came to the gathering determined to adopt a radical agenda. When Washington loyalists monopolized the proceedings, Du Bois quit in disgust.

The Talented Tenth

Du Bois, joined by a small cadre of black intellectuals, then set out to organize an aggressive effort to secure the rights of black citizens. He was convinced that the advancement of black people was the responsibility of the black elite, those he called the Talented Tenth, meaning the upper 10 percent of black Americans. Education, he believed, was the key:

> Work alone will not do it unless inspired by the right ideals and guided by intelligence. Education must not simply teach work—it must teach Life. The Talented Tenth of the Negro race must be made leaders of thought and missionaries of culture among people. No others can do this work, and Negro colleges must train men for it. The Negro race, like all other races, is going to be saved by its exceptional men.

The Niagara Movement

In 1905 Du Bois carried the anti-Washington crusade a step further and invited a select group to meet at Niagara Falls, in Canada. The twenty-nine delegates to this meeting insisted that black people no longer quietly accept the loss of the right to vote. "We believe that [Negro] American citizens should protest emphatically and continually against the curtailment of their political rights." They also demanded an end to segregation, declaring, "All American citizens have the right to equal treatment in places of public entertainment." They appealed for better schools, health care, and housing; protested the discrimination endured by black soldiers; and criticized the racial prejudice

The founders of the Niagara Movement posed in front of a photograph of the falls when they met at Niagara Falls, Ontario, Canada, in 1905. W. E. B. Du Bois is second from the right in the middle row.

Photographs and Prints Division, Schomburg Center for Research in Black Culture, The New York Public Library, Astor, Lenox, and Tilden Foundations

of most churches as "wrong, unchristian and disgraceful to the twentieth century civilization." Perhaps most important, the Niagara gathering insisted that white people did not know what was best for black people. "We repudiate the monstrous doctrine that the oppressor should be the sole authority as to the rights of the oppressed."

The Niagara Movement that emerged from this meeting attracted four hundred members and remained active for several years. Du Bois composed annual addresses to the nation designed to arouse black and white support. But the Niagara Movement was no match for the powerful, efficient, and well-financed Tuskegee Machine. Washington used every means at his disposal to undermine the movement. Black newspaper editors like the *Washington Bee's* W. Calvin Chase, who had earlier attacked Washington's Atlanta Compromise address, were paid to attack Du Bois and to praise Washington. Washington dispatched spies to Niagara meetings to report on the organization's activities.

There were also internal problems among Niagara members. Du Bois was an inexperienced leader, and difficulties developed between Du Bois and Trotter. In 1908 the Niagara Movement virtually collapsed. Most black and white Americans were not prepared to support an organization that seemed so uncompromising in its demands.

THE NAACP

As the Niagara Movement expired, the National Association for the Advancement of Colored People (NAACP) came to life. There was no direct link between the demise of the Niagara Movement and the rise of the NAACP. But the relatively small numbers of people—black and white—who felt comfortable with the Niagara Movement's assertive stance on race were inclined to support the NAACP. In its early years the NAACP was a militant organization dedicated to racial justice. White leaders dominated it and white contributors largely financed it.

A few white progressives were deeply concerned about the rampant racial prejudice manifested so graphically in lynchings, Jim Crow, black disfranchisement, and a vicious riot in 1908 in Springfield, Illinois—Abraham Lincoln's hometown. After a gathering of leaders in January 1909 in New York City, Oswald Garrison Villard issued a call on February 12—Lincoln's Birthday—to "all believers in democracy to join a national conference to discuss present evils, the voicing of protests, and the renewal of the struggle for civil and political liberty."

Villard was the president and editor of the New York *Evening Post* and the grandson of abolitionist William Lloyd Garrison. Prominent progressives endorsed the call, including social workers Lillian Wald and Jane Addams, literary scholar Joel E. Spingarn, and respected attorneys Clarence Darrow and Moorfield Storey.

W. E. B. Du Bois, Ida Wells Barnett, and Mary Church Terrell were the black leaders most involved in the formation of the NAACP.

The NAACP was determined that black citizens should fully enjoy the civil and political rights the Constitution guaranteed to all citizens. It relied on the judicial and legislative systems in what would be a persistent and decades-long effort to secure those rights. The NAACP won its first major legal victory in 1915 when the Supreme Court overturned Oklahoma's grandfather clause in *Guinn v. United States*. But poll taxes and literacy tests continued to disfranchise black citizens.

In 1917, in a case brought by the Louisville NAACP branch and argued before the Supreme Court by Moorfield Storey, the court struck down a local law that enforced residential segregation by prohibiting black people and white people from selling real estate to people of the other race. The NAACP also tried in 1918 to secure a federal law prohibiting lynching. With the assistance of Congressman Leonidas Dyer, a white St. Louis Republican, the antilynching measure—the Dyer bill—passed in the House of Representatives in 1922 over vigorous Democratic opposition. But the Senate blocked it, and it never became law.

W. E. B. Du Bois was easily the most prominent black figure associated with the NAACP during its first quarter century. He became director of publicity and research and edited the NAACP publication, *The Crisis*, while largely leaving leadership and administrative tasks to others.

With *The Crisis*, Du Bois the scholar became Du Bois the propagandist. In the pages of *The Crisis*, he denounced white racism and atrocities and demanded that black people stand up for their rights. "Agitate, then, brother; protest, reveal the truth and refuse to be silenced. . . . A moment's let up, a moment's acquiescence, means a chance for the wolves of prejudice to get at our necks." He would not provoke violence, but he would not tolerate mistreatment either. "I am resolved to be quiet and law abiding, but to refuse to cringe in body or in soul, to resent deliberate insult, and to assert my just rights in the face of wanton aggression." These were not the even-tempered, cautious words of Booker T. Washington to which so many Americans had grown accustomed. *The Crisis* became required reading in many black homes. By 1913 it had thirty thousand subscribers when the membership of the NAACP was only three thousand.

THE EMERGENCE OF NATIONAL AFRICAN-AMERICAN ORGANIZATIONS

1889	Afro-American League organized in Chicago
1892	Colored Women's League of Washington formed
1893	New Era Club founded in Boston
1895	National Federation of Afro-American Women organized in Boston
1896	National Association of Colored Women (NACW) formed in Washington
1897	American Negro Academy founded in Washington
1897	First Phillis Wheatley home established in Detroit
1900	National Negro Business League established in Boston
1905	Niagara Movement organized in Niagara Falls, Ontario,Canada
1909	National Association for the Advancement of Colored People (NAACP) founded in New York City
1910	National League on Urban Conditions among Negroes (Urban League) formed in New York City

Washington versus the NAACP

In 1909, with the founding of the NAACP, Oswald Garrison Villard tried to reassure Washington the organization posed no threat and to gain his support for the new association. "It is not to be a Washington movement, or a Du Bois movement. The idea is that there shall grow out of it, first, an annual conference . . . for the discussion by men of both races of the conditions of the colored people, politically, socially, industrially and educationally."

Many black leaders and members of the NAACP, however, despised Washington and his ideology, and Washington returned the sentiment. With the assistance of his followers, he worked to subvert the new organization. Washington looked on Du Bois as little more than the puppet of white people, who dominated the leadership of the NAACP, and the Tuskegee leader declined to debate Du Bois. One of Washington's aides commented that "it would be entirely out of place for Dr. Washington to enter into any discussion with a man occupying the place that Dr. Du Bois does, for the reason that Dr. Washington is at the head of a large institution. . . . Dr. Du Bois, on the other hand, is a mere hired man, as it were, in an institution completely controlled by white people."

Washington told an alumnus of Tuskegee that the main aim of the NAACP was to destroy Washington and Tuskegee. "As a matter of straight fact, this organization is for the purpose of tearing down our work wherever possible and I think none of our friends should give it comfort."

Washington became so obsessed with the NAACP that he was not above manipulating white supremacists to damage those connected with the association. When he learned that a group of black and white progressives associated with the NAACP were going to gather at the Café Boulevard in New York City in 1911, he allowed Charles Anderson to alert the hostile white press, which gleefully described the multiracial dinner in the most inflammatory terms. "Fashionable White Women Sit at Board with

Negroes, Japs and Chinamen to Promote 'Cause' of Miscegenation" proclaimed one headline. The New York *Press* added, "White women, evidently of the cultured and wealthier classes, fashionably attired in low-cut gowns, leaned over the tables to chat confidentially with negro men of the true African type."

Ultimately, Washington's efforts to ruin the NAACP and to reduce the influence of its supporters failed. By the time of his death in 1915, the NAACP had grown steadily to over six thousand members and fifty local branches. Its aggressive campaign for civil and political rights replaced Washington's strategy of progress through conciliation and accommodation.

THE URBAN LEAGUE

In 1910 the National League on Urban Conditions among Negroes was founded in New York City. The goal of this social welfare organization, soon known simply as the Urban League, was to alleviate conditions black people encountered as they moved into large cities in ever-increasing numbers in the early twentieth century. Like the NAACP, the Urban League was created by black and white progressives. It worked to improve housing, medical care, and recreational facilities among black residents who lived in segregated neighborhoods in New York, Philadelphia, Atlanta, Nashville, Norfolk, and other cities. The league also assisted youngsters who ran afoul of the law, and it helped establish the Big Brother and Big Sister movements.

BLACK WOMEN AND THE CLUB MOVEMENT

Years before the Urban League and the NAACP were founded, black women began creating clubs and organizations. The local groups that began forming in the 1870s and 1880s, such as the Bethel Literary and Historical Association in Washington, D.C., were mainly concerned with cultural, religious, and social matters. But many of the mostly middle-class women active in these clubs eventually became less interested in tea and gossip and more involved with community problems. In 1893 black women in Boston founded the New Era Club. They published a monthly magazine, *Woman's Era*, that featured articles on fashion, health, and family life.

In 1895 a New Era Club member, Josephine St. Pierre Ruffin, enraged by white journalist James W. Jack's vilification of black women as "prostitutes, thieves, and liars" who were "altogether without character," issued a call to "Let Us Confer Together" that drew 104 black women to a meeting in Boston. The result was the formation of the National Federation of Afro-American Women, which soon included thirty-six clubs in twelve states. In the meantime, the Colored Women's League of Washington, D.C., which had been founded in 1892, published an appeal in *Woman's Era* for black women to organize a national association at the 1895 meeting of the National Council of Women. At that gathering, representatives from several local black women's clubs organized the National Colored Woman's League.

The two groups—The National Federation of Afro-American Women and the National Colored Woman's League—merged in 1896 to form the National Association of Colored Women (NACW) with Mary Church Terrell elected the first president. The

NACW adopted the self-help motto "Lifting as We Climb," and in the reforming spirit of the progressive age, they stressed moral, mental, and material advancement. By 1914 there were fifty thousand members of the NACW in one thousand clubs nation-wide. The NACW clubs worked to eradicate poverty, end racial discrimination, and promote education, including the formation of kindergartens and day nurseries. Members cared for older people, especially former slaves. They aided orphans; assisted working mothers by providing nurseries, health care, and information on child rearing; and established homes for delinquent and abandoned girls.

Black women also formed Phillis Wheatley clubs and homes across the nation (named in honor of the eighteenth-century African-American poet). The residences offered living accommodations for single, black working women in many cities where they were refused admittance to YWCA facilities. Some Phillis Wheatley clubs also provided nurseries and classes in domestic skills. In Cleveland, nurse Jane Edna Hunter organized a residence for single, black working women who could not find comfortable and affordable housing. In 1911 she formed the Working Girls' Home Association for cleaning women, laundresses, and private duty nurses. With association members contributing five cents a week, Hunter opened a twenty-three-room residence in 1913 that expanded to a seventy-two-room building in 1917.

Anna Julia Cooper and Black Feminism

"Only the BLACK WOMAN can say 'when and where I enter, in the quiet, undisputed dignity of my womanhood, without violence and without suing or special patronage, then and there the whole Negro race enters with me.'" So wrote Anna Julia Cooper in the late nineteenth century. Not only was Cooper convinced that black women would play a decisive role in shaping the destiny of their people, she labored to dispel the stereotype that black women lacked refinement, grace, and morality.

Cooper was born a slave in Raleigh, North Carolina, in 1858 and graduated from St. Augustine's School. She then earned a bachelor's degree from Oberlin College in 1884. Speaking and writing with increasing confidence and authority, she published *A Voice from the South by a Black Woman of the South* in 1892. In this collection of essays she stressed the pivotal role that black women would play in the future, and she chastised white women for their lack of support. In 1900 she addressed the Pan African Conference in London.

Cooper was principal of Washington's famed M Street Colored High School (later Paul Laurence Dunbar High School) from 1901 to 1906. She was forced out in 1906 amid allegations that supporters of the powerful Tuskegee Machine resented Cooper's emphasis on academic preparation over vocational training. She went on to teach for four years at Missouri's Lincoln University before returning to M Street High as a teacher. Fluent in French, she earned a Ph.D. at the Sorbonne in Paris. She was active with the NACW, the NAACP, and YWCA. She died in 1964 at age 105.

Women's Suffrage

Historically, many black women had supported women's suffrage. Before the Civil War, many abolitionists, including Mary Ann Shadd Cary, Sojourner Truth, and Frederick Douglass, had also backed women's suffrage. Cary and Truth tried unsuccessfully to vote after the war. Black women, such as Caroline Remond Putnam of Massachusetts, Lottie Rollin of South Carolina, and Frances Ellen Watkins Harper of Pennsylvania, attended conventions of the mostly white American Woman's Suffrage Association in the 1870s.

Black women were also involved in the long struggle for women's suffrage on the state level. Ida Wells Barnett was a leader in the Illinois suffrage effort. By 1900 Wyoming, Utah, Colorado, and Idaho permitted women to vote, and by 1918 women in seventeen northern and western states had gained the vote. But as more women won voting rights, women's suffrage became more controversial. The proposed Nineteenth Amendment to the U.S. Constitution drove a wedge between black and white advocates of women's political rights. Many opponents of women's suffrage, especially white Southerners, warned that granting women the right to vote would increase the number of black voters. Some white women advocated strict literacy and educational requirements for voting in an effort to limit the number of black voters, both women and men.

As it turned out, only two southern states—Kentucky and Tennessee—ratified the Nineteenth Amendment before its adoption in 1920. Black suffragists understood that the right to vote meant political power, and political power could be exercised to acquire civil rights, improve education, and gain respect. White Southerners also grasped the importance of voting rights. Thus despite the Nineteenth Amendment, large numbers of black people in the South—both men and women—remained unable to vote.

THE BLACK ELITE

Many of the black leaders described by W. E. B. Du Bois as the Talented Tenth formed protest organizations, joined reform efforts, and organized self-help groups. The leaders were middle- and upper-class black people who were better educated than most Americans—black or white.

The American Negro Academy

In 1897 Episcopal priest Alexander Crummel met with sixteen other black men in Washington, D.C., to form the American Negro Academy. This scholarly organization was made up of "men of African descent" who assembled periodically to discuss and publish works on history, literature, religion, and science. Among those who attended the initial gathering were W. E. B. Du Bois, Paul Laurence Dunbar, Kelly Miller, and Francis Grimke.

Crummel was an elderly but a dynamic and distinguished leader who did not hesitate to express his deeply felt convictions on race, religion, and Africa. He had been born in 1818 in New York and spent several years in Liberia in the 1850s and 1860s as an Episcopal missionary. Crummel died in 1898, but the Academy survived as a vibrant intellectual and elitist society.

Carter G. Woodson, Alain Locke, Arthur Schomburg, and James Weldon Johnson subsequently joined its ranks before it eventually disbanded in 1928. It afforded black intellectuals an opportunity to ponder what it meant to be black in America and to develop their racial consciousness, thus nurturing ideas and concepts that would mature during the Harlem Renaissance.

Most members of the Academy supported women's rights and women's suffrage. Consequently it was exceedingly ironic that black women were not invited to become members of the Academy, although several black women, including Anna Julia Cooper, Ida Wells Barnett, and Mary Church Terrell, were easily the intellectual equals of the male participants.

By the early twentieth century, there were several hundred wealthy African Americans. These black aristocrats were as sophisticated, refined, and conscious of their status as any group in American society. They distanced themselves from less affluent black and white people and lived in expensive houses. Many of them possessed fair complexions. They were medical doctors, lawyers, and businessmen.

The black elite formed exclusive organizations that jealously limited membership to the small black upper class. In the 1860s the Ugly Fishing Club was transformed into an organization made up of New York City's wealthiest black men. It soon came to be known simply as the Ugly Club, and its membership spread to Newport, Rhode Island, Baltimore, and Philadelphia. In 1904 two wealthy Philadelphia physicians, a dentist, and a pharmacist formed Sigma Pi Beta, better known as Boulé. It was restricted to male college graduates, and it aimed to provide "inspiration, relaxation, intellectual stimulation, and brotherhood." Boulé expanded to seven chapters in cities that included Chicago and Memphis, but its membership totaled a mere 177.

Organizations like the Diamondback Club and the Cosmos Club in Washington, the Loendi Club in Pittsburgh, and the Bachelor-Benedict Club in New York sponsored luxurious banquets, dances, and debutante balls. Several of these groups owned ornate clubhouses. These elite societies and cliques typically competed to demonstrate social exclusivity and preeminence.

Among the black elite were also the African Americans who established the Greek letter black fraternities and sororities. In 1906 seven students at Cornell University formed Alpha Phi Alpha, the first college fraternity for black men. Within a few years, it had chapters at the University of Michigan, Yale, Columbia, and Ohio State. The first black sorority, Alpha Kappa Alpha, was founded in 1908 at Howard University. Several other Greek letter organizations were subsequently launched at Howard: Omega Psi Phi fraternity in 1911, Delta Sigma Theta sorority in 1913, Phi Beta Sigma in 1914, and Zeta Phi Beta sorority in 1920. In addition, in 1911 Kappa Alpha Psi fraternity was founded at Indiana University, and Sigma Gamma Rho sorority was formed in Indianapolis in 1922.

Besides providing college students with an opportunity to enjoy each other's company, the black fraternities and sororities stressed scholarship, social graces, and community involvement.

PRESIDENTIAL POLITICS

Since Reconstruction, black voters had loyally supported the Republican Party and its presidential candidates. "The Party of Lincoln" welcomed that support and periodically rewarded black men with federal jobs. Republican presidents Theodore Roosevelt (1901–1909) and William Howard Taft (1909–1913) continued that policy.

But other presidential actions more than offset whatever goodwill these appointments generated. Roosevelt discharged three companies of black soldiers after the Brownsville incident in 1906, and Taft tolerated restrictions on black voters in the South and encouraged the development of a "lily white" Republican Party, removing black people from federal jobs in the region.

In 1912 the Republican Party split in a bitter feud between President Taft and Theodore Roosevelt, and a third political party—the Progressive Party—emerged. The Progressives nominated Roosevelt to run against Taft and the Democratic candidate, Woodrow Wilson. But as the delegates at the Progressive convention in Chicago sang the "Battle Hymn of the Republic," southern black men who had come to the gathering stood outside the hall, denied admission by white Progressives.

It was not a complete shock that militant black leaders like William Monroe Trotter and W. E. B. Du Bois urged black voters to support Woodrow Wilson, the Democrat, in the 1912 presidential election. Wilson was the reform governor of New Jersey, and he had been president of Princeton University. Trotter and Du Bois were impressed with Wilson's academic background and his promise to pursue a progressive policy toward black Americans.

But as president, Wilson proved to be no friend of black people. Born in Virginia and raised in South Carolina, Wilson had thoroughly absorbed white southern racial views. Federal agencies and buildings were fully segregated early during Wilson's tenure. In 1914 Trotter and a black delegation met with Wilson to protest segregation in the treasury department and the post office. Wilson defended separation of the races as a means to avoid friction. Trotter vehemently disagreed, and Wilson became visibly irritated. The president warned that he would no longer meet with the group if Trotter remained their spokesman.

BLACK MEN AND THE MILITARY IN WORLD WAR I

In 1915–1916 Wilson faced more than problems with dissatisfied black people. United States–Mexican relations had steadily deteriorated after a revolution and civil war in Mexico. War in Europe threatened to draw the United States into conflict with Germany.

The Punitive Expedition to Mexico

In 1914 war almost broke out between the United States and Mexico when U.S. marines landed at Vera Cruz after an attack on American sailors. Then, in March 1916, Francisco "Pancho" Villa, one of the participants in Mexico's civil war, led a force of Mexican rebels across the border into New Mexico in an effort to provoke war between Mexico and the United States. Fifteen Americans were killed, including seven U.S. soldiers. In response, Wilson dispatched a "punitive expedition" that eventually numbered 15,000 U.S. troops under the command of General John J. "Black Jack" Pershing. Pershing acquired the nickname "Black Jack" after commanding black troops in Cuba during the Spanish-American War.

United States forces, including the black 10th Cavalry (see Chapter 15), spent ten months in Mexico in a futile effort to capture Villa. The 10th Cavalry was, as had been the case with black troops since the Civil War, commanded by white men. But Lieutenant Colonel Charles Young, an 1889 black graduate of the U.S. Military Academy at West Point, helped lead the regiment.

Young led the black troops against a contingent of Villa's rebels who had ambushed an element of the 13th Cavalry, a white unit, at Santa Cruz de Villegas. Major Frank Tompkins of the 13th was so relieved to be rescued that he reportedly exclaimed to Young, "By God, Young, I could kiss every black face out there." Young supposedly replied, "If you want to, you may start with me." U.S. troops were withdrawn from Mexico in 1917 as the probability increased that the United States would enter World War I against Germany.

World War I

When World War I erupted in Europe in August 1914, Woodrow Wilson and most Americans had no intention and no desire to participate. Wilson promptly issued a proclamation of neutrality. Running for reelection in 1916 on the appealing slogan "He Kept Us Out of War," Wilson narrowly defeated Republican candidate Charles Evans Hughes. Repeated German submarine attacks on civilian vessels and the loss of American lives infuriated Wilson and many Americans. On April 6, 1917, Congress declared war on Germany. Most African Americans supported the war effort. As in previous conflicts, black people sought to demonstrate their loyalty and devotion to the country through military service. "If this is our country," declared W. E. B. Du Bois, "then this is our war. We must fight it with every ounce of blood and treasure."

Some white leaders were less enthusiastic about the participation of black men. One southern governor wondered about the wisdom of having the military train and arm thousands of black men at southern camps and posts. General Pershing argued for the use of black troops, but insisted on white leadership. "Under capable white officers and with sufficient training, Negro soldiers have always acquitted themselves creditably."

Black Troops and Officers

There were about 10,000 black regulars in the U.S. Army in 1917: the 9th and 10th Cavalry regiments and the 24th and 25th Infantry regiments. There were more than 5,000 black men in the navy, but virtually all of them were waiters, kitchen attendants, and stokers for the ships' boilers. The Marine Corps did not admit black men. During World War I, the newly formed Selective Service system drafted more than 370,000 black men—13 percent of all draftees—although none of the local draft boards had black members. Several all-black state National Guard units were also incorporated into federal service.

Although the military remained rigidly segregated, there was political pressure from black newspapers and the NAACP to commission black officers to lead black troops. The War Department created an officer training school at Fort Des Moines, Iowa. Nearly 1,250 black men enrolled—1,000 were civilians and 250 were enlisted men from the regular regiments—and over 1,000 received commissions. Black officers, however, were confined to the lower ranks. None of these new black officers were promoted above captain, and the overall command of black units remained in white hands.

Lieutenant Colonel Charles Young was eligible to lead black and white troops in World War I. He had already served in Cuba, the Philippines, Haiti, and Mexico. Several white soldiers complained, however, that they did not want to take orders from a black man, and over Young's protests, military authorities forced him to retire by claiming he had high blood pressure. Young insisted he was in good health, and he rode a horse from his home in Xenia, Ohio, to Washington, D.C., to prove it. But Young remained on the retired list until he was given command of a training unit in Illinois five days before the war ended.

Discrimination and its Effects

Most white military leaders, politicians, and journalists embraced racial stereotypes and expected little from black soldiers. As in earlier American wars, black troops were discriminated against, abused, and neglected. Some were compelled to drill with picks and shovels rather than rifles. At Camp Hill, Virginia, black men lived in tents with no floors, no blankets, and no bathing facilities through a cold winter. White men failed to salute black officers, and black officers were denied admission to officers' clubs. Morale among black troops was low, and their performance sometimes reflected it.

Military authorities did not expect to use black troops in combat. The army preferred to employ black troops in labor battalions, as stevedores, in road construction, and as cooks and bakers. Of more than 380,000 black men who served in World War I, only 42,000 went into combat. Black troops represented 3 percent of U.S. combat strength. The army did not prepare black soldiers adequately for combat, but military leaders complained when black soldiers who did face combat performed poorly in battle.

The 368th Infantry Regiment of the 92nd Division came in for especially harsh criticism. Fighting alongside the French in September 1918, the second and third battalions fell back in disorder. Some black officers and enlisted men ran. The white regimental commander blamed black officers, and thirty of them were relieved of command. Five officers were court-martialed for cowardice; four were sentenced to death and one to life in prison. All were later freed. But black Lieutenant Howard H. Long agreed that the perceptions of white officers caused the poor performance. "Many of the [white] field officers seemed far more concerned with reminding their Negro subordinates that they were Negroes than they were in having an effective unit that would perform well in combat."

Even the white commander of the 92nd Division, General Charles C. Ballou, identified white officers as the main problem. "It was my misfortune to be handicapped by many white officers who were rabidly hostile to the idea of a colored officer, and who continually conveyed misinformation to the staff of the superior units, and generally created much trouble and discontent. Such men will never give the Negro the square deal that is his just due."

White officials stressed the weaknesses of the 368th Infantry Regiment and mostly ignored the commendable records of the 369th, 370th, 371st, and 372nd Regiments. The 369th compiled an exemplary combat record. Sent to the front for ninety-one consecutive days, these "Men of Bronze"—as they came to be known—consisted mainly of soldiers from the 15th New York National Guard. They fought alongside the French and were given French weapons, uniforms, helmets, and food. They had an outstanding military band led by Jim Europe, one of the finest musical leaders of the early twentieth century. The 369th lived up to their motto, "Let's Go," as they took part in some of the war's heaviest fighting. They never lost a trench or gave up a prisoner. By June 1918 French commanders were asking for all the black troops the Americans could send.

Most French civilians and troops praised the conduct of black soldiers and accepted them as equals. Following the triumph of the Allies in World War I, French authorities awarded the Croix de Guerre, one of France's highest military medals, to the men of the 369th, the 371st, and the 372nd Regiments.

Black troops returned to America on segregated ships. The 15th New York National Guard Unit from the 369th Regiment and its famed band were not permitted to join the farewell parade in New York City. Even when white Americans offered praise, it was riddled with racist stereotypes. The Milwaukee *Sentinel* offered a typical compliment: "Those two colored regiments fought well, and it calls for special recognition. Is there no way of getting a cargo of watermelons over there?"

Du Bois's Disappointment

Black leaders who had supported American entry in the war were embittered at the treatment of black soldiers. During the war in 1918, Du Bois appealed to black people in *The Crisis* to "close ranks" and support the war:

> We of the colored race have no ordinary interest in the outcome. That which the German power represents today spells death to the aspirations of Negroes and all darker races for equality, freedom and democracy. Let us not hesitate. Let us, while this war lasts, forget our special grievances and close ranks with our own white fellow citizens and the allied nations that are fighting for democracy.

Du Bois's unequivocal support may well have been connected to his effort to secure an officer's commission in military intelligence through the intervention of Joel E. Spingarn, chairman of the NAACP board of directors. Du Bois did not get his commission. What he did get was criticism for his "close ranks" editorial. His former ally, William Monroe Trotter, said that Du Bois had "finally weakened, compromised, deserted the fight, [and] betrayed the cause of his race." To Trotter, Du Bois was "a rank quitter in the cause for equal rights."

In 1930 Du Bois confessed that he should not have supported U.S. intervention in the war:

> I was swept off my feet during the world war by the emotional response of America to what seemed to be a great call to duty. The thing that I did not understand is how easy and inevitable it is for an appeal to blood and force to smash to utter negation any ideal for which it is used. Instead of a war to end war, or a war to save democracy, we found ourselves during and after the war descending to the meanest and most sordid of selfish actions.

By the end of World War I, Du Bois—who had visited black troops in France—could see that black loyalty and sacrifice had not eroded white racism. He wrote defiantly in

The Crisis that black people were determined to make America yield to its democratic ideals:

> But by the God of heaven, we are cowards and jackasses if now that the war is over, we do not marshal every ounce of our brain and brawn to fight a sterner, longer, more unbending battle against the forces of hell in our own land.
> We return.
> We return from fighting.
> We return fighting.
> Make way for Democracy! We saved it in France, and by the Great Jehovah, we will save it in the United States of America, or know the reason why.

RACE RIOTS

Despite the reformist impulse of the progressive era and the democratic ideals trumpeted as the United States went to war against Germany, most white Americans clung to social Darwinism and white supremacy. White people reacted with contempt and violence to demands by black people for fairer treatment and equal opportunities in American society. The campaigns of the NAACP, the efforts of the black club women, and the services and sacrifices of black men in the war not only failed to alter white racial perceptions but were sometimes accompanied by a backlash against African Americans. Ten black men still in uniform were lynched in 1919.

The racial violence that had permeated southern life in the late nineteenth century expanded into northern communities as many white Americans responded with hostility to the arrival of black migrants from the South. Black people defended themselves, and casualties among both races escalated (see Map 16–1).

Atlanta 1906

In 1906—eleven years after Booker T. Washington delivered his Cotton States Exposition address there—white mobs attacked black residents in Atlanta. Several factors aggravated white racial apprehensions in the city. In 1902 four black and four white people had been killed in a riot there. Many rural black people, attracted by economic opportunities, had moved to Atlanta. But white residents considered the newcomers more lawless and immoral than the longtime black residents. The Atlanta newspapers—*The Constitution, The Journal,* and *The Georgian*—ran inflammatory accounts about black crime and black men who brutalized white women. Many of these stories were false or exaggerated. Two white Democrats—Hoke Smith and Clark Howell—were engaged in a divisive campaign for a U.S. Senate seat in 1906, and both candidates stirred up racial animosity. There were also determined and ultimately successful efforts under way to disfranchise black voters in Georgia.

On a warm Saturday night, September 22, 1906, a white man jumped on a box on Decatur Street, one of Atlanta's main thoroughfares, and waved an Atlanta newspaper emblazoned with the headline THIRD ASSAULT. He hollered, "Are white men going to

MAP 16–1   Major Race Riots, 1900–1923. In the years between 1900 and 1923, race conflicts and riots occurred in dozens of American communities as black people migrated in increasing numbers to urban areas. The violence reached a peak in the immediate aftermath of World War I during the Red Summer of 1919. White Americans—in the North and South—were determined to keep black people confined to a subordinate role as menial laborers and restricted to well-defined all-black neighborhoods. African Americans who had made significant economic and military contributions to the war effort and who had congregated in large numbers in American cities insisted on participating on a more equitable basis in American society.

stand for this?" The crowd roared, "No! Save our women!" "Kill the niggers." A five-day orgy of violence followed.

The mayor, police, and fire departments vainly tried to stop the mob. Thousands of white people roamed the streets in search of black victims. Black people were indiscriminately tortured, beaten, and killed. White men pulled black passengers off streetcars. They destroyed black businesses. As white men armed themselves, the police disarmed black men. Black men and women who surrendered to marauding white mobs in hopes of mercy were not spared. Black men who fought back only further infuriated the crazed white crowd. Twenty-five black people and one white person died, and hundreds were injured in the riot.

Du Bois hurried home to Atlanta from a trip to Alabama to defend his wife and child. He waited on his porch with a shotgun for a mob that never came. He later explained, "I would without hesitation have sprayed their guts over the grass." In New York, black editor T. Thomas Fortune called for a violent black response: "It makes my blood boil. I would like to be there with a good force of armed men to make Rome howl." Fortune demanded retribution. "I cannot believe that the policy of non-resistance in a situation like that of Atlanta can result in anything but contempt and massacre of the race."

Booker T. Washington looked for a silver lining in the awful affair by noting that "while there is disorder in one community there is peace and harmony in thousands of others." He said that black resistance would merely result in more black fatalities. Washington went to Atlanta and appealed for racial reconciliation.

A Committee of Safety of ten black and ten white leaders was formed. Charles T. Hopkins, an influential white Atlantan, warned in strong paternalist terms, "If we let this dependent race be butchered before our eyes, we cannot face God in the judgement day." But little real racial cooperation resulted. No members of the white mob were brought to justice. Black Georgia voters were disfranchised. Atlanta's streetcars were segregated. The city had no public high school for black youngsters. The Carnegie Library did not admit black people, and the Atlanta police force had no black officers.

Springfield 1908

Two years later in August 1908, white citizens of Springfield, Illinois, attacked black residents in an episode that led to the creation of the NAACP in 1909. George Richardson, a black man, was falsely accused of raping a white woman. The sheriff managed to save Richardson by getting him out of town. But an angry mob tore into Springfield's small black population. Six black people were shot and killed, two were lynched, dozens were injured, and damage in the thousands of dollars was inflicted on black homes and businesses. About two thousand black people were driven out of the community.

There was even more violence in the second decade of the twentieth century as major racial conflicts occurred between 1917 and 1921 in East St. Louis, IL; Houston, TX; Chicago; Elaine, AR; and Tulsa, OK. Smaller violent confrontations occurred at Washington, D.C.; Charleston, SC; Knoxville, TN; Omaha, NE; and Waco and Longview, TX. Although different incidents sparked each riot, the underlying causes tended to be similar. White residents were concerned that recently arrived black migrants would compete for jobs and housing.

East St. Louis 1917

East St. Louis, Illinois, was a gritty industrial town of nearly sixty thousand across the Mississippi River from St. Louis, Missouri. About 10 percent of the inhabitants were black. The town's schools, public facilities, and neighborhoods were segregated. Racial tensions increased in February 1917 after 470 black workers were hired to replace white members of the American Federation of Labor who had gone on strike against the Aluminum Ore Company. On July 1 several white people drove through a black neighborhood firing guns. Shortly after, two white plainclothes police officers drove into the same neighborhood and were shot and killed by residents who may have believed the drive-by shooters had returned.

Angry white mobs then sought revenge. Black people were mutilated and killed, and their bodies were thrown into the river. Black homes, many of them little more than cabins and shacks, were burned. Hundreds of black people were left homeless. The police joined the rioters. Thirty-five black people and eight white people died in the violence.

The NAACP sent W. E. B. Du Bois and Martha Gruening to East St. Louis. They compiled a twenty-four-page report, "Massacre at East St. Louis," that documented instance after instance of brutality. "Negroes were 'flushed' from the burning houses, and ran for their lives, screaming and begging for mercy. A Negro crawled into a shed and fired on the white men. Guardsmen started after him, but when they saw he was armed, turned to the mob and said: 'He's armed boys. You can have him. A white man's life is worth the lives of a thousand Negroes."

To protest the riot, the NAACP organized a silent march in New York City and thousands of well-dressed black people marched to muffled drums down Fifth Avenue.

Houston 1917

A month after the East St. Louis riot, black soldiers in Houston attacked police officers and civilians. The Third Battalion of the 24th Infantry recently had been transferred from Wyoming and California to Camp Logan near Houston where the black troops came face to face with Jim Crow. Streetcars and public facilities were segregated. Local white and Hispanic people regularly called the black troops "niggers."

On July 28, 1917, the NAACP organized a silent march in New York City to protest the East St. Louis, Illinois, race riot in which thirty-five black people died as well as to denounce the ongoing epidemic of lynchings. The marchers were accompanied by the beat of muffled drums.
Courtesy of the Library of Congress

On August 23 a black soldier tried to prevent a police officer, Lee Sparks, from beating a black woman. Sparks clubbed the soldier and hauled him off to jail. Corporal Charles W. Baltimore later attempted to determine what had happened, and he was also beaten and incarcerated. Both soldiers were later released. But a rumor circulated that Baltimore had been slain. Led by Sergeant Vida Henry, black men sought revenge.

About one hundred armed black soldiers mounted a two-hour assault on the police station. Fifteen white residents—including five policemen—one Mexican American, four black soldiers, and two black civilians were killed. The army charged 63 black soldiers with mutiny. The NAACP retained the son of Texas legend Sam Houston to help defend them. Eight black men, however, agreed to testify against the defendants. Thirteen black troops were hanged (including Corporal Baltimore) after the first court-martial. Later seven more were executed, seven others were acquitted, and the remainder were sentenced to prison terms ranging from two years to life. Lee Sparks remained on the Houston police force and killed two black people later that year.

Chicago 1919

Between 1916 and 1919, the black population of Chicago doubled as migrants from the South moved north in search of jobs, political rights, and humane treatment. Many encountered a violent reception. A severe housing shortage strained the boundaries between crowded, segregated black neighborhoods and white residential areas. In the months after World War I ended in November 1918, racial tensions increased as black men were hired to replace striking white workers in several industries in Chicago.

The Chicago riot began on Sunday, July 27, 1919—one day after black troops were welcomed home with a parade down the city's Michigan Avenue. Eugene Williams, a young black man, was swimming in Lake Michigan and inadvertently crossed the invisible boundary that separated the black and white beaches and bathing areas. He was stoned by white people and drowned. Instead of arresting the alleged perpetrators, the police arrested a black man who complained about police inaction.

Williams's death set off a week of violence that left twenty-three black people and fifteen white people dead. More than five hundred were injured, and nearly one thousand were left homeless after fire raged through a Lithuanian neighborhood. Not only did police fail to stem the violence, they often joined roaming white mobs as they attacked black pedestrians and streetcar passengers. Black men formed a barrier along State Street to stop the advance of white gangs from the stockyard district. Three regiments of the Illinois National Guard were sent into the streets, but the violence ended only on Saturday, August 1, as heavy rains kept people indoors.

During the riot, the Chicago *Defender*, the city's black newspaper, reported many violent incidents. "In the early [Tuesday] morning a thirteen-year-old lad standing on his porch at 51st and Wabash Avenue was shot to death by a white man who, in an attempt to get away, encountered a mob and his existence became history. A mounted policeman, unknown, fatally wounded a small boy in the block of Dearborn Street and was shot to death by some unknown rioter."

Elaine 1919

In the fall of 1919, black sharecroppers in and around Elaine, Arkansas, attempted to organize a union and withhold their cotton from the market until they received a higher price. Deputy sheriffs tried to break up a union meeting in a black church, and one of the deputies was killed. In retaliation, white people killed dozens of black people. No white people were prosecuted, but twelve black men were convicted of the deputy's murder. They were sentenced to death, and sixty-seven other black men received prison terms of up to twenty years. Many were tortured and beaten while they were held in jail. Ida Wells Barnett and the Equal Rights League generated enormous publicity about the case. The NAACP appealed the convictions, and in 1923 the Supreme Court overturned them. The court agreed with NAACP attorney Moorfield Storey that the defendants had not received a fair trial.

Tulsa 1921

Violence erupted in Tulsa, Oklahoma, on May 31, 1921, after still another black man was accused of rape. Dick Rowland allegedly assaulted a white woman elevator operator, and rumors circulated that white men intended to lynch him. To protect Rowland, who was later found innocent, black men assembled at the courthouse jail where white men also gathered. Angry words were exchanged, and shooting erupted. Several black and white men died in the chaos that ensued.

Black men retreated to their neighborhood, known as Greenwood, to protect their families and homes. The governor dispatched the National Guard, and the sheriff removed Rowland from the jail to an unknown location. By the morning of June 1, some five hundred white men confronted about one thousand black men across a set of railroad tracks. White men in sixty to seventy automobiles were also cruising around the black residential area. Approximately fifty armed black people defended themselves in a black church near the edge of their neighborhood as white men advanced on them. The attackers set fire to the church. As black people fled the burning building, they were shot. More fires were set. About two thousand black residents managed to escape to a convention hall. Forty square blocks and more than one thousand of Greenwood's homes, churches, schools and businesses went up in flames. White men even utilized aircraft to drop incendiary devices on Greenwood. As many as three hundred black people and twenty white people may have perished in what was perhaps the worst episode of civilian violence in American history until September 11, 2001.

Following a three and a half year investigation, an eleven-member commission in 2001 made a series of recommendations to the Oklahoma legislature to offer a measure of restitution. The legislators declined to set aside funds for survivors, but they did appropriate $750,000 to formulate plans for a museum and memorial. They also created a Greenwood Redevelopment Authority and instituted a scholarship program.

Rosewood 1923

During the first week of January 1923, the small town of Rosewood, Florida, was destroyed and its black residents driven out or killed. Rosewood was a mostly black community—it had a few white inhabitants—located in the pinewoods of west central Florida not far from the Gulf of Mexico. On New Year's Day, Fannie Taylor, a married white woman from a nearby town, claimed she had been raped and beaten by a black man. Many white people quickly assumed Jessie Hunter was responsible. Other white people believed Mrs. Taylor wanted to divert attention from herself because she had a white lover who was not her husband.

White men sought Hunter and vengeance. Unable to locate him, they brutally beat Aaron Carrier, who may have helped Taylor's white lover escape. The mob shot and killed Samuel Carter after savagely mutilating him. Tensions dramatically escalated.

On January 4 a band of angry white men invaded Rosewood. Black people were prepared to defend themselves. Led by Sylvester Carrier and his mother Sarah, many townspeople had congregated in the Carrier home. The mob unleashed a hail of gunfire into the residence, killing Sarah Carrier. Two white men who attempted to gain entry into the home were shot and killed. Shooting continued until the mob's supply of ammunition was depleted on January 5.

The following day a mob of 250, including Ku Klux Klan members from Gainesville, invaded, burned, and destroyed Rosewood. The community's black residents fled to the nearby woods and swamps with little more than the clothes on their backs, never to return. Rosewood was no more.

The precise number of black people who died will never be known. It may have been well over one hundred. In 1994 the Florida legislature appropriated $2.1 million to survivors of Rosewood and to families who lost property in the assault. Although seven decades had elapsed, ten survivors were still alive and collected $150,000 each. But it proved impossible for many black people to verify they had been in Rosewood in 1923 or that they were kin to people who had owned property in the town. Much of the money was not disbursed.

THE GREAT MIGRATION

The great migration of African Americans from the rural South to the urban North began as a trickle of people after the Civil War and became a flood of human beings by the second decade of the twentieth century. Between 1910 and 1940, 1.75 million black people left the South. As a result, the black population outside the South doubled by 1940. Most of the initial wave of migrants were younger people born in the 1880s and 1890s, who had no recollection of slavery but anticipated a better future for themselves and their families in the North.

People moved for many reasons. Often they were both pushed from their rural circumstances and pulled toward urban areas. The push resulted from disasters in southern agriculture in the 1910s. The boll weevil destroyed cotton crops across the South from Mexico to the Carolinas, and floods devastated Mississippi and Alabama in 1915. The pull resulted from labor shortages created by World War I in northern industry and manufacturing. The war all but ended European immigration to the United States, eliminating a main source of cheap labor. At the same time, European governments and the United States placed huge orders for war material with northern factories. Thousands of jobs became available in steel mills, railroads, meatpacking plants, and the automobile industry. Northern businessmen sent labor agents to recruit southern workers.

Many southern white people reacted ambivalently to the loss of black residents. They welcomed the departure of people they held in such low regard, but they also worried about the loss of tenants and sharecroppers.

Black newspapers, such as the Pittsburgh *Courier* and especially the Chicago *Defender*, encouraged black Southerners to move north. Black railroad porters and dining car employees distributed thousands of copies of the *Defender* throughout the South. One unnamed black man wrote in the *Defender* that sensible men would leave the poverty, injustice, and violence of the South for the cold weather of the North. "To die from the bite of frost is far more glorious than that of the mob. I beg of you, my brothers, to leave that benighted land. You are free men."

A black resident of one of South Carolina's Sea Islands explained in 1917 that he left to earn more money. "I could work and dig all year on the Island and best I could do would be to make $100 and take a chance of making nothin'. Well, I figured I could make 'roun' thirty or thirty-five dollars every week and at that rate save possibly $100 every two months." Like many migrants, he moved more than once. He first went to Savannah, and then to Philadelphia, before finally settling in Brooklyn, New York.

Black people who departed the South escaped the most blatant forms of Jim Crow and the injustice in the judicial system. Black women fled the sexual exploitation of white and black men. Black people in the North could vote. The North offered better public schools. In the early twentieth century the South had almost no public high schools for black youngsters, and the longer school year in the urban North was not tied to the demands of planting and harvesting crops.

Some black people migrated to escape the dull, bleak, impoverished life and culture of the rural South. One young woman left South Carolina's St. Helena Island in 1919. "[I] got tired of the Island. Too lonesome. Go to bed at six o'clock. Everything dead. No dances, no moving picture show, no nothing. 'Coz every once in a while they would have a dance, but here you could go to 'em every Saturday night. That's why people move more than anything else."

The decision to migrate could take years of pondering and planning. To depart was to leave family, friends, and familiar surroundings behind for the uncertainty, confusion, and rapid pace of urban communities. Migrants often first moved to southern towns or cities and then headed for a larger city. Poet and writer Langston Hughes was born in Joplin, Missouri, in 1902 and moved to Lincoln, Illinois. "I had no sooner graduated from grammar school in Lincoln than we moved from Illinois to Cleveland. My stepfather sent for us. He was working in a steel mill during the war, and making lots of money. But it was hard work, and he never looked the same afterwards."

Some people made the decision to move impulsively. After she was fired from her nursing position at Hampton Institute in Virginia in 1905, Jane Edna Hunter decided to go to Florida, but changed her mind:

En route, I stopped at Richmond, Virginia, to visit with Mr. and Mrs. William Coleman, friends of Uncle Parris. They were at church when I arrived; so I sat on the doorstep to await their return. After these good friends had greeted me, Mrs. Coleman said, 'Our bags are packed to go to Cleveland, Jane. We are going to take you with us.' I was swept off my feet by the cheerful determination of the Colemans. My trunk, not yet removed from the station, was rechecked to Cleveland.

Most migrants maintained a genuine fondness for their southern homes and kin-folk. They returned regularly for holidays, weddings, and funerals. Kelly Miller, who had grown up in South Carolina, spent years as a scholar and teacher at Howard University in Washington, D.C., but he still had "an attachment for the old state that time and distance cannot destroy. After all, we love to be known as a South Carolinian." Thousands of black migrants routinely sent money home to the South.

Destinations

Although many black Southerners went to Florida, most migrants from the Carolinas and Virginia settled in Washington, Philadelphia, and New York (see Map 16–2). Black people who left Georgia, Alabama, and Mississippi tended to move to Pittsburgh, Cleveland, and Detroit. Migrants from Louisiana, Mississippi, and Arkansas often rode the Illinois Central Railroad to Chicago. Once they experienced a metropolis, many black people then resettled in smaller communities. Migrants to Philadelphia, for

MAP 16–2   The Great Migration and the Distribution of the African-American Population in 1920. Although several hundred thousand black Southerners migrated north in the second and third decades of the twentieth century, most African Americans remained in the southern states.

example, moved on to Harrisburg or Altoona, Pennsylvania, or to Wilmington, Delaware.

Few black Southerners moved west to California, Oregon, or Washington. There were only 22,000 thousand black residents of California in 1910. Substantial black migration west did not occur until the 1930s and 1940s. But in 1920 Mallie Robinson made the long trek west. Deserted by her husband Jerry, she set out with her five children (including one-year-old Jackie who would become a baseball legend) and eight other relatives. They boarded a train in Cairo, Georgia, traveled to Los Angeles, and settled in nearby Pasadena. Mallie's half brother, who had already moved west, assured her she would be closer to heaven in California.

However, most black migrants found their destination was neither near heaven nor the Promised Land. Black people congregated in all-black neighborhoods— Harlem in New York City, Chicago's South Side, Paradise Valley in Detroit, Cleveland's East Side, and the Hill District of Pittsburgh—that later would be called ghettoes. White property owners resisted selling or renting real estate to black people outside the confines of these neighborhoods. And many southern black migrants themselves, wary of white hostility, preferred to live among black people, often friends and family who had preceded them north.

Migration from the Caribbean

Many descendants of Africans who had been slaves in the sugarcane fields of the West Indies joined the migration of black Southerners to towns and cities in the North. Between 1900 and 1924, 102,000 West Indians came to the United States. Most came from British colonies including Jamaica, Barbados, and Trinidad and Tobago. But people also arrived from French-held Guadaloupe and Martinique; Dutch colonies of Aruba, Curacao, and Montserrat; the Danish Virgin Islands (which the United States acquired in 1917). Some of these migrants were middle-class professionals and skilled workers, but a sizable number were black men from Barbados, Jamaica, and elsewhere who had been employed as laborers on the construction of the Panama Canal from 1904 until 1914.

Although white Americans tended to lump all people of color together, regardless of their complexion or origin, the West Indians often did not mix easily or comfortably with African Americans. Some spoke Dutch and French. Those who came from British islands were usually members of the Anglican Church and not Baptists or Methodists. Almost all of the newcomers sent money home to family members who remained in the West Indies. Moreover, many of the Caribbean arrivals were temporary residents. As many as one-third of them would return to the West Indies. In 1924 Congress imposed rigid restrictions on immigration to the United States, and migration from the Caribbean dropped drastically.

NORTHERN COMMUNITIES

Even before the Civil War, most northern cities had small free black populations. By the late nineteenth century, southern migrants began to gravitate to these urban areas and make their presence felt. Black residents established churches, social organizations, businesses, and medical facilities. They gained representation in community and political affairs.

There was less overt segregation in the North. Most northern states, as well as California, had enacted laws in the late nineteenth century that prohibited racial discrimination in public transportation, hotels, restaurants, theaters, and barbershops. Most of these states also forbade segregated schools. However, passage of such laws and their enforcement were two different matters. Many white businesses and communities ignored the statutes and embraced Jim Crow, especially in areas along the Ohio River in southern Ohio, Indiana, and Illinois.

Chicago

As early as 1872, Chicago had a black policeman, and in 1876 John W. E. Thomas became the first black man elected to the Illinois Senate. Black physician Daniel Hale Williams established African-American-staffed Provident Hospital on Chicago's South Side in 1891. By 1900 black Chicagoans were the twelfth largest ethnic group in the city, behind such European immigrant groups as the Irish, Poles, and Germans.

Chicago's black population surged during the first three decades of the twentieth century as migrants poured into the city. Black institutions flourished. In 1912 an NAACP branch was established. By 1920 black Chicago had 80 Baptist and 36 Methodist churches. The Olivet Baptist Church grew from 3,500 members in 1916 to 9,000 by 1922. Because the downtown YMCA barred black men, black people raised $50,000 and Julius Rosenwald of Sears, Roebuck, and Company contributed $25,000 to build the Wabash YMCA for the black community in 1913. However, many black Chicagoans considered this a surrender to segregation and insisted that black men should be admitted to the white YMCA.

The Chicago *Defender* was the city's leading black newspaper. Its founder, Robert S. Abbott, the son of slaves, began publishing the *Defender* in 1905, and by 1920 it had a nationwide circulation of 230,000. Chicago's first black bank, Jesse Binga's State Bank, was established in 1908, and in 1919 Frank L. Gillespie organized the Liberty Insurance Company.

In 1915 black Chicago's political influence expanded when Oscar DePriest was elected second ward alderman. Two other black men were elected to the city council by 1918. DePriest was then elected to the U.S. House of Representatives as a Republican in 1928, becoming the first black congressman since North Carolina's George White left the House in 1901.

As the number of black people in Chicago swelled, racial tensions increased and exploded in the 1919 race riot. Competition for jobs was a critical issue. White employers, such as the meatpacking companies, regularly replaced white strikers with black workers. Black men usually did not hesitate to take such jobs because most labor unions would not admit them. But a few weeks before the riot in 1919, the Amalgamated Meatcutters Union tried to sponsor a unity parade of black and white stockyard workers. The police prohibited it because, some observers believed, the meatpacking companies feared that black and white workingmen might unite.

Housing was an even more divisive issue than employment. Chicago's black population was almost entirely confined to an eight-square-mile area on the South Side east of State Street. Prosperous black people who could afford more expensive housing outside the area could not purchase it because of their race. As the black population grew, housing became more congested, and crime and vice increased.

Langston Hughes described the similar housing situation his family experienced in Cleveland:

> Rents were very high for colored people in Cleveland, and the Negro district was extremely crowded, because of the great migration. It was difficult to find a place to live. We always lived, during my high school years, either in an attic or a basement, and paid quite a lot for such inconvenient quarters. White people on the east side of the city were moving out of their frame houses and renting them to Negroes at double and triple the rents they could receive from others. An eight room house with one bath would be cut up into apartments and five or six families crowded into it, each two-room kitchenette apartment renting for what the whole house had rented for before.

Harlem

Harlem was a white community in upper Manhattan that had declined by the latter 1800s. It then enjoyed an incredible building boom that occurred in anticipation of the construction of the subway that would link upper Manhattan to downtown New York City by the early twentieth century. But real estate speculators overbuilt and were left with empty houses and apartments. Facing foreclosure, many white property owners sold or rented to black people in Harlem. In 1904 Philip A. Payton formed the Afro American Realty Company that sold homes and rented apartments to black clients before it failed in 1908.

Harlem's white residents opposed the influx of black people. Some of them formed the Harlem Property Owners' Improvement Corporation in 1910 to block black settlement. Its founder, John G. Taylor, warned in 1913, "We are approaching a crisis, it is a question of whether the white man will rule Harlem or the Negro." However, many white property owners—eager for a profit—preferred to sell to black people than to maintain white unity.

As thousands of black people moved to Harlem, many left the "Tenderloin" and "San Juan Hill" areas of Manhattan's West Side where New York's black residents had lived in the nineteenth century. The construction of Pennsylvania Station forced many to vacate the "Tenderloin." Black churches took the lead in the "On to Harlem" movement as they occupied churches formerly used by white denominations. Some of the black churches were among the largest property owners in Harlem.

St. Philip's Protestant Episcopal Church, the wealthiest black church in the United States and noted for its solemn services and elite parishioners, moved from West 25th Street in the "Tenderloin" in 1910 to Harlem. In 1911 St. Philip's purchased ten apartment houses on West 135th Street between Lenox and Seventh Avenues for $640,000. The Reverend Adam Clayton Powell Sr. and the Abyssinian Baptist Church, St. Mark's Episcopal Church, and the African Methodist Episcopal Zion Church ("Mother Zion") also moved to Harlem and acquired extensive real estate holdings there. The black churches helped make Harlem a black community.

As the black population increased in Harlem, large houses and apartments were often subdivided among working families that could not rent or buy in other areas of New York. They paid higher prices for real estate than white people did. The average Harlem family paid $9.50 a room per month; white working families paid $6.50 for similar accommodations elsewhere in New York.

By 1920, 75,000 black people lived in Harlem. Harlem became the "Negro Capital of the World." Black businesses and institutions, including the Odd Fellows, Masons, Elks, Pythians, the NAACP, the Urban League, and the YMCA and YWCA moved to Harlem. Black newspapers—the *New York News* and *Amsterdam News*—opened in Harlem to compete with the older *New York Age*. One resident observed, "If my race can make Harlem, good lord, what can't it do?"

FAMILIES

Migration placed black families under enormous strains. Relatives frequently moved north separately. Fathers or mothers would leave a spouse and children behind as they sought employment and housing. Children might be left with grandparents for extended periods. In other instances, extended family members—cousins, in-laws, brothers and sisters—crowded into limited living space.

Men generally found more opportunities for work in northern industries than women did. There was a huge demand for unskilled labor during and after World War I. In 1915 Henry Ford astounded industrial America when he began to pay employees of the Ford Motor Company in Detroit the unprecedented sum of $5 per day, and that included black men and occasionally black women. Rarely, however, would a black man be promoted beyond menial labor. Except for some opportunities in manufacturing during the war, black women were confined to domestic and janitorial work. Mary Ellen Washington recalled the experience in her family. "In the 1920s my mother and five aunts migrated to Cleveland, Ohio, from Indianapolis and, in spite of their many talents, they found every door except the kitchen door closed to them."

Black women employed as domestics lived with white families, worked long hours, and saw more of their white employer's children than they did their own. Some vulnerable younger women were lured into prostitution in the intimidating urban environment. Black women's organizations worked to prevent newly arrived migrants from falling prey to sexual exploitation. They did not always succeed. Some women made a calculated decision to turn sex to their economic advantage. Sara Brooks caustically commented, "Some women woulda had a man to come and live in the house and had an outside boyfriend too, in order to get the house paid for and the bills. They meet a man and if he promises 'em four or five dollars to go to bed, they's grab it. That's called sellin' your own body, and I wasn't raised like that."

Despite the stresses and pressures, most black families survived intact. Most northern black families, although hardly well to do, were two-parent households. Women headed comparatively few families. Fathers were present in seven of ten black families in New York City in 1925. But the great migration transformed southern peasants into an urban proletariat.

TIMELINE

AFRICAN-AMERICAN EVENTS	NATIONAL EVENTS
1895	
1895 Frederick Douglass dies; Booker T. Washington delivers Cotton States Exposition address **1896** *Plessy v. Ferguson* is decided **1898** Riot erupts in Wilmington, N.C.	**1896** William McKinley is elected president **1898** Spanish-American War begins **1899** Philippine insurrection begins
1900	
1900 New Orleans riot **1903** W. E. B. Du Bois publishes *The Souls of Black Folk*	**1900** William McKinley reelected **1901** McKinley is assassinated; Theodore Roosevelt becomes president **1903** Boston defeats Pittsburgh in the first World Series **1904** Theodore Roosevelt is elected president
1905	
1905 Niagara Movement is founded at Niagara Falls, Ontario; The *Defender* is founded in Chicago **1906** Brownsville affair occurs; Atlanta riot occurs **1908** Springfield riot occurs **1909** NAACP is founded	**1905** Thomas Dixon publishes *The Clansman*. The film *Birth of a Nation* is based on the novel. **1906** Upton Sinclair publishes *The Jungle* The San Francisco earthquake kills nearly 700 people **1908** William Howard Taft is elected president **1909** Robert E. Peary and Matthew Henson, an African American, reach the North Pole with four Eskimos
1910	
1910 National Urban League is founded in New York City	**1910** The Mann Act prohibits the transporation of a woman across state lines for immoral purposes

continued

AFRICAN-AMERICAN EVENTS	NATIONAL EVENTS
1912 W.E.B. Du Bois endorses Woodrow Wilson for President	**1912** Woodrow Wilson is elected president **1914** World War I breaks out in Europe
1915	
1915 *Guinn v. United States* overturns the Oklahoma grandfather clause Booker T. Washington dies **1917** East St. Louis riot occurs; Houston riot occurs **1919** Chicago riot occurs; Elaine, Arkansas, riot occurs	**1915** A German submarine sinks the British liner, *The Lusitania* **1916** United States sends punitive expedition in Mexico; Woodrow Wilson is reelected **1917** United States enters World War I **1918** World War I ends **1919** Treaty of Versailles is negotiated
1920	
1920 Harlem becomes "The Negro Capital of the World" **1921** Tulsa riot occurs **1923** Rosewood destroyed	**1920** Nineteenth Amendment (Women's Suffrage) is ratified; Warren Harding is elected president
1925	

CONCLUSION

In 1900 Booker T. Washington was the nation's most influential black leader. He soothed white people and reassured black Americans as he counseled conciliation, patience, and agricultural and mechanical training as the most effective means to bridge the racial divide. His 1895 speech at the Cotton States Exposition in Atlanta elicited support and praise from both white and black listeners.

The Wizard of Tuskegee, as Washington was known, had little appreciation for criticism and did not hesitate to attack his opponents, including William Monroe Trotter and W. E. B. Du Bois. He worked to subvert the Niagara Movement and the NAACP. But support for Washington and his conservative strategy gradually diminished as the

NAACP openly confronted racial discrimination. Washington died in 1915. By 1920 the NAACP assumed the lead in the struggle for civil rights as it fought in the courts and legislatures.

The Talented Tenth of black Americans, distinguished by their educational and economic resources, promoted "self-help" through a variety of organizations—from women's groups to fraternities and sororities—to enhance their own status and to help less affluent black people.

As black men served in World War I and as thousands of black Southerners migrated north, many white Americans became alarmed that African Americans were not as content with their subordinate and isolated status as Booker T. Washington had suggested they were. Some white Americans responded with violence in race riots as they attempted to prevent black Americans from assuming a more equitable role in American society. By 1920, despite white opposition, black Americans had demonstrated they would not accept economic subservience and the denial of their rights.

REVIEW QUESTIONS

1. Compare and evaluate the strategies promoted by Booker T. Washington with those of W. E. B. Du Bois and the NAACP.

2. On which issues did Washington and Du Bois agree and disagree?

3. Assess Washington's contributions to the advancement of black people.

4. To what extent did middle-class and prosperous black people contribute to progress for their race? Were their efforts effective?

5. Why did most African Americans support U.S. participation in World War I? Was that support justified?

6. What factors contributed to race riots and violence in the World War I era?

7. Why did many black people leave the South in the 1920s? Why didn't this migration begin earlier or later?

8. What factors affected the decision to migrate or stay?

RECOMMENDED READING

W. E. B. Du Bois. *The Souls of Black Folk.* New York: Library of America, 1903. An essential collection of superb essays.

John Hope Franklin and August Meier. *Black Leaders of the Twentieth Century.* Urbana: University of Illinois Press, 1982. A series of "mini biographies" of fifteen people including Washington, Du Bois, T. Thomas Fortune, and Ida Wells Barnett.

Willard Gatewood. *Aristocrats of Color: The Black Elite, 1880–1920.* Bloomington: Indiana University Press, 1990. An examination of the lives and activities of well-to-do black people.

Lawrence Otis Graham. *One Kind of People: Inside America's Black Upper Class.* New York: HarperCollins, 1999. An informative history and analysis of black America's wealthiest families and organizations.

Louis R. Harlan. *Booker T. Washington: The Making of a Black Leader, 1856–1901.* New York: Oxford University Press, 1972, and *Booker T. Washington: The Wizard of Tuskegee, 1901–1915.*

New York: Oxford University Press, 1983. The definitive two-volume biography of Washington.

David Levering Lewis. *W. E. B. Du Bois: Biography of a Race, 1868–1919.* New York: Henry Holt and Co., 1993; *W. E. B. Du Bois: The Fight for Equality and the American Century, 1919–1963.* New York: Henry Holt and Co., 2001. A magisterial and exhaustive account of the 95-year life and times of Du Bois.

Deborah Gray White. *Too Heavy a Load: Black Women in Defense of Themselves.* New York: Norton, 1999. An exploration of the contours of black women's history in the twentieth century.

AFRICAN AMERICANS AND THE 1920s

STRIKES AND THE RED SCARE

In 1919 and 1920, Americans were bewildered and angered by labor unrest and afraid the communists (or "Reds") in the new Soviet Union would try to incite a revolution in America. There were 3,600 strikes in 1919 as workers who had deferred demands during the war for pay raises and improved working conditions walked off their jobs. More than 300,000 steel workers in Pittsburgh and Gary, Indiana, struck, including 7,000 unskilled black steel workers in Pittsburgh. In a demonstration of solidarity with striking shipyard workers, most of Seattle's working people shut the city down in a general strike. Americans were even more alarmed when police officers in Boston went on strike.

Political leaders exacerbated these feelings by warning that communists and foreign agents were plotting to overthrow the government. Woodrow Wilson's attorney general A. Mitchell Palmer ordered 249 aliens deported and some six thousand arrested and imprisoned in gross violation of their rights, but it was an action that many Americans warmly approved. Palmer went too far, however, when he predicted the Red revolution would begin in the United States on May 1, 1920. There was no revolution, and confidence in Palmer waned.

Prompted in part by the Red Scare, xenophobia (fear of foreigners) swept the nation in the 1920s. Two Sicilian immigrants, Nicola Sacco and Bartolomeo Vanzetti, who were anarchists, were charged in 1920 with a murder that had occurred during a payroll robbery near Boston. They were found guilty, and after a prolonged controversy they were executed in 1927. But their supporters believed the guilty verdict was due more to their foreign origins and radical beliefs than to conclusive proof they had committed the murder.

VARIETIES OF RACISM

The entrenched racism of American society found continued expression in more than one form in the 1920s. There was the sophisticated racism associated with supposedly scholarly studies that reflected the ideology of social Darwinism. There was also the raw bigotry that manifested itself in various aspects of popular culture and in the ideology of the increasingly popular Ku Klux Klan.

Scientific Racism

Many white Americans believed the United States was under siege as European immigrants and black migrants flooded American cities. Pseudoscholars gravely warned about the peril these "inferior" peoples posed. In 1916 Madison Grant published *The Passing of the Great Race*. Grant warned that America was committing "race suicide" because northern Europeans and their descendants—the Great Race—were being diluted by inferior people from eastern and southern Europe. Lothrop Stoddard's *The Rising Tide of Color* in 1920 argued that people of color would never be equal to white Americans.

These racist claims were cloaked in the trappings of legitimate scholarship, and they strengthened the cause of white supremacy in the 1920s and helped "protect" America from the "threat" of immigration. In 1921 and in 1924, Congress imposed quotas that severely restricted immigration from southern and eastern Europe, Latin America, and the Carribean, and prohibited it entirely from Asia.

The Birth of a Nation

In 1915 D. W. Griffith released *The Birth of a Nation*, a cinematic masterpiece and historical travesty based on Thomas Dixon's 1905 novel *The Clansman*. Both the book and the film purported to depict Reconstruction in South Carolina authentically. In this account, immoral and ignorant Negroes joined by shady mulattoes and greedy white Republicans ruthlessly seize control of state government until the heroic and honorable Ku Klux Klan saves the state and rescues its white womanhood. The film grossed $18 million (254 million in 2000 dollars) and helped to distort public perceptions about Reconstruction and black Americans.

The NAACP was enraged by *The Birth of a Nation* and fought to halt its presentation. W. E. B. Du Bois complained in *The Crisis* that in the film "the Negro [was] represented either as an ignorant fool, a vicious rapist, a venal or unscrupulous politician or a faithful but doddering idiot." The motion picture unleashed racist violence. After seeing the film in Lafayette, Indiana, an infuriated white man killed a young black man. In Houston, white theatergoers shouted, "Lynch him!" during a scene in which a white actor in blackface pursued the film's star, Lillian Gish. In front of a St. Louis theater, white real estate agents passed out circulars calling for residential segregation.

Thanks largely to NAACP opposition, the film was banned in Pasadena, California; Wilmington, Delaware; and Boston. With an election looming in Chicago, Republican mayor "Big Bill" Thompson appointed AME bishop Archibald Carey to the board of censors, which temporarily banned the film there. When the sound version of *The Birth of a Nation* was released in 1930, the NAACP renewed its opposition. Ironically, the NAACP campaign may have provided publicity that attracted more viewers to the film. By the same token, however, the campaign also helped increase NAACP membership.

The Ku Klux Klan

The Ku Klux Klan (KKK), which disappeared after Reconstruction, was resurrected a few months after *The Birth of a Nation* was released. On Thanksgiving night in 1915, William J. Simmons and thirty-four other men gathered at Stone Mountain near Atlanta, and in the flickering shadows of a fiery cross, they brought the Klan back to life.

The Ku Klux Klan that rose to prominence and power in the 1920s stood for white supremacy—and more. Klansmen styled themselves as "100 percent Americans" who opposed perceived threats from immigrants as well as black Americans. The Klan claimed to represent white, Anglo-Saxon, Protestant America. With European immigrants flocking to America, William Simmons announced the United States was no melting pot. "It is a garbage can! . . . When the hordes of aliens walk to the ballot box and their votes outnumber yours, then that alien horde has got you by the throat."

The Klan found enormous support among apprehensive white middle-class Americans in the North and West. Many of these people believed the liberal, immoral, and loose lifestyles they associated with urban life, immigrants, and African Americans threatened their religious beliefs and conservative cultural values. The Klan attacked the theory of evolution, fought for the prohibition of alcoholic beverages, and claimed to uphold the "sanctity" of white womanhood. The KKK opposed Jews, Roman Catholics, and black people. Klansmen often used violent intimidation to convey their patriotic, religious, and racial convictions. They burned synagogues and Catholic churches. They beat, branded, and lynched their opponents.

By 1925 the Klan had an estimated 5 million members, and 40,000 of them marched in Washington, D.C., that year. The Klan attracted small businessmen, shopkeepers, clerks, Protestant clergymen, farmers, and professional people. It was open only to native-born white men, but it also had a Women's Order, a Junior Order for boys, and a Tri K Klub for girls. The Klan was active in Oregon, Colorado, Illinois, and Maine, and it became a potent political force in Indiana, Oklahoma, and Texas. In those three states in particular, candidates for public office who refused to support or join the Klan stood little chance of election.

The Klan was also a highly effective moneymaking machine. Its leaders collected millions of dollars in initiation fees, membership dues, and income from selling Klan paraphernalia. But the Klan declined rapidly in the late 1920s when its leaders fought among themselves. Its claim to uphold the purity of white womanhood was damaged when one of its leaders, D. C. Stephenson, was arrested in Indiana and charged with raping a young woman who subsequently committed suicide. Stephenson was sentenced to life in prison, and the Klan never fully recovered.

Protest, Pride, and Pan-Africanism: Black Organizations in the 1920s

African Americans responded to racism and to larger cultural and economic developments in the 1920s in several ways. The NAACP forged ahead with its efforts to secure constitutional rights and guarantees by advocacy in the political and judicial systems. Many working-class black people who had migrated to northern cities were attracted to the racial pride promoted by Marcus Garvey and the Universal Negro Improvement Association. There were also ongoing attempts to foster racial cooperation among peoples of African descent and to exert diplomatic influence through the work of several Pan-African congresses that were held during the first three decades of the twentieth century.

The NAACP

During its second decade, the NAACP expanded its influence and increased its membership. In 1916 James Weldon Johnson (who wrote "Lift Every Voice and Sing") joined the NAACP as field secretary. He played a pivotal role in the organization's development and in its growth from 9,000 members in 1916 to 90,000 in 1920. Johnson traveled tirelessly, recruiting members and establishing branches. He journeyed to rural southern communities, to northern cities, and to the West Coast.

Johnson impressed both black and white people. He got along well with W. E. B. Du Bois and was an excellent diplomat. He methodically reported the gruesome details of lynchings, and when some NAACP directors complained in 1921 that these graphic descriptions offended people, Johnson stood his ground. "What we need to do is to root out the thing which makes possible these horrible details. I am of the opinion that this can be done only through the fullest publicity."

In 1918 Johnson hired Walter White to assist him. White was from Atlanta and, like Johnson, a graduate of Atlanta University. White's very fair complexion permitted him to move easily among white people to investigate racial discrimination and violence. Although his domineering personality offended some NAACP officials and supporters, White devoted his life to the organization and to racial justice.

Johnson and the NAACP fought hard in Congress to secure passage of the Dyer anti-lynching bill in 1921 and 1922 (see Chapter 16). The legislation ultimately failed, but the NAACP succeeded in publicizing the persistence of barbaric behavior by mobs in a nation supposedly devoted to fairness and the rule of law. It was the first campaign by a civil rights organization to lobby Congress, and—like the attempt to block *The Birth of a Nation*—it won favorable publicity and goodwill for the NAACP.

Johnson blamed the Dyer bill's failure on Republican senators. He charged that the Republican Party took black support for granted: "The Republican Party will hold the Negro and do as little for him as possible, and the Democratic Party will have none of him at all." He warned, however, that black voters in the North would abandon the Republicans. Johnson pointed out that black voters in Harlem had elected a black Democrat to the state legislature.

The NAACP continued to rely on the judicial system to protect black Americans and enforce their civil rights. By the 1920s the Democratic Party in virtually every southern state barred black people from membership, which excluded them from voting in Democratic primary elections. The result was what was known as "white primaries." Because the Republican Party had almost ceased to exist in most of the South, victory in the Democratic primary elections led invariably to victory in the general election. In 1924 the NAACP, in cooperation with its branch in El Paso, filed suit over the exclusion of black voters from the Democratic primary in Texas. In 1927 the Supreme Court ruled in *Nixon v. Herndon* that the Democratic primary was unconstitutional—the first victory in what would become a twenty-year legal struggle to permit black men and women to vote in primary elections across the South.

In Detroit in 1925, black physician Ossian Sweet and his family moved into an all-white neighborhood. For several nights a mob threatened the Sweet family and other people who joined in their defense. One evening, shots were fired from the Sweet home that killed a white man. Twelve occupants of the house were charged with murder.

The NAACP retained Clarence Darrow and Arthur Garfield Hayes, two of the nation's finest criminal attorneys, to defend the Sweets. The Sweets pleaded self-defense, and after two trials, they were acquitted.

"Up You Mighty Race": Marcus Garvey and the UNIA

With several million loyal and enthusiastic followers, Marcus Garvey's Universal Negro Improvement Association (UNIA) became the largest mass movement of black people in American history. The UNIA enabled people—often dismissed by the white majority for having no genuine history or culture—to celebrate one another and their heritage and to anticipate a glorious future. Garvey was an energetic, charismatic, and flamboyant leader who wove racial pride, Christian faith, and economic cooperation into a black nationalist organization that had spread throughout the United States by the early 1920s.

Garvey was born in 1887 in the British colony of Jamaica, the eleventh child in a rural family. He quit school at age fourteen and became a printer in Kingston, the island's capital; he was promoted to foreman before he was fired in 1907 for prolabor activities during a strike. He traveled to Costa Rica, Panama, Ecuador, and Nicaragua and became increasingly disturbed over the conditions black workers endured in fields, factories, and mines. He returned to Jamaica and with a growing appreciation of the power of the written and spoken word, he set out to educate himself. He spent two years in London where he sharpened his oratorical and debating skills discussing the plight of black people with Africans and people from the Caribbean.

He returned to Jamaica and founded the UNIA in 1914. With the slogan "One God! One Aim! One Destiny!" he stressed the need for black people to organize for their own advancement. Garvey had read Booker T. Washington's *Up from Slavery* and was much impressed with Washington's emphasis on self-help and on progress through education and the acquisition of skills. Garvey also—like Washington—could criticize black people for their lack of progress: "The bulk of our people are in darkness and are really unfit for good society." They had no right to aspire to equality because they had "done nothing to establish the right to equality."

Garvey came to the United States in 1916 just as thousands of African Americans were migrating to cities. A dynamic speaker whose message resonated among the disaffected urban working class, Garvey quickly built the UNIA into a major movement. He urged his listeners to take pride in themselves as they restored their race to its previous greatness. "We must canonize our own saints, create our own martyrs, and elevate to positions of fame and honor black men and women who have made their distinct contributions to our racial history." He reminded people that Africa had a remarkable past. "Africa was peopled with a race of cultured black men, who were masters in art, science and literature; men who were cultured and refined; men, who, it was said, were like the gods. . . . Black men, you were once great; you shall be great again." He insisted that his followers change their thinking. "We have outgrown slavery, but our minds are still enslaved to the thinking of the Master Race. Now take these kinks out of your mind, instead of out of your hair."

With the formation of the New York division of the UNIA in Harlem in 1917, Garvey exhorted, "Up you mighty race!" as he commanded black people to take control of their destiny. Still, he blamed them for their predicament. "That the Negro race became a race of slaves was not the fault of God Almighty . . . it was the fault of the race." Their salvation would result from their own exertion and not from concessions by white people.

Garvey's message and the UNIA spread to black communities large and small. He regularly couched his rhetoric in religious terms, and he came to be known as the Black Moses, a messiah. Garvey dwelled on Christ's betrayal as he identified himself with Jesus. "If Garvey dies, Garvey lives." "Christ died to make men free, I shall die to give courage and inspiration to my race."

Garvey and the UNIA established businesses that employed nearly one thousand black people. The weekly newspaper, *Negro World*, promoted Garvey's ideology. In New York City, the Negro Factories Corporation operated three grocery stores, two restaurants, a printing plant, a steam laundry, and a factory that turned out uniforms, hats, and shirts for UNIA members. The association also owned buildings, vehicles, and facilities in other cities. Garvey proudly declared to white Americans that the UNIA "employs thousands of black girls and black boys. Girls who could only be washer women in your homes, we made clerks, stenographers. . . . You will see from the start we tried to dignify our race."

Although Garvey and the UNIA are most frequently associated with urban communities in the North, the UNIA also spread rapidly through the rural South in the 1920s. Black farmers and sharecroppers established UNIA chapters from Virginia to Louisiana, and the Garvey movement and the *Negro World* could be found in such remote communities as Kinston, North Carolina; Ty Ty, Georgia; and Cotton Plant, Arkansas.

Garvey may be best remembered for his proposal to return black people to Africa by way of the Black Star Line, a steamship company he founded in 1919. Garvey sold stock in the company for five dollars a share, and he hoped to establish a fleet with black officers and crew members. In 1920 the company purchased the *Yarmouth*, a dilapidated vessel that became the first ship in the fleet. Garvey raised enough capital to buy two additional ships, the *Kanawha* and the *Booker T. Washington*, but he lacked the financial resources to maintain them or to transport anyone to Africa.

Moreover, Garvey knew it was unrealistic to expect several million black residents of the Western Hemisphere to join the back-to-Africa enterprise, but he genuinely believed the UNIA could liberate Africa from European colonial rule. "Wake up Ethiopia! Wake up Africa! Let us work towards the one glorious end of a free, redeemed and mighty nation." The UNIA adopted a red, green, and black flag for the proposed African republic that represented the blood, land, and race of the people of the continent.

The UNIA attempted to establish a settlement on the Cavalla River in southern Liberia. Garvey also petitioned the League of Nations to permit the UNIA to take possession of the former German colony of Tangaruyka (today's Tanzania) in East Africa. But the major colonial powers in Africa—Britain and France—and the United States thwarted Garvey's plans, and the UNIA never gained a foothold on the continent.

The U.S. government and several black American leaders also undermined the UNIA and Garvey. J. Edgar Hoover and the Bureau of Investigation (the predecessor of

Jamaican-born Marcus Garvey arrived in the
United States in 1916 and quickly rose to
prominence as the head of the Universal
Negro Improvement Association. Garvey
appears here in a 1924 parade in Harlem
attired in a uniform similar to those worn by
British colonial governors in Jamaica,
Trinidad, and elsewhere.
Corbis/Bettmann

the FBI) considered Garvey a serious threat to the racial status quo. Hoover employed
black agents to infiltrate the UNIA and compile information that could be used to de-
port Garvey, who had never become an American citizen.

Garvey had few friends or admirers among African-American leaders because he
and they differed fundamentally on strategy and goals. Garvey deplored efforts to gain
legal and political rights within the American system. By appealing to the black masses,
he rejected Du Bois's notion that the Talented Tenth would lead the race to liberation.
He mocked the NAACP as the National Association for the Advancement of Certain
People. Not long after he arrived in the United States, Garvey visited the NAACP office
in New York, and he commented sourly that it was essentially a white organization.
"There was no representation of the race there that any one could recognize. . . .
[Y]ou had to be as near white as possible, otherwise there was no place for you as ste-
nographer, clerk or attendant in the office of the National Association for the
Advancement of 'Colored' People."

Unlike African-American leaders, Garvey believed black and white people had
separate destinies, and he regarded interracial cooperation as absurd. Thus Garvey
considered a meeting he had with Ku Klux Klan leaders in Atlanta in 1922 consistent
with his racial views. He praised the white supremacist organization. "They are better
friends to my race, for telling us what they are, and what they mean, thereby giving us
a chance to stir for ourselves." He added that "every whiteman is a Klansman . . . and
there is no use lying about it."

In 1922 Garvey and three other UNIA leaders were arrested and indicted on
twelve counts of fraudulent use of the U.S. mail to sell stock in the Black Star Line.

Eight African-American leaders wrote to the U.S. attorney general to condemn Garvey and insist on his prosecution. Although Garvey was guilty of no more than mismanagement and incompetence, he was eventually found guilty and sent to the federal penitentiary in Atlanta in 1925. President Calvin Coolidge commuted his sentence in 1927, and he was deported.

The UNIA barely survived the loss of its inspirational leader, and it declined steadily in the late 1920s and the 1930s. The various UNIA businesses closed, and its property—including the *Yarmouth*—was sold. Garvey was never permitted to return to the United States, and he died in London in 1940. However, his legacy persisted.

Pan-Africanism

As diametrically opposed as Garvey and Du Bois were on most matters, they shared an abiding interest in Africa. Garvey, Du Bois, and other black leaders believed people of African descent from around the world should come together to share their heritage, discuss their ties to the continent, and explore ways to moderate—if not eliminate—colonial rule in Africa.

By 1914 Britain, France, Germany, Portugal, Belgium, Spain, and Italy had established colonies across almost all of Africa. Only Liberia and Ethiopia (then called Abyssinia) remained independent. The Europeans assumed the "white man's burden" in their imperialist "scramble" for Africa. Christian missionaries sought to convert Africans, and European companies exploited Africa's human and natural resources. As they gained control over the continent, the European powers confirmed their conviction that they represented a superior race and culture.

The first Pan-African Congress had convened in London in 1900 and was organized principally by Henry Sylvester Williams, a lawyer from Trinidad who had resided in Canada and then London. Du Bois attended and chaired the Committee on the Address to the Nations of the World. He called for the creation of "a great central Negro state of the world." But Du Bois did not insist on the immediate withdrawal of the European powers from Africa. Instead he offered a modest recommendation that would provide "as soon as practicable the rights of responsible self-government to the black colonies of Africa and the West Indies."

The second Pan-African Congress met in Paris for three days in February 1919, near Versailles, where the peace conference ending World War I was assembled. There were fifty-eight delegates from sixteen nations. Du Bois was among the sixteen African Americans in attendance. (None of them had been to Africa.) Marcus Garvey did not attend. The delegates took seriously the Fourteen Points that U.S. president Woodrow Wilson had proposed to fashion the postwar world. They were especially interested in the fifth point, which called for the interests of colonial peoples to be given "equal weight" in the adjustment of colonial claims after the war. The congress recommended that the League of Nations assume authority over the former German colonies in East Africa. The League later established mandates over those colonies but delegated authority to administer those mandates to Britain, France, and Belgium. Two more Pan-African Congresses in the 1920s met in Brussels and London but also failed to influence the policies of the colonial powers.

LABOR

The arrival of thousands of black migrants in American cities during and after World War I changed the composition of the industrial workforce and intensified pressure on labor unions to admit black members. By 1916 twelve thousand of the nearly fifty thousand workers in the Chicago stockyards were black people. In Detroit, black laborers made up nearly 14 percent of the workforce in the automobile industry. The Ford Motor Company employed 50 black people in 1916 and 2,500 by 1920.

Yet even with the industrial revolution and the great migration, more than two-thirds of black workers in 1920 were employed in agriculture and domestic service (see Figure 17–1). Less than 20 percent were engaged in manufacturing. Those who were part of industrial America disproportionately worked in the dreary, dirty, and sometimes dangerous unskilled jobs that paid the least. Still, work in the factories, mills, and mines paid more than agricultural labor.

Most of the major labor unions would not admit black workers. Since its founding in 1886, the American Federation of Labor (AFL) officially prohibited racial discrimination, but most of its local unions were all white and all male. The AFL was made up of skilled laborers, and less than 20 percent of black workers were skilled (see Figure 17–2). But even those with skills were usually not admitted to the local craft unions that made up the AFL. More than fifty trade unions within the AFL had no black members. Unions that did admit black workers included those representing cigar makers, coal miners, garment workers, and longshoremen.

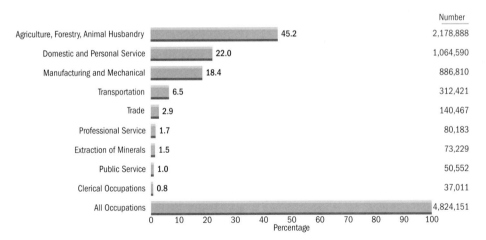

Figure 17–1 **Black Workers by Major Industrial Group, 1920.**
By 1920 thousands of African Americans had moved to northern cities and were employed in a variety of mostly unskilled and low-paying industrial jobs that nonetheless paid more than farm labor. Still, agriculture remained the largest single source of employment among black people, and agriculture and domestic service together employed more than two-thirds of African-American men and women. About 5 percent were employed in "white-collar" jobs.
Source: Sterling D. Spero and Abram L. Harris, *The Black Worker: The Negro and the Labor Movement* (1928), 81.

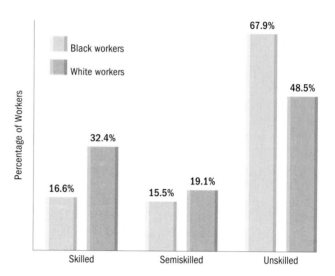

Figure 17–2 **Black and White Workers by Skill Level, 1920.** Only one-third of black workers, compared to slightly more than one-half of white workers, found employment in skilled or semiskilled jobs in 1920. Source: Sterling D. Spero and Abram L. Harris, *The Black Worker: The Negro and the Labor Movement* (1928), 85.

By the World War I years, the NAACP and the Urban League regularly appealed to employers and unions to accept black laborers. The Urban League attempted to convince business owners that black employees would be efficient and reliable. But many employers preferred to divide black and white workers by hiring black men and women as strikebreakers, thereby enraging striking white workers. In 1918 Urban League officials met with Samuel Gompers, the longtime president of the AFL, and he agreed to bring more black people into the federation, but there were few tangible results. The Urban League did succeed in persuading the U.S. Department of Labor to establish a Division of Negro Economics to advise the secretary of labor on issues involving black workers.

The Brotherhood of Sleeping Car Porters

By the 1920s the Pullman Company, which owned and operated passenger railroad coaches, was the single largest employer of black people in the United States. More than twelve thousand black men worked as porters on Pullman railroad cars. After founding the Pullman Palace Car Company in 1867, George Pullman decided to employ only black men as porters—on the assumption that prosperous white people were accustomed to being waited on by black servants. Furthermore, black employees could be and were paid less than white workers.

Pullman porters toiled for upward of four hundred hours each month to maintain the coaches and serve the passengers. Porters had to prepare the cars before the train's departure and service them after the train arrived at its destination, although they were paid only for the duration of the trip. They assisted passengers, shined shoes (they had to purchase the polish themselves), and arranged sleeping compartments. Considered mere servants by most passengers, porters had little time for rest. To add to the indignity, white travelers invariably referred to these black men as "George," no matter what their actual name was. Porters were paid an average of $67.50 per month—about $810 per year. But with tips, they earned more, occasionally as much as $300 a month, but usually far less. They were required to buy their own uniforms during their first ten years of employment.

Although strenuous and time consuming, Pullman employment was the most satisfactory work many black men could hope to achieve. Barred from business and industry, black men with college degrees worked as sleeping car porters. As poorly paid as they were compared with many white workers, they still earned more than most black schoolteachers. Most of these Pullman employees regarded themselves as solid, respectable members of the middle class.

It seemed unlikely that men as subservient and unobtrusive as the Pullman porters would form a labor union to challenge one of America's most powerful corporations. But they did. The key figure in this effort was A. Philip Randolph. In 1925 a gathering of Pullman porters in Harlem invited Randolph to become their "general organizer" as they formed the Brotherhood of Sleeping Car Porters (BSCP). Randolph accepted the invitation.

A. Philip Randolph

Randolph was a socialist with superb oratorical skills who had earned a reputation as a radical on the streets of Harlem. He was born in 1889 in Crescent City, Florida. He attended high school at Cookman Institute (later Bethune-Cookman College) and migrated to New York City in 1911 where he attended City College and joined the Socialist Party. With Chandler Owen, he founded *The Messenger*, a monthly socialist journal that drew the attention of federal agents. Randolph vigorously opposed American involvement in World War I. In 1919 Department of Justice officials arrested Randolph and Owen for their radical activities and held them briefly.

Randolph was an improbable militant. He was handsome, dignified, impeccably dressed, and aloof. He maintained an unwavering commitment to economic and racial change. He became one of the nation's foremost protest leaders and remained so for more than five decades.

Randolph faced the daunting task of recruiting support for the brotherhood, winning recognition from the Pullman Company, and gaining the union's acceptance by the AFL. There was considerable opposition, much of it from within the black community. Many porters were too frightened to join the brotherhood. Black clergymen counseled against union activities. Black newspapers, including the Chicago *Defender*, editorially opposed the BSCP.

But Randolph persevered with the assistance of Milton Webster, who became vice president of the brotherhood after Randolph assumed the presidency. With the slogan "Service not servitude," the two men recruited members, organized the brotherhood, and attempted to negotiate with the Pullman Company. Pullman executives ignored Randolph's overtures. They fired porters who joined the union, infiltrated union meetings with company agents, and organized the Employees' Representation Plan, an alternative company union that they claimed actually represented the black employees.

Although the NAACP and the Urban League strongly supported the BSCP, progress was painfully slow. In 1928 Randolph threatened to call a strike against the Pullman

Company, but he called it off after AFL president William Green promised modest assistance to the as-yet unrecognized union. Green's offer simply saved face for Randolph. It is unlikely that a strike would have succeeded or that most porters would have followed Randolph's leadership and left the trains. The Great Depression of the 1930s brought layoffs and mass resignations from the brotherhood. The AFL barely responded to repeated charges of discrimination by Randolph, the NAACP, and the Urban League. The BSCP nearly collapsed. Not until the passage of legislation during President Franklin D. Roosevelt's New Deal in the mid-1930s did the BSCP make substantial gains.

THE HARLEM RENAISSANCE

For most of American history, most black and white Americans have shown little interest in serious literature or intellectual developments. The 1920s were no exception. People were far more fascinated by sports, automobiles, the radio, and popular music than they were by poetry, plays, museums, or novels. Still, the 1920s witnessed a proliferation of creative works by a remarkable group of gifted writers and artists. Among white writers, T. S. Eliot, Ezra Pound, Edith Wharton, Ernest Hemingway, Sinclair Lewis, Eugene O'Neill, Willa Cather, and F. Scott Fitzgerald produced literary works that explored a range of themes but were mostly critical of American life and society. Eliot, Pound, Wharton, Fitzgerald, and Hemingway found American culture so unappealing that they exiled themselves in Europe.

Black intellectuals congregated in Manhattan and gave rise to the creative movement known as the Harlem Renaissance. Alain Locke promoted *The New Negro*. Poets, novelists, and painters probed racial themes and grappled with what it meant to be black in America. There was no precise beginning to this renaissance. As early as 1920, W. E. B. Du Bois wrote in *The Crisis* that the nation was on the verge of a "renaissance of American Negro literature." In 1925 the New York *Herald Tribune* declared that America was "on the edge, if not already in the midst of, what might not improperly be called a Negro renaissance." No matter when it began, the Harlem Renaissance produced a stunning collection of artistic works, especially in creative writing, that continued into the 1930s.

Before Harlem

There had certainly been serious cultural developments among African Americans before the 1920s. From 1897 to 1928, the American Negro Academy functioned as a forum for the Talented Tenth as men such as Alain Locke, Kelly Miller and Du Bois reflected on race and color.

At the turn of the century, novelist Charles W. Chestnutt depicted a young black woman's attempt to pass for white in *The House behind the Cedars*, and he wrote about racist violence in the post-Reconstruction South in *The Marrow of Tradition*. Ohio poet Paul Laurence Dunbar wrote evocatively of black life, frequently relying on black dialect, before he died at age thirty-four in 1906. Henry Ossawa Tanner attended the Pennsylvania Academy of Fine Arts and had an illustrious career as a painter. Shortly after he produced "The Banjo Lesson" in 1893, Tanner left for Paris and spent most of the rest of his life in Europe. He died there in 1937.

Carter G. Woodson, the son of Virginia slaves, earned a Ph.D. at Harvard in history and founded the Association for the Study of Negro Life and History in 1915. He stressed the need for the scholarly examination of Negro history and established the *Journal of Negro History* and the *Negro History Bulletin*. He also founded Associated Publishers to publish books on black history. Woodson wrote several major works, including *The Negro in Our History*. In 1926 he established Negro History Week during February. Not surprisingly, Woodson became known as the "father of Negro history."

During the bloody Red Summer of 1919 when racial violence erupted in Chicago and elsewhere, Claude McKay, a Jamaican who settled—like Marcus Garvey—in New York City, wrote a powerful poem, "If We Must Die," in response to the brutal attacks by white people in Chicago on black residents:

> If we must die, let it not be like hogs
> Hunted and penned in an inglorious spot,
> While round us bark the mad and hungry dogs,
> Making their mock at our accursèd lot.
> If we must die, O let us nobly die,
> So that our precious blood may not be shed
> In vain; then even the monsters we defy
> Shall be constrained to honor us though dead!
> O kinsmen! We must meet the common foe!
> Though far outnumbered let us show us brave,
> And for their thousand blows deal one deathblow!
> What though before us lies the open grave?
> Like men we'll face the murderous, cowardly pack,
> Pressed to the wall, dying, but fighting back!

McKay left the United States for the Soviet Union in 1922 and spent the next twelve years in Europe. In 1928, while in France, he wrote *Home to Harlem*, a novel that depicted life among pimps, prostitutes, loan sharks, and petty criminals. McKay was not on cordial terms with the African-American intellectuals who formed the core of the Harlem Renaissance, and he did not consider himself part of the Talented Tenth. He later commented, "I was an older man and not regarded as a member of the renaissance, but more as a forerunner."

Writers and Artists

Few white Americans and still fewer black Americans had access to a college education in the early twentieth century. Only slightly more than two thousand African Americans were pursuing college degrees by 1920. Yet the writers and artists who came to be associated with the Harlem Renaissance were the products of some of the nation's finest schools, and with the exception of Zora Neale Hurston, they did not come from isolated, rural southern communities. Hurston was born in Notasulga, Alabama, and raised in the all-black town of Eatonville, Florida, near Orlando. She attended Morgan State University and Howard University, and graduated from Barnard College. Alain Locke was a native of Philadelphia and Phi Beta Kappa graduate of Harvard. He was the first African American to win a Rhodes scholarship to Oxford

University, and he also earned a Ph.D. in philosophy from Harvard. Aaron Douglas was born in Kansas and was an art major at the University of Nebraska.

Langston Hughes was born in Joplin, Missouri, graduated from high school in Cleveland, and attended Columbia University before he graduated from Pennsylvania's Lincoln University. Jessie Fauset came from a prominent Philadelphia family of color. She was a graduate of Cornell University and a member of Phi Beta Kappa; she earned an M.A. from the University of Pennsylvania in romance languages. Jean Toomer was born in Washington, D.C., and he was raised largely by his grandparents in a fashionable white neighborhood. Toomer went to the University of Wisconsin and then the Massachusetts College of Agriculture. Wallace Thurman was born in Salt Lake City and attended both the University of Utah and the University of Southern California. Countee Cullen was a native of Lexington, Kentucky, and a Phi Beta Kappa graduate of New York University. Nella Larsen was the only major writer connected to the Harlem Renaissance who did not have a college degree. A native of Chicago, she graduated from the nurse training program at New York City's Lincoln Hospital.

The Renaissance gradually emerged in the early 1920s and then expanded dramatically later in the decade as more creative figures were drawn to Harlem. In 1923 Jean Toomer published *Cane*, a collection of stories and poetry about southern black life. It sold a mere five hundred copies, but it had a major impact on Jessie Fauset and Walter White. Fauset was the literary editor of *The Crisis*, and in 1924 she finished *There Is Confusion*, the first novel published during the Renaissance. Her novels explored the manners and color consciousness among well-to-do Negroes. Walter White, who was James Weldon Johnson's assistant at the NAACP, published *The Fire in the Flint* in 1924, a novel that dealt with a black physician who confronted white brutality in Georgia.

In the meantime, *The Crisis*, as well as *Opportunity*, a new publication of the Urban League, published the poetry and short stories of black authors, including Langston Hughes, Countee Cullen, and Zora Neale Hurston. White publishers were also attracted to black literary efforts. In 1925 *Survey Graphic* published a special edition devoted to black life and culture called "Harlem: Mecca of the New Negro." Howard University professor Alain Locke then edited *The New Negro*, which drew much of its material from *Survey Graphic* as well as *Opportunity* and included silhouette drawings with Egyptian motifs by Aaron Douglas. In his opening essay, Locke explained Harlem's literary significance: "Harlem has the same role to play for the new Negro as Dublin has had for the New Ireland or Prague for the New Czechoslovakia."

Sharp disagreements erupted during the Harlem Renaissance over the definition and purpose of black literature. Some, such as Alain Locke, W. E. B. Du Bois, Jessie Fauset, and Benjamin Brawley, wanted black writers to promote positive images of black people in their works. They hoped inspirational literature could help resolve racial conflict in America, and they believed black writers should be included in the larger (and mostly white) American literary tradition. Claude McKay, Langston Hughes, and Zora Neale Hurston disagreed. They portrayed the streets and shadows of Harlem and the lives of poor black people in their poetry and stories. In *The Ways of White Folks*, Hughes ridiculed the notion that writers could promote racial reconciliation. One of his characters derisively declares, "Art would break down color lines, art would save the race and prevent lynchings! Bunk!"

Black critic George Schuyler's "The Negro Art Hokum" in *The Nation* ridiculed black writers who contended that black people even had their own expressive culture that was separate from that of white people. "As for the literature, painting, and sculpture of Afroamericans—such as there is—it is identical in kind with the literature, painting, and sculpture of white Americans."

Langston Hughes meanwhile defended the authenticity of black art and literature but insisted the approval or disapproval of white people and black people was of little consequence:

> We younger Negro artists who create now intend to express our individual dark-skinned selves without fear or shame. If white people are pleased, we are glad. If they are not, it doesn't matter. We know we are beautiful. And ugly too. The tom-tom cries and the tom-tom laughs. If colored people are pleased we are glad. If they are not, their displeasure doesn't matter either. We build our temples for tomorrow, strong as we know how, and we stand on top of the mountain, free within ourselves.

Hughes pursued racial themes in *Fine Clothes to the Jew* (1927), which contained "Red Silk Stockings," a poem that depicted young black women who were tempted by liaisons with white men, a subject that offended some readers.

Even more upsetting to those who wanted to safeguard the reputation of black people was Wallace Thurman, who arrived in New York in 1925. Thurman worked briefly at *The Messenger*, the socialist publication that had been absorbed by A. Philip Randolph's Brotherhood of Sleeping Car Porters. He was a voracious reader with a brilliant mind and an eccentric personality who attracted many loyal admirers.

In 1926 Thurman published *Fire*, a journal that lasted only one issue but managed to incite enormous controversy and leave Thurman deeply in debt. *Fire* included Thurman's short story "Cordelia the Crude," about a prostitute, and a one-act play by Zora Neale Hurston, *Color Struck*. Hurston effectively replicated the speech of rural black Southerners while depicting the jealousy a darker woman feels when a light-skinned rival tries to take her man. Black critic Benjamin Brawley complained that with *Fire* "vulgarity had been mistaken for art."

Thurman antagonized still more people when *The Blacker the Berry* . . . was published in 1929. In it he described the tribulations and sorrows of Emma Lou, a young woman who did not mind being black, "but she did mind being too black." The book made it plain that many black people had absorbed a color prejudice that they did not hesitate to inflict on darker members of their own race.

Unlike Thurman, Nella Larsen wrote about black people who were indistinguishable from white people. Her novel, *Quicksand*, depicted the life of Helga Crane who, like Larsen herself, had a Danish mother and a black father. In *Passing*, Larsen dealt with a young black woman who passed for white and, indeed, married a white racist.

White People and the Harlem Renaissance

Like many of the writers associated with the Harlem Renaissance, Zora Neale Hurston had a pen that sliced like a scalpel. She called the white people who took an interest in Harlem "Negrotarians," and she labeled her black literary colleagues the "Niggerati."

But no matter how they were described, black and white people developed pleasant but often uneasy relationships during the Renaissance.

No white man was more attracted to the cultural developments in Harlem than photographer and writer Carl Van Vechten. In 1926 he caused a furor with his novel *Nigger Heaven*. Many people were offended by the title, which referred to the balcony where black patrons had to sit in segregated theaters and auditoriums. The novel dealt with the coarser aspects of life in Harlem, which irritated Du Bois, Fauset, and Countee Cullen. But Van Vechten's purpose was in part a call for a more honest depiction of the black experience, and James Weldon Johnson, Walter White, and Langston Hughes approved of the novel.

Most black writers and artists welcomed the encouragement, support, and financial backing they received from white authors, critics, and publishers. White writers, including Eugene O'Neill, Sherwood Anderson, Sinclair Lewis, and Van Wyck Brooks, were fascinated by black people and interested in the works of black authors. Major publishers, such as Alfred A. Knopf, brought out the works of Harlem writers. Black and white literary figures sometimes gathered for cocktails, small talk, and music at Carl Van Vechten's spacious apartment on West 55th Street.

The attention and support of white people were sometimes accompanied by condescension and disdain. Too many "Negrotarians" considered Harlem and its inhabitants exotic, curious, and uncivilized. They found life in Harlem—its clubs, music, and entertainers, as well as its poetry, prose, and painting—energetic, lively, and sensual compared to white life and culture. Black culture was also—many white people believed—unsophisticated and primitive, which is what made it so fascinating. Black writers like Langston Hughes, Claude McKay, and Countee Cullen wanted to depict black life realistically—from its gangsters to its gamblers. But they and other black artists resented the notion that black culture was inherently crude and unrefined.

White patrons like Amy Spingarn, whose husband Joel was president of the NAACP board of directors, and Charlotte Osgood "Godmother" Mason supported black writers and artists. Spingarn helped finance Langston Hughes's education at Lincoln University. "Godmother" Mason was a wealthy widow who offered substantial amounts of money to black artists. She worked closely with Alain Locke, who helped identify Langston Hughes, Zora Neale Hurston, and Aaron Douglas, among others, who became her "godchildren."

Mason wanted no publicity for herself, but the acceptance of her money had its costs. Mason gave Hughes $150 a month and Hurston $200 a month, as well as an automobile. She also gave Hughes expensive clothing and writing supplies. In return, Mason demanded that the black writers keep her fully informed about their activities, and she did not hesitate to tell them when they were not productive enough. She also tried to influence what they wrote. She preferred that black writers confine themselves to exotic themes. As helpful as Mason's financial assistance and personal encouragement were, she created a system of dependency, and Hughes and Hurston finally broke free from the arrangement. Hughes later fondly recalled, "I can only say that those months when I lived by and through her were the most fascinating and fantastic I have ever known."

Harlem's cultural icons sometimes congregated away from the curiosity and paternalism of white admirers. The plush twin town houses of A'Lelia Walker at 108–110 West 136th Street also attracted Harlem's literary figures as well as entertainers. Walker was the daughter of black cosmetics millionairess Madam C. J. Walker. Although she read little herself, A'Lelia Walker enjoyed hosting musicians, writers, and artists at "The Dark Tower," as she called it. Her home was named for Countee Cullen's column, "The Dark Tower," that appeared regularly in *Opportunity*. But Harlem artists also gathered in the much less luxurious surroundings of "Niggerati Manor" on 267 West 136th Street. This was a rooming house where Thurman, Hurston, and Hughes resided in the late 1920s.

The profusion of literary works associated with the Harlem Renaissance did not so much end as fade away. Black writers remained active into the 1930s. Zora Neale Hurston wrote her two most important works then—*Mules and Men* in 1935 and *Their Eyes Were Watching God* in 1937. Claude McKay and Langston Hughes continued to write and have their work published. But the Great Depression that began in 1929 devastated book and magazine sales. Subscriptions to *The Crisis* and *Opportunity* declined, and both journals published fewer works by creative writers. Many black intellectuals left Harlem. James Weldon Johnson and Aaron Douglas went to Fisk University in Nashville.

HARLEM AND THE JAZZ AGE

As powerful and important as these black literary voices were, they were less popular than the entertainers, musicians, singers, and dancers who were also part of the Harlem Renaissance. Without Harlem, the 1920s would not have been the Jazz Age. From wailing trumpets, beating drums, dancing feet, plaintive and mournful songs, Harlem's clubs, cabarets, theaters, and ballrooms echoed with the vibrant and soulful sounds of African Americans. By comparison, white American music seemed sedate and bland.

Black and white people flocked to Harlem to enjoy themselves—and to break the law. In 1919–1920, the Eighteenth Amendment and the Volstead Act prohibited the manufacture, distribution, and sale of alcoholic beverages. But liquor flowed freely in Harlem's fancy establishments and smoky dives. Musicians and entertainers, such as Harlem's working-class residents, had migrated there from elsewhere. The blues and their sorrowful tales of troubled and broken relationships arrived from the Mississippi Delta and rural South. Jazz had its origins in New Orleans, but it drew on ragtime and spirituals as it moved up the Mississippi River to Kansas City and Chicago on its way to Harlem.

The Cotton Club was Harlem's most exclusive and fashionable nightspot. Opened in 1923 by white gangster Owney Madden to peddle illegal beer, it catered to well-to-do white people who regarded a trip to Harlem as a foreign excursion. The Cotton Club's entertainers and waiters were black, but the customers were white. Black patrons were not admitted. The club featured well-choreographed and fast-paced two-hour revues that included a chorus line of attractive young women—all brown skinned, all under twenty-one years old, and all over 5'6" tall. No dark women appeared. Music was provided by assorted ensembles. Cab Calloway might sing "She's Tall, She's Tan and She's Terrific" or "Cotton Colored Gal of Mine."

In 1928 Edward K. "Duke" Ellington and his orchestra began a twelve-year association with the Cotton Club. Although Ellington had not yet begun to compose his own music in earnest, his band already had an elegant, sophisticated, and recognizable

African-American sound. Another club, Connie's Inn, also served a mostly white clientele. Thomas "Fats" Waller played a rambunctious piano at Connie's. Waller's father was the deacon at the Abyssinian Baptist Church in Harlem, and his mother was the organist. The songs and music their son wrote, including "Honeysuckle Rose" and "Ain't Misbehavin," were hardly sacred, but they were popular. Connie's also put on stunning musical revues, perhaps the best known of which was *Hot Chocolates.* Dancers who performed at Connie's included the legendary Bill "Bojangles" Robinson and Earl "Snakehips" Tucker. A young cornetist from New Orleans, Louis Armstrong, played briefly at Connie's. Armstrong amazed listeners with his virtuoso trumpet and his gravelly singing voice.

Harlem's black residents avoided the Cotton Club or Connie's Inn. They were more likely to step into one of Harlem's less pretentious and less expensive establishments, such as the Sugar Cane. The beer and liquor were cheap. The food was plentiful. The music was good, and there were no elaborate production numbers. Even less impressive clubs and bars remained open after the legal closing hour of 3 A.M. "Arrangements" were made with the police who looked the other way as the music and alcohol continued through the night. Musicians from "legal" clubs drifted into the after-hours joints and played until dawn.

Another popular—and sometimes necessary—form of entertainment among Harlemites was the rent party. Housing costs in Harlem were extravagant, and white people and real estate agents refused to rent or sell to black people in most other areas of New York City. To make the steep monthly rent payments, apartment dwellers would push the furniture aside, begin cooking chicken, chitterlings, rice, okra, and sweet potatoes. They would distribute a few flyers and hire a musician or two. The party was usually on a Saturday or a Thursday night. (Most domestic servants had Thursdays off.) Partygoers paid ten cents to fifty cents admission. Food and liquor were sold. With a decent crowd, the month's rent was paid.

Song, Dance, and Stage

Black women became popular as singers and dancers in Harlem and then often appeared in Broadway shows and revues. Florence Mills entranced audiences with her diminutive singing voice in several Broadway productions including *Plantation Review, Dixie to Broadway,* and *Blackbirds* before she died of appendicitis in 1927. Adelaide Hall also appeared in Blackbirds and later opened her own nightclubs in London and Paris. Ethel Waters worked her way up from smoky gin joints in Harlem basements, where she sang risqué and comic songs, to Broadway shows, and then to films. Many years later she toured with Billy Graham's religious crusades and revivals.

White men wrote many of the popular Broadway productions that starred black entertainers. In 1921, however, Eubie Blake and Noble Sissle put on *Shuffle Along,* which became a major hit. Its most memorable tune was "I'm Just Wild about Harry." Sissle and Blake wrote several more shows, including *Chocolate Dandies* in 1924. It was created especially for a thin, lanky, dark, and funny young lady named Josephine Baker. But in 1925 Baker left New York and moved to Paris where she starred in the *Revue Nègre,* which created a sensation in the French capital. She remained in France for the rest of her life.

White playwright Eugene O'Neill wrote serious drama involving black people. Charles Gilpin and then Paul Robeson appeared in O'Neill's *Emperor Jones*. He appeared in numerous productions, including O'Neill's *All God's Chillun Got Wings*, Shakespeare's *Othello*, Gershwin's *Porgy and Bess*, and Kern and Hammerstein's *Showboat*. He often sang spirituals in his magnificent, rich voice and later recorded many of them.

SPORTS

Sports flourished in America in the 1920s. Americans worshiped their athletic heroes. Professional athletics, especially baseball and boxing, expanded dramatically. Professional football and basketball emerged later. Black men had been banned from major league baseball in 1887 (see Chapter 15). Nevertheless, in 1901 New York Giants' manager John J. McGraw signed a black man, Charlie Grant, to play second base. McGraw claimed that Grant was "Chief Tokohoma," a full-blooded Cherokee Indian. Chicago White Sox owner Charles Comiskey knew otherwise, and Grant did not play in the major leagues.

Playing among themselves, black baseball players barely made a living as they moved from team to team in an ever-fluctuating and disorganized system that saw teams come and go with monotonous regularity. No leagues functioned effectively for the black teams and players. Black players crisscrossed the country on trains and in automobiles as they played each other in small towns and large cities for meager amounts of money shared from gate receipts. It was an insecure and nomadic life.

Rube Foster

Andrew "Rube" Foster was the father of black baseball in twentieth-century America. He was a crafty pitcher from Texas who combined athletic skills with mental dexterity. In 1911 he founded the Chicago American Giants, and he pitched with them regularly until 1915 and then mainly managed after that. As fine an athlete as Foster was, he was an even more talented organizer and administrator.

In 1920 he was the catalyst in the formation of the eight-team Negro National League and became its president and secretary. It was the first stable black league, with franchises in Kansas City, St. Louis, Indianapolis, Detroit, Dayton, and two teams in Chicago. The eighth team was the Cuban Stars.

Foster and the new league took advantage of the migration of black people to northern cities. The black ball clubs usually played late in the afternoon or in the early evening so fans could attend after a day's work. Sunday doubleheaders in Chicago or Kansas City might draw eight thousand to ten thousand people. Players were paid regularly, and athletes on Foster's Giants earned at least $175 a month. The biggest obstacle black teams faced was the lack of their own fields or stadiums. They were forced to rent, often at exorbitant rates, from major league clubs, which frequently kept the profits from concessions.

Black baseball thrived—more or less—in the 1920s, thanks mostly to Foster's force of personality and dedication. He was a tireless worker and strict disciplinarian, but the pressure may have been too much. In 1926 he suffered a mental breakdown and died in 1930. Foster's loss—combined with the impact of the Depression—severely disrupted the league system.

College Sports

Football, baseball, basketball, and track and field were popular at the collegiate level. Amateur sports were not as rigidly segregated as professional baseball. Black men continued to play for white northern universities, although few teams had more than one black player.

Black players on white teams encountered discrimination when the teams traveled. Spectators taunted and threatened them. The Big Ten had an unwritten agreement that basketball coaches would not accept black players. All-white college teams sometimes refused to play against schools with black players.

Sports in black colleges and universities thrived in the 1920s. Baseball and football were the most popular spectator events. With the migration of black people to the North, black colleges began to play football in northern cities. Howard and Lincoln played to a scoreless tie before eighteen thousand people in Philadelphia on Thanksgiving in 1925. Hampton and Lincoln played at New York's Polo Grounds on the edge of Harlem in 1929 in a game won by Lincoln 13–7 before ten thousand spectators.

T I M E L I N E

AFRICAN-AMERICAN EVENTS	NATIONAL EVENTS
1919	
1919	**1919**
Pan-African Congress meets in Paris	Aliens rounded up and deported by A. Mitchell Palmer
Black Star Line is founded by Marcus Garvey and the UNIA	Eighteenth Amendment (Prohibition) is ratified
	Volstead Act is passed
1920	
1920	**1920**
Rube Foster organizes the Negro National League in baseball	U.S. Senate rejects the Treaty of Versailles
	Nineteenth Amendment is ratified; women gain the right to vote
	Warren Harding is elected president
1921	
1921	**1921**
Tulsa, Oklahoma, race riot occurs	Congress establishes quotas to limit immigration

continued

AFRICAN-AMERICAN EVENTS	NATIONAL EVENTS

1922

1922

Dyer Anti-Lynching bill passes in U.S. House, fails in Senate

Marcus Garvey meets with KKK leaders in Atlanta

KKK virtually takes over the state of Oklahoma

1923

1923

President Harding dies in office

Investigation of government corruption in the Teapot Dome scandal begins

1924

1924

Calvin Coolidge is elected

Congress grants citizenship to Native Americans

1925

1925

Ossian Sweet case is tried in Detroit Tennessee

A. Philip Randolph founds the Brotherhood of Sleeping Car Porters

1925

John T. Scopes "Monkey" trial is heard in Dayton, Tennessee

KKK is at peak of prominence

1926

1926

Carter Woodson establishes Negro History Week

1927

1927

U.S. Supreme Court rules against the white primary in *Nixon v. Herndon*

Marcus Garvey is deported from the United States

1927

Charles Lindbergh flies nonstop from New York to Paris

Babe Ruth hits sixty home runs

1928

1928

Herbert Hoover is elected president

1929

1929

Stock market crashes

CONCLUSION

For African Americans who lived through it, the 1920s must have seemed little more than a depressing continuation of earlier decades. Little appeared to have changed. Racial violence and lynching persisted. *The Birth of a Nation* mocked black people and inflamed racial animosity. "Experts" offered "proof" that people of color were inferior and threatened America's ethnic purity. The Ku Klux Klan became a formidable organization again. Millions of white men joined the Klan, and millions of other Americans supported it.

Nevertheless, some genuinely positive developments in the 1920s gave hope for a more promising future. The NAACP became an organization to be reckoned with as it fought for antilynching legislation in Congress and for civil and political rights in the courts. Its membership exceeded 100,000 during the 1920s. Although many black and white Americans ridiculed Marcus Garvey for his flamboyant style and excessive rhetoric, he offered racial pride and self-respect as he enrolled hundreds of thousands of black people in the UNIA.

Black workers made very little progress as they sought concessions from big business and representation within the ranks of organized labor. A. Philip Randolph founded the Brotherhood of Sleeping Car Porters and began a struggle with the Pullman Company and the American Federation of Labor that would begin to pay off in the 1930s.

The Harlem Renaissance was a cultural awakening in literature and the arts that was unprecedented in African-American history. A torrent of words poured forth from novelists, essayists, and poets. Although they disagreed—sometimes vehemently—on the purposes of black art, the writers and artists who were a part of the Renaissance had an enduring impact. The Renaissance allowed thoughtful and creative men and women to grapple with what it meant to be black in a society in which the white majority had defined the black minority as inferior, incapable, and culturally backward. Hereafter African Americans were less likely to let other people characterize them in demeaning ways.

Black musicians, dancers, singers, entertainers, and athletes made names for themselves and contributed to popular culture in a mostly urban environment. As the nation moved into the 1930s, it remained to be seen whether the modest but real progress of the 1920s would be sustained.

REVIEW QUESTIONS

1. To what extent, if any, had the intensity of white supremacy changed by the 1920s from what it had been two to three decades earlier?

2. What examples of progress could leaders like W. E. B. Du Bois, James Weldon Johnson, A. Philip Randolph, and Marcus Garvey point to in the 1920s?

3. Why did so many African-American leaders reject Marcus Garvey?

4. How did the black nationalism of the Universal Negro Improvement Association differ from the white nationalism of the Ku Klux Klan?

5. What economic opportunities existed for African Americans who had migrated to northern cities?

6. How do you explain the emergence of the literary and artistic movement known as the Harlem Renaissance?

7. How distinctive were black writers, artists, and musicians? Were their creative works essentially a part of American culture or separate from it?

8. Were there any genuine reasons for optimism among African Americans by the late 1920s?

RECOMMENDED READING

William H. Harris. *Keeping the Faith: A. Philip Randolph, Milton P. Webster and the Brotherhood of Sleeping Car Porters, 1925–1937.* Urbana: University of Illinois Press, 1977. This is an excellent account of the struggle of Randolph and the BSCP for recognition.

David Levering Lewis. *When Harlem Was in Vogue.* New York: Alfred A. Knopf, 1981. Lewis captures the life and vitality of Harlem in the 1920s.

David Levering Lewis, ed. *The Portable Harlem Renaissance Reader.* New York: Penguin Books, 1994. Essays, poems, and excerpts from the works of virtually every writer associated with the Renaissance are contained in this volume.

Nancy MacLean. *Behind the Mask of Chivalry: The Making of the Second Ku Klux Klan.* New York: Oxford University Press, 1994. This is the most recent study of the revived KKK.

Arnold Rampersad. *The Life of Langston Hughes, Vol. 1, 1902–1941: I, Too, Sing America.* New York: Oxford University Press, 1986. Here is a rich study of a complex and extraordinary man and writer.

Judith Stein. *The World of Marcus Garvey: Race and Class in Modern Society.* Baton Rouge: Louisiana State University Press, 1991. This is an effective examination of Garvey and the Universal Negro Improvement Association.

BLACK PROTEST, THE GREAT DEPRESSION, AND THE NEW DEAL

THE CATACLYSM, 1929–1933

The Great Depression was a cataclysm. National income fell from $81 billion in 1929 to $40 billion in 1932. Americans lost faith in banks, and the resulting panic deepened the despair. Overnight millions of Americans lost their life savings in bank closings and foreclosures. Individual Americans responded by buying fewer consumer goods and, in turn, businesses cut back production, investment, and payrolls. The result was a downward spiral of economic activity made worse by increasing numbers of unemployed. According to the American Federation of Labor (AFL), the number of unemployed people increased from 3,216,000 in January 1930 to 13,689,000 in March 1933. The standard of living of nearly everyone from farmers to small businessmen and entrepreneurs to wage laborers dropped to a fraction of what it had been before 1929.

Most people blamed the stock market crash and Republican president Herbert Hoover for the hard times, but the explanation is more complicated. Although still a hotly debated issue, the Great Depression was probably caused by a combination of factors, including rampant speculation, corporate capitalism's drive for markets and profits unchecked by federal regulation, the failure of those in the government or private sector to understand the workings of the economy, a weak international trading system, and, most important, the great inequality of wealth and income that limited the purchasing power of millions of Americans.

Harder Times for Black America

The collapse of the American economy hit African Americans particularly hard. Most black people remained in the rural South mired in an increasingly exploitive agricultural system. Indeed, the Depression exacerbated the key problems besetting cash-crop production in the 1920s. Consumer demand for cotton and sugar fell with the economy, but as farmers grew more of these crops to make ends meet, the supply of these staples increased. The result was a catastrophe, with prices for cotton—still the mainstay of the southern economy—plunging from eighteen cents a pound in 1929 to six cents in 1933. Families of black sharecroppers and tenant farmers, nearly powerless in the rural South, found themselves reduced to starvation or thrown off the land.

The hard times also struck those 1.5 million African Americans who had escaped the South for northern urban communities (see Table 18–1). Even during the height

Table 18–1
Demographic Shifts: The Second Great Migration, 1930–1950

Year	Region	Black Population	Total Population	% Black
1930	Northeast	1,146,985	34,427,091	3.33
	Midwest	1,262,234	38,594,100	3.27
	Southeast	7,079,626	25,680,803	27.57
	South Central	2,281,951	12,176,830	18.74
	Mountain	30,225	3,701,789	0.82
	Pacific	90,122	8,622,047	1.05
1950	Northeast	2,018,182	39,477,986	5.11
	Midwest	2,227,876	44,460,762	5.01
	Southeast	7,793,379	32,659,516	23.86
	South Central	2,432,028	14,517,572	16.73
	Mountain	66,429	5,074,998	1.31
	Pacific	507,043	15,114,964	3.35

Source: U.S. Bureau of the Census Release, 1991 and Statistical Abstract, 1990. Also see Schomburg Center, The New York Public Library: African American Desk Reference (New York: John Wiley & Sons, 1999), 100–1.

of the prosperous 1920s, black Americans suffered layoffs and witnessed a steady deterioration in their living standards. After 1929 the same forces that impoverished those in the countryside swept those in urban areas further toward the economic margins as waves of refugees from the farms crowded into the cities. By 1934, when the federal government noted that 17 percent of white citizens could not support themselves, the figure for black Americans had increased to 38 percent overall. In Chicago the jobless rate for African-American men was 40 percent, in Pittsburgh 48 percent, in Harlem 50 percent, in Philadelphia 56 percent, and in Detroit 60 percent. The figures were even more dire for black workers in southern cities. In Atlanta, Georgia, 65 percent of black workers needed public assistance, and in Norfolk, Virginia, a stunning 80 percent had to apply for welfare.

African Americans lost jobs in those parts of the economy where they had gained a tenuous foothold. Before 1929 jobs in low-status or poorly paid occupations such as garbage collection, foundries, or domestic service had been regarded as "Negro work" and hence were generally immune from white competition. As desperation set in, white Southerners not only competed for these jobs, but they also used the old tactics of terror and intimidation to compel employers to fire black people. Unions, north and south, continued to exclude African Americans from membership and pressured manufacturers to hire white people.

Black women workers, overwhelmingly concentrated in domestic service and laundry work, were affected even more than black men. There were fewer jobs because many families could no longer afford domestic help. With many impoverished women coming into the cities, those white people with the money to hire help found they could pay almost nothing and still employ these desperate women. In 1935 two black women, Marvel Cooke and Ella Baker, published an exposé of the exploitation of these women laborers in *The Crisis*. They entitled the article "The Bronx Slave

Market" because the buying and selling of labor reminded them of the old slave marts in the antebellum South. Cooke and Baker described how the street corner market worked: "The Simpson avenue block exudes the stench of the slave market at its worst. Not only is human labor bartered and sold for a slave wage, but human love also is a marketable commodity." The black women gathered on particular street corners and waited as well-to-do white women selected them for a day's labor. They received "wages as low as 15 to 25 cents an hour, some working only two or three hours a day." Some black people were hired but never paid.

African Americans were no strangers to adversity, and many used the survival strategies developed through centuries of hardship to eke out an existence during the first years of the Great Depression. Survival demanded that black women pool their resources and adhere to a collective spirit that found such fertile ground in segregated northern neighborhoods. In Chicago, for example, women and their families lived in crowded tenements in which they shared bathrooms and other facilities including hot plates, stoves, and sinks. They bartered and exchanged goods and services because money was so scarce. One woman might dress the hair of a neighbor in return for permission to borrow her dress or use her pots and pans. Another woman might trade bread and sugar or some other household staple for milk, beans, or soap. Grandmothers watched over children as their mothers went to look with rising futility for a domestic job. They helped each other as best they could.

Rural black women, like their urban sisters, had to rely on their individual and collective ingenuity to survive. As one observer of black women household heads in rural Georgia noted, "In their effort to maintain existence, these people are catching and selling fish, reselling vegetables, sewing in exchange for old clothes, letting out sleeping space, and doing odd jobs. They understand how to help each other. Stoves are used in common, wash boilers go their rounds, and garden crops are exchanged and shared." Nonetheless, the depth and duration of this downturn pressed these mutual aid strategies to the breaking point. By 1933 the clock seemed to have been turned back to 1865 when many African Americans could claim to own little more than their bodies.

Black Businesses in the Depression: Collapse and Survival

Members of the black business and professional class also experienced economic losses. African Americans who had built successful businesses and professional practices in medicine and law, for example, faced the same Depression-borne problems as other businesses, but they suffered even more because the communities on which they depended were poorer. A description of two kinds of business, banking and insurance, illustrates how black enterprises stood or fell during the economic crisis.

The Binga Bank, Chicago's first black-owned-and-operated financial institution, had been founded in 1908 by its president Jesse Binga (1865–1950). Binga had managed the bank so effectively that by 1930 its deposits had grown to more than $1.5 million. The Binga Bank was, during its early years, an important symbol of successful black capitalism. But the bank's assets were too heavily invested in mortgage loans to black churches and fraternal societies, many of which could not meet their payments after their members lost their jobs. Binga refused to seize the properties of these community institutions, but his restraint, coupled with financial improprieties, led to the bank's

This photograph by Margaret Bourke-White captures the contrast between the American dream of prosperity—for white families—and the harsh realities of life for black Americans during the Depression.

Getty Images/Time Life Pictures. Margaret Bourke-White/LIFE magazine © TimePix

failure. On July 31, 1930, Illinois state bank auditors padlocked the institution and filed a federal misuse-of-funds charge against the once proud financier. Sentenced to prison in 1932, Binga was pardoned by President Franklin Delano Roosevelt a year later. However, he never rebuilt his bank or his fortune.

Some black businesses did survive the economic cataclysm. Atlanta Life Insurance Company, for example—founded by a former Georgia slave, Alonzo Franklin Herndon, in 1905—not only survived the Depression but recorded substantial profit. Between 1931 and 1936, the company's assets increased by more than $1 million. This was in part because insurance companies such as Atlanta Life provided an essential service for African Americans, particularly in an era before government provided social security, and could thus depend on a continued flow of premiums. And unlike Binga Bank, the officers of the Atlanta Life Insurance Company drastically reduced the percentage of their investment capital that secured mortgage loans in the black community.

The Failure of Relief

Before Franklin Roosevelt's New Deal, private charities or, as a last resort, state and local governments were responsible for providing relief from economic hardships. Even in good times these institutions provided too little for all those in need. Moreover,

African Americans had a much harder time getting aid than white people and were given less when they did get it. The Depression made it impossible for the nation's charitable organizations to meet the needs of more than a small portion of the hungry, homeless, and unemployed millions. In turn, state and local governments could not or would not provide unemployment insurance or increased welfare benefits to ease the pain and suffering of those most vulnerable to the economic disaster.

Despite the great need to alleviate the economic disaster, President Herbert Hoover hesitated to act. Steeped in the free-market orthodoxy of his time, he believed government should do little to interfere with the workings of the economy. Nevertheless, he did more to counteract a depression than any previous president had done. Hoover tried to convince businesses to retain employees and not to cut wages, believing companies would understand that by doing so they would contribute to the health of the general economy and promote their own long-term interests. The president also approved loans to banks, railroads, and insurance companies by the Reconstruction Finance Corporation, a federal agency set up to rescue large corporations. He hoped these businesses would reinvigorate production, create new jobs, and restore consumer spending. His faith was misplaced; businesses, seeking to save themselves, took the government loans and still laid off workers.

Hoover's reluctance to use the federal government to intervene in the economy extended to the provision of relief. He suggested that local governments and charities should address the needs of the unemployed, the homeless, and the starving masses. Hoover was not a callous person, but he was trapped in a rigid ideology. He watched with dismay the wandering groups of men, women, and children who began settling into what they called, with grim humor, "Hoovervilles," sordid clusters of shacks made of tin, cardboard, and burlap adjacent to railroad tracks and dumps. Still, he refused to allow the federal government to provide relief directly.

Hoover's inactivity was bad enough, but his politics were as racist as that of the Democratic Party. He wanted to create a white Republican Party in the South and cultivated white Southerners by attempting to appoint judge John Parker of North Carolina, who believed in "separate but equal," to the U.S. Supreme Court and by displacing black Republican Party leaders. Hoover's policy was not new; for decades the national Republican Party had treated black voters with contempt and often declined to reward them with patronage appointments. This policy took on a different meaning during the early 1930s against the backdrop of black suffering.

BLACK PROTEST DURING THE GREAT DEPRESSION

During the 1930s the NAACP developed a new effectiveness as an advocate for African-American civil rights. The biracial organization took the lead in pressing the government to protect African-American rights and to eliminate the blatant racism in government programs. Part of the reason for this new dynamism was the astute leadership of Walter White who became an insistent voice of protest, personally investigating forty-two lynchings and eight race riots. He was an ardent lobbyist for civil rights legislation and racial justice. Throughout the 1930s African Americans of all hues moved into leadership positions in the NAACP and added their names to the membership roles of its many branches.

The new dynamism of the NAACP became apparent in 1930 when Walter White took a prominent role in the successful campaign to defeat Hoover's nomination of circuit court judge John J. Parker of North Carolina to a seat on the U.S. Supreme Court. Parker had infuriated the organization because he openly embraced white supremacy, stating, for example, that the "participation of the Negro in politics is a source of evil and danger to both races." The NAACP formed a coalition with the American Federation of Labor to derail the Parker nomination. Although the NAACP could take only part of the credit, White trumpeted the victory and let it be known that African Americans would not be silent while "the Hoover administration proposed to conciliate southern white sentiment by sacrificing the Negro and his rights."

Du Bois Ignites a Controversy

The NAACP had critics, even within its own ranks. Many younger black people criticized its focus on civil liberties and deplored it for ignoring the economic misery of most African Americans. In 1934 W. E. B. Du Bois, editor of the NAACP's journal *The Crisis*, joined the chorus. Criticizing what he considered the group's overemphasis on integration, Du Bois advocated a program of self-determination he hoped would permit black people to develop "an economic nation within a nation." Du Bois acknowledged that this internal economy could only meet part of the needs of the African-American community. But he insisted it could be developed and expanded in many ways.

The black intellectual community quickly attacked Du Bois for advocating "voluntary segregation." Sociologist E. Franklin Frazier, for example, called the idea of black businesses succeeding within a segregated economy a black upper-class fantasy and social myth. Nevertheless, Du Bois held fast to his position that the NAACP should continue to oppose legal segregation yet combine that opposition with vigorous support to improve segregated institutions as long as discrimination persisted. He was eventually forced from the editorship of *The Crisis*, but his resignation did not end the controversy. By the late 1930s the NAACP had developed, alongside its older activities, a much greater emphasis on economic policy and worked to develop stronger ties to the burgeoning labor movement.

Challenging Racial Discrimination in the Courts

A dramatic expansion of its legal campaign against racial discrimination enhanced the NAACP's effectiveness. Central to this project was the hiring of Charles Hamilton Houston, a Harvard-trained African-American lawyer and scholar, to lead it. Houston had been vice dean of Howard University Law School, which he had transformed into a powerful institution for training black attorneys in the intricacies of civil rights law. At the NAACP, Houston laid out a plan for a legal program to challenge inequality in education and the exclusion of black people from voting in the South. Houston used lawsuits both to force state and local governments to live up to the Constitution and to inspire community organization.

Houston did not focus directly on eliminating segregation but rather sought to force southern states to equalize their facilities. Studies by the NAACP had revealed

Thurgood Marshall (1908–1993), Charles Hamilton Houston (1895–1950), and Donald Gaines Murray. In 1935, attorneys Marshall and Houston handled Donald Murray's suit against the University of Maryland Law School. In 1938 Murray became the first African American to graduate from a southern state school. Thus began the relentless black attack against segregated education in America.
Courtesy of the Library of Congress

great disparities in per capita expenditures for white and black students, and huge differences in salaries paid to white and black teachers. Houston was no supporter of segregation. He hoped to use litigation to secure judgments that would so increase the cost of separate institutions that states would be forced to abandon them.

To execute his agenda, Houston convinced Walter White to hire his former student at the Howard University Law School, Thurgood Marshall, in 1936. Marshall was born in Baltimore in 1908. His father was a dining-car waiter and club steward; his mother had been a teacher before her marriage. During the 1930s Marshall and Houston focused on bringing greater parity between black and white teachers, a project they hoped would increase NAACP membership among teachers, their students, and parents. The two men, working with a remarkable network of African-American attorneys, also attempted to end discrimination against black men and women in professional and graduate schools. Inequalities were obvious here because many southern states offered no graduate facilities of any kind to black students.

Like other campaigns, this focus on graduate education was intended to establish precedents that might be used to gain equality in other areas. The first significant accomplishment in the NAACP's legal campaign against segregation in graduate and professional education was the U.S. Supreme Court's 1938 decision in *Gaines v.*

Canada. The Supreme Court ordered the state of Missouri to provide black citizens an opportunity to study law in a state-supported institution. Failure to do so, the Court held, would violate the equal protection of the law clause of the Fourteenth Amendment to the U.S. Constitution. Although Lloyd Gaines, the prospective student for whom the case was brought, disappeared before the final resolution of this challenge, Missouri hastily established a law school for African Americans at the historically black Lincoln University. In the 1940s several southern states, including North Carolina, Texas, Oklahoma, and South Carolina, followed Missouri's lead and established law schools for their black citizens.

Thurgood Marshall and the NAACP were encouraged by the *Gaines* decision to persist in challenging the constitutionality of the "separate but equal" doctrine. The case of *Sipuel v. Board of Regents of the University of Oklahoma* (1947) was another such effort. In this case Ada Lois Sipuel sought admission to the law school of the University of Oklahoma at Norman. In accordance with state statutes she was refused admission but granted an out-of-state tuition award. Thurgood Marshall argued that this arrangement failed to meet the needs of the state's black citizens. The Supreme Court declared that Oklahoma was obliged under the equal protection clause of the Fourteenth Amendment to provide a legal education for Sipuel. The case established the principle that the state had to provide a separate law school for African-American students in their home states.

Heman Sweatt, a black mail carrier, tested this principle in a suit against the University of Texas Law School. In *Sweatt v. Painter* (1950), the U.S. Supreme Court again sided with the NAACP lawyers. In response to Sweatt's initial challenge, Texas had created a separate law school that had inadequate library facilities, faculty, and support staff. It was separate but hardly equal. Marshall and local Texas black lawyers argued that the legal education offered Sweatt at the black law school was so inferior it violated the equal protection clause of the Fourteenth Amendment. The victories registered in these early cases laid the legal foundation for the 1954 *Brown v. Topeka Board of Education* decision.

The fight against political disfranchisement also helped mobilize local and state communities and branches. Nowhere was this more apparent than in Texas. In 1923 the Texas legislature enacted the Terrell law, which expressly declared, "In no event shall a Negro be eligible to participate in a Democratic primary election . . . in . . . Texas." In the one-party South, the primary elections were more important than the general elections, which often merely rubber-stamped the choice made in the primary. Thus to be denied the right to vote in Democratic Party primary elections was to be disfranchised. The NAACP developed a case to test the constitutionality of the Terrell law and commenced a twenty-year battle through the courts. The Texas branches of the NAACP raised money and coordinated local involvement in the campaign to overthrow the Democratic white primary that disfranchised so many black Texans.

The Texas white primary fight was the most sustained and intense effort that any NAACP chapter undertook during the interwar period. It began in the 1920s and won its first victory when the Supreme Court ruled in 1927 in *Nixon v. Herndon* that the Texas Democratic primary was unconstitutional (see Chapter 17). At the national headquarters, Charles H. Houston and Thurgood Marshall orchestrated the assault. Their efforts were rewarded in subsequent decisions that further chipped away at the legal basis for the white primary. Finally, in 1944 the U.S. Supreme Court issued a ruling in *Smith v. Allwright* that ended the white primary altogether. It was the NAACP's greatest legal victory to that time. Many more would soon follow.

Black Women and Community Organizing

Black women made exceptional contributions to the NAACP during the 1930s through their successful fund-raising efforts and membership drives. Three agitators for racial justice were Daisy Adams Lampkin (c. 1884–1965), Juanita Mitchell (1913–1992), and Ella Baker (1903–1986). These women worked closely with White and the NAACP throughout the Depression and World War II. Lampkin, a native of Washington, D.C., in 1915 became the president of the Negro Women's Franchise League, a group dedicated to fighting for the vote. In 1930 Walter White enlisted her as regional field secretary of the NAACP, a post she held until she was made national field secretary in 1935. She continued raising funds for the NAACP and played leading roles within organized black womanhood.

Juanita E. Jackson was born in Hot Springs, Arkansas, and raised in Baltimore, Maryland. She earned a degree in education from the University of Pennsylvania in 1931, then returned to Baltimore, where she helped found the City-Wide Young People's Forum. This organization encouraged young people to discuss and plan attacks on such scourges as unemployment, segregation, and lynching. The success of the group, which she headed from 1931 to 1934, attracted Walter White's attention, and he subsequently offered her the leadership of the NAACP's new youth program. From 1935 to 1938 she served as NAACP national youth director. In 1950 she received

The NAACP in the 1930s and 1940s depended on the formidable fund-raising talents of black women like Daisy Lampkin (shown here in a black Baptist church), Ella Baker, and Juanita Mitchell. These women played a major role in building NAACP membership.

Courtesy Mary McLeod Bethune Council House National Historic Site, Washington, DC a law degree from the University of Maryland. As the first black woman admitted to practice law in Maryland, she embarked on a series of cases that helped destroy racial segregation on the state's public beaches and in its public schools.

Ella Baker, who became one of the most important women in the civil rights movement of the 1950s and 1960s, began her life's work during the Depression. Born in Norfolk, Virginia, Baker moved to New York City in 1927 and worked as a waitress and as an organizer involved in radical politics. She was also on the staff of two local newspapers, *The American West Indian News* and the *Negro National News.* Within two years after her arrival she had cofounded with George Schuyler the Young Negroes' Cooperative League in Harlem. The group practiced collective decision making and attempted to involve all segments of the community in the cooperatives. Meanwhile, she also worked with women's and labor groups. She served as publicity director of the Sponsoring Committee of the National Negro Congress and worked with the WPA. Walter White was impressed with her relentless organizing and management skills. After much persuasion Baker accepted, in 1941, White's offer to become an assistant field secretary of the NAACP. After resigning from the NAACP she joined the staff of the New York Urban League.

Other black women organized outside the NAACP. Black women in Detroit provide a potent illustration of this kind of activity. On June 10, 1930, fifty black women responded to a call issued by Fannie B. Peck, wife of Reverend William H. Peck, pastor of the two-thousand-member Bethel African Methodist Episcopal Church and the president of the Booker T. Washington Trade Association. Out of this initial meeting emerged the Detroit Housewives' League, an organization that combined economic nationalism and black women's self-determination to help black families and businesses survive the Depression.

The Detroit organization grew rapidly. By 1934 ten thousand black women belonged to it. According to Peck, the black woman had finally realized "that she has been traveling through a blind alley, making sacrifices to educate her children with no thought as to their obtaining employment after leaving school." The only requirement for membership was a pledge to support black businesses, buy black products, and patronize black professionals, thereby keeping money in the community. The league quickly spread to other cities. Housewives' leagues in Chicago, Baltimore, Washington, Durham (North Carolina), Harlem, and Cleveland used boycotts of merchants who refused to sell black products and employ black children as clerks or stock persons to secure an estimated 75,000 new jobs for black people.

African Americans and the New Deal

In 1932, the third year of the Great Depression, voters elected New York governor Franklin Delano Roosevelt to the presidency with a total of nearly 23 million votes. Roosevelt's lopsided victory over Hoover, who received fewer than 16 million votes, demonstrated the country's loss of faith in the Republican Party and its economic philosophy and heralded the emergence of a new electoral coalition. The new president appealed to the Democratic Party's base of support in the white South, but to this group he added a coalition of western farmers, industrial workers, urban voters from the white ethnic groups in northern cities, and reform-minded intellectuals. For the time being, however, black Americans still clung to the Republican banner. In Chicago, for example, less than 25 percent of black voters cast their ballots for Roosevelt. But this was the last election in which the party of Lincoln could take them for granted. In his first term Roosevelt inaugurated a multitude of programs to counter the Depression—collectively known as the New Deal—which would shift the allegiance of African Americans. Initially his programs continued past patterns of discrimination against African Americans. But by 1935 the New Deal was providing more equal benefits and prompting profound social changes. The result was a new political order that ultimately undermined key portions of the edifice of American racism.

Roosevelt and the First New Deal, 1933–1935

During his first one hundred days in office, Franklin Roosevelt pressed through Congress a profusion of bold new economic initiatives that came to be known as the first New Deal. To combat the Depression, Roosevelt, unlike Hoover, followed no predetermined plan. Instead he favored experimentation—tempered by political expediency—over ideology as the guide to federal action. With little resistance Congress passed the president's sprawling and complex laws aimed at overhauling the nation's financial, agricultural, and industrial systems. Most hoped, vainly as it turned out, that these changes would eventually bring a return to prosperity. In the meantime Roosevelt moved forcefully to counter the immediate suffering of the unemployed with a massive emergency federal relief effort. Many of the first New Deal's programs benefited both white and black people, but the strength of white Southerners in the Democratic Party and the nearly complete lack of African-American political power in the South caused much of this early program to be unfairly administered.

The Agricultural Adjustment Act (AAA), designed to protect farmers by giving them subsidies to limit production and thereby stabilize prices, illustrates the key benefits and problems African Americans experienced during the first New Deal. The theory underlying the AAA was that creating scarcity would increase agricultural prices. So farmers would be paid to grow less. The program provided for sharecroppers and tenant farmers to get part of the subsidies and allowed new rural relief agencies to dispense supplementary income to off-season wageworkers.

This program helped many African Americans, mainly because it pumped billions of dollars into an economic sector on which over 4.5 million black people relied for their livelihood. The flow of money from the AAA did, for a time, slow the exodus of black people from farming. During the 1930s only 4.5 percent of African Americans abandoned farming, compared with 8.6 percent who did so during the 1920s.

But the AAA was often administered unfairly and corruptly. Local control of the AAA resided in the hands of the Extension Service and County Agricultural Conservation Committees, which were supposed to represent all farmers. The county agents, however, were often the planters themselves, and the committees mirrored southern politics by excluding black people. During the first two years of the AAA, black farmers complained bitterly that white landlords simply grabbed and pocketed the millions of dollars of benefit checks they were supposed to forward to tenants. To compound the injury, some planters then evicted the sharecroppers and tenants from the land.

The experience of African Americans with the National Industrial Recovery Act (NIRA) mimicked the problems with the AAA. The NIRA was intended to promote the revival of manufacturing by allowing various industries to cooperate in establishing codes of conduct governing prices, wage levels, and employment practices, all of which were to be overseen by a National Recovery Administration (NRA). The NRA oversaw the drafting of the codes but faced tremendous resistance from employers and unions in eliminating racial disparities in wage rates and working conditions. Even when African-American advocates did win wage increases for occupations in which black people predominated, the result was often a shift to white labor. These policies prompted some African-American newspapers and protest organizations to claim that "NRA" really stood for the "Negro Removal Agency" or "Negroes Robbed Again." To the relief of many African-American advocates and workers, the U.S. Supreme Court declared the NIRA unconstitutional in spring 1935.

The New Deal's national welfare programs included the Federal Emergency Relief Administration (FERA), the Civilian Conservation Corps (CCC), Public Works Administration (PWA), and Civil Works Administration (CWA). Although inadequate and unfairly administered on local levels, these programs were often the only thing standing between black people and starvation. FERA provided funds for local and state relief operations to restart and expand their programs. The program pulled millions of people back from the brink of starvation. Because African Americans suffered greater economic devastation, they received benefits at a higher rate than whites. In most cities north and south, 25 to 40 percent of African Americans were on relief rolls that FERA funded wholly or in part. Direct welfare, however, was deemed by many in the Roosevelt administration to be debilitating, so it emphasized hiring the unemployed for public works projects. The CWA was a temporary agency created to help people through the winter of 1933–1934. The Civilian Conservation Corps (CCC) built segregated camps to employ young men and to take them away from the poverty and hopelessness of urban areas. By the time it was abolished in 1945, more than 200,000 African-American youth had taken part in the program.

These relief programs helped many African Americans through the worst parts of the Depression. But the programs also tended to be less helpful to black people than they were to whites. In its early days, the CCC, for example, was a tightly segregated institution, with only about 5 percent of its slots going to black youths during its first year. Likewise, although FERA tended to be administered fairly in northern cities, in the South it reached few of those in need.

Black Officials in the New Deal

The first New Deal was not completely bleak for African Americans. In addition to the benefits, however grudgingly disbursed, that they derived from New Deal relief programs, African Americans also gained new influence and allies within the Roosevelt administration. Their experience reflected both the growing availability of highly trained African Americans for government service and the emerging consciousness among white liberals about the problems—and potential electoral power—of black people.

Black people found a staunch ally in First Lady Eleanor Roosevelt. She was revered for her relentless commitment to racial justice. She arranged meetings at the White

House for some black leaders. She cajoled her husband to consider legislation on behalf of black rights. She personally defied Jim Crow laws by refusing to sit in a "white only" section while attending a meeting in the South. Moreover, she wrote newspaper columns calling for "fair play and equal opportunity for Negro citizens." Roosevelt further endeared herself to black Americans when she resigned her membership in the Daughters of the American Revolution after that organization refused to allow a young black opera singer, Marian Anderson, to perform at its Constitution Hall in Washington in 1939. (Administration officials subsequently arranged for Anderson to perform in front of the Lincoln Memorial on Easter Sunday before a crowd of 75,000.)

Eleanor Roosevelt was joined by other liberals to press the cause of racial justice and to seek the appointment of African Americans throughout the government. The result was that doors to the government began opening in an unprecedented way. For the first time, the government employed professional black architects, lawyers, engineers, economists, statisticians, interviewers, office managers, social workers, and librarians. The Department of Commerce hired Eugene K. Jones, on leave from the National Urban League. The National Youth Administration brought in Mary McLeod Bethune, and the Department of Interior employed William H. Hastie and Robert Weaver. Ira De A. Reid joined the Social Security Administration, and Lawrence W. Oxley worked for the Department of Labor, with Ambrose Caliver serving in the Office of Education.

A core of highly placed African Americans became linked in a network called the Federal Council on Negro Affairs, more loosely known as Roosevelt's "Black Cabinet." Mary McLeod Bethune was the undisputed leader of this body, which consisted primarily of "New Deal race specialists." It numbered twenty-seven men and three women working mostly in temporary emergency agencies such as the Works Progress Administration (WPA) and included such stalwarts as housing administrator Robert Weaver. This cadre of advisers pressured the president and the heads of federal agencies to adopt and support color-blind policies and lobbied to advance the status of black Americans.

Black Social Scientists and the New Deal

Many black intellectuals, scholars, and writers believed the social sciences could be used to adjudicate race relations in the country, and during the New Deal they found greater receptiveness to their work than ever before. Nearly two hundred African Americans received Ph.D.s during the 1930s, more than four times the combined total from the first three decades of the century. Several of these young scholars reached the top ranks of the social sciences studying the problems of black people with a depth of experience and theoretical sophistication lacking in earlier generations of scholars. In sociology E. Franklin Frazier and Charles S. Johnson took the lead. Frazier's pioneering studies of black families placed him at the forefront of debates on social policy. As the editor of *Opportunity*, the journal of the Urban League, throughout the 1930s, Johnson published insightful critiques of American racial practices and policies, as well as the work of emerging black novelists, poets, and playwrights. Meanwhile Ralph Bunche became well known within the field of political science, and Abram Harris and Robert Weaver gained renown in economics.

Historians such as Carter G. Woodson, Lorenzo Greene, Benjamin Quarles, and John Hope Franklin advanced the idea that black people had been active agents in the

Roosevelt's "Black Cabinet" in a 1938 photograph. Mary McLeod Bethune is in the center of the front row. The advisers included Robert Weaver, Eugene Kinckle Jones, Ambrose Caliver, and William H. Hastie, among many others.
Scurlock Studios

past and not simply the passive objects of white people's actions. Their scholarly emphasis on racial pride, achievement, and autonomy helped raise black morale.

The increasing importance of black scholars became apparent late in the 1930s when the Carnegie Corporation, a philanthropic foundation, sponsored a major study of black life. Although the study was led by Gunnar Myrdal, a Swedish social scientist, nearly half the large staff of scholars were African Americans, and several, particularly Bunche, had a major impact on the work. Published in 1944 as *An American Dilemma*, this massive study profoundly affected public understanding of how racism undermined the progress of African Americans. It helped set the agenda for the civil rights movement.

African Americans and the Second New Deal

By late 1935, after two years marked by a slow recovery, much of the first New Deal lay in shambles. The U.S. Supreme Court had invalidated major parts of it, and a conservative backlash was emerging against the Roosevelt administration. In response Roosevelt pressed for a second burst of legislation marked by the passage of the Social Security Act (SSA), the National Labor Relations Act (NLRA), the creation of the Works Progress Administration (WPA), and other measures considerably more radical than those that had come in 1933. The NLRA, for example, helped unions get established and grow. The SSA provided the rudiments of a social welfare system as well as unemployment and retirement insurance. This new set of laws, known as the second New Deal, survived legal challenges and changed the United States, particularly by strengthening the role of the federal government.

Roosevelt's leftward political shift helped him win the 1936 presidential election in a landslide. This election cemented a new electoral coalition that yoked the southern wing of the Democratic Party with more liberal farmers and working-class voters who were labor union members in the North and West. The Democratic Party began to win the votes of the large African-American populations in the great cities of the North. The great migration had effectively relocated tens of thousands of prospective black voters in northern urban centers, traditional strongholds of Democratic Party machines, such as in Chicago. Institutionalized housing segregation combined with the often conscious choice to live in their own neighborhoods concentrated the black electorate and increased its political power. In 1934, reflecting a shift in partisan allegiance, Chicago's black voters elected Democrat Arthur W. Mitchell to Congress, who thus became the first black Democrat ever to win a seat in the House of Representatives.

Mitchell's election was only the beginning of the change in black people's political party identification. The powerful black press fanned the shifting winds and many more black urban dwellers developed an intense interest in politics. They began to connect political power with the prospect of improving their economic conditions. By the end of the decade, black urban voters garnered noteworthy influence in key states such as Illinois, Ohio, Pennsylvania, and New York. This political consciousness led to the election of black state legislators in California, Illinois, Indiana, Kansas, Kentucky, New Jersey, New York, Ohio, Pennsylvania, and West Virginia.

In another indication of change, some Democrats began supporting antilynching legislation. Congressman Mitchell gave a strong speech printed in the *Congressional Record* in 1935 supporting President Roosevelt as an antilynching advocate. "No President," he declared, "has been more outspoken against the horrible crime of lynching than has Mr. Roosevelt. In speaking of lynching some time ago he characterized it as 'collective murder' and spoke of it as a crime which blackens the record of America." Mitchell told black audiences, "Let me say again, the attitude of the administration at the White House is absolutely fair and without prejudice, insofar as the Negro citizenry is concerned."

There are many complex reasons for the revolutionary transformation in black political allegiance. The shift to the Democratic Party did not occur without anxiety. Some black people feared that by joining the party they would open the door for even more white southern Democrats to assume national political power and thwart black advancement. But by 1936 most African-American voters were willing to take the risk.

The tension between black Democrats and white conservative Democrats erupted at the party's 1936 convention in Philadelphia. The seating of thirty-two black Democratic Party delegates provoked the wrath of southern politicians. The selection of a black Baptist minister to open one session with a prayer especially outraged South Carolina senator Ellison D. "Cotton Ed" Smith. Accompanied by Mayor Burnet Maybank of Charleston, South Carolina, and one or two other delegates, he marched ostentatiously off the floor proclaiming that they refused to support "any political organization that looks upon the Negro and caters to him as a political and social equal." Smith declared he was "sick of the whole damn thing." Undaunted, the black minister simply observed that "Brother Smith needs more prayer."

The South Carolina delegation subsequently adopted a protest resolution denouncing the appearance of black men on the convention's program. The protests of southern white politicians, however, had no effect on the political decisions of black men and women. Heeding the advice of the NAACP, they voted their personal interests.

Despite the rise of black people in the Democratic Party, southern congressmen succeeded in excluding many African Americans from key government programs. For example, they insisted on denying the benefits of the National Labor Relations Act and Social Security Act to agricultural laborers and domestic servants. These white Southerners could not, however, stop the tilt toward fairer administration of programs or the revival of the push for equal rights, which had lain all but dormant since the end of the Reconstruction era.

An examination of the Works Progress Administration (WPA) illustrates the changes that the second New Deal and the increasing shift of African Americans to the Democratic Party wrought. The WPA, with Harry Hopkins (1890–1946) as its head, was created to employ the unemployed. Under Hopkins's direction, and sustained with $1.39 billion in federal funds, the WPA put thousands of men and women to work building new roads, hospitals, city halls, courthouses, and schools. Larger scale projects included the Lincoln Tunnel under the Hudson River connecting New York and New Jersey, the Triborough Bridge system linking Manhattan to Long Island, and the Bonneville and Boulder Dams. (Boulder Dam was later renamed the Hoover Dam by a Republican-controlled Congress in 1946.)

The WPA was administered far more fairly than were the first New Deal programs. The national government explicitly rejected racial discrimination and worked to make sure local officials complied. Although far from perfect, by 1939 it provided assistance to one million black families on a far more equitable basis than ever before.

The same pattern prevailed in the WPA's four arts programs—the Federal Art Project, the Federal Music Project, the Federal Theater Project, and the Federal Writers Project—which employed thousands of musicians, intellectuals, writers, and artists. A fifth program, the Historical Records Survey, created in 1937, sent teams of writers, including Zora Neale Hurston, to collect folklore and study various ethnic groups. One team collected the life histories and reminiscences of some two thousand former slaves.

Between 1935 and 1943, the WPA helped artists display their talents and made their work widely available. Among the black artists hired to adorn government buildings, post offices, and public parks were Aaron Douglas, Charles Alston, Richmond Barthe, Sargent Johnson, Archibald Motley Jr., and Augusta Savage. Savage became the first director of the Harlem Community Art Center in 1937.

The Federal Theater Project established sixteen black theater units. Among their most notable productions was a version of *Macbeth* set in Haiti with an all-black cast. White actor John Houseman and black actress Rose McClendon directed the Harlem Federal Theater Project. This project—more than the others—proved controversial due to the fear of communist influence and the leftist political views of some African-American writers and performers.

ORGANIZED LABOR AND BLACK AMERICA

The relationship of African Americans to labor unions changed profoundly during the 1930s. The New Deal, especially after 1935, did much to transform the labor movement. The National Labor Relations Act and the militancy of workers provided the opportunity to organize the nation's great mass production industries. Still, leaders of the AFL dragged their feet, unwilling to incorporate into their unions the masses of un-skilled workers, many of whom were African American or recent European immigrants. Frustrated by this situation, in 1935 John L. Lewis (1880–1969), head of the United Mine Workers, and his followers formed the Committee for Industrial Organization (CIO) to take on the task.

Unlike the AFL, the CIO was committed to interracial and multiethnic organizing and so enabled more African Americans to participate in the labor movement. Its leaders knew it was in organized labor's best interest to admit black men and women to membership. As one black union organizer said, "We colored folks can't organize without you and you white folks can't organize without us." But it took a massive change in outlook to achieve this unity. By 1940 the CIO had enlisted approximately 210,000 black members.

A. Philip Randolph's Brotherhood of Sleeping Car Porters (BSCP) remained with the AFL, but it also benefited from New Deal legislation. In 1934 Congress had amended the Railway Labor Act in a way that helped the BSCP overcome the opposi-tion of the Pullman Company. The law required that corporations bargain in good faith with unions if the unions could demonstrate through elections monitored by the National Mediation Board that they genuinely represented the corporations' employ-ees. In 1937, long after an election certified the BSCP as the workers' representative, the Pullman company finally recognized the brotherhood. Then—and only then—did the AFL grant the BSCP full membership as an international union. After more than twelve years, A. Philip Randolph and thousands of black men won their struggles against a giant corporation and a powerful labor organization. These were no small victories.

Although most black people in unions were men, some unions also represented and helped improve the lives of black working women. For example, there had been a rigid hierarchy among workers in the tobacco industry since the early nineteenth cen-tury, one of the few areas of the economy outside agriculture or domestic service that employed many black women. Jobs were assigned on the basis of race and gender, with black women receiving the most difficult and tedious job, that of "stemmer." In 1939 stemmer Louise "Mama" Harris instigated a series of walkouts at the I. N. Vaughn Company in Richmond. The strikes, which were supported by CIO affiliates, including the white women of the International Ladies Garment Workers Union, led to the for-mation of the Tobacco Workers Organizing Committee, another CIO affiliate. In 1943 black women union leaders and activists, including Theodosia Simpson and Miranda Smith, were involved in a strike against the R. J. Reynolds tobacco company to force it to the negotiating table. Smith later became southern regional director of the Food, Tobacco, Agricultural, and Allied Workers of America. It was the highest position held by a black woman in the labor movement up to that time.

THE COMMUNIST PARTY AND AFRICAN AMERICANS

Throughout the 1930s the Communist Party intensified its support of African Americans' efforts to address unemployment and job discrimination and to seek social justice. Some African Americans were attracted to the party because of its militant antiracism and its determination to be interracial. The party expelled members who exhibited racial prejudice and gave black men key leadership positions. James Ford, an African American, ran as the party's vice-presidential candidate in the election of 1932. Although few black men and women actually joined the Communist Party, some became increasingly sympathetic to left-wing ideas and prescriptions as the Depression wore on.

Many black workers were drawn to the Communist Party because it criticized the refusal of organized white labor to include them. The communists maintained that "the low standard of living of Negro workers is made use of by the capitalists to reduce the wages of the white workers." They chided "the mis-leaders of labor, the heads of the reformist and reactionary trade union organizations" for refusing to organize black workers. They insisted "this anti-Negro attitude of the reactionary labor leaders helps to split the ranks of labor, allows the employers to carry out their policy of 'divide and rule,' frustrates the efforts of the working class to emancipate itself from the yoke of capitalism, and dims the class-consciousness of the white workers as well as of the Negro workers." Indeed, much of the push for racial equality within the CIO emanated from those connected with the party.

The International Labor Defense and the "Scottsboro Boys"

The Scottsboro case brought the Communist Party to the attention of many African Americans. The case began when nine black youths who had caught a ride on a freight train in Alabama were tried, convicted, and sentenced to death for allegedly raping two white women. Their ordeal began on the night of March 25, 1931, when they were accosted by a group of young white hobos. A fight broke out. The black youths threw the white youths off the train. The losers filed a complaint with the Scottsboro, Alabama, sheriff, charging that black hoodlums had viciously assaulted them. The sheriff ordered his deputies to round up every black person on the train. The sweep netted the nine young black men: Ozie Powell, Clarence Norris, Charlie Weems, Olen Montgomery, Willie Robertson, Haywood Patterson, Eugene Williams, Andy Wright, and Roy Wright. The police also discovered two young white women: nineteen-year-old Victoria Price and seventeen-year-old Ruby Bates.

Afraid of being arrested, and perhaps ashamed of being hobos, Price and Bates falsely claimed that the nine black youths had sexually assaulted them. On the basis of that accusation, the "Scottsboro Boys" (ranging in ages from thirteen to twenty) were given a hasty trial. Three days after the trial started, and fifteen days after their arrest, the jurors found all of them guilty. Eight received the death sentence, and the youngest, a thirteen-year-old, was sentenced to life imprisonment, even though medical examinations of Price and Bates proved that neither had been raped.

While other organizations either dawdled or refused to intervene, the Communist Party's International Labor Defense (ILD) rushed to the aid of the "boys" by appealing the conviction and death sentence to the U.S. Supreme Court. The case produced two important decisions that reaffirmed black people's right to the basic protections that all other American citizens enjoyed. In *Powell v. Alabama* (1932), the Court ruled that the nine Scottsboro defendants had not been given adequate legal counsel and the trial had taken place in a hostile and volatile atmosphere. Asserting the youths' right to due process as set forth in the Fourteenth Amendment had been violated, the Court ordered a new trial. Alabama did as instructed, but the new trial resulted in another guilty verdict and sentences of death or life imprisonment. The ILD promptly appealed, and in *Norris v. Alabama* (1935) the Supreme Court decided that all Americans have the right to a trial by a jury of their peers. The systematic exclusion of African Americans from the Scottsboro juries, the Court held, denied the defendants equal protection under the law, which the Fourteenth Amendment guaranteed. Chief Justice Charles Evans Hughes pointed out that no black citizens had served on juries in the Alabama counties for decades, even though many were qualified to serve. The Court noted that the exclusion was blatant racial discrimination and called for yet another trial.

Despite these stunning defeats and increasing evidence that the "boys" had been falsely convicted, Alabama still pursued the case. Even when Ruby Bates publicly admitted the rape charge had been a hoax, white Alabamians ignored her. Finally, in 1937 Alabama dropped its charges against five of the nine men, and in the 1940s the state released those still in jail. Altogether, nine innocent black men had collectively served some three-quarters of a century in prison. Clarence Willie Norris, however, escaped and fled to Michigan, returning decades later to receive a ceremonious pardon from Governor George Wallace.

Debating Communist Leadership

Throughout the Scottsboro case, the NAACP tried unsuccessfully to wrest control from the Communist Party. Indeed, as the case evolved, tensions and competition between the Communist Party and the NAACP for leadership of black America flared into open hostility. At first, the NAACP had hesitated to defend accused rapists, but it moved more decisively after the Communist Party had taken the lead.

The contest between the NAACP and the communists reveals the differences between the two groups. The party organized protest marches and demonstrations and used its press to denounce more cautious middle-class organizations. In Harlem, for example, the communists staged a 1931 protest march that attracted over three thousand black men and women and ended with an address by Ada Wright, the mother of two of the defendants, who praised the ILD for its help. The NAACP countered with a carefully orchestrated campaign that questioned the sincerity and effectiveness of the communists and sought to repair its own reputation as a respectable and effective advocate for African Americans.

Black public opinion divided in its evaluation of the party. Some black men and women applauded the communists. Historian Carter G. Woodson praised the Communist Party in the *New York Age*:

> I have talked with any number of Negroes who call themselves Communists, and I have never heard one express a desire to destroy anyone or anything but oppression. . . . Negroes who are charged with being Communists advocate the stoppage of peonage, equality in employment of labor. . . . If this makes a man 'Red,' the world's greatest reformers belong to

this class, and we shall have to condemn our greatest statesmen, some of whom have attained the presidency of the United States.

Although most African Americans applauded the antiracist work that the Communist Party supported and performed, there was no chance they would defect from the traditional American political system as W. E. B. Du Bois wrote in 1931:

> American Negroes do not propose to be the shock troops of the Communist Revolution, driven out in the front to death, cruelty and humiliation in order to win victories for white workers.... Negroes know perfectly well that whenever they try to lead revolution in America, the nation will unite as one fist to crush them and them alone.

The National Negro Congress

The infighting between the Communist Party and other groups doomed a major attempt to unite all the disparate African-American protest groups into the National Negro Congress (NNC). John P. Davis, a Washington-based economist, organized the NNC, modeling it on his experience as the executive secretary of the Joint Committee on National Recovery (JCNR), a coalition of black groups that pressed for fairness in the early New Deal. The NNC was to be a federation of organizations on a national scale supported by regional councils. Over 800 delegates representing 585 organizations attended its first meeting, held in Chicago in 1936. However, prominent black activists, leaders, and intellectuals were conspicuously absent, notably those associated with the NAACP. A. Philip Randolph was elected president, and Davis became the executive secretary. The group resolved not to be dominated by any one political faction and to build on the strength of all parts of the black community. Although handicapped by lack of funds, the NNC initially worked effectively at the local or community level. With branches in approximately seventy cities, the organization gained for its members increased employment opportunities, better housing, and adequate relief work.The NNC also prodded labor unions, in particular the CIO, to fight for better conditions and higher wages for black workers.

At the NNC's second meeting in Philadelphia in 1937, a skeptical Davis maintained that the Democratic Party would never allow black people to benefit justly and fairly from the New Deal. Eventually the increasing importance of communists in the NNC alienated most other groups and reduced the organization's ability to speak for the majority of black people. By 1940 it was greatly weakened. Randolph was voted out of office, and the once-promising NNC became little more than a front group for the Communist Party.

THE TUSKEGEE STUDY

The 1930s marked the rising prominence of black scholars and intellectuals, but paradoxically, the decade also witnessed the worst manifestation of racism in American science. This most shocking episode of virulent bigotry and racial mistreatment occurred in Macon County, Alabama. There, in 1932, U.S. Public Health Service (USPHS) officials initiated a major study of syphilis, a sexually transmitted disease that can cause paralysis, insanity, and heart failure. For the subjects of its program—entitled the Tuskegee Study of Untreated Syphilis in the Male Negro—the USPHS recruited 622 black men, all of them poor sharecroppers and the majority illiterate. Of these men, 431 had advanced cases of syphilis; the rest were free of the disease and served as controls for comparison.

The Tuskegee Study was called a treatment program, but it turned out to be an experiment, designed to chart the progression and development of a potentially fatal disease. To gain the trust of the men, the government doctors centered their work at Tuskegee Institute and hired a black nurse, Eunice Rivers, who convinced the men they had "bad blood" and needed special treatment. Although the drug penicillin, which could cure the disease, became available in the 1940s, the sharecroppers never received it. Instead, they were given ineffective placebos, which they were told would cure them.

Initially the Tuskegee Study was to last only six to twelve months, but it was repeatedly extended. The men received regular physical examinations, which included a painful lumbar puncture. This insertion of a needle into the spinal cord to obtain fluid for diagnosis often caused the men severe headaches, and in a few isolated cases it resulted in paralysis and even death. For almost forty years, Tuskegee Study doctors observed the men, keeping careful records of their health and performing autopsies on those who died; but they never treated them for syphilis. So little understood was the Tuskegee Study that men not only remained in the program but believed they were fortunate to have the physical examination, the hot lunches provided on examination days, and the burial allowance the government guaranteed their families. The medical community knew of the Tuskegee experiment, but the general public learned of it only in 1972 when a reporter broke the story. Black attorney Fred D. Gray of Alabama sued the U.S. government on behalf of the participants and their families, but before the case went to trial, the government made a $9 million settlement to the Tuskegee survivors and the descendants of those who had died.

T I M E L I N E

AFRICAN-AMERICAN EVENTS	NATIONAL EVENTS
1929	
	1929 October, Stock Market on Wall Street crashes
1930	
1930 Fannie Peck forms Detroit Housewives' League NAACP campaigns successfully to block John J. Parker's appointment to the Supreme Court	

continued

AFRICAN-AMERICAN EVENTS	NATIONAL EVENTS

1931

1931
The "Scottsboro Boys" are arrested

1932

1932	**1932**
In *Powell v. Alabama*, Supreme Court rules Scottsboro defendants lacked adequate counsel	Franklin D. Roosevelt elected president
The Tuskegee experiment begins	

1933

1933	**1933**
The "Black Cabinet" is formed	Roosevelt launches the First New Deal

1934

1934
Elijah Muhammad becomes leader of the Nation of Islam

W. E. B. Du Bois resigns from the NAACP

1935

1935	**1935**
Mary McLeod Bethune forms the National Council of Negro Women	The CIO is formed
Norris v. Alabama establishes right to trial by a jury of one's peers	Roosevelt's Second New Deal—Social Security Act, National Labor Relations Act, and the Works Progress Administration
Free Angelo Herndon Campaign begins	
The National Negro Congress is formed	

1936

1936	**1936**
African Americans shift allegiance to the Democratic Party	FDR is reelected in a landslide
Mary McLeod Bethune is named director of the Division of Negro Affairs	

1937

1937
William Hastie is named first black federal judge

Bethune organizes conference on Problems of the Negro and Negro Youth

CONCLUSION

Notable political changes occurred during the early 1930s: the NAACP came of age, black women found their voice, white left-wing leaders joined with black men and women in interracial alliances, organized labor bridged the race chasm, and black men and women switched from the Republican Party to the Democratic Party. The New Deal had stimulated some economic recovery and, more important, laid the basis for a strong national state and a political coalition that, beginning with World War II, would sharply challenge the nation's racial system.

REVIEW QUESTIONS

1. How did President Roosevelt entice black people to identify with the Democratic Party and abandon their long association with the Republican Party?

2. How did black people respond to and survive the Great Depression? How did the experiences of black women during the Depression reflect their race, class, and gender status in American society?

3. How did the New Deal agencies and programs affect the lives of African Americans and their communities? How did the New Deal adversely affect black sharecroppers, tenants, and farmers?

4. What were the political, social, and economic repercussions of the large-scale migration of African Americans out of the South during the 1930s?

5. What role did racism play in the Tuskegee experiment and the "Scottsboro Boys" case?

6. Why were W. E. B. Du Bois's Crisis editorials "on segregation" so divisive and explosive? How did black activists and scholars respond to the idea of voluntary self-segregation?

RECOMMENDED READING

John Egerton. *Speak Now against the Day: The Generation before the Civil Rights Movement in the South.* New York: Alfred A. Knopf, 1994. An excellent survey of the period before the southern civil rights era, with chapters on the Depression in the South and black and white Southerners' reactions to it.

Darlene Clark Hine. "The Corporeal and Ocular Veil: Dr. Matilda A. Evans (1872–1935) and the Complexity of Southern History," *Journal of Southern History,* 70, no. 1 (February 2004): 1–34. A case study of the strategies pursued by a black woman physician to provide health care for impoverished African Americans in Columbia, South Carolina, during the opening decades of the twentieth century.

James H. Jones. *Bad Blood: The Tuskegee Syphilis Experiment.* New York: Free Press, 1981. The best and most comprehensive study of the Tuskegee experiment.

Robin D. G. Kelley. *Hammer and Hoe: Alabama Communists during the Great Depression.* Chapel Hill: University of North Carolina Press, 1990. A splendid study of the radicalizing activism of working people in the steel industry and on the farm during the 1930s. Kelley does an excellent job of showing why the communists appealed to black workers.

Mark Naison. *Communists in Harlem during the Depression.* Urbana: University of Illinois Press, 1983. A well-researched and clear-sighted study of the Communist Party in Harlem and the history of the National Negro Congress.

Susan Reverby. *Tuskegee Truths: Rethinking the Tuskegee Syphillis Study.* Chapel Hill: University of North Carolina Press, 2000.

Harvard Sitkoff. *A New Deal for Blacks: The Emergence of Civil Rights as a National Issue, Vol. I: Depression Decade.* New York: Oxford University Press, 1978. An important work that covers the New Deal era and presents it as a period when the groundwork for the civil rights movement was laid.

Patricia Sullivan. *Days of Hope: Race and Democracy in the New Deal Era.* Chapel Hill: University of North Carolina Press, 1996. An invaluable study showing how the ideas of civil rights and democracy were forged in the New Deal South.

Raymond Wolters. *Negroes and the Great Depression: The Problem of Economic Recovery.* Westport, CT: Greenwood, 1974. A solid survey of African Americans in the Depression that covers its impact on African Americans, the workings of the Black Cabinet, and the effects of the New Deal agencies on the lives of black Americans.

MEANINGS OF FREEDOM

CULTURE AND SOCIETY IN THE 1930s AND 1940s

BLACK CULTURE IN A MIDWESTERN CITY

During the 1930s and 1940s, black migrants flocked to St. Louis, swelling its population to make it the fifth largest city in the United States. Yet because of segregation and discrimination, the black community in St. Louis developed institutions to address their own educational and cultural needs. St. Louis is in the heart of a region often considered remote from the nation's cultural centers. Yet it has produced outstanding jazz musicians, and Chuck Berry virtually invented rock and roll there. A closer look at black support for classical music in St. Louis during the 1930s and 1940s reveals the interior diversity of black community life; even though white St. Louisians marginalized or ignored the contributions of black artists in the city.

Schools, churches, labor, and media within the St. Louis black community had to create opportunities for black children to study, appreciate, and perform classical music. The two largest black newspapers, the St. Louis *Argus* and the St. Louis *American,* publicized recitals and concerts. Two all-black institutions supported classical music education: Lincoln University in Jefferson City (founded in 1866 as a school created by and for black Civil War veterans and their families) and Sumner High School (founded in 1875 as the first secondary school for black people west of the Mississippi).

By the 1940s Lincoln University had become the institution for training St. Louis musicians, and its music instructors were active in the black community's cultural affairs. Sumner High School had orchestras, bands, choirs, and glee clubs. Many of its music teachers had advanced degrees from prestigious music departments. The most influential teacher was Kenneth Billups, an arranger, composer, and founding director of the Legend Singers, a black professional chorus.

The Legend Singers appeared with the St. Louis Symphony and with the Municipal Opera Company (MUNY) in productions of *Show Boat,* where they dressed in demeaning slave costumes. Billups's response to criticism of these appearances indirectly addressed the dilemma of black artists in a racially restrictive environment:

> I've seen situations where I felt inwardly . . . I might have had to do some things; for example, let's take this Showboat thing at MUNY Opera. There is the need of a black chorus to go there, and I had the privilege of doing that with my Legend Singers, simply because one of the first requirements was to have a black chorus.

Black churches, including Antioch Baptist, Central Baptist, and Berea Presbyterian, sponsored religious programs highlighting the works of both black and white composers. Local 197 of the American Federation of Musicians and the St. Louis Music Association, which was the local branch of the National Association of Negro Musicians, promoted black performing organizations and training. These groups sponsored choirs, orchestras, and other musical organizations and devoted part of their members' dues to scholarships and summer choirs for boys and girls.

THE BLACK CULTURE INDUSTRY
AND AMERICAN RACISM

Black American artists had to confront institutional racism in the culture industry. Individual black creative artists could rarely afford to produce and disseminate their work. This power often resided in the hands of record companies, publishers, and the owners of radio stations and film studios. Yet black artists in the 1930s and 1940s were shaping a new black consciousness that would erupt in the 1950s as the modern civil rights movement.

The political content of black art provoked heated debates among black artists. Many black Americans expected black artists not only to create beauty, but also to use their art to further black freedom from white oppression. The involvement of white people in the marketing and use of black culture created tension among black artists during these decades. Although many white Americans had long appreciated black culture, some had also appropriated it for their own profit.

During the late 1930s and 1940s, corporate America recognized the money that could be made in producing and marketing black culture. But there was a problem: black artists had to be made "acceptable" if they were to be successfully marketed to affluent white consumers. These artists had to compromise, mask, and subordinate their true feelings and expressiveness if they wanted to earn income from their work. Artists who exhibited the right combination of showmanship, charm, and talent could reap some of the financial rewards their creativity generated. The paradox of the black performer—using your art to entertain your oppressor—was nowhere more apparent than in music.

THE MUSIC CULTURE FROM SWING TO BEBOP

Ironically, the very creativity that white Americans valued and often appropriated depended on the artists' ability to preserve some intellectual and emotional autonomy. Black artists had to juxtapose the requirements of earning a living with the need to remain true to their art. Black musicians continuously had to refine, expand, and perfect their art not only for themselves and each other but also for a white-dominated marketplace. In many respects black music is virtually synonymous with black culture, and segregation or self-imposed separation often made possible the creation of new cultural expressions. Music encapsulates and reflects the core values and underlying tensions and anxieties in black communities. In black music we witness cultural producers developing strategies of resistance against white domination.

The Great Depression wrought havoc on the vibrant black culture industry of the 1920s. Record sales in 1932 were only a sixth of those in 1927. Black musicians like Louis Armstrong had enjoyed a golden age of creativity during the 1920s. The record companies had their separate black music labels and sold thousands of records to southern migrants to the big cities. New bands sprouted up from Kansas City to Chicago; Memphis to Detroit; Washington, D.C., to New York. The territorial (traveling) bands took the music to the outposts of black America, and the big bands under Fletcher Henderson, Duke Ellington, Count Basie, and Cab Calloway played in white urban dance halls and ballrooms that admitted black people only as staff or entertainers.

New York was where black musicians felt they had to go to prove themselves. After entertaining affluent white people or providing backup music for the Apollo Theater in Harlem, black musicians discarded their masks of docility and deference and made a different sound in their own space and on their own time in late-night jam sessions. The small clubs became the most fertile sites for innovation. In them a new kind of jazz was born.

The big band swing style that became popular in the 1930s transformed white American culture. Swing emerged as white bands reduced the music of the more innovative black bandleaders to a broadly appealing formula based on a swinging 4/4 beat, well-blended saxophone sections, and pleasant-sounding vocals. The big swing bands of the 1930s played written-out, completely arranged music. The popularity of swing helped boost the careers of black and white bandleaders, but it also led to a creative slump that disheartened many of the younger black musicians. Tired of swing's predictability, they began improvising in the jazz clubs, sharpening their reflexes, ears, and minds.

In the 1940s at least seven musicians were among the men most responsible for making a revolution in jazz, ushering in a new sound and dimension that became known, scornfully at first, as bebop. These musicians were Charlie Parker, Dizzy Gillespie, Thelonious Monk, Bud Powell, Kenny Clarke, Max Roach, and Ray Brown. Bebop featured complex rhythms and harmonies and highlighted improvisation. Gillespie (1917–1993) said that Kansas City–born Charlie "Yardbird" and then just "Bird" Parker (1920–1955) was "the architect of the style."

Bebop met resistance from white America. The nation was about to enter World War II and was too preoccupied to switch from the big band swing ballroom dancing music to bebop. Moreover, because jazzmen played in small, intimate clubs, not big bands, they had more freedom from the expectations of white society. Bebop music was of such enduring quality, however, that it shaped the contours of American popular culture and style for two generations. Before long, bebop became the principal musical language of jazz musicians around the world.

Bebop was a way of life and had its own attendant styles whose nuances depended on class status and, perhaps, age. Gillespie helped create one side of bebop style in dress, language, and demeanor. He began to wear dark glasses on stage to reduce the glare from lights after he had cataract surgery. He grew a goatee because shaving every day irritated his bottom lip. He wore pegged pants, jackets with wide lapels, and a beret when men were still wearing hats with brims. Other bebop musicians emulated and modified this attire. Beboppers also created their own slang, hip Black English that mingled colorful and obscene language. They challenged convention in other ways too, engaging in a freewheeling lifestyle that often included love across the color line. There was also a downside to bebop. Some musicians became drug addicts, engaged in parasitical relationships with women, and spent their money recklessly. Black working-class young men adopted their own style of talking and of hip dressing, reflected in their zoot suits and conked hair. Zoot suits featured high-waisted, baggy, pegged pants and long draped coats.

Bebop was the dominant black music of the war decade, but after 1945 returning veterans preferred a slower-paced music, simple love songs, and melodies. This contributed to bebop's waning and led to more transformations. All artistic innovation extracts a high price. Bebop was no exception. Many of the most talented musicians, like Billie Holiday, discussed later in this chapter, paid that price in lives decimated by drugs, poverty, sickness, and broken relationships. Few black musicians received the respect, recognition, and financial rewards from white America that their creativity warranted. Ultimately, white Americans wanted the art, but not the artists.

POPULAR CULTURE FOR THE MASSES: COMIC STRIPS, RADIO, AND MOVIES

The masses of African Americans participated in more accessible black popular culture outlets. Everyone needed relief from the bleakness and despair of the Depression years. Comic strips, radio programs, and movies were affordable forms of artistic creativity that allowed momentary escape. Newspapers were widely shared, passing from hand to hand, and whole families gathered around the radio for nightly programs of comedy and music. For black city dwellers, the movies offered momentary escape from poverty and want.

The Comics

African Americans quickly noted the difference between the fun that black people made of each other and the mockery white people made of them. These differences were reflected in tone, intent, and sympathetic versus derisive laughter. During the Depression, comic strips in newspapers and comic books featuring superheroes diverted millions of Americans. Comic strips in black newspapers entertained, but also affirmed, the values and ideals of black people. They portrayed humorous situations and elaborated tales of intrigue and action.

The Philadelphia *Independent*, a black paper, ran a serial in the 1930s called "The Jones Family." This strip, drawn by an editorial cartoonist named Branford, was a good example of the dual function of entertaining and affirming. The strip emphasized black people's desire for achievement and respectability. The plot centered around the young Jones boy's search for the "good life" of money, success, love, and a happy marriage. But at every turn he confronts a harsh environment. Unable to get a job because of the Depression, he becomes an outlaw and narrowly escapes jail. He is constantly "on the run" from oppression. His only consolations are his family and his beautiful, ever-faithful girlfriend.

"The Jones Family" illuminates the gray areas that most African Americans, regardless of their class, faced when attempting to live rational and coherent lives in the northern cities. Although they espoused and cherished middle-class values, they often had to live among poverty, crime, and racial oppression. The black comic strips sought to provide entertaining, nonjudgmental prescriptions and blueprints for middle-class life, but to more cynical and alienated black people they seemed to be promoting unattainable values and lifestyles.

Radio and Race

Although there were individual exceptions, during the Depression black performers in radio and film were marginalized, exploited, or excluded. Commercial radio operated to deliver an audience of white consumers to white advertisers, and it denied black people jobs as announcers, broadcast journalists, or technicians. White entertainers schooled in blackface minstrelsy portrayed black radio characters. The major labor unions involved in the entertainment side of the radio industry restricted membership to white people. Still—with its offerings of vaudeville, big bands, drama, and comedy—radio provided relief from the miseries of the Depression to all Americans, black as well as white.

The most popular comedy radio program in the early 1930s was *The Amos 'n' Andy Show*. The title roles were played by two white performers, Charles Correll and Freeman Gosden, who wrote and performed scripts laced with oxymorons and malapropisms. Skillful showmen, Correll and Gosden ingratiated themselves in Chicago's black community, appearing at parades and posing with black children. The Chicago *Defender* endorsed them and they received standing ovations at the Regal Theater in Chicago's black South Side. Part of the amusement they generated derived from their mispronounced words, garbled grammar, and their show's minstrel ambience. Each episode highlighted an improbable situation involving the black cab driver (Amos) and his gullible overweight friend (Andy). Other characters included the scheming con artist Kingfish, his overbearing wife Sapphire, and his domineering mother-in-law, Mama. The characters and their humor reinforced unflattering racial and gender stereotypes, but the show was not mean spirited. Some of the characters conducted themselves with dignity, modeling such positive values as marital fidelity, strong families, hard work, and economic independence.

Black audiences recognized the minstrel stereotyping in *Amos 'n' Andy*, yet many among them still enjoyed the show. A vocal component of the ever more sophisticated and urbanized black population, however, complained that this show, and other radio programs, reinforced negative images—of black women as bossy Sapphires or Mammies and black men as childish clowns—in the nation's consciousness. Educator and activist Nannie Helen Burroughs considered the show demeaning. Robert L. Vann, editor of the Pittsburgh *Courier*, argued that it exploited African Americans for white commercial gain. Vann sponsored a petition to the Federal Communications Commission to ban the show, but his efforts were futile. By the 1940s *The Amos 'n' Andy*

Show was less popular. In the early 1950s, it had a brief life as a television series, this time with black actors.

For almost two decades, *Amos 'n' Andy* was the only depiction of black people on the nation's airwaves. Its negative stereotypes of African Americans buttressed white people's notions of their own superiority. The show never demonstrated how the characters' race affected their lives or the psychological or economic costs of racism. It taught white America that it was permissible to laugh at striving black men and women.

The best-known and most successful African American on network radio in the late 1930s was Eddie Anderson, who played Jack Benny's sidekick Rochester in NBC's *The Jack Benny Show*. Like the characters in *Amos 'n' Andy*, Anderson's character reinforced negative racial stereotypes. Anderson rationalized his role in a way that suggests discomfort with it:

> I don't see why certain characters are called stereotypes. The Negro characters being presented are not labeling the Negro race any more than "Luigi" is labeling the Italian people as a whole. The same goes for "Beulah," who is not playing the part of thousands of Negroes, but only the part of one person, "Beulah." They're not saying here is the portrait of the Negro, but here is "Beulah."

Race, Representation, and the Movies

In the 1930s and 1940s—after the introduction of sound in motion pictures—black and white producers began to make what were known as race films for African-American audiences. Except for these race films, white film executives, since the beginning of the film industry, had cast black men and women in roles designed to comfort, reassure, and entertain white audiences. Continuing this trend, African Americans in Hollywood movies of the 1930s were usually cast in servile roles and often portrayed as buffoons. For example, the first black actor to receive major billing in American films, Stepin Fetchit (1902–1985, born Lincoln Theodore Monroe Perry), purportedly earned $2 million in ten years playing a cringingly servile, dim-witted, slow-moving character.

Black performers appeared as servants in many other box office successes during the Depression era. Among them were Gertrude Howard and Libby Taylor, who played servants to Mae West's characters in *I'm No Angel* (1933) and *Belle of the Nineties* (1934). In *Imitation of Life* (1934), Louise Beavers played a black servant whose light-skinned daughter, played by Fredi Washington, tries to pass for white. The black tap dancer and stage performer Bill "Bojangles" Robinson was featured in four popular films—*The Little Colonel* (1935), *The Littlest Rebel* (1935), *Just around the Corner* (1938), and *Rebecca of Sunnybrook Farm* (1938)—as a servant to white child star Shirley Temple.

The film that most firmly cemented the role of black Americans as servants in the American consciousness was *Gone With the Wind* (1939). Hattie McDaniel and Butterfly McQueen were the black "stars" in this epic adaptation of Margaret Mitchell's romanticized literary salute to the Old South. McDaniel had played servant or "Mammy" roles throughout the 1930s. The image of Mammy, the headscarf-wearing, obese, dutiful black woman who preferred nurturing white families to caring for her own children, appealed to white America. But in *Gone With the Wind*, McDaniel gave the performance of a lifetime and in 1940 became the first African American to win an Oscar. Many in the black community criticized her for playing "female Tom" roles. Defensively, McDaniel retorted she would rather play a maid and earn $700 a week than be one and earn only $7 a week. Some black actors such as McDaniel, dismayed by their relegation to demeaning roles, formed the Fair Play Committee (FPC) to lobby the white-dominated movie industry for more substantial roles, to get rid of dialect speech, and to ban the term *nigger* from the screen. But in the *Beulah* radio show, which premiered in 1947, McDaniel again played a wise but subservient maid who provides the family that employs her with advice, guidance, and direction.

Eventually, during and after World War II, Hollywood developed more sophisticated race-directed movies. Of particular significance was the positive, even romanticized, portrayal of black Americans in a movie financed by the War Department to gain support among African Americans for the U.S. role in World War II. *The Negro Soldier*, directed by Frank Capra in 1944, played to vast audiences of enthusiastic black people. But even before the *The Negro Soldier*, some motion pictures had displayed African Americans positively. Paul Robeson made two movies, *The Emperor Jones* (1933) and *Show Boat* (1936), in which he attempted to change how black men and women were represented on screen. Robeson's films, however, were not box office successes, and he left the United States to pursue his career in Europe. There his commitment to communism and leftist politics made him a target of the anticommunist hysteria that gripped the United States as the Cold War took hold in the late 1940s (see Chapter 20).

To succeed commercially, African-American filmmakers had to disguise their dissent or create art purely for other black people. One of the most enterprising black filmmakers, Oscar Micheaux (1884–1951), made films aimed primarily at the black public, a group that Hollywood directors and producers of race movies ignored or insulted with stereotypical representations. Unlike the dominant Hollywood stereotypes, the black men and women in Micheaux's films were often educated, cultured, and prosperous. Micheaux endowed black Americans with cinematic voice and subjectivity. His films featured middle-class or identity issues such as "passing for white."

Micheaux produced more than thirty feature films between 1919 and 1948. In 1932, he released *The Exile*, the first sound motion picture to be made by, with, and for black Americans. The following year he produced *Veiled Aristocrats*, about passing for white among Chicago's black professional class. The characters in the film are considered "aristocrats" because they are descended from the white gentry of the Old South and Europe; they are "veiled" because of their color.

Micheaux tried to transform Hollywood without changing it, much as members of the black bourgeoisie struggled to be included in American society. His films capture the dilemma of black double consciousness. Black culture existed within and was shaped by, while simultaneously transforming, American culture. To the degree that black Americans had been assimilated, white American culture was their culture as well.

The white ethnic immigrants who created Hollywood were determined to help marginal and excluded groups like Jews and Italians assimilate into the American mainstream. Hollywood sought to create the illusion that these groups belonged to the power elite. However, these Hollywood entrepreneurs did not do the same for African Americans. Their films during the Depression represented black people as unassimilable. A small cadre of black filmmakers and actors created independent films and showed them in cinema houses exclusively for black patrons. Following the lead of pioneers like Micheaux, they created an alternative cinema in which they introduced nuanced and fully human characters.

THE BLACK CHICAGO RENAISSANCE

Black culture flourished during the 1930s and 1940s, decades otherwise noted for economic depression and global warfare. African-American musicians thrived in cities as far from Harlem as Kansas City (Missouri), Dallas, Denver, and Oklahoma City. They created a southwestern style of jazz with blues inflection. Jazz pianist Mary Lou Williams (1910–1981) worked in Kansas City during the 1930s. She recalled, "I found Kansas City to be a heavenly city—music everywhere in the Negro section of town, and fifty or more cabarets rocking on Twelfth and Eighteenth Streets." The southwestern musical style rivaled the West Coast jazz scene (that often included black and Latino musicians) that radiated from Los Angeles to Portland, Seattle, San Francisco, and Oakland, and reached as far as Honolulu and found patrons in such Asian cities as Yokohama in Japan, Shanghai and Hong Kong on the coast of China, and Manila in the Philippines.

But in many respects, Chicago was the center of black culture during the 1930s and 1940s. In contrast to some of the artists of the "Harlem Renaissance," the leading writers in Chicago harbored no illusions that art would solve the problems caused by white supremacy and black subordination. Although a western regional literary aesthetic did not emerge during these decades, a middle western renaissance did flourish. The Chicago writers of the 1930s and 1940s emphasized the idea that black art had to combine aesthetics and function. It had to serve the cause of black freedom.

Arna Bontemps (1902–1973) was to the Chicago Renaissance what Alain Locke had been to the Harlem Renaissance. Born in Louisiana, Bontemps migrated in 1935 from California to Chicago where he met Richard Wright and joined the South Side Writers Group, which Wright founded in 1936. After 1935 his novels and short stories reflected a militant restlessness and revolutionary spirit. In 1936 he published *Black Thunder* about the nineteenth-century slave conspiracy led by Gabriel and in 1939 *Drums at Dusk* about the Haitian Revolution and Toussaint L'Ouverture (1746–1803). Richard Wright's writings also celebrated resistance, but with more nuance. He published *Uncle Tom's Children* in 1938 and his masterpiece, *Native Son*, in 1940.

Among the artists who launched their careers on WPA funds were Margaret Walker and Willard Motley. Walker attracted widespread attention when her collected poems appeared as the book *For My People* in the Yale Series of Younger Poets. Willard Motley worked with a radio group while writing his powerful novel *Knock on Any Door* (1947), which depicted the transformation of an Italian-American altar boy into a criminal headed for the electric chair. The novel invited comparisons with Wright's *Native Son*.

Before the 1930s several black intellectuals misjudged the potential of Chicago to become a vibrant center of black culture. In the late 1920s, black social scientists Charles S. Johnson and E. Franklin Frazier expressed disdain for black Chicago's artistic and intellectual prospects. Frazier proclaimed that "Chicago has no intelligentsia," and in 1923 Johnson asked rhetorically,

> Who can write of lilies and sunsets in the pungent shadows of the stockyards? . . . It is no dark secret why literary societies fail, where there are no Art exhibits or libraries about, why periodicals presuming upon an I.Q. above the age of 12 are not read, why so little literature comes out of the city. No, the kingdom of the second ward [the black neighborhood] has no self-sustaining intelligentsia, and a miserably poor acquaintance with that of the world surrounding it.

Johnson did, however, admit that Chicago had "perhaps, the best musical school in the race, as these go."

Johnson and Frazier were too harsh. Just as Chicago's industrial economy attracted working-class black people, it also nurtured artists who drew inspiration from and reflected this stratum of moving and striving, strolling and styling black people who wanted to transgress class and geographical lines. These working-class people aspired to enjoy the middle-class life of accomplishment and consumption. A critical pulse point on Chicago's South Side came to be known as Bronzeville. It measured and reflected the reality of the lives of ordinary working-class people. As Harlem had its 125th Street, Chicago had 35th and State Street and 47th and South Park (now Martin Luther King Jr. Drive).

Chicago was heir to the Harlem Renaissance. In 1930 Langston Hughes published *Not without Laughter*, the first major novel about the black experience in Chicago. Hughes moved to the city himself in 1941 and wrote often for the widely read Chicago *Defender*. The city epitomized urban industrial America. As the northern terminus of the Illinois Central Railroad and the home of the *Defender*, it had long attracted displaced agricultural workers from the southern cotton fields, and by 1930 it had a black population of 233,903. The migrants arrived eager to absorb Chicago's hard-driving blues and jazz culture.

During the 1920s a discernible class structure among African Americans emerged in Chicago, fueled in part by the new migrants. These men and women expanded the consumer base and gave rise to a cadre of educated professionals and entrepreneurs who developed an appreciation for the arts. Chicago's South Side, became a black city within a city. Black businesses, such as banks and insurance companies, formed the financial foundation. Entrepreneur Walter L. Lee started Your Cab Company and each day put on the streets a half-dozen chauffeur-uniformed drivers of vehicles. In the late 1940s, John Johnson would launch a publishing empire with such magazines as *Negro Digest, Jet*, and *Ebony*. These businesses depended on black support. It was in their best interest to support the arts.

Chicago was a pioneering center both for recording and performing music. As black music became a commodity, influential black disk jockeys like Al Benson appeared on radio in Chicago. Benson proved to be as skilled a businessman as he was a cultural impresario.

Art and Culture Gallery II

Archibald Motley, Jr., *Barbecue*, 1934. Oil on canvas, 36 ¼" x 40 ⅞". The Howard University Gallery of Art, Washington, D.C. Photo: Jarvis Grant/Howard University.

Archibald Motley (1891–1981) was raised in Chicago where his father was a Pullman employee active in the Brotherhood of Sleeping Car Porters. Motley attended the Art Institute of Chicago and graduated in 1918. In works like *Barbecue*, painted in 1934 when he was employed by a New Deal arts program, Motley vividly captured the exuberance and vitality of nightlife in Chicago's Bronzeville.

Augusta Savage, *Gamin*, 1929, Plaster, 9 ¼" x 6" x 3 ½". Photo Manu Sassoonian. Schomburg Center for Research in Black Culture, Art & Artifacts Division, The New York Public Library, Astor, Lenox and Tilden Foundations.

As the child of an impoverished preacher near Jacksonville, Florida, Augusta Savage (1892–1962) learned to shape clay figures into farm animals. She eventually moved to New York City and furthered her artistic education at Cooper Union. In 1923 she was rejected for a summer school program in Paris because French officials feared her presence might offend Southern white students. During the New Deal she was an active teacher and administrator with the Works Progress Administration. Only a small number of her works survive. The model for *Gamin* (1929) was a boy from Savage's Harlem neighborhood.

William H. Johnson (1901–1970) was born and raised in Florence, North Carolina. He moved to New York at the age of seventeen and put himself through art school on his earnings as a stevedore. Gaining recognition from his teachers as a young artist of great promise, he moved to Europe in 1926 to pursue his career. Fleeing the growing Nazi menace on the eve of World War II, he returned to New York with his Danish wife in 1938. In his later paintings, including *Lamentation or Descent from the Cross*, (1944), he adopted a flat, deliberately "primitive" style and began documenting African-American life and religion.

Every American is familiar with the work of Selma Burke (1900–1995) without knowing it. She created the profile of President Franklin D. Roosevelt that appears on the Roosevelt dime. Burke's original bronze plaque of the president—which the U.S. mint relied on when it designed the coin—was made for the Recorder of Deeds Building in Washington in 1945. Born in Mooresville, North Carolina, Burke earned a master of fine arts degree from Columbia University. *Jim*, an undated work, captures the quiet dignity of its subject.

Jacob Lawrence. *The Migration of the Negro Panel No. 1*. 1940–1941. Tempera on masonite 12" x 18". (30.5 x 45.7 cm). Acquired 1942. The Phillips Collection, Washington, D.C.

Though he quit high school and had little artistic training, Jacob Lawrence (born 1917) emerged as one of the most prominent artists of the twentieth century. During the Depression he attended a Works Progress Administration art program in Harlem administered by Augusta Savage. Lawrence was fascinated by black history and enjoyed storytelling. *Migration of the Negro, Panel 1* (1940–1941) is the first of 60 panels documenting the migration of black Southerners to the North.

Romare Bearden, *Watching the Trains Go By*, 1964. Photograph by Sharon Goodman. ©Romare Bearden Foundation/Licensed by VAGA, New York, NY.

Romare Bearden, (1911–1988) a self-taught artist, grew up in Charlotte, North Carolina. In photomontages like *Watching the Trains Go By* (1964), he celebrated rural black folk traditions and rituals. "I use the train," Bearden explained, "as a symbol of the other civilization—the white civilization and its encroachment upon the lives of blacks. The train was always something that could take you away and could also bring you to where you were. And in the little towns it's the black people who live near the trains."

Elizabeth Catlett (born 1919) grew up in Washington, DC. Her father died before she was born, leaving her mother to support three children. Catlett studied art at Howard University. After a brief stint as a high school teacher she attended graduate school at the University of Iowa. *Malcolm X Speaks For Us* (1969), a linoleum block print, is part of her series on African-American heroes.

Steve Prince (born 1968) draws on themes from black history in his work. *Noble Sounds* (1995), addresses the issues of black identity and gender relations within the context of domination and resistance. "The three central characters represent dispossessed populations of the diaspora," Prince explains. "Their mental, physical, and spiritual power is unleashed as they remove the mask that grins and lies" while they dance in front of a white house, symbolic of the master's house on a plantation, with menacing white-hooded figures in the windows.

Jazz in Chicago

Within the confines of the South Side of Chicago, black musical giants, such as trumpeter Louis Armstrong (1898–1971) and his wife, Lillian Hardin Armstrong (1898–1971), a well-known and respected jazz pianist, performed and nurtured a distinct jazz culture. "Lil" Armstrong was born in Memphis, Tennessee, and received formal music training at Fisk University, the Chicago College of Music, and the New York College of Music. "Lil" Hardin Armstrong led her own band and was talented at arranging, composing, and singing. She and Louis Armstrong were married in 1924. Lil Armstrong eventually encouraged her husband to leave King Oliver's Creole Jazz Band and to join Fletcher Henderson in New York. The Armstrongs were divorced in 1938. She continued her recording career with Decca records under the name Lil Hardin.

Duke Ellington in his autobiography, *Music Is My Mistress*, remarked,

> Chicago always sounded like the most glamorous place in the world to me when I heard the guys in Frank Holliday's poolroom talking about their travels.... They told very romantic tales about nightlife on the South Side. By the time I got there in 1930, it glittered even more ... the Loop, the cabarets ... city life, suburban life, luxurious neighborhoods—and the apparently broken-down neighborhoods where there were more good times than any place in the city.

At this point Ellington was recording some of his best jazz, such as *Mood Indigo* (1930) and *Ko-Ko* (1940).

The seeds that blossomed into full-bodied jazz culture were planted across America at the turn of the century. The most famous musicians, however, all went to or passed through Chicago. As the Chicago Jazz Age came into its own, the beguiling tune *Pretty Baby* became the city's theme song. It was written by Tony Jackson, whom Jelly Roll Morton (the self-proclaimed "inventor of jazz") called "maybe the best entertainer the world has ever seen." The South Side, specifically along State Street between 31st and 35th, was the beating heart of the city's Jazz Age. Although Chicago did not replace New York as the major location for the aspiring jazz musician, it was the place you went to prove you had what it took to make a name for yourself.

Gospel in Chicago: Thomas Dorsey

The term *gospel* designates the traditional religious music of the black church. It was nurtured and flourished in Chicago's churches. Gospel music became the backbone of urban and contemporary black religion and is deeply entrenched in worship. The use of instruments—tambourines, drums, pianos, horns, guitars, and Hammond organs—characterizes gospel and distinguishes it from the earlier spiritual and black folk music. During the 1930s and 1940s, it developed its own idioms and performance techniques.

In Chicago, Thomas Dorsey (1899–1993)—one of Chicago's leading composers of the blues since the mid-1920s—was most responsible for developing black urban gospel. Dorsey's genius lay in his ability to synthesize elements of the blues with religious hymns to create a gospel blues. His gospel pieces, performed with a ragtime-derived, boogie-woogie piano accompaniment, radiated an urban religious spirit. In 1930 Dorsey gained widespread attention when gospel singer Willie Mae Ford Smith

(1904–1994) performed his "If You See My Savior, Tell Him That You Saw Me" at the National Baptist Convention meeting in Chicago. Two years later, in 1932, Dorsey's place in musical history was assured when Theodore Frye, with Dorsey at the piano, performed in the Ebenezer Baptist Church in Chicago his now classic gospel song, "Take My Hand, Precious Lord." The song had a profound impact on gospel performers and their audiences. Dorsey's abundant works provided a foundation for shout worship in the urban Protestant churches formed by transplanted black Southerners in the 1930s and succeeding decades.

One of the greatest gospel singers, Chicago-based Mahalia Jackson (1911–1972), sang and promoted Dorsey's songs all over the country on the church circuit and at religious conventions between 1939 and 1944. Jackson once said of the music, "Gospel songs are the songs of hope. When you sing them you are delivered of your burden." During the Depression and World War II, gospel became big business.

Chicago in Dance and Song: Katherine Dunham and Billie Holiday

The influence of the WPA in Chicago was especially reflected in dance. Dance has always been an integral part of African-American life, and the dances of black people have always been important in the American theater. The first performances by black dancers given within and taken seriously by the concert dance world occurred in the 1930s. The first "Negro Dance Recital in America" was performed in 1931 by the New Negro Art Theater Dance Company, co-founded by Edna Buy and Hemsley Winfield. In that same year, Katherine Dunham (1909–) founded the Negro Dance Group in Chicago, which survived thanks to WPA support. As Dunham later recalled, "Black dancers were not allowed to take classes in studios in the '30s. I started a school because there was no place for blacks to study dance. I was the first to open the way for black dancers and I was the first to form a black dance company."

Dunham was unique. Trained in anthropology, she studied African-based ritual dance in the Caribbean. In 1938 her troupe stunned an audience with the sexual vitality of its performance of one of her works. When the company, now renamed the Katherine Dunham Dance Company, performed in February 1940, audiences and critics were awed. The *New York Times* declared:

> Her performance with her group at the Windsor Theater may very well become a historic occasion, for certainly never before in all efforts of recent years to establish the Negro dance as a serious medium has there been so convincing and authoritative approach. . . . The potential greatness of the Negro dance lies in its discovery of its own roots and the crucial nursing of them into growth and flower. . . . It is because she has showed herself to have both the objective quality of the student and the natural instinct of the artist that she has done such a truly important job.

What kept audiences returning to Dunham dance performances, however, was the dancer's bold sensuality. A reviewer of *Tropical Revue*, for example, wrote that it was "Tempestuous and torrid, raffish and revealing." The *New York Sun* marveled, "Shoulders, midsections and posteriors went round and round. Particularly when the cynosure was Miss Dunham, the vista was full of pulchritude."

One of America's premier dance artists, the internationally acclaimed Katherine Dunham (1909–) performed in the Bobli Gardens in Florence, Italy, in 1950. A talented choreographer, anthropologist, and writer, Dunham founded one of the first black dance companies. She was an outspoken critic of Jim Crow segregation.
© David Lees/Corbis/Bettmann

The success in New York led to film offers. The producers of the all-black musical extravaganza *Cabin in the Sky* hired the dance troupe and gave the feature role of Georgia Brown to Dunham. The role gave Dunham, as the *Times* dance critic wrote, the chance "to sizzle." But it also undermined her seriousness, allowing white audiences to view her as the stereotypical sultry black sexpot.

In 1943 Dunham moved to New York and opened the Katherine Dunham School of Arts and Research, which trained artists not only in dance, but in theater, literature, and world cultures.

Dunham was not afraid to protest racial segregation, even though it hurt her popularity. In the early 1940s, she denounced discrimination. In 1944 in Louisville, Kentucky, after a performance, Dunham announced, "We are glad we have made you happy. We hope you have enjoyed us. This is the last time I shall play Louisville because the management refuses to let people like us sit by people like you. Maybe after the war we shall have democracy and I can return." Dunham was a gifted and talented pioneer in dance who underscored the responsibility that a black artist had to the black community to fight racism.

Billie Holiday (1915–1959), another great performer whose career took shape during the Depression, also used her art to challenge the oppression of black people. Holiday, popularly known as "Lady Day," began singing at age fifteen and was discovered three years later by John Hammond, a Chicago jazz producer and promoter. In 1934 she made her debut at the Apollo Theater in Harlem. An incomparable singer known for subtle and artful improvisation, she left a wealth of recordings.

BLACK GRAPHIC ART

Chicago artists, such as Charles White, Elizabeth Catlett, and Eldzier Cortor, and Harlem's Jacob Lawrence, celebrated both rural and urban working-class black people while implicitly criticizing the racial hierarchy of power and privilege. Their art belonged to the social realism school that flourished in the United States in the 1930s. Social realist art was intensely ideological. It strove to fuse propaganda—both left wing and right wing—to art to make it socially and politically relevant.

As the Depression worsened, black artists became even more determined to use their art to portray the crisis in capitalism. This involved depicting social and racial inequality. Chicago's Charles White wrote that "paint is the only weapon I have with which to fight what I resent. If I could write I would write about it. If I could talk I would talk about it. Since I paint, I must paint about it."

Defense Worker, a painting by Dox Thrash, reflects these concerns. Completed in 1942, just after the United States had entered World War II, it shows an isolated black worker looming over the horizon. The heroic proletarian imagery alludes to the dream of a racially integrated labor force, equal opportunity, and social reform in the wake of the New Deal and the sudden demand for labor triggered by the war.

The Harmon Foundation sponsored five juried exhibitions (1926–1931, 1933) of the work of black artists. The William E. Harmon Awards for Distinguished Achievement among Negroes celebrated black artists in the hope they would serve as role models for others. William E. Harmon, a real estate investor from Iowa, established the New York–based foundation in 1925. In the 1930s the WPA established art workshops and community art centers in black urban communities to teach art to neighborhood young people and provide work for artists. Sculptor Augusta Savage, as the first director of the Harlem Community Art Center, presided over more than 1,500 students enrolled in day and evening classes in drawing, painting, sculpture, printmaking, and design. Among the teachers was Selma Burke (1900–1995), who sculpted the relief of Franklin D. Roosevelt that appears on the dime.

One of the initiatives of the Federal Arts Project, another New Deal agency, was to sponsor the creation of murals in public buildings, such as post offices and schools, that celebrated American ideals. Murals by black artists celebrated the heritage, contributions to society, and struggles of African Americans.

Douglas and other black artists pressed the WPA to appoint more African Americans to its local boards and to hire them for more projects. The Harlem Artists Guild and the Arts and Crafts Guild in Chicago provided forums where black artists could meet and plan strategies to foster the visual arts and support the social and political issues that affected black people's lives.

BLACK LITERATURE

Black literature, like black art, has been assessed in terms of what it reveals about the social, cultural, and political landscape at a given historical moment. The most distinguishing feature of black literature may be the way that black writers have attempted to create spaces of freedom in their work, to liberate place, a trait that also marks black religious culture and folk cultural practices, such as storytelling. Black literature, like all black cultural production, is valued both for aesthetic reasons on its own and for the way it represents the struggles of black people to attain freedom. In their work black writers in the 1930s and 1940s felt obliged to address questions of identity and to define and describe urban life to the dispossessed and impoverished black migrants to the cities. They tried to delineate the dimensions of a shared American heritage by portraying the specific contributions that African Americans had made to American society. Finally, and perhaps most ambitiously, black writers explored the issue of the rights African Americans were entitled to as Americans and the demands they could and should make on the state and society.

Richard Wright's *Native Son*

In 1940 Richard Wright (1908–1960) published *Native Son*, the first of many important novels by Depression-generation black authors. Reviewers hailed it as "the new American tragedy." Its tale of the downfall of the young Bigger Thomas could be read as a warning about how economic hardship combined with segregation and discrimination could lead young black men to lash out in violence and rage. Setting out for an interview for a job as a chauffeur, Bigger meets with his neighborhood friends who want him to help them rob a grocery store. Bigger's fear of whites prevents him from going along. Instead, he picks a fight to camouflage his fear and avoid committing the crime. Bigger gets the chauffeur's job, which requires him to drive the wealthy Dalton family. On his first assignment, he is supposed to drive young Mary Dalton to a university lecture. But she talks him into picking up her boyfriend, Jan—a communist—and taking them to a restaurant in the black neighborhood. Jan and Mary are oblivious to the offensively patronizing way they treat Bigger. After dinner Bigger drives them around the city while they drink and make love in the back seat.

When Jan leaves, Bigger takes an intoxicated Mary home. Because Mary is too drunk to walk, Bigger carries her to her room and is putting her to bed when blind Mrs. Dalton comes to check on her daughter. Bigger panics. He covers Mary's head with a pillow to keep her quiet. When Mrs. Dalton leaves, Bigger discovers he has inadvertently smothered Mary. He then burns her body in the basement furnace. Not fully grasping what he has done, Bigger writes a ransom note signed with a phony name to make it seem that Mary has been kidnapped. When Mary's remains are discovered, Bigger flees. Fearing she might betray him, Bigger then murders his girlfriend, Bessie. Bigger is captured, tried, and condemned. The remainder of the novel explores the hysteria and bigotry that envelop the case, the harsh criminal justice system, the insensitivity of the Communist Party, which seeks to exploit Bigger's plight, and the poverty and social ills that plagued Chicago's African-American communities during the Depression.

At the center of the drama is Wright's exploration of how Bigger comes to terms with his murder of Mary and Bessie. In conversations with Max, his communist lawyer, he realizes his irrational fear of white people had caused him to kill the two women. Bigger realizes he was in fact a product of his experiences in the ghetto. At the end of the novel he says, "What I killed for I am."

Wright's novel poignantly and chillingly thrust the impact of urbanization and racism on black men and women into the collective consciousness of the American people. One white critic declared, "Speaking from the black wrath of retribution, Wright insisted that

Richard Wright (1908–1960), the first black writer to commandeer serious attention in mainstream American literature. In *Native Son* (1940) and *Black Boy* (1945) Richard Wright provided incisive critiques of American racism. He received support from the Federal Writers Project and in his early works he poignantly portrayed the pathos of black southern migrants to the urban industrial north.
Courtesy of the Library of Congress

history can be punishment. He told us the one thing even the most liberal whites preferred not to hear: that Negroes were far from patient or forgiving, that they were scarred by fear, that they hated every moment of their suppression even when seeming most acquiescent, and that often enough they hated us the decent and cultivated white men who from complicity or neglect shared in the responsibility of their plight."

In his closing arguments, the lawyer, Max, describes the psychological conditions that led Bigger to kill and warns of the destructive potential of suppressed black rage:

> The hate and fear which we have inspired in him, woven by our civilization into the very structure of his consciousness and into his blood and bones, into the hourly functioning of his personality, have become the justification of his existence. . . . Kill him and swell the tide of pent up lava that will some day break loose, not in a single, blundering crime, but in a wild cataract of emotion that will brook no control.

Native Son was an immediate success. It became a Book-of-the-Month Club selection and has sold millions of copies.

James Baldwin Challenges Wright

Wright's influence on American literature has been immense. He was the first African-American writer to enjoy an international reputation and showed that success and militancy were not mutually exclusive. A younger generation of black writers, however, especially James Baldwin (1924–1987), took issue with Wright. African Americans, they argued, need not all be portrayed as hapless victims of American racism. In a famous short essay, "Everybody's Protest Novel," in 1949, Baldwin argued that Bigger's tragedy was not that he was black, poor, and scared, but that he had accepted "a theology that denies him life, that he admits the possibility of his being sub-human and feels constrained, therefore, to battle for his humanity according to those brutal criteria bequeathed him at his birth." Baldwin concluded, "The failure of the protest novel lies in its rejection of life, the human being, the denial of his beauty, dread, power, in its insistence that it is his categorization alone which is real and which cannot be transcended." In turn, Wright accused Baldwin of trying to destroy his reputation and of betraying all African-American writers who wrote protest literature. "What do you mean, protest!" Wright demanded. "All literature is protest. You can't name a single novel that isn't protest."

Baldwin answered Wright in a second essay in 1951 entitled, "Many Thousand Gone." "Wright's work," Baldwin declared, "is most clearly committed to the social struggle. . . . [T]hat artist is strangled who is forced to deal with human beings solely in social terms; and who has, moreover, as Wright had, the necessity thrust on him of being the representative of some thirteen million people. It is a false responsibility (since writers are not congressmen) and impossible, by its nature, of fulfillment."

The controversy ended the budding friendship between Wright and Baldwin. Baldwin, whose work would soon include many powerful and revealing novels and insightful essays, inherited the mantle of "best-known black American male writer." (See Chapter 22.)

Ralph Ellison and *Invisible Man*

The most intricate novel about the black experience in America written during this era was Ralph Ellison's (1914–1994) *Invisible Man*, which won the National Book Award for fiction in 1952. Partially autobiographical, it traces the life of a young black man from his early years in a southern school (a thinly disguised Tuskegee Institute) through his migration to New York City. The novel explores class tensions within American society and within the black community. It illuminates the interaction between white and black Americans with a balanced incisive perspective.

Although he wrote many essays, *Invisible Man* was Ellison's only completed novel. He argued that the black tradition teaches one "to deflect racial provocation and to master and control pain. . . . It is a tradition which abhors as obscene any trading on one's own anguish for gain or sympathy. . . . It takes fortitude to be a man and no less to be an artist. Perhaps it takes even more if the black man would be an artist." He concluded, "It would seem to me, therefore, that the question of how the 'sociology of his existence' presses upon the Negro writer's work depends upon how much of his life the individual writer is able to transform into art."

Echoing Du Bois's now classic characterization of the "twoness" of the African-American character, Ellison observed, "[Black people] are an American people who are geared to what is and who yet are driven by a sense of what it is possible for human life to be in this society."

AFRICAN AMERICANS IN SPORTS

It is in the arena of professional sports that black Americans have demonstrated what human life can achieve when unconstrained by racism. The experiences of black men and women in American sports are a microcosm of their lives in American society. The

AFRICAN-AMERICAN MILESTONES IN SPORTS	
1934	The Negro National League is revived.
1936	Jesse Owens wins four gold medals at Berlin Olympics.
1937	Joe Louis defeats James J. Braddock to win world heavyweight title. The Negro American League is formed.
1938	Joe Louis defeats the German Max Schmeling.
1947	Jackie Robinson signs with the Brooklyn Dodgers to become the first black major-league baseball player. Dodgers win the National League Pennant.
1948	Alice Coachman wins a gold medal in the high jump to become the first black woman Olympic champion.
	Larry Doby joins the Cleveland Indians, becoming the first black player in the American League.
	Brooklyn Dodgers hire their second black player, Roy Campanella.
1949	Jackie Robinson wins the National League's Most Valuable Player Award.

privileges whites enjoyed in sports in this era paralleled the disadvantages and exclusions that were a constant part of black life. In the 1930s two black athletes, Jesse Owens and Joe Louis, captured the world's attention and inspired African Americans with pride, hope, and pleasure.

Jesse Owens and Joe Louis

Jesse Owens (1913–1980) was born on an Alabama sharecropping farm but grew up in Cleveland, Ohio. A talented runner, he studied at Ohio State University and prepared for the 1936 Olympics, which were to be held in Berlin, the capital of Nazi Germany. Many African-American leaders objected to participating in the games because they believed this would help legitimate the Nazi myth of the superiority of the so-called Aryan race. Owens participated to debunk that myth and he succeeded, becoming the first Olympian ever to win four gold medals. Although Hitler left the stadium to avoid congratulating Owens, his snub meant little to African Americans who relished Owens's victory over racism.

Joe Louis Barrow (1914–1981), like Owens, was the son of Alabama sharecroppers. His family migrated to Detroit, Michigan, when he was twelve. Although his mother wanted him to be a violinist, Joe Louis—he dropped the name Barrow—had other interests. As a youth, Louis displayed impressive boxing ability and won a string of local victories. In 1935 he faced former heavyweight champion Primo Carnera. A record crowd of 62,000 attended the fight in New York. The fight had political overtones. Louis was fighting an Italian-American at a time when Benito Mussolini, the Fascist dictator of Italy, was about to invade Ethiopia; this was the oldest black independent nation in Africa, whose ruler, Emperor Haile Selassie, many black Americans admired. Louis beat Carnera in the sixth round.

Louis held the world heavyweight title from 1937 to 1949.

Breaking the Color Barrier in Baseball

Although African Americans were integrated in track and in boxing, professional base-ball remained strictly segregated until after World War II. Despite the hardships of the Depression, however, virtually every major black community tried to field its own base-ball team. The Negro National League, which had folded in 1932, was revived in 1934, and a second league, the Negro American League, formed in 1937. Many of the play-ers in the Negro leagues, including such legends as Josh Gibson, Satchel Paige, Leon Day, and Cool Papa Bell, would have equaled or excelled their white counterparts in the major leagues, but, except for Paige, they never had the chance.

In 1947, however, major-league baseball, which had been a white man's game since the departure of Fleetwood Walker in 1887, became integrated again when Jackie Robinson (1919–1972) signed to play with the Brooklyn Dodgers. In 1945 Branch Rickey, the general manager of the Dodgers, decided to sign a black ball player to improve the Dodgers' chances of winning the National League pennant and the World Series. After scouting the Negro Leagues, he signed twenty-six-year-old Jackie Robinson.

Robinson was the ideal choice. He was a superb athlete and a man of fortitude and immense determination. Born in Georgia and raised in southern California, he had been an All-American running back in football at UCLA and then had played baseball for the legendary Kansas City Monarchs of the Negro leagues. Robinson was also com-mitted to black people and racial progress. Robinson played the 1946 season for the Brooklyn Dodgers minor-league team in Montreal where he and his wife Rachel were warmly received by the Canadians. But spring training in segregated Florida was diffi-cult to endure.

Jackie Robinson (1919–1972) broke baseball's color barrier when he joined the Brooklyn Dodgers in 1947. He silently endured considerable hostility and threats from angry white citizens.
Corbis/Bettmann

Robinson broke the color barrier when he opened at first base for the Dodgers in April 1947. Taunted, ridiculed, and threatened by some spectators and players, he responded by playing spectacular baseball. He won the Rookie of the Year honors in 1947, and the Dodgers won the National League pennant. Robinson retired in 1957 but remained outspoken on racial issues until his death from diabetes in 1972.

In July 1947 Larry Doby became the first black player in the American League when he joined the Cleveland Indians. As other major-league teams also signed black players, the once-popular Negro Leagues withered.

BLACK RELIGIOUS CULTURE

Just as black religion was the "invisible institution" that helped African Americans survive slavery, the black church was the visible institution that helped hundreds of thousands of migrants adjust to urban life while affirming an enduring set of core values consisting of freedom, justice, equality, and an African heritage. There was of course, no single "black church." The term is a shorthand way of referring to a pluralistic collection of institutions, including most prominently seven independent, historic, and black-controlled denominations: the African Methodist Episcopal Church, the African Methodist Episcopal Zion Church; the Christian Methodist Episcopal Church; The National Baptist Convention, Incorporated; the National Baptist Convention of America, Unincorporated; the Progressive National Baptist Convention; and the Church of God in Christ. Together, these denominations account for more than 80 percent of all black Christians.

The black church helped black workers make the transition from being southern peasants to being part of a northern urban proletariat. Yet the relationship between black religious tradition and the secular lives of black people was always changing. The blues and jazz performed in nightclubs were transformed into urban gospel music. Many of the nightclub musicians and singers received their training and first public performances in their churches. During the Depression, the black church helped black people survive by enabling them to pool their resources and by offering inspiration and spiritual consolation. Here we focus on alternative religious groups that became prominent during the 1930s and 1940s and addressed specific needs growing out of the Depression and the traumatic experience of relocating to alien and often hostile northern cities. Elijah Muhammad's Nation of Islam and Father Divine's Peace Mission Movement combined secular concerns with sacred beliefs. Both strengthened a sense of identity, affirmation, and community among their members.

The Nation of Islam

The Nation of Islam emerged in 1929, the year Timothy Drew died. Drew, who took the name Nobel Drew Ali, was founder of the Moorish Science Temple of America, which flourished in Chicago, Detroit, and other cities in the 1920s. After his death, a modified version of the Moorish Science Temple emerged in 1930 in Detroit. It was led by a mysterious door-to-door peddler of silks and other items that supposedly originated in Africa, known variously as Wallace D. Fard, Master Farad Muhammad, or Wali Farad. His teachings that black people were the true Muslims attracted many poor residents in Depression-era Detroit. In addition to the beliefs of Nobel Drew Ali, Fard's Nation of Islam also taught a mixture of Koranic principles, the Christian Bible, his own beliefs, and those of nationalist Marcus Garvey.

In 1934, after establishing a Temple of Islam, Fard disappeared, and one of his disciples, Elijah Poole (1897–1975), renamed Elijah Muhammad by Fard, became leader of the Detroit temple and then of a second temple in Chicago. The Nation attracted the attention of federal authorities during World War II when its members refused to serve in the military. Muhammad was arrested in May 1942 on charges of inciting his followers to resist the draft and was imprisoned in Milan, Michigan, until 1946. After his release he settled in Chicago and began to expand his movement.

The Nation of Islam taught that black people were the earth's original human inhabitants who had lived, according to Elijah Muhammad, in the Nile Valley. Approximately six thousand years ago, a magician named Yakub produced white people. These white people proved so troublesome that they were banished to Europe where they began to spread evil. Their worst crime was their enslavement of black people. Elijah Muhammad taught that white supremacy was ending and black people would rediscover their authentic history and culture. To prepare for the coming millennium, he instructed members to adhere to a code of behavior that included abstaining from many traditionally southern black foods, especially pork. Members subscribed to a family-centered culture in which women's role was to produce and rear the next generation. The Nation also demanded part of the South for a black national state.

Father Divine and the Peace Mission Movement

Father Major Jealous Divine (ca. 1877–1965) was born George Baker in Savannah. He captured attention in 1919 when he settled with twenty followers in Sayville, New York, and began what became known in the 1930s as the Peace Mission Movement. Divine secured domestic jobs for many of his followers on the surrounding estates and preached a gospel of hard work, honesty, sobriety, equality, and sexual abstinence. He provided free, or nearly free, meals and shelter for anyone who asked. In 1930 he changed his name to Father Divine. His Peace Movement espoused a racially neutral and economically empowering dogma that appealed to poor and needy black and white urbanites by offering them spiritual guidance and mental and physical healing. Hundreds of people traveled to see Father Divine on weekends, feast at his communal banquet table, and listen to his promises of heaven on earth.

In 1931 the police arrested Divine and eighty followers on charges of being a "public nuisance." Three days after a judge sentenced Divine to a year in jail and a $500 fine, the judge died of a heart attack. Divine was quoted as saying, "I hated to do it." The conviction was reversed, and Divine's reputation as a master of cosmic forces soared. Some of his followers now believed he was God. Aside from the belief in the divinity of Father Divine, members of the Peace Movement were drawn to the mission's strong emphasis on ending racial prejudice and economic inequalities.

In 1933 Divine moved his headquarters to Harlem, where his Peace Mission Movement prospered, eventually purchasing key real estate and housing projects called "heavens." His businesses enhanced Divine's ability to provide shelter, jobs, and incomes for his followers. He launched a journal entitled *New Day* in 1937 and used it to disseminate his teachings. Divine also protested social injustice and encouraged his followers to become politically engaged. Between 1936 and 1940, he lobbied strenuously for a federal antilynching law. At the time of Divine's death in 1965, the holdings of the Peace Mission were estimated to be worth $10 million. Father Divine's movement echoed the Protestant ethic: work hard, keep both your mind and body healthy; eat right; dress properly; keep good company; and avoid all manner of evil and vice.

T I M E L I N E

AFRICAN-AMERICAN EVENTS	NATIONAL EVENTS
1932	
1932 Thomas Dorsey's "Take My Hand, Precious Lord"	**1932** Franklin D. Roosevelt elected president
1933	
	1933 Approximately thirteen million Americans out of work
1934	
1935	
1935 Donald Murray and NAACP file suit to integrate University of Maryland School of Law	**1935** Committee for Industrial Organization (CIO) established; WPA created
1936	
1936 Jesse Owens wins four gold medals in the Berlin Olympics	
1937	
1937 Joe Louis becomes heavyweight champion; Katherine Dunham receives Guggenheim Award to investigate dance in Haiti, Jamaica, Trinidad, and Martinique	
1938	
	1938 CIO separates from the AFL

continued

AFRICAN-AMERICAN EVENTS	NATIONAL EVENTS
1939	
1939	**1939**
Billie Holiday sings "Strange Fruit" for the first time; Marian Anderson performs at Lincoln Memorial after DAR bars her from Constitution Hall; "Bojangles" Robinson organizes the Black Actors' Guild	World War II begins in Europe
1940	
1940	
Richard Wright publishes *Native Son;* Hattie McDaniel receives an Oscar for her role in *Gone with the Wind*	
1941	
1941	**1941**
Mary Lucinda Cardwell Dawson founds the National Negro Opera Company	United States enters World War II
1942	
1942	
Margaret Walker publishes For *My People;* Dox Thrash paints *Defense Worker;* Johnson Publishing launches *Negro Digest*	
1943	
1944	
1945	
1945	**1945**
Nat King Cole becomes first black star with his own network (NBC) radio variety show; Johnson Publishing launches Ebony Magazine	Roosevelt dies, Truman becomes president; United States drops atomic bombs on Hiroshima and Nagasaki; World War II ends
1946	
1947	
1947	
Jackie Robinson becomes the first black major-league baseball player	

continued

AFRICAN-AMERICAN EVENTS	NATIONAL EVENTS
1948	
1948 Alice Coachman becomes first black woman Olympic champion	

CONCLUSION

The Depression ushered in a period of intense hardship, but as this chapter indicates, it was also a period in which black Americans had an unprecedented impact on American culture. Black people excelled in sports, arts, drama, and music. The Works Progress Administration (WPA) funded a wide spectrum of artists whose cultural productions were accessible, inclusive, and populist.

The Chicago Black Renaissance reflected the impact of the WPA on the lives and fortunes of hundreds of artists. A new generation of black jazz musicians transformed black music into an art form that won worldwide admiration and emulation. Black musicians weaned Americans from swing to bebop, and gospel music became a dynamic genre that satisfied the needs of the black urban migrants to express their spiritual and communal feelings.

These positive changes were made against a backdrop of entrenched racism. Although some African Americans found satisfying jobs in film and radio, many others were excluded or relegated to demeaning, stereotypical roles. This bias and negative typecasting motivated innovative filmmakers to develop alternative films and artistic institutions that allowed a more balanced and accurate representation of black life and culture to develop. Such creative ventures seldom produced the profits that white entrepreneurs reaped from marketing black cultural productions to white consumers. The mass appeal and unparalleled success of entertainers such as Louis Armstrong and Duke Ellington should not obscure the fate of those artists who refused to entertain white America and instead sought to oppose racism and social and economic injustice. They remained poor and unnoticed by the dominant culture.

Still, black counterculture artists had a tremendous impact on America and on the spread of black internationalism. Black artists reflected a growing pride and a determination to resist complete assimilation into white culture. The comic strips, the Semple stories of Langston Hughes, the black press, and the black church preserved black people's dignity. Black culture prepared black people for the next level of struggle against the American Jim Crow regime and against all ideologies of white supremacy across the black diaspora.

REVIEW QUESTIONS

1. How did the Great Depression affect black culture? What role did the New Deal's Works Progress Administration (WPA) play in democratizing black culture? How did black religious culture change during this era?

2. How did black artists, musicians, filmmakers, and writers negotiate the dilemma of dual consciousness as articulated by W. E. B. Du Bois? Which parts of black art did white corporate executives find easiest to appropriate and shape for white consumption?

3. How did swing era big band music lead to bebop? What problems did the bebop musicians encounter? How did black music affect American culture?

4. How did Hollywood films portray black Americans during the 1930s and 1940s? How did these images affect white Americans' attitudes and behavior toward black Americans? How did these representations contribute to the emergence of an alternative or independent black cinema?

5. How did the cultural production of the Chicago Renaissance compare with that of the Harlem Renaissance? Why did black athletes become prominent during the 1930s and 1940s? What was their impact on American culture? How did the experiences of black sports figures reflect the status of race relations in the United States?

RECOMMENDED READING

William Barlow. *Voice Over: The Making of Black Radio*. Philadelphia: Temple University Press, 1999. A lucidly written, informative cultural history of the evolution of black radio and the personalities who made it a powerful instrument for disseminating black music, culture, language, and politics, and for constructing an African-American public sphere.

Scott DeVeaux. *BeBop: A Social and Musical History*. Berkeley: University of California Press, 1997. A perceptive study of the creative artistry and lives of the pivotal black professional musicians in the jazz world during the 1930s and 1940s and how they made bebop into a commercially successful art movement.

Manthia Diawara, ed. *Black American Cinema*. New York: Routledge, 1993. A collection of provocative essays. Three examine the work of filmmaker Oscar Micheaux. Others provide fresh interpretations of the recent independent cinema movement.

Melvin Patrick Ely. *The Adventures of Amos 'N' Andy: A Social History of an American Phenomenon*. New York: Free Press, 1991. A subtle and penetrating examination of the complexities of racial stereotyping in one of the most influential and controversial radio and television programs in the history of media race relations.

Samuel A. Floyd Jr. *The Power of Black Music: Interpreting Its History from Africa to the United States*. New York: Oxford University Press, 1995. An excellent overview of the history of black music with an insightful comparison of the Harlem and Chicago flowerings.

· C H A P T E R   T W E N T Y ·

THE WORLD WAR II ERA
AND THE SEEDS OF A REVOLUTION

ON THE EVE OF WAR, 1936–1941

As the world economy wallowed in the Great Depression, the international order collapsed in Europe and Asia. Germany under the dictatorship of Adolf Hitler (1889–1945) and Italy under the dictatorship of Benito Mussolini (1883–1945) created an alliance, known as the Axis, aimed to take economic and political control of Europe. These fascist dictators advocated a political program based on extreme nationalism that brutally suppressed internal opposition and used violence to gain their will abroad. Hitler was driven by a virulent form of racism and Anglo-Saxon supremacy. Unlike racists in the United States, he focused his hatred on Jews, blaming them for all Germany's social and economic problems. But the Nazis also despised black people and considered them inferior human beings. They discriminated against Germans with African ancestors. Through the late 1930s, the Germans and Italians embarked on a series of military campaigns that placed much of Central Europe under their power. In August 1939 Germany signed a nonaggression pact with the Soviet Union, a prelude to a September 1 attack on Poland by Germany, which the Soviets joined a few weeks later. Britain and France reacted to the invasion by declaring war on Germany, thus beginning World War II.

During the 1930s, the Empire of Japan sought to extend its power and territory in Asia. The Japanese wanted to drive out Britain, France, and the Netherlands, and the United States, which had extensive economic interests and colonial possessions in Asia. Japan's aggressive and expansionist policies also led to conflict with the Soviet Union in Manchuria and with the Nationalist regime in China, against which the Japanese became involved in a long and bloody struggle in the 1930s. The United States supported China and encouraged the European powers to resist Japanese demands for economic and territorial concessions in their Asian colonies. Japan's alliance with Nazi Germany and Fascist Italy further aggravated United States–Japanese relations. These tensions led to war on December 7, 1941, when the Japanese bombed American warships at Pearl Harbor, Hawaii, and launched a massive offensive against British, Dutch, and American holdings throughout the Pacific.

African Americans and the Emerging World Crisis

Many African Americans responded to the emerging world crisis with growing activism. When Ethiopia was invaded by Italy in 1935, it was, along with Liberia and Haiti, one of three black-ruled nations in the world, and black communities throughout the United

432

States organized to send it aid. Mass meetings in support of the embattled Ethiopians were held in New York City. Similar rallies occurred in other large cities while reporters from black newspapers brought the horror of this war home to their readers. Despite fierce resistance, the Italians won the war, in part, by using poison gas. The conflict alerted many African Americans to the dangers of fascism, reawakened interest in, and identification with, Africa.

A civil war in Spain had stimulated renewed activism among leftist African Americans. In 1936 the left-leaning Spanish Republic became embroiled in a civil war against a Fascist movement led by General Francisco Franco (1892–1975) whom Germany and Italy supported. About a hundred African Americans traveled to Spain in 1936–1937 to serve with the Abraham Lincoln Battalion, an integrated fighting force of three thousand American volunteers. Support of the Abraham Lincoln Battalion reflected a commitment by a few African Americans to the communists' vision of internationalism. Mobilization for war, however, would soon bring most black people and their organizations into the fight against fascism abroad and for equality and justice in the United States.

A. Philip Randolph and the March on Washington Movement

In 1939 and 1940, the American government, along with the governments of France and Britain, spent so much on arms that the U.S. economy was finally lifted out of the Depression. But the United States mobilized its economy for war and rebuilt its military in keeping with past practices of discrimination and exclusion. As unemployed white workers streamed into centers of war production, most jobless African Americans were left waiting at the gate. Most aircraft manufacturers, for example, would hire black people only in janitorial positions no matter what their skills. Many all-white AFL unions enforced closed-shop agreements that prevented their employers from hiring black workers who were not members of the labor organization. Government-funded training programs regularly rejected black applicants, often reasoning that training them would be pointless given their poor prospects of finding skilled work. The United States Employment Service (USES) filled "whites-only" requests for defense workers. The military itself made it clear that although it would accept black men in their proportion to the population, about 11 percent at the time, it would put them in segregated units and assign them to service duties. The navy limited black servicemen to menial positions; the Marine Corps and the Army Air Corps refused to accept them altogether.

When a young African-American man wrote the Pittsburgh *Courier* and suggested a "Double V" campaign—victory over fascism abroad and over racism at home—the newspaper adopted his words as the battle cry for the entire race. Fighting this struggle in a nation at war would be difficult, but the effort led to the further development of black organizations and transformed the worldview of many African-American soldiers and civilians.

Embodying the spirit of the "Double V" campaign, African-American protest groups and newspapers criticized discrimination in the defense program. Two months before the 1940 presidential election, the NAACP, Urban League, and other groups pressed President Roosevelt to take action. The president listened to their protests, but he responded with little of substance. As a result, during late 1940 the NAACP and other groups staged mass protest rallies around the nation. With the election safely won, the president, anxious not to offend white southern politicians he needed to back his war program, refused even to meet with black leaders.

In January 1941 A. Philip Randolph, who was president of the Brotherhood of Sleeping Car Porters and who had been working with other groups to get Roosevelt's attention, called on black people to unify their protests and direct them at the national government. He suggested that ten thousand African Americans march on Washington under the slogan "We loyal Negro-American citizens demand the right to work and fight for our country." In the coming months Randolph helped create the March on Washington Movement (MOWM), which soon became the largest mass movement of black Americans since the activities of Marcus Garvey's Universal Negro Improvement Association of the 1920s. The MOWM's demands included a presidential order forbidding companies with government contracts from engaging in racial discrimination, eliminating race-based exclusion from defense training courses, and requiring the USES to supply workers on a nonracial basis. Randolph also wanted an order to abolish segregation in the armed forces and the president's support for a law withdrawing the benefits of the National Labor Relations Act from unions that refused to grant membership to black Americans. Departing from the leadership tactics of most other African-American protest groups of the time, Randolph prohibited white participation and encouraged the participation of the black working class.

Randolph's powerful appeal captured the support of many African Americans who had not before taken part in the activities of middle-class-dominated groups like the NAACP. Roosevelt, fearing the protest would undermine America's democratic rhetoric, met with Randolph and other black leaders. The president offered a set of superficial changes, but the African Americans stood firm and raised the stakes by increasing their estimate of the number of black marchers coming to Washington to 100,000. By the end of June 1941, the president capitulated and had his aides draft Executive Order #8802, prompting Randolph to call off the march. It was a grand moment. "To this day," NAACP leader Roy Wilkins wrote in his autobiography, "I don't know if he would have been able to turn out enough marchers to make his point stick . . . but, what a bluff it was. A tall, courtly black man with Shakespearean diction and the stare of an eagle had looked the patrician Roosevelt in the eye—and made him back down."

Executive Order #8802

On the surface at least, the president's order marked a significant change in the government's stance. It stated in part:

> I do hereby affirm the policy of the United States that there shall be no discrimination in the employment of workers in the defense industry or government because of race, creed, color, or national origin.

The order instructed all agencies that trained workers to administer such programs without discrimination. To ensure full cooperation with these guidelines, Roosevelt created the Fair Employment Practices Committee (FEPC) with the power to investigate complaints of discrimination. The order said nothing about desegregation of the military, but private assurances were made that the barriers to entry in key services would be lowered.

Black excitement with the order soon soured as many industries, particularly in the South, evaded its clear intent and engaged in only token hirings. Mere articulation of antidiscrimination principles and the establishment of commissions and committees did not lead to eradication of inequalities. Moreover, the order did not mention union discrimination. Nonetheless, the threat of the march, the issuance of the executive order, and the creation of the FEPC marked the formal acknowledgment by the federal government that it bore some responsibility for protecting black and minority rights in employment. Black activists and their allies would have to continue their fight if the order was to have any meaning. Randolph sought to lead them but would find it difficult to do so because of the opposition of key government agencies—notably the military—the political power of southern congressmen, and a belief among white people that winning the war took precedent over racial issues.

RACE AND THE U.S. ARMED FORCES

The demands of A. Philip Randolph and other black leaders and health-care professionals to end segregation in the armed forces initially met stiffer resistance than their pleas for change in the civilian sector. Black men were expected to serve their country, but at the beginning of the war, most were assigned to segregated service battalions, relegated to noncombat positions, kept out of the more prestigious branches of the service, and faced tremendous obstacles to appointment as commissioned officers.

During the prewar mobilization period, 1940–1941, black physicians and leaders of their black professional organization, the National Medical Association (NMA), remembering the segregation they experienced during World War I, queried the War Department about their status. In a new war, would black physicians be integrated into the medical corps or required to practice in separate facilities set aside for sick and wounded black soldiers? In a 1940 speech, Dr. G. Hamilton Francis underscored the concerns of black doctors: "Our nation is again preparing to defend itself against aggression from without. Today, we are ready and willing to contribute all of our skill and energy and to wholeheartedly enlist our services as members of the medical profession, but we must be permitted to take our right places, as evidenced by our training, experience, and ability."

Institutional Racism in the American Military

Much of the armed forces' racial policy derived from negative attitudes and discriminatory practices common in American society. Reflecting this ingrained racism, a 1925 study by the American War College concluded that African Americans were physically unqualified for combat duty, were by nature subservient and mentally inferior, believed themselves to be inferior to white people, were susceptible to the influence of crowd psychology, could not control themselves in the face of danger, and did not have the initiative and resourcefulness of white people.

Based on this and later studies, the War Department laid out two key policies in 1941 for the use of black soldiers. Although they would be taken into the military at

This World War II War Department recruitment poster recognizes the heroism of Dorie Miller (1919–1943) at Pearl Harbor. His bravery, however, did not alter the navy's policy of restricting black sailors to the kitchens and boiler rooms of navy vessels.
Courtesy of the Library of Congress

the same rate as white inductees, African Americans would be segregated and would serve primarily in noncombat units.

In creating these policies, the army and navy ignored evidence of the fighting ability that African Americans had shown in previous wars, confirmed by the heroism of Dorie Miller during the attack on Pearl Harbor. Miller was the son of Texas sharecroppers who had enlisted in the navy in 1938 and, like all black sailors in the navy at the time, he had been assigned as a cook and a waiter. When the Japanese air force attacked the naval base on December 7, 1941, the twenty-two-year-old Miller was below decks on the battleship *Arizona*. When his captain was seriously wounded, Miller braved bullets to help move him to a more protected area of the deck. He then took charge of a machine gun, shooting down at least two and perhaps six enemy aircraft before running out of ammunition. Miller had never before fired the gun. On May 27, 1942, the navy cited him for "distinguished devotion to duty, extraordinary courage and disregard for his own personal safety" and awarded him a Navy Cross. The navy then sent Miller back to mess duty without a promotion.

The Costs of Military Discrimination

Although the War and Navy Departments held to the fiction of "separate but equal" in their segregation program, their policies gave black Americans inferior resources or excluded them entirely. Segregation at army camps most often meant that black soldiers were placed in the least desirable spots and denied the use of officers' clubs, base stores, and recreational areas. Four-fifths of all training camps were located in the South, where black soldiers were harassed and discriminated against off base as well as on. For southern African Americans, even going home in uniform could be dangerous. For example, when Rieves Bell of Starkville, Mississippi, was visiting his family in 1943, three young white men cornered him on a street and attempted to strip off his uniform. Bell fought back and injured one of them with a knife. The local civilian authorities sentenced Bell to three and a half years in the notorious Parchman state penitentiary for the crime of self-defense.

Perhaps most galling was to see German prisoners of war accorded better treatment than African-American soldiers. Dempsey Travis of Chicago saw "German prisoners free to move around the camp, unlike black soldiers who were restricted. The Germans walked right into the doggone places like any white American. We were wearin' the same uniform, but we were excluded."

Most of the nearly one million African Americans who served during World War II did so in auxiliary units, notably in the transportation and engineering corps. Soldiers in the transportation corps, almost half of whom were black, loaded supplies and drove them in trucks to the front lines. As they drove toward Germany in 1944 and 1945, African Americans braved enemy fire and delivered the fuel, ammunition, and other

Black women Army nurses, like black male servicemen, served in all-black units in the U.S. military during World War II. The War Department assigned them to care for German prisoners of war but initially prohibited them from caring for sick and wounded white Americans. Under the leadership of Mabel Staupers, black nurses successfully fought against enlistment quotas and other discriminatory treatment.
NAACP Collection/Library of Congress

goods that made the fight possible. Black engineers built camps and ports, constructed and repaved roads, and performed many other tasks to support frontline troops.

Black soldiers performed well in these tasks but were often subject to unfair military discipline. In Europe, black soldiers were executed in vastly greater numbers than whites even though African Americans made up only 10 percent of the total number of soldiers. One of the most glaring examples of unfair treatment was the navy's handling of a "mutiny" at its Port Chicago base north of San Francisco. On July 17, 1944, in the worst home-front disaster of the war, an explosion at the base killed 320 American sailors, of whom 202 were black ammunition loaders. In the following month 328 of the surviving ammunition loaders were sent to fill another ship. When 258 of them refused to do so, they were arrested. Eventually the Navy charged fifty men with mutiny, convicted them, and sentenced them to terms of imprisonment ranging from eight to fifteen years at Terminal Island in Southern California. The NAACP's Thurgood Marshall filed a brief on behalf of the fifty men arguing that they had been railroaded into prison because of their race, but to no avail.

Black American leaders identified a formidable but vulnerable target. Employing a variety of strategies they mobilized the black civilian workforce, black women's groups, college students, and an interracial coalition to participate in resistance to this blatant inequality. They provoked a public dialogue with government and military officials at a pivotal moment when America's leaders most desired to present a united democratic front to the world.

Examples of black protest abound. In 1942 the NAACP's *Crisis*, and *Opportunity*, the organ of the National Urban League, published numerous editorials denouncing the army's segregation policy. Walter White inundated the War Department and the president with letters citing examples of improper, hostile, and humiliating treatment of black servicemen by military personnel and in the white communities in which bases were located.

Black Women in the Struggle to Desegregate the Military

The role of black women in the struggle to desegregate the military has often been overlooked, but their militancy contributed to the effort. A 1942 editorial in the Crisis suggested why:

> [T]he colored woman has been a more potent factor in shaping Negro society than the white woman has been in shaping white society because the sexual caste system has been much more fluid and ill-defined than among whites. Colored women have worked with their men and helped build and maintain every institution we have. Without their economic aid and counsel we would have made little if any progress.

The most prominent example of black women's struggle is found in the history of the National Association of Colored Graduate Nurses (NACGN). Mabel K. Staupers, its executive director, led an aggressive fight to eliminate quotas established by the U.S. Army Nurse Corps. Although many black nurses volunteered their services during World War II, they were refused admittance into the navy, and the army allowed only a few to serve. To draw attention to the unfairness of quotas, Staupers requested a meeting with Eleanor Roosevelt. In November 1944 the First Lady and Staupers met, and Staupers described black nurses' troubled relationship with the armed forces. She informed the First Lady that 82 black nurses were serving 150 patients at the all-black station hospital at Fort Huachuca, Arizona, at a time when the army was complaining of a dire nursing shortage and debating the need to draft nurses. Staupers expounded on the practice of using black women to care for German prisoners of war. She asked, rhetorically, if this was to be the special role of the black nurse in the war? Staupers elaborated, "When our women hear of the great need for nurses in the Army and when they enter the service it is with the high hopes that they will be used to nurse sick and wounded soldiers who are fighting our country's enemies and not primarily to take care of these enemies."

Soldiers and sailors also resisted segregation and discrimination while in the service. Their action included well-organized attempts to desegregate officers' clubs. At Freeman Field, Indiana, for example, one hundred black officers refused to back down when their commanders threatened to arrest them for seeking to use the officers' club. In other bases African-American soldiers responded with violence to violence, intimidation, and threats. Their actions, although put down with dispatch, prompted the army brass to reevaluate their belief in the military efficiency of discrimination.

The Beginning of Military Desegregation

In response to the militancy of black officers, civil rights leaders, and the press, the War Department made changes and began to take on the challenge of reeducating soldiers, albeit in a limited fashion. The Advisory Committee on Negro Troop Policies was charged with coordinating the use of black troops and developing policy on social questions and personnel training. In 1943 the War Department also produced its own propaganda film—*The Negro Soldier*, directed by Frank Capra—to alleviate racial tensions. This patronizing film emphasized the contributions black soldiers had made in the nation's wars since the American Revolution and was designed to appeal to both black and white audiences.

The War Department also attempted to use propaganda to counter black protest groups and the claims of discrimination found in the black press. The key to this effort was fighter Joe Louis, whom the army believed was "almost a god" to most black Americans. "The possibilities for using him," a secret internal report stated, "are almost unlimited, such as touring the army camps as special instructor on physical training; exhibition bouts, for use in radio or in movies; in a movie appearance a flashback could be shown of Louis knocking out Max Schmeling, the champion of the Germans." The same report also mentioned other prominent black men and women who had "great value in any propaganda programs. Other athletes like Ray Robinson, also track athletes, etc.; name bands like Cab Calloway, [Jimmy] Lunceford; stage, screen and concert stars like Ethel Waters, Bill Robinson, Eddie Anderson, Paul Robeson, etc." The effect of this propaganda barrage is impossible to gauge, but it did little to counter the real incidents of prejudice and discrimination that most black people experienced in their daily lives.

Racism remained strong throughout the war, but the persistent push of protest groups and the military's need for soldiers gradually loosened its grip. After the attack on Pearl Harbor, nearly all the services had to relax their restrictions on African Americans. The navy, previously the most resistant service, began to accept black men as sailors and noncommissioned officers. By 1943 it allowed African Americans into officer training schools. The Marine Corps, exclusively white throughout its history, began taking African Americans in 1942. Black officers were trained in integrated settings in all services except the Army's Air Corps. The War Department even acted to compel recalcitrant commanding officers to recommend black servicemen for admission to the officer training schools, and soon, over two thousand a year were graduated.

Many African Americans also saw combat, although under white officers. Several African-American artillery, tank destroyer, antiaircraft, and combat engineer battalions fought with distinction in Europe and Asia. Military prejudice seemed to be borne out by the poor showing of the all-black 92nd Combat Division, but investigation revealed that its failure was the result of poor training and leadership by a white officer with no confidence in his men. After the Battle of the Bulge, a massive late-1944 German counterattack, 2,500 black volunteers fought in integrated units. The experiment would not be repeated during the war, but its success laid the groundwork for later changes. Although subject to many of the same kinds of discrimination as African-American men, African-American women also found expanded opportunities in the military. Approximately four thousand black women served in the Women's Army Auxiliary Corps (WAACs).

The Tuskegee Airmen

The most visible group of black soldiers served in the Army Air Force. In January 1941 the War Department announced the formation of an all-black Pursuit Squadron and the creation of a training program at Tuskegee Army Air Field, Alabama, for black pilots.

Unlike all other units in the army, the 99th Squadron and the 332nd Group, made up of the 100th, 301st, and 302nd Squadrons, had black officers. The 99th went to North Africa in April 1943 and flew its first combat mission against the island of Pantelleria on June 2. Later the squadron participated in the air battle over Sicily, operating from its base in North Africa, and supported the invasion of Italy. The squadron regularly engaged German pilots in aerial combat. General Benjamin O. Davis Jr. commanded the 332nd Group when it was deployed to Italy in January 1944. In July the 99th was added to the 332nd and the Group participated in campaigns in Italy, France, Germany, and the Balkans.

The Tuskegee Airmen amassed an impressive record. They flew over 15,500 sorties and completed 1,578 missions. During the two hundred missions in which they escorted heavy bombers deep into Germany's Rhineland, not one of the "heavies" was lost to enemy fighter opposition. They destroyed 409 enemy aircraft, sank an enemy destroyer, and knocked out numerous ground installations. They were well regarded and recognized for their heroism. They accumulated 150 Distinguished Flying Crosses, a Legion of Merit, a Silver Star, 14 Bronze Stars, and 744 Air Medals. Tuskegee pilot Coleman Young (1919–1997; mayor of Detroit 1973–1993) recalled, "once our reputation got out as to our fighting ability, we started getting special requests for our group to escort their group, the bombers. They all wanted us because we were the only fighter group in the entire air force that did not lose a bomber to enemy action. Oh, we were much in demand."

The Transformation of Black Soldiers

A new generation of African Americans became soldiers during World War II and many would emerge from the experience with an enhanced sense of themselves and a commitment to the fight for black equality. They returned home with a broader perception of the world and a transformed consciousness. Unlike the black soldiers in World War I, a greater percentage of those drafted at the outset of World War II had attended high school and more were either high school or college graduates. Some black soldiers brought so-called radical ideas with them as they were drafted and sent to segregated installations. The urban and northern black servicemen and women and many of the southern rural recruits had a strong sense of their own self-worth and dignity. In their study of Chicago, sociologists St. Clair Drake and Horace Cayton noted the following:

> At least half of the Negro soldiers—and Bronzeville's men fall into this class—were city people who had lived through a Depression in America's Black Ghettoes, and who had been exposed to unions, the Communist movement, and to the moods of racial radicalism that occasionally swept American cities. Even the rural southern Negroes were different this time—for the thirty years between the First and Second World War has seen a great expansion of school facilities in the South and distribution of newspapers and radios.

Serving in the armed forces first exposed many African Americans to a world outside the segregated South and nurtured a budding internationalism among them. Douglas Conner, a Mississippi veteran, captured the collective understanding of the social and political meaning of the war shared by the men in his unit, the 31st Quartermaster Battalion stationed in Okinawa: "The air people in Tuskegee, Dorie Miller, and the others gave the blacks a sense that they could succeed and compete in a world that had been saying that 'you're nothing.'" Conner insisted that "because of the world war, I think many people, especially blacks, got the idea that we're going back, but we're not going back to business as usual. Somehow we're going to change this nation so that there's more equality than there is now." The personal transformation that Conner and others experienced, combined with a number of international, national, and regional forces, laid the foundation for a modern movement for freedom of opportunity.

BLACK PEOPLE ON THE HOME FRONT

Just as they did in the military, African Americans on the home front fought a dual war against the Axis and discrimination. Black workers and volunteers helped staff the factories and farms that produced goods for the fight while also purchasing war bonds and participating in other defense activities. The changes brought on by the war also created new points of conflict while exacerbating preexisting problems and occasionally igniting full-scale riots. Throughout the war, protest groups and the black press continued to fight employment discrimination and political exclusion.

Black Workers: From Farm to Factory

The war accelerated the migration of African Americans from rural areas to the cities. Even though the farm economy recovered during the war, the lure of high-paying defense jobs and other urban occupations tempted many black farmers to abandon the land. By the 1940s the bitter experiences of the previous decades had made it clear there was little future in the cotton fields. Boll weevils, competition from other parts of the world, and mechanization reduced the need for black labor. Indeed, by the end of the war, only 28 percent of black men worked on farms, a decline of 13 percent since 1940. More than 300,000 black men left agricultural labor between 1940 and 1944 alone.

The wartime need for workers, backed by pressure from the government, helped break down some of the barriers to employing African Americans in industry. During the war the total number of black workers in nonfarm employment rose from 2,900,000 to 3,800,000. Nearly all industries relaxed their resistance to hiring African-American workers, and thousands moved into previously whites-only jobs.

With so many of their men away at war, black women increasingly found work outside the laundry and domestic service that had previously been their lot. Nationally 600,000 black women—400,000 of them former domestic servants—shifted into industrial jobs. As one aircraft worker wryly put it, "Hitler was the one that got us out of the white folks' kitchen." Even those women who stayed in domestic work often saw their wages improve as the supply of competing workers dwindled.

The abundance of industrial jobs helped spur and direct the migration of African Americans during and after World War II. Some 1.5 million migrants, nearly 15 percent of the population, left the South, swelling the black communities in northern and western cities that had significant war industries. By 1950 the proportion of the nation's black population living in the South had fallen from 77 percent to 68 percent. The most dramatic rise in black population was in southern California. Because of its burgeoning aircraft industry and the success of civil rights groups and the federal government in limiting discrimination, Los Angeles saw its relatively small African-American community increase by more than 340,000 during the war.

During the war many unions became more open to African-American workers. Between 1940 and 1945, black union membership rose from 200,000 to 1.25 million. Those unions connected to the CIO, particularly the United Automobile Workers, were the most open to black membership, whereas AFL affiliates were the most likely to treat African Americans as second-class members or to continue to exclude them altogether. Some white unionized workers continued to oppose hiring black workers, even going on strike to prevent it, but their resistance was often deflected by the union leadership, the government, or employers. The growth in black membership did not end racism in unions, even in the CIO, but it did provide African Americans a stronger foundation upon which to protest continuing discrimination in employment.

The FEPC During the War

Responding to the ineffectiveness of the Fair Employment Practices Committee during the first years of the war, in May 1943 President Roosevelt issued Executive Order #9346. The order established a new Committee on Fair Employment Practice, increased its budget, and placed its operation directly under the Executive Office of the President. Roosevelt appointed Malcolm Ross, a combative white liberal, to head the committee. Ross proved to be more effective than the committee's previous leadership. He initiated nationwide hearings of cases concerning discrimination in the shipbuilding and railroad industries. These proceedings brought some compliance with the FEPC's orders. Resistance, however was more common. In Mobile, Alabama, for example, the white employees of the Alabama Dry Dock and Shipbuilding Company opposed the FEPC's efforts to pressure the company to promote twelve of the 7,000 African Americans it employed in menial positions to racially mixed welding crews. The white workers went on a rampage, assaulting fifty African Americans. The FEPC thereupon withdrew its plan and acquiesced in the traditional Jim Crow arrangements for all work assignments. White workers retained their more lucrative positions. As a result of this kind of intransigence, the committee failed to redress most of the grievances of black workers. A concerted effort to continue the committee after the war was defeated.

Anatomy of a Race Riot: Detroit, 1943

One of the bloodiest race riots in the nation's history took place in 1943 in Detroit, Michigan, where black and white workers were competing fiercely for jobs and housing. Relations between the two communities in the city had been smoldering for months, with open fighting in the plants and on the streets. White racism, housing segregation, and economic discrimination were part of the problem. The brutality of white police officials was an especially potent factor. Tensions were so palpable that weeks before the riot NAACP leader Walter White had warned the city could explode in violence at any moment.

The immediate trigger for the riot was a squabble on June 20 between groups of white and black bathers at the segregated city beaches on the Detroit River. Within hours, two hundred white sailors from a nearby base joined the white mob that pursued and attacked individual black men and women. A rumor that white citizens had killed a black woman and thrown her baby over the bridge spread across the city. The riot spread quickly along Woodward Avenue, the city's major thoroughfare, into Paradise Valley where some 35,000 southern black migrants had, in the spring of 1943, joined the city's already crowded black population. By Monday morning downtown Detroit was overrun with white men roaming in search of more victims.

Six thousand federal troops had to be dispatched to Detroit to restore order. When the violence ended, 34 people had been killed (25 black and 9 white people) and more than 700 injured. Of the 25 black people who died, the Detroit police killed 17. The police did not kill any of the white men who assaulted African Americans or committed arson. Property damage exceeded $2 million and one million man-hours were lost in war production.

In the aftermath, the city created the Mayor's Interracial Committee, the first permanent municipal body designed to promote civic harmony and fairness. Despite the efforts of labor and black leaders, many white people in Detroit, including Wayne County prosecutor William E. Dowling, blamed the black press and the NAACP for instigating the riot. Dowling and others accused the city's black citizens of pushing too hard for economic and political equality and insisted that they operated under communist influence. One of many commissioned reports concluded that black leaders provoked the riot because they had compared "victory over the axis . . . [with] a corresponding overthrow in the country of those forces which . . . prevent true racial equality." In contrast, black leaders, radical trade unionists, and members of other ethnic organiza-tions, especially Jewish groups, blamed, "the KKK, the Christian Front, the Black Dragon Society, the National Workers League, the Knights of the White Camelia, the Southern Voters League, and similar organizations based on a policy of terror and . . . white supremacy."

Old and New Protest Groups on the Home Front

The NAACP grew tremendously during the war, and by its end stood poised for even greater achievements. Under the editorial direction of Roy Wilkins, the circulation of the NAACP's *Crisis* grew from 7,000 to 45,000. During the war, the *Crisis* was one of the most important sources for information on the status of black men and women. The NAACP's membership increased from 50,000 in 1940 to 450,000 at the end of the war. Even more important, much of this growth occurred in the South, which had more than 150,000 members by 1945. Supreme Court victories and especially close monitoring of the "Double V" campaign help explain these huge increases.

With success, however, came conflict and ambivalence. Leaders split over the value of integration versus self-segregation and questioned the benefit of relying so heavily on legal cases rather than paying more attention to the concerns and needs of working-class black men and women. Wilkins acknowledged the organization's uncertainty and indecisiveness:

> The war was a great watershed for the NAACP. We had become far more powerful, and now the challenge was to keep our momentum. Everyone knew the NAACP stood against discrimination and segregation, but what was our postwar program to be? Beyond discrimination and segregation, where would we stand on veterans, housing, labor-management relations, strikes, the Fair Employment Practices Commission, organizations at state levels, education? What would we do to advance the fight for the vote in the South? . . . We had a big membership . . . but we didn't know how to use them.

In 1944 southern white liberals joined with African Americans to establish the Southern Regional Council (SRC). This interracial coalition, an important example of the local initiative of private citizens, was devoted to expanding democracy in a region better known for the political and economic oppression and exploitation of its black citizens. The SRC conducted research and focused attention on the inequalities endemic to black life in the South and challenged the facade of southern white supremacy.

In 1942 a far more strident group called the Congress of Racial Equality (CORE) had been formed in Chicago when an interracial group of Christian pacifists gathered to find ways to make America live up to the ideals of equality and justice on which it based its war program. Activists James Farmer and Bayard Rustin were key in getting the group off the ground. Unlike the NAACP, CORE was a decentralized, intensely democratic organization. CORE dedicated itself to the principles of nonviolent direct action as expounded by Indian leader Mohandas Gandhi. Over the course of the war this pacifist organization challenged segregation in the North with sit-ins and other protest tactics that the civil rights movement would later adopt.

African Americans found many ways to fight discrimination. Throughout the 1940s, in countless communities across the South and the Middle West, black women organized women's political councils and other groups to press for integration of public facilities—hospitals, swimming pools, theaters, and restaurants—and for the right to pursue collegiate and professional studies. Others created lasting works in the arts, literature, and popular culture. Women whose names would become virtually synonymous with the modern civil rights movement in the 1950s and 1960s helped lay its foundation in the World War II era. Ella Baker served as the NAACP field secretary. Rosa Parks began resisting segregation laws on Montgomery, Alabama, buses in the 1940s.

Black college students also began protesting segregation in public accommodations. The spark that ignited the Howard University campus civil rights movement came in January 1943. Three sophomore women, Ruth Powell from Massachusetts and Marianne Musgrave and Juanita Morrow from Ohio, sat at a lunch counter near the campus and were refused service. They demanded to see the manager and vowed to wait until he came. Instead of the manager, two policemen arrived who instructed the waitress to serve them. When the check arrived the trio learned they had been charged 25 cents each instead of the customary 10 cents. They placed 35 cents on the counter, turned to leave, and were arrested. Ruth Power later reported that "the policemen who arrested us told us we were being taken in for investigation because he had no proof that we weren't 'subversive agents.'" No charges were lodged against the women. The purpose of their arrest had been to intimidate them, but the incident instead fanned the smoldering embers of resentment in the Howard University student body.

THE TRANSITION TO PEACE

After first Germany and then Japan surrendered in 1945, the United States began the transition to peace. Many of the gains of black men and women were wiped away as the armed forces demobilized and the factories began reinstituting the discriminatory hiring systems in place before the conflict. It was clear segregation and discrimination would face a huge challenge in the coming years and that the African-American community was ready, willing, and able to fight in ways undreamed of in earlier eras.

THE COLD WAR AND INTERNATIONAL POLITICS

In early 1945, the United Nations began planning for the peace. However, the opposing interests of the Soviet Union and the United States led to a long period of intense hostility that became known as the Cold War. The overriding goal of the United States and its allies was the "containment" of communism. To this end, the North Atlantic Treaty Organization (NATO) was formed in 1949 to provide a military counterforce to Soviet power in Europe while American dollars helped rebuild Western Europe's war-shattered economy. The United States forged a similarly close relationship with Japan. Much of the rest of the world, however, became contested terrain.

As the nations of Asia and Africa gained independence from colonial domination over the ensuing decades, the United States struggled to keep them out of the Soviet orbit. It did so through foreign aid, direct military force, and, occasionally, through clandestine operations run by the Central Intelligence Agency (CIA). These military interventions were matched by a rising diplomatic and propaganda effort to convince the emerging nations of the world that the United States was a model to be emulated and an ally to be trusted.

The Cold War had an enormous influence on American society precisely when the powerful movement for African-American rights was beginning to emerge. The long conflict resulted in the rise of a permanent military establishment in the United States. Small in scope before World War II, the reorganized American military enlisted millions of men and women by the early 1950s and claimed most of the national budget. The federal government also grew in power during the war and provided a check on the control that white Southerners had so long exercised over race relations in their region. American policy makers also became concerned about the nation's ability to win the allegiance of Africans and other nonwhite people who formed the population of the emerging nations. The Soviet Union could discredit American sincerity by pointing to the deplorable state of race relations within the United States. Hence, during the Cold War, external pressures reinforced efforts to change American racial policy.

African Americans in World Affairs: W. E. B. Du Bois and Ralph Bunche

The Cold War gave new importance to the voices of African Americans in world affairs. Two men, W. E. B. Du Bois and Ralph Johnson Bunche (1904–1971), represent alternative strategies for responding to this opportunity. Du Bois took a highly critical approach to American policy. For half a century he had linked the fate of African Americans with that of Africans, and by 1945 was widely hailed as the Father of Pan-Africanism. In that year he directed the Fifth Pan-African Congress, which met in Manchester, England. The Africans who had been radicalized by World War II dominated the conference and encouraged it to denounce Western imperialism. Du Bois considered the United States a protector of the colonial system and opposed its stance in the Cold War. On returning from the Manchester congress, he declared,

> We American Negroes should know . . . until Africa is free, the descendants of Africa the world over cannot escape their chains. . . . The NAACP should therefore put in the forefront of its program the freedom of Africa in work and wage, education and health, and the complete abolition of the colonial system.

In contrast to Du Bois, scholar diplomat Ralph Bunche opted to work within the American system. Bunche held a Harvard doctorate in government and international relations and had spent much of the 1930s studying the problems of African Americans. During World War II Bunche became one of the key policy makers for Africa and he was an adviser to the U.S. delegation at the San Francisco conference that drafted the United Nations (UN) Charter. In 1948 he served as acting mediator of the UN Special Committee on Palestine, and in 1949 he negotiated an armistice between Egypt and Israel. He received the Spingarn Medal of the NAACP in 1949, and in 1950 he became the first African American to receive the Nobel Peace Prize. Bunche was committed to winning independence for African nations and freedom for his own people. As he wrote,

> Today, for all thinking people, the Negro is the shining symbol of the true significance of democracy. He has demonstrated what can be achieved with democratic liberties even when grudgingly and incompletely bestowed. But the most vital significance of the Negro . . . to American society . . . is the fact that democracy which is not extended to all of the nation's citizens is a democracy that is mortally wounded.

Anticommunism at Home

The rising tensions with the Soviet Union affected all aspects of domestic life in the United States. Conservatives used fears of communist subversion to attack anyone who advocated change in America. This included people who were, or had been, members of the Communist Party, union members, liberals, and people who had fought for African-American rights. The Truman administration (1945–1952) responded to fears of subversion by instituting government loyalty programs. Government employees were dismissed for the merest suspicion of disloyalty. Militant American anticommunism reached a feverish peak in the immediate postwar years and gave rise to an explosion of red-baiting hysteria that led to the rise of Wisconsin Republican senator Joseph McCarthy (1909–1957) and the House Un-American Activities Committee (HUAC). The relentless pursuit of "communist sympathizers" by McCarthy and HUAC ruined many lives. HUAC in particular hounded people in the media and in the entertainment industry. Even so prominent a figure as W. E. B. Du Bois was ripe for attack. On February 8, 1951, HUAC indicted him for allegedly serving as an "agent of a foreign principal" in his work with the Peace Information Center. In November a federal judge dismissed all charges against Du Bois. The government had been unable to prove he was an agent of communism. Despite Du Bois's past contributions, fear and personal malice prevented most African-American leaders from defending him.

Paul Robeson

Paul Robeson was one of the most tragic victims of these anticommunist witch-hunts. During the 1930s he worked closely with the Communist Party (although he was never a member), becoming one of the most famous defenders of the Soviet Union. Many leftists of the time became disaffected with the USSR after its 1939 pact with Hitler and after its brutal repressiveness became clear. Robeson, however, doggedly stuck to his belief in Soviet communism.

In the late 1940s, Robeson's pro-Soviet views and inflammatory statements aroused the ire of the U.S. government and its red hunters. A statement he made at the communist-dominated World Congress of the Defenders of Peace in Paris in 1949 provoked particular outrage. "It is unthinkable," Robeson said, "that American Negroes would go to war on behalf of those [the United States] who have oppressed us for generations against a country [the Soviet Union] which in one generation has raised our people to full human dignity of mankind." Later in 1949 crowds of rock-throwing locals twice disrupted a Robeson concert in Peekskill, New York, the first time preventing the concert from being held, the second time terrorizing performers and audience members at the concert's conclusion.

Throughout the 1940s Robeson consistently linked the struggles of black America with the struggles of black Africa, brown India, yellow Asia, the black men and women of Brazil and Haiti, and oppressed workers throughout Latin America. Robeson also refused to sign an affidavit concerning past membership in the Communist Party. In response, the U.S. State Department revoked his passport in 1950, explaining "the action was taken because the Department considers that Paul Robeson's travel abroad at this time would be contrary to the best interest of the United States." The travel ban remained in effect until ruled unconstitutional by the Supreme Court in 1958.

Robeson had combined his art and his politics to launch a sustained attack against racial discrimination, segregation, and the ideology of white supremacy and black inferiority as practiced in American society. During the Cold War the state would tolerate no such dissent by even a world-acclaimed black artist.

Henry Wallace and the 1948 Presidential Election

Robeson's struggles illustrate how conservative attacks choked off left-wing involvement in the struggle for black equality. The attacks destroyed Robeson's brilliant singing career. The increasing importance of black votes to Democrats, however, meant that key elements of the African-American liberation struggle remained at the center of national politics. Nowhere was this more apparent than in the 1948 presidential election.

President Harry S Truman was not expected to win this election because he faced a strong challenge from Thomas Dewey, the popular and well-financed Republican governor of New York. Truman's problems were compounded by a challenge from his former secretary of commerce Henry Wallace, who had been Roosevelt's vice president from 1941 to 1945. Wallace ran on the ticket of the communist-backed Progressive Party, which sought to take the votes of liberals, leftists, and civil rights advocates disappointed by Truman's moderation. Wallace also supported a peaceful accommodation with the Soviet Union. To undercut Wallace's challenge, Truman began to press Congress to pass liberal programs.

Black votes in key northern states were central to Truman's strategy for victory. African Americans in these tightly contested areas could make the difference between victory and defeat, so Truman, to retain their allegiance, sought to demonstrate his administration's support of civil rights. In January 1948 he embraced the findings of his biracial Committee on Civil Rights and called for their enactment into law. The committee's report, "To Secure These Rights," was a blueprint for changing the racial caste system in the United States. It recommended passage of federal antilynching legislation, ending discrimination at the ballot box, abolishing the poll tax, desegregating the military, and a whole range of other measures.

The reaction of white southern politicians was swift and threatening, causing Truman to pause; but as the election neared, fear of black abandonment at the polls became so great that the Democratic convention passed a strong pro–civil rights plank. Many white Southerners, led by South Carolina's governor Strom Thurmond, bolted the convention and formed their own States' Rights, or "Dixiecrat," party. The Dixiecrats carried South Carolina, Alabama, Mississippi, and Louisiana in the election; Wallace carried no state. The failure of the bulwark of white supremacy to prevent the Democratic Party from advocating African-American rights, and Truman's ultimate victory despite the defection of hard-line racists, represented a profound turning point in American politics.

Desegregating the Armed Forces

The importance of the black vote, the fight for the allegiance of the emerging nations, and the emerging civil rights movement hastened the desegregation of the military. In February 1948 a communist coup in Czechoslovakia raised the possibility of war between the United States and the Soviet Union and heightened concerns among military leaders about the willingness of African Americans to serve yet again in a Jim Crow army. When President Truman reinstated the draft in March 1948, A. Philip Randolph, who, in a replay of the March on Washington scenario, had formed the League for Non-Violent Civil Disobedience against Military Segregation in 1947, warned the nation that black men and women were fed up with segregation and Jim Crow and would not take a Jim Crow draft lying down. New York congressman Adam Clayton Powell Jr. also supported this stance. He declared there weren't enough jails in America to hold the black men who would refuse to bear arms in a Jim Crow army. On June 24, 1948, the Soviet Union heightened tensions even further when it imposed a blockade on West Berlin. On July 26 Truman, anticipating war between the superpowers and hoping to shore up his support among black voters for the approaching November elections, issued Executive Order #9981, officially desegregating the armed forces.

Executive Order #9981, which mandated "equality of treatment and opportunity for all persons in the armed services without regard to race, color, religion, or national origin," signaled the victorious culmination of a decades-long struggle by black civilians and soldiers to win full integration into the nation's military. After Truman signed the order, Randolph and Grant Reynolds, a former minister and co-chair of the League for Nonviolent Civil Disobedience against Military Segregation, disbanded the organization and called off marches planned for Chicago and New York.

Not until 1950 and the outbreak of the Korean War, however, was Truman's order fully implemented. The war reflected the American Cold War policy of containment, which was intended to stop what American leaders believed to be a worldwide conspiracy orchestrated by Moscow to spread communism. In 1950 North Koreans, allied to the Soviets, attacked the American-supported government in South Korea and launched the "hot war" in the midst of the Cold War. After the North Koreans invaded South Korea, the United States under UN auspices intervened. Heavy casualties early in the war depleted many white combat units. Thus, early in 1951, the army acted on Truman's executive order and authorized the formal integration of its units in Korea. By 1954 the army had disbanded its last all-black units, and the armed forces became one of the first sectors of American society to abandon segregation.

TIMELINE

AFRICAN-AMERICAN EVENTS	NATIONAL AND WORLD EVENTS
1936	
	1936
	Abraham Lincoln Brigade goes to Spain to resist Franco
1938	
	1938
	German troops overrun Austria
	1939
	Germany invades Poland, beginning World War II
1940	
1941	**1940**
Dorie Miller, hero of Pearl Harbor, receives Navy Cross	Benito Mussolini and Hitler form Axis
	Germany conquers most of Western Europe
A. Philip Randolph organizes March on Washington Movement	Selective Training and Service Act begins
	Roosevelt wins reelection to third term
	1941
	Executive Order #8802 is issued
	Japan attacks Pearl Harbor; America joins World War II
1942	
1942	**1942**
Congress of Racial Equality (CORE) is founded in Chicago	100,000 Japanese Americans interred in camps
	1943
Charity Adams (Early) becomes first black woman commissioned officer in the Women's Army Auxiliary Corps (WAACs)	Roosevelt signs GI Bill
	Servicemen's Readjustment Act provides funds for housing and education after the war
First black cadets graduate from flying school at Tuskegee, Alabama	
1943	
William H. Hastie resigns in protest from War Department	
Race riots in Mobile, Detroit, and Harlem	
The black 99th Pursuit Squadron flies its first combat mission	
1944	
1944	**1944**
Adam Clayton Powell Jr. is elected to U.S. House of Representatives, from Harlem	D-Day, Allied invasion of German-occupied France begins
U.S. Supreme Court overthrows the white primary in *Smith v. Allwright*	Roosevelt wins his fourth term

continued

AFRICAN-AMERICAN EVENTS	NATIONAL AND WORLD EVENTS
1945 Mabel Staupers secures an end to discrimination against black nurses in the military Du Bois, Bethune, White, and Bunche attend U.N. founding Paul Robeson receives NAACP Spingarn Medal	The Battle of the Bulge begins last major German counteroffensive **1945** United Nations founded FDR dies; Truman becomes president Germany surrenders U.S. bombs Hiroshima and Nagasaki; Japan surrenders
1946	
1947 The Journey of Reconciliation project begins. It is the precursor to the 1961 Freedom Rides	**1946** President Truman creates the Committee on Civil Rights
1948	
1948 *Ada Lois Sipuel v. Board Regents* is decided Truman's Executive Order 9981 desegregates the millitary **1949** Whites riot against Robeson concerts in Peekskill, New York	**1948** Truman wins presidential election with support of black voters
1950	
1950 *Sweatt v. Painter* is decided *McLaurin v. Oklahoma* is decided	**1950–53** Korean War is fought
1952	
1952 Colonel Benjamin O. Davis Jr. is appointed commander of the 51st Fighter Interceptor Wing in Korea	
1954	
1954 *Brown v. Board of Education* declares the "separate but equal" doctrine unconstitutional	

CONCLUSION

The years between 1940 and 1954 were a dynamic period of black activism and witnessed a rising international consciousness among African Americans. The quest for racial justice in the military and on the home front became an integral part of the ongoing struggle for economic, political, and social progress. President Roosevelt's Executive Order #8802 was a significant victory for A. Philip Randolph's March on Washington Movement and for black workers who were able to appeal racial discrimination in defense industries to the Fair Employment Practices Commission. The rise of fascism in Europe alarmed black and white Americans who correctly perceived ideologies based on racial tyranny and state dominance to be inimical to individual freedom and democracy. World War II also had far-reaching consequences. It profoundly transformed black servicemen and servicewomen.

Following victory in World War II, the Cold War created a climate in America that was both hospitable and hostile to the African-American freedom movement. Radicals such as Paul Robeson and W. E. B. Du Bois found no place in the movement or in American society. Moderate organizations, such as the NAACP-LDEF, pursuing their goals within the ideological and legal constraints of the nation, would meet with some success. The coming civil rights movement would, however, soon expand this narrow field of action and pave the way for a more varied, vibrant, and successful challenge to racism.

REVIEW QUESTIONS

1. How did World War II alter the status of African Americans? What were some of the consequences of so many black servicemen fighting in Europe against fascism and Nazism?

2. How did black women participate in the campaign to desegregate the U.S. military and in the Abraham Lincoln Brigade? How did Mabel Staupers win acceptance of black women into the military nurses corps?

3. What were the consequences of the "Double V" campaign? How did African-American civilians indicate their support of black servicemen? What institutional resources were African Americans able to marshal in their campaign for victory against racism at home?

4. How did World War II affect the status of black workers in America? What was the significance of A. Philip Randolph's March on Washington Movement, and how did President Roosevelt respond to it?

5. Why did the Cold War originate, and what is its significance for black activism? How did the World War II era promote the rising internationalization of African-American consciousness? How did the State Department attempt to downplay black dissent in America and why?

6. Why did President Harry S Truman decide to desegregate the U.S. military?

RECOMMENDED READING

John D'Emilio. *Lost Prophet: The Life and Times of Bayard Rustin.* New York: Simon & Schuster, 2003. A first-rate, well-written, thoughtful biography of a key, although often underappreciated, leader in the long struggle for social justice for all Americans.

Mary L. Dudziak. *Cold War Civil Rights: Race and the Image of American Democracy.* Princeton, NJ: Princeton University Press, 2000. An excellent study of the intricacies of Cold War diplomacy and the centrality of race issues and a splendid analysis of the Truman administration's commitment to civil rights.

Darlene Clark Hine. "Black Professional and Race Consciousness: Origins of the Civil Rights Movement, 1890–1950." *The Journal of American History*, 89, no. 4 (2003): 1279–94. A detailed discussion of the struggle of black physicians and nurses to end the racial segregation of medicine in the armed forces during World War II.

Paula F. Pfeffer. *A. Philip Randolph, Pioneer of the Civil Rights Movement.* Baton Rouge: Louisiana State University Press, 1990. A richly insightful biography of a pioneering labor leader and activist whose March on Washington Movement in 1941 was essential to the formation of the first Fair Employment Practices Committee and the integration of the armed services.

William R. Scott. *The Sons of Sheba's Race: African-Americans and the Italo-Ethiopian War, 1935–1941.* Bloomington: Indiana University Press, 1993. A detailed and illuminating account of African-American responses to the Italian invasion of Ethiopia and the growth of black internationalism.

Laura Wexler. *Fire in a Canebrake: The Last Mass Lynching in America.* New York: Scribner's, 2003. A riveting and sobering account of the lynching by a white mob of four victims on July 25, 1946, in Walton County, Georgia, at Moore's Ford Bridge. The book is a poignant study of the pernicious power of racism in the wake of the global holocaust of World War II.

CHAPTER TWENTY ONE

THE FREEDOM MOVEMENT

1954–1965

THE 1950s: PROSPERITY AND PREJUDICE

For most white Americans, the 1950s ushered in an era of unparalleled prosperity, heightened consumer consumption, and a patriarchal business culture. Affluent white Americans fled to the suburbs, and by 1960 52 percent of Americans owned their own homes. The decade is remembered nostalgically as a time of large stable nuclear families, wives and mothers who stayed at home, and communities untroubled by drugs and juvenile delinquency.

For most black Americans, however, the 1950s were less blissful. American society remained rigidly segregated in housing and in education. Despite the gains African Americans made during the World War II era, Jim Crow still reigned. Jim Crow restrictions and the ever-present threat of white violence kept millions of African Americans from voting in the deep South. Violence and extralegal practices still made housing integration a distant dream.

THE ROAD TO *BROWN*

In 1954, with the U.S. Supreme Court's decision in *Brown v. Board of Education of Topeka, Kansas*, progress in the desegregation of American society moved from the military into the civilian realm. Ultimately, the *Brown* decision would undermine state-sanctioned segregation in all aspects of American life. The NAACP's legal program of the 1920s and 1930s was largely responsible for this turn of events. In 1940 the NAACP set up the Legal Defense and Educational Fund (NAACP-LDEF) to pursue its assault on the legal foundations of race inequality in American education. Thereafter, NAACP-LDEF fought segregation and discrimination in education, housing, employment, and politics. In the first years of its existence, attorneys for the fund won stunning victories including a 1944 U.S. Supreme Court decision, *Smith v. Allwright*, declaring white primaries unconstitutional, and the *Shelley v. Kramer* (1948) decision outlawing restrictive residential covenants. The life and career of one of the NAACP-LDEF lawyers, Constance Baker Motley, symbolizes the struggle that black professionals, both men and women, waged to overcome racial and gender exclusion and the coalescence of

454

disparate forces that carried the seeds of the coming revolution. Motley is our guide on the road to *Brown*.

Constance Baker Motley and Black Lawyers in the South

Constance Baker Motley was born in 1921 to immigrant parents, Rachel Huggins and Willoughby Alva Baker, from Nevis, in the British West Indies. She grew up in a tightly knit West Indian community in New Haven, Connecticut. Baker attended integrated schools and developed a strong racial consciousness. She recalled, "[M]y interest in civil rights [was] a very early interest which developed when I was in high school. The fact that I was a Black, a woman, and a member of a large, relatively poor family was also the base of this great ambition [to enter the legal profession]."

The most important event in her early life was the lecture that George Crawford, a 1903 Yale Law School graduate, who worked as an NAACP lawyer in New Haven, gave at the local Dixwell Community Center. The talk concerned the Supreme Court decision in *State of Missouri ex rel. Gaines v. Canada*. Crawford explained that the University of Missouri's law school had denied Gaines admission but had offered to pay his tuition expenses to an out-of-state school. The NAACP Legal Committee under Charles H. Houston's leadership won a victory before the U.S. Supreme Court when it ruled that the state had violated the clause in the Fourteenth Amendment mandating that state laws provide equal protection regardless of race. After *Gaines*, states were required to furnish within their borders facilities for legal education for black people equal to those offered white citizens.

Baker desperately wanted to go to law school, but her family could not even afford to send her to college. In 1940 Baker came to the attention of Clarence Blakeslee, a local white businessman and philanthropist who offered to finance her education. She attended Fisk University until 1942 and then transferred to New York University, where she earned a bachelor's degree in economics in 1943. She then became the second black woman ever to attend Columbia University Law School. In 1946, shortly after she finished her legal training she married former New York University law student Joel Motley and went to work with the NAACP's LDEF.

Constance Baker Motley first met Thurgood Marshall in October 1945 when he hired her as a law clerk during her second year in law school. Marshall assigned her to work on the hundreds of army court-martial cases filed after World War II.

In the late 1940s, the NAACP-LDEF's attack on inequality in graduate education provided the basis for a full-scale assault on segregation. No longer would the organization

THE ROAD TO *BROWN*	
1938	*Missouri ex rel. Gaines v. Canada*
1948	*Sipuel v. Oklahoma State Board of Regents*
1950	*McLaurin v. Oklahoma; Sweatt v. Painter*
1954	*Brown v. Board of Education of Topeka*

be satisfied only to push for fulfillment of the promise of "separate but equal" facilities. In 1948 Ada Lois Sipuel was denied admission to the University of Oklahoma Law School because she was black. The U.S. Supreme Court ordered Oklahoma, in *Sipuel v. Board of Regents of the University of Oklahoma*, to "provide [a legal education] for [Sipuel] in conformity with the equal protection clause of the Fourteenth Amendment and provide it as soon as it does for applicants of any other group." Another case, *Sweatt v. Painter*, which the Supreme Court decided in 1950, began when the University of Texas at Austin attempted to circumvent court orders to admit Heman Sweatt into its law school by creating a separate facility consisting of three basement rooms, a small library, and a few instructors who would lecture to him alone. The court ruled that the University of Texas had deprived Sweatt of intangibles such as "the essential ingredient of a legal education . . . the opportunity for students to discuss the law with their peers and others with whom they would be associated professionally in later life." On the same day the justices ruled in *Sweatt*, they also declared illegal the University of Oklahoma's segregation of George W. McLaurin from white students attending the Graduate School of Education. The University of Oklahoma had admitted McLaurin but made him sit in the hallway at the classroom door, study in a private part of the balcony of the library, and eat in a sequestered part of the lunch room. When he finally

This black student at the University of Oklahoma was not allowed to sit in a classroom with white students. It took two Supreme Court decisions to end such segregation at the University of Oklahoma.
CORBIS

gained a seat in the classroom, it was marked "reserved for colored." These cases were important stepping-stones on the road to *Brown*.

A year after the *Sweatt* and *McLaurin* decisions, black parents and their lawyers filed suits in Kansas, South Carolina, Virginia, Delaware, and the District of Columbia asking the courts to apply the qualitative test of the *Sweatt* case to elementary and secondary schools and to declare the "separate-but-equal" doctrine invalid in public education.

Brown and the Coming Revolution

Black lawyers in the South handling civil rights cases were frequently assaulted. On February 27, 1942, for example, NAACP attorney Leon A. Ransom was attacked by a former deputy sheriff in the hall of the Davidson County Courthouse in Nashville, Tennessee.

It was no less difficult for a black woman lawyer to venture into the South in search of justice. Black attorney Derrick Bell, who also worked for the LDEF, said of Motley's work,

> Nothing in the Southern lawyers' background could have prepared them for Connie. To them Negro women were either mammies, maids, or mistresses. None of them had ever dealt with a Negro woman on a peer basis, much less on a level of intellectual equality, which in this case quickly became superiority.

Motley was keenly aware of her precarious situation. "Often a southern judge would refer to men attorneys as Mister, but would make a point of calling me 'Connie,' since traditionally Black women in the South were only called by their first name." Housing was another problem. Motley recalled that when in a southern town for a long trial, "I knew that it was going to be impossible to stay in a decent hotel." These lawyers had to depend on the good graces and courage of local people. Motley explained, "Usually in these situations a Black family would agree to put you up. But there was so much publicity involved with civil rights cases that no Black family dared have us—they were too afraid. I wonder how many lawyers have had the experience of preparing for trial in a flophouse. That was the only room I could get."

In the late 1940s, the black parents of Scott's Branch School in Clarendon County, South Carolina, approached Roderick W. Elliott, the chairman of the school board, with a modest request. There were 6,531 black students and only 2,375 whites students enrolled in the county's schools. Although the county had thirty buses to convey the white students to their schools, not one bus was available to black schoolchildren. Some of the black students had to walk eighteen miles round trip each day. Once they arrived they entered buildings heated by wood stoves and lit by kerosene lamps. For a drink of water or to go to the toilet they had to go outdoors.

The parents mustered the courage and resolve to petition the school board for buses. Elliott's reply was short: "We ain't got no money to buy a bus for your nigger children." In 1949 DeLaine went to the NAACP officials in Columbia, and Thurgood Marshall was there. On December 20, 1950, Harry Briggs, a navy veteran, and twenty-four other Clarendon County residents sued the Summerton School District (Clarendon District

22). The case, *Briggs v. Elliott*, was the first legal challenge to elementary school segregation to originate in the South. Meanwhile, however, four other cases in different parts of the country were inexorably advancing through the federal courts. These would be combined into one case that would decide the fate of the *Plessy* doctrine of "separate but equal."

The years of preparation and hardship paid off. Motley worked with the dream team of black lawyers and academics, an inner circle of advisers that included Louis Redding from Wilmington, Delaware; James Nabrit from Washington, D.C.; Robert Ming from Chicago; psychologist Kenneth Clark from New York; and historian John Hope Franklin to prepare the case, *Brown v. Board of Education of Topeka*, and argue it before the U.S. Supreme Court. Motley, Robert Carter, Jack Greenberg, and Marshall also sought assistance from Spottswood Robinson and Oliver Hill of Richmond, Virginia, and read papers prepared by historians C. Vann Woodward and Alfred Kelly about the original equalitarian intentions of the post–Civil War amendments and other legislation. In his argument, Marshall appealed to the U.S. Supreme Court to meet the *Plessy* doctrine head on and declare that it is erroneous.

By the time Marshall made this argument, black intellectuals, scholars, and activists and their progressive white allies had closed ranks in support of integration. To suggest alternatives as the goal for African Americans was to find oneself swimming against the current.

During late 1953 and early 1954, Chief Justice Earl Warren brought the court in support of Marshall's position. On May 17, 1954, the court ruled unanimously in favor of the NAACP lawyers and their clients that a classification based solely on race violated the Fourteenth Amendment to the U.S. Constitution.

The *Brown* decision would eventually lead to the dismantling of the entire structure of Jim Crow laws that regulated important aspects of black life in America: movement, work, marriage, education, housing, even death and burial. The *Brown* decision, more than any other case, signaled the emerging primacy of equality as a guide to constitutional decisions. This and subsequent decisions helped advance the rights of other minorities and women. As Motley reflected, "In the *Brown* case and in the decisions that followed, we blazed a trail for others by showing the competence of Black lawyers."

BROWN II

A year after the 1954 *Brown* decision, in May 1955, the Supreme Court issued a second ruling, commonly known as *Brown II*, which addressed the practical process of desegregation. The Court underscored that the states in the suits should begin prompt compliance with the 1954 ruling, but that this should be done with "all deliberate speed." Many black Americans interpreted this to mean "immediately." White Southerners hoped it meant a long time, or never. Ominously, President Eisenhower seemed displeased with the Court's rulings and refused to put the moral authority of his office behind their enforcement.

Nevertheless, in 1955 and early 1956, desegregation proceeded without hindrance in Maryland, Kentucky, Delaware, Oklahoma, and Missouri. Many other moderate white southern politicians counseled calm and worked to head off a full-scale conflict between their region and the federal government.

Massive White Resistance

White moderates, however, soon found themselves a shrinking minority, as extremists, determined to maintain white supremacy at any cost, prepared for mass resistance to the Court's decisions. The rhetoric of these extremists bordered on hysteria but found a receptive audience among many white people. A young minister from Virginia named Jerry Falwell, for example, explained that black people were the descendants of Noah's son Ham and destined to be servants because of a curse God had put on him. Falwell also claimed the Supreme Court's decisions were inspired by Moscow. In 1955 leading businessmen, white-collar professionals, and clergy began organizing White Citizens' Councils in virtually every southern city; these were groups dedicated to preserving the southern way of life and the South's "sacred heritage of freedom." The councils used their economic and political power to intimidate black people who challenged segregation. They fired people from their jobs, evicted them from their homes, and refused them credit.

Many white politicians took up the banner of massive resistance. Senator James O. Eastland, from Mississippi, called the *Brown* decision a "monstrous crime." The Virginia legislature closed all public schools in Prince Edward County to thwart integration. Most dramatically, on March 12, 1956, ninety-six southern congressmen led by North Carolina's senator Sam Ervin Jr. and South Carolina's senator Strom Thurmond issued "The Southern Manifesto," vowing to fight to preserve segregation and the southern way of life. The manifesto called the *Brown* decisions an "unwarranted exercise of power by the court, contrary to the Constitution." The only southern senators who refused to sign the "Manifesto" were Albert Gore Sr. of Tennessee and Lyndon B. Johnson of Texas.

The NAACP came under siege after the *Brown* decision as southern states tried to wipe it out of existence. By 1957 nine southern states had filed suit to eradicate the organization. Some states, alleging the NAACP was linked to a worldwide communist conspiracy, made membership illegal. Membership plummeted from 128,716 to 79,677, and the association lost 246 branches in the South.

Under these pressures, desegregation ground to a halt. Massive resistance successfully challenged the possibility of achieving change through court action alone.

The Lynching of Emmett Till

The violent reaction of white Southerners to the growing assertiveness of black people found expression in the summer of 1955 in the lynching of fourteen-year-old Emmett Till of Chicago, an event that helped galvanize the emerging civil rights movement. Till was visiting relatives in the small town of Money, Mississippi. On a dare from his friends, he entered Bryant's grocery store, bought candy, and said "Bye, baby" to Carolyn Bryant, the wife of the owner, as he left. Till was unaware how far white people in the town would go to avenge this small breach of white supremacy's racial etiquette. In the middle of the night a few days after the incident, Bryant's husband and brother-in-law arrived at the small home where Till was staying and kidnapped him at gunpoint. His body was subsequently found in the Tallahatchie River tied to a heavy cotton gin fan. Till had a bullet in his head and had been tortured before his murder. Despite overwhelming evidence and the brave testimony of Mose Wright, Till's uncle, and other local black people, an all-white jury acquitted the two men who lynched Till. In early 1956 the murderers sold their confession to *Look* magazine and gloated over their escape from justice. In 2004, new evidence surfaced indicating that ten people may have been involved in the Till lynching.

The Till lynching shaped the consciousness of an entire generation of young African-American activists. Partly this was due to the efforts of Till's mother, Mamie Bradley. Unwilling to let America turn away from this crime, Till's mother had her son's mangled body displayed in an open casket in Chicago. Thousands of mourners paid their respects, and many committed themselves to fighting the system that made this crime possible. Bradley also traveled around the nation speaking to groups on whom her grief had a profound impact.

NEW FORMS OF PROTEST: THE MONTGOMERY BUS BOYCOTT

Strong local communities formed the core of the civil rights movement and they were often sparked to action by the deeds of brave and committed individuals. The first and one of the most important expressions of this process occurred in Alabama's small capital city of Montgomery (see Map 21–1). The city's African-American community of 45,000 was poised to make history.

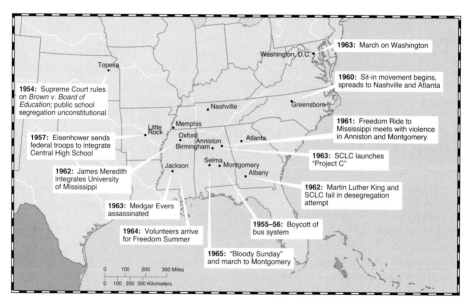

MAP 21–1   Major Events of the Civil Rights Movement. This map shows the location of key events in the struggle for civil rights between 1954 and 1965.

The Roots of Revolution

The movement in Montgomery was the result of years of organization and planning by protest groups. In addition to its numerous churches, two black colleges, and other social organizations, the Alabama capital had a strong core of protest groups. One, the Women's Political Council (WPC), had been founded in 1946 by Mary Frances Fair Burks, chair of Alabama State College English Department, after the all-white League of Women Voters had refused to allow black women to participate in its activities. Although the WPC had only forty members, all middle-class women, its courageous and competent leaders were willing to stand up to powerful white people. The WPC was joined by a chapter of the NAACP led by E. D. Nixon, a Pullman train porter and head of the Alabama chapter of the Brotherhood of Sleeping Car Porters. In 1943 Nixon had founded the Montgomery Voters League, an organization dedicated to helping African Americans navigate Alabama's tortuous voter registration process. In the decade after 1945 these groups searched for a way to mobilize the black community to challenge white power.

Four days after the 1954 *Brown* decision was announced, Jo Ann Robinson, a professor at Alabama State College, wrote a letter to Montgomery's mayor on behalf of the WPC. In it she reiterated the complaints of the black community concerning conditions on the city's buses and ended, "Please consider this plea, for even now plans are being made to ride less, or not at all, on our buses." The mayor ignored the warning and the buses remained as segregated as before. All seemed quiet on the surface, but Montgomery's black lawyers and NAACP chapter began laying the groundwork for a test case challenging segregation of the city's bus lines.

On March 2, 1955, a fifteen-year-old girl, Claudette Colvin, was arrested for refusing to give up her seat on a bus to a white person. The WPC was ready to use this incident to initiate the threatened bus boycott, but Nixon dissuaded them. He felt that Colvin, who was unmarried and pregnant, would not be an appropriate symbol around which to organize. He and other activists resolved to wait for another chance.

Rosa Parks

On Thursday, December 1, 1955, Rosa Parks, a forty-three-year-old department store seamstress and civil rights activist, boarded a city bus and moved to the back where African Americans were required to sit. All seats were taken so she sat in one toward the middle of the bus. When a white man boarded the bus, the driver ordered Parks to vacate her seat for him, but Rosa Parks refused to move. She had not planned to resist on that day, but, as she later said, she had "decided that I would have to know once and for all what rights I had as a human being and a citizen. . . . I was so involved with the attempt to bring about freedom from this kind of thing . . . I felt just resigned to give what I could to protest against the way I was being treated, and felt that all of our meetings, trying to negotiate, bring about petitions before the authorities . . . really hadn't done any good at all." With this act of resistance launched the Montgomery bus boycott movement and inspired the modern civil rights struggle for freedom and equality.

The plans of the WPC and NAACP came into play after Parks's arrest for violating Montgomery's transportation laws. She was ordered to appear in court on the following Monday. Meanwhile, E. D. Nixon bailed her out of the city jail and began mobilizing the leadership of the black community behind her. Working in tandem with

Nixon, Robinson wrote and circulated a flyer calling for a one-day boycott of the buses followed by a mass meeting of the community to discuss the matter. Robinson took the flyer to the Alabama State College campus, stayed up all night, and, with the help of a colleague, mimeographed thirty thousand copies of it. The WPC had planned distribution routes months earlier, and the next day, Robinson and nearly two hundred volunteers distributed bundles of flyers throughout black neighborhoods.

Montgomery Improvement Association

On December 5, 1955, the black community did not ride the buses, and the movement had begun. Nixon and other community leaders decided to form a new organization, the Montgomery Improvement Association (MIA), to coordinate the protest; they also selected a twenty-six-year-old minister, Martin Luther King Jr., to act as its president. That evening there was an overflowing mass meeting of the black community at the large Holt Street Baptist church to decide whether to continue the boycott. King, with barely an hour to prepare, spoke to the crowd and delivered a message that would define the goals of the boycott and the civil rights movement that followed. In his dramatic voice he connected the core values of America and of the Judeo-Christian tradition to the goals of African Americans nationwide as well as in Montgomery.

Martin Luther King Jr.

King's speech electrified the meeting, which unanimously decided to stay off the city's buses until the MIA's demands were met. The speech also marked the beginning of King's role as a leader of the civil rights movement. King had been raised in a prominent ministerial family with a long history of standing up for African-American rights. King's grandfather had led a protest to force Atlanta to build its first high school for African Americans. King's father spoke out for African-American rights as pastor of Ebenezer Baptist Church. At age fifteen, King had entered Morehouse College but did not embrace the ministry as his profession until he came under the influence of its president, Dr. Benjamin E. Mays. By age twenty-five, King had been awarded a Ph.D. in theology from Boston University. He moved to Alabama with his wife, Coretta Scott King, to become pastor of Dexter Avenue Baptist Church in Montgomery.

In addition to his verbal artistry, King had the ability to inspire moral courage and to teach people how to maintain themselves under excruciating pressure. King merged Gandhian nonviolence with black Christian faith and church culture to create a unique ideology well suited for the civil rights struggle. King declared that the boycott would continue with or without its leaders because the conflict was not "between the white and the Negro" but "between justice and injustice." He explained to the boycotting community, "If we are arrested every day, if we are exploited every day, if we are trampled over every day, don't ever let anyone pull you so low as to hate them. . . . We must realize so many people are taught to hate us that they are not totally responsible for their hate."

Walking for Freedom

Although men occupied the top leadership positions in the boycott, women were the key to its effectiveness. The boycott lasted more than a year—381 days—and over its course nearly all the black women previously dependent on the buses to get to work refused to ride them. Some walked twelve miles a day. Others had the support of their white women employers, who provided transportation. And many helped organize an efficient car pool of two hundred vehicles that proved critical to sustaining the boycott. The community at large participated in mass meetings held nightly in local churches. Robinson edited the MIA newsletter. Other women supported the boycott in dozens of ways. Some organized bake sales, and others made door-to-door solicitations to raise the $2,000 per week needed to keep the car pools going.

The boycott took 65 percent of the bus company's business, forcing it to cut schedules, lay off drivers, and raise fares. White merchants also suffered. The bus company, however, could scarcely afford to break the laws of the city that chartered it, and despite the company's losses, the city government refused to capitulate. Officials would not even accede to such a modest demand as a "first come, first served" seating arrangement—like that proposed by the Montgomery Women's Political Council before the boycott began—in which black riders would sit from back to front and white riders from front to back.

Impressive as it was, the boycott by itself could not end segregation on the buses. Black Montgomery needed a two-pronged strategy of mass local pressure and legal recourse through the courts. The legal backing of the federal government was necessary to end Jim Crow. Thus NAACP lawyers and MIA's lawyer Fred Gray filed a suit in the names of Claudette Colvin, Mary Louise Smith, and three other women.

Friends in the North

The Montgomery movement was not without allies outside the South. Money poured into the MIA's coffers from concerned Americans. Many northern activists who had long been hoping black Southerners would begin just this kind of resistance also swung into action to help. Two people were particularly important at this juncture: Bayard Rustin and liberal Jewish lawyer Stanley Levison. Two and a half months into the boycott, Montgomery officials indicted King and one hundred other leaders on charges of conspiracy to disrupt the bus system. At this juncture Bayard Rustin arrived in Montgomery and immediately encouraged the leaders to follow Gandhian practice and submit freely to arrest. Rustin continued working behind the scenes as one of King's most trusted advisers on nonviolent principles and tactics.

Levison was a wealthy attorney committed to social justice. He had worked with the Communist Party, and Rustin had a long history of association with radical groups. Their influence soon attracted the attention of the Federal Bureau of Investigation, which had long been obsessed with black leaders and organizations. King was not a communist, but FBI director J. Edgar Hoover developed an intense hatred of him and other black leaders. At one point Hoover called King "the most dangerous man in America," and he pressed his subordinates to prove King was a communist and that the civil rights movement was a Moscow-inspired conspiracy. Hoover and his men began tapping King's telephone and hotel rooms and even threatened to expose his extramarital affairs if he did not commit suicide. By the early 1960s, the FBI had stopped warning King when it uncovered threats to his life.

Victory

As the bus boycott reached the one-year mark, King and others grew discouraged. Their hopes seemed to fade in November 1956 when it became clear the state courts would soon move to declare the car pools illegal. Salvation for the movement came from the cases local women and the NAACP had taken to the federal courts. On November 13, 1956, the Supreme Court ordered an end to Montgomery's bus segregation. The *Gayle v. Browder* decision, unlike the *Brown* decision, expressly overturned the 1896 *Plessy v. Ferguson* decision, because like *Plessy* it applied to transportation. The bus company agreed not only to end segregation but also to hire African-American drivers and to treat all passengers with equal respect. On the morning of December 21, 1956, black citizens of Montgomery boarded the buses and sat wherever they pleased.

No Easy Road to Freedom: 1957–1960

The victory at Montgomery set an example for future protests. It was the result of a highly organized black community led by committed and capable black leaders. These local efforts were bolstered by the advice and involvement of activists outside the South, the attention of a sympathetic national press, and, crucially, intervention from the federal courts. But local victories could only go so far, particularly as white resistance intensified. In the three years following the boycott, black Southerners and their allies across the nation prepared for a broader movement. At the same time, federal officials outside the judiciary found they could not ignore the white South's incipient rebellion without grave consequences for the nation and their own power.

Martin Luther King and the SCLC

By the end of the campaign in Montgomery, Martin Luther King Jr. had emerged as a moral leader of national stature. On the advice of Levison, Rustin, and Ella Baker, he helped create a new organization, the Southern Christian Leadership Council (SCLC), to provide an institutional base for continuing the struggle. The SCLC was a federation of civil rights groups, community organizations, and churches that sought to coordinate all the burgeoning local movements. King assumed leadership of the SCLC, crisscrossing the nation in the ensuing years to build support for the organization and to raise money to fund its activities. Members of the organization also began training black activists, particularly on college campuses, in the tactics of nonviolent protest. Because the ballot was deemed the critical weapon needed to complete school desegregation and secure equal employment opportunity, adequate housing, and equal access to public accommodations, the SCLC focused on securing voting rights for black people. In the three years after the Montgomery bus boycott, the SCLC also aided black communities in applying the lessons of that struggle to challenge bus segregation in Tallahassee (Florida) and Atlanta.

The NAACP's leadership doubted the effectiveness of the protest tactics favored by the SCLC. They resented having to divert resources away from work on important court cases to defend people arrested in protests and were troubled by the left-wing connections of King's advisers. Despite their differences, the SCLC and the NAACP worked together, but the tensions over tactics were never far from the surface.

Civil Rights Act of 1957

Despite President Eisenhower's tepid response to *Brown*, Congress proved willing to take a modest step toward ending racial discrimination when it enacted the Civil Rights Act of 1957, the first such legislation since the end of Reconstruction. In a departure from the past, liberals in the Senate were able to end a filibuster by Southerners, but the bill they passed was, for all its symbolic import, weak. It created a commission to monitor violations of black civil rights and to propose remedies for infringements on black voting. It upgraded the Civil Rights Section into a division within the Justice Department and gave it the power to initiate civil proceedings against those states and municipalities that discriminated on the basis of race. This act disappointed black activists because it was not strong enough to counter white reaction and because they felt the Eisenhower administration would not enforce it.

Little Rock, Arkansas

Eisenhower may have had little inclination to support the fight for black rights, but the defiance of Arkansas governor Orville Faubus would soon force him to. At the beginning of the school year in 1957, Faubus posted 270 soldiers from the Arkansas National Guard outside Little Rock Central High School to prevent nine black youths from entering. Faubus was determined to flout the *Brown* ruling and to maintain school segregation. When a federal district court order forced the governor to allow the children into the school, he simply withdrew the state guard and left the children alone to face a hate-filled mob.

   To defend the sovereignty of the federal court and the Constitution, Eisenhower had to act. He sent in 1,100 paratroopers from the 101st Airborne to Little Rock and put the state national guard under federal authority. It was the first time since Reconstruction that troops had been sent to the South to protect the rights of African-American citizens. The troops remained in Little Rock Central High School for the rest of the school year. Governor Faubus closed the Little Rock public schools in 1958–1959. Eight of the nine black students valiantly withstood the abuse, harassment, and curses of segregationists both inside and outside the facility and eventually desegregated the high school. Other young African Americans throughout the South would show similar courage.

BLACK YOUTH STAND UP BY SITTING DOWN

Beginning in 1960 motivated black college students adapted a strategy that CORE had used in the 1940s—the sit-in—and emerged as the dynamic vanguard of the civil rights movement. Their contributions to the black protest movement accelerated the pace of social change. Before long the movement would inspire an even larger number of northern black and white students.

Sit-Ins: Greensboro, Nashville, Atlanta

Early on the morning of February 1, 1960, Ezell Blair Jr., Joseph McNeil, Franklin McCain, and David Richmond, all freshmen at North Carolina Agricultural and Technical College (A & T), decided to desegregate local restaurants by sitting at the

Four students—from the left they are Joseph McNeil, Franklin McCain, Billy Smith, and Clarence Henderson—sit patiently at Woolworth's lunch counter on February 2, 1960, the second day of the sit-in in Greensboro, North Carolina. Although not the first sit-in protest against segregated facilities, the Greensboro action triggered a wave of sit-ins by black high school and college students across the South.
News & Record Library/John G. Moebes

lunch counter of Greensboro, North Carolina's Woolworth five-and-dime store. Although black people were welcome to spend their money in the store, they were not permitted to dine at the lunch counter, making it a painful symbol of white supremacy. At 4:30 in the afternoon the students sat at the counter. They received no service that day but sat quietly doing their school work until the store closed. The action of these four young men electrified their fellow students, and the next day many others joined them. Soon, black women students from Bennett College and a few white students from the University of North Carolina Women's College joined the protest, and by the fifth day hundreds of young, studious, neatly dressed African Americans crowded the downtown store demanding their rights.

Like the black people of Montgomery, the students in Greensboro acted with forethought and with the support of their community. Although they began the sit-in on their own, it quickly gained the support of the black community. Many people in the North and West—both black and white—also joined the campaign by picketing local stores of the national chains that approved of segregation in the South. After facing the collective power of the black community and their allies for many months, white businessmen and politicians finally gave in to the black community's demands.

The students at Greensboro were not alone in their desire to strike out at discrimination. Indeed, at Fisk University in Nashville, Tennessee, Diane Nash, John Lewis,

Marion Barry, James Bevel, Curtis Murphy, Gloria Johnson, Bernard Lafayette, and Rodney Powell had begun organizing nonviolent workshops before the Greensboro sit-in. Even better organized than their comrades in North Carolina, they had been undergoing intensive training for a sit-in campaign. Twelve days after the first sit-ins began, the Nashville group swung into action. Hundreds were arrested, and those who sat suffered insults, mob violence, beatings, arrest, and torture while in jail. Nonetheless, they compelled major restaurants to desegregate by May 1960.

Atlanta, Martin Luther King Jr.'s home base and the site of a large African-American community, spawned an even more dramatic movement. It began after Spelman College freshman Ruby Doris Smith persuaded her friends and classmates to launch sit-ins in the city. On March 15, 1960, at Atlanta University, two students, Julian Bond and Lonnie King, executing a carefully orchestrated plan, deployed two hundred sit-in students to ten different eating places. They targeted government-owned property and public places, including bus and train stations and the state capitol, that should have been willing to serve all customers. At the Federal Building, Bond and his classmates attempted to eat in the municipal cafeteria and were arrested. The Atlanta sit-in students broadened their campaign demands to include desegregation of all public facilities, black voting rights, and equal access to educational and employment opportunities. On September 27, 1961, the Atlanta business and political elite gave in.

By April 1960 more than two thousand students from black high schools and colleges had been arrested in seventy-eight southern towns and cities. Local people demonstrated their allegiance to them in numerous ways, but their most effective tactic was the economic boycott. When business began to suffer as a result of the protests, white leaders proved willing to negotiate the racial status quo. By the summer, more than thirty southern cities had set up community organizations to respond to the complaints of local black citizens.

The Student Nonviolent Coordinating Committee

Recognizing the significance of the regionwide student action and fearing it would soon melt away, the SCLC's Ella Baker organized a conference for 150 students at her alma mater, Shaw University, in Raleigh, North Carolina. Baker, who managed operations in the SCLC's Atlanta headquarters, chafed under the rigid male leadership of the organization. In contrast, she advocated decentralized leadership and celebrated participatory democracy. Her skepticism about the SCLC struck a chord with the students.

On April 15–17, 1960, delegates representing over fifty colleges and high schools from thirty-seven communities in thirteen states arrived and began discussing how to keep the movement going. Baker addressed the group in a speech entitled "More Than a Hamburger" and became the midwife of a new organization named the Student Nonviolent Coordinating Committee (SNCC). The newest addition to the roster of civil rights associations adhered to the ideology of nonviolence, but it also acknowledged the possible need for increased militancy and confrontation. More accommodating black leaders, even some of those in the SCLC, objected to the students' use of direct confrontational tactics that disrupted race relations and community peace.

Freedom Rides

The sit-in movement paved the way for the "Freedom Rides" of 1961. CORE's James Farmer and Bayard Rustin resolved it was time for a reprise of their 1947 mission to ride interstate buses and trains in the upper South. That early effort—a planned bus trip from Washington, D.C., to Kentucky—reached only as far as Chapel Hill, North Carolina. There the group of interracial riders met violent resistance, were arrested, and were sentenced to thirty days on a road gang. This new journey tested the Justice Department's willingness to protect the rights of African Americans to use bus terminal facilities on a nonsegregated basis.

The Freedom Rides showed the world how far some white Southerners would go to preserve segregation. The first ride ran into trouble on May 4, 1961, when John Lewis, one of the seven black riders, tried to enter the white waiting room of the Greyhound bus terminal in Rock Hill, South Carolina, and was brutally beaten by local white people in full view of the police. The interracial group continued through Alabama toward Jackson, Mississippi, but repeated acts of white violence made escape from Alabama difficult. At Anniston, Alabama, a mob firebombed the bus and beat the escaping riders. A group of local African Americans led by the Reverend Fred Shuttlesworth took many of the shocked and injured riders to Birmingham.

With the police offering no protection, CORE abandoned the Freedom Rides, and all but a few of the original riders left Alabama. But SNCC activists and students in Nashville refused to let the idea die. At least twenty civil rights workers went to Birmingham where they vowed on May 20 to ride on to Montgomery. John Lewis remained with the group that arrived in Montgomery. Awaiting them was another angry mob of more than a thousand white people, and not a policeman in sight. This time Lewis was knocked unconscious, and all the riders had to be hospitalized. Even a presidential aide assigned to monitor the crisis was injured.

News services flashed graphic images of the violence around the world, and the federal government resolved to end the bloodletting. Attorney General Robert Kennedy sent four hundred federal marshals to restore law and order. Martin Luther King Jr. and Ralph Abernathy joined the conflict on May 21, as 1,200 men, women, and children met at Abernathy's church. The federal marshals averted further bloodshed by surrounding the building. Only then did Governor John Patterson order the National Guard and state troopers to protect the protesters. When the group arrived in Jackson, Mississippi, white authorities promptly arrested them. By summer's end, more than three hundred Freedom Riders had served time in Mississippi's notorious prisons.

A SIGHT TO BE SEEN: THE MOVEMENT AT HIGH TIDE

Between 1960 and 1963, the civil rights movement developed the techniques and organization that would finally bring America face to face with the conflict between its democratic ideals and the racism of its politics. Day after day the movement squared off against the die-hard resistance of the white South and created a situation that demanded the president and Congress take action.

The Election of 1960

One of the persistent fears of white Southerners was that black Americans, if armed with the ballot, would possess the balance of political power. The presidential election of 1960 proved this to be the case. Initially, many African Americans favored the Republican Party's nominee, Richard Nixon, who had advocated strong civil rights legislation. Baseball star Jackie Robinson was a Nixon supporter as were many other well-known African Americans. It seemed as if the New Deal coalition had weakened and black citizens would reverse their move into the Democratic Party. The Democratic nominee, Massachusetts senator John F. Kennedy, in contrast, had done little to distinguish himself to black Americans in the struggles of the 1950s. As the campaign progressed, however, Kennedy made more sympathetic statements in support of black protests. Meanwhile, Nixon attempted to strengthen his position with white southern voters and remained silent about civil rights issues, even though the Republican Party had a strong pro–civil rights record.

Shortly before the election, Martin Luther King was sentenced to four months in prison for leading a nonviolent protest march in Atlanta. Kennedy seized the opportunity to telephone King's wife, Coretta Scott King, to offer his support while his brother Robert F. Kennedy used his influence to obtain King's release. These acts impressed African Americans and won their support. African-American voters in key northern cities provided the crucial margin that elected John F. Kennedy. In Illinois, for example, with black voters casting 250,000 ballots for Kennedy, the Democrats carried the state by merely 9,000 votes.

The Kennedy Administration and the Civil Rights Movement

Early in his administration John F. Kennedy grew concerned about the mounting violence occasioned by the civil rights movement. As the Freedom Rides continued across the deep South, the activists provoked crises and confrontations and forced the federal government to intervene in their behalf. Kennedy's primary interest at this point was to prevent disorder from getting out of hand and to avoid compromising America's position with the developing nations. But Kennedy had little room to maneuver given the continued power of white Southerners in his party and in Congress.

Despite these limitations, Kennedy did aid the cause of civil rights. He issued Executive Order 11063, which required government agencies to discontinue discriminatory policies and practices in federally supported housing, and he named Vice President Lyndon B. Johnson to chair the newly established Committee on Equal Employment Opportunity. Kennedy also pleased black Americans when he nominated Thurgood Marshall to the Second Circuit Court of Appeals on September 23, 1961. He named journalist Carl Rowan deputy assistant secretary of state. More than forty African Americans took positions in the new administration, including Robert Weaver, director of the Housing and Home Finance Agency; Mercer Cook, ambassador to Norway; and George L. P. Weaver, assistant secretary of labor. Moreover, Kennedy's brother Robert put muscle into the Civil Rights Division of the Justice Department by hiring an impressive team of lawyers headed by Washington attorney Burke Marshall.

On June 25, 1962, one year after James Meredith had filed a complaint of racial discrimination against the University of Mississippi, the U.S. Circuit Court of Appeals for the Fifth Circuit ruled that the university had to admit him. Mississippi governor Ross Barnett vowed to resist the order, but Kennedy sent three hundred federal marshals to uphold it. Thousands of students rioted at the campus; two people died, two hundred were arrested, and nearly half the marshals were injured. Kennedy did not back down. He federalized the Mississippi National Guard to ensure Meredith's admission. Although isolated and harassed throughout his time at Ole Miss, Meredith eventually graduated. Likewise, in June 1963, the Kennedy administration compelled Governor George Wallace of Alabama to allow the desegregation of the University of Alabama.

Voter Registration Projects

On June 16, 1961, Robert Kennedy met with student leaders and urged them to redirect their energies to voter registration projects and to lessen their concentration on direct-action activities. He and the Justice Department aides persuaded the students that the free exercise of the ballot would result in profound and significant social change. James Foreman, SNCC's executive director, followed Kennedy's lead. By October 1961 SNCC had joined forces with the NAACP, SCLC, and CORE in the voter education project funded by major philanthropic foundations and administered by the Southern Regional Council. SNCC was responsible for Alabama and Mississippi. Drawing heavily on the expertise of Robert Moses and working closely with a cadre of local leaders like Amzie Moore, head of the NAACP in Mississippi's Cleveland county, and Fannie Lou Hamer of Ruleville, SNCC opened a series of voter registration schools. The "graduates" thereupon attempted to register to vote. These attempts unleashed a wave of white violence and murder across Mississippi.

THE ALBANY MOVEMENT

In Albany, Georgia, the movement began in the summer of 1961 when SNCC members moved into the city to conduct a voter registration project. Soon representatives of various local groups decided to form a coalition called the Albany Movement and elected osteopath William G. Anderson as its president. The movement's goal quickly expanded from securing the vote to the total desegregation of the town.

In Laurie Pritchett, Albany's police chief, the movement faced an uncommonly sophisticated opponent. Pritchett studied the past tactics of SNCC and King and resolved not to confront the federal government directly and to avoid the kind of violence that brought negative media attention. When students from a black college decided to begin demonstrations by desegregating the bus terminal, Pritchett immediately arrested them after they entered the white waiting room and attempted to eat in the bus terminal dining room. Shrewdly, he charged the students with violating a city ordinance for failing to obey a law enforcement officer.

The Albany Movement decided to invite King and the SCLC to aid them and to overwhelm the police department by filling the jails with protesters. King answered the call. On December 16, 1961, he and more than 250 demonstrators were arrested, joining the 507 people already in jail. The plan was to stay in jail in order to, as Charles Sherrod explained, "break the system down from within. Our ability to suffer was somehow going to overcome their ability to hurt us." King vowed to remain in jail until the city desegregated. Sheriff Pritchett, however, made arrangements to house almost two thousand people in surrounding jail facilities and trained his deputies in the use of nonviolent techniques. Thus Pritchett avoided confrontation, violence, and federal intervention.

On December 18, 1961, two days after King's arrest, the city and the Albany Movement announced a truce. King returned to Atlanta, and the city refused to implement the terms of the agreement. When King and Ralph Abernathy returned to Albany in July 1962 for sentencing on their December arrests, they chose forty-five days in jail rather than admit guilt by paying a fine. The mass marches resumed, but again Pritchett thwarted King by having him released from jail to avoid negative publicity. The city's attorney then secured a federal injunction to prevent King and the other leaders from demonstrating. Given his dependence on the federal government, King felt he could not violate the injunction and abandoned the protest. For King, the Albany Movement was a failure, his most glaring defeat, and one that called into question the future of the movement.

THE BIRMINGHAM CONFRONTATION

Black communities in many parts of the South were strong and well organized, but their enormous efforts had achieved only modest changes. National politicians, including President Kennedy, remained reluctant to act unless faced with open defiance by white people or televised violence against peaceful protesters. King and other black leaders knew that if city governments throughout the South followed the model of Sheriff Pritchett in Albany, the civil rights movement might lose momentum. To rejuvenate the movement, the SCLC decided to launch a massive new campaign during 1963, the year of the one hundredth anniversary of the Emancipation Proclamation.

Birmingham, Alabama, a large, tightly segregated industrial city, was chosen as the site for the action. The city was ripe for such a protest, in part because its black community suffered from severe police brutality as well as economic, educational, and social discrimination. The Ku Klux Klan terrorized people with impunity. The black community had, however, developed a strong phalanx of protest organizations called the Alabama Christian Movement for Human Rights (ACMHR) led by the Reverend Fred Shuttlesworth. The ACMHR and SCLC planned a campaign of boycotts, pickets, and demonstrations code-named Project C for Confrontation. Their program would be far more extensive than any before, with demands to integrate public facilities, for guarantees of employment opportunities for black workers in downtown businesses, to desegregate the schools, to improve services in black neighborhoods, and to provide low-income housing. Organizers hoped to provoke the city's public safety commissioner Eugene T. "Bull" Connor, who, unlike Sheriff Pritchett, had a reputation for viciousness. Civil rights leaders believed Connor's conduct would horrify the nation and compel Kennedy to act.

Project C began on the third of April with college students conducting sit-ins. Days later, marches began, and Connor, following the lead of Pritchett, arrested all who participated but avoided overt violence. When the state courts prohibited further protests, King and Abernathy, among others, violated the ruling. They were arrested and jailed on Good Friday, April 12, 1963.

While in jail, King received a letter from eight local Christian and Jewish clergymen who objected to what they considered the "unwise and untimely" protest activities of black citizens. King had smuggled a pen into jail and on scraps of paper, including toilet paper and the margins of the Birmingham *News*, he wrote an eloquent treatise on the use of direct action. His "Letter from Birmingham Jail" was widely published in newspapers and magazines. In it, King dismissed those who called for black people to wait.

King's letter had a powerful national impact, but the Birmingham movement was beginning to lose momentum because many of the protesters were either in jail or could not risk new arrests. At this juncture James Bevel of the SCLC proposed using schoolchildren to continue the protests. Many observers criticized this idea, as did some of those in the movement. But King and other leaders believed it was necessary to risk harm to children in order to ensure their freedom. Thus, on May 2 and 3, 1963, a "children's crusade" involving thousands of youths, some as young as six, marched. This tactic enraged "Bull" Connor and his officers. The police not only arrested the children but flailed away with nightsticks and set vicious dogs on them. On Connor's order, firefighters aimed their powerful hoses at the youngsters, ripping the clothes from backs, cutting flesh, and tumbling children down the street. In the ensuing days many of the children and their parents began to fight back, hurling bottles and rocks at their uniformed tormentors. As the violence escalated, white businessmen became concerned, and the city soon came to the bargaining table.

President Kennedy deployed Assistant Attorney General for Civil Rights Burke Marshall to negotiate a settlement. On May 10, 1963, white businessmen agreed to integrate downtown facilities and to hire black men and women. The following night the KKK bombed the A. G. Gaston Motel, where the SCLC had its headquarters, and the house that belonged to King's brother, the Reverend A. D. King. Black citizens in turn burned cars and buildings and attacked the police. Only intervention by King and other movement leaders prevented a riot. White moderates delivered on the promises and the agreement stuck.

Although the SCLC did not win on every demand, Birmingham was a major triumph and a turning point in the movement. The summer of 1963 saw a massive upsurge in protests across the South with nearly eight hundred marches, demonstrations, and sit-ins. Ten civil rights protesters were killed and twenty thousand arrested as the white South desperately sought to stem the tide. In one of the most tragic losses for the movement, white extremist Byron de la Beckwith gunned down Medgar Evers in the driveway of his home on June 12, 1963, in Jackson, Mississippi. Evers had been the executive secretary of the NAACP's Mississippi organization and the center of a powerful movement in that city. His cold-blooded murder dramatized the depth of hatred among some white Southerners and the lengths to which they would go to prevent change.

A HARD VICTORY

The sacrifices in Birmingham and the intensification of the movement throughout the South set the stage for Congress to pass legislation for a Second Reconstruction that would at last fulfill the promise of the first.

The March on Washington

The lingering image of Birmingham and the growing number of demonstrations throughout the South compelled action from President Kennedy. On June 11, 1963, he addressed the nation with his strongest statement about civil rights. He declared, "We face . . . a moral crisis as a country and a people. It cannot be met by repressive police action. It cannot be left to increased demonstrations in the streets. It cannot be quieted by token moves or talk. It is a time to act in the Congress, in your state and local legislative body, and above all, in all our daily lives. A great change is at hand, and our task, our obligation, is to make that revolution . . . peaceful and constructive for all." Kennedy subsequently proposed the strongest civil rights bill the country had yet seen, but despite the public's heightened awareness of discrimination, he still could not muster sufficient support in Congress to counter the powerful southern bloc within his own party.

To demonstrate their support for Kennedy's civil rights legislation, a coalition of civil rights organizations—SCLC, NAACP, CORE, SNCC, and the National Urban League—and their leaders resurrected the idea of organizing a march on Washington that A. Philip Randolph had first proposed in 1941. In 1962 Randolph and Bayard Rustin had proposed a march to protest black unemployment. Their call received a tepid response, but after Birmingham many of the major civil rights organizations reconsidered. Reflecting renewed hope, Randolph christened it a march for "Jobs and Freedom."

In August 1963 nearly 250,000 marchers gathered before the Lincoln Memorial to show their support for the civil rights bill and the movement at large. Throughout the day they sang freedom songs and listened to speeches from civil rights leaders. Finally, late in the afternoon, Martin Luther King Jr. arose, and casting aside his prepared remarks, he delivered an impassioned speech. Most powerfully, King spoke of this vision of the future:

> I say to you today, my friends, that in spite of the difficulties and frustrations of the moment I still have a dream. It is a dream deeply rooted in the American dream. I have a dream that one day this nation will rise up and live out the true meaning of its creed: "We hold these truths to be self-evident; that all men are created equal." I have a dream that one day on the red hills of Georgia the sons of former slaves and the sons of former slave owners will be able to sit down together at the table of brotherhood. I have a dream that one day even the state of Mississippi, a desert state sweltering with the heat of injustice and oppression, will be transformed into an oasis of freedom and justice. I have a dream that my four children will one day live in a nation where they will not be judged by the color of their skin but by the content of their character. I have a dream today. I have a dream that one day the state of Alabama, whose governor's lips are presently dripping with the words of interposition and nullification, will be transformed into a situation where little black boys and black girls will be able to join hands with little white boys and white girls and walk together as sisters and brothers. I have a dream today . . .

King's words did not still the angry opposition of some white Southerners. On September 15, 1963, only days after the march on Washington, white racists bombed the 16th St. Baptist Church in Birmingham and killed four little girls attending Sunday

At the height of his moral authority, Martin Luther King Jr. (1929–1968) delivers the memorable "I Have A Dream" speech at the 1963 March on Washington. He conveyed a vision of a future America free of the evil of racism where all God's children would be judged by the content of their character, not the color of their skin. King received the Nobel Peace Prize in 1964, and since 1986 the nation honors him with a holiday in his name.
AP Wide World Photos

school: Addie Mae Collins, Denise McNair, Carole Robertson, and Cynthia Wesley. Chris McNair, the father of the youngest victim, pleaded for calm out of the depth of his own pain: "We must not let this change us into something different than who we are. We must be human." In a similar vein, Martin Luther King sadly intoned, "The innocent blood of these little girls may well serve as the redemptive force that will bring new light to this dark city. . . . Indeed, this tragic event may cause the white South to come to terms with its conscience." The event shook the nation, and combined with the reaction to the assassination of John F. Kennedy in November 1963, set the stage for real change.

The Civil Rights Act of 1964

Kennedy's successor Lyndon B. Johnson lobbied hard to secure passage of the landmark Civil Rights Act. Many in the civil rights movement feared that Johnson, a Southerner, would back his region's defiance. Nonetheless, only four days after taking the oath of office, Johnson told the nation he planned to support the civil rights bill as a memorial for the slain president. A master politician, Johnson pushed the bill through Congress despite a marathon filibuster by its opponents.

The Civil Rights Act of 1964 was the culmination of the civil rights movement to that time. The act banned discrimination in places of public accommodation, including restaurants, hotels, gas stations, and entertainment facilities, as well as schools, parks, playgrounds, libraries, and swimming pools. The desegregation of public accommodations irrevocably changed the face of American society. The issue of legally mandated racial separation was now settled. The act also banned discrimination by employers, of labor unions on the basis of race, color, religion, national origin, and sex in regard to hiring, promoting, dismissing, or making job referrals. The act had strong provisions for enforcement. Most important, it allowed government agencies to withhold federal money from any program permitting or practicing discrimination. This provision had particular import for the desegregation of schools and colleges across the country. The act also gave the U.S. attorney general the power to initiate proceedings against segregated facilities and schools on behalf of people who could not do so on their own. Finally it created the Equal Employment Opportunity Commission to monitor discrimination in employment.

Mississippi Freedom Summer

While Congress considered the Civil Rights Act, movement activists renewed their focus on voter registration in the deep South. In the fall of 1963, many CORE and SNCC workers saw segregation crumbling, but they knew that without the ballot, African Americans could never drive racist politicians from office, gain a fair hearing in court, reduce police and mob violence, or get equal services from state and local governments. CORE took responsibility for running registration campaigns in Louisiana, South Carolina, and Florida while SNCC took on the two most repressive states, Alabama and Mississippi. Mississippi was widely known in the movement as the "toughest nut to crack"—the symbolic center of American racism and white violence. By the summer of 1964, national attention had shifted from Alabama to Mississippi, the site of a massive project known as "Freedom Summer."

The voter registration campaign in Mississippi began in late 1963 when Robert "Bob" Moses mobilized the Council of Federated Organizations (COFO), which had been established in 1961 to aid imprisoned freedom riders. Moses convinced the members of COFO (CORE, SNCC, SCLC, and the NAACP) to sponsor a mock Freedom Election in Mississippi. On Election Day, eighty-thousand disfranchised black people cast ballots for COFO candidates. Impressed with the turnout, Moses and other COFO members believed a massive effort to register voters during the summer of 1964 might break the white monopoly on the ballot box.

After much debate, COFO decided to invite northern white students to participate in the Mississippi project. These students, about one thousand in all, were to be drawn primarily from the nation's most prestigious universities. COFO leaders calculated that the presence of elite white students in the Magnolia State would attract increased media attention and pressure the federal government to provide protection.

Shortly after the project began, three volunteers, two white New Yorkers—twenty-four-year-old Michael Schwerner and twenty-one-year-old Andrew Goodman—and a black Mississippian, twenty-one-year-old James Chaney, disappeared. Unknown at the time, Cecil Price, deputy sheriff of Philadelphia, Mississippi, had arrested the three on a trumped-up speeding charge. That evening the young men were delivered to a deserted road where three carloads of Klansmen waited. Schwerner and Goodman were shot to death. Chaney was beaten with chains and then shot.

These events were not publicly known until Klan informers, enticed by a $30,000 reward, led investigators to the earthen dam in which Goodman, Schwerner, and Chaney had been buried. The disappearance of the three nonetheless focused national attention on white terrorism. In the face of this violence, uncertainty, and fear, many SNCC activists rejected Martin Luther King's commitment to nonviolence, the inclusion of white activists in the movement, and the wisdom of integration. Divisions over these issues greatly increased tensions among the groups that made up the movement.

Despite the problems it encountered, the Freedom Summer organized dozens of Freedom Schools and community centers throughout Mississippi. Its efforts mobilized the state's black people to an extent not seen since the first Reconstruction. Many communities began to develop the rudiments of a political movement, one that would grow in coming years.

The Mississippi Freedom Democratic Party

Freedom Summer intersected with national politics at the Democratic Party's national convention in August 1964 in Atlantic City, New Jersey. White Mississippians routinely excluded African Americans from the political process, and Robert Moses encouraged COFO to set up the Mississippi Freedom Democratic Party (MFDP) to challenge the state's regular Democratic delegation at the convention. Under the leadership of veteran activists Fannie Lou Hamer, Victoria Gray, Annie Divine, and Aaron Henry, the MFDP held its first state convention on August 6. Approximately eighty thousand citizens put their names on the rolls. The convention elected sixty-four delegates who traveled to the national convention to present their credentials.

The MFDP challenge caused considerable difficulty for the Democratic Party. Many liberals wanted to seat the civil rights delegation, but President Lyndon Johnson, who was running for reelection, did not want to alienate white Southerners, fearing they would vote for Barry Goldwater, his Republican opponent. Liberal Democratic senator Hubert H. Humphrey, from Minnesota, worked out a compromise calling for Mississippi regulars to be seated if they swore loyalty to the national party and agreed to cast their forty-four votes accordingly. The compromise also provided for the creation of two "at-large" seats to be filled by MFDP members Aaron Henry and Ed King. The rest of the Freedom Democrats could attend the convention as nonvoting guests.

Martin Luther King Jr., Bayard Rustin, and other black leaders counseled acceptance of this compromise. Johnson and the Democrats, they argued, had achieved much of the legislative program favored by the movement, and if the party were returned to power they could do much more. But most of the MFDP delegation, fed up with the violence of Mississippi and unwilling to settle for token representation, rejected the compromise. Many members of SNCC, bitter and angry, turned their backs on liberalism and cooperation with white people of any political persuasion.

Selma and the Voting Rights Act of 1965

The Civil Rights Act of 1964 contained provisions for helping black voters to register, but white resistance in the deep South had rendered them ineffective. In Alabama, for example, at least 77 percent of black citizens were unable to vote. Their cause was taken up by businesswoman Amelia P. Boynton, owner of an employment and insurance agency in Selma, along with her husband and a high school teacher, the Reverend Frederick Reese, who also led the Dallas County Voters League. These three, with others, fought for black enfranchisement and an end to discriminatory treatment. Their struggle would help pass the Voting Rights Act of 1965, which finally ended the systematic exclusion of African Americans from southern politics.

Selma's sheriff James G. Clark worked to block the voter registration activity sponsored by the Boyntons, Reese, and SNCC suffrage workers. By 1964 fewer than four hundred of the fifteen thousand eligible African Americans had registered to vote in Dallas County. President Lyndon Johnson refused requests to deploy federal marshals to the county to protect voter registration workers. Seeking reinforcements, the workers sent a call to Martin Luther King Jr. and the SCLC. King came and was promptly arrested.

The SCLC announced plans for a mass march from Selma to Montgomery, the state capital, to begin on Sunday, March 7, 1965. As the marchers approached the Edmund Pettus Bridge, state troopers and Sheriff Clark's county police, in a shocking display of aggression, teargassed and beat the retreating marchers while their horses trampled the fallen. Captured in graphic detail by television cameras, this battle became known as "Bloody Sunday." Seizing the moment, King and the activists rescheduled a pilgrimage for March 9. The SCLC leader soon found himself in a dilemma. A federal judge, who was normally supportive of civil rights, had issued an injunction against the march. Moreover, President Johnson and many other key figures in the government urged King not to go through with it. King was reluctant to violate a federal injunction, and he knew he needed Johnson's support to win strong voting rights legislation.

When the day of the march came, 1,500 protesters marched to the bridge singing "Ain't Gonna Let Nobody Turn Me 'Round" and other freedom songs. To their surprise, King crossed the Pettus Bridge, prayed briefly, and turned around. He had privately made a face-saving compromise with the federal authorities. SNCC workers felt betrayed, and King's leadership suffered. That evening a white Unitarian minister from Boston, James Reeb, was clubbed to death by local white people. His martyrdom created a national outcry and prompted Johnson to act. On March 15 the president, in a televised address to Congress, announced he would submit voter registration legislation. In his address he praised civil rights activists, electrifying them when he invoked the movement's slogan to declare, in his Texas drawl, "We shall overcome."

The protests at Selma and the massive white resistance spurred Congress to pass the Voting Rights Act of 1965, which President Johnson signed on August 6. The act outlawed educational requirements for voting in states or counties where less than half the voting age population had been registered on November 1, 1964, or had voted in the 1964 presidential election. It also empowered the attorney general to have the Civil Rights Commission assign federal registrars to enroll voters. The attorney general, Nicholas Katzenbach, immediately deployed federal registrars in nine southern counties. Within months, they had registered approximately 80,000 new voters. In Mississippi, black registrants soared from 28,500 in 1964 to 251,000 in 1968.

Southern state legislators resisted the act. They instituted a dazzling array of disfranchisement devices such as gerrymandering, at-large elections, more appointive offices, and higher qualifications for candidates. But the era when white supremacy lay at the core of southern politics was over.

TIMELINE

AFRICAN-AMERICAN EVENTS	NATIONAL EVENTS
1954	

May 17	**July 11**
Supreme Court's *Brown v. Board of Education* decision declares separate but equal education unconstitutional	First White Citizens Council in Mississippi
May 21	
Jo Ann Robinson of the Women's Political Council in Montgomery writes to Mayor W. A. Gayle, warning of a possible bus boycott	

1955	

Supreme Court's *Brown II* decision calls for school districts to desegregate immediately or "with all-deliberate speed"	The American Federation of Labor and Congress of Industrial Organizations merge to form the AFL-CIO
The Interstate Commerce Commission outlaws segregated buses and waiting rooms for interstate passengers	
August 28	
Emmett Till is lynched	
December 1	
Rosa Parks is arrested for refusing to give up her seat on a Montgomery, Alabama, city bus, beginning Montgomery bus boycott	

1956	

November 13	Segregationists in Congress issue the "Southern Manifesto"
The Supreme Court, in *Gayle v. Browder*, bars segregation in intrastate travel	**November**
	President Dwight D. Eisenhower wins second term as president

1957	

May	
Congress passes the Civil Rights Act of 1957, the first in 87 years	
September 24	
President Eisenhower enforces integration of Little Rock's Central High School with federal troops	

continued

AFRICAN-AMERICAN EVENTS	NATIONAL EVENTS

1958

January

Martin Luther King Jr. and other religious leaders organize the SCLC

1959

1960

February 1	**November**
Black students sit in at Woolworth lunch counter in Greensboro, North Carolina, launching the sit-in movement	John F. Kennedy elected president
April	
SNCC founded	
November	
Black vote critical to Kennedy's election	

1961

May

Freedom Riders attacked in Alabama and Mississippi

September 23

Kennedy names Thurgood Marshall to the Second Circuit Court of Appeals

September 25

Herbert Lee, a local activist, is killed in Amite County, Mississippi

1962

February

The Council of Federated Organizations (COFO) is formed

June 25

James Meredith desegregates the University of Mississippi with federal support

July

The Albany Movement fails

August

Voter Education Project launched

continued

AFRICAN-AMERICAN EVENTS	NATIONAL EVENTS
1963	
April–May	**November 22**
Project C highlights racial injustices in Birmingham	President Kennedy is assassinated
King writes his celebrated "Letter from Birmingham Jail"	Lyndon Johnson succeeds to the presidency
June	
Federal government compels Alabama governor George C. Wallace to desegregate the University of Alabama	
June 12	
Medgar Evers is murdered	
August 17	
W. E. B. Du Bois dies in Ghana, Africa, at 95	
August 28	
The March on Washington; Martin Luther King Jr. delivers his "I Have a Dream" speech	
September 15	
Ku Klux Klan bombs the 16th Street Baptist Church in Birmingham, Alabama, killing four girls	
December	
Malcolm X breaks with Elijah Muhammad and the Nation of Islam and founds his own movement, Muslim Mosque	
1964	
SNCC launches the Mississippi Freedom Summer Project to promote voter registration	Equal Employment Opportunity Commission established
January	
Twenty-fourth Amendment to the U.S. Constitution is ratified, outlawing the poll tax	
June 21	
James E. Chaney, Michael Schwerner, and Andrew Goodman murdered in Mississippi	
July 2	
Civil Rights Act of 1964 enacted	
August	
The Mississippi Freedom Democratic Party denied seating at the Democratic National Convention	
December	
Martin Luther King Jr. wins the Nobel Peace Prize	

continued

AFRICAN-AMERICAN EVENTS	NATIONAL EVENTS
1965	
March 21 Civil rights marchers walk from Selma to Montgomery after violent confrontation in Selma **August 6** Voting Rights Act of 1965 enacted	Lyndon Johnson outlines the Great Society Program to attack poverty

CONCLUSION

The two *Brown* decisions ended the legal underpinning of segregation and discrimination and set in motion events that would irrevocably transform the political and social status of African Americans. White southerners resisted the changes unleashed by *Brown*, and as their massive resistance gained momentum, violence against African Americans and their allies exploded. Still the civil rights movement achieved major successes that depended on many factors. The federal government intervened at crucial moments to enact historic civil rights legislation, issue judgments on behalf of the civil rights protesters, and protect the rule of law with federal marshals and soldiers. Black leaders deliberately pursued strategies to provoke confrontations that would ensure intervention by the federal government and garner widespread media coverage. For more than a decade, the victorious freedom fighters of the civil rights movement stormed the legal barricades of segregation. The uncompromising struggle of African Americans, their organizations, and their white allies pressured federal officials in the legislative, executive, and judicial branches of government to enact major civil rights legislation, issue executive orders, and deliver judicial decisions that dismantled segregation in the South.

The victories of this era were far reaching, but as they were achieved, new issues arose that would fracture the movement. The civil rights movement had largely been focused on the South. Black Northerners already had many of the rights granted by the federal legislation of the era; nonetheless, they still suffered from many forms of discrimination. Addressing their problems required different techniques and new ways of thinking that would emerge over the coming decade.

REVIEW QUESTIONS

1. What role did "ordinary" or local people play in the civil rights movement? How did children contribute to the overall struggle for social change?

2. What key issues and events led the federal government to intervene in the civil rights movement? What were the major pieces of legislation enacted, and how did they dismantle legalized segregation?

3. What were the ideologies, objectives, and tactics of the major civil rights organizations and their leaders?

4. What were the human costs of the civil rights movement? Who were some of the people who lost their lives in the struggle?

5. What were the major successes and failures of the freedom movement? What intergenerational tensions plagued the movement? How did the movement transform American politics and society?

RECOMMENDED READING

Taylor Branch. *Parting the Waters: America in the King Years, 1954–63.* New York: Simon & Schuster, 1988. Richly researched, lively study that places King at the center of American politics during a critically transformative decade.

Clayborne Carson. *In Struggle: SNCC and the Black Awakening of the 1960s.* Cambridge, MA: Harvard University Press, 1981. One of the best historical studies of SNCC and the contributions students made to galvanize the civil rights movement.

Vickie Crawford, Jacqueline Rouse, and Barbara Woods, eds. *Women in the Civil Rights Movement: Trailblazers and Torchbearers.* Brooklyn, NY: Carlson Publishing, 1990. An anthology of essays presented at a symposium. The meeting was designed to draw attention to the women whose contributions to the freedom struggle of the 1950s and 1960s are often overlooked or neglected.

Henry Hampton and Steve Fayer, eds. *The Voices of Freedom: An Oral History of the Civil Rights Movement from the 1950s through the 1980s.* New York: Bantam Books, 1990. A remarkable and indispensable oral history of all the participants in the civil rights movement, from the least well known to the internationally celebrated.

Richard Kluger. *Simple Justice: The History of "Brown v. Board of Education" and Black America's Struggle for Equality.* New York: Knopf, 1976; new ed., 2004. An excellent treatment of the historical events leading up to *Brown* and the local individuals whose lives were forever changed because of their resistance to Jim Crow segregation. The new edition includes an illuminating assessment of the fifty years since *Brown.*

Steven F. Lawson. *Running for Freedom: Civil Rights and Black Politics in America since 1941.* Philadelphia: Temple University Press, 1991. A succinct analysis of the politics, legislative measures, and individuals that figured in the successes and failures of the civil rights movement.

Aldon D. Morris. *The Origins of the Modern Civil Rights Movement: Black Communities Organizing for Change.* New York: Free Press; London: Collier Macmillan, 1984. An important and insightful analysis of the mobilization and organizing strategies pursued by diverse communities for social change that paved the way for the modern civil rights movement.

THE STRUGGLE CONTINUES

1965–1980

THE FADING DREAM OF RACIAL INTEGRATION: WHITE BACKLASH AND BLACK NATIONALISM

Even though President Johnson easily defeated Republican senator Barry Goldwater, the 1964 election was hardly a mandate for civil rights. When, in 1966, Johnson asked Congress for federal legislation to ban discrimination in housing, white opposition to civil rights helped elect Republicans, including former movie actor Ronald Reagan as governor of California. Meanwhile, Alabama governor George Wallace, an outspoken opponent of racial integration and civil rights legislation, was emerging as a national political figure.

With many white Americans increasingly reluctant to support the goals of the civil rights movement, many black Americans began searching for new approaches to their problems. The reign of terror experienced by COFO (Council of Federated Organizations) workers in Mississippi had undermined the commitment to integration and nonviolence of the civil rights movement and would help radicalize a new, younger generation of activists. Men like Floyd McKissick of the Congress of Racial Equality (CORE) and Stokely Carmichael of the Student Nonviolent Coordinating Committee (SNCC) became disillusioned, rejecting King's moderation, nonviolence, and universalism. In 1965, after the Selma-to-Montgomery march, he helped found the Lowndes County (Mississippi) Freedom Organization (LCFO). It became the first political organization in the civil rights movement to adopt the symbol of the black panther.

Black residents of northern and western cities also lost patience with the slow pace of change. Increasing numbers of young black churchmen castigated mainstream white religious groups for their complicity with racism, demanded reparations, and agitated for substantive power or leadership roles within the governing structures of the National Council of Churches. Out of the interracial conflict and tension emerged a black theology that critiqued racism within white religious groups. It was followed by a black feminist theology that offered searing critiques of sexism within the black church. Leaders in the development of Black Theology and the expression of a black nationalist Christianity were theologians James H. Cone, author of *Black Theology and Black Power* (1969) and the Reverend Albert Cleage Jr. of Detroit who was pastor of the Shrine of the Black Madonna. Black Christian nationalism argued for black symbols of

483

religious faith and asserted the importance of conjoining religious practice and faith with political activism and social change. Growing numbers of young African Americans, along with diverse black religious leaders, dismayed by the great political and economic disparities between themselves and white Americans, became catalysts for an increasingly radical turn in the civil rights movement.

Malcolm X

After 1965, the year in which he died, no one had more influence on young black activists and the residents of America's ghettoized inner cities than Malcolm X. The son of a Baptist preacher, he was born Malcolm Little in Omaha, Nebraska, and grew up in Lansing, Michigan. His family's home was burned by Klan terrorists, and his father was murdered two years later. His mother was subsequently committed to a mental institution, and welfare agencies separated the children. Malcolm was sent to a juvenile detention home, quit school after the eighth grade, and moved to Boston to live with his sister. There he became involved in the street life of gambling, drugs, and burglary. He was arrested and sentenced to a ten-year prison term in 1946. During the six and a half years he spent in prison, he embraced the teachings of Elijah Muhammad of the Nation of Islam and renounced what he considered his "slave name" to become Malcolm X. In 1954 he became minister of Harlem's Temple Number 7. Articulate, charismatic, and forceful, Malcolm did not believe in nonviolence or advocate integration. His was the voice of the northern urban "second ghettoes." In 1961 he began publishing *Muhammad Speaks*, the official newspaper of the Nation. In *The Autobiography of Malcolm X*, published in 1965 by the writer Alex Haley of *Roots* fame, Malcolm declared,

> Few white people realize that many black people today dislike and avoid spending any more time than they must around white people. This "integration" image, as it is popularly interpreted, has millions of vain, self-exalted white people convinced that black people want to sleep in bed with them—and that's a lie! Oh you can't tell the average white man that the Negro man's prime desire isn't to have a white woman—another lie! Like a black brother recently observed to me, "Look, you ever smell one of them wet?"

Malcolm's dismissal of the goal of racial integration and King's message of redemption through brotherly love resonated with many younger civil rights workers disillusioned by white violence. "The day of nonviolent resistance is over," Malcolm insisted. And in 1964 he declared, "Revolutions are never based upon love-your-enemy, and pray-for-those-who-despitefully-use-you. And revolutions are never waged by singing 'We Shall Overcome.' Revolutions are based on bloodshed."

Malcolm X's popularity created tensions between himself and the leadership of the Nation of Islam. He grew disillusioned with Elijah Muhammad's aversion to political activism, and Elijah Muhammad grew jealous of Malcolm's success. When Malcolm described the Kennedy assassination as a case of "the chickens coming home to roost" (meaning Kennedy was a victim of the same kind of violence that afflicted black people), Elijah Muhammad suspended him. In 1964 Malcolm broke with the Nation of Islam and founded his own organization, the Muslim Mosque, Inc. That same year he went on a pilgrimage to Mecca that profoundly influenced him. He changed his name to El-Hajj Malik El-Shabazz, founded the Organization for Afro-American Unity (after the Organization of African Unity), repudiated the Nation of Islam doctrine that all white people are evil, and began lecturing on the connection between the civil rights struggle in the South and the struggle against colonialism in Africa. On February 14, 1965, assassins associated with the Nation of Islam killed Malcolm X as he addressed an audience in Harlem.

Stokely Carmichael and Black Power

In 1966 Stokely Carmichael, a native of Trinidad who had been raised in New York City and educated at Howard University, became chairman of SNCC. He was determined to move SNCC toward black nationalism and dismissed its few white staffers.

About this time, James Meredith began a one-man "march against fear" from Tennessee to Jackson, Mississippi, to encourage black Southerners to register and vote. On this march, he was shot and wounded by white gunmen. In June 1966, after this incident, SNCC and Carmichael joined with other organizations to complete the march. It was at this time that Carmichael popularized the slogan "Black Power" that was to become SNCC's rallying cry. "The only way we gonna stop them white men from whippin' us," he announced to a cheering crowd, "is to take over. We been saying freedom for six years and we ain't got nothin'. What we gonna start saying is Black Power."

Critics accused advocates of black power of reverse racism, but Carmichael argued on the contrary that they were promoting positive self-identity, racial pride, and the development of independent political and economic power. All of the organizations suffered internal problems concerning gender roles, relations between white women and black men, and separatism versus integration. In 1968 CORE followed SNCC's example and ejected its white members with a resulting loss of financial resources. For various reasons both organizations began to decline, and by the end of the 1960s, SNCC had virtually disappeared.

Stokely Carmichael (1941–1998) changed his name to Kwame Ture, a combination of the names of two major African leaders, Kwame Nkrumah and Ahmed Sekou Toure. After he settled in Guinea in 1969, he founded the All-African People's Revolutionary Party.
© Bettmann/Corbis

Martin Luther King had mixed feelings about the ideology of black power. He welcomed its promotion of black political and economic strength, psychological assertiveness, and cultural pride. But when black power degenerated into a mantra of taunts against white people, King denounced it as "a nihilistic philosophy born out of the conviction that the Negro can't win." King also objected to black power's "implicit and often explicit belief in black separatism."

In May 1967 Hubert G. Brown followed Carmichael as head of SNCC. "H. Rap" Brown, as he became known, raised the militancy of the black power movement's rhetoric to a new level, calling white people "honkies" and the police "pigs." "Violence," he said, was "as American as apple pie." In August 1967 Brown told enthusiastic listeners in the black neighborhood of Cambridge, Maryland, that "black folks built America, and if America don't come around, we're going to burn America down." When a few hours later, a fire erupted in a dilapidated school in the heart of the city's black community, white firemen refused to fight it. Police charged Brown with inciting a riot and committing arson, but he posted bail and fled. Later he was arrested on other charges.

The National Council of Churches

Black and white leaders of mainstream religious organizations were transformed by black power. In 1946 the Federal Council of Churches, composed of Protestants, Catholics, and Jews, pledged to work for "a non-segregated church and a non-segregated society." Between 1963 and 1965, the National Council of Churches (NCC) contributed financial and moral support to the civil rights movement. In 1963 the NCC founded its Commission on Religion and Race to support the black freedom movement. Although a white-controlled and managed operation, three of the eight staff members of the commission were African American: Anna Hedgeman, J. Oscar Lee, and James Breeden. The NCC supported events such as the March on Washington and lobbied for passage of the Civil Rights Act of 1964 and the Voting Rights Act of 1965.

In 1965 the NCC appointed Benjamin Payton as director of the Commission on Religion and Race. Payton, a native of Orangeburg, South Carolina, had been educated at Harvard Divinity School and had earned a Ph.D. at Yale. Payton had taught at Howard University and he was a member of the National Baptist Convention, U.S.A., the largest African-American denomination. Under his stewardship the Commission on Religion and Race was incorporated into the Division of Christian Life and Mission and later became part of the NCC's Department of Social Justice that included five other special task forces.

The black power movement spurred the creation of black caucuses within the predominantly white churches. In February 1968 James Lawson headed the Black Methodists for Church Renewal, a caucus that crystallized within the United Methodist Church. In the same year, the United Presbyterian Church witnessed the formation of the Black Presbyterian United that replaced the Presbyterian Interracial Council. The Episcopal Society for Racial and Cultural Unity, an interracial group, was replaced by an Episcopal Union of Black Clergy and Laity. By the early 1970s, there were nine such caucuses. Within the Roman Catholic Church, black Catholics insisted that the church demonstrate more respect for African-American patterns of worship. All these black religious groups pressed for more black leadership within the denominations. Thus the stage was set for James Forman's black manifesto.

In April 1969 James Forman, a former Chicago schoolteacher renowned for his work with SNCC, addressed the National Black Economic Development Conference in Detroit, sponsored by the Interreligious Foundation for Community Organizations (which was supported by predominantly white churches). Forman demanded that white churches pay $500 million in reparations for their participation in and benefit from American slavery and racial exploitation. His sharply secular critique of American religion precipitated the withdrawal of mainstream white religion groups from active participation in the civil rights movement. These white groups were offended by Forman's black power rhetoric and revolutionary Marxist ideology. Black and other minority groups wanted to share real power within the white-dominated churches. Relations between Blacks and Jews also deteriorated as countercharges circulated of "Jewish racism" and "Black anti-Semitism."

THE BLACK PANTHER PARTY

The most institutionalized expression of the new black militancy was the Black Panther Party for Self-Defense created by Huey P. Newton and Bobby Seale in Oakland, California, in October 1966. Newton and Seale took the name of the party from the black panther symbol of the Lowndes County Freedom Organization (LCFO). The Black Panthers combined Black Nationalist ideology with Marxist-Leninist doctrines. Working with white radicals, they hoped to fashion the party into a revolutionary vanguard dedicated to overthrowing capitalist society and ending police brutality. For a few months Stokely Carmichael, who had become estranged from SNCC, aligned himself with the Panthers and was named the party's prime minister. (However, Carmichael soon shifted his interest to pan-Africanism. He moved to Africa and changed his name to Kwame Turé.) Eldridge Cleaver, the Panther's minister of education, helped formulate the party's ideology. Cleaver had spent most of his youth in prison, where he became a follower of Malcolm X and began writing the autobiographical essays that would be published as *Soul on Ice* in 1968, the year the party dropped "Self-Defense" from its name. Black people, Cleaver maintained, were victims of colonization, not just disfranchised American citizens. Thus integrationism could not meet their needs. They needed, instead, like other colonized peoples, to be liberated. Cleaver and other top Panther leaders were arrested after a shoot-out with Oakland police in 1968. Cleaver escaped and fled into exile. While abroad, he abandoned his radicalism and became involved with the Republican Party and fundamentalist Christianity after his return to the United States in 1975.

Police Repression and the FBI'S Cointelpro

The Panthers alarmed white Americans when they took up arms for self-defense and patrolled their neighborhoods to monitor the police. A series of bloody confrontations and shoot-outs in Oakland distracted attention from the Panthers' broader political objectives and community service projects. In Oakland and Chicago, the Panthers arranged free breakfast and health-care programs, worked to instill racial pride, lectured and wrote about black history, and launched some of the earliest drug education programs. These activities were captured in the slogan "Power to the People."

FBI director J. Edgar Hoover was determined to infiltrate, harass, destabilize, and destroy all nationalist groups and their leaders. The FBI cooperated with local law enforcement officials to ridicule and discredit leaders and to undermine and weaken the Black Panther Party. In August 1967 Hoover distributed an explanatory memorandum that detailed the FBI's Counterintelligence Program directed toward black nationalist groups. The purpose, according to the memo, of this new "counterintelligence (COINTELPRO) endeavor is to expose, disrupt, misdirect, discredit, or otherwise neutralize the activities of black nationalist, hate-type organizations and groupings, their leadership, spokesmen, membership, and supporters, and to counter their propensity for violence and civil disorder." Undercover agents infiltrated the Panthers and provoked violence and criminal acts. The FBI and its counterintelligence agents may have provoked much of the mayhem and violence that became associated with the Black Panther Party. Certainly, COINTELPRO helped shape negative public opinion of black nationalist ideology.

In their effort to destroy the party, law enforcement officials killed an estimated 28 Panthers and imprisoned 750 others. In perhaps the most egregious incident, police in Chicago killed Fred Hampton and Mark Clark in their sleep in a predawn raid on the Illinois Black Panther Headquarters on December 4, 1969. While the police fired hundreds of rounds, only two shots were fired from within the apartment.

Prisoners' Rights

Despite such repression, black militancy survived in many forms, including the prisoners' rights movement. One of the Black Panthers' social programs had focused on the conditions of black prisoners. By 1970 more than half the inmates in U.S. prisons were African American. In New York State, black Americans were around 70 percent of the prison population. Black activists argued that many African Americans were in jail for political reasons and suffered from unfair sentences and deplorable conditions because of racism and class exploitation.

Angela Davis, an assistant professor of philosophy at the University of California at Los Angeles, became the first black woman to be listed on the FBI's Ten Most Wanted list because of her involvement in prisoners' rights. In 1969 UCLA's board of regents refused to renew her contract citing her lack of a Ph.D., but in fact they objected to her membership in the Communist Party. During the late 1960s, she had worked on behalf of the Soledad Brothers, three prisoners—George Jackson, John Clutchette, and Fleeta Drumgo—accused of murdering a white guard at Soledad Prison. On August 7, 1970, George Jackson's younger brother, seventeen-year-old Jonathan Jackson, staged a one-man raid on the San Rafael courthouse in Marin County, California, to try to seize hostages to trade for the Soledad Brothers. In the ensuing shoot-out, Jonathan Jackson, two prisoners, and a judge were killed. Angela Davis, accused of supplying the weapons for the raid, was charged with murder, kidnapping, and conspiracy. She escaped and lived as a fugitive, but she was eventually captured and spent over a year in jail. After a long ordeal and a national "Free Angela" campaign, a jury acquitted Davis. On August 21, 1971, George Jackson was shot and killed at San Quentin Prison by guards who claimed he was trying to escape.

Across the country, prisoners at Attica, a maximum-security prison in northern New York State, began a fast in memory of George Jackson that within days erupted into a full-scale rebellion. On September 9, 1971, 1,200 inmates seized control of half of

Attica and took hostages. Four days later, state police and prison guards suppressed the uprising.

THE INNER-CITY REBELLIONS

The militant nationalism of Malcolm X and Stokely Carmichael and the radicalism of the Panthers reflected growing alienation and anger in America's impoverished inner cities. In 1965, 29.1 percent of black households, compared with only 7.8 percent of white households, lived below the poverty line. Almost 50 percent of nonwhite families lived in substandard housing compared with 18 percent of white families. Despite a drop in the number of Americans living in poverty from 38.0 million in 1959 to 32.7 million in 1965, the percentage of poor black people increased from 27.5 percent to 31 percent. In 1965 the black unemployment rate was 8.5 percent, almost twice the white unemployment rate of 4.3. For black teenagers the unemployment rate was 23 percent compared with 10.8 percent for white teenagers. As psychologist Kenneth Clark declared in 1967, "The masses of Negroes are now starkly aware of the fact that recent civil rights victories benefited a very small percentage of middle-class Negroes while their predicament remained the same or worsened."

The passage of civil rights legislation did not resolve these disparities or diminish inner-city alienation. As jobs moved increasingly to suburbs to which inner-city residents could neither travel nor relocate, inner-city neighborhoods sank deeper into poverty. School dropout rates reached epidemic proportions, crime and drug use increased, and fragile family structures weakened. It was these conditions that led militants like the Panthers to liken their neighborhoods to exploited colonies kept in poverty by repressive white political and economic institutions. Few white Americans understood the depths of the black despair that flared into violence each summer between 1965 and 1969, beginning with the Watts rebellion of 1965.

Watts

In the summer of 1965, a section of Los Angeles called Watts exploded. Watts was 98 percent black. Its residents suffered from overcrowding, unemployment, inaccessible health-care facilities, inadequate public transportation, and increasing crime and drug addiction. Almost 30 percent of the black male population was unemployed. The poverty, combined with anger at the often-brutal behavior of Los Angeles's police force in Watts, proved to be an incendiary combination. On August 11, 1965, a policeman pulled over a young black man to check him for drunk driving. The man was arrested, but not before a crowd gathered. The policeman called for reinforcements, and when they arrived, the crowd pelted them with stones, bottles, and other objects. Within a few hours, Watts was in a total riot.

Governor Pat Brown, a Democrat, sent in the National Guard to restore order, but by the sixth day of the conflagration, Watts had been reduced to rubble and ashes. Thirty-four people had been killed; more than 900 injured; and 4,000 arrested. Total property damage was more than $35 million, equivalent to hundreds of millions of dollars today. The Watts rebellion was the beginning of four summers of uprisings that would engulf cities in the North and Midwest. There were riots in the summer of 1966, but even worse ones erupted in Newark and Detroit in 1967.

The first major urban uprising of the 1960s was in the Watts neighborhood of East Los Angeles in August 1965. It lasted nearly a week and left thirty-four people dead.
AP/Wide World Photos

Newark

Newark, New Jersey, had more than 400,000 inhabitants in 1967. As was true in many other urban areas, white flight to the suburbs in the 1950s and 1960s made Newark a majority black city, but one that operated on an inadequate tax base and under white political control. The city lacked the means to meet its inhabitants' social needs. The school system deteriorated as unemployment had increased. In 1967 Newark had the highest unemployment rate among black men in the entire nation. As tensions flared and police brutality escalated, white officials paid little attention to black people's complaints. On July 12, after a black cab driver in police custody was beaten, protesters gathered at the police station near the Hayes Homes housing project. When a firebomb hit the wall of the station house, the police charged, clubbing the crowd. This triggered one of the most destructive civic rebellions of the period. During four days of rioting, the police and National Guard killed twenty-five black people—most of them innocent bystanders, including two children; a white policeman and fireman were also killed. Widespread looting and arson caused millions of dollars in property damage.

Detroit

When Detroit erupted a few days after Newark, it caught everyone by surprise except the residents of its inner-city neighborhoods. On the surface Detroit seemed like a model of prosperity and interracial accord. Some of the country's most dynamic popular music flowed from Detroit's Motown recording company. Owned by the astute Berry Gordy, Motown was a classic up-by-the-bootstraps success story. Gordy and his wife Raynoma and their extended family had, by 1967, produced such stars as Diana Ross and Mary Wells. "Before Motown," said Wells, "there were three careers available to a black girl in Detroit—babies, the factories or daywork."

But success like Gordy's was rare among the black migrants and their children, who poured into Detroit during and after World War II. The parents held their disappointment in check, but the children, particularly young men aged between seventeen and thirty-five, sought an outlet for their anger and alienation. Some joined the

Nation of Islam; others embraced the Panthers or formed even more radical organizations calling for an all-black nation.

On the night of Saturday, July 23, police raided an after-hours drinking establishment in the center of the black community where more than eighty people were celebrating the return of two veterans from Vietnam. Police efforts to clear the club triggered five days of rioting. Congressman John Conyers, the black U.S. representative for Michigan's First District, knew many of the people in the area and tried to get them to disperse, but they refused. Later, Conyers said, "People were letting feelings out that had never been let out before, that had been bottled up. It really wasn't that they were that mad about an after-hours place being raided and some people being beat up as a result of the closing down of that place. It was the whole desperate situation of being black in Detroit."

Of the fifty-nine urban rebellions that occurred in 1967, Detroit's was the deadliest. Forty-three black people died, most of them shot by members of the National Guard, which had been sent in by Republican governor George Romney. But even the National Guard, combined with 200 state police and 600 Detroit police, could not restore order. A reluctant President Johnson had to order 4,700 troops of the elite 82nd and 101st Airborne units to Detroit.

The Kerner Commission

On July 29, 1967, in the wake of the Newark and Detroit riots, Johnson established the National Advisory Commission on Civil Disorders, headed by Illinois governor Otto Kerner. The commission included two black members, Republican senator Edward W. Brooke of Massachusetts (elected in 1966 and the first black senator since Reconstruction) and Roy Wilkins, executive director of the NAACP. In a speech explaining why he had set up the commission, Johnson declared,

> The only genuine, long-range solution for what has happened lies in an attack—mounted at every level—upon the conditions that breed despair and violence. All of us know what those conditions are: ignorance, discrimination, slums, poverty, disease, not enough jobs. We should attack these conditions—not because we are frightened by conflict, but because we are fired by conscience. We should attack them because there is simply no other way to achieve a decent and orderly society in America.

In its final report, released in 1968, the Kerner Commission indicted white racism as the underlying cause of the riots and warned that America was "moving towards two societies, one white, one black—separate and unequal." The commission emphasized that "Negroes firmly believe that police brutality and harassment occur repeatedly in Negro neighborhoods. This belief is unquestionably one of the major reasons for intense Negro resentment against the police." The report added, "Physical abuse is only one source of aggravation in the ghetto. In nearly every city surveyed, the Commission heard complaints of harassment of interracial couples, dispersal of social street gatherings and the stopping of Negroes on foot or in cars without objective basis." The report called for massive government aid to the cities, including funds for public housing, better and more integrated schools, two million new jobs, and funding for a "national system of income supplementation." None of its major proposals was enacted.

DIFFICULTIES IN CREATING THE GREAT SOCIETY

The urban riots of the late 1960s undercut support for the broadest attack the federal government had yet waged on the problems of poor Americans, what President Johnson in his election campaign in 1964 had called "the Great Society." Much of the legislation Johnson pushed through Congress in 1964 and 1965—the Medicare program, for example, which provided medical care for the elderly and disabled under the Social Security system, or federal aid to education from elementary through graduate schools—remained popular. But the most ambitious Great Society programs—what Johnson called "an unconditional war on poverty"—were controversial and tested the limits of American reform.

Johnson's concern for the disadvantaged showed itself in the cornerstone of his War on Poverty, the Economic Opportunity Act of 1964. This act created an Office of Economic Opportunity that administered several programs: Head Start to help disadvantaged preschoolers, Upward Bound to prepare impoverished teenagers for college, and Volunteers in Service to America (or VISTA) to serve as a domestic peace corps to help the poor and undereducated across the country. These programs included community-governing boards on which black men and women gained representation, learning such essential political skills as bargaining and organizing.

The War on Poverty was the first government-sponsored effort to involve poor African Americans directly in designing and implementing programs to serve low-income communities. For example, in the New Careers program, residents of poor neighborhoods found jobs as community organizers, day care workers, and teacher aides. The program provided meaningful work, access to education, and critical material resources to poor people, so they would become leaders in their own communities and run for office. The Community Action Programs (CAPs) insisted on "maximum feasible participation" by the poor. On another level, the Education Act increased federal funding to colleges and universities and provided low-interest student loans. This initiative increased college enrollments and put higher education within the reach of many more Americans than before.

Johnson faced considerable opposition to CAPs and other Great Society programs. Local politicians, fearing the federal government was subsidizing their opponents and undercutting their power, were especially threatened by programs that empowered the previously disfranchised and dispossessed. Others, reflecting persistent white stereotypes of African Americans, complained that Johnson was rewarding lawlessness and laziness with handouts to the undeserving poor. The black residents of America's inner cities, for their part, had their expectations raised by the promises of the Great Society only to be frustrated by white backlash and minimal gains. They felt as betrayed by its programs as Johnson's white critics felt robbed by them.

No one will ever know whether Lyndon Johnson could have won his War on Poverty had he been given the resources to do so. As it turned out, the nation's resources were increasingly going into his other war, the war in Vietnam. Statistics tell the story. Government spending, including spending for domestic programs, increased dramatically under Johnson. But most of the money spent on domestic programs during Johnson's presidency, $44.3 billion, went to social security benefits, which now included Medicare. Appropriations for the War on Poverty came to only $10 billion. The war in Vietnam, in contrast, consumed $140 billion.

JOHNSON AND THE WAR IN VIETNAM

Vietnam was a French colony from the 1860s until the Japanese seized it during World War II. After the war the Vietnamese communists, led by Ho Chi Minh, declared independence, but the French, with massive U.S. financial aid, fought to reassert their control from 1945 until they were finally defeated in 1954. In retrospect it is easy to argue that American policy makers should have been more impressed by the failure of the French to defeat the communists in Vietnam. But in 1954, with the French pulling out, the Americans arranged a temporary division of the country into a communist-controlled North Vietnam and a U.S.-supported South Vietnam (which, however, contained many communist guerrillas, called by the Americans "Viet Cong"). The United States ignored the possibility that as guarantor of South Vietnam, it would replace the French as targets for those Vietnamese who were determined to end white colonial domination and unify their country.

For nine years, under Presidents Eisenhower and Kennedy, American aid and advisers propped up the corrupt and incompetent South Vietnamese government in Saigon. By the time Johnson became president, only the dramatic escalation of American involvement—the bombing of North Vietnam and the introduction of large numbers of American troops into combat in South Vietnam—could keep the South Vietnamese government in power. Johnson himself doubted the advisability of a wholesale American commitment and did not want a foreign war to distract the public's attention or take away resources from the Great Society programs about which he cared so much. And so, half aware he was entering a quagmire but determined to slug through it, Johnson intervened in Vietnam—gradually, massively, and inexorably.

After an incident involving an alleged North Vietnamese attack on U.S. Navy destroyers in the Gulf of Tonkin in August 1964, Johnson pushed a resolution through Congress that gave him authority to escalate American involvement in Vietnam. In the spring of 1965, he authorized the bombing of selected North Vietnamese targets, but the bombing failed to stop the North Vietnamese from resupplying and reinforcing their forces in the south. The American military presence in South Vietnam then grew rapidly. By the end of 1966, more than 385,000 U.S. troops were there, and by 1968 more than 500,000.

Black Americans and the Vietnam War

In the mid-1960s, black Americans made up 10 percent of the armed forces. This percentage increased during America's involvement in the Vietnam War. (In the Persian Gulf War in 1991, African Americans were 25 percent of the troops deployed.) Black overrepresentation among the U.S. troops in Vietnam resulted, in large part, from draft deferments for college and graduate students who were predominantly white and middle class (such as Dan Quayle and George W. Bush). Black men and women entered the military for many compelling reasons, in addition to the draft. One was patriotism. Another was that the military offered educational and vocational opportunities that the children of the working black poor could not otherwise obtain. Still another was Project 100,000.

Project 100,000

In 1966 the U.S. Defense Department launched Project 100,000 to reduce the high rejection rate of African Americans by the military. The project enabled recruitment officers to accept applicants whom they otherwise would have rejected because of criminal records or lack of skills. The project supplied more than 340,000 new recruits for Vietnam, 136,000 of whom were African Americans. As some have argued, this made the Vietnam War a white man's war but a black man's fight. Although the recruits were promised training and "rehabilitation," they saw more combat duty than regular recruits.

JOHNSON: VIETNAM DESTROYS THE GREAT SOCIETY

By the end of 1967, the nation seemed to be heading toward total racial polarization. In their rage against economic exploitation and police brutality, some inner-city black people had destroyed many of their own neighborhoods. Frightened white people, unable to comprehend black anger, rallied behind those who promised to restore order by any means. The two men who, only a few years before, had seemed the most effective advocates of racial reconciliation—Lyndon Johnson and Martin Luther King Jr.—were both trying to regain the initiative. Each, tragically, ended by alienating himself from the other.

By 1967 Johnson's situation was untenable. He had escalated the war in Vietnam without convincing many Americans it was worth fighting. Johnson hoped that, with more bombing and more troops, the Vietnamese communists would give up, but he knew that if Congress had to choose between spending on the war and spending on domestic programs, it would choose the war. After Johnson asked for a tax increase, his Great Society programs met increasing resistance.

An even more dramatic example of the ugly mood on Capitol Hill was the House of Representatives expulsion in 1967 of the most prominent African-American politician in the United States, Adam Clayton Powell Jr. (1908–1972). Pastor of the Abyssinian Baptist Church in Harlem and a longtime civic activist, Powell had first been elected to represent his Harlem district in 1944 and became the foremost champion of civil rights in the House. Because of his seniority he became chairman of the Education and Labor Committee in 1961 and had been instrumental in passing Johnson's education and antipoverty legislation.

Powell gave ammunition to his enemies. He mismanaged the committee's budget, took numerous trips abroad at government expense, and was exiled from his district when threatened with arrest there because of his refusal to pay a slander judgment against him. Yet the sentiment behind his ouster owed much to the dislike he inspired as a champion of minorities and the poor and as a flamboyant black man. The Supreme Court, overruling the House action, upheld his right to his seat, and his Harlem constituents kept him in office until his death.

Despite opposition in Congress, Johnson did not give up on the Great Society. He knew he could initiate no major programs while the Vietnam War lasted, but he continued to push a variety of measures, including a law to prohibit discrimination in housing. He also named the architect of the NAACP's attack on segregation, Thurgood Marshall, to the Supreme Court in 1967.

Vietnam trapped Johnson. As the hundreds of thousands of people who demonstrated against the war reminded him, Vietnam was incontestably "Lyndon Johnson's war." It was not, he would have replied, the war he had wanted to fight—that was the war against poverty and discrimination—but he was committed to seeing it through.

He believed his and the nation's honor were at stake. Even though objective commentators considered the conflict a stalemate, optimistic reports in 1967, from military commanders and intelligence agents, convinced the president he might yet prevail.

Then, on January 30, 1968, at the start of the Vietnamese new year (called Tet), communist insurgents attacked thirty-six of the forty-four provincial capitals in South Vietnam as well as its national capital, Saigon, where they penetrated the grounds of the American embassy. Although American and South Vietnamese forces quickly recaptured all the territory that was lost and inflicted massive casualties on the enemy, the Tet Offensive was a major psychological blow for the American public.

On March 31, 1968, President Johnson told the nation he would halt the bombing of North Vietnam to encourage the start of peace negotiations, which began in Paris in May. Then, as if an afterthought, he added he would not seek renomination as president. Worn out by Vietnam, frustrated in his efforts to achieve the Great Society, the target of bitter criticism, and dispirited by a poor showing in the New Hampshire primary, Lyndon Johnson ended his public career rather than engage in a potentially bruising renomination battle.

KING: SEARCHING FOR A NEW STRATEGY

Like President Johnson, Martin Luther King was attacked on many fronts. Many white people considered him a dangerous radical, whereas black militants considered him an ineffectual moderate. His first response to the urban rebellions in 1965 and 1966 had been to move his campaign to the North to demonstrate the national range of the civil rights movement. In 1966 King and the SCLC set up operations in Chicago at the invitation of the Chicago Freedom Movement. King was confident he would receive the support of the city's white liberals and the entire black community. James Bevel, King's Chicago lieutenant, declared, "We are going to create a new city. . . . Nobody will stop us." His optimism proved unwarranted.

Chicago's powerful, wily mayor Richard Daley viewed King suspiciously from the outset, but he treated him with respect and cautioned the police not to use violence against King's civil rights demonstrators. Because King's movement depended on provoking confrontation, not much happened until King attempted to march into the white ethnic enclave of Marquette Park and the all-white suburb of Cicero.

The ensuing violence attracted the nation's television cameras. Chicago's white liberals joined with King and Daley in negotiating the Summit Agreement on housing, which amounted to a hasty retreat by King in the face of virulent white rage and black militancy. The Chicago strategy was a dismal failure.

But Chicago reinforced two important lessons for King. First, racial discrimination was more than a southern problem: in Chicago he witnessed an intensity of hatred and hostility that surpassed even that of Birmingham. Second, racial discrimination was inextricably intertwined with the country's economic structure. And so he began to think more critically about the need not only to eradicate poverty but to end systemic economic inequality. In the fall of 1967, he announced plans for his most ambitious and militant project, an integrated, nonviolent "Poor People's Campaign" the following spring.

According to the plan, tens of thousands of the nation's dispossessed would descend on Washington to focus attention on the disadvantaged members of American society. Among other things, King and his aides wanted a federally guaranteed income policy.

King on the Vietnam War

While planning the Poor People's Campaign, King began to attack the war in Vietnam. King rejected what he considered the hypocrisy of the federal government's determination to send black and white men to Vietnam "to slaughter, men, women, and children" while failing to protect black American civil rights protesters in places like Albany, Birmingham, and Selma. His statements that the president was more concerned about winning in Vietnam than winning the "war against poverty" in America turned Johnson against him and further alienated King from many of Johnson's black supporters, including the more traditional civil rights leaders who supported the war in Vietnam. At the same time, the young militants in SNCC, who had already condemned the war, did not rush to embrace him. But King persisted, and by 1968 he had become one of the war's most trenchant critics.

King's Murder

His search for a new strategy led King to a closer involvement with labor issues. In February 1968, attempting to gain union recognition for municipal workers in Memphis, 1,300 members of a virtually all-black sanitation workers local went on strike and together with the local black community boycotted downtown merchants. But Memphis mayor Henry Loeb refused to negotiate. On March 18, 1968, responding to a call from James Lawson, a longtime civil rights activist and the minister of Centenary Methodist Church in Memphis, King went to Memphis to address the striking sanitation workers.

The occasion was marked by violence. Nevertheless, King returned to Memphis on April 3 and delivered his last and perhaps most prophetic speech:

> I would like to live a long life. Longevity has its place. But I'm not concerned about that now. I just want to do God's will. And He's allowed me to go up to the mountaintop, and I've looked over. And I've seen the promised land. I may not get there with you. But I want you to know tonight that we as a people will get to the promised land. So I'm happy tonight. I'm not worried about anything. I'm not fearing any man. "Mine eyes have seen the glory of the coming of the Lord."

The next day King was murdered by James Earl Ray as he stood on the balcony of the Lorraine Motel in Memphis. His assassination unleashed a torrent of civic rage in black communities. More than 125 cities experienced uprisings. By April 11, forty-six people were dead, 35,000 were injured, and more than 20,000 had been arrested.

In what seemed to many a belated gesture of racial reconciliation, within days of King's assassination, Congress passed the Civil Rights Act of 1968. Proposed by Johnson two years before, the act outlawed discrimination in the sale and rental of housing and gave the Justice Department authority to bring suits against such discrimination.

King's assassination also boosted support for the SCLC's faltering Poor People's Campaign. The campaign began in May when more than two thousand demonstrators settled into a shantytown they called Resurrection City in Washington, D.C. For more than a month, they marched daily to various federal offices and took part in a mass demonstration on June 19. On June 24, police evicted them, and the campaign ended, leaving an uncertain legacy.

THE BLACK ARTS MOVEMENT AND BLACK CONSCIOUSNESS

The years between 1967 and 1975 witnessed some of the most intense political and cultural discussions in the history of the black freedom struggle. Black power stimulated debate about both the future of black politics in the post–civil rights era and the role of black art and artists in the quest for black liberation. Creative people revisited the long-standing issue of whether black art is political or aesthetic. For a decade, discussion about black culture and identity focused on the relationship between art and the artist, and the political movement within the black community. This period became known as the black arts movement. Among the outstanding poets who helped shape the revolutionary movement, introducing new forms of black writing and delivering outspoken attacks on "the white aesthetic" while stressing black beauty and pride, were Sonia Sanchez, Nikki Giovanni, and Don L. Lee (Haki Madhubuti). Sanchez captured the violence and turbulence of the era. In 1970 she published a major collection of poetry entitled, *We a BaddDDD People*. Of equal significance in the development and evolution of this creative flowering was playwright and poet LeRoi Jones.

The formal beginning of the movement was the founding in 1965 of the Black Arts Repertory Theater by LeRoi Jones, who changed his name to Imamu Amiri Baraka in 1967. Jones was the bridge that linked the political and cultural aspects of black power. He had been closely associated with the white avant-garde poets in New York in the 1950s and early 1960s, but he began to change in 1965 from an integrationist to a black cultural nationalist.

The guiding ethos of the black arts movement was the determination of black artists to produce black art for black people and thereby to accomplish black liberation. In 1968 he coedited with Larry Neal the anthology *Black Fire*, which revealed the extent to which black writers and thinkers had rejected the premises of integration in favor of a new black consciousness and nationalist political engagement.

The black arts movement was criticized because of its celebration of black maleness, its racial exclusivity, and its homophobia. It was never a unified movement in the sense of all black artists speaking in one voice. There was creative dissent and competing visions of freedom. In 1970 Maya Angelou published an autobiographical novel, *I Know Why the Caged Bird Sings*, that unveiled her experience with sexual abuse and the silencing of black women within black communities. Other black women writers would follow suit and in the 1970s create a black women's literary renaissance. Still, prominent integrationist writers agreed with some of the black arts movement's fundamental tenets and were converted to its principles.

The works of Langston Hughes, Lorraine Hansberry, Gwendolyn Brooks, and James Baldwin linked the black cultural renaissances of the 1930s, 1940s, and 1950s to the black arts movement. Brooks, for example, stressed the commitment of artist to community and the importance of the relationship between the artist and her audience.

She had consistently supported community-based arts programs, and it seemed natural that she should "convert" to a Black Nationalist perspective during the 1960s and join forces with younger artists.

But the most popular black writer of the era, especially among white audiences, was James Baldwin. Baldwin was an integrationist. In his work he had resisted the simple inversion of racial hierarchies that characterized some parts of the black power and black arts movements. He wrote, "I think all theories are suspect, that the finest principles may have to be modified, or may even be pulverized by the demands of life, and that one must find therefore, and move through the world hoping that center will guide one aright." Yet in many ways, Baldwin was as alienated and angry as some of the artists identified with black arts.

In *The Fire Next Time* (1963), he concluded with a phrase that echoed through discussions of the rebellions in Watts, Newark, and Detroit. "If we do not now dare everything, the fulfillment of that prophecy, recreated from the bible in song by a slave, is upon us: 'God gave Noah the rainbow sign, No more water, the fire next time!'"

Baldwin was also an unflinching commentator on white racism and had a major impact on public discourse. At one point he told his white readers, "There appears to be a vast amount of confusion on this point, but I do not know many Negroes who are eager to be 'accepted' by white people, still less to be loved by them; they, the blacks, simply don't wish to be beaten over the head by the whites every instant of our brief passage on this planet." And in *No Name in the Street*, Baldwin declared, "I agree with the Black Panther position concerning black prisoners: not one of them has ever had a fair trial, for not one of them has ever been tried by a jury of his peers." He explained: "White middle-class America is always the jury, and they know absolutely nothing about the lives of the people on whom they sit in judgment: and this fact is not altered, on the contrary it is rendered more implacable by the presence of one or two black faces in the jury box."

Poetry and Theater

The black arts movement had its greatest and most significant impact in poetry and theater. The movement had three geographical centers: Harlem, Chicago and Detroit, and San Francisco.

The Chicago-based *Negro Digest/Black World*, edited by Hoyt Fuller and published by John Johnson, promoted many of the works of the new generation of creative artists. Fuller, a well-connected intellectual with an exhaustive command of black literature, became editor of the monthly magazine in 1961. In 1970 he changed the name of the magazine to *Black World* to signal the rejection of "Negro" and the adoption of "black" to designate people of African descent. The name change identified African Americans with both the African Diaspora and Africa itself.

In Detroit, Naomi Long Madgett's Lotus Press and Dudley Randall's Broadside Press republished the previous generation of black poets, notably Gwendolyn Brooks, Margaret Walker, and Sterling Brown. In Chicago, poet and literary critic Don L. Lee, who changed his name to Haki Madhabuti, launched Third World Press, which published many of the black arts poets and writers.

The Chicago-Detroit publishing nexus promoted new poets like Nikki Giovanni, Etheridge Knight, and Sonia Sanchez. These and other poets produced some of the most accomplished and experimental work of the black arts movement. It resonated with the sounds of the African-American vernacular, combining the rhythmic cadences of sermons with popular music and black "street speech" into a spirited new form of poetry that was free, conversational, and militantly cool.

Theater was another prominent genre of the black arts movement. Playwright Ed Bullin edited a special issue of the journal *Drama Review* in the summer of 1968 that featured essays and plays by most of the major activists in black arts, including Sonia Sanchez, Ron Milner, and Woodie King Jr. This volume became the textbook of black arts. In his plays Bullins, who was greatly influenced by Baraka, portrayed ordinary black life and explored the inner forces that prevented black people from realizing their own liberation and full potential. He showed how racism had deformed the black experience and consciousness. Across the country local black communities formed their own theater groups, including Val Gray Ward's Kuumba Workshop in Chicago and Baraka's Spirit House Theater in New Jersey. These groups reached out to people by hosting seminars, guest appearances, fashion shows, art exhibits, dance recitals, parades, and mass media parties. On the West Coast, in 1969, Robert Chrisman and Nathan Hare launched *The Black Scholar*, the first serious journal to promote black studies.

Music

The cultural nationalists in the black arts movement cultivated an appreciation for modern jazz musicians, making them icons of the quest for black freedom. Baraka argued that jazz and other black music was the language that black people developed to give uncensored accounts of their experiences. He and other cultural nationalists believed music could promote black identity and encourage the pride that was vital for political struggle. The music of the jazzmen was often dense and austere, but it could also be powerfully primitive and dazzlingly complex. Above all, the music appeared to challenge Western conceptions of harmony, rhythm, melody, and tone. In jazz you have to improvise, to create your own form of expression by using whatever information inspires you. The emphasis is not on the original, but on individual articulation.

Cultural nationalists perceived jazz to be a self-consciously engaged, economically independent, politically useful art form. Novelist Ralph Ellison put it most succinctly:

> True jazz is an art of individual assertion within and against the group. Each true jazz moment (as distinct from the uninspired commercial performance) springs from a contest in which each artist challenges all the rest; each solo flight, or improvisation, represents (like the successive canvases of a painter) a definition of his identity: as individual, as member of the collectivity and as a link in the chain of tradition.

This outlook explains why Miles Davis's legendary album *Kind of Blue* (1959), one of the most progressive jazz albums ever produced, also became one of the most popular. Davis showed that art could be accessible without sacrificing excellence and rigor. Davis, in the words of one admirer, was able to "dance underwater and not get wet." For black cultural nationalists, Davis projected an image of uncompromising and uncompromised black identity.

Among other intensely celebrated jazzmen were Charlie Parker, Archie Shepp, Ornette Coleman, Pharoah Sanders, Eric Dophy, Thelonious Monk, and John

Coltrane. Playwright Ronald Milner described Coltrane as "a man who through his saxophone before your eyes and ears completely annihilates every single western influence." Coltrane also played the deep, and deeply political, blues of "Alabama" written in response to the Birmingham church bombings.

Jazz, however, tended to appeal to intellectuals. Most black people preferred rhythm and blues, gospel, and soul. During the height of the black consciousness movement, black popular musicians gave performances and concerts to raise funds and to assert racial pride. Aretha Franklin and Ray Charles, for example, allowed SNCC workers to attend their concerts free. Just as the freedom songs had done, the soul music of the black power era helped unify black people.

No history of the era would be complete without mentioning the performances of the "Godfather of Soul," James Brown, the "Queen of Soul," Aretha Franklin's powerful rendition of the song "R.E.S.P.E.C.T.," and the financial contributions of Berry Gordy of Motown. James Brown's "Say It Loud, I'm Black and I'm Proud" became an anthem for the era. Brown linked sound commercial marketing to social commentary, confronting American racism with racial pride and righteous indignation. He confessed, "I may not do as much as some other individuals who have made it big," but, "you can bet your life that I'm doing the best I can. . . . I owe it to the black community to help provide scholarships, to help children stay in school, to help equip playgrounds and recreation centers, and to keep kids off the streets." Brown was "totally committed to black power, the kind that is achieved not through the muzzle of a rifle but through education and economic leverage."

Berry Gordy contributed to black freedom struggles both artistically and financially. To support King's Chicago movement, Gordy arranged for Stevie Wonder to give a benefit concert at Soldier Field in Chicago. He made cash contributions to black candidates, to the NAACP and its Legal Defense and Educational Fund, and to the Urban League. With Gordy's encouragement, his performers flirted just enough with black radicalism to gain a patina of militancy. During the late 1960s and early 1970s, the musical and lyrical innovations of the Temptations, Stevie Wonder, and Marvin Gaye reflected Motown's politicization.

THE SECOND PHASE OF THE BLACK STUDENT MOVEMENT

The most dramatic expression of militant assertiveness after 1968 occurred among black college students. The black power generation of students was committed to transforming society, although those on predominantly white campuses often, but not always, seemed to be more reformist than revolutionary. Some observers describe the period of activism between 1968 and 1975 as the "second phase" of the black students' movement.

The Orangeburg Massacre

The first phase, in this view, was launched by students at southern black colleges in the early 1960s. It began with the sit-ins in Greensboro, North Carolina, and the Freedom Rides, and it culminated in the Mississippi Freedom Summer of 1964. By 1968, however, many of the student organizations that had grown out of the civil rights movement, notably SNCC, were in decline. The massacre of black students at South Carolina State College in Orangeburg on February 8, 1968, marks the end of the first phase and the beginning of the second. Students attending the historically black institution had protested a local bowling alley's whites-only admission policy. When the tension and protests escalated, state officials deployed the highway patrol and National Guard. On the evening of February 8, the students assembled at the front of the campus and taunted the officers; some threw rocks, bricks, and bottles. One officer was hit by a piece of lumber. Later, without warning, nine highway patrolmen opened fire on the students with shotguns. The officers killed three young men and wounded twenty-seven. Most of them were shot in the back. All the officers involved were later acquitted, but a young black activist and SNCC leader, Cleveland Sellers, was convicted of rioting and served nearly a year in prison. He was pardoned in 1993. On February 8, 2001, South Carolina governor James Hodges apologized to a group of survivors who had assembled in Orangeburg.

Black Studies

The second phase owed much of its inspiration to the black power and black arts movements. It began when significant numbers of black students enrolled in predominantly white institutions for the first time. The black students at the white campuses demanded courses in black history, culture, literature, and art as alternatives to the "Eurocentric" bias of the average university curriculum. Many black students also formed all-black organizations.

Black students understood that education was essential to empowerment. In 1967 black students accounted for only 2 percent of the total enrollment at predominantly white colleges and universities. This meant that only 95,000 African Americans were among the approximately 5 million full-time undergraduates at these schools. Federal legislation—especially the Civil Rights Act of 1964 and the Higher Education Act of 1965—outlawed discrimination or segregation in higher education, and by instituting an array of financial aid programs, it spurred colleges and universities to take affirmative action to recruit black students.

On the national level, the overall status of black people in education reflected the accomplishments of the classic phase of the civil rights movement, but the black power generation was determined to make its own mark on the struggle. In 1960 only 227,000 black Americans attended the nation's colleges (including those at predominantly black institutions). By 1977, 1.1 million black students attended America's universities. They shared the sense of being strangers in a white-controlled environment. They resolved to change this situation.

At San Francisco State College, Nathan Hare, formerly a professor at Howard University, and black students demanded not only curriculum changes but the structural transformation of the college. In the 1966–1967 academic year, the Black Student Union (BSU) orchestrated a strike that involved thousands of students of diverse ethnic and racial backgrounds. The students deliberately chose to strike, rather than take over buildings, so they could circulate freely on the campus, increasing their support and maintaining their momentum. Among their demands were the creation of an autonomous degree-granting black studies department and the admission of more black students. The college ultimately did create the first black studies department in 1968, with Hare as its head.

Black students also took over administration buildings at other institutions, demanding not only that the schools offer more black studies courses and programs and hire more black faculty, but often that classrooms and facilities also be made available to local black communities.

In 1968 Yale University's Black Student Alliance sponsored a symposium to discuss the need, status, and function of Afro-American Studies. Conference organizer Armstead Robinson saw it as the first attempt to create a viable program of Afro-American Studies. In December 1968 the faculty voted to make Yale one of the first major universities in the country to institute a degree-granting African-American Studies program. In 1969 Harvard University created an Afro-American Studies Department, and other schools soon followed. In 1969 the Institute of the Black World in Atlanta conducted a project to define the methods and purpose of black studies and then sponsored a black studies directors' seminar. Ron Karenga wrote what remains a major textbook for the new field, *Introduction to Black Studies*. By 1973 some two hundred black studies programs existed in the United States. By the late 1980s, several of the programs, such as those at Cornell, Yale, and UCLA, offered master's degrees in African-American studies. In 1988 Temple University, under the leadership of Molefi Kete Asante, became the first university to offer a Ph.D. in African-American Studies. In 2002, Michigan State University became the sixth to offer the doctorate in the discipline.

Still, there was no universally accepted definition of black studies. James E. Turner, founder of Africana Studies at Cornell, viewed it as a collective, interdisciplinary scholarly approach to the experiences of people of African descent throughout the world. History, in black studies, constituted the foundation for the analysis of common patterns of life that reflected the social conditions of black people. Africana studies or black studies theoreticians have generally agreed on four goals for this new scholarly field: (1) It should develop solutions to the problems facing black people in the African Diaspora; (2) it should provide an analysis of black culture and life that challenges and replaces preexisting Eurocentric models; (3) it should promote social change and educational reform throughout the academy; and (4) it should institutionalize the study of black people as a field with its own theories, methods, ideologies, symbols, language, and culture. In short, the first generation of advocates envisioned black studies as a revolutionary, historically grounded educational reform movement that sought to make the study of African descendants—their culture, problems, worldviews, and spirituality—a serious scholarly endeavor with practical implications for improving black people's lives.

THE ELECTION OF 1968

In the presidential campaign of 1968, the Democrats provided the excitement but lost the election. In late 1967 Senator Eugene McCarthy of Minnesota entered the race as the antiwar alternative to Lyndon Johnson, but few politicians took him seriously, even though he won several primaries. Robert Kennedy, U.S. senator from New York, was taken seriously, even though by the time he entered the race in mid-March, most of the convention delegates were already pledged to Johnson, and, after Johnson's withdrawal, they quickly transferred their allegiance to Vice President Hubert Humphrey. Whether Kennedy could have gained the nomination will never be known because—in the second traumatic assassination of 1968—he was murdered in June. Grief over his death, bitterness over the war, and personal rivalries spilled over to produce the most tumultuous political convention in modern American history, with Chicago policemen clubbing and gassing antiwar demonstrators.

In November, Republican Richard Nixon narrowly defeated Humphrey 43.1 percent to 42.7 percent in the popular vote and 301 to 191 in the electoral vote. George Wallace, the segregationist ex-governor of Alabama won 13.5 percent of the popular vote and forty-six electoral votes. Wallace denounced civil rights legislation and court-ordered desegregation. He also endorsed the repression of demonstrators and rioters and promised to stamp out communism in Southeast Asia.

THE NIXON PRESIDENCY

Of all modern presidents, Richard Nixon is probably the hardest to pin down with neat ideological labels. By the standards of the early twentieth-first century, much of his record seems progressive. He created the Environmental Protection Agency, endorsed an equal rights amendment to the Constitution that would have prohibited gender discrimination, and signed more regulatory legislation than any other president. His willingness to innovate in policy affecting African Americans can be illustrated by his naming of Daniel Patrick Moynihan, one of Johnson's experts on social policy, to be his domestic policy adviser. But Nixon also pursued a "Southern Strategy" that realigned the Republican Party with the white southern backlash to civil rights and weakened the New Deal coalition.

The "Moynihan Report" and Fap

Moynihan first attracted national attention as assistant secretary of labor in the Johnson administration when a confidential memorandum he wrote—loosely organized and full of sweeping generalizations—was leaked to the press. It would later be published as "The Negro Family: The Case for National Action" and is popularly known as the "Moynihan Report." Moynihan's guiding assumption was that civil rights legislation, necessary as it was, would not address the problems of the inner city. There, he argued, the breakdown of the "lower-class" black family had led to the "pathology" of juvenile delinquency, illegitimacy, drug addiction, and poor performance in school. He attributed the vulnerability of the black family to "three centuries of almost unimaginable treatment" by white society: exploitation under slavery, the strain of urbanization, and persistent unemployment.

These forces, he argued, weakened the role of black men and resulted in a disproportionate number of dysfunctional female-headed families. In the most-often repeated passage in the report, Moynihan declared that the black community had been forced into "a matriarchal structure, [which] because it is so out of line with the rest of American society, seriously retards the progress of the group as a whole, and imposes a crushing burden on the Negro male. . . . Obviously, not every instance of social pathology afflicting the Negro community can be traced to the weakness of family structure . . . [but] once or twice removed, it will be found to be the principal source of most of the aberrant, inadequate, or anti-social behavior that did not establish, but now serves to perpetuate the cycle of poverty and deprivation."

Although based on the work of earlier black scholars, such as E. Franklin Frazier, Moynihan's condemnation of "matriarchy" drew fire. Black social scientists countered that the structure of the black family reflected a functional adaptation that black people had made to survive in a hostile and racist American society. Historians Herbert Gutman and John Blassingame argued that Moynihan underestimated the prevalence of two-parent black families in the past. Although many of the criticisms of the report were deserved, they diverted attention from its positive thrust. Moynihan wanted to eliminate poverty and unemployment in the black community, and he recommended vigorous enforcement of the civil rights laws to achieve equality of opportunity. Moynihan was one of the first to appreciate how white resentment of the Community Action Program (CAP) and the expansion of the welfare rolls would make both programs politically unfeasible.

Intrigued with Moynihan's independence, Nixon told him to develop a plan to assist poor families. Under the Family Assistance Plan (FAP) that Nixon unveiled in the summer of 1969, each family of four with no wage earner would receive an annual payment of $1,600 plus $800 of food stamps.

Had it passed, FAP would have preserved and promoted two-parent families by removing the prohibition against assistance to dependent children whose fathers were alive, well, and living at home. It would also have encouraged work by requiring able-bodied recipients to accept jobs or vocational training and by providing benefits to those accepting low-paying jobs. But the Senate, under pressure both from conservatives who objected to any government programs for the poor and from welfare-rights advocates who complained the payments were too low, killed it.

Busing

Nixon was acutely aware that he moved in a changed political environment and particularly in a far more conservative Republican Party than he had when he ran against and lost to John F. Kennedy in 1960. Then, as a presidential candidate, he had had to appease Eastern, pro–civil rights liberals led by New York governor Nelson Rockefeller (1908–1979). But in 1968 an influx of southern segregationists whom Barry Goldwater had attracted to the Republican Party in 1964 had to be appeased. Now Nixon chose to court closer relations with South Carolina senator Strom Thurmond, a Republican who had abandoned the Democratic Party in 1964. Thurmond and his allies had demanded that, if elected, Nixon would slow down the process of court-ordered school desegregation in the South. Finally, Nixon could hardly ignore George Wallace, with his racist appeals. In another three-way race in 1972, Wallace might ensure Nixon's defeat.

As a result of these pressures, the Nixon administration perfected its southern strategy and embarked on a collision course with civil rights organizations such as the NAACP, which supported busing to achieve school integration. Thus the major battle over civil rights in the early 1970s was over the federal courts' willingness to implement desegregation goals by busing students across district lines. Nixon used the busing controversy to lure Wallace voters. In 1971 he had advised federal officials to stop pressing to desegregate schools through "forced busing." He argued that such efforts were ultimately "counterproductive, and not in the interest of better race relations."

Educational segregation in the North reflected residential segregation. In Boston, site of some of the most acrimonious busing protests, schools in black neighborhoods received less funding than their white counterparts. Buildings were derelict, seriously overcrowded, and deficient in supplies and equipment, even desks. In 1974 U.S. district judge W. Arthur Garrity ruled in favor of a group of black parents who had filed a class action suit against the Boston School Committee. The ruling found the school committee guilty of violating the equal protection clause of the Fourteenth Amendment. To achieve racial balance in the Boston schools, the judge ordered the busing of several thousand students between mostly white South Boston, Hyde Park, and Dorchester, and mostly black Roxbury.

White people who opposed busing organized demonstrations and boycotts to prevent their children from being bused into black communities and black children from being bused into white schools. Violence and hostilities continued for weeks.

Nixon and the War

Meanwhile, the war in Vietnam seemed to drag on endlessly, with the peace negotiations that had begun in Paris in May 1968 making no apparent progress. Nixon realized that what most Americans disliked about the war was that it was killing their sons and husbands. So in 1969 he began to phase out direct U.S. involvement in the war. This "Vietnamization," he claimed, was made possible by the growing ability of the South Vietnamese to fight for themselves. What Nixon did not say was that another reason for troop withdrawals was that the morale of American soldiers was plunging rapidly. Drug abuse among troops was widespread, some soldiers had killed their officers, and some of those incidents had racial overtones. Along with his domestic record, Nixon's promise to "wind down the war" was widely popular and assured his reelection. In 1972 he defeated South Dakota senator George McGovern in a landslide.

Few in the Nixon administration, however, took South Vietnamese military capability seriously, and Nixon was unwilling to "lose" Vietnam. Between 1969 and 1971, Nixon stepped up the war. Antiwar demonstrations kept Nixon off balance and may have deterred him from further escalation.

The most dramatic response to Nixon's escalation in the Vietnam War came after the invasion of Cambodia in April 1970. The invasion triggered antiwar protests on many campuses. In one such protest, on May 4, Ohio National Guardsmen shot and killed four white students at Kent State University. The response of students across the country was electric: the first nationwide student strike in American history. Ten days later in Mississippi, the shooting and killing of two black students at Jackson State University attracted much less attention from either white students or the media. Three years later, at the beginning of 1973, the United States and North Vietnam signed a peace agreement. Congress then prohibited the reintroduction of American troops and the resumption of bombing, and in 1974 began cutting off military aid to the South Vietnamese government. The result of this loss of American support was predictable: in 1975 the communists launched their final offensive, and South Vietnam collapsed.

Nixon's Downfall

If Nixon assumed the presidency in 1969 with any popular mandate, it was to restore law and order. The disorder that irritated the American public included many things: the inner-city riots, the antiwar demonstrations and campus protests, and the rise in crime. Responding to this mood, Nixon pushed legislation through Congress that gave local law enforcement officials expanded power to use wiretaps and enter premises without advance warning.

But Nixon's personality—a combination of paranoia and ruthlessness—pushed him beyond what the public would tolerate, and even beyond the law itself. He increasingly confused ordinary criminals with principled protesters and his political opponents, and he decided to punish them all. One method was to create an extralegal ring of burglars, operating out of the White House to gather incriminating information. In June 1972 they were discovered breaking into Democratic National Committee headquarters in the Watergate apartment complex in Washington. Full details emerged in a Senate investigation in 1973–1974, and on August 9, 1974, threatened with impeachment, Nixon resigned. His downfall, however, left no one of his stature or with his flexible attitude toward public policy to resist the takeover of the Republican Party by more ideologically dogmatic conservatives. One early intimation of this was the difficulty Nixon's successor, Gerald Ford, had in securing the 1976 Republican presidential nomination against the right's new hero, former California governor Ronald Reagan.

THE RISE OF BLACK ELECTED OFFICIALS

Just as King searched for a new strategy after the victories of the early phase of the civil rights movement, other black leaders mobilized the newly enfranchised black electorate to win political office. After the adoption of the Voting Rights Act of 1965, Vernon Jordan, director of the Voter Education Project, coordinated registration drives and workshops across the South. As he explained, "Too many of these people have been alienated from the political process for too long a time . . . and so we have to . . . teach them what a local government is, how it operates, and try to relate their votes to the things they want."

By 1974 there were 1,593 black elected officials outside the South, and by 1980 the number had risen to 2,455. Although black people in northern cities had been able to vote for a century and had been slowly developing political muscle and winning representation in state legislatures and on municipal councils, they had not been able to command an equal voice in city governance. The rise of black power and the inspiration of the Voting Rights Act, however, signaled a new departure. People now eagerly engaged in the electoral process to achieve a political influence to which their numbers entitled them. In 1967 in Cleveland, where the black population had skyrocketed after

World War II, Carl Stokes became the first black mayor of a major American city, winning election with the support of white business leaders and the solid backing of the black community. In the same year prosecutor Richard G. Hatcher became mayor of Gary, Indiana, where the black population had also increased greatly after the war. Hatcher won by a mere 1,389 votes, garnering 96 percent of the black vote and 14 percent of the white vote.

The Gary Convention and the Black Political Agenda

These victories made possible one of the most significant events of recent black political history, the Gary convention of 1972. The co-chairs of the convention were Detroit congressman Charles Diggs, Hatcher, and writer and cultural nationalist Amiri Baraka of Newark, New Jersey. The nationalists interpreted "black power" to mean that black people should control their own communities and create separate cultural institutions distinct from those of white society. These views clashed with the ideas espoused by the black elected officials represented by Stokes and Hatcher.

Hatcher observed that "people had come to Gary from communities all over the United States where they were politically impotent, but. . . they went back home and rolled up their sleeves and dived into the political arena." Approximately eight thousand people gathered to develop an agenda for black empowerment. The discussions about bloc voting, the efficacy of coalitions, and the feasibility of a third party inspired scores of individual African Americans to run for local office. The convention was not homogeneous, however, and no unified black consensus emerged.

Several discussions over strategies to secure common interests revealed deep-seated internal divisions that allowed ancillary issues to provoke even more impassioned disagreement. Coleman Young and other Michigan delegates walked out to protest a proposal calling for African Americans to reject "discriminatory" unions and form their own. Others walked out over a resolution condemning Israel for its "expansionist policy" toward the Palestinians. Others opposed "forced racial integration of schools" through busing, arguing that such practices insulted black students and would cost black teachers their jobs.

The Gary convention was important because it signaled a shift in the political focus of the black community toward electoral politics and away from mass demonstrations and protest measures. Unity continued to elude subsequent conventions, however, and delegates attending the last National Black Convention at Little Rock, Arkansas, in 1974 abandoned the idea of a black political party. Deep ideological differences and institutional cleavages precluded coalitions and cooperation between black nationalists and the rising numbers of black elected officials. These same differences prevented some nationalists and elected officials from taking seriously the 1972 Democratic Party presidential bid of New York congresswoman Shirley Chisholm.

Black People Gain Local Offices

Despite the demise of the National Black Convention movement, African Americans continued to register impressive gains in electoral politics. A few statistics indicate the success of black politicians. When the leaders first convened the Gary convention, there were 13 African-American members of Congress; by 1997 there were 40. In 1972 there were 2,427 black elected officials; by 1993 there were 8,106. An amendment to the Voting Rights Act in 1975 enabled minorities to mount court challenges to at-large voting practices that diluted the impact of bloc voting; this helped increase the number of black elected officials. Districts were redrawn with race as the predominant factor in their reconfiguration. On November 5, 1985, state senator L. Douglas Wilder was elected lieutenant governor in Virginia, making him the first African-American lieutenant governor in a southern state since Reconstruction. In 1989 he was elected governor, making him the first black governor of any state since Reconstruction.

Between 1971 and 1975, the number of African-American mayors rose from 8 to 135, leading to the founding of the National Conference of Black Mayors in 1974. In 1973 Coleman Young in Detroit and Thomas Bradley in Los Angeles became the first African-American mayors of cities of more than a million citizens. Bradley won in Los Angeles even though black people made up only 15 percent of the city's electorate. Ten years later, in 1983, Chicago swore in its first black mayor, Harold Washington. The era of the black elected official had arrived.

ECONOMIC DOWNTURN

The 1970s were a decade of recessions and economic instability. Many black people experienced this economic downturn as a depression. During the 1970s, as the gap between the incomes of the upper 20 percent of African Americans and their white counterparts narrowed, the gap between black men and women at the bottom of the economic ladder and their counterparts expanded. Poor black people were losing ground. In 1969 approximately 10 percent of white men and 25 percent of black men earned less than $10,000 (in 1984 constant dollars). In 1984 about 40 percent of black men between twenty-five and fifty-five earned less than $10,000 compared with 20 percent of comparable white men. Put a different way, between 1970 and 1986, the proportion of black families with incomes of less than $10,000 grew from 26.8 to 30.2 percent. Still, there were some improvements. The black middle class grew. In 1970, 4.7 percent of black families had incomes of more than $50,000; by 1986 the number had almost doubled to 8.8 percent. But in general, the relative economic status of black workers did not improve.

BLACK AMERICANS AND THE CARTER PRESIDENCY

In 1976 the United States celebrated its bicentennial. Flags flew from every flagpole, and fire hydrants were painted red, white, and blue. Tall ships sailed into New York harbor from around the world, and there were more parades than anyone could count. For African Americans, it was an important year, but for another reason. For the first time since 1964, the man most of them voted for was elected president—Jimmy Carter, a former governor of Georgia. Ninety percent of African-American voters favored the soft-spoken, religious Georgia Democrat over incumbent president

Gerald Ford. As in 1960 their votes were crucial; without them, Carter could not have even carried his native South.

Black Appointees

Carter acknowledged his debt to the black electorate by appointing African Americans to highly visible posts. He named Patricia Harris secretary of Housing and Urban Development, making her the first black woman to serve in the Cabinet. Carter appointed Andrew Young, former congressman from Georgia and a longtime political ally, ambassador to the United Nations. (Young was forced to resign in 1979.) Clifford Alexander Jr. became the secretary of the army. Eleanor Holmes Norton became the first woman to chair the Equal Employment Opportunity Commission (EEOC). Ernest Green, who had been one of the nine students to desegregate Little Rock's Central High School, was appointed assistant secretary of the Department of Labor. Wade McCree was appointed solicitor general in the Justice Department. Drew Days III became assistant attorney general for civil rights. Historian and former University of Colorado chancellor Mary Frances Berry was appointed assistant secretary for education. Carter also named Louis Martin his special assistant, making him the first African American in a position of influence on the White House staff.

Carter's Domestic Policies

There are many ways to judge the significance of the Carter presidency to African Americans. Carter's black appointments were practically and symbolically important. Never had so many black men and women occupied positions that had direct and immediate impact on the day-to-day operations of the federal government. Carter also helped cement gains for civil rights. When Congress passed legislation to stop busing for schoolchildren as a means of integrating the schools, Carter vetoed it. He tried to improve fair employment practices by strengthening the enforcement powers of the EEOC. His Justice Department chose cases to prosecute under the Fair Housing Act that involved widespread discrimination, to make the greatest possible impact.

Yet Carter's overall record proved unsatisfactory to most African Americans. Despite a Public Works Employment Act that directed 10 percent of public works funds to minority contractors and helped spur the creation of 585,000 jobs, Carter failed to help Democrats in Congress pass either full-employment or universal health-care bills. He also cut social welfare programs in an attempt to balance the budget, including school lunch programs and financial aid to black students.

Although the sluggish economy undermined Carter's popularity, the event that proved his undoing was the Iran hostage crisis that began in the fall of 1979. For many black people, however, Carter had become a disappointment long before that. They believed he had done little to help them achieve social justice and economic advancement. Still, the nomination of the conservative Ronald Reagan by the Republicans left black voters no alternative to Carter. In the election of 1980, 90 percent of black voters again supported him, but this time they could not prevent his defeat. Carter pulled down scores of Democrats with him, and the Republicans regained the Senate for the first time since 1954.

TIMELINE

AFRICAN-AMERICAN EVENTS	NATIONAL EVENTS
1965	
1965	**1965**
Malcolm X assassinated	President Johnson authorizes the bombing of North
Watts Riot	Vietnam
Voting Rights Act of 1965 enacted	**1966**
1966	National Organization for Women (NOW) is formed
Black Panther Party formed	
Stokely Carmichael coins the slogan "black power"	
Chicago campaign begins	
Edward William Brooke of Massachusetts elected the first black U.S. senator since Reconstruction	
Robert C. Weaver becomes first black cabinet officer	
Strike at San Francisco State University results in first black studies program	
1967	
1967	**1968**
Uprisings in Newark, Detroit, and other cities	North Vietnam launches Tet Offensive
Muhammad Ali refuses to be drafted	U.S. and North Vietnam begin peace talks
Thurgood Marshall confirmed as first black Supreme Court justice	Johnson declines to run for another term
Adam Clayton Powell Jr. denied his seat in Congress	Robert Kennedy assassinated
1968	Richard M. Nixon elected president
Kerner Commission Report released	Secret bombing of Cambodia
Poor People's Campaign in Washington, D.C.	
Orangeburg Massacre	
Martin Luther King Jr. assassinated	
Shirley Chisholm elected to the U.S. House of Representatives	
Carl Stokes elected major of Cleveland and Richard Hatcher elected mayor of Gary, Indiana	
1969	
1969	**1970**
Harvard establishes an Afro-American Studies program	U.S. incursion into Cambodia
	Kent State killings

continued

AFRICAN-AMERICAN EVENTS	NATIONAL EVENTS
Maulana Karenga publishes *Introduction to Black Studies*	
Black Panther leaders Fred Hampton and Mark Clarke killed in Chicago police raid	
1970	
Jackson State killings	
Angela Davis placed on the FBI's Ten Most Wanted list	

1971

1971	**1972**
Angela Davis arraigned	Watergare break-in
Jesse Jackson founds People United to Save Humanity (PUSH)	Nixon reelected president
Busing to achieve integration begins	
1972	
First National Black Political Convention held in Gary, Indiana	
Shirley Chisholm makes a bid for the Democratic presidential nomination	
Barbara Jordan elected to the House of Representatives	
Angela Davis acquitted	

1973

1973	**1974**
Thomas Bradley elected mayor of Los Angeles	Watergate hearings
Coleman Young elected mayor of Detroit	Nixon resigns
1974	
National Council for Black Studies formed	

1975

1975	**1975**
Antibusing protests break out in Boston	South Vietnam falls
1976	**1976**
Andrew Young named U.S. ambassador to the United Nations	Jimmy Carter elected president

1979

1979	**1979**
Andrew Young resigns as U.S. ambassador	Iran hostage crisis begins
	1980
	Ronald Reagan elected president

CONCLUSION

The civil rights movement's victories changed African-American life in particular and American culture in general. The black power and black arts movements continued the struggle for freedom in northern and western urban areas where housing segregation, rising unemployment, and persistent police brutality sparked rebellions that resulted in many deaths and widespread destruction in Watts, Newark, Detroit, and other cities. The black political convention movement did not create a black third party. But one of the most enduring legacies of the era was the rise of black elected officials. Black student militancy persisted despite the destruction of the Black Panther Party. Throughout the late 1960s and 1970s, black students fought to create and institutionalize black studies as a new academic field. The black arts and black consciousness movement opened up new avenues for the expression of black unity and positive black identity. A new generation of black poets, dramatists, and musicians found receptive audiences.

The legislative successes of the early phase of the civil rights movement illuminated how much more needed to be done to achieve a truly egalitarian society. Poor people, black and white, needed jobs, housing, medical care, and education. To varying degrees, Presidents Johnson, Nixon, and Carter attempted to address these needs. Their efforts produced mixed results in the face of a disastrous war in Vietnam and a massive white backlash. In the 1980s Republicans would reap the benefit of the Democratic Party's disarray, and the plight of the poor would deteriorate.

Still, some black intellectuals chose a long view in their assessment of the significance of the post–World War II decades of struggle. Historian and theologian Vincent Harding put it most eloquently:

> It may be that the greatest discovery . . . was the fact that there is no last word in the human struggle for freedom, justice, and democracy. Only the continuing word, lived out by men, women, and children who dance and rest, who wrestle with alligators and stand firm before tanks, and presidents, and drug lords and deep, deep, fears. We learn again that the continuing word remains embedded in those who determined not to be moved, who know, against all odds, that they will overcome, will continue to create a more perfect union, a more compassionate world. The world remains with those who discover, in the midst of unremitting struggle, deep amazing powers within their own lives, power from, power for, the planet.

REVIEW QUESTIONS

1. Why did African-American residents of Watts, Newark, and Detroit rebel in 1965–1966? What did these rebellions suggest about the value of the civil rights movement victories?

2. How did the visions and ideals, successes and failures of Martin Luther King Jr. compare with those of Lyndon B. Johnson? Why were these men at odds with each other?

3. What role did African Americans play in the Vietnam War?

4. In what ways can the presidency of Richard Nixon be considered progressive? Which reforms initiated by President Lyndon B. Johnson did Nixon advance once he took office?

5. What were the major ideological concerns of the artists of the black arts movement? To what extent did Baldwin and Amiri Baraka have similar views about art, consciousness, aesthetics, and politics?

6. Why did African Americans not form a third political party? What was the significance of the rise of black elected officials?

7. Why were African Americans disappointed with the presidency of Jimmy Carter?

RECOMMENDED READING

Stokely Carmichael and Charles V. Hamilton. *Black Power: The Politics of Liberation in America.* New York: Vintage Books, 1967. One of the most important books of the era of black power, by Carmichael, who popularized the slogan, and political scientist Hamilton.

Theodore Cross. *The Black Power Imperative: Racial Inequality and the Politics of Nonviolence.* New York: Faulkner Books, 1984. Provides a useful critique of the black power movement and explores the persistence of racial inequality.

Robert Dalleck. *Flawed Giant: Lyndon B. Johnson and His Times 1961–1973.* New York: Oxford University Press, 1998. A definitive biography of President Lyndon Johnson with fresh insights, grounded in exhaustive research.

Henry Hampton and Steve Fayer, eds. *Voices of Freedom: An Oral History of the Civil Rights Movement from the 1950s through the 1980s.* New York: Bantam Books, 1990. Contains the recollections of all the key participants in the critical battles and movements of the three decades that transformed race relations in America.

Michael D. Harris. *Colored Pictures: Race and Visual Representation.* Chapel Hill: University of North Carolina Press, 2003. A splendid study of how race has been represented and visualized with insightful analyses of arts movements and informative discussions of black painters.

Robert C. Smith. *We Have No Leaders: African Americans in the Post–Civil Rights Era.* New York: State University of New York Press, 1996. A thoughtful critique of the successes and failures of black politics beginning with the National Black Political Convention in Gary, Indiana, in 1972.

Wallace Terry. *Bloods: An Oral History of the Vietnam War by Black Veterans.* New York: Ballantine Books, 1984. One of the best sources for firsthand accounts of the Vietnam War as experienced by black soldiers.

Brian Ward. *Just My Soul Responding: Rhythm and Blues, Black Consciousness, and Race Relations.* Berkeley: University of California Press, 1998. An excellent study of black popular culture during the civil rights and black power movement era.

Craig Hansen Werner. *Playing the Changes: From Afro-Modernism to the Jazz Impulse.* Urbana: University of Illinois Press, 1994. An insightful study of the gospel, blues, and jazz impulse in the writings of key black writers, including James Baldwin and Leon Forrest, during the post–civil rights movement era.

BLACK POLITICS, WHITE BACKLASH

1980 TO THE PRESENT

RONALD REAGAN AND THE CONSERVATIVE REACTION

Beginning in the late 1970s, American politics took a hard turn to the right. This shift profoundly affected African Americans, particularly the poor. With the election of Ronald Reagan (1911–2004) to the presidency in 1980, the executive branch ceased to support expanded civil rights. It also sought to reduce welfare programs, and it staffed key agencies and the federal judiciary with opponents of affirmative action. The now overwhelmingly white Republican Party became increasingly entrenched in the South, ending the Democratic Party's long dominance in that region. The political landscape of the 1980s and 1990s was thus marked by a realignment and a hardening of ideological conflict between liberal and progressive Democrats on one side and conservative Republicans on the other.

Ronald Reagan's defeat of Jimmy Carter in the 1980 presidential election marked the emergence of the New Right as the dominant force in American politics. Over the previous decade, many groups unhappy with the changes of the 1960s had developed powerful political organizations that found a home in the Republican Party. These groups included those opposed to equal rights for women, to abortion rights, to the Supreme Court's decisions protecting the rights of the accused and banning compulsory prayer from the public schools, and a range of other issues. White Southerners opposed to the changes wrought by the civil rights movement, and white Northerners angry at school busing, affirmative action programs, and the tax burden they associated with welfare were a key part of this coalition.

Dismantling the Great Society

One of the New Right's goals was to reverse the growth of social welfare programs created during and after the New Deal. To this end, from 1981 to 1992, Reagan and his Republican successor George H. W. Bush cut federal grants to cities in half and terminated programs crucial to the stability of many black families. As a result, inner-city neighborhoods, where 56 percent of poor residents were African American, became more unstable.

Reagan advanced a trickle-down theory of economics. He believed if the financial position of the wealthiest Americans improved, their increased prosperity would percolate through the middle and working classes to the poor. Unemployment statistics soon challenged this theory. By December 1982, the unemployment rate had risen to 10.8, and the rate for African Americans was twice that of white Americans. The real income of the highest paid 1 percent of the nation, meanwhile, increased from $312,206 to $548,970 during the 1980s.

Reagan and Bush often cloaked their intent to undermine rights-oriented policies by appointing black conservatives to key administrative positions. Reagan chose William Bell as chair of the Equal Employment Opportunity Commission (EEOC). Because Bell was a conservative with few qualifications for the post, civil rights leaders and organizations immediately protested his appointment. Reagan simply replaced Bell the following year with yet another black conservative, Clarence Thomas, who strongly opposed affirmative action. Thomas reduced the commission's staff and allowed the backlog of affirmative action cases to grow to 46,000 and processing time to increase to ten months.

Reagan similarly tried to change the direction of the U.S. Commission on Civil Rights (CCR), but in this case he met with resistance. Since its creation in 1957, the commission had served as a civil rights watchdog, with no real enforcement powers but with considerable influence on public opinion. Soon after Reagan took office, the CCR began to issue reports critical of his civil rights policies. Reagan responded by trying to load the commission with members sympathetic to his perspective. He replaced the commission's chair, Arthur S. Flemming, who was white, with a black Republican, Clarence Pendleton, former executive director of the San Diego Urban League. The vice chair, however, was Mary Frances Berry, a well-respected, longtime civil rights activist and historian who had been appointed by Carter and who frequently clashed with the new president. In 1984 Reagan tried to remove Berry from the CCR, but she resisted, suing in court to retain her position. When her suit was successful, she became known as "the woman the president could not fire." Even with Berry, however, the CCR declined to virtual insignificance under Pendleton during the Reagan years.

Men like Bell, Thomas, and Pendleton were part of a vocal cadre of black, middle-class, conservative intellectuals, professionals, and politicians who gained prominence during the Reagan years. To augment their influence in the Republican Party, these conservatives cultivated a small, well-educated, articulate group of black men and women intellectuals in addition to black politicians. Prominent black proponents of conservative ideology include Thomas Sowell, Walter Williams, Shelby Steele, Armstrong Williams, Ward Connerly, and, until he broke with the others in the late 1990s, Glenn Loury. Black Republican politicians rarely exercised meaningful power within the party. In contrast, elite black Democratic politicians could, and often did, make their influence felt. Moreover, they represented a large and essential constituency within the party.

The Thomas–Hill Controversy

The role of black conservatives acquired its greatest visibility when, in 1991, President George H. W. Bush nominated Clarence Thomas to the U.S. Supreme Court. Thomas was born in 1948 in rural Georgia. He graduated from Holy Cross College in Massachusetts and Yale Law School. The symbolism of Thomas, who opposed the expansion of civil rights, replacing Thurgood Marshall, the greatest civil rights lawyer of the twentieth century, could not have been more dramatic.

George Bush's nomination of Thomas precipitated the most public exposure of gender conflict within the black community in history. Marshall had been one of the Court's great liberals and a staunch defender of civil rights. Thomas was a black conservative whose record on civil rights did not endear him to white liberals, or for that matter, to many within the black community. His credentials for the position were also open to question: he had served only fifteen months as an appellate court judge. However, he was a black man, and the black community was loath publicly to contest his nomination or to challenge the cynical tokenism of the Bush administration. Still, civil rights organizations expressed grave reservations about the Thomas nomination. The Urban League declared, "We welcome the appointment of an African-American jurist to fill the vacant seat left by Justice [Thurgood] Marshall. Obviously, Judge Thomas is no Justice Marshall. But if he were, this administration would not have appointed him. We are hopeful that Judge Thomas' background of poverty and minority status will lead him to greater identification with those in America who today are victimized by poverty and discrimination. And [we] expect the Senate, in the confirmation hearings, to explore whether he is indeed likely to do so."

The anticipated easy confirmation process derailed when black law professor Anita Hill agreed to appear before the Senate Judiciary Committee, which heard testimony on Thomas's confirmation. Hill accused Thomas of sexually harassing her when she worked for him at the Equal Employment Opportunity Commission.

Some senators questioned her own character and integrity. Thomas countered her charges with charges of his own. He declared he was a victim of a "high-tech lynching" in the media and that Hill's accusations were false. Although many in the black community supported Thomas, progressive feminists, white liberals, and some black people supported Hill. Activist black women were especially incensed by the treatment that Hill received from the Senate and were determined to voice their opposition to Thomas's political views. Despite the opposition, Clarence Thomas won confirmation to the U.S. Supreme Court by a narrow 52 to 48 majority. On the Court, Thomas has proved to be an archconservative who consistently votes against progressive or liberal causes such as affirmative action.

Debating the "Old" and the "New" Civil Rights

The Reagan and Bush administrations distinguished between what might be called the "old civil rights law," which they claimed to support, and the "new civil rights law," which they opposed. Developed in the decade between the *Brown* decision and the Voting Rights Act of 1965, the old civil rights law prohibited intentional discrimination, be it legal segregation in the schools, informal discrimination in the workplace, or racially biased restrictions on voting. The new civil rights law is concerned with discriminatory outcomes, as measured by statistical disparities, rather than with discriminatory intent. If, for example, black children overall are disproportionately in all-black schools, or if the workforce in a given firm, compared with the community in which it is located, is disproportionately white (or male), or if elected officials in a multiracial state or municipality are disproportionately white, discrimination is assumed.

The remedies for such historic discrimination, collectively labeled "affirmative action," tend to be statistical in nature. They include increasing the number of minority pupils, minority employees, or (by redrawing the districts from which they were elected) minority elected officials to correspond to the percentage of the relevant minority population. In employment (and in admissions to colleges and universities), the methods used in reaching these goals became known as affirmative action "guidelines." Sometimes guidelines were imposed by court order; more often they were the result of voluntary efforts by legislatures, government agencies, business firms, and colleges and universities to comply with civil rights laws and court rulings.

Affirmative Action

Few civil rights policies in the twentieth century have proved more persistently controversial than affirmative action. Many white Americans oppose affirmative action, arguing it runs contrary to the concept of achievement founded on objective merit and amounts to reverse racial or sexual discrimination. Ironically, because gender discrimination in employment was made illegal in the 1964 Civil Rights Act, prompting federal agencies to scrutinize the percentage of women in a given workforce, white women have been among the major beneficiaries of affirmative action. But the major advocates of affirmative action have been African Americans, most of whom see it as a remedy for centuries of discrimination. The debate over affirmative action has thus, inevitably, led to racial polarization, and it even divided the black community.

The term *affirmative action* was first used by President Lyndon Johnson in a 1965 executive order that required federal contractors to "take affirmative action" to guarantee that job seekers and employees "are treated without regard to their race, color, religion, sex, or national origin." Much of the credit for compliance with affirmative action belongs to conservative Republican president Richard Nixon. In 1969 Arthur A. Fletcher, a black assistant secretary of labor in the Nixon administration, developed the "Philadelphia Plan," in which firms with federal government contracts in the construction industry would have to set and meet hiring goals for African Americans or be penalized. The plan became a model for subsequent "set-aside" programs that reserved some contracts for minority-owned businesses or that favored the hiring of women and minorities. The process of setting goals and timetables to achieve full compliance with federal civil rights requirements appealed to large corporations and accounted for the early success of affirmative action initiatives.

The Backlash

Although it has produced more litigation, affirmative action in employment has been less controversial than affirmative action in college and university admissions. State higher education institutions have been at the center of the controversy both because they are narrowly bound by the Fourteenth Amendment's prohibitions on racial discrimination and because they represent, far more than do elite private institutions, the gateways to upward mobility for millions of Americans, white and black. As the 1970s progressed, in the interest both of aiding disadvantaged minorities and of increasing racial and cultural diversity on campus, admissions offices began using different criteria for white and minority admissions. Conservatives called these criteria "racial preferences." They argued that such policies did more harm than good and created new unfairness and white resentment of African Americans.

Negative reaction to affirmative action mushroomed in the late 1970s. The case of *Regents of the University of California v. Bakke* was a key part of this backlash. The medical school at the University of California, as a form of affirmative action, had set aside sixteen of its one hundred places in each entering class for disadvantaged and minority students. They were considered for admission in a separate system. A white male student named Alan Bakke sued the university for discrimination after it rejected his application for admission. In 1976 the California Supreme Court ruled he should be admitted to the university, but the university appealed the ruling to the U.S. Supreme Court, which also ruled in Bakke's favor in 1978. Of the nine justices, five agreed the university violated Bakke's rights. However, other related legal issues were involved, and the court split without a majority on nearly every one of them. Only one justice declared that affirmative action cases should be judged on the same strict level of scrutiny applied to "invidious" discrimination. All the other justices stated that race-conscious remedies could be used in some circumstances to correct past discrimination.

California remains the center of the affirmative action storm because of its multiracial population. In 1995 Republican governor Pete Wilson ended affirmative action in state employment. In 1996 California voters approved Proposition 209, the so-called California Civil Rights Initiative, which banned all state agencies from implementing affirmative action programs. The campaign for the proposition was led by Ward Connerly, a conservative black entrepreneur. Born in 1939 in rural Louisiana, he had earned a B.A. from Sacramento State College and had received over $140,000 from state contracts set aside for minority businesses. Nonetheless, Connerly maintained that affirmative action exacerbated the negative stereotyping of African Americans. He and his supporters insisted moreover that affirmative action had failed to address problems of poverty, unemployment, and inadequate education that beset the truly disadvantaged. Instead, it had merely elevated to higher status those least in need of assistance, especially middle-class white women. Finally, Connerly accepted the broader argument that affirmative action assaulted the concept of individual merit and violated core American values of equality and opportunity. Since the proposition was upheld by the U.S. Supreme Court, the numbers at Berkeley, U.C.'s most prestigious campus, fell precipitously.

On June 23, 2003, the U.S. Supreme Court, in two separate decisions, handed the University of Michigan both a major victory, when it upheld the law school's practice of using race as a criterion in admissions procedures to create a diverse student body, and a defeat, when it banned the university from awarding points based on race as a criterion for admitting undergraduates. In the first case, *Grutter v. Bollinge*, a 5–4 decision declared that the University of Michigan Law School could use race to achieve diversity, thus firmly endorsing the long-standing *Bakke* decision written by Justice Powell. Justice Sandra Day O'Connor was persuaded that the law school acted out of a compelling interest to obtain the educational benefits that accrued from a diverse student population and meaningful integration. However, writing for the majority in the second case, *Gratz v. Bollinger*, Chief Justice Rehnquist maintained that in admitting undergraduates the university crossed the line of what was permissable by giving points to black applicants.

BLACK POLITICAL ACTIVISM IN THE AGE OF CONSERVATIVE REACTION

Presidents Reagan and Bush did not completely reverse or halt the advancement of the civil rights agenda. The increased participation of black men and women in the upper echelons of the Democratic Party reflected the extent to which they had overcome political exclusion. In 1964 there were only 103 black elected officials in the nation; by 1994 there were nearly 8,500. Forty-one African Americans were serving in Congress by 1996. By the mid-1990s, black men and women held the mayor's office in four hundred towns and cities. The days of black political powerlessness had ended. Or had they?

During the Reagan–Bush era, one house of Congress—and often both—was in the hands of the Democratic Party. Reflecting the importance of African-American voters to the party, that house used its power to pass many equal rights laws. Among the most important of these statutes were the Voting Rights Act of 1982, the Civil Rights Restoration Act of 1988, and the Fair Housing Act of 1988. The Civil Rights Restoration Act of 1988 authorized the withholding of federal funds from an entire institution if any program within it discriminated against women, racial minorities, the aged, or the disabled. The Fair Housing Act of 1988 provided for enforcing fair housing laws. It stipulated that either an individual or the Department of Housing and Urban Development (HUD) could bring a complaint of housing discrimination and authorize administrative judges to investigate housing complaints, issue injunctions and fines, and award punitive damages. With both laws, Congress was responding to Supreme Court decisions that had narrowed the scope of earlier legislation. The Civil Rights Act of 1991 was likewise a response to a spate of restrictive Supreme Court decisions. In it, Democrats secured the protection of many of the defenses of civil rights the court had called into question.

The King Holiday

Many African Americans invested symbolic importance in an effort to make Martin Luther King Jr.'s birthday a national holiday, elevating him to the stature of Presidents George Washington and Abraham Lincoln, both of whom are honored with a holiday. At first Reagan resisted the effort, but he eventually gave in to pressure from African Americans and their white allies. On November 2, 1983, Reagan signed a law designating the third Monday in January to honor the great civil rights leader. On January 20, 1985, the United States officially observed Martin Luther King Jr. Day for the first time. In 1988 more than sixty thousand people made the pilgrimage to Washington, D.C., to commemorate the twenty-fifth anniversary of the 1963 March on Washington and to remember Martin Luther King Jr.'s "I Have a Dream" speech.

Transafrica and the Antiapartheid Movement

Black activism persisted on the international as well as the national front. Much of this effort focused on ending the oppressive conditions of apartheid—the complete social, political, and economic isolation of black people—in South Africa. Randall Robinson, a native of Richmond, Virginia, and a graduate of Harvard Law School sought to link African-American liberation struggles with those waged by Africans in South Africa and elsewhere. In 1977 he founded TransAfrica to lobby for black political prisoners in South Africa, chief among them Nelson Mandela.

The antiapartheid movement became a major priority for African-American activists. They were able to enlist the sympathy and help of white Americans on college campuses and to pressure many universities into divesting their investments in South Africa. In 1986 the Black Congressional Caucus persuaded their colleagues to enact a U.S. trade embargo against South Africa and sustain it over President Reagan's veto.

In 1990, bowing to international pressure and a souring domestic economy, South African president F. W. de Klerk removed the ban on the African National Congress, the key opposition party, and a few days afterward ended the twenty-eight-year prison term of its leader, Nelson Mandela. Soon thereafter, South Africa was transformed into a multiracial democracy, and Mandela was elected its president.

JESSE JACKSON AND THE RAINBOW COALITION

As Reagan's first term ended, Jesse Jackson made history by announcing he would campaign for the presidency of the United States. The first African American to seek the presidential nomination of a major political party was congresswoman Shirley Chisholm, in 1972. Chisholm had little money and only a small campaign organization, and she was never taken as a serious candidate by her male competitors or the press. Her campaign had nonetheless helped raise the visibility of African-American voters. She captured more than 150 votes on the first ballot at the Democratic National Convention. In the thoroughly male world of presidential politics, however, a black man was a more credible contender.

Jesse Jackson's preparation for political battle was not the traditional climb from one elective office to another. Rather, he came up through the ranks of the civil rights movement, working alongside Martin Luther King Jr. in the Southern Christian Leadership Conference (SCLC) and heading Operation Breadbasket, an organization that attempted to mobilize Chicago's black poor. After King's death, Jackson founded People United to Save (later Serve) Humanity (PUSH). This Chicago-based organization induced major corporations with large markets in the black community to adopt affirmative action programs. PUSH-EXCEL, which focused on education, succeeded in raising students' test scores and was given a large grant by the Carter administration.

In 1983, angered by the effects of Reagan's social welfare and civil rights rollbacks, Jackson and PUSH began a successful drive to register black voters. Jackson's charismatic style engendered enthusiasm, especially as the Democratic Party searched for a presidential candidate who could challenge Reagan's popularity.

On November 4, 1983, Jackson declared his candidacy for the Democratic nomination and honed an already effective style of grassroots mobilization. He began by appealing to what he would call a "rainbow coalition" of people who felt politically marginalized and underrepresented. Jackson developed a comprehensive economic policy focusing on tax reform, deficit reduction, industrial policy, and employment. The centerpiece of his plan was "Rebuilding America," a program to coordinate

In 1988 the Reverend Jesse Jackson (1941–) addressed the Democratic National Convention. He made two unsuccessful bids for the White House (1984, 1988) but remained a powerful force in the Democratic Party because of his tremendous zeal in registering voters and building coalitions.
Paul Conklin, PhotoEdit

government, business, and labor in a national industrial policy. Jackson eventually garnered almost one-fourth of the votes cast in the Democratic primaries and caucuses and one-eighth of the delegates to the convention. His speech to the convention cemented his position as a voice for progressive change and a spiritual heir to both Martin Luther King Jr. and Robert Kennedy.

In November 1984 black voters overwhelmingly favored the Democratic ticket, but Reagan nonetheless won by a landslide with 59 percent of the popular vote. Mondale carried only his home state of Minnesota and the largely black District of Columbia. Clearly, most white Americans backed Reagan's conservative policies. Undeterred by defeat, Jackson worked to build his Rainbow Coalition, reaching out to a variety of constituencies, including the unemployed, militant trade unionists, small farmers, and gay people. He criticized the Democratic Party's timid opposition to Reagan. Perhaps most important, he continued to promote voter registration and indeed inspired the registration of enough new voters to affect several races in the 1986 midterm elections. Democrats held control of the House and regained a majority in the Senate.

By the time Jackson announced he would again run for president in October 1987, he had become a serious contender. He won fifteen presidential primaries and caucuses and garnered seven million votes, one-third of all those cast. His Rainbow Coalition, however, never materialized. His victories in the primaries were based on mobilizing his black supporters; almost all his white support tended to come from college towns and the highly educated. Michael Dukakis, governor of Massachusetts, won the 1988 Democratic nomination.

Despite Jesse Jackson's voter registration drive and the hopes of the black community, Reagan's vice president, George H. W. Bush, triumphed in the 1988 election. The most memorable feature of his campaign was a polarizing ad that featured Willie Horton, a black convict who had raped a white woman while on furlough from a

Massachusetts prison as part of a program approved by Dukakis and his Republican predecessor as governor. Jackson and other black leaders criticized the ad as a blatant appeal to white racism, but Bush would not renounce it.

The general white perception of black men as criminals increased following Bush's election. The perceptions of black youths as criminals acquired potent political currency, resulting in the mass incarceration of young black men and a rising incidence of police brutality and racial profiling. After the disputed 2000 presidential election, the black community became even more aware of the adverse consequences of mass incarceration because most states deny the right to vote to convicted and incarcerated felons, and 1.8 million of the 4.7 million felons and former felons in the United States are black. Moreover, black people, especially black men, are incarcerated in astonishingly high numbers. Not only are African Americans seven times more likely than whites to be in prison, but in 2001, 10 percent of black men in their late twenties were in prison, and more than 30 percent of the young black men who had dropped out of high school had spent time in prison or jail, many for drug-related offenses.

Prison reform activists have sought to draw attention to the brutal conditions that exist within U.S. prisons. Yet they have achieved little.

POLICING THE BLACK COMMUNITY

In March 1991 Los Angeles police pulled Rodney Glen King from his car after a high-speed chase and beat him with nightsticks. A bystander, George Holliday, captured the incident on videotape. Television newscasts broadcast the tape repeatedly, increasing long-simmering anger over police brutality among African Americans in Los Angeles. When a jury of eleven white Americans and one Hispanic American acquitted the four police officers involved in the incident of all but one of the charges brought against them, south-central Los Angeles burst into flames of protest. The verdict highlighted the gulf between the perceptions of white and black Americans about the police and the criminal justice system. Fifty-two people were killed in the outbreak that followed the verdict. Arsonists and looters devastated much of the community. Thousands of people were injured, four thousand were arrested, and an estimated half-billion dollars worth of property was damaged or destroyed. The four officers were later retried in federal court on charges of violating King's civil rights. This time juries found two of them guilty and acquitted the other two. Meanwhile, a jury in King's civil suit ordered the city of Los Angeles to pay him $3.8 million in damages.

Several such high-profile cases focused public attention on the relation of black communities to white police authorities throughout the 1980s and 1990s. In the late 1990s, the issue exploded into national consciousness with three cases. In 1997 a Haitian immigrant, Abner Louima, was beaten and sodomized while in custody at a Brooklyn police station. In 1999 New York police shot Amadou Diallo, a West African immigrant, forty-one times when they mistook his reaching for a wallet for going for a gun. A jury in Albany acquitted the four police officials charged in the Diallo killing. Finally, also in 1999, Patric Dorismond (a Haitian immigrant) was shot and killed after he refused to purchase drugs from, and got into an argument with, a team of undercover antinarcotic police officers. In each instance an enraged black community protested the police profiling as one more instance of biases toward black men and one that targeted other minorities for illegal detention.

Human Rights in America

In October 1998 the human rights group Amnesty International, known for its condemnation of human rights abuse in countries with repressive governments, published a report on police brutality in the United States. The report covered the actions of local and state police, the Federal Bureau of Investigation, the Immigration and Naturalization Service, and the prison system. Its contents came as no surprise to most black Americans or, indeed, to anyone who lived in America's poor urban neighborhoods. The report detailed violations of the UN Code of Conduct for Law Enforcement Officials and the UN Basic Principles on the Use of Force and Firearms. Among the violations reported were the following:

- the shooting of unarmed suspects fleeing a minor crime scene
- excessive force used on mentally ill or disturbed people
- multiple shootings of a suspect, sometimes after the suspect was apprehended or disabled
- the beating of unresisting suspects
- the misuse of batons, chemical sprays, and electroshock weapons

These violations all involved the misuse of force during arrests, traffic stops, searches, and so forth. This was by far the greatest area of concern. The report also cited sexual abuse of prisoners and the denial of food and water to them. One of the most important points in the Amnesty International report was that most victims of American law enforcement abuse were members of racial and ethnic minorities, and most police officers were white.

It is far too easy to interpret these findings as showing that American police officers, as a group, are racists who purposefully use their authority to oppress people they do not like. In fact, the issue of police brutality is not nearly so simple. Police officers are under tremendous pressure and live dangerous lives, in part because of the wide availability of guns in American society. No one can be expected to have perfect judgment about using force, and the cumulative effect of years of dealing with violence can destroy a person's sense of perspective and moral equilibrium.

Neither is the problem of crime by black Americans a simple one. The level of crime in black communities is extremely high. The murder rate, for example, for African Americans in 1997 was seven times that of whites, and black victims accounted for 49 percent of all those murdered, even though African Americans make up only 12 percent of the population. Over 90 percent of those who murder, rape, and assault black people are black people themselves. The murder rate for young black men between the ages of fourteen and seventeen tripled between 1976 and 1993. Although this rate, like the rate of violent crime in the country in general, fell in the 1990s, the security of many African Americans remains imperiled.

Crime devastates black neighborhoods. High crime rates raise the costs of business, driving jobs and investment dollars out of those areas most in need of them. Fear of violence leads many in the inner cities to barricade themselves inside their homes. The result has been a transformation of once vibrant neighborhoods into virtual ghost towns where the silence of the streets is punctuated only by the sound of gunfire.

Being disproportionately the victims of crime, most African Americans have looked to the nation's police departments for aid. Because of their growing political power they have sought, not always successfully, to make the police both responsive to crime and fair in enforcing the laws. One key device for changing the behavior of law enforcement officials has been the appointment of black police chiefs.

Police Director Hubert Williams of Newark

Black mayor Kenneth Gibson appointed Hubert Williams as the police director in Newark, New Jersey, and Williams served from 1974 to 1985. Upon assuming command, Williams demoted and transferred several entrenched deputy chiefs and captains. He implemented a 911 system to increase police response to citizens' calls for assistance and placed police decoys on city streets to thwart muggers. Among the many innovations that the reform-minded Williams introduced were police sweeps of high-crime sections, roadblocks to deter drunken drivers, a truancy task force to discourage teenage crime, and police storefronts to foster the image of law enforcement officers as community service workers. Williams also acknowledged that he would use "color-conscious" policies in promoting and assigning officers. He argued that in a city where black people made up more than 50 percent of the population, it was good policy to assign detectives and administrators who reflected the racial composition of specific neighborhoods.

Williams received high marks for his performance, and soon white mayors in other cities also began appointing black officers—like Benjamin Ward in New York City; Lee P. Brown in Houston; William H. Moore in Pittsburgh, Pennsylvania; and Reuben Greenberg in Charleston, South Carolina—to head their police departments. By 1982 there were black police chiefs in fifty American cities, and in the 1990s the number increased to more than 130.

THE CLINTON PRESIDENCY

During his first campaign for the presidency, in 1992, black Americans welcomed the Democratic Party candidate, Arkansas governor Bill Clinton, into their churches, schools, and homes. Incumbent George H. W. Bush had done little to win their loyalty, nominating conservatives to the federal courts and attacking civil rights legislation. White Americans, too, were dissatisfied with the Bush presidency. By early 1992 his ratings had slumped in the face of an economic downturn.

Clinton positioned himself as a a centrist, solidly within the mainstream of American politics. Undeterred by charges of womanizing, draft evasion, and marijuana smoking, Clinton attacked Bush's record and promised to make government more responsive to the needs of everyday Americans. The strategy catapulted him into the White House. Clinton won in November 1992 with just 43 percent of the popular vote to Bush's 38 percent and third-party candidate H. Ross Perot's 19 percent. However, Clinton garnered 78 percent of the black vote and 39 percent of the white vote in key states including New Jersey, Michigan, New York, Illinois, and California. The election did not present the Democrats with a clear mandate. Although maintaining control of Congress, they gained no seats in the Senate and lost seats in the House. Republicans used the ambiguous outcome to oppose most of Clinton's economic programs and launched a relentless campaign to undermine his presidency.

Most black people, however, considered Clinton, despite major disappointments, the best president on race issues since Lyndon Johnson. Writer Toni Morrison called Clinton the first black president, and in some circles he was called the first woman president because of his support for equal rights for all women, both black and white. Clinton appointed women, including many black women, to 37 percent of the five hundred upper-level positions in the White House and federal bureaucracy. Clinton created a cabinet that mirrored the diversity of the American population—in some cases, such as Hazel O'Leary as secretary of the Department of Energy, Alexis Herman as secretary of labor, and Ron Brown as secretary of commerce, appointing black people to posts that had nothing to do with race. Clinton also gave Washington, D.C., delegate to Congress Eleanor Holmes Norton the prerogative, normally reserved to U.S. senators, of selecting U.S. district court judges, U.S. marshals, and the U.S. attorney for the District of Columbia. Clinton was the first American president to visit Africa.

"It's the Economy, Stupid!"

In 1996 Clinton became the first Democratic president to win a second term since Franklin Roosevelt. Throughout his two terms in office, Clinton focused attention on the economy, a strategy that won grudging support from moderate Republicans. His objectives were to strengthen the economy and to make more opportunities available for black Americans and other previously excluded groups. He supported a new tax bill that increased the taxes of higher income Americans. He also advocated expansion of the earned income tax credit to help improve the lives of working-poor and very poor Americans. His college student-aid program made available increased federal loan benefits. The economy boomed during the Clinton presidency, and when he left office in 2001, the country had the lowest poverty rate in twenty years. The Congressional Black Caucus (CBC) provided critical support for his economic programs. In 1993 CBC chairman Representative Kweisi Mfume of Maryland and the highest ranking black congressman, Representative John Lewis, delivered the caucus vote that saved Clinton's $500 billion economic budget in both the House and Senate. In return, black congressmen gained financial support for inner-city neighborhood development, poor families, children, and the elderly. Representative Mfume credited the CBC, for example, for saving the $2.5 billion allocation for food stamps that the Senate phased out and $3.5 billion for empowerment zones in cities and rural areas.

Unemployment plummeted from 7.2 percent when Clinton took office to 5.5 percent in 1995 and continued to decline in ensuing years. American businesses created 10 million new jobs, and many black people who feared they would never gain a foothold in the economy found work, some for the first time. Reduced federal spending and the 1993 tax increase helped cut the annual federal deficit in half. As interest rates fell and the stock market soared, optimistic Americans increased their consumer spending.

Clinton Signs the Welfare Reform Act

Shortly before his reelection, in August 1996, Clinton signed the Personal Responsibility and Work Opportunity Reconciliation Act, a welfare reform bill. This disappointed many African Americans and political progressives in general. The legislation combined Clinton's own ideas with others espoused in the Republicans' "Contract with America" blueprint for conservative changes. The Republicans had used this platform to win control of both houses of Congress in 1994. The main target of the Personal Responsibility Act was Aid to Families of Dependent Children (AFDC), a program created in 1935 as part of the Social Security Act to prevent children from suffering because of the poverty of their parents. Critics claimed AFDC stipends discouraged poor mothers from finding work, that it was responsible for the breakdown of the family among the nation's poor and did little to reduce poverty. The conservative welfare "reform" measure ended guarantees of federal aid to poor children, turning control of such programs over to the states along with allocations of block grants. The act denied benefits to legal immigrants, called for drastic reductions in food stamp appropriations, and limited families to five years of benefits. The law also required most adult welfare recipients to find employment within two years.

Clinton's support of the welfare act was politically astute and consistent with his centrist ideology. It also immunized him from Republican attacks on the issue and had little impact on his support among African Americans. Black support for him remained strong, and Clinton easily defeated his Republican opponent, Senator Robert Dole of Kansas, in the election of 1996.

The preliminary results of the new welfare reform strictures indicated that within a couple of years half of those who had taken jobs had returned to lives of unemployment, poverty, and quiet desperation. As the economy took a downturn in the closing months of Clinton's second term and in the opening years of the new millennium, conditions of poor mothers and children deteriorated steadily. The debate over welfare policy receded to the back burner during the 2000 election campaign and disappeared completely after George W. Bush took office, superseded by the emphasis on tax cuts for the wealthy.

Republicans Challenge Clinton

Congressional Republicans and radical conservatives hated Clinton's presidency and many of them hated Clinton himself. They vowed to take back the White House. The Democrats seemed demoralized and did little to mobilize their base, especially in the black community. Many African Americans did not vote in the midterm congressional elections in 1994, and the Democrats lost control of Congress. For the first time in forty years, the Republicans could implement their conservative legislative agenda, which included rolling back environmental protection policies, reducing the capital gains tax for the rich, and cutting benefits for the elderly. Belatedly awake to the peril of black political alienation, some younger Democratic Party leaders began to fight back. In 1994 thirty-year-old Jesse Jackson Jr. won a seat in Congress representing a southside Chicago district. But Democrats were now in a minority.

Republicans drew further strength from the appointment of Kenneth Starr as an independent counsel to investigate allegations surrounding Bill and Hilary Clinton's investment in an Arkansas land development deal known as Whitewater. Although no proof was found that the Clintons had broken the law, Starr relentlessly pursued every hint or rumor of misdeed. Clinton made the tactical mistake of denying sexual involvement with a White House intern, Monica Lewinsky. On December 19, 1998, the Republican majority in the House of Representatives narrowly voted to impeach Clinton for perjury and obstruction of justice for tampering with witnesses to conceal his relationship with Lewinsky. But the Senate refused to convict him, and he remained in office. In the midst of the turmoil, Clinton derived solace from the unwavering support of black people, the Congressional Black Caucus, and his friends, including Vernon Jordan and Jesse Jackson.

BLACK POLITICS IN THE NEW MILLENNIUM: THE CONTESTED 2000 PRESIDENTIAL ELECTION

Within the American electorate, the election of 2000 revealed fault lines of culture, geography, race, class, and gender. The campaign focused largely on economic issues—social security, taxes, health care (HMO reform and a prescription-drug benefit for seniors), and education. Black community leaders and organizations worked hard to register voters and to increase turnout for the 2000 election.

Gore v. Bush

In a hotly contested election, the outcome hung on one state: Florida. In the end, the U.S. Supreme Court, in a 5-to-4 ruling [*Bush v. Gore*, 121 S. Ct. 525 (2000)], decided the issue by halting the recount of ballots in Florida. The Court's majority based its ruling on the Fourteenth Amendment's prohibition of states denying citizens equal protection of the law. The Court insisted the recount had to be stopped because the Florida Supreme Court, which had authorized it, had failed to provide uniform standards for determining the intent of the voters. Bush was declared the winner in Florida by fewer than six hundred votes, which gave him a four-vote majority in the electoral college.

Bill Clinton called *Gore v. Bush* "an appalling decision" and compared its impact on African-Americans to the infamous Dred Scott and *Plessy v. Ferguson* decisions of the nineteenth century. Indeed, African Americans reported serious discrimination and interference with their voting in Florida. A lawsuit filed in Jacksonville, Florida, claimed that many votes were thrown out as "undervotes" or "overvotes," especially in four districts with the highest concentration of African Americans in the state. According to the lawsuit, 26,000 ballots were not counted in Duval County, and more than 9,000 of those were cast in largely African-American precincts where Gore had captured more than 90 percent of the vote. Indeed, the U.S. Civil Rights Commission found that tens of thousands of African Americans were disfranchised in Florida. More black and low-income voters, who tended to vote Democratic, had their ballots invalidated.

REPUBLICAN TRIUMPH

In the 2000 elections, Republicans also retained narrow majorities in both the House and the Senate. *Gore v. Bush* thus not only put George W. Bush in the White House. It also meant that for the first time since the early 1950s, the Republican Party was in control of the presidency and of both houses of Congress.

President George W. Bush's Black Cabinet

President Bush was aware that few African Americans had voted for him. But this did not prevent him from appointing well-educated, articulate, and accomplished black men and women to key posts within his administration. Such appointments tended to mute black criticism, and they also placated white swing voters who disdained racial exclusion. Bush named the highly regarded General Colin L. Powell to be secretary of state. Powell had served as chairman of the Joint Chiefs of Staff (1989–1993), the highest military position in the Department of Defense. During his tenure he oversaw Operation Desert Storm, the victorious 1991 Persian Gulf War. Secretary Powell not only assisted in the formulation of foreign policy, but he also "represented the race."

Bush also tapped a black woman, Condoleezza Rice, to be his national security adviser. Rice was the first African American and the first woman to hold this post. During the 2000 election, Rice had formed a strong personal bond with Bush, and this relationship became the foundation of her power in his administration.

An expert on European affairs, especially the Soviet Union, Rice had been sharply critical of the Clinton administration's policies and peacekeeping efforts in Bosnia and

Well educated, accomplished, and loyal, Colin Powell and Condoleezza Rice occupied high-ranking positions within George W. Bush's first administration. They put a more positive face on Republican conservatism and represent the party's racial diversity.
© AFP/Corbis. Photo by Stephen Jaffe

Haiti. Foreign policy under Clinton, she charged, had "assiduously failed" to separate "the important from the trivial . . . we don't need to have the 82nd Airborne escorting kids to kindergarten." But Rice should have paid closer attention to Samuel Berger, Clinton's national security adviser, when he warned, "America is in a deadly struggle with a new breed of anti-Western jihadist—nothing less than a war . . . as a nation . . . we are engaged in a wholly new battle against an international terrorist network in dozens of countries, which is deeply committed to injuring and destroying the United States and its allies. This is one of the most serious threats the next administration will face." As September 11, 2001, was to show, Rice should have heeded Berger's warning.

Education Reform: Leave No Child Behind

Bush had made many pledges during the 2000 presidential campaign, none more important than his vow to reform public education. This was an issue of vital importance to both black and white families. Black parents were especially alarmed over the de facto resegregation of black children in urban schools.

As secretary of education, Texan Rod Paige introduced the Leave No Child Behind Act, an education reform that Bush ardently embraced. This legislation spoke directly to the concerns of white working- and middle-class Americans. It underscored their demand for student and teacher use of testing as an assessment tool to measure performance. The legislation required all schools to test students at regular intervals in reading, math, and science. States also have to publish the test results and sanction schools whose students fail to do well on the tests. Implicitly the measure rejected integration as a primary social policy objective and retreated from mandatory busing while promoting parents' freedom to enroll their children in the schools of their choice through voucher programs.

Some African Americans, such as Anthony Williams, the mayor of Washington, D.C., supported the school voucher program, arguing that competition with strong schools would force weaker schools to improve their performance. However, Reginald Weaver, the black president of the National Educational Association, argued the voucher program ignored the needs of most of the students in poor schools. Leave No Child Behind was soon mired in controversy. Critics, including many conservatives, blasted the measure for setting unrealistic goals and for not including sufficient federal funding to help schools meet the higher standards.

Reparations

While party politics attracted attention, many African Americans shifted their focus to specific issues including reparations for slavery and the spread of HIV/AIDS in the United States and in Africa. In 1969 James Foreman, in his "Black Manifesto," called on America's churches and synagogues to collect $500 million as "a beginning of the reparations due us as a people who have been exploited and degraded, brutalized, killed, and persecuted." Although Foreman's call was widely publicized, churches made no serious effort to respond to his demand. Four years later, Boris Bittker, a Yale Law School professor, raised the issue again and argued in *The Case for Black Reparations* that slavery and the persistence of government-sanctioned racial discrimination justified the creation of a program to provide compensation to black Americans. Since

1993 John Conyers, a black Democratic congressman from Detroit, has introduced a bill in every session of Congress—not to pay reparations, but to establish a federal commission to investigate slavery and the legacy of racial discrimination. The bill has never come to the floor of the House of Representatives for a vote.

In 2000 the issue of reparations for slavery was resurrected and finally received widespread attention when Randall Robinson, founder and president of TransAfrica, published *The Debt: What America Owes to Blacks*. Robinson reasoned that because Jews and Japanese Americans have been compensated for the indignities and horrors they experienced in World War II, African Americans were also due financial indemnification for slavery, for "246 years of an enterprise murderous both of a people and their culture." Robinson maintained that many African Americans still bear the scars of slavery in terms of poor housing, inadequate health care, and insufficient educational opportunities. He insists that reparations would remedy the effect of such inequalities. Temple University professor and Afrocentrist Molefi Asante proposed that instead of "a one-time cash payout" that the American government make long-term commitments for "educational, health care, land or property grants, and a combination of such grants."

Some black writers and journalists adamantly reject arguments that reparations are a realistic resolution of the nation's slave and racist legacy. Two black journalists, William Raspberry and Juan Williams, object to the very idea of reparations. Instead, Raspberry favors a greater investment in education for African Americans, "not because of debts owed to or incurred by our ancestors, but because America needs its citizens to be educated and productive."

HIV/AIDS in America and Africa

As he had done repeatedly in the preceding three decades, Jesse Jackson, along with scholars, health-care professionals, social activists, and others, drew attention to the HIV/AIDs epidemic and its disastrous impact on black America and in Africa. Jackson believed HIV/AIDs was as much a political issue as it was a matter of health care. His words reflected a mature black internationalism that emphasized the bonds of health and disease across the African Diaspora. He declared,

> As it is in Africa, AIDS is now the leading cause of death for African Americans between twenty-five and forty-four in the United States. Almost two-thirds (63 percent) of all women reported with AIDS are African American; 62 percent of all reported pediatric cases are African-American children; 1 in 50 African-American men and 1 in 160 African-American women are estimated to be HIV infected. Like Africans, many African Americans do not know their HIV status; like Africans, many African Americans cannot access care or afford adequate treatment. Like Africans, many African Americans are in poverty, and many of their communities lack the infrastructure needed to meet the needs of those infected and afflicted by AIDS. Simply speaking, as we begin to understand our commonalities, our differences will no longer be a continent away.

Of the fifteen leading causes of death, African Americans have the highest incidence rates in thirteen. Paraphrasing Martin Luther King Jr., Hood concluded, "Of all forms of inequity, injustice in health care is the most shocking and inhumane." (For more on African Americans and health care, see Chapter 24.)

September 11, 2001

Americans of virtually every racial, religious, and ethnic background were stunned on a Tuesday morning in September 2001, when four commercial airliners were commandeered by terrorists and crashed into New York's World Trade Center, the Pentagon in Washington, and rural Pennsylvania. Several hundred African Americans perished among the three thousand people who died that day.

If the debate over reparations dramatized the separate pasts that black and white Americans have experienced, then the tragedy of September 11, 2001, reminded them of their common future. But the sense of national unity did not last. Less than two years later, as the United States prepared to invade Iraq, activist and scholar Manning Marable wrote of the lessons he had learned from the 9/11 tragedy: "No political ideology, no crusade, no belief in a virtuous cause, can justify the moral bankruptcy of terror. Yet, because of the military actions of our own government, any claims to moral superiority have now disintegrated, in the minds of much of the black and brown world."

The War in Iraq

Following September 11, Americans expected President Bush to devise an effective strategy against the Taliban regime in Afghanistan and to destroy Osama bin Laden and the al-Qaeda network. The president and Secretary of Defense Donald Rumsfeld pledged retribution, and the war in Afghanistan began on October 7, 2001. The Taliban government was easily overthrown, but bin Laden and the Taliban leader, Mullah Omar, proved elusive.

Still, the Bush administration called its Afghan foray a success even though the Taliban soon launched a new guerrilla war, and much of Afghanistan remained in the control of warlords and insurgents. However, critics argued that the Bush adminstration's real target after 9/11 was not Afghanistan and al-Qaeda but Saddam Hussein's Iraq and that Bush and National Security Adviser Condoleezza Rice had failed to take seriously the reports of a planned terrorist attack before September 11, 2001. Al-Qaeda, which claimed responsibility for the bombing of U.S. embassies in Kenya and Tanzania in 1998 and for an attack on the USS *Cole* in Yemen in 2000, should have been the national security priority. Rice strenuously denied these charges, but early in 2002 the administration began to shift the nation's attention from Afghanistan to war with Iraq.

In a speech before the UN Security Council in February 2003, Secretary of State Colin Powell argued, based on what turned out be misleading intelligence reports, that Saddam not only had weapons of mass destruction, but he also had ties to international terrorist networks, including al-Qaeda. The Security Council was not convinced and voted against the invasion, but the United States invaded Iraq anyway on March 19, 2003. Only Britain gave it significant support.

As in Afghanistan, victory in Iraq appeared to come quickly, and Bush declared the mission had been accomplished when Baghdad was occupied after a few weeks of fighting. However, it proved easier to overthrow Saddam than to secure peace in Iraq. Much of the country quickly descended into chaos. By August 2004 over nine hundred U.S. service men and women had died, Iraq remained in turmoil, and there were renewed threats of terror attacks against U.S. cities. Critics blasted the administration for failing to develop an effective and coherent peace plan. The war, they charged, had actually strengthened terrorism while the failure to secure UN support or to find weapons of mass destruction or establish ties between Saddam and al-Qaeda had damaged America's reputation and credibility and weakened the fabric of international cooperation.

THE 2004 PRESIDENTIAL ELECTION

Massachusetts senator John F. Kerry won the Democratic Party's nomination to be its presidential candidate. Kerry selected Senator John Edwards from North Carolina to be his running mate against incumbents George W. Bush and Dick Cheney. While these men campaigned, African Americans registered an important, but subtle, shift in their status within the Democratic Party as it became clear that they would play a key role in determining the outcome of the 2004 presidential election.

The process of political transformation begun in the 1960s peaked in the 2004 presidential primaries. In these contests African Americans emerged as the most reliable base of the Democratic Party and made their views heard and their power acknowledged. They wanted Americans to understand that little divided blacks and whites when it came to regaining the White House. In so doing, African-American leaders skillfully moved from being considered spokespersons for a small special interest group. In 2004 they demanded acknowledgment of their central role as Democratic Party standard-bearers. Two of the nine contenders for the Democratic Party's nomination were African Americans: Carol Moseley Braun, former U.S. senator from Illinois, and Reverend Al Sharpton of New York. Braun and Sharpton participated in all of the primary debates before throwing their support to Kerry.

In the spirit of presenting a united front, Braun, Sharpton, and Jesse Jackson addressed the delegates at the Democratic National Convention in Boston. While praising Kerry and attacking Bush, they reiterated their concerns about high black unemployment, the lack of national health-care insurance, and the deteriorating physical plant of the nation's schools, especially those that served the poor and inner-city residents. And they emphatically expressed their objections to the war in Iraq.

The black star of the convention, however, was the little known forty-two-year-old state senator from Illinois, Barack Obama, who was running for the U.S. Senate. Obama's keynote speech, claiming that good and efficient government would improve the life chances of all Americans, catapulted him into the nation's limelight. The *Chicago Tribune's* black columnist Clarence Page called Obama "the quintessential crossover candidate, a Colin Powell for the party of the Revs. Jesse Jackson and Al Sharpton." In the passage of his speech that received the most sustained applause, Obama asserted,

> Yet even as we speak, there are those who are preparing to divide us, the spin masters and negative ad peddlers who embrace the politics of anything goes. Well, I say to them tonight, there's not a liberal America and a conservative America; there's the United States of America. There's not a black America and white America and Latino America and Asian America; there's the United States of America.

Obama's personal history captures the complexity of identity in new millennium America. As he reminded his listeners, "I live in the African-American community but I am not limited by it." Obama's father was an immigrant from Kenya who married a white American from Kansas. Obama was raised in Hawaii, attended Harvard Law

School, and taught law at the University of Chicago before entering the political arena. As a state senator, Obama voted to ban racial profiling and supported increased funding for child health care, among other issues of great importance to African Americans. In 2004 he won the Democratic primary for the U.S. Senate. When a scandal forced his white Republican opponent to withdraw from the race, the Republican state committee selected black conservative Alan Keyes to run against Obama. For the first time in American history, both major candidates in a U.S. Senate race were African Americans.

On November 4, 2004, Americans reelected George W. Bush by a 3 million vote margin. After the election Secretary of State Colin Powell tendered his resignation. In repayment for her loyalty and experience in international affairs, President Bush appointed Condoleezza Rice to replace Powell as Secretary of State. Significant developments also occurred on the state level. The wildly popular "rising star" of the Democratic Party, Obama became the second African American to serve in the Senate from Illinois; the first had been Carol Mosely Braun. As 2004 faded into 2005, politics in America had become even more important and outcomes difficult to anticipate.

T I M E L I N E

AFRICAN-AMERICAN EVENTS	NATIONAL EVENTS
1978	
1978 U.S. Supreme Court decides *Regents of the University of California v. Bakke*	
1980	
	1980 Ronald Reagan is elected president **1981** Recession settles in Economic Recovery Tax Act is passed
1982	
1984	
1984 Jesse Jackson creates Rainbow Coalition and seeks Democratic nomination for president	**1984** Reagan is reelected
1986	
1987 August Wilson wins Pulitzer prize for his play *Fences*	
1988	
1988 Jesse Jackson makes second run for the Democratic nomination for president	**1988** George H. W. Bush is elected president of the United States

continued

AFRICAN-AMERICAN EVENTS	NATIONAL EVENTS
1989 Ron Brown is elected chairman of the Democratic Party, the first African American to lead a major national political party	
1990	
1991 Clarence Thomas wins Senate confirmation to the U.S. Supreme Court John Singleton's *Boyz N the Hood* wins box office success Rodney King is beaten by four white Los Angeles policemen	**1991** Operation Desert Storm—against Iraq—is initiated and ended
1992	
1992 Los Angeles riots after King's police assailants are acquitted Carol Mosley-Braun of Illinois is the first black woman elected to the U.S. Senate **1993** Clinton names Ron Brown and Hazel O'Leary to Cabinet	**1992** William Jefferson Clinton is elected president
1994	
1994 Jesse Jackson Jr. elected to Congress	**1994** Midterm elections give Republican Party control of Congress
1996	
	1996 Clinton is reelected Clinton signs welfare reform legislation
1998	
	1998 Clinton is impeached by the House of Representatives **1999** The U.S. Senate acquits Clinton
2000	
2000 Donna Brazile manages the presidential campaign of Al Gore	**2000** George W. Bush becomes president of the United States

continued

AFRICAN-AMERICAN EVENTS	NATIONAL EVENTS
	2001
	Bush names Condoleezza Rice national security adviser and Colin Powell secretary of state
	Sept. 11
	Terrorists demolish the World Trade Center in New York City and attack the Pentagon in Washington
	United States invades Afghanistan
	No Child Left Behind Act becomes law
2002	
2003	**2003**
Supreme Court upholds use of racial preferences in admission to University of Michigan Law School	United States invades Iraq
2004	
2004	**2004**
Carol Mosely Braun and Al Sharpton run for president	George W. Bush reelected President of the United States
Barack Obama elected to U.S. Senate	
Condoleezza Rice appointed Secretary of State	

CONCLUSION

Jesse Jackson, whose Rainbow Coalition of the 1980s reflected a quest for unity amid diversity, asked at the 1988 Democratic convention, "Shall we expand, be inclusive, find unity and power; or suffer division and impotence?" The 2004 Democratic Party primary campaign illustrated the political importance of black Americans and the extent to which the Democratic Party had embraced its diverse constituency. African Americans remained committed to a progressive political agenda that emphasized universal health care, quality education, urban economic development, job training, safe environments, an end to racial profiling and police brutality, and reform of the prison-industrial complex that had disenfranchised so many black Americans and members of other minority groups. At the dawn of the new millenium, black political power had come of age. It marked another stage in the black odyssey toward freedom and the transformation of American society.

REVIEW QUESTIONS

1. To what extent and in what key areas did the Reagan and Bush presidencies nullify or dismantle Great Society legislation? How did African Americans respond to the era of Republican conservative reaction?

2. What was the significance of Jesse Jackson's campaigns for the Democratic presidential nomination?

3. Compare and contrast the effects on African Americans of the welfare reform legislation passed during Clinton's administration and the education reform policies of George W. Bush's No Child Left Behind Act.

4. Why did affirmative action become one of the most contested issues of the 1990s? How did affirmative action in the workplace differ from affirmative action in education?

5. How did the Rodney King case illuminate the different perceptions of black and white Americans of the police and the justice system?

6. What were some of the major concerns of black Americans during the 2004 presidential campaigns? To what extent have African Americans become the base of the Democratic Party?

7. What are the main arguments of black conservative ideology?

RECOMMENDED READING

Martha Biondi. "The Rise of the Reparations Movement." *Radical History Review*, 87 (Fall 2003): 5–18. A superb historical overview of the black reparations movement from the Civil War to the present.

Cathy J. Cohen. *The Boundaries of Blackness: AIDS and the Breakdown of Black Politics.* Chicago: University of Chicago Press, 1999. A black political scientist provides a sophisticated and provocative exploration into the social, political, and cultural impact of the AIDS epidemic on the African-American community.

Mary Pattillo, David Weiman, and Bruce Western, eds. *Imprisoning America: The Social Effects of Mass Incarceration.* New York: Russell Sage Foundation, 2004. Important essays that explore the sociological, political, and economic consequences of the mass incarceration of African-American men and other minorities. These studies demonstrate the need for new policies to deal with ex-prisoners, their families, and communities.

Brenda Gayle Plummer, ed. *Window on Freedom: Race, Civil Rights, and Foreign Affairs, 1945–1988.* Chapel Hill: University of North Carolina Press, 2003. An anthology of wide-ranging essays that explore how race and ethnicity complicated U.S. foreign relations during the Cold War.

Deborah Gray White. *Too Heavy a Load: Black Women in Defense of Themselves, 1894–1994.* New York: Norton, 1998. A brilliant study by a black woman historian of black women and the organizations they founded to fight for the ballot, against segregation, and against the sexism and misogyny of contemporary black nationalism.

AFRICAN AMERICANS AT THE DAWN OF A NEW MILLENNIUM

PROGRESS AND POVERTY: INCOME, EDUCATION, AND HEALTH

After the triumphs of the civil rights era, many African Americans made great strides in overcoming the economic and educational disadvantages that had plagued their ancestors. Partly as a result of this progress, they also lived longer, healthier lives. Yet the disparities between the levels of wealth, schooling, and health of African Americans and the white majority, although narrowed, have persisted as a stubborn legacy from centuries of racial oppression.

High-Achieving African Americans

The years after 1970 witnessed the consolidation of black economic, civic, and political progress. In part, this was exemplified by the prominence of such visible African Americans as entertainer Oprah Winfrey, Bill Clinton's secretary of commerce Ronald Brown, chairman of the Joint Chiefs of Staff and later secretary of state Colin Powell, professional golfer Tiger Woods, and public intellectual Henry Louis Gates. These people, and many other African Americans, rose to the top of their fields.

As with the American population as a whole, the ultrarich remain rare in the black community, but their ranks have grown. Oprah Winfrey, Bill Cosby, Michael Jackson, and Michael Jordon acquired immense fortunes as entertainers or athletes. Others in this fortunate few include businessman Robert L. Johnson, founder of Black Entertainment Television (BET), who became the first African American to own a professional basketball team, the Charlotte, North Carolina, Hornets; John H. Johnson, publisher of *Ebony* and *Jet* magazines; Berry Gordy, founder of Motown Records; and Russell Simmons, a recording and fashion entrepreneur.

The career of Reginald Lewis illustrates the possibilities open to black people in other industries. Armed with a degree from Harvard Law School, he first purchased the McCall Pattern Company, and then in 1987 bought Beatrice Foods, an international packaged goods company, for $2.5 billion. At the time it was the largest leveraged buyout in U.S. history, and Lewis became the wealthiest African American. Before his death in 1993, Lewis demonstrated an understanding of the need to give back to his community by donating millions of dollars to Howard University and the NAACP.

African Americans' Growing Economic Security

The achievements of the most successful African Americans are impressive, but more significant is the increase in job opportunities, income, and wealth for a broad cross section of working African Americans. Before the 1960s nearly all black men worked in the lower rungs of agriculture, construction, transportation, and manufacturing. Black women were predominantly caged in domestic and food service jobs. Few black men or women had a chance to move to higher paid and more prestigious skilled or managerial positions, and the wages for all African Americans remained low.

Antidiscrimination laws and affirmative action programs allowed millions of black people to begin climbing off the bottom rungs of career ladders. In 1940, for example, only 5.2 percent of black men and 6.4 percent of black women worked in white-collar occupations. By 2000 those figures had risen to 35.3 percent for black men and 62.3 percent for black women. Black people moved in large numbers into jobs in government, education, finance, and such professions as the law and medicine, which had largely excluded them.

As a result of these changes, black family income has increased dramatically. In 1940 only 1 percent of black families, compared with 12 percent of white families, had incomes at least twice as high as the government's poverty line: by 1998, 50 percent of black families did, compared with 73 percent of white families. The disparity of income between similar families also decreased. In 1960 two-parent black families earned 61 percent as much as two-parent white families, but by 1998 they earned 87 percent as much. This figure is even more impressive when one considers that a larger proportion of black people live in the low-wage South than do white people. On average black women now make 94 percent of what white women earn. The economic boom of the Clinton years from 1993 to 2000 particularly benefited black people. Although the median income of black families remains substantially below that of white families, it rose at more than twice the rate over this period (see Table 24–1).

Although many African-American families have made progress in closing the income gap, their average wealth remains far behind that of whites. This is due partly to the centuries-long heritage of poverty during which most black people accumulated little property or other forms of wealth to hand on to their children. It is also closely tied to differences in the proportions of blacks and whites who own their own homes because home ownership is most American families' primary asset. Only 35 percent of African-American families owned their homes in 1950. This was partly due to low incomes but also to systematic discrimination.

Table 24–1
Median Income of Black and White Households, 1992–2001

	1992	2001	Change	Percentage Increase
White	$39,825	$44,517	$4,692	11.6
Black	$23,190	$29,470	$6,280	27.0

Source: U.S. Census Bureau Historical Income Tables—Households

The Persistence of Black Poverty

Although most African Americans enjoyed greater absolute and relative increases in income, many remained mired in poverty. The poverty rate (in 2001 this meant having an annual income below $18,104 for a family of four) for blacks dipped to a low of 22.7 percent during the Clinton boom, but it climbed back to 24.1 percent during the first years of George W. Bush's presidency. Most poor black people are trapped in inner-city neighborhoods plagued by gang warfare, crime, drug and alcohol addiction, and high rates of HIV/AIDS infection. There they are cut off from meaningful participation in the social and economic life of the nation and experience fewer educational and other opportunities that might allow them to escape from poverty. A second large concentration of black poverty is found in depressed rural areas, especially in the South, where mechanization and declining commodity prices for crops have long limited African-American opportunities. Despite cherished myths about rural life, these areas see many of the same social problems as the inner cities.

The high rate of poverty in the black community disproportionately affects children. In the year 2000, 53.3 percent of all African Americans under age eighteen lived in families with only one parent, generally with their mother. Partly for this reason, 55.6 percent of black children lived in families at or near the poverty level. Many, if not most, single-parent families headed by females suffer from limited earning capacity, meager public assistance, poor housing, and inferior schools. These conditions often handicap children for the rest of their lives, helping perpetuate poverty from generation to generation. Given their proportion among African-American youth, this is an ominous sign for the future.

Poverty persists among urban African Americans in part because of the national economic restructuring that has been under way since the 1960s. Deindustrialization, relentless advances in laborsaving technology, and the development of low-wage offshore production have wiped out many jobs that African Americans with limited education and skills once held.

Racial Incarceration

The growth in criminal activity in inner-city districts during the 1980s and 1990s and an overwhelming national shift toward aggressive policing and harsher sentencing for those convicted of breaking the law led to a vast increase in the imprisonment rates of African-American men. Incarceration is an increasingly common experience for poor young black men, compounding the barriers to advancement they already face. (For more on black imprisonment, see Chapter 23.)

Education One-Half Century After *Brown*

Educational attainment is the key factor that distinguishes the African Americans who achieve economic success from those who do not. Black rates of school completion have advanced tremendously in the past half century. Many more black youths graduate from high school than ever before. In 1960 only 37.7 percent of African Americans between ages twenty-five and twenty-nine had completed high school, but by 2000, 86.8 percent had, which is close to the 94 percent for white Americans. Black enrollment in college also rose from a mere 136,000 in 1960 to 1,548,000 in 2000. Although still behind white Americans, these rates of achievement place African Americans among the most highly educated groups of people in the world. African Americans between the ages of twenty-five and thirty-four are now more likely than young adults in Canada, France, Italy, and the United Kingdom to have completed high school, and they are more likely than those in Italy, the United Kingdom, Germany, and France to have completed college.

Yet despite these encouraging figures, black people who want an education, particularly those in poor inner-city and rural areas, still face severe problems. Schools starved of funds by regressive tax policies and the movement of wealthier people—both black and white—to the suburbs are almost predestined to fail. Affirmative action programs that made a place for African-American students have been cut in California, Texas, and elsewhere, resulting in declining enrollments among black students at the top schools.

The Health Gap

As in income and education, African Americans have made significant progress toward living longer, healthier lives, but they still suffer greater incidence of disease and mortality for most major illnesses. In 1970, the first year for which we have statistics, life expectancy was 60 years for black men and 68.3 years for black women. By 2000 it had risen to 68.3 and 75.2 years, respectively. Improvements in the quality of care accessible to blacks are partly responsible for these increases, but higher infant mortality rates and greater numbers of deaths from diseases kept them well below the 74.9-year life span for white men and 80.1 years for white women.

Cancer and HIV/AIDS infections are currently among the greatest threats to black health. African-American men are significantly more likely than white men to develop cancer and to die from the disease within five years of diagnosis. Black women have a somewhat lower incidence of cancer than do white women, but those black women who do get the disease die at a higher rate from it than white women do. Cancer is a complicated disease caused by a variety of factors. Some of the higher rate of its incidence among African Americans is related to risky behaviors common to all impoverished people. These include smoking, heavy drinking, obesity, and a general lack of knowledge about health. A lack of access to health insurance or quality providers compounds the impact of these behaviors. Evidence also indicates that many African Americans mistrust the health-care system and, on the other side, that medical workers tend to treat black cancer patients less aggressively than white patients.

African Americans are more likely to have HIV/AIDS than any other group in the United States. Black people comprise 38 percent of all HIV/AIDS cases despite making up less than 13 percent of the U.S. population. For new cases of the disease, the disparity is even greater: 47 percent of all reported new cases of HIV/AIDS were among African Americans, and 63 percent of the American women newly diagnosed with the disease were black. Although HIV/AIDS first spread in the United States primarily among gay men, and unprotected sex between men is still the primary form of transmission, only about one-third of African Americans contract the disease in this manner. More acquire HIV/AIDS through intravenous drug use and unprotected heterosexual sex.

Although African Americans have had high rates of HIV infection from the beginning of the epidemic, consciousness that this was an important black problem only began to rise in the 1990s. At first the disease was perceived by many black leaders to affect only gay white men and to be relatively less important than the many other crises affecting their community during the 1980s. This began to change when Los Angeles Lakers' star Earvin "Magic" Johnson told the world he had HIV. The deaths of tennis star Arthur Ashe and the young rapper Eric "Eazy-E" Wright also shocked the black community into action.

Identity issues that concerned sexual orientation, feminine and masculine roles, and male/female relationships acquired a new urgency when 2003 reports indicated that African-American women registered more new cases of HIV/AIDS than any other sector of the population. Clearly, heterosexual African-American women sought testing to a greater extent than men. While women received treatment and understanding, their male partners remained in denial and avoided such active engagement in programs that could prolong their lives. Eventually questions about the sexual experiences of black men illuminated practices known as the Down Low. While denying they were gay or bisexual, self-described straight men were having sex with both men and women and spreading the virus that causes HIV/AIDs to their unsuspecting female partners. The future of the black community in the new millennium demands open conversation and creative measures to address the HIV/AIDS crisis.

AFRICAN AMERICANS AT THE CENTER OF ART AND CULTURE

Cultural triumphs are among the most positive recent developments for black Americans. Beginning in the 1980s, a cultural renaissance emerged in every American community with a substantial African-American presence. Black consciousness institutions proliferated and flourished. They included black history and culture museums, festivals, expositions, publishing houses, bookstores and boutiques, concerts, theaters, and dance troupes. In 1996 *Publishers Weekly* reported that bookstores specializing in African-American books had increased from a dozen a few years earlier to more than two hundred. By 1994 there were seventy-five African-American publishing companies. In 1998 the National Literary Hall of Fame for Writers of African Descent opened at Chicago State University. Black painters used outdoor murals to celebrate the black experience.

Black playwrights were in the vanguard of this cultural explosion and helped revitalize the American theater. August Wilson had begun writing overtly political work in the 1960s and 1970s but focused on broader themes of race and personality as his work matured. His first great success came in 1984 with the Broadway production of *Ma Rainey's Black Bottom* that explored the impact of racism in the music industry. He won praise for his powerful use of the rhythmic and symbolic power of black speech. He has since had four other plays on Broadway, two of which won Pulitzer prizes—*Fences* in 1987 and *The Piano Lesson* in 1990. Charles Fuller has also made race the center of his plays, attacking stereotypes and exploring the complexity of racial identity in modern America. His most well-known play was the 1982 *A Soldier's Tale* that also won a Pulitzer Prize. George C. Wolfe is a playwright, director, and producer whose achievements helped demolish racial barriers in the theater. His plays, such as *The Colored Museum* and *Jelly's Last Jam,* have won critical acclaim, and he received a Tony Award as best director for *Angels in America* in 1994. His talent and energy are credited with returning the New York Shakespeare Festival to its former glory after his appointment as its director. Anna Deavere Smith has pioneered new forms of theater with her powerful one-woman plays derived from interviews. Her first major success was *Fires in the Mirror* about tensions between blacks and Jews in Brooklyn's Crown Heights neighborhood. This was followed by *Twilight: Los Angeles 1992,* a powerful portrayal of the Rodney King riots. Smith's achievements in drama and her gifted teaching were rewarded with a MacArthur genius grant in 1996.

The new cultural renaissance differed from the black arts movement of the 1960s and 1970s. The contemporary flowering was more inclusive and more appreciative of women artists. It also included the work of openly gay and lesbian artists, such as documentary filmmaker Marion Riggs, dance choreographer Bill T. Jones, and novelist E. Lynn Harris. Whereas poets and dramatists dominated earlier movements, novelists took center stage in the 1980s. Much of the new work in all fields appeals to white as much as to black audiences, providing new insights into the lives of people of African heritage in a predominantly Eurocentric society.

There were signs of the emergence of a new wave of African-American novelists as early as 1977 when Toni Morrison's *Song of Solomon* became a Book-of-the-Month-Club selection, the first by a black author since Richard Wright's *Native Son* in 1940. Then Barbara Chase-Riboud made waves with *Sally Hemings* (1979), a fictional treatment of a woman who was both slave to and mistress of President Thomas Jefferson. In 1980 Toni Cade Bambara won the American Book Award for *The Salt Eaters.* At least as significant as these individual books was the founding in 1981 of a new publishing house, Kitchen Table: Women of Color Press. Then, in 1982, Alice Walker won the Pulitzer Prize and the American Book Award for *The Color Purple.* In 1987 poet Rita Dove won the Pulitzer Prize for poetry. In 1993 she became America's poet laureate, and in the same year Toni Morrison became the first African American to win the Nobel Prize for Literature. President Bill Clinton invited Maya Angelou to read one of her poems during his first inauguration.

Critics were not the only ones to take an interest in these works. In 1992 novels by three African-American women—Morrison, Walker, and Terry McMillan—made the *New York Times* best-seller list at the same time. In 2001 the works of four African Americans made the *Times* best-seller list and revealed the expanding readership and growing appreciation of black literature across the racial spectrum.

The Hip-Hop Nation

Rap is the most recent musical genre to arise out of black urban communities. Since the 1980s it has been emblematic of the younger generation of African Americans, known collectively as the hip-hop nation. Rap is a form of rhythmic speaking in rhyme: hip-hop refers to the backup music for rap that is often composed of excerpts or "samples" from other songs. Rap's roots lie in long traditions of street boasting, in the preaching style of black clergy, and in Afro-Caribbean rhythmic traditions.

Origins of a New Music: A Generation Defines Itself

The rap musical style arose in the early 1970s in poverty-stricken South Bronx neighborhoods in New York City. Its original purpose was to substitute musical and dance competition for gang violence. Rap pioneer Kool Herc (aka Clive Campbell) began using simple raps to cover a mix of beats played from two turntables. At the same time, former gang leader Afrika Bambaataa developed a political version of rap by merging the ideology of the Nation of Islam with the Black Panthers' cultural nationalism. Bambaataa's Zulu Nation promoted competition in break dancing, rapping, and graffiti art and helped spread rap among poor black and Latino neighborhoods.

The first commercial rap hit, "Rapper's Delight" by the Sugar Hill Gang, came out in 1979 and popularized the term *hip-hop*. This was followed by the rise to stardom of Grandmaster Flash and the Furious Five, which grew out of 1970s funk but added rap vocals and the technique of *scratching*—moving a record back and forth under a needle to produce a rhythmic, jarring sound, and manipulating turntable speeds.

Hip-hop music provided African American youths with a creative medium in which they could discuss the things that mattered most to them, especially their lives in cities burdened by racial poverty and all that that entailed. In the Reagan years (1981–1989), few middle-class Americans cared to acknowledge the millions left behind in urban decay. Conditions in inner cities worsened during this period when crack flooded neighborhoods and gang warfare erupted over drug turfs. The "keeping it real" lyrics of hip-hop artists helped forge a sense of community and common destiny among members of an often-ignored generation.

Rap Music Goes Mainstream

Ironically, white indifference allowed the first hip-hop entrepreneurs to take control of the production, dissemination, and profits connected with this new musical genre. Russell Simmons saw the potential of rap street music in the mid-1970s and recognized that the mainstream entertainment industry was not aware of it. He became a concert promoter, encouraging early rap groups to stay close to the dress styles and language of the inner-city African-American community. In 1984 he and a partner formed Def Jam Records. Their bands, such as RunDMC and Public Enemy, became enormously popular, and many of their albums sold millions of copies. Simmons expanded his business to include marketing hip-hop clothing under the label Phat Pharm and promoting poetry and comedy acts. In 2000 he sold his share of Def Jam for over $100 million. Like Simmons, P. Diddy (aka Sean "Puff Daddy" Combs) found success by working within the mainstream recording industry. In 1993 he formed his own company, Bad Boy Records, which was an immediate success.

Commercial success brought new groups to the fore, and the genre changed and grew tremendously during the 1980s and 1990s. Hard-core rap bands such as RunDMC, which dominated the charts in the mid-1980s, brought the sound to MTV and to a larger public, which soon came to include white suburban teens. Hip-hop culture quickly spread beyond New York to other African-American urban centers, and each developed a distinctive, and often more graphic, variant of the original. With the music came changes in clothing style, such as baggy, loose-fitting jeans, that trend-hungry fashion designers quickly adopted.

Gansta Rap

The southern California group NWA (Niggas With Attitude) was one of the most successful of the new rap bands coming out in the late 1980s. Their 1988 release of the album *Straight Out of Compton* heralded the rise of *gangsta rap*. Its song "Gansta, Gansta" shocked many observers with its sexist and violent lyrics. Particularly troubling, however, is the persistent objectification of women in hard-core rap music and related films.

Gansta rap, however, is only part of the story. The rap genre is so broad that it includes many bands that explicitly reject hard-core obscenity and violence. Artists like Queen Latifah, for example, avoid putting down other African Americans even as they put forward a message of empowerment for black women and men. Other black female hip-hop artists were also in the game. Many, such as Lil' Kim, resolved to make sexuality their signature in ways that left little to the imagination.

Hip-hop quickly moved beyond the shores of the United States and has influenced music worldwide, particularly across the African Diaspora. France, for example, has a thriving rap music scene. Most of its artists are of Arab, African, or Spanish descent whose music focuses on ethnic and racial discrimination and social criticism. Africa, the Caribbean, and Latin America have also developed rap that builds on indigenous traditions of African music. The ability of rap to combine with other musical forms to create compelling hybrids and the global penetration of American popular culture ensures that it will continue to thrive and evolve.

African-American Intellectuals

The struggles of the civil rights and black power movements forced predominantly white academic and cultural institutions to open their doors to African Americans. With a beachhead established, a number of black scholars gained a level of prominence as public intellectuals unknown in earlier eras. These individuals go beyond their roles as academics to participate in public debate on major issues. In the past four decades many of the most prominent public intellectuals to emerge have been African American. Among them are Cornel West, Henry Louis Gates Jr., Molefi Kete Asante, Shelby Steele, William Julius Wilson, Michele Wallace, Ishmael Reed, Stanley Crouch, Charles Johnson, Vonnie McLoyd, John Edgar Wideman, Manning Marable, Adolph Reed, Thomas Sowell, Robin D. g. Kelley, Michael Eric Dyson, Nell Irvin Painter, bell hooks, and Anthony Appiah. Their views range across the ideological gamut from Marxist to extreme conservative, but they all strive to define black identity in the United States and to explore the role of race in its social, economic, and political life.

Many African-American scholars are connected to the black studies programs founded in the late 1960s and early 1970s. Initially marginalized and few in number, these programs now exist in nearly every major university or college. They have become institutionalized—even prized—by institutions that once resisted them. Doctoral degrees are now offered at Temple University, the University of Massachusetts at Amherst, Harvard, Michigan State University, and the University of California at Berkeley. Yale and Cornell offer masters' degrees in the field.

Afrocentricity

In the 1980s and 1990s, a philosophy of culture referred to as "Afrocentricity" captured widespread media and academic attention. The philosophy and practice of Afrocentricity had been a prominent feature in the political movement that created black studies but the emergence of Temple University professor Molefi Kete Asante gave it a presence and a personality. In the 1980s Asante published three books, *Afrocentricity*, *Kemet, Afrocentricity and Knowledge*, and *The Afrocentric Idea* in which he argued that an African-centered perspective was needed to re-orient African Americans from the Eurocentric periphery to a centered place in their own history. In its most extreme form, Afrocentrists argue that much of European civilization arose out of African origins, particularly the culture of ancient Egypt. They also point to evidence of advanced cultures in other parts of the continent to refute assertions of African cultural inferiority.

Many black educators enthusiastically embraced Afrocentricity as a way to celebrate and reclaim a positive African identity and to unite the peoples of the African Diaspora. Afrocentrists rejected the idea of America as a melting pot. Assimilation, they argued, meant a rejection of their African cultural heritage. At the heart of this position is an indictment of American ideas and institutions for their complicity in the long oppression of black people.

Many black scholars insist that Afrocentricity is regressive and fosters self-segregation. Writer Earl Ofari Hutchinson, for example, concedes that Asante's ideas merit attention, but he is skeptical about the claims of some Afrocentrist academics. "In their zeal to counter the heavy handed 'Eurocentric imbalance of history,' some have crossed the line between historic fact and fantasy. They've constructed groundless theories in which Europeans are 'Ice People,' 'suffer genetic defects,' or are obsessed with 'color phobias.' They've replaced the shallow European 'great man' theory of history with a feel-good interpretation of history." White and black critics alike caution that the Afrocentrist desire to fabricate "a glorious past" for black people did a disservice to the truth and fostered a narrow notion of race ill suited as a platform for pursuing the study of Africans in America.

African-American Studies Matures

While the African-American studies department at Temple is the center of the Afrocentric approach and remains one of the largest black studies programs in the nation, many other programs adopt a more ideologically flexible approach. Under the leadership of literary scholar Henry Louis Gates Jr., Harvard University now has the premier program in the integrationist tradition. His goals for the department focus less on recovering a usable past and more on the rigorous multidisciplinary study of the black experience. Apart from intellectual rigor, what binds the department together is a belief that race is a malleable category of identity to be analyzed critically and that effective scholarship in the area is not fundamentally limited by the racial identity of the scholar.

As with American intellectual life as a whole, African-American studies has been influenced by the emergence of scholarship that questions prevailing gender assumptions.

Just as the black studies movement challenged racial ideology, women's studies have forced a reconsideration of deeply held gender beliefs and raised historical and social science questions that went unasked in an earlier era. African-American scholars in *womanism* studies, a term popularized by Alice Walker to describe the intellectual project of women of color, have paid particular attention to the intersections of gender with racial and class hierarchies in shaping the lives of black women. As more black women enrolled in college, courses with titles like "Black Women Writers" and "Black Women's History" became part of black studies curricula. The field of black women's history has grown rapidly. These historians have productively explored the role of race, class, and gender in the oppression of marginalized people in American society.

Perhaps most importantly, scholars have begun to flesh out the larger picture of the black Diaspora. Building on the important work of Philip Curtin, Colin Palmer, and others who have studied the development of the Atlantic slave-labor economy, scholars have begun serious comparisons of the centuries-old African-descended communities throughout the New World and those of more recent African immigrants to Europe. This project is enriching our understanding of African-American history by placing it in the context of a larger global story.

BLACK RELIGION AT THE DAWN OF THE MILLENNIUM

Religion remains at the heart of the African-American experience. Black churches, claiming over 25 million members, remain by far the largest black-controlled institutions in the nation. Houses of worship ranging in size from small storefront operations with a few dozen congregants to massive "mega churches" with many thousands of members are the sinew that binds together nearly every African-American community. The major denominations remain those with ties going back to the nineteenth century. Among the largest are the African American National Baptist Convention of America, Inc., Progressive National Baptist Convention, Inc., African Methodist Episcopal Church, National Missionary Baptist Convention of America, Churches of Christ, and the African Methodist Episcopal Zion Church. Due to immigration from the Caribbean and Africa, African Americans are becoming a larger part of some predominantly white denominations.

African-American men and women have had great success in occupying leadership positions within a variety of predominantly white denominations since the 1960s. Harold R. Perry was consecrated a bishop in the American Roman Catholic Church in 1966, and Bishop Wilton Gregory became the first African American to head the American Catholic bishops in 2002. Recognizing the importance of Africans and African Americans to the future of the church, in 1993 Pope John Paul II apologized for the Catholic Church's support of slavery. African-American John M. Burgess was installed as the first black bishop to head an Episcopal diocese in America in Massachusetts in 1970, followed by John T. Walker in Washington, D.C., in 1977.

Despite this continuity with the past and the successes of black religious leaders, African-American religious life has changed in the last several decades. Most African Americans remain Protestants, but demographic and social changes within the community have challenged the mainline denominations. One difficulty is the move of middle-class parishioners out of the close-knit urban communities that once supported churches with people from many different walks of life. Greater levels of education and different life experiences combine with geographical distance to create large suburban mega churches with a distinct character and worship practice. Often Pentecostal, these churches espouse a theology that emphasizes the individual's relationship to God. Their ministers speak to the tensions and anxiety of people with stressful lives and careers or with specific problems such as substance abuse or difficulty with relationships. They also provide community institutions with tremendous services for their parishioners.

Black Christians on the Front Line

Faced with the problems of the black community in the United States and with a changing population, African-American Christians in both traditional and nontraditional religious institutions have developed outreach programs to create supportive communities for the embattled and vulnerable. Some of the new mega churches are located in or near the black inner-city communities and retain a commitment to local action.

Reverend Eugene Rivers has developed a different approach from that of the mega churches. Along with like-minded former students at Harvard University, he founded the small Azusa Christian Community in a crime-plagued neighborhood in Boston. Its primary goal, Rivers says, is to keep children from killing one another. He and fellow black clergy formed the 10-Point Coalition and entered into a partnership with the police. The collaboration helped eliminate juvenile murders for two-and-a-half years. Rivers advocates a pragmatic black nationalism aimed at developing a rich, viable black civil society centered on the church.

Tensions in the Black Church

Tensions have arisen within many black churches over their socially conservative message, patriarchal structure, staid ritual, and lack of social engagement. Gender and sexuality are two key areas in which this has been expressed. The black church has long been in accord with other conservative Christian churches in advocating the subordination of women to men. Although most black churchgoers are women, men overwhelmingly dominate visible church leadership. Although a few voices, both male and female, have always challenged patriarchal assumptions in the churches, only in recent decades has the chorus grown too loud to ignore. As theologian, sociologist and ordained Baptist minister Cheryl Townsend Gilkes puts it, "[t]he cultural maxim 'If it wasn't for the women, you wouldn't have a church,' rises up against male attempts to exclude, ignore, trivialize, or marginalize women in a number of capacities." Some African-American women, particularly of the younger generations, have left the church because of this marginalization. Others, like Gilkes, have stayed to challenge sexism in individual churches and the denominations.

The African Methodist Episcopal (AME) Church has been at the forefront of this movement for reform. Although it has ordained women since 1898, the number of

With the support of the Delta Sigma sorority, family, and the Baltimore, Maryland, church community, Vashti Murphy McKenzie broke through "the stained-glass ceiling" (her words) to become the first woman to be appointed a bishop in the history of the AME Church. She is a graduate of the University of Maryland and earned a master of divinity from Harvard University's Divinity School and a doctorate in ministry at the United Theological Seminary in Dayton, Ohio.
AP/Wide World Photos

women ministers has only recently grown significant. Now 3,000 of its 8,000 ministers are female, and in 2000 it elected Reverend Vashti M. McKenzie bishop of its Southern African district. She took the post after a successful ten-year stint as pastor of Baltimore, Maryland's Payne Memorial Church, whose membership she increased from 300 to 1,700. The achievements of women in the churches have not come without conflict, and this promises to be at the center of the black religious life in the twenty-first century.

Black churches also face conflicts over sexuality. Their theology has traditionally limited legitimate sexual activity to monogamous, heterosexual marriages. Of all of these challenges, those surrounding the HIV/AIDS crisis are most pressing but also the most difficult to address, given the church's traditional refusal to do more than denounce, or remain silent about, nontraditional sexualities.

Black Muslims

Although still a relatively small phenomenon in African America, Islam has been gaining a significant number of converts. The Nation of Islam is the best known of the many groups comprising African-American Muslims, but in fact its 20,000 to 40,000 members make up only a small percentage of the estimated 1.5 million black American Muslims. After the death of founder Elijah Muhammad in 1975, the Nation of Islam was led by his son Wraith Deen Muhammad, who rejected the racialist aspects of his father's theology for more orthodox, mainstream Sunni Muslim beliefs. He eventually left the organization to found the Muslim American Society, the largest group of African-American Muslims with perhaps 500,000 members. Many black Muslims have rejected Christianity for what they perceive as its Eurocentric bias and for its former tolerance of slavery, although Islam also had a long history of slave trading in Africa. The clarity and discipline of the Muslim faith and the solidarity they feel with Muslims around the world also attract converts, estimated at about 18,000 per year in the United States.

With growing immigration from Islamic countries, African Americans have become more closely connected to the larger trends of the religion. This is evident in the rise of more orthodox Islam among American blacks. Tensions have arisen between African-American and immigrant Muslims, who make up three-quarters of all American Muslims.

The aftermath of the attacks on the World Trade Center and the Pentagon on September 11, 2001, has left many African-American Muslims conflicted. On the one hand, most deplore the attacks and the ideology that led to them. On the other hand, many African Americans are troubled by what they perceive to be an indiscriminate anti-Muslim feeling in the United States and are concerned the nation's war on terror might become a holy war against Islam.

LOUIS FARRAKHAN AND THE NATION OF ISLAM

Beginning in the 1980s, the Nation of Islam's minister Louis Farrakhan became a potent source of racial division in the United States. Farrakhan was the younger of two sons of immigrant parents from the West Indies. As a young man, Farrakhan attended a black teachers' college in Winston-Salem, North Carolina, but he dropped out to become a Calypso singer known as the Charmer. In 1955, while performing in Chicago, he heard Elijah Muhammad preach at the Nation of Islam's mosque. This marked a turning point in his life. Farrakhan joined the Nation and quickly ascended within its hierarchy in the wake of Malcolm X's rupture with Elijah Muhammad and subsequent murder in February 1965. Farrakhan became minister of the Harlem Mosque No. 7 and Muhammad's national representative. Farrakhan opposed Wraith Muhammad's move to a more orthodox Islam and was able to take leadership of the Nation of Islam by 1978. In 1982 he purchased a building to publish the Nation of Islam's newspaper, *The Final Call,* and in 1985 he bought and moved into Elijah Muhammad's mansion in Chicago. Under Farrakhan's direction, the Nation developed a number of economic enterprises, including media ventures, restaurants, clothing stores, and companies to provide security for apartment buildings, distribute soap and cosmetics, and manufacture pharmaceuticals. Farrakhan recruited among poor and marginalized urban African Americans and within the black prison population. The national move to the right during the Reagan era complemented the reconstituted Nation's conservative social ideas, which harked back to those advanced by Booker T. Washington at the turn of the century.

Until 1984 most white Americans were barely aware of Farrakhan's existence. In that year, however, he broke the Nation of Islam's long-standing tradition of abstaining from politics to support Jesse Jackson's bid for the Democratic presidential nomination and soon ignited a firestorm of controversy. When some Jews took offense at Jackson's off-the-record reference to New York as "Hymietown" during a conversation with two African-American reporters, Farrakhan, whose Fruit of Islam provided security for Jackson's campaign, rose to his defense and made matters worse. In 1984, as in the past, Farrakhan's verbal assaults against Jews attracted support from ultra-right-wing anti-Semitic forces and condemnation from Jewish Americans and the Anti-Defamation League. Jewish Americans, many of whom had been among the principal allies of African Americans during the civil rights movement, called on African-American organizations and leaders to repudiate Farrakhan and his rhetoric of "Jewish domination and control."

MILLENNIUM MARCHES

In recent years Farrakhan has attempted to move beyond his extremist ideas and reach out to a broader group of African Americans. To this end he called for a Million Man March in Washington, D.C. Farrakhan framed this march as a "Holy Day of Atonement and Reconciliation." The estimated 400,000-strong crowd at the October 16, 1995, march made it a symbolic success and generated positive coverage even in the mainstream media. It inspired many black men to become more engaged with their communities and to speak out more forcefully against oppression. Many marchers reported that even though they did not support the Nation of Islam's program, they drew hope from the peaceful solidarity of the gathering.

Yet the goodwill dissipated when, three months after the march, Farrakhan embarked on a World Friendship Tour to Africa and the Middle East. To the consternation of many, he met with the leader of the brutally repressive military regime in Nigeria, General Sani Abacha. At home, Farrakhan's intemperate rhetoric continued to attract attention. In the wake of the Million Man March, however, he failed to forge a coherent strategy to resolve African America's continuing social problems.

The Million Man March inspired women to organize their own march. Initiated by two Philadelphia women—Phile Chionesu, a small-business owner, and Asia Coney, a public housing activist—on October 25, 1997, an estimated 300,000 black women gathered in Philadelphia to listen to speeches by California congresswoman and president of the Congressional Black Caucus Maxine Waters, rapper Sister Souljah, and South African activist Winnie Mandela. The march was a celebration, a call to unity, and a forum for black women to speak out against domestic violence, and inadequate access to quality health care and educational opportunities. The march did not garner nearly as much media attention as the Million Man March, perhaps because the organizers were relatively unknown. The March nonetheless symbolized the ongoing struggle of black women to be seen and heard in American society and to counter negative stereotypes and derogatory images of black womanhood. Like the Million Man March, there was little in the way of specific policy demands, but the women marchers did gain a feeling of solidarity. As Detroit real estate agent Gloria Graves put it, "I thought that it was very important that we as black women come together in prayer and unity and the belief that we can bring back the family unit that has been lost. I wanted to meet other strong black women who had the same agenda and be united. It has been just great."

COMPLICATING BLACK IDENTITY
IN THE TWENTY-FIRST CENTURY

The 2000 U.S. census counted 281,421,906 Americans, a 13.2 percent increase from 1990. African-American numbers stood at 34.7 million, or about 12 percent of the total. For the first time in U.S. history, African Americans were no longer the largest minority group: the 35.3 million Americans who identified themselves as Hispanic slightly outnumbered them.

One of the most important changes in the census was the ability of respondents to choose more than one racial designation for themselves. Since the first census, such classifications have been shaped by the politics of race. During the early civil rights movement, some groups like the ACLU attempted to remove racial classifications altogether from the census data, reasoning that the only purpose of such distinctions was to disadvantage black people.

The civil rights laws of the 1960s changed the purpose of gathering data by racial classification. It was now necessary to have reliable statistics on racial characteristics of people to combat discrimination. With the rise of affirmative action programs, an individual's identity as an African American could actually be a benefit. The black power movement led many to embrace their identity as African Americans and reject the assimilation implied by abandoning racial categories.

In 1977 the Office of Management and Budget addressed the U.S government's need for standard racial categories with its Statistical Policy Directive 15. This set up the familiar racial classifications: white, black, Asian and Pacific Islander, and Native American. "Hispanic" was chosen to denote an ethnicity and could be chosen in addition to one of the four racial categories. Because there is no scientific backing for any biological racial distinctions, these categories are bureaucratic approximations of socially relevant distinctions designed to serve administrative needs. They were not necessarily meant to reflect the complex identities of many individuals included in them. For example, "Asian and Pacific Islander" encompasses individuals from nations with vastly different histories and cultures. The white category included people descended from Arabs and Turks as well as Europeans. In terms of ethnicity, people now called Hispanic had formerly thought of themselves in terms of national identities, such as Mexican American, Cuban American, and so on, and overlapped with the "black" category for Dominicans and other African-descended people from the former Spanish colonial regions. Over the quarter century after its adoption, these categories became incorporated into identities and social understandings and, in important ways, influenced business and government programs.

Two groups sought to change the categories. The first group saw an end to racial categories as the true legacy of the civil rights movement. These advocates point to the rhetoric of Martin Luther King Jr. and the plain language of the Civil Rights Act of 1964, which forbade any discrimination on the basis of race, as evidence of the need to eliminate racial classifications by the government. Some adherents to this view want to do away with the notion of race altogether. Their goal is a colorblind society that they believe will not be achieved until an individual's race ceases to have a positive or negative impact on access to education, government programs, or employment. Others who advocate this position, however, are ideologically driven conservatives who want to limit the power of the federal government to redress inequality. They have bankrolled state referendums and court cases to end racial classifications and see this as a way to roll back the gains of the civil rights era.

Those who are biracial form a second group opposed to the old classification scheme. Racial mixing is nothing new in America. Under slavery many black women were compelled to bear children to their white masters. There have also been consensual sexual relationships and marriages between African Americans and other ethnic and racial groups. The number of such unions and their social acceptance as legitimate relationships have grown precipitously, however, since the civil rights movement destroyed many of the old racial barriers and the U.S. Supreme Court cast down the last antimiscegenation laws in *Loving v. Virginia* in 1967. Although still a small percentage of the total, there are now more than 1.5 million mixed-race marriages in the United States and an increasing number of children growing up in these households. The proportion of mixed-race marriages is much higher among younger generations and seems likely to increase rapidly in the future.

The debate over biracial and multiracial identities rages in the African-American community. One of the most significant concerns is that to make fundamental changes in the classification system will undermine the project they were designed to advance. As poverty researcher John A. Powell put it, "Without racial statistics, we will not know how distributions of resources affect racial and ethnic groups. Without them, racism, which is still very much a part of our society, will be that much more difficult to eradicate, and that much more likely to remain a societal norm." The programs that use these statistics include the Equal Employment Opportunity Act, the Civil Rights Act of 1964, the Voting Rights Act of 1965, the Public Health Act, the Job Partnership Training Act, the Equal Credit Opportunity Act, the Fair Housing Act, and many others. Some argue that offering mixed-race people the option of not being black might undermine the racial solidarity that has been the basis for black advances. As historian Ibrahim K. Sundiata puts it, "[t]he disaggregation of Blacks would drive a wedge into the community that would only increase the isolation of its most disadvantaged members."

Although only 1.8 million Americans opted for the biracial designation in the 2000 census, its existence does bring into question the nature of racial identity itself. Clearly racism exists, and black Americans experienced centuries of discrimination that distinguishes them from other groups. At the same time, many who would have been considered black under the American system of racial classification no longer think of themselves in the same way and may be increasingly able to assert a multiple identity. The larger pattern of recent immigration that the United States is undergoing undermines what had once been a largely biracial dynamic.

Immigration and African Americans

Because of immigration restrictions and the general oppression of people of African descent in America, few blacks, either from the Western Hemisphere or Africa, immigrated to the United States before the last few decades. Changes in immigration laws, particularly the landmark 1965 Hart-Cellar Act, which abandoned the racially exclusive restrictions of the past, helped open the door. Military, economic, health, and environmental crises that have roiled Africa and the Caribbean in these years have pushed substantial numbers from these regions through it. These new African Americans often do not fit their identity neatly into the traditional African-American category.

Black people from the West Indies have a long history of immigration to the United States, but their numbers increased dramatically since the 1960s. During the entire decade of the 1950s, only 123,000 Caribbean people immigrated, but during the 1990s nearly one million did so. The Caribbean islands were one of the main areas of importation for African slaves. The islands' sugar production served as the economic engine of the Spanish, French, and British New World empires well into the nineteenth century. These empires all abandoned slavery by the late 1800s, and the retreat of colonialism from the Caribbean in the twentieth century has left a number of micro-nations largely populated by people of African descent whose cultures have remained more influenced by Africa than was true of the United States. Hence African cultural practices were fused with those of the British in Jamaica, the French in Haiti, and the Spanish in Santo Domingo and Cuba. Although a racial hierarchy is not unknown in these societies, racial identity is less important than class and merit-based achievement. Upon immigration to mostly New York, Florida, and other parts of the East Coast, immigrants from the Caribbean soon learn the importance of race in the United States, but at the same time they have carved out a separate identity from other African Americans. First-generation West Indians tend to have more economic success than native African Americans, in part because employers often favor them. The second generation has tended to have a more difficult time as the effects of racial discrimination and poor schools take their toll.

Black Feminism

The feminist and gay rights movements have challenged traditional ideas of racial identity in recent decades. Both arose as part of the broader "rights revolution" that began with the civil rights movement, but each highlights a different aspect of an individual's identity—gender or sexuality—in addition to race.

A new wave of feminism emerged on the American political landscape in the 1960s and 1970s and transformed gender relations. This movement arose, in part, out of the successes of the African-American civil rights struggle. The 1964 Civil Rights Act outlawed sexual as well as racial discrimination in employment. Although this had not been a goal of the civil rights movement at that time, and its inclusion was meant in part to lessen the law's chance of passage, it helped open discussions of gender oppression that had laid dormant for decades. Many white women activists in SNCC and other civil rights groups assumed leading roles in the emerging feminist movement, often using the same strategies and tactics that had worked in the fight against racism.

Second Wave Feminism achieved many important changes as it gathered adherents in the 1960s and 1970s. The National Organization for Women (NOW), founded in 1966, spearheaded efforts to end job discrimination against women, to expand access to safe and effective birth control, to legalize abortion, and to secure federal and state support for child care. One of the movement's most important early successes was Title IX of the Educational Amendments Act of 1972, which required colleges and universities to ensure equal access for women. Another was the Supreme Court's decision in *Roe v. Wade*, legalizing abortion. Beyond these legislative and judicial victories, the feminist movement has opened up choices for women on nearly every aspect of their lives that traditional gender roles had precluded. It has also engendered a backlash as conservative men and women organized to fight against passage of the Equal Rights Amendment to the Constitution, access to abortion, sex education in schools, and a variety of related issues. This fight has driven much of the political conflict in the United States since the 1970s.

Prolific writer, accomplished actress, and renowned poet, Maya Angelou (1928–) read an original poem, "On the pulse of the Morning" at President Clinton's first inauguration in 1993. In 1970 she published her now classic autobiography, *I Know Why the Caged Bird Sings*, that describes her childhood in Stamps, Arkansas. She is the Reynolds Professor of American Studies at Wake Forest University in Winston-Salem, North Carolina.
Corbis/Bettmann

Black women were involved from the start in shaping modern feminism. The core of black feminist thinking is a dual critique of the women's and black liberation movements' core ideology. Black women scholars and writers argued that a critique of patriarchy was incomplete without attention to race and class. Whereas white leaders of the women's movement were silent on race, many male leaders in the African-American freedom movement were all too forthright about their views on gender. Many believed racial oppression was the primary evil to be fought and that feminism was either a distraction or, by encouraging women to be strong and self-reliant, actually undermined the efforts of black men to overcome the emasculating effects of white male power. Black feminists such as Frances Beale countered that racism and sexism had oppressed black women.

Responding to sexism in the black power movement, many black women writers and activists sought to make the struggle against it as important as that against racism. Between 1973 and 1975, the National Black Feminist Organization (NFBO) articulated many of the concerns specific to black women, from anger with black men for dating and marrying white women, to internal conflict over skin color, hair texture, and facial features, to sexual violence and harassment against black women, to differences in the economic mobility of white and black women. Black feminists also attacked the myth of black matriarchy and stereotypical portrayals of black women in popular culture. Although the organization was short lived, it did break the silence imposed on black women by black liberation movements. Black feminists also helped others talk openly about domestic violence, rape, and sexual harassment in employment.

Gay and Lesbian African Americans

The success of the civil rights movement encouraged gays and lesbians to fight openly against the discrimination they had faced for centuries. Their movement was small and quiet until 1969 when gay men at the Stonewall Inn in New York's Greenwich Village violently resisted a police raid. The multiracial crowd's refusal at this bar to go on submitting to the kind of police harassment that homosexuals had long been subjected to in the United States sparked an explosion of activism. By the end of the 1970s, many states and cities had decriminalized homosexual behavior and lifted employment policies that discriminated on the basis of sexuality. Although tensions arose between the lesbian and gay wings of the movement, they worked together to pursue the full range of civil rights enjoyed by heterosexuals despite a persistent and powerful opposition from conservative groups.

Gay, bisexual, lesbian, and transgender African Americans have struggled against their marginality within the larger gay rights movement and homophobia in their own communities. Like the women's movement, the early gay and lesbian rights movement tended to be predominantly white and middle class. Although not explicitly racist, it tended to see racial issues as secondary to or separate from the goal of ending discrimination based on sexual preference.

Despite hostility toward the gay and lesbian rights movement by some African Americans, many black leaders, such as Jesse Jackson, Eleanor Holmes Norton, and John Lewis, and civil rights organizations, such as the NAACP, have embraced its agenda. They do so in part because they accept the analogy between the struggle against repression based on sexual preference and that based on race. The debate between black feminists and gay rights activists, who argue that gender and class identities must be taken into account in political and scholarly analysis, and nationalists, who focus on black identity as primary, continues to rage and will influence our understanding of African-American life in the twenty-first century.

T I M E L I N E

AFRICAN-AMERICAN EVENTS	NATIONAL EVENTS
1960	
	1964 Civil Rights Act outlaws sexual discrimination in employment

continued

AFRICAN-AMERICAN EVENTS	NATIONAL EVENTS
	1966
	National Organization for Women founded
	1969
	Stonewall Riot in New York
1970	
1973	
National Black Feminist Organization founded	
1978	
Louis Farrakhan becomes head of Nation of Islam	
1980	
1982	**1980**
Alice Walker and Charles Fuller win Pulitzer Prizes in fiction and drama	Ronald Reagan is elected president
1984	**1981**
Russell Simmons forms Def Jam Records	Recession settles in
	Economic Recovery Tax Act is passed
1987	**1984**
August Wilson wins Pulitzer Prize for drama	President Reagan is reelected
1988	**1988**
"Straight Out of Compton" marks rise of gangsta rap	George Bush is elected president of the United States
1990	
1990	**1990**
Anna Deveare Smith and August Wilson win Pulitzer Prizes for poetry and drama	1.4 million Caribbean and African immigrants move to the United States
1993	**1991**
Toni Morrison becomes the first black woman to win Nobel Prize for literature	Operation Desert Storm against Iraq is initiated and ended
1995	**1992**
Million Man March	William Jefferson Clinton is elected president of the United States
1997	**1994**
Million Woman March	Midterm elections give Republican party control of Congress
	1996
	Clinton is reelected
	Clinton signs welfare reform legislation
	1998
	Clinton is impeached by the House of Representatives

continued

AFRICAN-AMERICAN EVENTS	NATIONAL EVENTS
	1999 The U.S. Senate acquits Clinton
2000	
2000 Vashti M. McKenzie elected first woman AME bishop African-American college enrollment tops 1.5 million	**2000** Hispanics become the largest minority group in the United States
2001 AIDS becomes a leading cause of death among young African-American men	George W. Bush is elected president of United States Bush names Condoleezza Rice national security advisor and Colin Powell secretary of state
2002 Wilton Gregory heads U.S. Catholic bishops	**September 11, 2001** Terrorists demolish the World Trade Center and attack the Pentagon

CONCLUSION

The closing of the twentieth century saw remarkable progress for African Americans even as part of the community remained mired in poverty and suffering. African Americans still experience the burden of racism that was so familiar to W. E. B. Du Bois, which prompts collective political action and the maintenance of predominantly black churches, colleges, and social action groups. The black soul that he thought had so much to give America now flows freely through its art, language, and popular culture. At the same time, increasing diversity in the ways that African Americans live their lives has led to differences in the ways in which individuals understand their identities. Some, like Anthony Appiah, long for the possibility of asserting those identities in ways not limited by race. The tension between racial and other identities will shape the African-American odyssey as it moves through the twenty-first century.

REVIEW QUESTIONS

1. What social, economic, and material gains did African Americans make after the civil rights era? Why did some black Americans do better than others during this period?

2. Why do white Americans tend to live longer than black Americans? How has the black community dealt with the problems of AIDS/HIV?

3. Who were some of the most important African-American writers in the late twentieth century? What is the hip-hop nation? How did rap music enter the American cultural mainstream?

4. What are the goals of the Afrocentricity movement? Why do many black intellectuals oppose Afrocentricity?

5. Why has the church remained so important to African Americans? How are women's roles changing in the black church? Why has Louis Farrakhan been such a controversial figure?

6. Were the Millenium Marches a success? What did the marches accomplish for those men and women who marched?

7. How has immigration from the Caribbean and Africa affected black America? What factors gave rise to black feminism? What problems do black gays and lesbians face in the black community?

RECOMMENDED READING

Patricia Hill Collins. *Black Feminist Thought: Knowledge, Consciousness, and the Politics of Empowerment.* Boston: Unwin Hyman, 1990. A classic text on black feminist theory and practice by one of black studies' foremost sociologists.

Robin D. G. Kelley. *Yo' Mama Is DysFunkshional!* Boston: Beacon Press, 1998. Insightful essays about America's culture wars and an excellent critique of scholarship about black working-class culture by one of this generation's finest historians.

J. L. King. *On the Down Low: A Journey into the Land of "Straight" Black Men Who Sleep with Men.* New York: Broadway Books, 2004. A provocative and disturbing account of the sexual behavior of closeted black gay men.

Ismael Reed. *Airing Dirty Laundry.* Reading, MA: Addison-Wesley, 1993. Provocative, iconoclastic, and entertaining essays by an insightful cultural critic.

"A NATION WITHIN A NATION"

Since the first Africans were brought to these shores in the seventeenth century, black people have been a constant and distinct presence in America. During the prolonged course of the Atlantic slave trade, approximately 600,000 Africans were sold into servitude in what became the United States. By the outbreak of the Civil War in 1861 there were nearly four million African Americans in this country. Today black people number over 30 million and make up slightly over 10 percent of the nation's population.

Initially regarded merely as an enslaved labor force to produce cash crops and not as a people who would or could enjoy an equal role in the political and social affairs of American society, African Americans constituted a separate ethnic, racial, and cultural group. For more than two centuries they remained outcasts.

People of African descent developed decidedly ambivalent relationships with the white majority in America. Never fully accepted and never fully rejected, black people relied on their own resources as they created their own institutions and communities. In 1852 Martin Delany declared, "We are a nation within a nation." A half century later W. E. B. Du Bois observed that the black man wanted to retain his African identity and to be an American as well. "He would not Africanize America, for America has too much to teach the world and Africa. He would not bleach his Negro soul in a flood of white Americanism, for he knows that Negro blood has a message for the world. He simply wishes to make it possible for a man to be both a Negro and an American, without being cursed and spit upon by his fellows, without having the doors of Opportunity closed roughly in his face."

Sometimes in desperation or disgust, some black people have been willing to abandon America or reject assimilation. The slaves who engaged in South Carolina's 1739 Stono rebellion attempted to reach Spanish Florida. As early as 1773, slaves in Massachusetts pledged to go to Africa after emancipation. From the 1790s to the start of the Civil War, visions of nationhood in Africa attracted a minority of African Americans. During the 1920s, Marcus Garvey and the Universal Negro Improvement Association glorified Africa while seeking black autonomy in the United States. By the 1950s, Elijah Muhammad, Malcolm X, and the Nation of Islam attracted black people by emphasizing a separate black destiny.

Yet in spite of the horrors of slavery, the indignity and cruelty of Jim Crow, and the unrelenting violence and discrimination inflicted on people of color, most African Americans have not rejected America but worked and struggled to participate fully in the American way of life. African slaves accepted elements of Christianity, and their descendants found solace in their spiritual beliefs. Black Americans have embraced American principles of brotherhood, justice, fairness, and equality before the law that are embedded in the Declaration of Independence and the Constitution. Again and again, African Americans have insisted that America be America, that the American majority live up to its professed ideals and values.

The nation within a nation has never been homogeneous. There have been persistent class, gender, and color divisions. There have been tensions and ideological conflicts among black leaders and organizations as they sought strategies to overcome racial inequities and white supremacy. Some leaders, such as Booker T. Washington, have emphasized self-reliance and economic advancement while others, including W. E. B. Du Bois and leaders of the NAACP, have advocated full inclusion in the nation's political, economic, and social fabric.

Furthermore, African Americans have been far more than victims, than an exploited labor force, than the subjects of segregation and stereotypes. They have contributed enormously to the development and character of American society and culture. As slaves, they provided billions of hours of unrequited labor to the American economy. Black people established churches, schools, and colleges that continue to thrive. Black people demonstrated a willingness to fight and die for a country that did not fully accept or appreciate their sacrifices. African Americans have made remarkable and innovative contributions to art, music, folklore, science, politics, and athletics that have shaped and enriched American society.

America is no longer what it was in 1700, 1800, or 1900. Chattel slavery ended in 1865. White supremacy is no longer fashionable or openly acceptable. Legal segregation was prohibited a generation ago. The capacity and willingness of Americans of diverse backgrounds and origins to live together in harmony has vastly improved in recent decades. Though we are now in the twenty-first century, the long odyssey of people of African descent has not ended nor will it end in the immediate future. Black people will continue to help mold and define this society, and they will continue to be "a nation within a nation."

Appendix

THE DECLARATION OF INDEPENDENCE

When in the course of human events it becomes necessary for one people to dissolve the political bands which have connected them with another and to assume, among the powers of the earth, the separate and equal station to which the laws of nature and of nature's God entitle them, a decent respect to the opinions of mankind requires that they should declare the causes which impel them to the separation.

We hold these truths to be self-evident, that all men are created equal; that they are endowed by their Creator with certain unalienable rights; that among these are life, liberty, and the pursuit of happiness. That, to secure these rights, governments are instituted among men, deriving their just powers from the consent of the governed; that, whenever any form of government becomes destructive of these ends, it is the right of the people to alter or to abolish it, and to institute a new government, laying its foundation on such principles, and organizing its powers in such form, as to them shall seem most likely to effect their safety and happiness. Prudence, indeed, will dictate that governments long established should not be changed for light and transient causes; and, accordingly, all experience hath shown that mankind are more disposed to suffer, while evils are sufferable, than to right themselves by abolishing the forms to which they are accustomed. But when a long train of abuses and usurpations, pursuing invariably the same object, evinces a design to reduce them under absolute despotism, it is their right, it is their duty, to throw off such government and to provide new guards for their future security. Such has been the patient sufferance of these colonies, and such is now the necessity which constrains them to alter their former systems of government. The history of the present King of Great Britain is a history of repeated injuries and usurpations, all having, in direct object, the establishment of an absolute tyranny over these States. To prove this, let facts be submitted to a candid world:

He has refused his assent to laws the most wholesome and necessary for the public good.

He has forbidden his governors to pass laws of immediate and pressing importance, unless suspended in their operation till his assent should be obtained; and, when so suspended, he has utterly neglected to attend to them.

He has refused to pass other laws for the accommodation of large districts of people, unless those people would relinquish the right of representation in the legislature, a right inestimable to them and formidable to tyrants only.

He has called together legislative bodies at places unusual, uncomfortable, and distant from the depository of their public records, for the sole purpose of fatiguing them into compliance with his measures.

He has dissolved representative houses, repeatedly for opposing, with manly firmness, his invasions on the rights of the people.

He has refused, for a long time after such dissolutions, to cause others to be elected; whereby the legislative powers, incapable of annihilation, have returned to the people at large for their exercise; the state remaining, in the meantime, exposed to all the danger of invasion from without and convulsions within.

He has endeavored to prevent the population of these States; for that purpose, obstructing the laws for naturalization of foreigners, refusing to pass others to encourage their migration hither, and raising the conditions of new appropriations of lands.

He has obstructed the administration of justice by refusing his assent to laws for establishing judiciary powers.

He has made judges dependent on his will alone for the tenure of their offices and the amount and payment of their salaries.

He has erected a multitude of new offices and sent hither swarms of officers to harass our people and eat out their substance.

He has kept among us, in time of peace, standing armies, without the consent of our legislatures.

He has affected to render the military independent of, and superior to, the civil power.

He has combined with others to subject us to a jurisdiction foreign to our Constitution and unacknowledged by our laws, giving his assent to their acts of pretended legislation—

For quartering large bodies of armed troops among us;

For protecting them, by mock trial, from punishment for any murders which they should commit on the inhabitants of these States;

For cutting off our trade with all parts of the world;

For imposing taxes on us without our consent;

For depriving us, in many cases, of the benefit of trial by jury;

For transporting us beyond seas to be tried for pretended offences;

For abolishing the free system of English laws in a neighboring province, establishing therein an arbitrary government, and enlarging its boundaries, so as to render it at once an example and fit instrument for introducing the same absolute rule into these colonies;

For taking away our charters, abolishing our most valuable laws, and altering, fundamentally, the powers of our governments.

For suspending our own legislatures and declaring themselves invested with power to legislate for us in all cases whatsoever.

He has abdicated government here by declaring us out of his protection and waging war against us.

He has plundered our seas, ravaged our coasts, burnt our towns, and destroyed the lives of our people.

He is, at this time, transporting large armies of foreign mercenaries to complete the works of death, desolation, and tyranny already begun with circumstances of cruelty and perfidy scarcely paralleled in the most barbarous ages, and totally unworthy the head of a civilized nation.

He has constrained our fellow citizens, taken captive on the high seas, to bear arms against their country, to become the executioners of their friends and brethren, or to fall themselves by their hands.

He has excited domestic insurrections amongst us and has endeavored to bring on the inhabitants of our frontiers, the merciless Indian savages, whose known rule of warfare is an undistinguished destruction of all ages, sexes, and conditions.

In every stage of these oppressions, we have petitioned for redress in the most humble terms; our repeated petitions have been answered only by repeated injury. A prince whose character is thus marked by every act which may define a tyrant is unfit to be the ruler of a free people.

Nor have we been wanting in attention to our British brethren. We have warned them, from time to time, of attempts made by their legislature to extend an unwarrantable jurisdiction over us. We have reminded them of the circumstances of our emigration and settlement here. We have appealed to their native justice and magnanimity, and we have conjured them, by the ties of our common kindred, to disavow these usurpations, which would inevitably interrupt our connections and correspondence. They, too, have been deaf to the voice of justice and consanguinity. We must, therefore, acquiesce in the necessity which denounces our separation, and hold them, as we hold the rest of mankind, enemies in war, in peace, friends.

We, therefore, the representatives of the United States of America, in general Congress assembled, appealing to the Supreme Judge of the world for the rectitude of our intentions, do, in the name and by the authority of the good people of these colonies, solemnly publish and declare, that these united colonies are, and of right ought to be, free and independent states: that they are absolved from all allegiance to the British Crown, and that all political connection between them and the state of Great Britain is, and ought to be, totally dissolved; and that, as free and independent states, they have full power to levy war, conclude peace, contract alliances, establish commerce, and to do all other acts and things which independent states may of right do. And, for the support of this declaration, with a firm reliance on the protection of Divine Providence, we mutually pledge to each other our lives, our fortunes, and our sacred honor.

Proposed clause on the slave trade omitted from the final draft of the Declaration

He has waged cruel war against human nature itself, violating its most sacred rights of life and liberty in the person of a distant people who never offended him; captivating and carrying them into slavery in another hemisphere, or to incur miserable death in their transportation thither. This piratical warfare, the opprobrium of infidel powers, is the warfare of the Christian king of Great Britain. Determined to keep open a market where men should be bought and sold, he has prostituted his negative for suppressing every legislative attempt to prohibit or restrain this execrable commerce.

SELECTED ARTICLES AND AMENDMENTS FROM THE CONSTITUTION OF THE UNITED STATES

The following selections from the Constitution are clauses and amendments that pertain specifically to the stature of African Americans within the United States.

THE PREAMBLE

We the people of the United States, in order to form a more perfect union, establish justice, insure domestic tranquility, provide for the common defense, promote the general welfare, and secure the blessings of liberty to ourselves and our posterity, do ordain and establish this Constitution for the United States of America. . . .

ARTICLE I

SECTION 2

3. Representatives and direct taxes shall be apportioned among the several States which may be included within this Union, according to their respective numbers, which shall be determined by adding to the whole number of free persons, including those bound to service for a term of years, and excluding Indians not taxed, three fifths of all other persons. The actual enumeration shall be made within three years after the first meeting of the Congress of the United States, and within every subsequent term of ten years, in such manner as they shall by law direct.

SECTION 9

1. The migration or importation of such persons as any of the States now existing shall think proper to admit, shall not be prohibited by the Congress prior to the year one thousand eight hundred and eight, but a tax or duty may be imposed on such importation, not exceeding ten dollars for each person.

AMENDMENT XIII [RATIFIED DECEMBER 6, 1865]

SECTION 1.   Neither slavery nor involuntary servitude, except as punishment for crime whereof the party shall have been duly convicted, shall exist within the United States, or any place subject to their jurisdiction.

SECTION 2.   Congress shall have power to enforce this article by appropriate legislation.

AMENDMENT XIV [RATIFIED JULY 9, 1868]

SECTION 1.   All persons born or naturalized in the United States, and subject to the jurisdiction thereof, are citizens of the United States and of the State wherein they reside. No State shall make or enforce any law which shall abridge the privileges or immunities of citizens of the United States; nor shall any State deprive any person of life, liberty, or property, without due process of law; nor deny to any person within its jurisdiction the equal protection of the laws.

SECTION 2.   Representatives shall be apportioned among the several States according to their respective numbers, counting the whole number of persons in each State, excluding Indians not taxed. But when the right to vote at any election for the choice of electors for President and Vice President of the United States, representatives in Congress, the executive and judicial officers of a State, or the members of the legislature thereof, is denied to any of the male inhabitants of such State, being twenty-one years of age, and citizens of the United States, or in any way abridged, except for participating in rebellion, or other crime, the basis of representation there shall be reduced in the proportion which the number of such male citizens shall bear to the whole number of male citizens twenty-one years of age in such State.

SECTION 3.   No person shall be a senator or representative in Congress, or elector of President and Vice President, or hold any office, civil or military, under the United States, or under any State, who having previously taken an oath, as a member of Congress, or as an officer of the United States, or as a member of any State legislature, or as an executive or judicial officer of any State, to support the Constitution of the United States, shall have engaged in insurrection or rebellion against the same, or given aid or comfort to the enemies thereof. But Congress may by a vote of two thirds of each House, remove such disability.

SECTION 4.   The validity of the public debt of the United States, authorized by law, including debts incurred for payment of pensions and bounties for services in suppressing insurrection or rebellion; shall not be questioned. But neither the United States nor any State shall assume or pay any debt or obligation incurred in aid of insurrection or rebellion against the United States, or any claim for the loss or emancipation of any slave; but all such debts, obligations, and claims shall be held illegal and void.

SECTION 5.   The Congress shall have the power to enforce, by appropriate legislation, the provisions of this article.

AMENDMENT XV [RATIFIED FEBRUARY 30, 1870]

SECTION 1.   The right of citizens of the United States to vote shall not be denied or abridged by the United States or by any State on account of race, color, or previous condition of servitude.

SECTION 2. The Congress shall have power to enforce this article by appropriate legislation.

AMENDMENT XXIV [RATIFIED JANUARY 23, 1964]

SECTION 1. The right of citizens of the United States to vote in any primary or other election for President or Vice President, for electors for President or Vice President, or for Senator or Representative in Congress, shall not be denied or abridged by the United States or any State by reason of failure to pay any poll tax or other tax.

SECTION 2. The Congress shall have power to enforce this article by appropriate legislation.

THE EMANCIPATION PROCLAMATION

BY THE PRESIDENT OF THE UNITED STATES OF AMERICA

Whereas, on the twenty-second day of September, in the year of our Lord one thousand eight hundred and sixty-two, a proclamation was issued by the President of the United States, containing, among other things, the following, to wit:

> That on the first day of January, in the year of our Lord one thousand eight hundred and sixty-three, all persons held as slaves within any State or designated part of a State, the people whereof shall then be in rebellion against the United States, shall be then, thenceforward, and forever free; and the Executive Government of the United States, including the military and naval authority thereof, will recognize and maintain the freedom of such persons, and will do no act or acts to repress such persons, or any of them, in any efforts they may make for their actual freedom.

> That the Executive will, on the first day of January aforesaid, by proclamation, designate the States and parts of States, if any, in which the people thereof, respectively, shall then be in rebellion against the United States; and the fact that any State, or the people thereof, shall on that day be, in good faith, represented in the Congress of the United States by members chosen thereto at elections wherein a majority of the qualified voters of such State shall have participated, shall, in the absence of strong countervailing testimony, be deemed conclusive evidence that such State, and the people thereof, are not then in rebellion against the United States.

Now, therefore I, Abraham Lincoln, President of the United States, by virtue of the power in me vested as Commander-in-Chief, of the Army and Navy of the United States in time of actual armed rebellion against the authority and government of the United States, and as a fit and necessary war measure for suppressing said rebellion, do, on this first day of January, in the year of our Lord one thousand eight hundred and sixty-three, and in accordance with my purpose so to do publicly proclaimed for the full period of one hundred days, from the day first above mentioned, order and designate as the States and parts of States wherein the people thereof respectively, are this day in rebellion against the United States, the following, to wit:

Arkansas, Texas, Louisiana, (except the Parishes of St. Bernard, Plaquemines, Jefferson, St. John, St. Charles, St. James Ascension, Assumption, Terrebonne, Lafourche, St. Mary, St. Martin, and Orleans, including the City of New Orleans), Mississippi, Alabama, Florida, Georgia, South Carolina, North Carolina, and Virginia, (except the forty-eight counties designated as West Virginia, and also the counties of Berkley, Accomac, Northampton, Elizabeth City, York, Princess Ann, and Norfolk, including the cities of Norfolk and Portsmouth), and which excepted parts, are for the present, left precisely as if this proclamation were not issued.

And by virtue of the power, and for the purpose aforesaid, I do order and declare that all persons held as slaves within said designated States, and parts of States, are, and henceforward shall be free; and that the Executive government of the United States, including the military and naval authorities thereof, will recognize and maintain the freedom of said persons.

And I hereby enjoin upon the people so declared to be free to abstain from all violence, unless in necessary self-defense; and I recommend to them that, in all cases when allowed, they labor faithfully for reasonable wages.

And I further declare and make known, that such persons of suitable condition, will be received into the armed service of the United States to garrison forts, positions, stations, and other places, and to man vessels of all sorts in said service.

And upon this act, sincerely believed to be an act of justice, warranted by the Constitution, upon military necessity, I invoke the considerate judgment of mankind, and the gracious favor of Almighty God.

In witness whereof, I have hereunto set my hand and caused the seal of the United States to be affixed. Done at the City of Washington, this first day of January, in the year of our Lord one thousand eight hundred and sixty-three, and of the Independence of the United States of America the eighty-seventh.

By the President: Abraham Lincoln

William H. Seward, Secretary of State

KEY PROVISIONS OF THE CIVIL RIGHTS ACT OF 1964

AN ACT

To enforce the constitutional right to vote, to confer jurisdiction upon the district courts of the United States to provide injunctive relief against discrimination in public accommodations, to authorize the Attorney General to institute suits to protect constitutional rights in public facilities and public education, to extend the Commission on Civil Rights, to prevent discrimination in federally assisted programs, to establish a Commission on Equal Employment Opportunity, and for other purposes.

TITLE I—VOTING RIGHTS

SECTION 101.   . . . (2) No person acting under color of law shall—

(A) In determining whether any individual is qualified under State law or laws to vote in any Federal election, apply any standard, practice, or procedure different from the standards, practices, or procedures applied under such law or laws to other individuals within the same county, parish, or similar political subdivision who have been found by State officials to be qualified to vote;

(B) deny the right of any individual to vote in any Federal election because of an error or omission on any record or paper relating to any application, registration, or other act requisite to voting, if such error or omission is not material in determining whether such individual is qualified under State law to vote in such election;

(C) employ any literacy test as a qualification for voting in any Federal election unless (i) such test is administered to each individual and is conducted wholly in writing, and (ii) a certified copy of the test and of the answers given by the individual is furnished to him within twenty-five days of the submission of his request made within the period of time during which records and papers are required to be retained and preserved . . .

TITLE II—INJUNCTIVE RELIEF AGAINST DISCRIMINATION IN PLACES OF PUBLIC ACCOMMODATION

SECTION 201.   (a) All persons shall be entitled to the full and equal enjoyment of the goods, services, facilities, and privileges, advantages and accommodations of any place of public accommodation, as defined in this section, without discrimination or segregation on the ground of race, color, religion, or national origin. (b) Each of the following establishments which serves the public is a place of public accommodation within the meaning of this title if its operations effect commerce, or if discrimination or segregation by it is supported by State action:

(1) any inn, hotel, motel, or other establishment which provides lodging to transient guests, other than an establishment located within a building which contains not more than five rooms for rent or hire and which is actually occupied by the proprietor of such establishment as his residence;

(2) any restaurant, cafeteria, lunchroom, lunch counter, soda fountain, or other facility principally engaged in selling food for consumption on the premises, including, but not limited to, any such facility located on the premises of any retail establishment; or any gasoline station;

(3) any motion picture house, theater, concert hall, sports arena, stadium or other place of exhibition or entertainment;

(4) any establishment (A)(i) which is physically located within the premises of any establishment otherwise covered by this subsection, or (ii) within the premises of which is physically located any such covered establishment, and (B) which holds itself out as serving patrons of such covered establishment. . . .

(d) Discrimination or segregation by an establishment is supported by State action within the meaning of this title if such discrimination or segregation

(1) is carried on under color of any law, statute, ordinance, or regulation; or

(2) is carried on under color of any custom or usage required or enforced by officials of the State or political subdivision thereof; or

(3) is required by action of the State or political subdivision thereof. . . .

SECTION 202.   All persons shall be entitled to be free, at any establishment or place, from discrimination or segregation of any kind on the ground of race, color, religion, or national origin, if such discrimination or segregation is or purports to be required by any law, statute, ordinance, regulation, rule, or order of a State or any agency or political subdivision thereof.

SECTION 203.   No person shall (a) withhold, deny, or attempt to withhold or deny, or deprive or attempt to deprive, any person of any right or privilege secured by section 201 or 202, or (b) intimidate, threaten, or coerce, or attempt to intimidate, threaten, or coerce any person with the purpose of interfering with any right or privilege secured by section 201 or 202, or (c) punish or attempt to punish any person for exercising or attempting to exercise any right or privilege secured by section 201 or 202.

TITLE III—DESEGREGATION OF PUBLIC FACILITIES

SECTION 301.   (a) Whenever the Attorney General receives a complaint in writing signed by an individual to the effect that he is being deprived of or threatened with the loss of his right to the equal protection of the laws, on account of his race, color, religion, or national origin, by being denied equal utilization of any public facility which is owned, operated, or managed by or on behalf of any State or subdivision thereof, other than a public school or public college as defined in section 401 of title IV hereof, and the Attorney General believes the complaint is meritorious and certifies that the signer or signers of such complaint are unable, in his judgment, to initiate and maintain appropriate legal proceedings for relief and that the institution of an action will materially further the orderly progress of desegregation in public facilities, the Attorney General is authorized to institute for or in the name of the United States a civil action in any appropriate district court of the United States against such parties and for such relief as may be appropriate. And such court shall have and shall exercise jurisdiction of proceedings instituted pursuant to this section. The Attorney General may implead as defendants such additional parties as are or become necessary to the grant of effective relief hereunder. . . .

TITLE VI—NONDISCRIMINATION IN FEDERALLY ASSISTED PROGRAMS

SECTION 601.   No person in the United States shall, on the ground of race, color, or national origin, be excluded from participation in, be denied the benefits of, or be subjected to discrimination under any program or activity receiving Federal financial assistance.

SECTION 602.   Each Federal department and agency which is empowered to extend Federal financial assistance to any program or activity, by way of grant, loan, or contract other than a contract of insurance or guaranty, is authorized and directed to effectuate the provisions of section 601 with respect to such program or activity by issuing rules, regulations, or orders of general applicability which shall be consistent with achievement of the objectives of the statute authorizing the financial assistance in connection with which the action is taken. No such rule, regulation, or order shall become effective unless and until approved by the President. Compliance with any requirement adopted pursuant to this section may be effected

> (1) by the termination of or refusal to grant or to continue assistance under such program or activity to any recipient as to whom there has been an express finding on the record, after opportunity for hearing, of a failure to comply with such requirement, but such termination or refusal shall be limited to the particular political entity, or part thereof, or other recipient as to whom such a finding has been made and, shall be limited in its effect to the particular program, or part thereof, in which such non-compliance has been so found . . .

TITLE VII—EQUAL EMPLOYMENT OPPORTUNITY . . .

Discrimination Because of Race, Color, Religion, Sex, or National Origin

SECTION 703.   (a) it shall be an unlawful employment practice for an employer—

(1) to fail or refuse to hire or to discharge any individual, or otherwise to discriminate against any individual with respect to his compensation, terms, conditions, or privileges of employment, because of such individual's race, color, religion, sex, or national origin; or

(2) to limit, segregate, or classify his employees in any way which would deprive or tend to deprive any individual of employment opportunities or otherwise adversely affect his status as an employee, because of such individual's race, color, religion, sex, or national origin.

(b) it shall be an unlawful employment practice for an employment agency to fail or refuse to refer for employment, or otherwise to discriminate against, any individual because of his race, color, religion, sex, or national origin, or to classify or refer for employment any individual on the basis of his race, color, religion, sex, or national origin.

(c) it shall be an unlawful employment practice for a labor organization—

(1) to exclude or to expel from its membership, or otherwise to discriminate against, any individual because of his race, color, religion, sex, or national origin;

(2) to limit, segregate, or classify its membership, or to classify or fail or refuse to refer for employment any individual, in any way which would deprive or tend to deprive any individual of employment opportunities, or would limit such employment opportunities or otherwise adversely affect his status as an employee or as an applicant for employment, because of such individual's race, color, religion, sex, or national origin; or

(3) to cause or attempt to cause an employer to discriminate against an individual in violation of this section.

(d) It shall be an unlawful employment practice for any employer, labor organization, or joint labor-management committee controlling apprenticeship or other training or re-training, including on-the-job training programs to discriminate against any individual because of his race, color, religion, sex, or national origin in admission to, or employment in, any program established to provide apprenticeship or other training . . .

Other Unlawful Employment Practices

SECTION 704.   (a) It shall be an unlawful employment practice for an employer to discriminate against any of his employees or applicants for employment, for an employment agency to discriminate against any individual, or for a labor organization to discriminate against any member thereof or applicant for membership, because he has opposed any practice made an unlawful employment practice by this title, or because he has made a charge, testified, assisted, or participated in any manner in an investigation, proceeding, or hearing under this title.

(b) It shall be an unlawful employment practice for an employer, labor organization, or employment agency to print or publish or cause to be printed or published any notice or advertisement relating to employment by such an employer or membership in or any classification or referral for employment by such a labor organization, or relating to any classification or referral for employment by such an employment agency, indicating any preference, limitation, specification, or discrimination, based on race, color, religion, sex, or national origin, except that such a notice or advertisement may indicate a preference, limitation, specification, or discrimination based on religion, sex, or national origin when religion, sex, or national origin is a bona fide occupational qualification for employment.

Equal Employment Opportunity Commission

SECTION 705.   (a) There is hereby created a Commission to be known as the Equal Employment Opportunity Commission, which shall be composed of five members, not more than three of whom shall be members of the same political party, who shall be appointed by the President by and with the advice and consent of the Senate. One of the original members shall be appointed for a term of one year, one for a term of two years, one for a term of three years, one for a term of four years, and one for a term of five years, beginning from the date of enactment of this title, but their successors shall be appointed for terms of five years each, except that any individual chosen to fill a vacancy shall be appointed only for the unexpired term of the member whom he shall succeed. The President shall designate one member to serve as Chairman of the Commission, and one member to serve as Vice Chairman. The Chairman shall be responsible on behalf of the Commission for the administrative operations of the Commission, and shall appoint, in accordance with the civil service laws, such officers, agents, attorneys, and employees as it deems necessary to assist it in the performance of its functions and to fix their compensation in accordance with Classification Act of 1949, as amended. . . .

Key Provisions of the Voting Rights Act of 1965

An Act

To enforce the fifteenth amendment to the Constitution of the United States, and for other purposes.

Be it enacted by the Senate and House of Representatives of the United States of America in Congress assembled, That this Act shall be known as the "Voting Rights Act of 1965."

SECTION 2.   No voting qualification or prerequisite to voting, or standard, practice, or procedure shall be imposed or applied by any State or political subdivision to deny or abridge the right of any citizen of the United States to vote on account of race or color.

SECTION 4.   (a) To assure that the right of citizens of the United States to vote is not denied or abridged on account of race or color, no citizen shall be denied the right to vote in any Federal, State, or local election because of his failure to comply with any test or device in any State with respect to which the determinations have been made under subsection (b) ... (1) demonstrate the ability to read, write, understand, or interpret any matter, (2) demonstrate any educational achievement or his knowledge of any particular subject, (3) possess good moral character, or (4) prove his qualifications by the voucher of registered voters or members of any other class. ...

SECTION 10.   (a) The Congress finds that the requirement of the payment of a poll tax as a precondition to voting (i) precludes persons of limited means from voting or imposes unreasonable financial hardship upon such persons as a precondition to their exercise of the franchise, (ii) does not bear a reasonable relationship to any legitimate State interest in the conduct of elections, and (iii) in some areas has the purpose or effect of denying persons the right to vote because of race or color. Upon the basis of these findings, Congress declares that the constitutional right of citizens to vote is denied or abridged in some areas by the requirement of the payment of a poll tax as a precondition to voting.

SECTION 11.   (a) No person acting under color of law shall fail or refuse to permit any person to vote who is entitled to vote under any provision of this Act or is otherwise qualified to vote, or willfully fail or refuse to tabulate, count, and report such person's vote.

(b) No person, whether acting under color of law or otherwise, shall intimidate, threaten, or coerce, or attempt to intimidate, threaten, or coerce any person for voting or attempting to vote, or intimidate, threaten, or coerce, or attempt to intimidate, threaten, or coerce any person for urging or aiding any person to vote or attempt to vote, or intimidate, threaten, or coerce any person for exercising any powers or duties under section 3 (a), 6, 8, 9, 10, or 12 (e).

Additional Bibliography

Chapter 1   Africa

Prehistory, Egypt, and Kush

William Y. Adams, *Nubia—Corridor to Africa*, Princeton, NJ: Princeton University Press, 1984.

Martin Bernal. *Black Athena; The Afroasiatic Roots of Classical Civilization*. New Brunswick, NJ: Rutgers University, 1987.

Nicholas C. Grimal. *A History of Ancient Egypt*. Oxford, England: Blackwell, 1993.

Donald Johanson, Lenora Johanson, and Blake Edgar. *Ancestors: In Search of Human Origins*. New York: Villard Books, 1994.

Susan Kent. *Gender in African Prehistory*. Walnut Creek, CA: Altamira, 1998.

Mary R. Lefkowitz and Guy MacLean Rogers, eds. *Black Athena Revisited*. Chapel Hill, NC: University of North Carolina Press, 1996.

Michael Rice. *Egypt's Making: The Origins of Ancient Egypt, 5000–2000 B.C.* New York: Routledge, 1990.

Derek A. Welsby. *The Kingdom of Kush: The Napatan and Merotic Empires*. Princeton, NJ: Markus Wiener, 1998.

Western Sudanese Empires

Nehemiah Levtzion. *Ancient Ghana and Mali*. London: Methuen, 1973.

Nehemiah Levtzion and J. F. Hopkins, eds. *Corpus of Early Arabic Sources for West African History*. New York: Cambridge University Press, 1981.

Roland Oliver and Brian M. Fagan. *Africa in the Iron Age*. New York: Cambridge University Press, 1975.

Roland Oliver and Caroline Oliver, eds. *Africa in the Days of Exploration*. Englewood Cliffs, NJ: Prentice Hall, 1965.

J. Spencer Trimington. *A History of Islam in West Africa*. New York: Oxford University Press, 1962.

The Forest Region of the Guinea Coast

I. A. Akinjogbin. *Dahomey and Its Neighbors, 1708–1818*. New York: Cambridge University Press, 1967.

Daryll Forde, ed. *African Worlds*. New York: Oxford University Press, 1954.

Samuel Johnson. *History of the Yorubas*. Lagos: C.M.S., 1921.

Robert W. July. *Precolonial Africa*. New York: Scribner's, 1975.

Robin Law. *The Oyo Empire, c. 1600–c. 1836*. Oxford: Clarendon, 1977.

R. S. Rattray. *Ashanti*. Oxford: Clarendon, 1969.

Walter Rodney. *A History of the Upper Guinea Coast, 1545–1800*. Oxford: Clarendon, 1970.

Culture

Harold Courlander, ed. *A Treasury of African Folklore*. New York: Marlowe, 1996.

Susan Denyer. *African Traditional Architecture: An Historical and Geographical Perspective*. London: Heinemann, 1978.

Ruth Finnegan. *Oral Literature in Africa*. 1970; reprint, Nairobi: Oxford University Press, 1976.

Werner Gillon. *A Short History of African Art*. New York: Viking, 1984.

Paulin J. Hountondji. *African Philosophy: Myth and Reality*. Bloomington: University of Indiana Press, 1984.

John S. Mbiti. *An Introduction to African Religion*. London: Heinemann, 1975.

J. H. Kwabena Nketia. *The Music of Africa*. New York: Norton, 1974.

Oyekan Owomoyela. *Yoruba Trickster Tales*. Lincoln: University of Nebraska Press, 1977.

Chapter 2   Middle Passage

The Slave Trade in Africa

Bernard Lewis. *Race and Slavery in the Middle East: An Historical Enquiry*. New York: Oxford University Press, 1990.

Patrick Manning. *Slavery and African Life: Occidental, Oriental, and African Slave Trades*. New York: Cambridge University Press, 1990.

Suzanne Miers and Igor Kopytoff, eds. *Slavery in Africa*. Madison: University of Wisconsin Press, 1977.

Suzanne Miers and Richard Roberts. *The End of Slavery in Africa*. Madison: University of Wisconsin Press, 1988.

Claire C. Robertson and Martin A. Klein, eds. *Slavery in Africa*. Madison: University of Wisconsin Press, 1983.

Elizabeth Savage, ed. *The Human Commodity: Perspectives on the Trans-Saharan Slave Trade*. London: Frank Cass, 1992.

John K. Thornton. *The Kingdom of Kongo: Civil War and Transition, 1641–1718*. Madison: University of Wisconsin Press, 1983.

The Atlantic Slave Trade

Paul Edwards, ed. *Equiano's Travels*. London: Heinemann, 1967.

Herbert S. Klein. *The Middle Passage: Comparative Studies in the Atlantic Slave Trade*. Princeton, NJ: Princeton University Press, 1978.

Paul E. Lovejoy. *Africans in Bondage: Studies in Slavery and the Slave Trade*. Madison: University of Wisconsin Press, 1986.

Rosemarie Robotham, ed. *Spirits of the Passage: The Transatlantic Slave Trade in the Seventeenth Century*. New York: Simon & Schuster, 1997.

Lief Svalesen. *The Slave Ship Fredensborg*. Bloomington: Indiana University Press, 2000.

Hugh Thomas. *The Slave Trade: The Story of the Atlantic Slave Trade, 1440–1870*. New York: Simon & Schuster, 1997.

Vincent Bakpetu Thompson. *The Making of the African Diaspora in the Americas, 1441–1900*. New York: Longman, 1987.

John Vogt. *Portuguese Rule on the Gold Coast, 1469–1682*. Athens: University of Georgia Press, 1979.

James Walvin. *Making the Black Atlantic: Britain and the African Diaspora*. New York: Cassell, 2000.

The West Indies

Edward Brathwaite. *The Development of Creole Society in Jamaica, 1770–1820*. New York: Oxford University Press, 1971.

William Claypole and John Robottom. *Caribbean Story: Foundations*. Kingston: Longman, 1980.

Melville J. Herskovits. *The Myth of the Negro Past*. Boston: Beacon, 1941.

Clarence J. Munford. *The Black Ordeal of Slavery and Slave Trading in the French West Indies, 1625–1715*. Lewiston, NY: Mellen, 1991.

Keith Albert Sandiford. *The Cultural Politics of Sugar: Caribbean Slavery and Narratives of Colonialism*. New York: Cambridge University Press, 2000. The Granger Collection, New York.

Chapter 3   Black People in Colonial, North America

Colonial Society

Wesley Frank Craven. *The Southern Colonies in the Seventeenth Century, 1607–1689*. Baton Rouge: Louisiana State University Press, 1949.

Jack P. Greene. *Pursuits of Happiness: The Social Development of Early Modern British Colonies and the Formatiosn of American Culture*. Chapel Hill: University of North Carolina Press, 1988.

John J. McCusker and Russell R. Menard. *The Economy of British America, 1607–1789*. Chapel Hill: University of North Carolina Press, 1985.

Gary B. Nash. *Red, White, and Black: The Peoples of Early America*, 3d ed. Englewood Cliffs, NJ: Prentice Hall, 1992.

Origins of Slavery and Racism in the Western Hemisphere

David Brion Davis. *The Problem of Slavery in Western Culture*. Ithaca, NY: Cornell University Press, 1966.

Seymour Drescher. *From Slavery to Freedom: Comparative Studies of the Rise and Fall of Atlantic Slavery*. New York: New York University Press, 1999.

David Eltis. *The Rise of African Slavery in the Americas*. New York: Cambridge University Press, 2000.

Ronald Sanders. *Lost Tribes and Promised Lands: The Origins of American Racism*. Boston: Little, Brown, 1978.

Frank Tannenbaum. *Slave and Citizen: The Negro in the Americas*. New York: Knopf, 1946.

Betty Wood. *The Origins of American Slavery: Freedom and Bondage in the English Colonies*. New York: Hill and Wang, 1997.

The Chesapeake

Barbara A. Faggins. *Africans and Indians: An Afrocentric Analysis of Contacts between Africans and Indians in Colonial Virginia*. New York: Routledge, 2001.

Allan Kulikoff. *Tobacco and Slaves: The Development of Southern Cultures in the Chesapeake, 1680–1800*. Chapel Hill: University of North Carolina Press, 1986.

Gloria L. Main. *Tobacco Colony: Life in Early Maryland, 1650–1720*. Princeton, NJ: Princeton University Press, 1982.

Edmund S. Morgan. *American Slavery, American Freedom: The Ordeal of Colonial Virginia.* New York: Norton, 1975.

Isaac Rhys. *The Transformation of Virginia, 1740–1790.* New York: Norton, 1982.

Mechal Sobel. *The World They Made Together: Black and White Values in Eighteenth-Century Virginia.* Princeton, NJ: Princeton University Press, 1987.

The Carolina and Georgia Low Country

Judith Ann Carney. *Black Rice: The African Origins of Rice Cultivation in the Americas.* Cambridge, MA: Harvard University Press, 2001.

Alan Gallay. *The Indian Slave Trade: The Rise of the English Empire in the American South, 1670–1717.* New Haven: Yale University Press, 2002.

Daniel C. Littlefield. *Rice and Slaves: Ethnicity and the Slave Trade in Colonial South Carolina.* Baton Rouge: Louisiana State University Press, 1981.

Julia Floyd Smith. *Slavery and Rice Culture in Low Country Georgia, 1750–1860.* Knoxville: University of Tennessee Press, 1985.

Betty Wood. *Slavery in Colonial Georgia, 1730–1775.* Athens: University of Georgia Press, 1984.

The Northern Colonies

Lorenzo J. Greene. *The Negro in Colonial New England, 1620–1776.* 1942; reprint, New York: Atheneum, 1968.

Leslie M. Harris. *In the Shadow of Slavery: African Americans in New York City, 1626–1863.* Chicago: University of Chicago Press, 2003.

Graham R. Hodges. *Root and Branch: African Americans in New York and East Jersey, 1613–1863.* Chapel Hill: University of North Carolina Press, 1999.

Edgar J. McManus. *Black Bondage in the North.* Syracuse, NY: Syracuse University Press, 1973.

William D. Piersen. *Black Yankees: The Development of an Afro-American Subculture in Eighteenth-Century New England.* Amherst: University of Massachusetts Press, 1988.

Spanish Borderlands and Louisiana

Lynn Robinson Bailey. *Indian Slave Trade and the Southwest: A Study of Slave-Taking and the Traffic in Indian Captives.* Los Angeles: Westernlore, 1966.

Gwendolyn Midlo Hall. *Africans in Colonial Louisiana: The Development of Afro-Creole Culture in the Eighteenth Century.* Baton Rouge: Louisiana State University Press, 1992.

Thomas N. Ingersoll. *Mammon and Manon in Early New Orleans: The First Slave Society in the Deep South, 1718–1819.* Knoxville: University of Tennessee Press, 1999.

John L. Kessell. *Spain in the Southwest: A Narrative History of Colonial New Mexico, Arizona, Texas, and California.* Norman: University of Oklahoma Press, 2002.

Jane Landers. *Black Society in Spanish Florida.* Urbana: University of Illinois Press, 1999.

Michael M. Swann. *Migrants in the Mexican North: Mobility, Economy, and Society in a Colonial World.* Boulder, CO: Westview, 1989.

Quintard Taylor. *In Search of the Racial Frontier: African Americans in the American West, 1528–1990.* New York: Norton, 1998.

African-American Culture

John B. Boles. *Black Southerners, 1619–1869.* Lexington: University Press of Kentucky, 1983.

Joanne Brooks. *American Lazarus: Religion and the Rise of African American and Native American Literature.* New York: Oxford University Press, 2003.

Dickson D. Bruce. *The Origins of African American Literature, 1680–1865.* Charlottesville: University Press of Virginia, 2001.

Margaret W. Creel. *A Peculiar People: Slave Religion and Community Culture among the Gullahs.* New York: New York University Press, 1988.

Sylviane A. Diouf. *Servants of Allah: African Muslims Enslaved in the Americas.* New York: New York University Press, 1998.

Michael Gomez. *Exchanging Our Country Marks: The Transformation of African Identities in the Colonial and Antebellum South.* Chapel Hill: University of North Carolina Press, 1998.

Melville J. Herskovits. *The Myth of the Negro Past.* 1941; reprint, Boston: Beacon, 1990.

Joseph E. Holloway, ed. *Africanisms in American Culture.* Bloomington: Indiana University Press, 1990.

Henry Mitchell. *Black Belief: Folk Beliefs of Blacks in America and West Africa.* New York: Harper & Row, 1975.

Sheila S. Walker, ed. *African Roots/American Culture: Africa and the Creation of the Americas.* Lanham: Rowman and Littlefield, 2001.

Joel Williamson. *New People: Miscegenation and Mulattoes in the United States.* New York: Free Press, 1980.

Black Women in Colonial America

Joan Rezner Gunderson, "The Double Bonds of Race and Sex: Black and White Women in a Colonial Virginia Parish," in Darlene Clark Hine, Wilma King, and Linda Reed, eds., *We Specialize in the Wholly Impossible: A Reader in Black Women's History.* Brooklyn, NY: Carlson, 1995.

Darlene Clark Hine and Kathleen Thompson. *A Shining Thread of Hope: The History of Black Women in America.* New York: Broadway, 1998, Chapter 1.

Jane Kamensky. *The Colonial Mosaic: American Women, 1600–1760: Rising Expectations from the Colonial Period to the American Revolution.* New York: Oxford University Press, 1995.

Jenny Sharpe. *Ghosts of Slavery: A Literary Archaeology of Black Women's Lives.* Minneapolis: University of Minnesota Press, 2003.

Resistance and Revolt

Herbert Aptheker. *American Negro Slave Revolts.* 1943; reprint, New York: International Publishers, 1974.

Thomas J. Davis. *A Rumor of Revolt: The "Great Negro Plot" in Colonial New York.* New York: Free Press, 1985.

Merton L. Dillon. *Slavery Attacked: Southern Slaves and Their Allies, 1619–1865.* Baton Rouge: Louisiana State University Press, 1990.

Eugene D. Genovese. *From Rebellion to Revolution: Afro-American Slave Revolts in the Making of the Modern World.* Baton Rouge: Louisiana State University Press, 1979.

Gerald W. Mullin. *Flight and Rebellion: Slave Resistance in Eighteenth-Century Virginia.* New York: Oxford University Press, 1972.

Michael Mullin. *Africa in America: Slave Acculturization and Resistance in the American South and the British Caribbean, 1736–1831.* Urbana: University of Illinois Press, 1992.

John K. Thornton. *African and Africans in the Making of the Atlantic World, 1400–1800.* New York: Cambridge University Press, 1992.

Chapter 4   Rising Expectations African Americans and the Struggle for Independence, 1763–1783

The Crisis of the British Empire

Stephen Conway. *The British Isles and the War of American Independence.* New York: Oxford University Press, 2000.

Edward Countryman. *The American Revolution.* New York: Hill and Wang, 1975.

Douglas E. Leach. *Roots of Conflict: British Armed Forces and Colonial Americans, 1677–1763.* Chapel Hill: University of North Carolina Press, 1986.

Pauline Maier. *From Resistance to Revolution: Colonial Radicals and the Development of American Opposition to Britain, 1765–1776.* New York: Knopf, 1972.

Peter David Garner Thomas. *Revolution in America: Britain and the Colonies, 1765–1776.* Cardiff, UK: University of Wales, 1992.

The Impact of the Enlightenment

Bernard Bailyn. *The Ideological Origins of the American Revolution.* Cambridge, MA: Harvard University Press, 1967.

Henry Steele Commager. *The Empire of Reason: How Europe Imagined and America Realized the Enlightenment.* Garden City, NY: Anchor, 1977.

Paul Finkelman. *Slavery and the Founders: Race and Liberty in the Age of Jefferson.* London: M. E. Sharpe, 1996.

J. G. A. Pocock. *The Machiavellian Moment: Florentine Political Thought and the Atlantic Republican Tradition.* Princeton, NJ: Princeton University Press, 1975.

Frank Shuffelton, ed. *The American Enlightenment.* Rochester, NY: University of Rochester Press, 1993.

African Americans and the American Revolution

Lerone Bennett Jr. *Before the Mayflower: A History of Black America,* 6th ed. Chicago: Johnson, 1987, Chapter 3.

Ira Berlin. "The Revolution in Black Life," in Alfred F. Young, ed., *The American Revolution: Explorations in the History of American Radicalism.* DeKalb: Northern Illinois University Press, 1976, 349–82.

Jeffrey J. Crow. *The Black Experience in Revolutionary North Carolina.* Raleigh: North Carolina Department of Cultural Resources, 1977.

Merton L. Dillon. *Slavery Attacked: Southern Slaves and Their Allies, 1619–1865.* Baton Rouge: Louisiana State University Press, 1990, Chapter 2.

Sylvia R. Frey. "Between Slavery and Freedom: Virginia Blacks in the American Revolution." *Journal of Southern History,* 69 (August 1983): 375–98.

Jack P. Greene. *All Men Are Created Equal: Some Reflections on the Character of the American Revolution.* Oxford: Clarendon, 1976.

Sidney Kaplan and Emma Nogrady Kaplan. *The Black Presence in the Era of the American Revolution.* Amherst: University of Massachusetts Press, 1989.

Peter Kolchin. *American Slavery, 1619–1877.* New York: Hill and Wang, 1993, Chapter 3.

Duncan McLeod. *Slavery, Race, and the American Revolution.* New York: Cambridge University Press, 1974.

Gary B. Nash. *Forging Freedom: The Formation of Philadelphia's Black Community, 1720–1840.* Cambridge, MA: Harvard University Press, 1988.

John W. Pulis. *Moving On: Black Loyalists in the Afro-Atlantic World.* New York: Garland, 1999.

Peter H. Wood. "'The Dream Deferred': Black Freedom Struggles on the Eve of White Independence," in Gary Y. Okihiro, ed., *In Resistance: Studies in African, Caribbean, and Afro-American History.* Amherst: University of Massachusetts Press, 1986, 166–87.

Antislavery and Emancipation in the North

Robin Blackburn. *The Overthrow of Colonial Slavery, 1776–1848.* New York: Verso, 1988, Chapter 3.

Merton L. Dillon. *The Abolitionists: The Growth of a Dissenting Minority.* New York: Norton, 1974, Chapter 1.

Dwight L. Dumond. *Antislavery: The Crusade for Freedom in America.* 1961; reprint, New York: Norton, 1966.

Joanne Pope Melish. *Disowning Slavery: Gradual Emancipation and "Race" in New England, 1780–1860.* Ithaca, NY: Cornell University Press, 1998.

Gary B. Nash. *Freedom by Degrees: Emancipation in Pennsylvania and Its Aftermath.* New York: Oxford University Press, 1991.

———. *Race and Revolution.* Madison, WI: Madison House, 1990.

James Brewer Stewart. *Holy Warriors: The Abolitionists and American Slavery.* Rev. ed. New York: Hill and Wang, 1997, Chapter 1.

Biography

Silvio A. Bedini. *The Life of Benjamin Banneker.* New York: Scribner, 1972.

Henry Louis Gates Jr. *The Trials of Phillis Wheatley.* New York: Basic Civitas Books, 2003.

William Henry Robinson. *Phillis Wheatley and Her Writings.* New York: Garland, 1984.

Chapter 5 African Americans in the New Nation, 1783–1820

Emancipation in the North

James D. Essig. *The Bonds of Wickedness: American Evangelicals against Slavery, 1770–1808.* Philadelphia: Temple University Press, 1982.

Joanne Pope Melish. *Disowning Slavery: Gradual Emancipation and "Race" in New England, 1780–1860.* Ithaca, NY: Cornell University Press, 1998.

Gary B. Nash and Jean R. Soderlund. *Freedom by Degrees: Emancipation in Pennsylvania and Its Aftermath.* New York: Oxford University Press, 1991.

Shane White. *Somewhat More Independent: The End of Slavery in New York City, 1770–1810.* Athens: University of Georgia Press, 1991.

Arthur Zilversmit. *The First Emancipation: The Abolition of Slavery in the North.* Chicago: University of Chicago Press, 1967.

Proslavery Forces

Paul Finkelman. *Slavery and the Founders: Race and Liberty in the Age of Jefferson.* Armonk: M. E. Sharpe, 1996.

Duncan J. MacLeod. *Slavery, Race, and the American Revolution.* New York: Cambridge University Press, 1974.

Donald G. Nieman. *Promises to Keep: African Americans and the Constitutional Order, 1776 to the Present.* New York: Oxford University Press, 1991.

Donald L. Robinson. *Slavery in the Structure of American Politics, 1765–1820.* New York: Harcourt Brace Jovanovich, 1971.

Larry E. Tise. *Proslavery: A History of the Defense of Slavery in America, 1701–1840.* Athens: University of Georgia Press, 1987.

Free Black Institutions and Migration Movements

Carol V. R. George. *Segregated Sabbaths: Richard Allen and the Emergence of Independent Black Churches, 1760–1840.* New York: Oxford University Press, 1973.

Eddie S. Glaude. *Exodus! Religion, Race, and Nation in Early Nineteenth-Century Black America.* Chicago: University of Chicago Press, 2000.

Sheldon H. Harris. *Paul Cuffe: Black America and the Africa Return.* New York: Simon & Schuster, 1972.

Leon Litwack. *North of Slavery: The Negro in the Free States.* Chicago: University of Chicago Press, 1961.

William A. Muraskin. *Middle-Class Blacks in a White Society: Prince Hall Freemasonry in America.* Berkeley: University of California Press, 1975.

Lamont D. Thomas. *Rise to Be a People: A Biography of Paul Cuffe.* Urbana: University of Illinois Press, 1986.

Julie Winch. *Philadelphia's Black Elite: Activism, Accommodation, and the Struggle for Autonomy,*

1787–1848. Philadelphia: Temple University Press, 1988.

———. *A Gentleman of Color: The Life of James Forten*. New York: Oxford University Press, 2002.

Carter G. Woodson. *The Education of the Negro Prior to 1861*. 1915; reprint, Brooklyn, NY: A&B Books, 1998.

The South

John Hope Franklin. *The Free Negro in North Carolina, 1790–1860*. 1943; reprint, New York: Russell and Russell, 1969.

Peter Kolchin. *American Slavery, 1619–1877*. New York: Hill and Wang, 1993.

John Chester Miller. *The Wolf by the Ears: Thomas Jefferson and Slavery*. 1977; reprint, Charlottesville: University Press of Virginia, 1991.

T. Stephen Whitman. *The Price of Freedom: Slavery and Manumission in Baltimore and Early National Maryland*. Lexington: University of Kentucky Press, 1997.

Slave Revolts, Resistance, and Escapes

Herbert Aptheker. *American Negro Slave Revolts*. 1943; reprint, New York: International, 1983.

Merton L. Dillon. *Slavery Attacked: Southern Slaves and Their Allies, 1619–1865*. Baton Rouge: Louisiana State University Press, 1990.

Eugene D. Genovese. *From Rebellion to Revolution: Afro-American Slave Revolts in the Making of the Modern World*. Baton Rouge: Louisiana State University Press, 1979.

John R. McKivigan and Stanley Harrold, eds. *Antislavery Violence: Sectional, Racial, and Cultural Conflict in Antebellum America*. Knoxville: University of Tennessee Press, 1999.

Gerald W. Mullin. *Flight and Rebellion: Slave Resistance in Eighteenth-Century Virginia*. New York: Oxford University Press, 1972.

James Sidbury. *Ploughshares into Swords: Race, Rebellion, and Identity in Gabriel's Virginia, 1730–1810*. New York: Cambridge University Press, 1998. The Library Company of Philadelphia.

Chapter 6   Life in the Cotton Kingdom

Slavery and Its Expansion

Stanley M. Elkins. *Slavery: A Problem in American Institutional and Intellectual Life*, 3d ed. Chicago: University of Chicago Press, 1976.

Eugene D. Genovese. *The Political Economy of Slavery: Studies in the Economy and Society of the Slave South*. 1961; reprint, New York: Random House, 1967.

Lewis C. Gray. *History of Agriculture in the Southern United States to 1860*. 1933; reprint, Clifton, NJ: A. M. Kelley, 1973.

Roger G. Kennedy. *Mr. Jefferson's Lost Cause: Land, Farmers, Slavery, and the Louisiana Purchase*. New York: Oxford University Press, 2003.

Larry Koger. *Black Slaveowners: Free Black Slave Masters in South Carolina, 1790–1860*. 1985; reprint, Columbia: University of South Carolina Press, 1994.

Donald P. McNeilly. *The Old South Frontier: Cotton Plantations and the Formation of Arkansas Society, 1819–1861*. Fayetteville: University of Arkansas Press, 2000.

John H. Moore. *The Emergence of the Cotton Kingdom in the Old Southwest*. Baton Rouge: Louisiana State University Press, 1988.

Larry Eugene Rivers. *Slavery in Florida: Territorial Days to Emancipation*. Gainsville: University Press of Florida, 2000.

Kenneth M. Stampp. *The Peculiar Institution: Slavery in the Antebellum South*. 1956; reprint, New York: Vintage Books, 1989.

Urban and Industrial Slavery

Ronald L. Lewis. *Coal, Iron, and Slaves: Industrial Slavery in Maryland and Virginia, 1715–1865*. Westport, CT: Greenwood, 1979.

Robert S. Starobin. *Industrial Slavery in the Old South*. New York: Oxford University Press, 1970.

Midori Takagi. *Rearing Wolves to Our Own Destruction: Slavery in Richmond, Virginia, 1782–1865*. Charlottesville: University Press of Virginia, 1999.

Richard C. Wade. *Slavery in the Cities: The South 1820–1860*. 1964; reprint, New York: Oxford University Press, 1967.

The Domestic Slave Trade

Frederic Bancroft. *Slave Trading in the Old South*. 1931; reprint, Columbia: University of South Carolina Press, 1996.

Walter Johnson. *Soul by Soul: Life inside the Antebellum Slave Market*. Cambridge, MA: Harvard University Press, 1999.

Michael Tadman. *Speculators and Slaves: Masters, Traders, and Slaves in the Old South*. 1989; reprint, Madison: University of Wisconsin Press, 1996.

The Slave Community

Ira Berlin. *Generations of Captivity: A History of African-American Slaves.* Cambridge, MA: Harvard University Press, 2003.

John W. Blassingame. *The Slave Community: Plantation Life in the Antebellum South,* 2d ed. New York: Oxford University Press, 1979.

Janet Duitsman Cornelius. *Slave Missions and the Black Church in the Antebellum South.* Columbia: University of South Carolina Press, 1999.

Wilma A. Dunaway. *The African-American Family in Slavery and Emancipation.* New York: Cambridge University Press, 2003.

Eugene D. Genovese. *Roll, Jordan, Roll: The World the Slave Made.* 1974; reprint, Vintage Books, 1976.

Herbert Gutman. *The Black Family in Slavery and Freedom.* 1976; reprint, Vintage Books, 1977.

Charles Joyner. *Down by the Riverside: A South Carolina Community.* Urbana: University of Illinois Press, 1984.

Ann Patton Malone. *Sweet Chariot: Slave Family and Household Structure in Nineteenth-Century Louisiana.* Chapel Hill: Univeristy of North Carolina Press, 1992.

Leslie Howard Owens. *This Species of Property: Slave Life and Culture in the Old South.* 1976; reprint, New York: Oxford University Press, 1977.

Todd L. Savitt. *Medicine and Slavery: The Diseases and Health Care of Blacks in Antebellum Virginia.* Urbana: University of Illinois Press, 1978.

Maria Jenkins Schwartz. *Born in Bondage: Growing Up Enslaved in the Antebellum South.* Cambridge, MA: Harvard University Press, 2000.

Enslaved Women

David Barry Gaspar and Darlene Clark Hine, eds. *More than Chattel: Black Women and Slavery in the Americas.* Bloomington: University of Indiana Press, 1996.

Darlene Clark Hine, Wilma King, and Linda Reed, eds. *"We Specialize in the Wholly Impossible": A Reader in Black Women's History.* Brooklyn, NY: Carlson, 1996.

Patricia Morton, ed. *Discovering the Women in Slavery: Emancipating Perspectives on the American Past.* Athens: University of Georgia Press, 1996.

Deborah Gray White. *Ar'n't I a Woman? Female Slaves in the Plantation South.* New York: Norton, 1985.

Jean Fagan Yellin. *Harriet Jacobs: A Life.* New York: Basic Civitas, 2003.

Slave Culture And Religion

John B. Boles, ed. *Masters and Slaves in the House of the Lord: Race and Religion in the American South, 1740–1870.* Lexington: University Press of Kentucky, 1988.

Janet Duitsman Cornelius. *When I Can Read My Title Clear: Literacy, Slavery, and Religion in the Antebellum South.* Columbia: University of South Carolina Press, 1991.

———. *Slave Missions and the Black Church in the Antebellum South.* Columbia: University of South Carolina Press, 1999.

Sharla M. Fett. *Working Cures: Healing, Health, and Power on Southern Slave Plantations.* Chapel Hill: University of North Carolina Press, 2002.

Lawrence W. Levine. *Black Culture and Black Consciousness: Afro-American Folk Thought from Slavery to Freedom.* New York: Oxford University Press, 1977.

Albert J. Raboteau. *Slave Religion: The "Invisible Institution" in the Antebellum South.* New York: Oxford University Press, 1978.

Chapter 7   Free Black People in Antebellum America

Community Studies

Tommy L. Bogger. *Free Blacks in Norfolk, Virginia, 1790–1860: The Darker Side of Freedom.* Charlottesville: University Press of Virginia, 1997.

Letitia Woods Brown. *Free Negroes in the District of Columbia, 1790–1846.* New York: Oxford University Press, 1972.

Leslie M. Harris. *In the Shadow of Slavery: African Americans in New York City, 1626–1863.* Chicago: University of Chicago Press, 2003.

Graham Russell Hodges. *Root and Branch: African Americans in New York and East Jersey, 1613–1863.* Chapel Hill: University of North Carolina Press, 1999.

———. *Slavery and Freedom in the Rural North: African Americans in Monmouth County, New Jersey, 1665–1865.* Madison, WI: Madison House, 1995.

James Oliver Horton. *Free People of Color: Inside the African-American Community.* Washington, DC: Smithsonian Institution Press, 1993.

James Oliver Horton and Lois E. Horton. *Black Bostonians: Family Life and Community Struggle in the Antebellum North.* New York: Holmes and Meier, 1979.

Gary B. Nash. *Forging Freedom: The Formation of Philadelphia's Black Community, 1720–1840.*

Cambridge, MA: Harvard University Press, 1988.

Christopher Phillips. *Freedom's Port: The African-American Community of Baltimore, 1790–1860.* Urbana: University of Illinois Press, 1997.

Bernard E. Powers Jr. *Black Charlestonians: A Social History, 1822–1885.* Fayetteville: University of Arkansas Press, 1994.

Harry Reed. *Platform for Change: The Foundations of the Northern Free Black Community, 1775–1865.* East Lansing: Michigan State University Press, 1994.

Judith Kelleher Schafer. *Becoming Free, Remaining Free: Manumission and Enslavement in New Orleans, 1846–1862.* Baton Rouge: Louisiana State University Press, 2003.

Julie Winch. *Philadelphia's Black Elite: Activism, Accommodation, and the Struggle for Autonomy, 1787–1848.* Philadelphia: Temple University Press, 1988.

State-Level Studies

Barbara Jeanne Fields. *Slavery and Freedom on the Middle Ground: Maryland during the Nineteenth Century.* New Haven, CT: Yale University Press, 1985.

John Hope Franklin. *The Free Negro in North Carolina, 1790–1860.* Chapel Hill: University of North Carolina Press, 1943.

John H. Russell. *The Free Negro in Virginia, 1619–1865.* 1913; reprint, New York: Negro Universities Press, 1969.

H. E. Sterkx. *The Free Negro in Antebellum Louisiana.* Rutherford, NJ: Fairleigh Dickinson University Press, 1972.

Marina Wilkramangrake. *A World in Shadow—The Free Black in Antebellum South Carolina.* Columbia: University of South Carolina Press, 1973.

Race Relations

Francis D. Adams. *Alienable Rights: The Exclusion of African Americans in a White Man's Land, 1619–2000.* New York: Harper Collins, 2003.

Eugene H. Berwanger. *The Frontier against Slavery: Western Anti-Negro Prejudice and the Slavery Expansion Controversy.* Urbana: University of Illinois Press, 1967.

Phyllis F. Field. *The Politics of Race in New York: The Struggle for Black Suffrage in the Civil War Era.* Ithaca, NY: Cornell University Press, 1982.

Noel Ignatiev. *How the Irish Became White.* New York: Routledge, 1995.

David Roediger. *The Wages of Whiteness: Race and the Making of the American Working Class.* New York: Verso, 1991.

Joel Williamson. *New People: Miscegenation and Mulattoes in the United States.* New York: Free Press, 1980.

Carol Wilson. *Freedom at Risk: The Kidnapping of Free Blacks in America, 1780–1865.* Lexington: University Press of Kentucky, 1994.

Women and Family

Herbert G. Gutman. *The Black Family in Slavery and Freedom, 1750–1925.* New York: Pantheon Books, 1977.

Lynn M. Hudson. *The Making of "Mammy Pleasant": A Black Entrepreneur in Nineteenth-Century San Francisco.* Urbana: University of Illinois Press, 2003.

Jacqueline Jones. *Labor of Love, Labor of Sorrow: Black Women, Work and the Family from Slavery to the Present.* New York: Basic Books, 1985.

Suzanne Lebsock. *The Free Women of Petersburg: Status and Culture in a Southern Town, 1784–1860.* New York: Norton, 1984.

Bert James Loewenberg and Ruth Bogin, eds. *Black Women in Nineteenth-Century American Life.* University Park: Pennsylvania State University Press, 1976.

T. O. Madden Jr., with Ann L. Miller. *We Were Always Free: The Maddens of Culpeper County, Virginia, a 200 Year Family History.* New York: Norton, 1992.

Dorothy Sterling, ed. *We Are Your Sisters: Black Women in the Nineteenth Century.* New York: Norton, 1984.

Institutions and The Black Elite

Vincent P. Franklin. *The Education of Black Philadelphia.* Philadelphia: University of Pennsylvania Press, 1979.

Carlton Mabee. *Black Education in New York State.* Syracuse, NY: Syracuse University Press, 1979.

Eileen Southern. *The Music of Black America,* 2d ed. New York: Norton, 1983.

Loretta J. Williams. *Black Freemasonry and Middle-Class Realities.* Columbia: University of Missouri Press, 1980.

Chapter 8   Opposition to Slavery, 1800–1833

The Relationship Among Evangelicalism, Reform, and Abolitionism

Robert H. Abzug. *Cosmos Crumbling: American Reform and the Religious Imagination.* New York: Oxford University Press, 1994.

Gilbert H. Barnes. *The Antislavery Impulse, 1830–1844.* 1933; reprint, Gloucester, MA: Peter Smith, 1973.

Ronald G. Walters. *American Reformers, 1815–1860.* Baltimore: Johns Hopkins University Press, 1978.

American Abolitionism Before 1831

David Brion Davis. *The Problem of Slavery in the Age of Revolution.* Ithaca, NY: Cornell University Press, 1975.

———. *The Problem of Slavery in Western Culture.* Ithaca, NY: Cornell University Press, 1966.

———. *Slavery and Human Progress.* Ithaca, NY: Cornell University Press, 1987.

Merton L. Dillon. *The Abolitionists: The Growth of a Dissenting Minority.* New York: Norton, 1974.

———. *Benjamin Lundy and the Struggle for Negro Freedom.* Urbana: University of Illinois Press, 1966.

Richard S. Newman. *The Transformation of American Abolitionism: Fighting Slavery in the Early Republic.* Chapel Hill: University of North Carolina Press, 2002.

Sean Wilentz, ed. *David Walker's Appeal.* 1829; reprint, New York: Hill and Wang, 1995.

Slave Revolts and Conspiracies

Herbert Aptheker. *American Negro Slave Revolts.* 1943; new ed., New York: International Publishers, 1974.

Douglas R. Egerton. *Gabriel's Rebellion: The Virginia Slave Conspiracies of 1800 & 1802.* Chapel Hill: University of North Carolina Press, 1993.

———. *He Shall Go Out Free: The Lives of Denmark Vesey.* Madison, WI: Madison House, 1999.

David P. Feggus, ed. *The Impact of the Haitian Revolution on the Atlantic World.* Columbia: University of South Carolina Press, 2001.

Alfred N. Hunt. *Haiti's Influence on Antebellum America: Slumbering Volcano in the Caribbean.* Baton Rouge: Louisiana State University Press, 1988.

John Lofton. *Denmark Vesey's Revolt: The Slave Plot That Lit a Fuse to Fort Sumter.* Kent, OH: Kent State University Press, 1983.

Stephen B. Oates. *The Fires of the Jubilee: Nat Turner's Fierce Rebellion.* New York: Harper & Row, 1975.

Black Abolitionism and Black Nationalism

Eddie S. Glaude. *Exodus!: Religion, Race, and Nation in Early Nineteenth-Century Black America.* Chicago: Unversity of Chicago Press, 2000.

Leroy Graham. *Baltimore: Nineteenth-Century Black Capital.* Washington, DC: University Press of America, 1982.

Vincent Harding. *There Is a River: The Black Struggle for Freedom in America.* New York: Harcourt, Brace, Jovanovich, 1981.

Floyd J. Miller. *The Search for Black Nationality: Black Colonization and Emigration, 1787–1863.* Urbana: University of Illinois Press, 1975.

Marilyn Richardson. *Maria W. Stewart: America's First Black Woman Political Writer.* Bloomington: Indiana University Press, 1987.

Sterling Stuckey. *Slave Culture: Nationalist Theory and the Foundations of Black America.* New York: Oxford University Press, 1987.

Lamont D. Thomas. *Rise to Be a People: A Biography of Paul Cuffe.* Urbana: University of Illinois Press, 1986.

Julie Winch. *Philadelphia's Black Elite: Activism, Accommodation, and Struggle for Autonomy, 1787–1840.* Philadelphia: Temple University Press, 1988.

Chapter 9   Let Your Motto Be Resistance, 1833–1850

General Studies of the Antislavery Movement

Herbert Aptheker. *Abolitionism: A Revolutionary Movement.* Boston: Twayne, 1989.

Merton L. Dillon. *The Abolitionists: The Growth of a Dissenting Minority.* New York: Norton, 1974.

Lawrence J. Friedman. *Gregarious Saints: Self and Community in American Abolitionism, 1830–1870.* New York: Cambridge University Press, 1982.

Stanley Harrold. *American Abolitionists.* Harlow, England: Longman, 2001.

———. *The Rise of Aggressive Abolitionism: Addresses to the Slaves.* Lexington: University Press of Kentucky, 2004.

James Brewer Stewart. *Holy Warriors: The Abolitionists and American Slavery,* 2d ed. New York: Hill and Wang, 1997.

The Black Community

John Brown Childs. *The Political Black Minister: A Study in Afro-American Politics and Religion.* Boston: G. K. Hall, 1980.

Leonard P. Curry. *The Free Black in Urban America, 1800–1850: The Shadow of a Dream.* Chicago: University of Chicago Press, 1981.

Martin E. Dann. *The Black Press, 1827–1890.* New York: Capricorn, 1971.

James Oliver Horton and Lois E. Horton. *In Hope of Liberty: Culture, Community, and Protest among Northern Free Blacks, 1700–1860.* New York: Oxford University Press, 1997.

Patrick Rael. *Black Identity and Black Protest in the Antebellum North.* Chapel Hill: University of North Carolina Press, 2002.

David E. Swift. *Black Prophets of Justice: Activist Clergy before the Civil War.* Baton Rouge: Louisiana State University Press, 1989.

Black Abolitionists

Howard Holman Bell. *A Survey of the Negro Convention Movement, 1830–1861.* New York: Arno, 1969.

————, ed. *Minutes of the Proceedings of the National Negro Conventions, 1830–1864.* New York: Arno, 1969.

R. J. M. Blackett. *Building an Antislavery Wall: Blacks in the Atlantic Abolitionist Movement, 1830–1860.* Baton Rouge: Louisiana State University Press, 1983.

Women

Blanch Glassman-Hersh. *Slavery of Sex: Feminist-Abolitionists in Nineteenth-Century America.* Urbana: University of Illinois Press, 1978.

Darlene Clark Hine, ed. *Black Women in American History: From Colonial Times through the Nineteenth Century.* 4 vols. New York: Carlson, 1990.

Julie Roy Jeffrey. *The Great Silent Army of Abolitionism: Ordinary Women in the Antislavery Movement.* Chapel Hill: University of North Carolina Press, 1998.

Jean Fagan Yellin. *Women and Sisters: Antislavery Feminists in American Culture.* New Haven, CT: Yale University Press, 1990.

Biography

Catherine Clinton. *Harriet Tubman: The Road to Freedom.* New York: Little, Brown, 2003.

William S. McFeely. *Frederick Douglass.* New York: Simon & Schuster, 1991.

Nell Irvin Painter. *Sojourner Truth: A Life, A Symbol.* New York: Norton, 1996.

Joel Schor. *Henry Highland Garnet: A Voice of Black Radicalism in the Nineteenth Century.* Westport, CT: Greenwood, 1977.

James Brewer Stewart. *William Lloyd Garrison and the Challenge of Emancipation.* Arlington Heights, IL.: Harlan Davidson, 1992.

Victor Ullman. *Martin R. Delany: The Beginnings of Black Nationalism.* Boston: Beacon, 1971.

Underground Railroad

Larry Gara. *The Liberty Line: The Legend of the Underground Railroad.* Lexington: University of Kentucky Press, 1961.

Stanley Harrold. *Subversives: Antislavery Community in Washington, D.C., 1828–1865.* Baton Rouge: Louisiana State University Press, 2003.

Wilbur H. Siebert. *The Underground Railroad from Slavery to Freedom.* 1898; reprint, New York: Arno, 1968.

William Still. *The Underground Railroad.* 1871; reprint, Chicago: Johnson Publishing, 1970.

Black Nationalism

Rodney Carlisle. *The Roots of Black Nationalism.* Port Washington, NY: Kennikat, 1975.

Floyd J. Miller. *The Search for Black Nationality: Black Emigration and Colonization, 1787–1863.* Urbana: University of Illinois Press, 1975.

Chapter 10   And Black People Were at the Heart of It: The United States Disunites over Slavery

California and the Compromise of 1850

Eugene H. Berwanger. *The Frontier against Slavery: Western Anti-Negro Prejudice and the Slave Extension Controversy.* Urbana: University of Illinois Press, 1967.

Holman Hamilton. *Prologue to Conflict: The Crisis and Compromise of 1850.* Lexington: University of Kentucky Press, 1964.

Rudolph M. Lapp. *Blacks in Gold Rush California.* New Haven, CT: Yale University Press, 1977.

The Fugitive Slave Law and Its Victims

Stanley W. Campbell. *The Slave Catchers: Enforcement of the Fugitive Slave Law, 1850–1860.* Chapel Hill: University of North Carolina Press, 1968.

Gary Collison. *Shadrach Minkins.* Cambridge, MA: Harvard University Press, 1998.

Albert J. von Frank. *The Trials of Anthony Burns.* Cambridge, MA: Harvard University Press, 1998.

Jonathan Katz. *Resistance at Christiana: The Fugitive Slave Rebellion at Christiana, Pennsylvania, September 11, 1851: A Documentary Account.* New York: Crowell, 1974.

Thomas P. Slaughter. *Bloody Dawn: The Christiana Riot and Violence in the Antebellum North.* New York: Oxford University Press, 1991.

The Late 1850s

Walter Ehrlich. *They Have No Rights: Dred Scott's Struggle for Freedom.* Westport, CT: Greenwood Press, 1979.

Don E. Fehrenbacher. *The Dred Scott Case: Its Significance in American Law and Politics.* New York: Oxford University Press, 1978.

Robert W. Johannsen. *Stephen A. Douglas.* New York: Oxford University Press, 1973.

Kenneth M. Stampp. *America in 1857: A Nation on the Brink.* New York: Oxford University Press, 1990.

John Brown and the Raid on Harpers Ferry

Paul Finkelman. *And His Soul Goes Marching On: Responses to John Brown and the Harpers Ferry Raid.* Charlottesville: University of Virginia Press, 1995.

Truman Nelson. *The Old Man John Brown at Harpers Ferry.* New York: Holt, Rinehart, & Winston, 1973.

Stephen Oates. *To Purge This Land with Blood: A Biography of John Brown.* New York: Harper & Row, 1970.

Benjamin Quarles. *Blacks on John Brown.* Urbana: University of Illinois Press, 1972.

Secession

William L. Barney. *The Road to Secession.* New York: Praeger, 1972.

Steven A. Channing. *Crisis of Fear: Secession in South Carolina.* New York: Simon & Schuster, 1970.

Kenneth M. Stampp. *And the War Came: The North and the Secession Crisis, 1860–1861.* Baton Rouge: Louisiana State University Press, 1950.

Abraham Lincoln

Gabor Boritt, ed. *The Lincoln Enigma.* New York: Oxford University Press, 2001.

David Herbert Donald. *Lincoln.* New York: Simon & Schuster, 1995.

Stephen B. Oates. *With Malice toward None: A Life of Abraham Lincoln.* New York: Harper & Row, 1977.

Benjamin Thomas. *Abraham Lincoln: A Biography.* New York: Alfred A. Knopf, 1952.

Novels

Martin R. Delany. *Blake or the Huts of America.* Boston: Beacon Press, 1970.

Harriet Beecher Stowe. *Uncle Tom's Cabin, or Life among the Lowly.* New York: Modern Library, 1985.

Chapter 11 Liberation: African Americans and the Civil War

Military

Joseph T. Glatthaar. *Forged in Battle: The Civil War Alliance of Black Soldiers and White Officers.* New York: The Free Press, 1990.

———. *The March to the Sea and Beyond: Sherman's Troops in the Savannah and Carolina Campaign.* New York: New York University Press, 1985.

Herman Hattaway and Archer Jones. *How the North Won: A Military History of the Civil War.* Urbana: University of Illinois Press, 1983.

Geoffrey Ward and Ken Burns. *The Civil War.* New York: Alfred A. Knopf, 1990.

Stephen R. Wise. *Gate of Hell: Campaign for Charleston Harbor, 1863.* Columbia: University of South Carolina Press, 1994.

African Americans and The War

Peter Burchard. *One Gallant Rush: Robert Gould Shaw and His Brave Black Regiment.* New York: St. Martin's Press, 1965.

Catherine Clinton. *Harriet Tubman: The Road to Freedom.* Boston: Little, Brown, 2004.

Ella Forbes. *African American Women during the Civil War.* New York: Garland, 1998.

Kate Clifford Larson. *Bound for the Promised Land: Harriet Tubman, Portrait of an American Hero.* New York: Ballantine, 2004.

Leon Litwack. *Been in the Storm So Long: The Aftermath of Slavery.* New York: Alfred A. Knopf, 1979.

Edward A. Miller. *Gullah Statesman: Robert Smalls from Slavery to Congress, 1839–1915.* Columbia: University of South Carolina Press, 1995.

Benjamin Quarles. *The Negro in the Civil War.* Boston: Little, Brown, 1953.

Willie Lee Rose. *Rehearsal for Reconstruction: The Port Royal Experiment.* Indianapolis: Bobbs Merrill, 1964.

Noah A. Trudeau. *Like Men of War: Black Troops in the Civil War, 1862–1865.* Boston: Little, Brown, 1998.

Bell I. Wiley. *Southern Negroes, 1861–1865.* New Haven, CT: Yale University Press, 1938.

Documents, Letters, and Other Sources

Virginia M. Adams, ed. *On the Altar of Freedom: A Black Soldier's Civil War Letters from the Front.* [Corporal James Henry Gooding]. Amherst: University of Massachusetts, 1991.

Ira Berlin et al., eds. "Freedom: A Documentary History of Emancipation, 1861–1867," Series 1, Volume I, *The Destruction of Slavery*. New York: Cambridge University Press, 1985.

———. "Freedom: A Documentary History of Emancipation, 1861–1867," Series 1, Volume III, *The Wartime Genesis of Free Labor: The Lower South*. New York: Cambridge University Press, 1990.

Robert F. Durden. *The Gray and the Black: The Confederate Debate on Emancipation*. Baton Rouge: Louisiana State University Press, 1972.

Michael P. Johnson and James L. Roark, eds. *No Chariot Letdown: Charleston's Free People of Color on the Eve of the Civil War*. Chapel Hill: University of North Carolina Press, 1984.

James McPherson. *The Negro's Civil War: How American Negroes Felt and Acted during the War for the Union*. New York: Pantheon, 1965.

Edwin S. Redkey, ed. *A Grand Army of Black Men: Letters from African American Soldiers in the Union Army, 1861–1865*. New York: Cambridge University Press, 1992.

Reminiscences

Thomas Wentworth Higginson. *Army Life in a Black Regiment*. Boston: Beacon Press, 1962.

Elizabeth Keckley. *Behind the Scenes: Or Thirty Years a Slave and Four Years in the White House*. New York: Oxford University Press, 1968.

Susie King Taylor. *Reminiscences of My Life in Camp*. Boston: Taylor, 1902.

Chapter 12   The Meaning of Freedom: The Promise of Reconstruction, 1865–1868

Education

James D. Anderson. *The Education of Blacks in the South, 1860–1935*. Chapel Hill: University of North Carolina Press, 1988.

Ronald E. Butchart. *Northern Schools, Southern Blacks, and Reconstruction: Freedmen's Education, 1862–1875*. Westport: Greenwood Press, 1981.

Edmund L. Drago. *Initiative, Paternalism, and Race Relations: Charleston's Avery Normal Institute*. Athens: University of Georgia Press, 1990.

Robert C. Morris. *Reading, 'Riting, and Reconstruction: The Education of the Freedmen in the South, 1861–1890*. Chicago: University of Chicago Press, 1981.

Joe M. Richardson. *Christian Reconstruction: The American Missionary Association and Southern Blacks, 1861–1890*. Athens: University of Georgia Press, 1986.

Willie Lee Rose. *Rehearsal for Reconstruction: The Port Royal Experiment*. Indianapolis: Bobbs Merrill, 1964.

Brenda Stevenson, ed. *The Journals of Charlotte Forten Grimke*. New York: Oxford University Press, 1988.

Land and Labor

Paul A. Cimbala and Randall M. Miller, eds. *The Freedmen's Bureau and Reconstruction*. New York: Fordham University Press, 1999.

Barbara J. Fields. *Slavery and Freedom on the Middle Ground: Maryland during the Nineteenth Century*. New Haven, CT: Yale University Press, 1985.

Jacqueline Jones. *Labor of Love, Labor of Sorrow: Black Women, Work and Family, from Slavery to the Present*. New York: Basic Books, 1985.

Edward Magdol. *A Right to the Land: Essays on the Freedmen's Community*. Westport, CT: Greenwood Press, 1977.

Claude F. Oubre. *Forty Acres and a Mule: The Freedmen's Bureau and Black Landownership*. Baton Rouge: Louisiana State University Press, 1978.

Dylan C. Penningroth. *The Claims of Kinfolk: African American Property and Community in the Nineteenth-Century South*. Chapel Hill: University of North Carolina Press, 2003.

Roger L. Ransom and Richard Sutch. *One Kind of Freedom: The Economic Consequences of Emancipation*. New York: Cambridge University Press, 1977.

Julie Saville. *The Work of Reconstruction: From Slave to Wage Labor in South Carolina, 1860–1870*. New York: Cambridge University Press, 1994.

James D. Schmidt. *Free to Work: Labor, Law, Emancipation, and Reconstruction, 1815–1880*. Athens: University of Georgia Press, 1998.

Leslie A. Schwalm. *A Hard Fight for We: Women's Transition from Slavery to Freedom in South Carolina*. Urbana: University of Illinois Press, 1997.

Black Communities

John W. Blassingame. *Black New Orleans, 1860–1880*. Chicago: University of Chicago Press, 1973.

Cyprian Davis. *The History of Black Catholics in the United States*. New York: Crossroad, 1990.

Robert F. Engs. *Freedom's First Generation: Black Hampton, Virginia, 1861–1890*. Philadelphia: University of Pennsylvania Press, 1979.

William E. Montgomery. *Under Their Own Vine and Fig Tree, The African American Church in the South 1865–1900*. Baton Rouge: Louisiana State University Press, 1993.

Bernard E. Powers, Jr. *Black Charlestonians: A Social History, 1822–1885*. Fayetteville: University of Arkansas Press, 1994.

Clarence E. Walker. *A Rock in a Weary Land: The African Methodist Episcopal Church during the Civil War and Reconstruction*. Baton Rouge: Louisiana State University Press, 1982.

James M. Washington. *Frustrated Fellowship: The Black Baptist Quest for Social Power*. Macon, GA: Mercer University Press, 1986.

Chapter 13   The Meaning of Freedom: The Failure of Reconstruction

Reconstruction in Specific States

Jane Dailey. *Before Jim Crow: The Politics of Race in Post Emancipation Virginia*. Chapel Hill: University of North Carolina Press, 2000.

Edmund L. Drago. *Black Politicians and Reconstruction in Georgia*. Athens: University of Georgia Press, 1982.

———. *Hurrah for Hampton: Black Red Shirts in South Carolina during Reconstruction*. Fayetteville: University of Arkansas Press, 1998.

Luther P. Jackson. *Negro Officeholders in Virginia, 1865– 1895*. Norfolk, VA: Guide Quality Press, 1945.

Peter Kolchin. *First Freedom: The Responses of Alabama's Blacks to Emancipation and Reconstruction*. Westport, CT: Greenwood, 1972.

Merline Pitre. *Through Many Dangers, Toils, and Snares: The Black Leadership of Texas, 1868–1900*. Austin, TX: Eakin Press, 1985.

Joe M. Richardson. *The Negro in the Reconstruction of Florida, 1865–1877*. Tallahassee: Florida State University Press, 1965.

Buford Stacher. *Blacks in Mississippi Politics, 1865–1900*. Washington, DC: University Press of America, 1978.

Ted Tunnell. *Crucible of Reconstruction: War, Radicalism and Race in Louisiana, 1862–1877*. Baton Rouge: Louisiana State University Press, 1984.

Charles Vincent. *Black Legislators in Louisiana during Reconstruction*. Baton Rouge: Louisiana State University Press, 1976.

Joel Williamson. *After Slavery: The Negro in South Carolina: 1861–1877*. Chapel Hill: University of North Carolina Press, 1965.

National Politics: Andrew Johnson and the Radical Republicans

Michael Les Benedict. *A Compromise of Principle: Congressional Republicans and Reconstruction*. New York: Norton, 1974.

Dan T. Carter. *When the War Was Over: The Failure of Self-Reconstruction in the South, 1865–1867*. Baton Rouge: Louisina State University Press, 1983.

Michael W. Fitzgerald. *The Union League Movement in the Deep South*. Baton Rouge: Louisiana State University Press, 1989.

Eric L. McKitrick. *Andrew Johnson and Reconstruction, 1865–1867*. Chicago: University of Chicago Press, 1960.

James M. McPherson. *The Struggle for Equality: Abolitionists and the Negro in the Civil War and Reconstruction*. Princeton, NJ: Princeton University Press, 1964.

Hans L. Trefousse. *The Radical Republicans: Lincoln's Vanguard for Racial Justice*. Baton Rouge: Louisiana State University Press, 1969.

Economic Issues: Land, Labor, and the Freedmen's Bank

Elizabeth Bethel. *Promiseland: A Century of Life in a Negro Community*. Philadelphia: Temple University Press, 1981.

Carol R. Bleser. *The Promised Land: The History of the South Carolina Land Commission, 1869–1890*. Columbia: University of South Carolina Press, 1969.

Sharon Ann Holt. *Making Freedom Pay: North Carolina Freed People Working for Themselves, 1865–1900*. Athens: University of Georgia Press, 2000.

Lynda J. Morgan. *Emancipation in Virginia's Tobacco Belt*. Athens: University of Georgia Press, 1992.

Donald G. Nieman. *To Set the Law in Motion: The Freedmen's Bureau and Legal Rights for Blacks, 1865–1869*. Millwood, NY: KTO, 1979.

Carl R. Osthaus. *Freedmen, Philanthropy and Fraud: A History of the Freedman's Savings Bank*. Urbana: University of Illinois Press, 1976.

Violence and The Ku Klux Klan

George C. Rable. *But There Was No Peace: The Role of Violence in the Politics of Reconstruction*. Athens: University of Georgia Press, 1984.

Allen W. Trelease. *White Terror: The Ku Klux Klan Conspiracy and Southern Reconstruction*. New York: Harper & Row, 1973.

Lou Falkner Williams. *The Great South Carolina Ku Klux Klan Trials, 1871–1872.* Athens: University of Georgia Press, 1996.

Autobiography and Biography

Mifflin Wistar Gibbs. *Shadow & Light: An Autobiography.* Lincoln: University of Nebraska Press, 1995.

Peter D. Klingman. *Josiah Walls.* Gainesville: University Presses of Florida, 1976.

Peggy Lamson. *The Glorious Failure: Black Congressman Robert Brown Elliott and Reconstruction in South Carolina.* New York: Norton, 1973.

Edward A. Miller. *Gullah Statesman: Robert Smalls: From Slavery to Congress, 1839–1915.* Columbia: University of South Carolina Press, 1995.

Loren Schweninger. James T. *Rapier and Reconstruction.* Chicago: University of Chicago Press, 1978.

Okon E. Uya. *From Slavery to Public Service: Robert Smalls, 1839–1915.* New York: Oxford University Press, 1971.

Chapter 14   White Supremacy Triumphant: African Americans in the South in the Late Nineteenth Century

State and Local Studies

Eric Anderson. *Race and Politics in North Carolina, 1872–1901: The Black Second.* Baton Rouge: Louisiana State University Press, 1981.

David Cecelski and Timothy B. Tyson, eds. *Democracy Betrayed: The Wilmington Race Riot and Its Legacy.* Chapel Hill: University of North Carolina Press, 1998.

Helen G. Edmonds. *The Negro and Fusion Politics in North Carolina, 1894–1901.* Chapel Hill: University of North Carolina Press, 1951.

William Ivy Hair. *Carnival of Fury: Robert Charles and the New Orleans Riot of 1900.* Baton Rouge: Louisiana State University Press, 1976.

Neil R. McMillen. *Dark Journey: Black Mississippians in the Age of Jim Crow.* Urbana: University of Illinois Press, 1989.

H. Leon Prather. *We Have Taken a City: Wilmington Racial Massacre and Coup of 1898.* Rutherford: Fairleigh Dickinson University Press, 1984.

David M. Oshinsky. *"Worse Than Slavery": Parchman Farm and the Ordeal of Jim Crow Justice.* New York: The Free Press, 1999.

George B. Tindall. *South Carolina Negroes, 1877–1900.* Columbia: University of South Carolina Press, 1952.

Vernon Wharton. *The Negro in Mississippi, 1865–1890.* Chapel Hill: University of North Carolina Press, 1947.

Biographies and Autobiographies

Albert S. Broussard. *African-American Odyssey: The Stewarts, 1853–1963.* Lawrence: University Press of Kansas, 1998.

Alfreda Duster, ed. *Crusade for Justice: The Autobiography of Ida B. Wells.* Chicago: University of Chicago Press, 1972.

Henry O. Flipper. *The Colored Cadet at West Point.* New York: Arno Press, 1969.

John F. Marszalek Jr. *Court Martial: The Army vs. Johnson Whittaker.* New York: Scribner, 1972.

Linda McMurry. *To Keep the Waters Troubled: The Life of Ida B. Wells.* New York: Oxford University Press, 1998.

Patricia A. Schechter. *Ida B. Wells-Barnett and American Reform, 1882–1930.* Chapel Hill: University of North Carolina Press, 2001.

Politics and Segregation

Grace Hale. *Making Whiteness: The Culture of Segregation in the South, 1890–1940.* New York: Pantheon Books, 1998.

J. Morgan Kousser. *The Shaping of Southern Politics: Suffrage Restriction and the Establishment of the One-Party South, 1880–1910.* New Haven, CT: Yale University Press, 1974.

Michael Perman. *Struggle for Mastery: Disfranchisement in the South, 1888–1908.* Chapel Hill: University of North Carolina Press, 2001.

Lynching

James Allen, Hinton Als, John Lewis, and Leon F. Litwack. *Without Sanctuary: Lynching Photography in America.* Santa Fe, NM: Twin Palms Books, 2000.

W. Fitzhugh Brundage, ed. *Under Sentence of Death: Lynching in the South.* Chapel Hill: University of North Carolina Press, 1997.

W. Fitzhugh Brundage. *Lynching in the New South: Georgia and Virginia, 1880–1930.* Urbana: University of Illinois Press, 1993.

Sandra Gunning. *Race, Rape, and Lynching: The Red Record of American Literature, 1890–1912.* New York: Oxford University Press, 1996.

National Association for the Advancement of Colored People. *Thirty Years of Lynching in the United States, 1889–1918.* New York: NAACP, 1919.

The West

Robert G. Athearn. *In Search of Canaan: Black Migration to Kansas, 1879–80.* Lawrence: Regents Press of Kansas, 1978.

Jacob U. Gordon. *Narratives of African Americans in Kansas, 1870–1992.* Lewiston, NY: Edward Mellon Press, 1993.

Nell Irvin Painter. *Exodusters: Black Migration to Kansas after Reconstruction.* New York: Alfred A. Knopf, 1977.

Quintard Taylor. *In Search of the Racial Frontier: African Americans in the American West, 1528–1990.* New York: Norton, 1998.

Migration, Mobility, and Land Ownership

William Cohen. *At Freedom's Edge: Black Mobility and the Southern White Quest for Racial Control, 1861–1915.* Baton Rouge: Louisiana State University Press, 1991.

Pete Daniel. *The Shadow of Slavery: Peonage in the South, 1901–1969.* Urbana: University of Illinois Press, 1972.

Edward Royce. *The Origins of Southern Sharecropping.* Philadelphia: Temple University Press, 1993.

Loren Schweninger. *Black Property Owners in the South, 1790–1915.* Urbana: University of Illinois Press, 1990.

Chapter 15 Black Southerners Challenge White Supremacy

Education

Eric Anderson and Alfred A. Moss Jr. *Dangerous Donations: Northern Philanthropy and Southern Black Education, 1902–1930.* Columbia: University of Missouri Press, 1999.

James D. Anderson and V. P. Franklin, eds. *New Perspectives on Black Education.* Boston: G. K. Hall, 1978.

Henry A. Bullock. *A History of Negro Education in the South from 1619 to the Present.* Cambridge, MA: Harvard University Press, 1967.

Religion

Stephen W. Angell. *Bishop Henry McNeal Turner and African American Religion in the South.* Knoxville: University of Tennessee Press, 1992.

Cyprian Davis. *The History of Black Catholics in the United States.* New York: Crossroad, 1990.

Harold T. Lewis. *Yet with a Steady Beat: The African American Struggle for Recognition in the Episcopal Church.* Valley Forge, PA: Trinity Press International, 1996.

Iain MacRobert. *The Black Roots and White Racism of Early Pentecostalism in the USA.* Basingstoke, England: Macmillan, 1988.

James M. O'Toole. *Passing for White: Race, Religion, and the Healy Family, 1820–1920.* Amherst: University of Massachusetts Press, 2002.

Edwin S. Redkey, ed. *The Writings and Speeches of Henry McNeal Turner.* New York: Arno Press, 1971.

Clarence E. Walker. *A Rock in a Weary Land: The African Methodist Episcopal Church during the Civil War and Reconstruction.* Baton Rouge: Louisiana State University Press, 1982.

The Military and the West

John M. Carroll, ed. *The Black Military Experience in the American West.* New York: Liveright, 1973.

Willard B. Gatewood, ed. *Smoked Yankees and the Struggle for Empire: Letters from Negro Soldiers, 1898–1902.* Urbana: University of Illinois Press, 1971.

William Loren Katz. *The Black West.* New York: Touchstone Books, 1996.

William H. Leckie. *The Buffalo Soldiers: A Narrative of the Negro Cavalry in the West.* Norman: University of Oklahoma Press, 1967.

Paul W. Stewart and Wallace Yvonne Ponce. *Black Cowboys.* Broomfield, CO: Phillips, 1986.

John D. Weaver. *The Brownsville Raid.* New York: Norton, 1971.

Labor

Tera W. Hunter. *To 'Joy My Freedom: Southern Black Women's Lives and Labors after the Civil War.* Cambridge, MA: Harvard University Press, 1997.

Gerald D. Jaynes. *Branches without Roots: Genesis of the Black Working Class in the American South, 1862–1882.* New York: Oxford University Press, 1986.

The Professions

V. N. Gamble. *The Black Community Hospital: Contemporary Dilemmas in Historical Perspective.* New York: Garland, 1989.

Darlene Clark Hine. *Speak Truth to Power: Black Professional Class in United States History.* Brooklyn, NY: Carlson, 1996.

J. Clay Smith Jr. *Emancipation: The Making of the Black Lawyer, 1844–1944.* Philadelphia: University of Pennsylvania Press, 1993.

J. Clay Smith Jr., ed. *Rebels in Law: Voices in History of Black Women Lawyers.* Ann Arbor: University of Michigan Press, 1998.

Susan L. Smith. *Sick and Tired of Being Sick and Tired: Black Women's Health Activism in America, 1890–1950.* Philadelphia: University of Pennsylvania Press, 1995.

Thomas J. Ward Jr. *Black Physicians in the Jim Crow South.* Fayetteville: University of Arkansas Press, 2003.

Music

W. C. Handy. *Father of the Blues: An Autobiography.* New York: Macmillan, 1941.

John Edward Hasse, ed. *Ragtime, Its History, Composers, and Music.* London: Macmillan, 1985.

Alan Lomax. Mr. *Jelly Roll: The Fortunes of Jelly Roll Morton, New Orleans Creole and "Inventor of Jazz."* New York: Grove Press, 1950.

Gunther Schuller. *Early Jazz: Its Roots and Musical Development.* New York: Oxford University Press, 1968.

Sports

Ocania Chalk. *Black College Sport.* New York: Dodd, Mead, 1976.

Neil Lanctot. *Negro League Baseball: The Rise and Ruin of a Black Institution.* Philadelphia: University of Pennsylvania Press, 2004.

Robert W. Peterson. *Only the Ball Was White: Negro Baseball: A History of Legendary Black Players and All-Black Professional Teams before Black Men Played in the Major Leagues.* New York: Prentice-Hall, 1970.

Andrew Ritchie. *Major Taylor: The Extraordinary Career of a Championship Bicycle Racer.* San Francisco: Bicycle Books, 1988.

Randy Roberts. *Papa Jack: Jack Johnson and the Era of White Hopes.* New York: Free Press, 1983.

Chapter 16   Conciliation, Agitation, and Migration: African Americans in the Early Twentieth Century

Leadership Conflicts and the Emergence of African-American Organizations

Charles F. Kellogg. *NAACP: A History of the National Association for the Advancement of Colored People.* Baltimore: Johns Hopkins University Press, 1967.

August Meier. *Negro Thought in America, 1880–1915.* Ann Arbor: University of Michigan Press, 1967.

Alfred A. Moss Jr. *American Negro Academy: Voice of the Talented Tenth.* Baton Rouge: Louisiana State University Press, 1981.

B. Joyce Ross. *J. E. Spingarn and the Rise of the N.A.A.C.P.* New York: Atheneum, 1972.

Lawrence C. Ross Jr. *The Divine Nine: The History of African-American Fraternities and Sororities.* New York: Kensington Books, 2000.

Elliott Rudwick. *W. E. B. Du Bois.* New York: Atheneum, 1968.

Nancy Weiss. *The National Urban League, 1910–1940.* New York: Oxford University Press, 1974.

Shamoon Zamir. *Dark Voices: W. E. B. Du Bois and American Thought, 1888–1903.* Chicago: University of Chicago Press, 1995.

African-American Women in the Early Twentieth Century

Elizabeth Clark-Lewis. *Living In, Living Out: African American Domestics in Washington, D.C., 1910–1940.* Washington, DC: Smithsonian Institution Press, 1994.

Anna Julia Cooper. *A Voice from the South.* New York: Oxford University Press, 1988.

Cynthia Neverdon-Morton. *Afro-American Women of the South and the Advancement of the Race, 1895–1925.* Knoxville: University of Tennessee Press, 1998.

Jacqueline A. Rouse. *Lugina Burns Hope: A Black Southern Reformer.* Athens: University of Georgia Press, 1989.

Stephanie J. Shaw. *What a Woman Ought to Be and to Do: Black Professional Women Workers during the Jim Crow Era.* Chicago: University of Chicago Press, 1996.

Rosalyn Terborg-Penn. *African American Women in the Struggle for the Vote, 1850–1920.* Bloomington: Indiana University Press, 1998.

African Americans in the Military in the World War I Era

Arthur E. Barbeau and Florette Henri. *Black American Troops in World War I.* Philadelphia: Temple University Press, 1974.

Edward M. Coffman. *The War to End All Wars: The American Military Experience in World War I.* Madison: University of Wisconsin Press, 1986.

Arthur W. Little. *From Harlem to the Rhine: The Story of New York's Colored Volunteers.* New York: Covici, Friede, 1936.

Bernard C. Nalty. *Strength for the Fight: A History of Black Americans in the Military.* New York: Free Press, 1986.

Cities and Racial Conflict

Michael D'Orso. *Rosewood.* New York: Boulevard Press, 1996.

St. Clair Drake and Horace R. Clayton. *Black Metropolis: A Study of Negro Life in a Northern City.* 2 vols. Chicago: Harcourt, Brace and Co., 1945.

Sherry Sherrod Dupree. *The Rosewood Massacre at a Glance.* Gainesville, FL: Rosewood Forum, 1998.

Scott Ellsworth. *Death in a Promised Land: The Tulsa Race Riot of 1921.* Baton Rouge: Louisiana State University Press, 1982.

Robert V. Haynes. *A Night of Violence: The Houston Riot of 1917.* Baton Rouge: Louisiana State University Press, 1976.

Hannibal Johnson. *Black Wall Street, From Riot to Renaissance in Tulsa's Historic Greenwood District.* Austin, TX: Eakin Press, 1998.

David M. Katzman. *Before the Ghetto: Black Detroit in the Nineteenth Century.* Urbana: University of Illinois Press, 1973.

Kenneth L. Kusmer. *A Ghetto Takes Shape: Black Cleveland, 1870–1930.* Urbana: University of Illinois Press, 1976.

Gilbert Osofsky. *Harlem: The Making of a Ghetto, 1890–1930.* New York: Harper & Row, 1966.

Christopher Reed. *The Chicago NAACP and the Rise of Black Professional Leadership, 1910–1966.* Bloomington: Indiana University Press, 1997.

Elliott M. Rudwick. *Race Riot at East St. Louis, July 2, 1917.* Cleveland: World Publishing, 1966.

Roberta Senechal. *The Sociogenesis of a Race Riot: Springfield, Illinois, in 1908.* Urbana: University of Illinois Press, 1990.

Allan H. Spear. *Black Chicago: The Making of a Negro Ghetto, 1890–1920.* Chicago: University of Chicago Press, 1967.

Joe William Trotter Jr. *Black Milwaukee: The Making of an Industrial Proletariat, 1915–1945.* Urbana: University of Illinois Press, 1985.

William Tuttle. *Chicago in the Red Summer of 1919.* New York: Atheneum, 1970.

Lee E. Williams. *Anatomy of Four Race Riots: Racial Conflict in Knoxville, Elaine (Arkansas), Tulsa, and Chicago, 1919–1921.* Hattiesburg: University and College Press of Mississippi, 1972.

The Great Migration

Peter Gottlieb. *Making Their Own Way: Southern Blacks' Migration to Pittsburgh, 1916–1930.* Urbana: University of Illinois Press, 1987.

James R. Grossman. *Land of Hope: Chicago, Black Southerners, and the Great Migration.* Chicago: University of Chicago Press, 1989.

Florette Henri. *Black Migration, 1900–1920.* Garden City, NY: Anchor Press, 1975.

Carole Marks. *Farewell—We're Good and Gone: The Great Black Migration.* Bloomington: Indiana University Press, 1989.

Milton C. Sernett. *Bound for the Promised Land: African American Religion and the Great Migration.* Durham, NC: Duke University Press, 1997.

Joe William Trotter Jr., ed. *The Great Migration in Historical Perspective.* Bloomington: Indiana University Press, 1991.

Autobiography and Biography

W. E. B. Du Bois. *Dusk of Dawn.* New York: Harcourt, Brace & Co., 1940.

———. *The Autobiography: A Soliloquy on Viewing My Life from the Last Decade of Its First Century.* New York: International Publishers, 1968.

Stephen R. Fox. *The Guardian of Boston: William Monroe Trotter.* New York: Atheneum, 1970.

Kenneth R. Manning. *Black Apollo of Science: The Life of Ernest Everett Just.* New York: Oxford University Press, 1983.

Linda O. McMurry. *George Washington Carver: Scientist and Symbol.* New York: Oxford University Press, 1981.

Arnold Rampersad. *The Art and Imagination of W. E. B. Du Bois.* Cambridge, MA: Harvard University Press, 1976.

Mary Church Terrell. *A Colored Woman in a White World.* New York: Arno Press reprint, 1940.

Emma Lou Thornbrough. *T. Thomas Fortune.* Chicago: University of Chicago Press, 1970.

Booker T. Washington. *Up from Slavery.* New York: Doubleday, 1901.

Chapter 17   African Americans and the 1920s

The Ku Klux Klan

David M. Chalmers. *Hooded Americanism: A History of the Ku Klux Klan.* New York: Franklin Watts, 1965.

Kenneth T. Jackson. *The Ku Klux Klan in the City.* New York: Oxford University Press, 1967.

The NAACP

Charles F. Kellogg. *NAACP: A History of the National Association for the Advancement of Colored People.* Baltimore: Johns Hopkins University Press, 1967.

Robert L. Zangrando. *The NAACP Campaign against Lynching, 1909–1950.* Philadelphia: Temple University Press, 1980.

Black Workers, A. Philip Randolph, and the Brotherhood of Sleeping Car Porters

Jervis B. Anderson. *A. Philip Randolph: A Biographical Portrait.* New York: Harcourt, Brace, Jovanovich, 1973.

Beth Tompkins Bates. *Pullman Porters and the Rise of Protest Politics in Black America, 1925–1945.* Chapel Hill: University of North Carolina Press, 2001.

David E. Bernstein. *Only One Place of Redress: African Americans, Labor Regulations and the Courts from Reconstruction to the New Deal.* Durham, NC: Duke University Press, 2001.

Jack Santino. *Miles of Smiles, Years of Struggle: Stories of Black Pullman Porters.* Urbana: University of Illinois Press, 1989.

Marcus Garvey and the Universal Negro Improvement Association

Randall K. Burkett. *Garveyism as a Religious Movement: The Institutionalization of a Black Civil Religion.* Metuchen, NJ: Scarecrow Press, 1978.

E. David Cronon. *Black Moses: The Story of Marcus Garvey and the Universal Negro Improvement Association.* Madison: University of Wisconsin Press, 1955.

Marcus Garvey. *Philosophy and Opinions of Marcus Garvey.* New York: Atheneum, 1969.

Theodore Kornweibel, Jr. *Seeing Red: Federal Campaigns against Black Militancy, 1919–1925.* Bloomington: Indiana University Press, 1998.

The Harlem Renaissance

Arna W. Bontemps, ed. *The Harlem Renaissance Remembered.* New York: Dodd, Mead, 1972.

Nathan Huggins. *Harlem Renaissance.* New York: Oxford University Press, 1971.

Bruce Kellner, ed. *The Harlem Renaissance: A Historical Dictionary of the Era.* Westport, CT: Greenwood Press, 1984.

Steven Watson. *The Harlem Renaissance: Hub of African American Culture, 1920–1930.* New York: Pantheon, 1995.

Biographies and Autobiographies

Pamela Bordelon, ed. *Go Gator and Muddy the Water: Writings by Zora Neale Hurston from the Federal Writers Project.* New York: Norton, 1999.

Robert C. Cottrell. *The Best Pitcher in Baseball: The Life of Rube Foster; Negro League Giant.* New York: New York University Press, 2001.

Thadious M. Davis. *Nella Larsen: Novelist of the Harlem Renaissance.* Baton Rouge: Louisiana State University Press, 1994.

Wayne F. Cooper. *Claude McKay, Rebel Sojourner in the Harlem Renaissance: A Biography.* Baton Rouge: Louisiana State University Press, 1987.

Robert Hemenway. *Zora Neale Hurston: A Literary Biography.* Urbana: University of Illinois Press, 1977.

Gloria T. Hull. *Color, Sex, and Poetry: Three Women Writers of the Harlem Renaissance.* Bloomington: Indiana University Press, 1987.

James Weldon Johnson. *Along the Way.* New York: Viking Press, 1933.

Cynthia E. Kerman. *The Lives of Jean Toomer: A Hunger for Wholeness.* Baton Rouge: Louisiana State University Press, 1987.

Eugene Levy. *James Weldon Johnson: Black Leader, Black Voice.* Chicago: University of Chicago Press, 1973.

Chapter 18   Black Protest, the Great Depression, and the New Deal

Politics

Adam Fairclough. *Better Day Coming: Blacks and Equality, 1890–2000.* New York: Viking, 2001.

Kenneth W. Goings. *"The NAACP Comes of Age": The Defeat of Judge John J. Parker.* Bloomington: Indiana University Press, 1990.

Charles V. Hamilton. *Adam Clayton Powell, Jr., the Political Biography of an American Dilemma.* New York: Atheneum, 1991.

Darlene Clark Hine. *Black Victory: The Rise and Fall of the White Primary in Texas.* New edition with essays by Darlene Clark Hine, Steven F. Lawson, and Merline Pitre. Columbia: University of Missouri Press, 2003.

John B. Kirby. *Black Americans in the Roosevelt Era: Liberalism and Race.* Knoxville: University of Tennessee Press, 1980.

Christopher R. Reed. *The Chicago NAACP and the Rise of Black Professional Leadership, 1910–1966.* Bloomington: Indiana University Press, 1997.

Bernard Sternsher, ed. *The Negro in Depression and War: Prelude to Revolution, 1930–1945.* Chicago: Quadrangle Books, 1969.

Mark V. Tushnet. *The NAACP's Legal Strategy against Segregated Education, 1925–1950.* Chapel Hill: University of North Carolina Press, 1987.

Nancy J. Weiss. *Farewell to the Party of Lincoln: Black Politics in the Age of Lincoln.* Princeton, NJ: Princeton University Press, 1983.

Labor

Lizabeth Cohen. *Making a New Deal: Industrial Workers in Chicago, 1919–1939.* New York: Cambridge University Press, 1990.

Dennis C. Dickerson. *Out of the Crucible: Black Steelworkers in Western Pennsylvania, 1875–1980.* Albany, NY: SUNY Press, 1986.

William H. Harris. *The Harder We Run: Black Workers since the Civil War.* New York: Oxford University Press, 1982.

August Meier and Elliott Rudwick. *Black Detroit and the Rise of the UAW.* New York: Oxford University Press, 1979.

Education

James D. Anderson. *The Education of Blacks in the South, 1860–1935.* Chapel Hill: University of North Carolina Press, 1988.

Horace M. Bond. *The Education of the Negro in the American Social Order.* New York: Octagon Books, 1934; rev. 1966.

Richard Kluger. *Simple Justice: The History of Brown v. Board of Education and Black America's Struggle for Equality,* 1976; new rev. ed., 2004. With a new chapter assessing the 50th year impact of *Brown.*

Mark V. Tushnet. *Making Civil Rights Law: Thurgood Marshall and the Supreme Court, 1935–1961.* New York: Knopf, 1994.

Black Radicalism

Dan Carter. *Scottsboro: A Tragedy of the American South.* Baton Rouge: Louisiana State University Press, 1969.

Vanessa Northington Gamble. *Making a Place for Ourselves: The Black Hospital Movement, 1920–1945.* New York: Oxford University Press, 1995.

Kenneth W. Goings. *Mammy and Uncle Mose: Black Collectibles and American Stereotyping.* Bloomington: Indiana University Press, 1994.

Michael K. Honey. *Southern Labor and Black Civil Rights: Organizing Memphis Workers.* Urbana: University of Illinois Press, 1993.

Jacqueline Jones. *Labor of Love, Labor of Sorrow: Black Women, Work, and the Family from Slavery to the Present.* New York: Basic Books, 1985.

Nicholas Natanson. *The Black Image in the New Deal: The Politics of FSA Photography.* Knoxville: University of Tennessee Press, 1992.

Richard H. Pells. *Radical Visions and American Dreams: Culture and Social Thought in the Depression Years.* New York: Harper & Row, 1973.

Daryl Michael Scott. *Contempt and Pity: Social Policy and the Image of the Damaged Black Psyche, 1880–1996.* Chapel Hill: University of North Carolina Press, 1997.

Mark Solomon. *The Cry Was Unity: Communists and African Americans, 1917–1936.* Jackson: University Press of Mississippi, 1998.

Richard W. Thomas. *Life for Us Is What We Make It: Building Black Community in Detroit, 1915–1945.* Bloomington: Indiana University Press, 1992.

Thomas J. Ward Jr. *Black Physicians in the Jim Crow South.* Fayetteville: University of Arkansas Press, 2003.

Economics

Charles T. Banner-Haley. *To Do Good and to Do Well: Middle Class Blacks and the Depression, Philadelphia, 1929–1941.* New York: Garland, 1993.

Abram L. Harris. *The Negro as Capitalist: A Study of Banking and Business among American Negroes.* Originally published by the American Academy of Political and Social Sciences, 1936; reprint, Chicago: Urban Research Press, 1992.

Alexa Benson Henderson. *Atlanta Life Insurance Company: Guardian of Black Economic Dignity.* Tuscaloosa: University of Alabama Press, 1990.

Robert E. Weems Jr. *Black Business in the Black Metropolis: The Chicago Metropolitan Assurance Company, 1924–1985.* Bloomington: Indiana University Press, 1996.

Biography and Autobiography

Andrew Buni. *Robert L. Vann of the Pittsburgh Courier.* Pittsburgh: University of Pittsburgh Press, 1974.

Henry Louis Gates, Jr. and Evelyn Brooks Higginbotham, eds. *African American Lives.* New York: Oxford University Press, 2004.

Wil Haywood. *King of the Cats: The Life and Times of Adam Clayton Powell, Jr.* Boston: Houghton Mifflin, 1993.

Spencie Love. *One Blood: The Death and Resurrection of Charles R. Drew.* Chapel Hill: University of North Carolina Press, 1996.

Genna Rae McNeil. *Groundwork: Charles Hamilton Houston and the Struggle for Civil Rights.* Philadelphia: University of Pennsylvania Press, 1983.

Nell Irvin Painter. *The Narrative of Hosea Hudson: His Life as a Negro Communist in the South.* Cambridge, MA: Harvard University Press, 1979.

Paula F. Pfeffer. *A. Philip Randolph, Pioneer of the Civil Rights Movement.* Baton Rouge: Louisiana State University Press, 1990.

Barbara Ransby. *Ella Baker and the Black Freedom Movement*. Chapel Hill: University of North Carolina Press, 2003.

George S. Schuyler. *Black and Conservative: The Autobiography of George S. Schuyler*. New Rochelle, NY: Arlington House, 1966.

Gilbert Ware. *William Hastie: Grace under Pressure*. New York: Oxford University Press, 1984.

Roy Wilkins with Tom Mathews. *Standing Fast: The Autobiography of Roy Wilkins*. New York: Da Capo Press, 1994.

Chapter 19   Meanings of Freedom: Culture and Society in the 1930s and 1940s

Art

Michael D. Harris and Moyo Okediji. *Colored Pictures: Race and Visual Representation*. Chapel Hill: University of North Carolina Press, 2003.

Sharon F. Patton. *African-American Art*. New York: Oxford University Press, 1998.

Richard J. Powell. *Black Art and Culture in the 20th Century*. New York: Thames and Judson, 1997.

William E. Taylor and Harriet G. Warkel. *A Shared Heritage: Art by Four African Americans*. Bloomington: Indiana University Press, 1996.

Black Chicago Renaissance

Robert Bone. "Richard Wright and the Chicago Renaissance." *Callaloo*, 9, no. 3 (1986): 446–68.

Craig Werner. "Leon Forrest, the AACM and the Legacy of the Chicago Renaissance." *The Black Scholar*, 23, no. 3/4 (1993): 10–23.

Culture

St. Clair Drake and Horace R. Cayton. *Black Metropolis: A Study of Negro Life in a Northern City*. New York: Harper & Row, 1962.

Gerald Early, ed. *"Ain't But a Place": An Anthology of African American Writing about St. Louis*. St. Louis: Missouri Historical Society Press, 1998.

Geneviève Fabre and Robert O'Meally, eds. *History and Memory in African-American Culture*. New York: Oxford University Press, 1994.

Kenneth W. Goings. *Mammy and Uncle Mose: Black Collectibles and American Stereotyping*. Bloomington: Indiana University Press, 1994.

Joseph E. Harris, ed. *Global Dimensions of the African Diaspora*. Washington, DC: Howard University Press, 1993.

Robin D. G. Kelley. *Race Rebels: Culture, Politics, and the Black Working Class*. New York: Free Press, 1994.

Lawrence Levine. *Black Culture and Black Consciousness: Afro-American Folk Thought from Slavery to Freedom*. New York: Oxford University Press, 1977.

Tommy L. Lott. *The Invention of Race: Black Culture and the Politics of Representation*. Malden, MA: Blackwell, 1999.

Daryl Scott. *Contempt and Pity: Social Policy and Image of the Damaged Black Psyche, 1880–1996*. Chapel Hill: University of North Carolina Press, 1997.

Mel Watkins. *On the Real Side: Laughing, Lying, and Signifying*. New York: Simon & Schuster, 1994.

Robert E. Weems Jr. *Desegregating the Dollar: African American Consumerism in the Twentieth Century*. New York: New York University Press, 1998.

Dance

Katherine Dunham. *A Touch of Innocence*. London: Cassell, 1959.

Terry Harnan. *African Rhythm–American Dance*. New York: Knopf, 1974.

Films

Donald Bogle. *Brown Sugar: Eighty Years of America's Black Female Superstars*. New York: Crown, 1980.

Thomas Cripps. *Making Movies Black: The Hollywood Message Movie from World War II to the Civil Rights Era*. New York: Oxford University Press, 1993.

Jane M. Gaines. *Fire and Desire: Mixed-Race Movies in the Silent Era*. Chicago: University of Chicago Press, 2001.

Literature

Ralph Ellison. "The World and the Jug." In Joseph F. Trimmer, ed., *A Casebook on Ralph Ellison's Invisible Man* (pp. 172–200). New York: T. Y. Crowell, 1972.

Michael Fabre. *The Unfinished Quest of Richard Wright*. Iowa City: University of Iowa Press, 1973.

Henry Louis Gates and Nellie Y. McKay, eds. *Norton Anthology of African American Literature*. New York: Norton, 1997.

Joyce Ann Joyce. *Richard Wright's Art of Tragedy*. New York: Warner Books, 1986.

Robert G. O'Meally. *The Craft of Ralph Ellison*. Cambridge, MA: Harvard University Press, 1980.

Arnold Rampersad. *The Life of Langston Hughes*. New York: Oxford University Press, 1986.

Margaret Walker. *Richard Wright, Daemonic Genius: A Portrait of the Man, a Critical Look at His Work.* New York: Morrow, 1988.

Music and Radio

William Barlow. *Looking Up at Down: The Emergence of Blues Culture.* Philadelphia: Temple University Press, 1989.

Thomas Brothers, ed. *Louis Armstrong: In His Own Words.* New York: Oxford University Press, 1999.

Jack Chalmers. *Milestones I: The Music and Times of Miles Davis to 1960.* Toronto, Canada: University of Toronto Press, 1983.

John Chilton. *The Song of the Hawk: The Life and Recordings of Coleman Hawkins.* Ann Arbor: University of Michigan Press, 1990.

Donald Clarke. *Wishing on the Moon: The Life and Times of Billie Holiday.* New York: Viking Penguin, 1994.

Linda Dahl. *Morning Glory: A Biography of Mary Lou Williams.* New York: Pantheon Books, 2000.

Miles Davis and Quincy Troupe. *Miles: The Autobiography.* New York: Simon & Schuster, 1989.

Duke Ellington. *Music Is My Mistress.* New York: Da Capo Press, 1973.

John Birks Gillespie and Wilmot Alfred Fraser. *To Be or Not . . . to Bop: Memoirs/Dizzy Gillespie with Al Fraser.* New York: Doubleday, 1979.

Michael Harris. *The Rise of Gospel Blues: The Music of Thomas Andrew Dorsey in the Urban Church.* New York: Oxford University Press, 1992.

Allan Keiler. *Marian Anderson: A Singer's Journey.* New York: Scribner, 2000.

Robert G. O'Meally. *Lady Day: The Many Faces of Billie Holiday.* New York: Arcade Publishers, 1991.

Thomas Owens. *Bebop: The Music and Its Players.* New York: Oxford University Press, 1955.

Barbara Dianne Savage. *Broadcasting Freedom: Radio, War, and the Politics of Race, 1938–1948.* Chapel Hill: University of North Carolina Press, 1999.

Jules Schwerin. *Got to Tell It: Mahalia Jackson, Queen of Gospel.* New York: Oxford University Press, 1992.

Alyn Shipton. *Groovin' High: The Life of Dizzy Gillespie.* New York: Oxford University Press, 1999.

Eileen Southern. *The Music of Black Americans: A History,* 2d ed. New York: Norton, 1983.

Quintard Taylor. *In Search of the Racial Frontier: African Americans in the American West, 1528–1900.* New York: Norton, 1998.

J. C. Thomas. *Chasin' the Trane: The Music and Mystique of John Coltrane.* Garden City, NY: Doubleday, 1975.

Dempsey J. Travis. *Autobiography of Black Jazz.* Chicago: Urban Research Press, 1983.

Sports

Arthur Ashe, with the assistance of Kip Branch, Ocania Chalk, and Francis Harris. *A Hard Road to Glory: A History of the African-American Athlete.* New York: Warner Books, 1988.

Richard Bak. *Joe Louis: The Great Black Hope.* New York: Da Capo Press, 1998.

Robert Peterson. *Only the Ball Was White: A History of Legendary Black Players and All-Black Professional Teams.* New York: McGraw-Hill, 1984.

Arnold Rampersad. *Jackie Robinson: A Biography.* New York: Alfred A. Knopf, 1997.

Jackie Robinson. *I Never Had It Made.* New York: G. P. Putnam's Son, 1972.

Jeffrey T. Sammons. *Beyond the Ring: The Role of Boxing in American Society.* Urbana: University of Illinois Press, 1988.

Religion

Claude Andrew Clegg III. *An Original Man: The Life and Times of Elijah Muhammad.* New York: St. Martin's Griffin, 1997.

C. Eric Lincoln and Lawrence H. Mamiya. *The Black Church in the African American Experience.* Durham, NC: Duke University Press, 1990.

Elijah Muhammad. *The True History of Elijah Muhammad: Autobiographically Authoritative.* Atlanta: Secretrius Publications, 1997.

Jill Watts. *God, Harlem USA: The Father Divine Story.* Berkeley: University of California Press, 1992.

Robert Weisbrot. *Father Divine and the Struggle for Racial Equality.* Urbana: University of Illinois Press, 1983.

Chapter 20   The World War II Era and the Seeds of a Revolution

African Americans and the Military

Robert Allen. *Port Chicago Mutiny: The Story of the Largest Mass Mutiny in U.S. Naval History.* New York: Warner Books-Amistad Books, 1989.

Richard Dalfiume. *Desegregation of the U.S. Armed Forces: Fighting on Two Fronts 1939–1953.* Columbia: University of Missouri Press, 1969.

Charles W. Dryden. *A-Train: Memoirs of a Tuskegee Airman.* Tuscaloosa: University of Alabama Press, 1997.

Charity Adams Earley. *One Woman's Army: A Black Officer Remembers the WAC.* College Station: Texas A & M University Press, 1989.

Darlene Clark Hine. *Black Women in White: Racial Conflict and Cooperation in the Nursing Profession,*

1890–1950. Bloomington: Indiana University Press, 1989.

Ulysses Lee. *The Employment of Negro Troops.* Washington, DC: Center of Military History, 1990.

Neil McMillen, ed. *Remaking Dixie: The Impact of World War II on the American South.* Jackson: University Press of Mississippi, 1997.

Mary Penick Motley. *The Invisible Soldier: The Experience of the Black Soldier, World War Two.* Detroit: Wayne State University Press, 1975.

Alan M. Osur. *Blacks in the Army Air Forces during World War II: The Problem of Race Relations.* Washington, DC: Office of Air Force History, 1977.

Lou Potter. *Liberators: Fighting on Two Fronts in World War II.* New York: Harcourt Brace Jovanovich, 1992.

Stanley Sandler. *Segregated Skies: All-Black Combat Squadrons of WWII.* Washington, DC: Smithsonian Institution Press, 1992.

Howard Sitkoff. "Racial Militancy and Interracial Violence in the Second World War," *Journal of American History,* 58, no. 3 (1971): 663–83.

Paul Stillwell, ed. *The Golden Thirteen: Recollections of the First Black Naval Officers.* Annapolis, MD: Naval Institute Press, 1993.

Black Urban Studies

Albert Broussard. *Black San Francisco: The Struggle for Racial Equality in the West, 1900–1954.* Lawrence: University of Kansas Press, 1993.

Dominic Capeci. *The Harlem Riot of 1943.* Philadephia: Temple University Press, 1977.

Dominic Capeci. *Race Relations in Wartime Detroit: The Sojourner Truth Housing Controversy of 1942.* Philadelphia: Temple University Press, 1984.

Dominic Capeci and Martha Wilkerson. *Layered Violence: The Detroit Rioters of 1943.* Jackson: University Press of Mississippi, 1991.

Lawrence B. DeGraaf. "Significant Steps on an Arduous Path: The Impact of World War II on Discrimination Against African Americns in the West." *Journal of the West,* 35, no. 1 (1996): 24–33.

St. Clair Drake and Horace R. Cayton. *Black Metropolis: A Study of Negro Life in a Northern City.* New York: Harcourt Brace, 1945.

August Meier and Elliott Rudwick. *Black Detroit and the Rise of the UAW.* New York: Oxford University Press, 1979.

Robert Shogan and Tom Craig. *The Detroit Race Riot: A Study in Violence.* New York: Chilton Books, 1964.

Richard W. Thomas. *Life for Us Is What We Make It: Building Black Community in Detroit, 1915–1945.* Bloomington: Indiana University Press, 1992.

Black Americans, Domestic Radicalism, and International Affairs

William C. Berman. *The Politics of Civil Rights in the Truman Administration.* Columbus: Ohio State University Press, 1970.

John Morton Blum. *V Was for Victory: Politics and American Culture during World War II.* New York: Harcourt Brace Jovanovich, 1996.

Richard M. Freeland. *The Truman Doctrine and the Origins of McCarthyism.* New York: New York University Press, 1985.

Herbert Garfinkel. *When Negroes March: The March on Washington Movement in the Organizational Politics for FEPC.* New York: Atheneum, 1973.

Joseph Harris. *African American Reactions to War in Ethiopia, 1936–1941.* Baton Rouge: Louisiana State University Press, 1994.

Gerald Horne. *Black and Red: W. E. B. Du Bois and the Afro-American Response to the Cold War.* Albany: State University of New York Press, 1986.

Sudarshan Kapur. *Raising Up a Prophet: The Afro-American Encounter with Gandhi.* Boston: Orbis, 1992.

Andrew Edmund Kersten. *Race and War: The FEPC in the Midwest, 1941–46.* Urbana: University of Illinois Press, 2000.

George Lipsitz. *Rainbow at Midnight: Labor and Culture in the 1940s.* Urbana: University of Illinois Press, 1994.

August Meier and Elliott Rudwick. *CORE: A Study in the Civil Rights Movement, 1942–1968.* Urbana: University of Illinois Press, 1975.

Gail Williams O'Brien. *The Color of the Law: Race, Violence and Justice in the Post–World War II South.* Chapel Hill: University of North Carolina Press, 1999.

Brenda Gayle Plummer. *Rising Wind: Black Americans and U.S. Foreign Affairs, 1935–1960.* Chapel Hill: University of North Carolina Press, 1996.

Linda Reed. *Simple Decency and Common Sense: The Southern Conference Movement, 1938–1963.* Bloomington: Indiana University Press, 1991.

Patricia Scott Washburn. *A Question of Sedition: The Federal Government's Investigation of the Black Press during World War II.* New York: Oxford University Press, 1986.

Autobiography and Biography

Andrew Buni. *Robert Vann of the Pittsburgh Courier.* Pittsburgh: University of Pittsburgh Press, 1974.

Martin Bauml Duberman. *Paul Robeson: A Biography.* New York: Ballantine Press, 1989.

Shirley Graham Du Bois. *His Day Is Marching On: A Memoir of W. E. B. Du Bois.* New York: Lippincott, 1971.

Kenneth R. Janken. *Rayford W. Logan and the Dilemma of the African-American Intellectual.* Amherst: University of Massachusetts Press, 1993.

Spencie Love. *One Blood: The Death and Resurrection of Charles Drew.* Chapel Hill: University of North Carolina Press, 1996.

Manning Marable. *W. E. B. Du Bois: Black Radical Democrat.* Boston: Twayne, 1986.

Constance Baker Motley. *Equal Justice under Law: An Autobiography.* New York: Farrar, Straus and Giroux, 1998.

Pauli Murray. *Song in a Weary Throat: An American Pilgrimage.* New York: Harper & Row, 1987.

Bayard Rustin. *Troubles I've Seen.* New York: HarperCollins, 1996.

Studs Terkel, ed. *The Good War.* New York: Pantheon, 1984.

Brian Urquhart. *Ralph Bunche: An American Life.* New York: Norton, 1993.

Gilbert Ware. *William Hastie: Grace under Pressure.* New York: Oxford University Press, 1984.

Roy Wilkins with Tom Mathews. *Standing Fast: The Autobiography of Roy Wilkins.* New York: Da Capo Press, 1994.

Chapter 21   The Freedom Movement, 1954–1965

General Overviews of Civil Rights Movement and Organizations

Robert Fredrick Burk. *The Eisenhower Administration and Black Civil Rights.* Knoxville: University of Tennessee Press, 1984.

Stewart Burns. *Daybreak of Freedom: The Montgomery Bus Boycott.* Chapel Hill: University of North Carolina Press, 1997.

John Dittmer. *Local People: The Struggle for Civil Rights in Mississippi.* Urbana: University of Illinois Press, 1994.

Adam Fairclough. *To Redeem the Soul of America: The Southern Christian Leadership Conference and Martin Luther King, Jr.* Athens: University of Georgia Press, 1987.

David R. Goldfield. *Black, White and Southern: Race Relations and the Southern Culture, 1940 to the Present.* Baton Rouge: Louisiana State University Press, 1991.

Martin Luther King Jr. *Stride Towards Freedom: The Montgomery Story.* New York: Harper, 1958.

Michael J. Klarman. *From Jim Crow to Civil Rights: The Supreme Court and the Struggle for Racial Equality.* New York: Oxford University Press, 2003.

Steven F. Lawson. *Black Ballots: Voting Rights in the South, 1944–1969.* New York: Columbia University Press, 1976.

Manning Marable. *Race, Reform, and Rebellion: The Second Reconstruction in Black America, 1945–1982.* Jackson: University Press of Mississippi, 1984.

August Meier and Elliot Rudwick. *CORE: A Study of the Civil Rights Movement, 1942–1968.* New York: Oxford University Press, 1973.

Anne Moody. *Coming of Age in Mississippi.* New York: Dial Press, 1968.

Donald G. Nieman. *Promises to Keep: African-Americans and the Constitutional Order, 1776 to the Present.* New York: Oxford University Press, 1991.

Robert J. Norrell. *Reaping the Whirlwind: The Civil Rights Movement in Tuskegee.* New York: Alfred A. Knopf, 1985.

James T. Patterson. *Brown v. Board of Education: A Civil Rights Milestone and Its Troubled Legacy.* New York: Oxford University Press, 2000.

Charles M. Payne. *I've Got the Light of Freedom: The Organizing Tradition and the Mississippi Freedom Struggle.* Berkeley: University of California Press, 1995.

Fred Powledge. *Free at Last? The Civil Rights Movement and the People Who Made It.* Boston: Little, Brown, 1991.

Howell Raines. *My Soul Is Rested: Movement Days in the Deep South Remembered.* New York: Putnam, 1977.

Belinda Robnett. *How Long? How Long? African-American Women in the Struggle for Civil Rights.* New York: Oxford University Press, 1997.

Juan Williams. *Eyes on the Prize: America's Civil Rights Years, 1954–1965.* New York: Viking, 1987.

Black Politics/White Resistance

Numan V. Bartley. *The Rise of Massive Resistance: Race and Politics in the South during the 1950's.* Baton Rouge: Louisiana State University Press, 1969.

Elizabeth Jacoway and David R. Colburn. *Southern Businessmen and Desegregation.* Baton Rouge: Louisiana State University Press, 1982.

Darlene Clark Hine. *Black Victory: The Rise and Fall of the White Primary in Texas* (Columbia: University of Missouri Press, 2nd ed. 2003.)

Doug McAdam. *Freedom Summer.* New York: Oxford University Press, 1988.

Neil R. McMillen. *The Citizen's Council: A History of Organized Resistance to the Second Reconstruction.* Urbana: University of Illinois Press, 1971.

Frank R. Parker. *Black Votes Count: Political Empowerment in Mississippi after 1965*. Chapel Hill: University of North Carolina Press, 1990.

Autobiography and Biography

Daisy Bates. *The Long Shadow of Little Rock: Memoir*. New York: David McKay Co., 1962.

Taylor Branch. *Pillar of Fire: America in the King Years, 1963–65*. New York: Simon & Schuster, 1998.

Eric R. Burner. *And Gently He Shall Lead Them: Robert Parris Moses and Civil Rights in Mississippi*. New York: New York University Press, 1994.

Septima Clark. *Ready from Within: Septima Clark and the Civil Rights Movement*. Navarro, CA: Wild Tree Press, 1986.

Robert S. Dallek. *Flawed Giant: Lyndon Johnson and His Times, 1961–1973*. New York: Oxford University Press, 1998.

Dennis C. Dickerson. *Militant Mediator: Whitney M. Young, Jr., 1921–1971*. Lexington: University Press of Kentucky, 1998.

James Farmer. *Lay Bare the Heart: An Autobiography of the Civil Rights Movement*. New York: Arbor House, 1985.

Cynthia Griggs Fleming. *Soon We Will Not Cry: The Liberation of Ruby Doris Smith Robinson*. Lanham, MD: Rowman & Littlefield, 1998.

David J. Garrow. *Bearing the Cross: Martin Luther King, Jr., and the Southern Christian Leadership Conference*. New York: William Morrow & Company, 1986.

———. *The FBI and Martin Luther King, Jr.* New York: Penguin Books, 1981.

Chana Kai Lee. *For Freedom's Sake: The Life of Fannie Lou Hamer*. Urbana: University of Illinois Press, 1999.

David Levering Lewis. *King: A Critical Biography*. New York: Praeger, 1970.

Genna Rae McNeil. *Groundwork: Charles Hamilton Houston and the Struggle for Civil Rights*. Philadelphia: University of Pennsylvania Press, 1983.

Barbara Ransby. *Ella Baker and the Black Freedom Movement*. Chapel Hill: University of North Carolina Press, 2003.

Jo Ann Gibson Robinson, with David Garrow. *The Montgomery Bus Boycott and the Women Who Started It*. Knoxville: University of Tennessee Press, 1987.

Mark V. Tushnet. *Making Civil Rights Law: Thurgood Marshall and the Supreme Court, 1936–1961*. New York: Oxford University Press, 1994.

Timothy B. Tyson. *Radio Free Dixie: Robert F. Williams and the Roots of Black Power*. Chapel Hill: University of North Carolina Press, 1999.

Juan Williams. *Thurgood Marshall: American Revolutionary*. New York: Times Books, 1998.

Reference Works

Charles Eagles, ed. *The Civil Rights Movement in America*. Jackson: University Press of Mississippi, 1986.

Charles S. Lowery and John F. Marszalek, eds. *Encyclopedia of African-American Civil Rights: From Emancipation to the Present*. New York: Greenwood Press, 1992.

Chapter 22   The Struggle Continues, 1965–1980

Black Panthers

Philip S. Foner, ed. *The Black Panther Speaks*. Philadelphia: Lippincott, 1970.

Toni Morrison, ed. *To Die for the People: The Writings of Huey P. Newton*. New York: Writers and Readers Publishing, 1995.

Kenneth O'Reilly. *Racial Matters: The FBI's Secret File on Black America, 1960–1972*. New York: Free Press, 1989.

Robert Scheer, ed. *Eldridge Cleaver: Post-Prison Writings and Speeches*. New York: Random House, 1969.

Black Power and Politics

Robert L. Allen. *Black Awakening in Capitalist America*. Trenton, NJ: Africa World Press, 1990.

Elaine Brown. *A Taste of Power: A Black Woman's Story*. New York: Pantheon, 1992.

James H. Cone. *Martin & Malcolm & America: A Dream or a Nightmare*. Maryknoll, NY: Orbis, 1991.

Sidney Fine. *Violence in the Model City: The Cavanagh Administration, Race Relations and the Detroit Riot of 1967*. Ann Arbor: University of Michigan Press, 1989.

James F. Finley Jr. *Church People in the Struggle: The National Council of Churches and the Black Freedom Movement, 1950–1970*. New York: Oxford University Press, 1993.

Frye Gaillard. *The Dream Long Deferred*. Chapel Hill: University of North Carolina Press, 1988.

B. I. Kaufman. *The Presidency of James E. Carter, Jr.* Lawrence: University of Kansas Press, 1993.

Steven Lawson. *In Pursuit of Power: Southern Blacks and Electoral Politics, 1965–1982*. New York: Columbia University Press, 1985.

C. Eric Lincoln. *The Black Muslims in America*. Boston: Beacon Press, 1961.

J. Anthony Lukas. *Common Ground*. New York: Knopf, 1985.

John T. McCartney. *Black Power Ideologies: An Essay in African-American Thought*. Philadelphia: Temple University Press, 1992.

William B. McClain. *Black People in the Methodist Church*. Cambridge, MA: Schenkman, 1984.

Larry G. Murphy. *Down by the Riverside: Readings in African American Religion*. New York: New York University Press, 2000.

William E. Nelson Jr. and Philip J. Meranto. *Electing Black Mayors: Political Action in the Black Community*. Columbus: Ohio State University Press, 1977.

Gary Orfield. *Must We Bus? Segregated Schools and National Policy*. Washington, DC: Brookings Institution, 1978.

Robert A. Pratt. *The Color of Their Skin: Education and Race in Richmond, Virginia, 1954–89*. Charlottesville: University Press of Virginia, 1992.

James R. Ralph Jr. *Northern Protest: Martin Luther King, Jr., Chicago, and the Civil Rights Movement*. Cambridge, MA: Harvard University Press, 1993.

Diane Ravitch. *The Great School Wars*. New York: Basic Books, 1974.

Wilbur C. Rich. *Coleman Young and Detroit Politics*. Detroit, MI: Wayne State University Press, 1989.

Bobby Seale. *Seize the Time*. New York: Random House, 1970.

James Melvin Washington. *Frustrated Fellowship: The Black Baptist Quest for Social Power*. Macon, GA: Mercer University Press, 1986.

Delores S. Williams. *Sisters in the Wilderness: The Challenge of Womanist God-Talk*. Maryknoll, NY: Orbis, 1993.

Gayraud S. Wilmore. *Black Religion and Black Radicalism*. New York: Anchor Press, 1973.

Black Studies and Black Students

Talmadge Anderson, ed. *Black Studies: Theory, Method, and Cultural Perspectives*. Pullman: Washington State University Press, 1990.

Jack Bass and Jack Nelson. *The Orangeburg Massacre*. Cleveland, OH: Word Publishing, 1970.

William H. Exum. *Paradoxes of Protest: Black Student Activism in a White University*. Philadelphia: Temple University Press, 1985.

Richard P. McCormick. *The Black Student Protest Movement at Rutgers*. New Brunswick, NJ: Rutgers University Press, 1990.

Cleveland Sellers, with Robert Terrell. *The River of No Return: The Autobiography of a Black Militant and the Life and Death of SNCC*. New York: William Morrow, 1987.

Class and Race

Jack M. Bloom. *Class, Race, and the Civil Rights Movement*. Bloomington: Indiana University Press, 1987.

Martin Gilens. *Why Americans Hate Welfare: Race, Media, and the Politics of Antipoverty Policy*. Chicago: University of Chicago Press, 1999.

Michael Katz. *The Undeserving Poor: From the War on Poverty to the War on Welfare*. New York: Pantheon Books, 1989.

Bart Landry. *The New Black Middle Class*. Berkeley: University of California Press, 1987.

William Julius Wilson. *The Truly Disadvantaged: The Inner City, the Underclass, and Public Policy*. Chicago: University of Chicago Press, 1987.

Black Arts and Black Consciousness Movements

William L. Andrews, Frances Smith Foster, and Trudier Harris, eds. *The Oxford Companion to African American Literature*. New York: Oxford University Press, 1997.

James Baldwin. *Notes of a Native Son*. New York: Dial Press, 1955.

———. *Nobody Knows My Name*. New York: Dial Press, 1961.

———. *The Fire Next Time*. New York: Dial Press, 1963.

———. *No Name in the Street*. New York: Dial Press, 1972.

Imamu Amiri Baraka. *Dutchman and the Slave, Two Plays by LeRoi Jones*. New York: William Morrow, 1964.

Samuel A. Hay. *African American Theater: An Historical and Critical Analysis*. Cambridge, MA: Cambridge University Press, 1994.

LeRoi Jones and Larry Neal, eds. *Black Fire: An Anthology of Afro-American Writing*. New York: William Morrow, 1968.

LeRoi Jones. *Blues People: Negro Music in White America*. New York: William Morrow, 1963.

Frank Kofsky. *Black Nationalism and the Revolution in Music*. New York: Pathfinder Press, 1970.

Larry Neal. *Visions of a Liberated Future: Black Arts Movement Writings*. New York: Thunder's Mouth Press, 1989.

Leslie Catherine Sanders. *The Development of Black Theater in America: From Shadow to Selves*. Baton Rouge: Louisiana State University Press, 1988.

Suzanne E. Smith. *Dancing in the Streets: Motown and the Cultural Politics of Detroit*. Cambridge, MA: Harvard University Press, 2000.

Autobiography and Biography

Imamu Amiri Baraka. *The Autobiography of LeRoi Jones.* New York: Freundlich Books, 1984.

Dennis C. Dickerson. *Militant Mediator: Whitney M. Young, Jr.* Lexington: University Press of Kentucky, 1998.

James Farmer. *Lay Bare the Heart: An Autobiography of the Civil Rights Movement.* New York: Arbor House, 1985.

Jimmie Lewis Franklin. *Back to Birmingham: Richard Arrington, Jr., and His Times.* Tuscaloosa: University of Alabama Press, 1989.

Elliott J. Gorn, ed. *Muhammad Ali: The People's Champ.* Urbana: University of Illinois Press, 1995.

Charles V. Hamilton. *Adam Clayton Powell, Jr.: The Political Biography of an American Dilemma.* New York: Atheneum, 1991.

Hil Haygood. *King of the Cats: The Life and Times of Adam Clayton Powell, Jr.* Boston: Houghton Mifflin, 1993.

David Remnick. *King of the World: Muhammad Ali and the Rise of an American Hero.* New York: Random House, 1998.

Mary Beth Rogers. *Barbara Jordan: American Hero.* New York: Bantam Books, 1998.

Kathleen Rout. *Eldridge Cleaver.* Boston: Twayne Publishers, 1991.

Bobby Seale. *Seize the Time.* New York: Random House, 1970.

Nancy J. Weiss. *Whitney M. Young, Jr., and the Struggle for Civil Rights.* Princeton, NJ: Princeton University Press, 1989.

Chapter 23   Black Politics, White Backlash, 1980 to the Present

Culture and Race Studies

Molefi Kete Asante. *Erasing Racism: The Survival of the American Nation.* New York: Prometheus Books, 2003.

Robin D. G. Kelley. *Race Rebels: Culture, Politics, and the Black Working Class.* New York: Free Press, 1994.

Jacob Levenson. *The Secret Epidemic: The Story of AIDS and Black America.* New York: Pantheon, 2004.

Manning Marable. *The Great Wells of Democracy: The Meaning of Race in American Life.* New York: Basic Books, 2002.

Terry McMillan. *Five for Five: The Films of Spike Lee.* New York: Stewart, Tabori & Chang, 1991.

Nikhil Pal Singh. *Black Is a Country: Race and the Unfinished Struggle for Democracy.* Cambridge: Harvard University Press, 2004.

Black Politics and Economics

Andrew Billingsley. *Climbing Jacob's Ladder: The Enduring Legacy of African-American Families.* New York: Simon & Schuster, 1993.

Barry Bluestone and Bennett Harrison. *The Deindustrialization of America: Plant Closings, Community Abandonment, and the Dismantling of Basic Industry.* New York: Basic Books, 1982.

Donna Brazile. *Cooking with Grease: Stirring the Pot in American Politics.* New York: Simon & Schuster, 2004.

Michael K. Brown. *Race, Money, and the American Welfare State.* Ithaca, NY: Cornell University Press, 1999.

Robert D. Bullard, Glenn S. Johnson, and Angel O. Torres, eds. *Highway Robbery: Transportation Racism and New Routes to Equity.* Cambridge, MA: South End Press, 2004.

Martin Carnoy. *Faded Dreams: The Politics and Economics of Race in America.* Cambridge, England: Cambridge University Press, 1994.

Dalton Conley. *Being Black, Living in the Red: Race, Wealth, and Social Policy in America.* Berkeley: University of California Press, 1999.

Robert Dallek. *Ronald Reagan: The Politics of Symbolism.* Cambridge, MA: Harvard University Press, 1984.

W. Avon Drake and Robert D. Holsworth. *Affirmative Action and the Stalled Quest for Black Progress.* Urbana: University of Illinois Press, 1996.

Robert Gooding-Williams, ed. *Reading Rodney King: Reading Urban Uprising.* New York: Routledge, 1993.

Lani Guinier. *Tyranny of the Majority: Fundamental Fairness and Representative Democracy.* New York: Free Press, 1995.

Andrew Hacker. *Two Nations: Black and White, Separate, Hostile, Unequal.* New York: Ballantine Books, rev., 1995.

Melissa Victoria Harris-Lacewell. *Barbershops, Bibles, and Bet: Everyday Talk and Black Political Thought.* Princeton: Princeton University Press, 2004.

Charles P. Henry. *Jesse Jackson: The Search for Common Ground.* Oakland, CA: Black Scholar Press, 1991.

Anita Faye Hill and Emma Coleman Jordan, eds. *Race, Gender, and Power in America: The Legacy of the Hill–Thomas Hearings.* New York: Oxford University Press, 1995.

James Jennings. *Welfare Reform and the Revitalization of Inner City Neighborhoods.* East Lansing: Michigan State University Press, 2003.

Norman Kelley. *The Head Negro in Charge Syndrome: The Dead End of Black Politics.* New York: Nation Books, 2004.

Douglas S. Massey and Nancy A. Denton. *American Apartheid: Segregation and the Making of the Underclass.* Cambridge, MA: Harvard University Press, 1993.

Adolph Reed Jr. *The Jesse Jackson Phenomenon: The Crisis in Afro-American Politics.* New Haven, CT: Yale University Press, 1986.

Condoleezza Rice. "Why We Know Iraq Is Lying," *New York Times,* January 23, 2003.

Andrea Y. Simpson. *The Tie That Binds: Identity and Political Attitudes in the Post–Civil Rights Generation.* New York: New York University Press, 1998.

Special Issue on Affirmative Action. *The Western Journal of Black Studies,* 27, no. 1 (Spring 2003).

William Julius Wilson. *The Bridge over the Racial Divide: Rising Inequality and Coalition Politics.* Berkeley: University of California Press, 1999.

Liberation Studies

Derrick Bell. *Faces at the Bottom of the Well: The Permanence of Racism.* New York: Basic Books, 1992.

Michael C. Dawson. *Behind the Mule: Race and Class in African-American Politics.* Princeton, NJ: Princeton University Press, 1994.

W. Marvin Dulaney. *Black Police in America.* Bloomington: Indiana University Press, 1996.

Henry Hampton and Steve Fayer. *Voices of Freedom: An Oral History of the Civil Rights Movement from the 1950s through the 1980s.* New York: Bantam Books, 1990.

Randall Robinson. *The Debt: What America Owes to Blacks.* New York: Plume, 2000.

Cornel West. *Democracy Matters: Wining the Fight Against Imperialism.* New York: The Penguin Press, 2004.

Black Conservatives

Thomas Sowell. *Preferential Policies: An International Perspective.* New York: William Morrow, 1990.

Shelby Steele. *A Dream Deferred: The Second Betrayal of Black Freedom in America.* New York: HarperCollins, 1998.

Shelby Steele/CCC. *The Content of Our Character: A New Vision of Race in America.* New York: St. Martin's Press, 1990.

Autobiography and Biography

Marshall Frady. *Jesse: The Life and Pilgrimage of Jesse Jackson.* New York: Random House, 1996.

Barack Obama, *Dreams from My Father: A Story of Race and Inheritance.* New York: Three Rivers Press, 1995, 2004.

Rev. Al Sharpton (with Karen Hunter). *Al on America.* New York: Kensington, 2002.

Chapter 24   African Americans at the Dawn of a New Millennium

Black Culture Studies

Anthony Bogues. *Black Heretics, Black Prophets: Radical Political Intellectuals.* New York: Doubleday, 2003.

Brian Cross. *It's Not about a Salary . . . Rap, Race and Resistance in Los Angeles.* London: Verso, 1993.

Michael Eric Dyson. *Between God and Gangsta Rap: Bearing Witness to Black Culture.* New York: Oxford University Press, 1996.

Patricia Liggins Hill, gen. ed. Call and Response: The Riverside Anthology of the African American Literary Tradition. New York: Houghton Mifflin, 1969.

bell hooks. *Outlaw Culture: Resisting Representations.* New York: Routledge, 1994.

Robin D. G. Kelley. *Race Rebels: Culture, Politics, and the Black Working Class.* New York: Free Press, 1994.

Terry McMillan. *Five for Five: The Films of Spike Lee.* New York: Stewart, Tabori & Chang, 1991.

Joan Morgan. *When Chickenheads Come Home to Roost: My Life as a Hip-Hop Feminist.* New York: Simon & Schuster, 1999.

Tricia Rose. *Black Noise: Rap Music and Black Culture in Contemporary America.* Hanover, NH: Wesleyan University Press, 1994.

Greg Tate. *Flyboy in the Buttermilk.* New York: Fire-side, 1992.

Deborah Willis. *Reflections in Black: A History of Black Photographers, 1840 to the Present.* New York: Norton, 2000.

Identity Studies

K. Anthony Appiah and Amy Guttman. *Color Conscious: The Political Morality of Race.* Princeton: Princeton University Press, 1996.

Molefi Kete Asante. *The Afrocentric Idea.* Philadelphia: Temple University Press, 1987.

Martin Bernal. *Black Athena: The Afroasiatic Roots of Classical Civilization: The Fabrication of Ancient*

Greece, 1785–1985. New Brunswick, NJ: Rutgers University Press, 1987.

Jonathan Betsch Cole and Beverly Guy Sheftall. *Gender Talk: The Struggle for Women's Equality in African-American Communities.* New York: Ballantine Books, 2003.

F. James Davis. *Who Is Black? One Nation's Definition.* University Park: Pennsylvania State University Press, 1991.

Charles Harmon, ed. *Double Exposure: Poverty and Race in America.* Armonk, NY: M. E. Sharpe, 1997.

Tsehloane Keto. *Vision, Identity and Time: The Afrocentric Paradigm and the Study of the Past.* Dubuque, IA: Kendall/Hunt, 1995.

Wilson Jeremiah Moses. *Afrotopia: The Roots of African American Popular History.* Cambridge, MA: Cambridge University Press, 1998.

Arthur M. Schlesinger Jr. *The Disuniting of America.* New York: Norton, 1992.

Clarence Walker. *You Can't Go Home Again.* New York: Oxford University Press, 2001.

Cornel West. *Race Matters.* Boston: Beacon Press, 1993.

Race, Gender, and Class

Paul M. Barrett. *The Good Black: A True Story of Race in America.* New York: Dutton, 1999.

Lois Benjamin. *The Black Elite: Facing the Color Line in the Twilight of the Twentieth Century.* Chicago: Nelson-Hall, 1991.

Douglas G. Glasgow. *The Black Underclass: Poverty, Unemployment, and Entrapment of Ghetto Youth.* New York: Random House, 1981.

Christopher Jencks. *Rethinking Social Policy: Race, Poverty, and the Underclass.* Cambridge, MA: Harvard University Press, 1992.

Jonathan Kozel. *Savage Inequalities: Children in America's Schools.* New York: Crown, 1991.

Haki R. Madhubuti. *Black Men—Obsolete, Single, Dangerous? Afrikan American Families in Transition: Essays in Discovery, Solution, and Hope.* Chicago: Third World Press, 1990.

Leith Mullings. *On Our Own Terms: Race, Class, and Gender in the Lives of African American Women.* New York: Routledge, 1997.

Autobiography and Biography

Amy Alexander, ed. *The Farrakhan Factor: African-American Writers on Leadership, Nationhood and Minister Louis Farrakhan.* New York: Grove Press, 1998.

E. Lynn Harris. *What Becomes of the Broken Hearted?* New York: Doubleday, 2003.

Randall Robinson. *Defending the Spirit: A Black Life in America.* New York: NAL/Dutton, 1998.

Index